UKRAINE AND EUROPE

Cultural Encounters and Negotiations

Ukraine and Europe

Cultural Encounters and Negotiations

Edited by Giovanna Brogi Bercoff,
Marko Pavlyshyn, and Serhii Plokhy

UNIVERSITY OF TORONTO PRESS
Toronto Buffalo London

ISBN 978-1-4875-0090-0

Printed on acid-free, 100% post-consumer recycled paper with
vegetable-based inks.

Library and Archives Canada Cataloguing in Publication

Ukraine and Europe : cultural encounters and negotiations
/ edited by Giovanna Brogi Bercoff, Marko Pavlyshyn, and Serhii Plokhy.

Includes bibliographical references and index.
ISBN 978-1-4875-0090-0 (cloth)

1. Ukraine – Civilization. 2. Ukraine – Relations – Europe –
History. 3. Europe – Relations – Europe – History. I. Pavlyshyn,
Marko, author, editor II. Brogi Bercoff, Giovanna, author,
editor III. Plokhy, Serhii, 1957–, editor

DK508.4.U45 2017   947.7   C2017-900719-X

Resources for the conference on which this collection is based were provided
by the Ukrainian Studies Support Fund (USSF) of the Association of Ukrainians
in Victoria (Australia), the Harvard Ukrainian Research Institute (HURI), and
the University of Milan. Publication of this book has been made possible in part
by the financial support of the USSF and HURI. The editors are grateful to Ms
Marta Olynyk for translating one of the volume's chapters and for her editorial
work on several of them, and to Ms Daniela Agostinelli for preparing the index.

University of Toronto Press acknowledges the financial assistance to its
publishing program of the Canada Council for the Arts and the Ontario Arts
Council, an agency of the Government of Ontario.

Canada Council   Conseil des Arts
for the Arts   du Canada

ONTARIO ARTS COUNCIL
CONSEIL DES ARTS DE L'ONTARIO
an Ontario government agency
un organisme du gouvernement de l'Ontario

Funded by the   Financé par le
Government   gouvernement
of Canada   du Canada

Contents

Note on Transliteration   viii

Introduction: Cultural Encounters and Negotiations   3
GIOVANNA BROGI BERCOFF, MARKO PAVLYSHYN,
AND SERHII PLOKHY

Prologue. Ukrainian Literature and Europe: Aporias,
Asymmetries, and Discourses   17
GEORGE G. GRABOWICZ

**Part One: Ukraine in the Common Cultural Space of
the European Baroque**

Plurilinguism and Identity: Rethinking Ukrainian Literature of
the Seventeenth Century   45
GIOVANNA BROGI BERCOFF

The Image of the Intercession of the Mother of God in Ukraine:
East versus West   72
MICHAEL S. FLIER

"Europe" in Seventeenth- and Early Eighteenth-Century Ukrainian
Texts: Between Geography and Ambivalent Judgments   101
NATALIA YAKOVENKO

Too Close to "the West"? The Ruthenian Language of the
Instruction of 1609   119

MICHAEL MOSER

Ukraine and the General Crisis of the Seventeenth Century: The
Khmel'nyts'kyi Uprising among the Early Modern "Revolutions"   136

FRANK E. SYSYN

Catherine of Alexandria's Crown of Golden Liberty   158

NATALIA PYLYPIUK

The Wisdom of Virtue: Iosyp Turobois'kyi's Praise of
Ioasaf Krokovs'kyi   182

GIOVANNA SIEDINA

Part Two: Recovering Europe: Ukraine's Romanticisms and Modernisms

Ukrainian Prose from the 1800s to the 1860s: In Quest of a
European Modernity   211

MARKO PAVLYSHYN

A Ticket to Europe: Collections of Ukrainian Folk Songs and
Their Russian Reviewers, 1820s–1830s   227

EDYTA M. BOJANOWSKA

Discovering "Little Russia": Victor Tissot and Ukraine's Image in
the West in the 1880s   249

GIULIA LAMI

Traditional or Modern, Nativist or Foreign, Ukrainian or European:
The Roots of Ivan Nechui-Levyts'kyi's Antimodernism   269

MAXIM TARNAWSKY

Rewriting Johann Wolfgang Goethe in the Poetry of Western
Ukrainian Modernism   283

STEFAN SIMONEK

Ivan Franko in Vienna: Towards Conflicting Concepts of Modernity   300

YAROSLAV HRYTSAK

**Part Three: Ukrainian Visions of Europe from Imperial
to Post-Soviet Times**

Institutionalizing "Europe": Imperial High Culture and the Ukrainian
Intelligentsia from Gogol' to Khvyl'ovyi   319
OLEH S. ILNYTZKYJ

The Train to Europe: Berlin as a Topos of Modernity in Ukrainian
Literature of the 1920s   340
TAMARA HUNDOROVA

Between Cultural Memory and Trauma: An Interpretation of
Mykola Khvyl'ovyi's "My Being"   361
ALEXANDER KRATOCHVIL

Literaturnyi iarmarok: Mediation between Nativist Tradition and
Western Culture   374
HALYNA HRYN

The Poetry of the Sixtiers and Europe: Between Culture and Politics   390
OXANA PACHLOVSKA

Waiting for Europe: Public Intellectuals' Visions and Political Reality
on the Eve of the Euromaidan   414
OLA HNATIUK

Epilogue. The EuroRevolution: Ukraine and the New Map
of Europe   433
SERHII PLOKHY

Index   449

Colour plates follow page 88.

Note on Transliteration

In general, transliteration of Cyrillic characters follows a simplified Library of Congress Romanization system (without ligatures). Bibliographical references adhere strictly to this norm. In the main text, a few proper nouns are rendered in spellings that have become conventional in English (e.g., Yushchenko, Lviv). Where transliteration of the possessive of nouns ending in a soft sign would result in a double apostrophe, a single apostrophe is used (e.g., Dal', but Dal's).

UKRAINE AND EUROPE

Cultural Encounters and Negotiations

Introduction: Cultural Encounters and Negotiations

GIOVANNA BROGI BERCOFF, MARKO PAVLYSHYN,
AND SERHII PLOKHY

In Western studies of the geopolitical and, to a lesser extent, civilizational predicament of Ukraine – and in no small part of the domestic Ukrainian scholarly commentary – it has become customary to invoke two relational spatial motifs: "Ukraine and…" and "Ukraine between…" The former usually announces an inquiry into Ukraine's relationship with Ukraine's significant others, both real and symbolic: Russia and Europe. The latter motif signals consideration of Ukraine as a liminal or transitional zone, an entity that itself cannot claim centrality and is thus either pulled towards one of the two neighbouring centres of gravity – or oscillates between them. Ukraine from this perspective lies between East and West, between Europe and Eurasia, between Western and Eastern Christianity, between the Roman and the Byzantine traditions, between the European Union and the Russian Federation. The problematic of Ukraine's Janus-faced identity is a rich source of sometimes picturesque scholarly metaphors: Ukraine is visualized as "torn apart" between Europe and Russia,[1] "trapped between East and West," or on a "meandering path between East and West";[2] "at a crossroads"[3] or "choosing"[4] a path, or on a "road"[5] to a "destination";[6] if not a "frontier,"[7] then part of a "neighborhood"[8] or a "space."[9] Only occasionally is Ukraine envisioned as being "in" Europe,[10] and less often still as the "keystone" of an arch.[11]

Inevitably, such spatial metaphors cannot but be inherited by a collection such as ours, which enters into an ongoing scholarly discussion and sets out to enrich a relatively neglected part of it: the cultural.[12] Much of the existing discussion focuses upon politics and geopolitics,[13] on economics and international relations,[14] or on society and social attitudes.[15] It privileges, overwhelmingly, a contemporary perspective; its cognitive interest is often driven by a pragmatic wish to understand and predict whose "side" Ukraine as a state will ultimately take in the competition between Western-style pluralist democracies and economic systems and Eurasian-style monolithic political and economic systems.

Interactions with Europe and with Russia, existing and ideal, are issues that bring into focus other questions concerning contemporary Ukraine. First among them is the unresolved matter of the collective identity – national, regional, ethnic, linguistic, and historical – of Ukraine's citizens. Closely related is the unique role of Ukraine in the collective imagination of its biggest neighbour, Russia, and of the disparate roles that Russia plays in the imaginations of different groups of Ukrainians. No less important is the asymmetry of the relationship between Ukraine and Europe. Many Ukrainians, intellectuals in particular, place emphasis upon their "choice of Europe," which for them represents a choice of civic values and political and ethical norms that they hope to see triumph in their country. Europe in its contemporary iteration as the European Union, on the other hand, has been relatively indifferent towards Ukraine.

All of these issues have traditions of different longevity. Their manifestations – in varying combinations and at disparate historical moments – are the subject matter of this book. Our collection takes as its theme Ukraine's relationship with one of its two principal interlocutors: Europe. It brings together inquiries that, in the majority of cases (not all), focus on the arts and on intellectual endeavours. Through this cultural prism our book examines the relationship between "Europe" and "Ukraine" or, to be precise, the historical entities or reverse-projected constructs that correspond to these terms (the first quite ancient, the latter rather more modern). The relationship emerges from these studies as complex and not necessarily best captured by the juxtaposition between a reified "Europe" and an equally reified "East," with Ukraine "torn" between the two.

This collection of articles is also inspired by, and is a continuation of, a rich and growing literature on the "invention" and imagining of Europe as a whole and its constituent parts, including Ukraine, produced largely by historians, political scientists, anthropologists, and literary scholars in the course of the last two decades.[16] The essays collected here seek, mainly through detailed inquiries into particular individuals, texts, and circumstances, to situate Ukrainian realities, historically defined, upon cognitive grids that highlight a variety of interethnic, interlingual, intercultural, and international relationships. The essays are arranged according to the chronological sequence of their subject matter. We have divided them into three parts: The first covers the early modern era, the second – the nineteenth and early twentieth centuries. The third part deals, in the main, with the Soviet and post-Soviet period. This division flows from the nature of the subject matter: each of the parts focuses on a period during which the Ukraine-Europe nexus was especially salient. In the early modern period Ukrainian high culture was caught up in the pan-European reappropriation of the legacy of classical antiquity, as well as in European struggles over religion; the latter were also a crucial element of the social and political tumult that characterized seventeenth-century Ukraine. Beginning with the early decades of the nineteenth century, Ukrainian culture organized itself as a response to one of Europe's most compelling ideas: that of the nation. The quest for a collective identity that would embrace the cultural wealth of the untutored majority; the development of a narrative of a shared glorious past; the nurturing of a national literary culture that could assert the right of Ukraine to an equal place at the imagined European round table of nations – these projects, inspired by the values and enthusiasms of romanticism, the Ukrainian educated class had in common with elites of stateless peoples throughout Europe. Finally, through most of the twentieth century and at the beginning of the twenty-first, many Ukrainians opposed to Soviet authoritarianism cherished Europe as a symbol of their ideal of civic and civilizational normality – of liberty in contrast to oppression.

There is a degree of continuity between the essays in each of the three sections, as there is between the three periods to which they correspond. The complexity and contingency of cultural and national identities; the role of language as an indicator of cultural orientation; and, above all, the determination of the educated part of society to participate in European modernity – these and other themes recur as leitmotifs in the essays gathered in this book. All three periods are crucial for understanding the development of Ukrainian writers', intellectuals', and artists' thinking about their country and its relations with the wider world, and each receives more or less equal attention in the collection.

The contributions come from a number of different disciplines. History, linguistics, and art history are represented. Some of the essays, in addition to their scholarly character, are interventions in contemporary cultural and political debates. But it is literature as a key venue for reflection upon, and reflection of, the cultural orientation of a society that takes centre stage in most of the essays. We were fortunate to gather under one cover contributions not only by representatives of different disciplines, but also by scholars working in distinct national traditions. The editors themselves come from three continents: Australia, Europe, and North America, while the authors are scholars working in Ukraine, countries of the European Union (Austria, Germany, and Italy), and the United States and Canada.

Beyond the chronological division that has served as the basis for the structural arrangement of the volume, our essays fall into a number of groups depending on the kinds of relationship that they investigate. Some articles focus on ways in which Ukraine may be seen, historically or at present, as *participating* in Europe. Others consider how Europe may be said to have *influenced* Ukrainian developments. A third group, closely related to the second, explores the ways in which ideas of Europe have exercised a *normative function* for Ukrainian educated elites, especially those involved in the project of nation-building. A fourth cluster brings together studies that test the validity of particular *theoretical models* for research into the relationship between Europe and Ukraine. Finally, a fifth group of chapters considers the actual and potential *meanings and uses* that the concept of Europe has had and continues to have for Ukrainian writers, intellectuals, and activists.

Participation

Several articles adopt a perspective that enables us to see Ukrainian historical and cultural developments as part of, or in relation to, overarching European processes. The tensions between the Europeanness and the non-Europeanness of Ukraine are the focal point of "Ukrainian Literature and Europe: Aporias, Asymmetries and Discourses," the survey of the literary and intellectual history of Ukraine by George Grabowicz that opens the collection. Grabowicz's wide-ranging discussion outlines the contexts and chief features of the interaction between the European and Ukrainian literary spheres in various phases of cultural history. At the same time it draws attention to the inevitably problematic nature of such an enterprise – the very terms of comparison, "Europe" and "Ukraine," are complex and mutable constructions. In the interface between these two entities "Europe" often presents itself to "Ukraine" through a mediating culture, in modern times most often that of Poland. Analogies between cultural phenomena in Western Europe and those that in Ukrainian cultural historiography bear the same names ("humanism," for example, or "Enlightenment") are at best approximate. Grabowicz is at pains to point out that resistance to Europe and a determination to protect and assert values perceived as autochthonous is just as much a motif of modern Ukrainian literary and cultural history as is a yearning to embrace Europe.

Participation is the leitmotif of a number of chapters dedicated to the premodern and early modern periods. It is no accident that our collection places emphasis on this period and the key Ukrainian cultural institution of this time, the Kyiv Mohyla Collegium (later Academy): it was during this period, and at this institution, that the awareness of the Ukrainian elite of the cultural world of Europe at large was most in evidence. Giovanna Brogi Bercoff in "Plurilinguism and Identity: Rethinking Ukrainian Literature of the Seventeenth Century" considers texts by churchmen associated through their education and

early formation with the Ukrainian lands as representatives of European plurilingual learned culture. This culture, shared throughout the Europe of humanism and the Renaissance, had not penetrated deeply into Muscovy; it became
the task of ecclesiastical intellectuals from Ukraine and Belarus, and their
texts, to transmit it to Muscovy and, subsequently, the Russian Empire. While
documenting the Europeanness of these Kyiv-gestated writings, Brogi Bercoff
draws attention to their connection to a particular Kyivan cultural, religious,
and historical context.

Giovanna Siedina and Natalia Pylypiuk advance similar arguments concerning the same period, though based on the detailed analysis of individual
texts. Siedina ("Wisdom of Virtue: Iosyp Turobois'kyi's praise of Ioasaf Krokovs'kyi") studies a panegyrical poem composed in Latin in 1699 by a cleric
of the Kyiv Mohyla Collegium who in the first decade of the eighteenth century was one of many from that institution who made imposing ecclesiastical
careers in Muscovy (from 1721 the Russian Empire) in the service of Tsar
Peter I. Close analysis of the laudatory poem's rhetorical structure, its artful
deployment of trope and figure, and its exhaustive reference to Greco-Roman
myth and to exempla from Roman history confirm the intimate connection of
the Mohylanian milieu to the learned humanist culture of Western, Mediterra-
nean, and Central Europe.

Pylypiuk's contribution, "Catherine of Alexandria's Crown of Golden Liberty," studies another Mohylanian text, the drama *Declamatio de S. Catharinae
Genio*, written in Polish by a group of students and included in a manual of
rhetoric in 1703–4. Comparison with the treatment of the martyrology of
St Catherine in a contemporaneous Polish drama and a Spanish dramatic text
composed one hundred years earlier enables Pylypiuk to demonstrate the con-
tiguity of the literary culture of Orthodox Kyiv at the time of Ivan Mazepa's
hetmancy with the humanist culture of Europe in its Jesuit redaction. Pylypiuk
also suggests the possibility of reading the drama politically as anti-Petrine and
sympathetic to the autonomist aspirations of Mazepa's circle.

Focusing not on the early modern period, but on the avant-gardism of
the 1920s during the brief period of "Ukrainianization" in Soviet Ukraine,
Halyna Hryn in "*Literaturnyi iarmarok*: Mediation between Nativist Tradition and Western Culture" examines the sophisticated and irreverent journal
Literaturnyi iarmarok (Literary Fair, 1928–30). Hryn analyses the journal's
parodic and intertextual structure, documenting its authors' deliberate and frequent references to artistic currents of Western and Central Europe and their
representative personalities and texts. The author interprets the jokes and
mystifications that accompany this use of Europe in *Literary Fair*, and the
journal's self-ironic mélange of European modernism and Ukrainian populist

traditionalism, as features of carnivalized literature – the literary embodiment of the ancient social and sociopsychological phenomenon of carnival widely attested throughout Europe and influentially theorized by Mikhail Bakhtin.

Dealing with the same period, Tamara Hundorova ("The Train to Europe: Berlin as a Topos of Modernity in Ukrainian Literature of the 1920s") confirms Hryn's observations concerning the simultaneity of modernist (and therefore Europe-oriented) and nativist impulses in Ukrainian literature of the 1920s. Hundorova studies the role of Berlin, one of the symbolic sites of urban modernity in the interwar period, in the lives and works of such Ukrainian writers as Valerian Pidmohyl'nyi, Mykola Khvyl'ovyi, Ievhen Cherniak, and Mykhailo Mohylians'kyi. On the one hand, Hundorova argues, many authors were disappointed in their hopes of finding in Berlin the "Faustian Europe" that Khvyl'ovyi, inspired by Oswald Spengler, had envisaged. Ultimately, they proved ready to rehabilitate a romantic vision of their homeland. On the other hand, their experiences of Berlin, both direct and literary, often led them to superimpose that city's urban atmosphere and architectural styles upon their literary portraits of Kharkiv and Kyiv.

Oxana Pachlovska's chapter, "The Poetry of the Sixtiers and Europe: Between Culture and Politics," reflects upon the (aesthetic, world view, and political) dissidents of 1960s Ukraine. Pachlovska draws attention to the way in which these "Sixtiers," as they were called, continued the traditions of the 1920s, including the 1920s orientation towards Europe. In contrast to George Grabowicz's scepticism as to the strength of this connection in the 1960s, Pachlovska reads the Sixtiers' attachment to the values of freedom, free choice, and individual responsibility as a fundamental, if often inexplicit, profession of European identity. She finds powerful parallels between the Sixtiers' refusal to accept the Soviet status quo – in the arts, historiography, and, most generally, civic morality – and the stance of the French Existentialists with respect to their post-war Western societies. Pachlovska seconds Václav Havel's definition of the whole of the dissident movement in Soviet-dominated East and Central Europe as an "existential revolution."

Influence

The metaphor of the cultural flow – of "influence" – structures some of our contributors' views of Ukrainian cultural phenomena. Michael Flier in his study of the icon of the Intercession of the Mother of God (the *Pokrova*) in the Ukrainian lands ("The Image of the Intercession of the Mother of God in Ukraine: East Versus West") examines the evolution of the iconography of the feast of the Protection of the Theotokos in Rus' and points to the accretion of both Byzantine and Western (late medieval and Renaissance) elements in the icon's tradition, their synthesis being a characteristic feature of the florescence of the *Pokrova* icon and cult in seventeenth- and eighteenth-century Ukraine.

Michael Moser ("Too Close to 'The West'? The Ruthenian Language of the *Instruction* of 1609") undertakes a detailed linguistic analysis of a text from 1609, the *Lamentation* that forms part of the *Instruction* that the Orthodox Ruthenian burghers of Lviv dispatched with their delegates to the diet or parliament of the Polish-Lithuanian Commonwealth. He does so to demonstrate the depth of Western influence (Polish, but also Latin and German mediated through Polish) upon the high-variety written language of the Ruthenians of the time, the *prosta mova*. This influence, Moser shows, is evidenced even by a text whose purpose is to assert and defend a separate Ruthenian identity against the alleged assault and intrigues of the Catholic West.

Observing Norms

A number of contributions inquire into Ukrainian responses to European cultural, intellectual, and implicitly political models felt to be so compelling as to require emulation. This concerns, above all, the model of the national high culture based on the culture of the ordinary people – a model indebted, preeminently, to the thought of Johann Gottfried Herder.

Edyta Bojanowska in "A Ticket to Europe: Collections of Ukrainian Folk Songs and Their Russian Reviewers, 1820s–1830s" gives an account of the proliferation of collections of Ukrainian folksongs in the Russian Empire in the first half of the nineteenth century. Bojanowska reads positive and negative appraisals of these publications as interventions into an implicit and sometimes explicit debate over the composition of future nations: would an overarching Russian nation encompass a Ukrainian (Little Russian) component or would the two be more properly viewed as separate?

Marko Pavlyshyn ("Ukrainian Prose from the 1800s to the 1860s: In Quest of a European Modernity") considers the evolution of modern literary prose in Ukrainian in the early and middle decades of the nineteenth century. He sees this process as enabling the emergence of Ukrainian as a communicative medium usable in the kind of modern public sphere, secular and national, that had become the European norm. The Ukrainian narratives of Marko Vovchok focused on the content of the message rather than its form, and opened the way to a multifunctional language available for the wide range of messages that need to be transmitted in such a context. This discourse overcame the limitations of the previously dominant paradigm of Ukrainian prose, the parodic or sentimentally folkloric, which, though indebted to European classicist and pre-romantic templates, had imposed the limitations of provincialism upon Ukrainian-language writing.

Maxim Tarnawsky ("Traditional or Modern, Nativist or Foreign, Ukrainian or European: The Roots of Ivan Nechui-Levyts'kyi's Antimodernism") takes for his subject a little-known and brief text by the Ukrainian novelist Ivan Nechui-Levyts'kyi, a champion of the realist aesthetic and of the nation-building role of literature. Tarnawsky's case study of the story "Bez puttia" (Going Nowhere, 1900) locates Nechui-Levyts'kyi between two norms, one as West European as the other: the positivist-realist and the modernist. Tarnawsky reads "Going Nowhere" as a satirical sally, grounded in a realist aesthetics of representation and a common-sense notion of "normal" social behaviour, against the Europe-wide fashion for fin-de-siècle aestheticism and hypersensi-tivity. He plausibly suggests that Nechui-Levyts'kyi's parody may be directed against a concrete instance of Ukrainian modernist writing: Lesia Ukraïnka's drama *Blaktyna troianda* (The Blue Rose).

European norms feature in Giulia Lami's contribution to the collection, "Dis-covering Little Russia: Victor Tissot and Ukraine's Image in the West in the 1880s." Here European norms figure not as objects of aspiration for Ukrainian culture builders, but as criteria for European judgments of Ukrainian realities. Lami's inquiry into a travelogue about the Ukrainian lands, *La Russie et les Russes* (Russia and the Russians, 1882) by the Swiss French-language writer Victor Tissot, reveals a European (postcolonially attuned scholars would say Ori-entalizing) gaze that measures Ukrainian social, cultural, and economic realities by European standards that, for the author, are the standards of civilization itself. Tissot finds the objects of his curiosity now charming, now deplorable. What is charming for Tissot fits the European template of romantic exoticism (rem-iniscences of the Cossacks freely roaming the steppes; the village culture and lifestyle of ordinary people, as well as their folklore) or confirms stereotypes pre-sented to Europe by Russian nineteenth-century literature (the gentility and sweet life of the landed nobility). Likewise, European prejudices prefigure what Tissot disdains: the small towns of Ukraine with their majority Jewish populations.

Theoretical Models

Against the background of an extensive review of the scholarship concerning seventeenth-century Europe and the Polish-Lithuanian Commonwealth, Frank Sysyn in "Ukraine and the General Crisis of the Seventeenth Century: The Khmel'nyts'kyi Uprising among the Early Modern 'Revolutions'" examines the political and social features of the Khmel'nyts'kyi rebellion. Sysyn details the ways in which this early modern revolt shared some, but not all, of its features with other European upheavals of the same period, affirming on balance the validity of regarding Bohdan Khmel'nyts'kyi's Cossack and peasant revolt as an instance of what many historians have called the European "general crisis of the seventeenth century."

Sysyn asks to what extent the nuances of historians' models of a seventeenth-century European crisis illuminate Ukrainian realia of the period. Yaroslav Hrystak does something similar with respect to the late nineteenth and early twentieth centuries. His inquiry ("Ivan Franko in Vienna: Toward Conflicting Concepts of Modernity") into the significance of the Habsburg capital for the Ukrainian writer, intellectual, and scholar Ivan Franko is a case study in the intersection between that quintessentially European artefact, modernity, and nationalism. Taking his cue from Ernst Gellner's classical reflections on the rise of the nationalisms of subject peoples in opposition to, but also within the framework of, imperial politics and culture, Hrytsak paints a complex portrait of Franko as a figure responding at different times to the activist, positivist model of modernity, and to the equally modern, but radically different modernity of the aestheticist fin-de-siècle.

Stefan Simonek's contribution, "Rewriting Johann Wolfgang Goethe in the Poetry of Western Ukrainian Modernism," applies to the Ukrainian cultural predicament a conceptual grid that is still underutilized in studies of East Central Europe: postcolonial studies. Simonek takes for his object of inquiry the work of Franko's younger contemporaries, the modernist poets of the "Moloda Muza" (Young Muse) group who were active in Eastern Galicia within the Habsburg Empire. Members of Young Muse proclaimed their orientation towards Europe and their reverence for the symbolic figures of European modernism (Nietzsche, Ibsen, Maeterlinck, and Baudelaire). Yet they also expressed resentment at the subaltern and marginal status of Ukrainian identity relative to the metropolitan ascendance enjoyed by German culture in their part of Europe, as Simonek shows in his analyses of Petro Karmans'kyi's and Bohdan Lepkyi's translations of some of Goethe's best-known poems.

The disciplines of memory studies and trauma studies provide the framework within which Alexander Kratochvil's chapter, "Between Cultural Memory and Trauma: An Interpretation of Mykola Khvyl'ovyi's 'My Being,'" interprets one of the most confronting texts of modern Ukrainian literature, Mykola Khvyl'ovyi's "Ia (Romantyka)" (I [A Romantic Tale], 1924, translated into English as "My Being"). This approach enables Kratochvil to position Khvyl'ovyi's short story – in which the first-person narrator, a confirmed Bolshevik, commits matricide out of revolutionary fervor – within the context of European trauma narratives of the First World War, notably the novels of Erich Maria Remarque and Ernst Jünger.

Meanings of Europe

A number of our studies discuss the use of the term "Europe" by Ukrainian (and other) literati and intellectuals. They examine the role of this symbolically weighty place name in shaping identities among the educated elites of Ukraine between early modern times and the present.

Natalia Yakovenko in her contribution, "'Europe' in Seventeenth and Early Eighteenth-Century Ukrainian Texts: Between Geography and Ambivalent Judgments," examines the invocation of "Europe," as well as the meaning attributed to this term and its variant, "all of Europe," in seventeenth- and early eighteenth-century Ukrainian texts. Her study of the library of the churchman and scholar Ioannikii Galiatovs'kyi, and of his annotations in the margins of his books, reveals Galiatovs'kyi's erudite familiarity with West European texts, mostly in Latin, though sometimes mediated by Polish translations. Yakovenko's examination of writings produced from the 1630s onward by the professoriate of the Kyiv Mohyla Academy shows that this milieu was familiar not only with Europe as a republic of letters, but also with a wide array of Western Europe's toponyms. These markers of cultural and geographical awareness signalled, whether spontaneously or by design, the Kyivan learned elite's determination to participate in an essentially Western European discursive and intellectual field.

In "Institutionalizing 'Europe': Imperial High Culture and the Ukrainian Intelligentsia from Gogol' to Khvyl'ovyi," Oleh S. Ilnytzkyj makes the concept of Europe – its presence or absence in literary and intellectual discourse, and then its invocation as a symbol of a desirable modern normality – the leitmotif of his excursion through Ukrainian intellectual history of the nineteenth and early twentieth centuries. Ilnytzkyj notes the relative insignificance of references to Europe in the writings of Ukrainians in the middle decades of the nineteenth century, when most Ukrainian intellectuals defined their role in the Russian Empire by differentiating themselves from the Russians, while at the same time arguing that Ukrainians and Russians were complementary parts of a single East Slavic ("all-Russian") whole. He follows the stepwise evolution of this model, characteristic, *inter alia*, of Nikolai Gogol's oeuvre, to the emphatically autarkic stance of the modernist writers grouped around the journal *Ukraïns'ka khata* (1909–14). Ilnytzkyj draws attention to the poorly studied figure of Andrii Tovkachevs'kyi, who articulated with great clarity the argument that the idea of an overarching all-Russian nation and the idea of a modern Ukrainian nation were mutually exclusive.

Ola Hnatiuk ("Waiting for Europe: Public Intellectuals' Visions and Political Reality") reflects on the uses of the notion of "Europe" in the discourse of

Ukrainian public intellectuals after the Orange Revolution of 2004. Members of this group, typified by the writer Yuri Andrukhovych whose interventions in public debates Hnatiuk considers in some detail, were the pre-eminent advocates of a European orientation for Ukraine. Their conception of Europe as the homeland of the political, civic, and cultural values that they treasured, however, did not correspond to the more pragmatic notion demonstrated by opinion polls of the time. According to those, most Ukrainians saw in Europe a symbol of high standards of living. Hnatiuk argues that the impact of public intellectuals, and therefore of the highbrow European vision that they promoted, was relatively minor. Available data show that the number of people who read intellectuals' commentary on social media, which became their favourite forum, was outweighed even by the readership of traditional print media, not to mention the audiences of television talk shows dedicated to politics and public affairs.

The final essay of the collection, Serhii Plokhy's "The EuroRevolution: Ukraine and the New Map of Europe," initiates discussion of the impact that the Euromaidan and the ongoing Russian aggression against Ukraine has had on the imagining of the map of Europe both in Ukraine and in the countries of the European Union. It comprises a proposal to scholars and others whose business it is to reflect on the strategic dimensions of geopolitics that the three countries wedged between the expanded European Union and the resurgent Russian Federation – Ukraine, Moldova, and Belarus – be thought of as a key region of Europe and not as its eastern frontier. Acknowledging the differences among the three, especially the contrast between the authoritarian regime in Belarus and the pluralist political system of Ukraine, Plokhy argues that the region is physically central in relation to a geographical picture of Europe that, since the Enlightenment, has located the border of the continent on the Urals. It would benefit both the elites and the public of the European Union and Ukraine, Plokhy submits, to think about Ukraine and its immediate region as an integral part of Europe on which will depend relations between the European Union and Russia in the near and longer-term future – a part of Europe where these relations are being tested today.

Our collection attests to the importance of the European idea in and for Ukraine. It does so from various perspectives and in relation to Ukraine's cultural history from early modern times to the present. In December 1991 more than 90 per cent of those voting endorsed Ukraine's declaration of independence. The Orange Revolution of 2004 and the Euromaidan protests of 2013–14 mobilized hundreds of thousands of Ukrainians in support of civic values and democratic political ideals that many of them identified as European. In 2013, Ukrainians went to the streets to defend their pro-European choice against their corrupt government and in the process transformed not only themselves but also the essence of European politics, in particular the EU's relations with Russia and the countries "in between." The relationship between Ukraine and Europe, then, is much more than a point of interest for scholars intent upon giving a plausible account of a selection of historical and contemporary data. It is a relationship that is changing the way in which not only Ukrainians but also the citizens of the EU countries think about the project called "Europe." The process of defining Ukraine's identity and finding its place on the map of Europe is far from over. We do not know where Ukraine will end up. But we trust that our volume will help readers to appreciate the importance and complexity of the cultural dilemmas that inform twenty-first-century debates and struggles in, and about, Ukraine.

July 2015

Notes

1 Fabian Niculae and Oana Popescu, *Ukraine: A Country Torn Apart between Europe and Russia* (Bucharest: Politeia-SNSPA, 2004).
2 Andrej N. Lushnycky and Mykola Riabchuk, eds., *Ukraine on its Meandering Path between East and West* (Bern: Lang, 2009).
3 *Ukraine at the Crossroads: Ten Years After Independence: Hearing Before the Commission on Security and Cooperation in Europe, One Hundred Seventh Congress, First Session, May 2, 2001* (Washington: U.S. G.P.O., 2001); Nicolas Hayoz and Andrej N. Lushnycky, eds., *Ukraine at a Crossroads* (Bern: Lang, 2005); *Ukraine at a Crossroads: What's at Stake for the U.S. and Europe? Hearing before the Subcommittee on European Affairs of the Committee on Foreign Relations, United States Senate, One Hundred Twelfth Congress, Second Session, February 1, 2012* (Washington: U.S. G.P.O., 2012).
4 Gwendolyn Sasse, "The EU Common Strategy on Ukraine: A Response to Ukraine's 'Pro-European Choice'?" in *The EU and Ukraine: Neighbours, Friends, Partners?* ed. Ann Lewis (London: Federal Trust, 2002); Marko Pavlyshyn, "Choosing a Europe: Andrukhovych, Izdryk, and the New Ukrainian literature," in *Contemporary Ukraine on the Cultural Map of Europe*, ed. Larissa M. L. Zaleska Onyshkevych and Maria G. Rewakowicz (Armonk, NY: M.E. Sharpe in co-operation with Shevchenko Scientific Society Inc., 2009), 249–63.
5 Giulia Lami, "Ukraine's Road to Europe: A Still Controversial Issue," in *Contemporary Ukraine on the Cultural Map of Europe*, 29–39.
6 Marta Dyczok, "Ukraine's Changing Communicative Space: Destination Europe or the Soviet Past?" in *Contemporary Ukraine on the Cultural Map of Europe*, 375–94.

7 *Frontiers and Horizons of the EU: The New Neighbors Ukraine, Belarus and Moldova. October 15th–17th, 2004, Lviv* (Hamburg: Körber-Stiftung, 2005); Oliver Schmidtke and Serhy Yekelchyk, eds., *Europe's Last Frontier? Belarus, Moldova, and Ukraine between Russia and the European Union* (New York: Palgrave Macmillan, 2008).

8 Ann Lewis, ed., *The EU and Ukraine: Neighbours, Friends, Partners?* (London: The Federal Trust, 2002); Alexander J. Motyl, "Ukraine, Europe, and Russia – Exclusion or Dependence?" in *Ambivalent Neighbors: The EU, NATO and the Price of Membership*, ed. Anatol Lieven and Dmitri Trenin (Washington, DC: Carnegie Endowment for International Peace, 2003).

9 A. I. Kudriachenko, ed., *Kul'turno-tsyvilizatsiinyi prostir Ievropy i Ukraïna: osoblyvosti stanovlennia ta suchasni tendentsiï rozvytku* (Kyiv: Universytet "Ukraïna," 2010); Andrii Portnov, *Mizh "Tsentral'noiu Ievropoiu" ta "Russkim mirom": Suchasna Ukraïna u prostori mizhnarodnykh intelektual'nykh dyskusii* (Kyiv: Natsional'nyi instytut stratehichnykh doslidzhen', 2009).

10 Richard W. Murphy, *Ukraine in Europe: Collected Papers* (Washington, DC: Center for Strategic and International Studies, 1999).

11 Sherman W. Garnett, *Keystone in the Arch: Ukraine in the Emerging Security Environment of Central and Eastern Europe* (Washington, DC: Carnegie Endowment for International Peace, 1997).

12 See, however: Petro Holubenko, *Ukraïna i Rosiia: u svitli kul'turnykh vzaiemyn* (Toronto: Naukovo-doslidnyi in-t im. O. Ol'zhycha, 1987); Ihor Ševčenko, *Ukraine Between East and West: Essays on Cultural History to the Early Eighteenth Century.* 2nd, rev. ed. (Edmonton: Canadian Institute of Ukrainian Studies Press, 2009); Oxana Pachlovska, "Finis Europae: Contemporary Ukraine's Conflicting Inheritances from the Humanistic 'West' and the Byzantine 'East' (A Triptych)," in *Contemporary Ukraine on the Cultural Map of Europe*, 40–68 and other essays in that collection.

13 Boris Shmelev, ed., *Ukraina i Rossiia: regional'nye napravleniia vneshnei politiki v 1990-e gody: materialy "kruglogo stola" rossiiskikh i ukrainskikh uchenykh, Odessa, 29–30 oktiabria 1998 g.* (Moscow: Epikon, 1999); Rawi Abdelal, "Lithuania: Toward Europe and the West; Ukraine: Between East and West; Belarus: Toward Russia and the East," *National Purpose in the World Economy: Post-Soviet States in Comparative Perspective* (Ithaca: Cornell University Press, 2001), 84–149; G.P.E. Walzenbach, "Ukraine Between the Orange Revolution and the EU: European Governance and Transformation in Ukraine," in *From Post-Communism Toward the Third Millennium: Aspects of Political and Economic Development in Eastern and South-Eastern Europe from 2000–2005*, ed. Josette Baer (Bern: Lang, 2011), 29–58.

14 Oleksiy Semeniy, "Ukraine's European Policy as an Alternative choice: Achievements, Mistakes and Prospects," in *Ukraine, the EU and Russia: History,*

Culture and International Relations, ed. Stephen Velychenko (Basingstoke: Palgrave Macmillan, 2007).

15 Evhen Golovakha, Andriy Gorbachyk, Natalia Panina, eds., *Ukraine and Europe: Outcomes of International Comparative Sociological Survey* (Kyiv: National Academy of Sciences of Ukraine, Institute of Sociology, 2007); H. M. Nadtoka, ed., *Ukraïna mizh Rosiieiu ta Ievropeis'kym Soiuzom: poshuk identychnosti. Materialy Mizhnarodnoï naukovoï konferentsiï 19 travnia 2011 roku* (Kyiv: Kyïvs'kyi universytet im. B. D. Hrinchenka, 2011).

16 See, for example, Gerard Delanty, *Inventing Europe* (New York: Palgrave Macmillan, 1995); Larry Wolff, *Inventing Eastern Europe: The Map of Civilization on the Mind of the Enlightenment* (Stanford: Stanford University Press, 1994); Larry Wolff, *The Idea of Galicia: History and Fantasy in Habsburg Political Culture* (Stanford: Stanford University Press, 2012); Maria Todorova, *Imagining the Balkans* (New York: Oxford University Press, 2009); Edward Ousselin, *The Invention of Europe in French Literature and Film* (New York: Palgrave Macmillan, 2009); Steven Seegel, *Mapping Europe's Borderlands: Russian Cartography in the Age of Empire* (Chicago: University of Chicago Press, 2012); Larissa M. L. Zaleska Onyshkevych and Maria Rewakowicz, eds., *Contemporary Ukraine on the Cultural Map of Europe* (Armonk, NY: M. E. Sharpe, 2014).

Prologue. Ukrainian Literature and Europe: Aporias, Asymmetries, and Discourses

GEORGE G. GRABOWICZ

Introduction

The idea of Europe, discussed and analysed at least since the end of the Second World War, but most intensely so in the decades leading up to and following the creation of the European Union, has given rise to dozens of books and hundreds if not thousands of articles, not to mention publications on the Internet.[1] Political and economic perspectives have shaped the vast majority of them; attention precipitously declines when intellectual history and literature are involved. The question of Ukraine and Europe yields an even more modest harvest of scholarly inquiries, reflecting the double bind of Ukrainian Studies: its generally small academic presence in the West on the one hand, and on the other the long night of Stalinism and post-Stalinist Sovietism that isolated Ukraine from the West, decimated its intellectual elite, and provincialized its discourse.[2] The revival of Ukrainian Studies in the West in the last three or four decades has made a significant difference, but the issue of Ukraine's relationship to Europe, especially in the area of literature, has seldom been directly addressed; the solitary publications in Ukraine that have approached this topic since independence exhibit partial and occluded vision.[3]

The very formulation of the topic as "Ukraine and Europe" suggests a fundamental dichotomy or opposition, which is then further complicated by multiple scenarios and ideologies of inclusion and exclusion. As intuitively true as this opposition may seem – and it draws on a thousand-year-old narrative and informs virtually all the studies that will be mentioned here – it is still subject to a range of qualifications. Each of its components, "Ukraine" and "Europe," as well as the way in which the relationship between them is perceived, are contingent and subject to further parsing. The terms of the subtitle of this discussion – aporias, asymmetries, and discourses – point to one such strategy of delimitation and interpretation, but others are possible. The deconstructionist and revisionist perspective that is implied here seems particularly timely for Ukrainian literary historiography as it emerges from its Soviet strictures and deeply ingrained colonial and postcolonial pathologies.[4]

What, then, is "Europe?" What is "Ukraine?" And what does one mean by "literary relations?" The simple answer is that these are quintessentially moving targets that defy simple definition. As Nietzsche succinctly put it: "definierbar ist nur das, was keine Geschichte hat" (only that can be defined which has no history).[5] One can begin, therefore, with the briefest of recapitulations of the "idea of Europe."

The Greek Europa, object of Zeus's mythological conquest, gave her name to one of the three known continents (the other two being Libya/Africa and Asia). She reminds us of the primacy of geography for identity. The first hypostasis of Europa as conscious self-definition is precisely in contrast to Persia and draws not just on geography but also culture and governance.[6] The distinction between the Greek (European) West and the Persian East became established in later antiquity, as Ihor Ševčenko notes, on the basis of the administrative division of the Roman Empire into its Western and Eastern parts, which was later echoed in the division of Christendom into two separate Christian Churches.[7] Two matters of consequence can be observed here: one is that from the beginning Europe is conceived of in opposition to another cultural and political entity, here Persia or "the East" (later it will be "the Turk" or "Russia"); the second is that those polarities will themselves shift with time, and what was once part of Europe – Byzantium – will become the East.[8]

The next and perhaps longest-lasting self-identification of Europe is through Christianity and the topos of its militant defence. The *antemurale Christianitatis* (bulwark of Christianity) establishes not just a border but also a competition as to who has attained the most merit in defending Europe or Christianity. (Among the major contenders were the Albanians, Croatians, Serbs, Poles, Hungarians, and Cossacks.)[9] A corollary to this is the fact that Byzantium, which vied for the title of "bulwark of Christianity,"[10] was also a victim of European Christianity, that is, of its militant projection, the Crusades. After the second of these (1145–9) the crusaders earned themselves the appellation of "wild beasts of the West," and during the fourth crusade (1203–4) the defenders of Christendom sacked the city that certainly considered itself to be (and arguably was) the bulwark of Christianity.[11]

The subsequent stages of the European idea – humanism and then the Enlightenment, Napoleonic Europe, and the recurring political ideal of European unification; the Europe of romanticism, of revolutions, and of the Holy

Alliance; nationalist Europe culminating in the twentieth-century European civil war conventionally known as the First and Second World Wars; and finally the ascendant utopia of the present-day European Union (a fiscally challenged utopia, as it turns out) – are all essentially congruent with European history itself; they have been conceptualized and examined in multifarious ways and require no elaboration here. But we will return to some of them, especially with respect to their universalistic, "Europe-projecting" functions.

While smaller in comparison, the question of Ukraine and, within that, of Ukrainian literature also bulks large and resists quick summation, and one is thus obliged to focus only on the overriding issues. The major issue, reflecting as it does a complex cultural and political history, is that Ukrainian literature is marked by profound discontinuities between its three fundamental historical periods – the Kyivan and later the Galician-Volhynian period (from the eleventh to the fourteenth century), the early modern (from the end of the sixteenth to the eighteenth century), and the modern (from the early nineteenth century to the present) – which are far more pronounced than in Western literatures or indeed in the neighbouring Polish and Russian cases. This discontinuity is manifest not only in political and state structures and institutions (an issue still plaguing Ukraine) but also in the arguably more basic matter of historical identity. Thus, at the beginning of the national revival in the nineteenth century, for one of its most enlightened and rationalist architects, Panteleimon Kulish (1819–97), it is a very real question whether the early modern period – which he himself is then studying and whose newly found sources he is publishing – truly fits the paradigm of the new Ukrainian literature in the vernacular: whether it is, in fact, Ukrainian.[12] If one considers the earliest, Kyivan period of Ukrainian literature, then its integration into Ukrainian literary historiography is a matter of the late nineteenth and early twentieth centuries, and its literary and artistic integration into the canon takes place as late as the interwar period of the twentieth century.[13]

A separate question concerns the reception of Ukrainian literature in or by Europe – which, of course, needs to be further differentiated, since the reception in the Austro-Hungarian Empire, of which Ukrainian (Ruthenian) territories are a constituent part throughout the nineteenth century, will arguably be significantly different from those of, say, France or Italy or England. The answers to this question will depend on cultural and political preconceptions prevailing in various parts of Europe, and also on the paradigms or modes of the reception – whether through the prism of exoticism or orientalism, as in Byron's *Mazeppa*, where Ukraine and Ukrainian history are assimilated into the general ambience of his "Eastern Tales,"[14] or of a no less prevalent nineteenth-century Rousseauism, which can be said to frame the early Russian, but even more the Polish and West European reception of Taras Shevchenko and, implicitly, much early nineteenth-century Ukrainian literature. A further qualification of the paradigm of the wildness or exoticism of all things Ukrainian is its conflation with an implicitly political mission of "civilizing" these "wild lands" (*dzikie pola*), with fire and sword if need be – an objective that is paradigmatically proclaimed in Henryk Sienkiewicz's *Ogniem i mieczem* (With Fire and Sword, 1884), but is already implied in Polish romanticism, particularly in the works of Henryk Rzewuski and Michał Grabowski.[15]

Situating Europe

The relational or instrumental axis is central: the sense of what Europe is and what it does for Ukraine emerges – especially in the initial, protean, pre-thematized, or pre-ideological stage – not from geography, or some variant of metaphysics, but from the polarity itself. In short, *for Ukraine*, Europe – functionally, as the source of literary models, standards, and influences – may well be not only Poland (which in the usual, Western order of things would itself only be "Eastern Europe," if not actually "almost Europe") but also Russia (which usually, "normally," is cast as Europe's antipode or "anti-matter"). As much as this is often conceded or taken for granted (and stoutly denied by the essentialists), it requires closer examination and is, of course, one of our first aporias.

It is generally understood that whole periods of early modern Ukrainian literature, especially the Renaissance and the baroque, are intimately connected with the Polish literature of that time, and that the latter serves Ukrainian literature as the conduit for Western, European literary standards and models.[16] (This pattern will be repeated in later periods as well, especially that of romanticism.) Yet the same may be said of Russian literature. This is best recognized in relation to particular cases: for example, it is through Pushkin and Lermontov that Shevchenko receives access to Byron and his radical innovations in poetry, prose, and the projection of self. But it is also true of the larger, general picture. Modern Ukrainian literature, beginning with Kotliarevs'kyi at the turn of the nineteenth century, programmatically projects itself as provincial and as marked by a particular stylistic modality – the largely burlesque idiom of the so-called *kotliarevshchyna*.[17] The frame that prevails here, particularly in the first two decades of the nineteenth century, is that of Ukrainian literature as an addendum to imperial Russian literature – and in that frame Russian literature *eo ipso* serves as the model and carrier of European literary modes and developments. (For its part, Russian literature, particularly in the massive translation

project of Vasilii Zhukovskii, is also undergoing an intense course of acceler-
ated Europeanization.) Similar patterns apply in Western Ukraine with respect
to Polish and, in part, Austrian literature.

What situates Europe as a cultural model and source of influence, however, projecting the idea of Europe not in terms of political structures or ideas
(individualism, freedom, the social contract, etc.) but of literary and cultural
values – is arguably the postulate of literary universalism, couched above all
in the model of the Enlightenment. As has been variously argued, this is the
idea of Europe par excellence: Europe as a republic of letters, with a conjoin-
ing of Enlightenment and modernism that is epitomized in the French *Encyclopédie* (1751–72), in which the universalistic postulates of reason, progress,
and enlightenment become fundamental human values and generate models
for social structures. (Soon this conjuncture will be replicated in the founding
documents of the United States.) The earlier version of this is the Renaissance
and the values and poetics of humanism.

For all the ways in which romanticism rejects various Enlightenment and
classicist values, it also continues the momentum of universalism, on the one
hand by thematizing and developing the idea of Europe,[18] and, more generally,
on the other, through new core values and modes that come to light through
the discovery of the individual, the psyche, and the unconscious; of the "night
world" and with it the Gothic, the exotic, and the Oriental; of Ossian and the
"poetry of the North"; and of the collective and of nations, the *narod* and the
folk, and with them of folklore and ethnography. These are all implicitly universalizing, and they each attain all but universal cultural and literary extension. The same can be said for the values, agendas, and topoi that came to
replace them – those of realism and positivism and, even more so, modernism.
The latter is a particularly productive period for Ukrainian literature and the
one during which it attains its full maturity, but also when it becomes the target
of a ruthless Stalinist and Soviet campaign to press Ukrainian literature into a
more manageable, provincial mould. In that process modernism emerges – and
is proscribed by the Soviet system – as an essentially European modality. After
Ukraine's achievement of independence the status of modernism as integral to
the Ukrainian literary tradition is seemingly reasserted, along with an admix-
ture of postmodernism. The tonic effects of this are more virtual than real,
however.

The archetypal comparative dilemma remains: what do you compare? Given
the range of national literatures, what specific literary connection provides that
enabling, if not altogether essential and exhaustive, ground for comparison that

then can shed light on the underlying issue of Europeanness? For as central as any one European literature may be, it can hardly represent Europe in total, although it may point to a typology or pattern. But, for Ukraine, one literature more than others may play such a role: that of neighbouring and at least nominally (although not self-avowedly) Slavic Poland. No other literature is both so highly and programmatically integrated into the Western European literary frame and values, and yet at the same time so organically close to the Ukrainian in historical, social, and political, if not always cultural, setting. In a word, for an extraordinarily long period, roughly for the duration of the Polish-Lithuanian Commonwealth from the fifteenth century to the eighteenth, Poland is both functionally and materially, indeed organically, Ukraine's Europe. In the *longue durée* Ukraine's connection to Poland is arguably as central as the Russian-Ukrainian interface, although the latter is crucial in that it coincides with the modern period and hence the period of nation formation. Indeed, the latter relationship continues into the present, whereas the Polish frame is for the most part historically closed by the mid-nineteenth century when the Ukrainian-Polish national divergence or divorce becomes politically conceptualized and then finalized in the course of the latter half of the century. But while specific periods, particularly romanticism and, more recently, the interwar period, have drawn their share of attention, the overall relationship has not been truly examined.

Varieties of Asymmetry

The earliest, Kyivan (and later Galician-Volhynian) Rus' period, which Soviet literary historians divided into an early and late medieval style, and which Dmytro Chyzhevs'kyi distinguished into separate "Monumental" and "Ornamental" periods, seems to project a surface parity with Europe, appearing as relatively rich and varied when compared to the Western literatures.[19] And its generic distortion – the overwhelming predominance of religious or church genres and themes – also does not seem all that peculiar. But this in fact hides a telling, "imprinted" or indeed "colonial" asymmetry. As argued first by the Ukrainian scholar Oleksandr Bilets'kyi in 1959 and the Russian scholar Igor' Eremin in 1964, a special and unique relationship was at play here between Rus'/Ukraine and Byzantium (which then functioned as its Europe).[20] The gist of the aporia here is that while in this period (the eleventh and twelfth centuries) Byzantium was experiencing, as Eremin put it, a remarkable renascence of the classics, with study and commentary of Homer, Pindar, Aristophanes, Plato, and Aristotle, and religious literature was itself experiencing exegesis and polemics, "this broad range of socio-literary activity ... in Byzantium passed without leaving a trace on contemporary Rus'. Not one of the more or less notable Byzantine authors of that period was translated, not even the most outstanding – Michael Psellus (1018–78), theologian and philosopher, historian and philologist, orator and poet."[21]

In short, what Rus' received were various medieval "Reader's Digests," various compilations, condensations, anthologies, and selections – all of them belonging, basically, to popular and "low" literature. As Bilets'kyi put it, "only that was translated which was absolutely indispensable for the new Christian cult, and which by its properties and content would further the hegemony of Byzantine culture over the 'barbarians' that it was civilizing."[22] The most portentous component of this cultural imperialism, the worst of the "poisoned pill" that this hypostasis of Europe was offering Rus'/Ukraine, however, was its official, "high" language. For Old Church Slavonic, the "sacred" language that came with the Cyrillo-Methodian mission by way of Bulgaria could only open the smallest of canons: the Gospels and some liturgical texts. The world of Greek and Latin was closed to it.[23] For Omeljan Pritsak the cultural low point for Ukrainian history was precisely the decision of the Kyivan Princes Volodymyr (958–1015) and his son Iaroslav (983–1054) to accept Byzantine cultural hegemony and this language with it; the fact that it came at the very outset, and that its basis was this radical cultural asymmetry, suggests that its workings would have multiple repercussions. This idea, however, is hardly to be identified only with Pritsak and the Harvard School he animated: it inheres in a "Europeanist" perspective that stretches back to the religious polemics of the late sixteenth and early seventeenth centuries – to Piotr Skarga, Meletii Smotryts'kyi, and Kasiian Sakovych – and continues to this day. The irony (or another aporia) is that this "Greek gift" also came from Europe. But not the right Europe, as it turned out.

The period of the Renaissance presents another striking case of asymmetry. The fundamental question that confronts the scholar is whether one can speak of a Ukrainian/Rus' Renaissance and humanism, or only of Renaissance and humanism on Ukrainian territories with putatively identifiable Ukrainian or Ruthenian authors, but within the overarching framework of the literature and culture of the Polish-Lithuanian Commonwealth. The issue is not only terminological or one of perspective. To the extent that one can speak of authorial self-identification[24] and of a cultural profile of Rus' in that period (the issue with Muscovy is simpler – it had almost no access to Renaissance or humanist thought), one can postulate that Rus' culture at that time was reflective only marginally – in selected, individual instances and certainly not in an institutional fashion – of the values and structures of the European Renaissance and humanism. Generalizations about this period are rendered difficult by a great paucity of sources. While some are now being recovered and the picture somewhat fleshed out, the period from the mid-thirteenth century to the late sixteenth is one approaching total silence which, when juxtaposed against the Europe of Dante, Boccaccio, Petrarch, and Chaucer, could not offer a starker contrast. This silence, however, cannot be read in traditional fashion as but the consequence of the ravages of the Mongol invasion of 1240, but must be seen as a product of a totalizing Orthodox Rus' religious mindset. (Orthodoxy is then the principal modality of Rus', and leaving it is tantamount to leaving Rus', as later writers will assert.)[25] This mindset was a consequence of various religious and, especially, monastic developments in the course of the fourteenth through sixteenth centuries, particularly hesychasm with its dualism and mysticism. It shaped an attitude that in large measure rejected not just secular learning but all things of this world, including literature and even writing itself.

A paradigmatic instance of this attitude is the first major Ukrainian writer of the early modern period, Ivan Vyshens'kyi (ca. 1545/50–1620?), whom Chyzhevs'kyi placed now in the Renaissance, now in the baroque. Both choices are schematic, and neither is correct, since Vyshens'kyi, the now canonical progenitor of early modern Ukrainian literature, is in fact unequivocally, in vivid textual form and message, not a part of either cultural or literary system: he categorically rejects not just the Europeanism of the Polish-Lithuanian Commonwealth, its Catholicism, learning, and institutions, but all things of this world – for they are all of the devil – and passionately argues for a different path for Rus'.[26] He writes as if constantly under duress and in protest against the exigency of having to write, to stoop to speech and intersubjectivity when the monastic ideal is silence and meditation, but his passion and unequivocal anti-Europeanism is a major wellspring of Ukrainian literature.

Around that time there are, of course, various other, more conventional and above all institutional sources for the literary revival, but none of them matches Vyshens'kyi for passion and spiritual gravitas. In their totality they all respond to the perceived threat to Rus' in the wake of the Church Union of Brest of 1596. In effect, that union with the Church of Rome galvanizes the sense that Europe and Europeanism is a form of deracination, self-abnegation, and an abandonment of Rus' identity in the face of a highly seductive European culture, more powerful and more enabling than one's own. Ivan Borets'kyi's *Perestoroha* (Warning, 1605–6) gives this full articulation:

> Not having any learning of their own, they [the Ruthenians] began to send their children to receive Roman instruction, and these children learned not only the instruction, but the [Latin] faith as well. And thus, step by step, by their learning they enticed all the Rus' lords into the Roman faith so that the descendants of the

Rus' princes were rebaptized from the Orthodox faith into the Roman one, and changed their family names and their Christian names as if they had never been descendants of their pious forebears. As a result, Greek Orthodoxy lost its fervor and was scorned and neglected.[27]

Just a few years later, in 1610, Meletii Smotryts'kyi in his powerful *ΘΡΗΝΟΣ to iest lament iedyney s. powszechney apostolskiej wschodniey cerkwie* (Threnos, or Lament of the Holy Universal Apostolic Eastern Church) gives on the opening pages a catalogue of dozens and dozens of noble, indeed magnate Rus' families – the Ostroz'ki, Sluts'ki, Zaslavs'ki, Zbaraz'ki, Vyshnevets'ki (Wiśniowiecki), Sangushky, Chartorys'ki, Solomyrets'ki, Masal's'ki, and many others – who left the Rus' faith and became Catholic and "Polish." These families would become the very backbone of the new Polish cultural elite for centuries to come. (In some instances, as with Jeremi Wiśniowiecki in the Khmel'nyts'kyi period of the mid-seventeenth century, they became fierce enemies of the Ukrainian political and national revival.) The stance that Smotryts'kyi adopts is the obverse of the European ideal, or rather its indictment from the point of view of a "weaker," "non-competitive," or colonized culture (one should also recall the centuries-old "Greek gift"). This colonized culture is, however, still able to articulate its hemorrhaging and the threat to its identity, and to bemoan the very concrete loss of its elite in the face of a hegemonic and triumphant Westernism. In effect, these foundational texts of early modern Ukrainian literature introduce a discourse of anti-Europeanism that will become a major component of Ukrainian literature in later periods. Characteristically, this discourse is not just nativist; rather, it also articulates universal cultural concerns (which recent scholarship has increasingly come to recognize) and starkly formulates the dilemma of Europe versus local or traditional identity. (It also reminds us that in cultural transactions nothing is for free.)

The highly developed Ukrainian baroque, extending from the early seventeenth to the late eighteenth century, has understandably drawn concerted scholarly attention. As rich and interesting as Ukrainian baroque literature is, however, it is still highly skewed and quite incomplete with respect to such typical Western (and Polish) baroque features or modes as erotic poetry, drama, epic poetry, and various forms of prose.[28] It addresses religious, as well as popular, themes and audiences, and thereby reveals its social and institutional bases. Characteristically, even a patriotic Ukrainian writer like Danylo Bratkovs'kyi (Daniel Bratkowski, mid-seventeenth century–1702), a nobleman who takes up arms with the Cossacks against the Polish side and loses his life for this, publishes his poetry in Polish, since the genre (secular, epigrammatic, ironic, and satiric verse) requires it; at the time, this genre-modality is simply not available in Ukrainian.[29]

The paradigmatic moment of asymmetry in our purview is the period of the Enlightenment. For Europe it signals both the formation of the universal values noted above and of modern states. For Ukraine, the eighteenth century and especially its second half is the time of its greatest cultural and political somnolence: it is the period of the gradual dissolution of Ukraine's political autonomy (vested in the Cossack Hetman State) after the defeat at Poltava in 1709, and of Ukraine's inexorable transformation (especially after the partitions of Poland) into a province of the Russian Empire. Given this *force majeur* of political history, the bulk of the Enlightenment discourse of Ukrainian literature is shifted into a later period, in effect the second half of the nineteenth century, when the Ukrainian nation-building process assumes critical mass and momentum. This incongruity or absence of chronological equivalency may be disconcerting, or add fuel to the claim that Ukraine's culture is "incomplete," but it should not distress our historiography: literary history is not an exact science and its laws are not Euclidian. This is a given in comparative studies where, for example, one gives full credence to Slavic romanticism even though it appears about three decades or so behind English romanticism.

In the eighteenth century the discourse of the Ukrainian Enlightenment is largely confined to the political and historical frame and to but a few works, most notably *Razhovor Malorosii z Velykorosiieiu* (Dialogue of Little Russia with Great Russia, 1762) and *Istoriia Rusov* (History of the Rus'), which by all indications was written sometime in the early nineteenth century. Both draw on the syncretic genre of the Cossack chronicles and the political and social thought of the Cossack elite. While qualifying as literature, they are also quintessentially political treatises; their hybridity is itself a feature of the transitional nature of late eighteenth- and early nineteenth-century thought in Ukraine.

The shift from Enlightenment to romantic thought and values occurs by way of Russian and Ukrainian pre-romanticism and especially through the Decembrists and their legacy. Most striking here, especially in the case of Kondratii Ryleev, but also of Orest Somov, Sergei Glinka, and other writers, is that in formulating their general historicist and reformist interests and articulating their values of freedom, republicanism, and self-sacrifice for the nation's cause, they take Ukraine and the history of the Cossacks as their prime historical models. For a curious, intense, and brief moment, more or less the decade between the fall of Napoleon and the Decembrist uprising of 1825, Ukraine becomes a major theme in Russian imperial discourse. Cossack history, folklore, ethnographic topics, local lifeways, and the old Kyivan past (which, however, is then seen as unquestionably Russian) occupy a prominent place in literature, particularly up to the 1830s when a different pattern begins to emerge.[30] A similar development occurs in the Polish literature of this time, above all in the writings of the pre-romantics Julian Ursyn Niemcewicz and Tymon Zaborowski and the subsequent "Ukrainian school of Polish poetry." This Ukrainian school is traditionally regarded as comprising Antoni Malczewski, Seweryn Goszczyński, and Józef Bohdan Zaleski, but it also includes the eminent poet Juliusz Słowacki. Ukraine, particularly Cossack Ukraine, becomes an integral and in its early stages perhaps the dominant theme in Polish romanticism. In both literatures and in the critical discourses attending them the Ukrainian material is treated as naturally belonging to, and merely a local part of, the dominant (Russian or Polish) cultural and literary tradition. Indeed, it is not only seen as highly colourful and exotic but is enthusiastically touted as the very essence of the new romantic spirit. Ukraine – its traditions, people (*narod/naród*, or *lud*), folklore, and heroic and turbulent past – become the "ticket" for cashing in on the fashionable, new, and quintessentially European romanticism. To the extent that both Polish and Russian literatures, each with its particular nuances, are then part of "European literature," Ukraine and Ukrainian literary topoi also become part of that European canon. They do so, however, as objects rather than subjects, as the contents of a literary portmanteau (Ukrainian subject matter is packed into Polish or Russian literature). Given subsequent developments, however (to continue with this metaphor of packing, conveyance, and borders), they are also a kind of contraband – material that, if not actually smuggled, soon comes to be claimed by its rightful owners.

Modern Ukrainian literature thus begins with a double aporia: it enters the public (European) stage not under its own power but packed into more established carriers like Polish and Russian literature, and it does so without a fully conscious or articulated literary identity, let alone programs or strategies of development. These were all to come later, and their creation was precisely the task of discourses and institutions. In the early decades of the nineteenth century, particularly in the Russian Empire, Ukrainian literature is all but explicitly cast by its own practitioners as a local or regional addendum to the all-Russian imperial literature, with a studied avoidance or fudging of the implicit claim to literary separatism that writing in another language conveys. The phenomenon of *kotliarevshchyna*, of Ukrainian writing in the vernacular and in the burlesque mode, was its prime early articulation.[31] Apart from political will and cultural readiness, which clearly required gestation and critical mass, it was also a matter of surviving in a police state – an empire that did not have genuine imperial ethnic or cultural tolerance; that was toying, then as now, with the contradictory notion of a Russian national empire; and that had been highly suspicious since the time of Mazepa in the early eighteenth century of Ukrainian separatism (and treachery). Not surprisingly, it soon cast the nascent Ukrainian literary revival as a form of political separatism and responded (in 1847, 1863, and 1876) with a series of trials and administrative measures officially banning or otherwise severely limiting the use of the Ukrainian language and the pursuit of its literature. Not surprisingly, too, as soon as Ukrainian literature began to assert itself in the late 1830s and early 1840s, the leading and "progressive" Russian literary critic of that time, Vissarion Belinskii, came out adamantly against it.[32] Such was the inhospitable political climate in which the bulk of nineteenth-century Ukrainian literature existed. A major, but only partial, antidote was provided by the Ukrainian literary scene in Galicia, in the constitutional Hapsburg monarchy. For its part, the synergy between Ukrainian literature under the Russian and the Austro-Hungarian Empires had a decisive impact on the eventual political unification of the modern Ukrainian nation.

Modern Terms of Engagement

As noted at the outset, Ukrainian literature's relationship with Europe – or, more precisely, its increasingly sophisticated and programmatic conceptualization of this relationship – becomes a fundamental mechanism for articulating its identity in the course of both the nineteenth and the twentieth centuries; as one can expect, this course was neither smooth nor consistent. Generally speaking, the process subtends five periods. Demarcations between them at times correspond to discrete historical or political markers, but to a much greater extent the periods overlap: 1) the romantic (from the 1830s to the 1860s and beyond), 2) the realist (from the mid-nineteenth century to the early twentieth century and into the present), 3) the modernist (from the turn of the twentieth century to the end of the 1920s and the very early 1930s, but also including interwar Western Ukrainian literature and post–Second World War émigré literature and then the revival of modernism in independent Ukraine), 4) Soviet socialist realism (from the late 1920s to the present), and 5) anti-Soviet, crypto-Soviet, and post-Soviet writing (from the 1960s to the present, with independence in 1991 serving as a significant but hardly all-important watershed). When looked at more closely, the process is more a kaleidoscope than a sequence of periods, but this mélange does reflect its fluid and institution-deprived nature.

The contribution of the romantic period lies both in the elemental and largely unreflecting assumption of Western models and practices – Byron, Sir Walter Scott, the collecting of folklore and oral material à la Thomas Percy and the

Brothers Grimm, disquisitions on poetry, the folk, and national character in the spirit of the German philosophers – and in the pointed and programmatic discussion of the relationship and the gap between Ukrainian literature and Europe. The appropriation of Western models may occur subliminally, as it did in the case of Levko Borovykovs'kyi's translations of Mickiewicz's "Farys" and "Sonety krymskie" (Crimean Sonnets) in the 1820s. The significance of these translations, excellent though they were, might have been modest enough were it not for the fact that their language is utterly modern mid- to high-level Ukrainian hardly distinguishable from the language of the Kyivan Neoclassicists of the 1920s. The impact they had on the development of the poetic language has never been adequately assessed, but it must have been groundbreaking; clearly, they constituted early assertions of the dignity of the language. For the most part the "elemental" or default tactic of Ukrainian writers was to adapt for Ukrainian literature existing Polish or Russian borrowings or translations from Western literatures. The intermediaries at first were such figures as Michał Grabowski in Polish literature (who subsequently articulated a theory of the Scottian novel as the national genre: the *powieść narodowa*, or novel of the people) and, in the Russian, Vasilii Zhukovskii (who programmatically translated a broad range of European poetry, especially ballads), and Aleksandr Pushkin, the major mediator of Byron. In time the process continues with other writers. While hardly inclined to a European-centred vision or program, Shevchenko mentions Walter Scott, Robert Burns, and the Panslavists Vuk Karadžić and Pavel Šafárik in his introduction to the ultimately unpublished *Kobzar* of 1847, explicitly stating that such international and implicitly European – and pointedly non-Russian, that is, non-regional and not self-marginalizing – standards need to be stringently applied to the writing and publishing of Ukrainian literature.[33]

The programmatic and polemical introduction of European values and achievements not only as a standard for emulation but as an indictment of the laziness and backwardness of Ukrainian literary culture is primarily associated with the name of Panteleimon Kulish, the second major figure in this period after Shevchenko. While his writings are voluminous and often contradictory, his emphasis on reaching back to the sources of culture and civilization, and hence absorbing the legacy of Europe, is constant and unvarying. It situates him both in the romantic and in the positivist traditions. Perhaps the most striking articulation of this position is to be found in the poem "Do ridnoho narodu" (To My Own Nation), subtitled "Podaiuchy iomu ukraïns'kyi pereklad Shekspirovykh tvoriv" (As I Present it with a Ukrainian Translation of the Works of Shakespeare), where the dedication turns into a forceful condemnation of a national tradition that, as Kulish sees it, values mindless exploits of bravery and self-destruction – the cult of "ruin" – over the task of building culture through universal values.[34]

Kulish's poem is perhaps the first programmatic and rationalist formulation of the cult of the Word, of language and literature as national bastion, and of the word-as-state (*derzhava slova*) that came to be the central leitmotif of modern Ukrainian literature, particularly in the twentieth century.[35] This cult would also draw on Shevchenko's mythical mode, his millenarian vision, and the centrality of the Word for his poetry.[36] But what stands out here is the harshness of Kulish's charge, later echoed by Ivan Franko in the introduction to his poem "Moisei" (Moses, 1905). It reveals not just an intellectual agenda or program but also barely concealed angst, self-flagellation, even self-abasement with respect to Europe, as well as a symbolic projection of the Other as a model of unachievable excellence and virtue.[37] The degree to which this attitude functions as a kind of collective neurosis and conceals resentments that may emerge in even stronger outbursts of antipathy is a subject for further inquiry.

What is particularly interesting in the case of Kulish, however, and substantiates the notion that Europe can assume various hypostases along the culture-barbarism axis (for Kulish this was the line between the values of Enlightenment on the one hand and the ravages of armed anarchy, ceaseless revolts, and "ruin" that characterize Ukrainian history on the other) is his belief that Russia and even the Russian tsars, particularly Peter I and Catharine II, can be a source of culture. For Shevchenko (and the earlier Cossack Hetmanate elite on which much of Shevchenko's intellectual model relied) and, under his impact, the Ukrainian national movement, Peter and Catherine were anathema as incarnations of the imperial policy of integration, homogenization, and subjugation. Kulish's revisionism, expressed in his program of *kul'turnytstvo* (enculturation), by placing universal culture and enlightenment over native culture and independence, laid the ground for his own eventual isolation within the very literature and national movement he did so much to further.

Before considering the central figure of the realist or positivist period, Mykhailo Drahomanov, one should note that the official Soviet prioritization of realism (or critical realism) had not only its avowed Marxian ideological cause but also its covert nationalist agenda. Soviet literary and cultural studies in effect propounded, even fetishized a traditional Russocentrism, promoting a colonial vision in which all things Ukrainian depended on the Russian model, the "older brother" of Soviet iconography. This process involved a simulacrum – the replacement of the model of Europe with that of Russia, not as the functional stand in for Europe that it was (and that it was seen to be by, say, Belinskii, who claimed that only through Russia and the Empire could Ukraine get a seat at the table of civilization), but in an essentialized, ideological, and ought-to-be-mode. In effect, stating Ukraine's functional subordination to Russia a) made it "eternally" subordinate to Russia in the guise of its provincial younger brother and b) circumscribed Ukraine's very ability to grow into a normal modern nation. This restriction of Ukraine's identity to that of a province, region, or "younger brother" and hedging on its autonomy and identity as a fully fledged subject of history and culture was also predicated on implicitly denying (and later limiting by administrative or police fiat) its right to external contacts, most specifically with Europe. Thus, to the very end of the Soviet Union to fly from Kyiv to Warsaw, let alone Paris or London, one had to go through Moscow. In the nineteenth century the restrictions were various and more subtle, but also directed at channeling in various institutional ways the ability of the Ukrainian discourse to engage freely with the Western, European one. Such constraints, applied through the institutions of censorship, education, canon formation, publishing, and the press, reached their symbolic high point in the 1876 Ems Ukase, which forbade most publishing in Ukrainian in the Russian Empire. These prohibitions struck at something fundamental: the right of the subject to exist in his own right, to enjoy self-determination and identity and, in particular, to use his own language. The full history of this process is yet to be written, and its repercussions are still to be fully conceptualized in terms of modern postcolonial thought.

In any serious discussion of Ukrainian literature and Europe, indeed of Ukraine in the modern, international context, the figure and legacy of Mykhailo Drahomanov (1841–95) must occupy centre stage. While he clearly dominates his period, beginning with the 1870s, his legacy extends far beyond it. His most general impact on Ukrainian and, indeed, Russian and East European thought rested on his articulation of a rational, progressive, largely socialist political philosophy that placed prime importance on civil and national rights and enlightened governance. In intellectual terms Drahomanov almost single-handedly – and then with a cohort of disciples – reoriented Ukrainian thought from romantic and affective populism to rational and critical analysis and, in the span of a generation, made it compatible with the European. In political terms his impact was even more far-reaching: through his writing, later continued by the foremost Western Ukrainian writer, Ivan Franko, he inscribed on the political consciousness of Western Ukrainians the imperative of *sobornist'* – the need to unite with their fellow countrymen in Eastern Ukraine ("Great Ukraine") in one nation (with the actual state structures to be worked out in time). In a few decades this imperative became fact as Ukrainian Galician society overwhelmingly accepted a Ukrainian identity – which was symbolically asserted in the union of Western Ukraine with the Ukrainian National Republic in the East in January 1919.

Remarkably, all of this came about as part of an integrated and consistent, although not explicitly formulated project, that conjoined a multifaceted, long-term goal of intellectual, artistic, and literary Europeanization of the Ukrainian cause and the Ukrainian discourse with the more fundamental cause of establishing Ukraine as a subject, not an object, of history. This was a nation-building project predicated on the universal (Enlightenment) postulate that all peoples have the right to self-determination; it antedated by a century and a half the axiom of today's Polish civil rights movement: *Nic o nas bez nas* (Nothing that concerns us will be done without us).[38] Several features define this agenda, and they all limn the central fact that the Ukrainianist and Ukraine-building agenda is also an essentially Europeanist one. For one, on the personal level, as a political émigré living first in Geneva (1876–89) and then in Sofia (from 1889 until his death in 1895), Drahomanov devoted all his multifaceted efforts – scholarly, publicistic, as editor, critic, publisher, and public intellectual – to the Ukrainian cause. He chose a programmatic pen name, "Ukraïnets'" (a Ukrainian), affirming the political and European usage of the new ethnonym, which had been in intellectual circulation only since the 1840s – the first to use it in a political sense was Panteleimon Kulish. With profound insight, and before this notion was fully crystallized, Drahomanov understood the Ukrainian cause to be not so much political (although it was that too) as discursive: it involved the shaping of public opinion, *y compris* European public opinion. It was paradigmatic for his outlook that his paper, "La littérature ucrainienne proscrite par le gouvernement Russe" (Ukrainian Literature, Proscribed by the Russian Government), later published as a pamphlet, was read at the 1878 International Literary Congress in Paris that was chaired by Victor Hugo, and that an Italian version, *La letteratura di una nazione plebea* (The Literature of a Plebeian Nation), was published in 1881. Drahomanov was a constant contributor (under a pseudonym, to be sure) to the liberal St Petersburg journal *Vestnik Evropy*, continually engaging with key issues and asserting the Ukrainian presence.

Second, this assertion and projection of Ukraine and Ukrainian studies was programmatically multifaceted, involving along with the fields already mentioned also the academic pursuit of folklore and ethnography, source studies, law and legal history, religion, and philosophy.[39] In effect, Drahomanov's work was the Ukrainian equivalent of the paradigmatic Enlightenment project, the French *Encyclopédie* – delayed by only about one century. Throughout, this was also an institution-building project, involving a diverse range of actors: political parties, publications, associations, research projects, and networks of activists. Finally, despite straitened circumstances, through a massive epistolary effort Drahomanov was able to recruit for this project followers and disciples from at least two subsequent generations: first Franko and his collaborator Mykhailo Pavlyk, thereby cementing its Galician base, and then his niece, Larysa Kosach. Under the pseudonym Lesia Ukraïnka, given to her by her mother (Drahomanov's sister), Larysa Kosach proceeded to become a pillar of turn-of-the-century Ukrainian literature, although in a modernist vein and not entirely according to her uncle's blueprint. By the time of Drahomanov's death in 1895 his vision of a European Ukraine – of a people and culture that were not an adjunct to or a fiefdom of either the Romanov or the Habsburg Empires but more like equals of other European nations – was bearing fruit. 1895 also marked the appearance of Iuliian Bachyns'kyi's *Ukraina irredenta* that, with great political rigor, argued the inevitability of Ukraine's political independence – and was a text that had earlier been shown to Drahomanov.

With modernism the picture is much brighter. In recent decades the topic has received increasing and sophisticated attention.[40] The range and depth of Ukrainian modernism is greater than what we may have supposed,[41] but its mass, extent, and quality are hardly comparable to those of various Western European modernisms; it is also more circumscribed when compared to its Polish and Russian counterparts. Despite that asymmetry, however, it is precisely with modernism and the avant-garde that Ukrainian literary and artistic culture attains basic parity with other national cultures and Ukraine in some key ways becomes part of Europe. This connection is especially evident in the first years of Soviet Ukraine, when the resources of a Ukrainian state are made available to support Ukrainian culture. That parity and the renascence of Ukrainian cultural life that animated it were short-lived: beginning with the onset of Stalinism in the late 1920s and early 1930s Ukrainian high culture was rolled back and marginalized. Characteristically, the campaign against modernism and against the presence or influence of Europe, with which it was identified, was much more intense in Ukraine than in Moscow or Leningrad. To be sure, the picture was qualified by the polycentric nature of Ukrainian literature of this time: Western Ukrainian literature under Poland in the interwar period and émigré literature after the Second World War. The modernist impulse in those settings, however, was constricted and largely defensive, the major exception being the New York Group of Ukrainian émigré poets (from the mid-1950s to the mid-1980s and beyond).

Apart from the *force majeur* of the political context, Ukrainian modernism was marked by other cultural and historical specificities. Internally, it manifested an East-West split into "spheres of influence." The poets of the "Moloda Muza" (Young Muse) and the prose writer Vasyl' Stefanyk, for example, were recipients of Polish-mediated Western influence, while Russian influence was especially evident around the end of the First World War in the poetry of Pavlo Tychyna and the writings of the Neoclassicists. With the establishment of Soviet Ukraine and the cultural renascence there in the 1920s, and given the basically moribund nature of Ukrainian literature in Poland in that decade, these distinctions become secondary. For its part, the seemingly "deracinated" nature of Ukrainian modernism in the post–Second World War émigré mode deserves further attention – as does, especially, its uneasy coexistence with the mainstream of Ukrainian émigré life.[42] Characteristically, in the immediate post–Second World War setting that mainstream was *in* Europe but not *of* it.

The socialist realism imposed under Stalin in the early 1930s can be seen as paradigmatic of Ukraine's forceful separation from Europe. The argument, fashionable in some quarters, that socialist realism is a variant of modernism, while plausible in some theoretical respects, is unpersuasive in its actual historical and cultural context and in the Ukrainian case in particular, where the enforcement of socialist realism led to unmitigated distortions of literary creativity and to basic suppression. Nonetheless, the nuances of the imposition of socialist realism, and the hybridity that resulted, can be very telling. While also evident in pictorial art, socialist realism is most provocatively present in the corpus of the outstanding Ukrainian writer of this period, the poet Pavlo Tychyna, whose middle and even late poetry – for example, the epic poem "Shablia Kotovs'koho" (The Sword of Kotovs'kyi, 1938) – shows a remarkable interpenetration of official cant and subtle modernist parody and decentring. While more evidence needs to be adduced and examined, the notion that the Europeanism introduced into Ukrainian literature in the relatively brief modernist interlude could be easily rolled back by ideological decree now seems to require rethinking. At the same time it seems clear that the wellsprings of inspiration for Tychyna and other important writers of the period were hardly confined to the Europeanist tradition, and that the native and the traditional were easily the more central.

Similar questions could be asked regarding the late Soviet phenomenon of dissident writing, or even the quasi-dissident writing of the so-called "Shistdesiatnyky" (the writers of the sixties). Do they articulate a form of Europeanism? Is any dissent against Sovietism and its strictures a form of Europeanism? The answer must be guarded. In its antitotalitarian pathos this discourse does share various core values with what we take as Europe, but it is also quite Soviet in other respects. As recent criticism has shown, its values were more Soviet than not. Its reliance on a range of collectivist and illiberal, not to say paleo- or archeo-realist assumptions about literature and the role of the writer, hardly associates it with modern Europe. In effect, all discussions about Europe are about values, ethical and esthetic values included. These late Soviet "anti-Soviet" articulations do perhaps constitute a form of Europeanism, but of an attenuated or "regional" kind.

While clearly interesting, the present state of Ukrainian literature vis-à-vis Europe should be left for a later discussion. As never before, Ukrainian writers, writing in both Ukrainian and Russian, are being translated into various European languages, especially Polish, German, and English, and are becoming commercially visible. Yuri Andrukhovych, Serhii Zhadan, Andrei Kurkov, Iurii Izdryk, Oksana Zabuzhko, and others are not perhaps household names, but for literary cognoscenti and critics they are on the map (again, especially in Poland and Germany); from a European perspective Ukrainian literature is not a *terra incognita*. The asymmetries discussed earlier are arguably smaller, although aporias abound. How well Ukrainian literature is actually understood and studied – the strength and depth of its academic or curricular presence – is another question. A still larger question is the meaning of Europe, or specifically of the interaction of Ukrainian literature with Europe, in the age of the Internet. How can one define the geopolitical or cultural reality of Europe in a medium that knows no political or cultural limitations?

In Ukraine, new light has been shed on competing discourses in contemporary Ukrainian literature. One essayist has argued that they are three in number: a conservative, basically traditionalist and largely retrograde "testimonial and rustic [TR] discourse" (for all practical purposes socialist realist in essence, but with admixtures of old-time nationalism and populism), a "neo-modernist" [NM] discourse, and a budding post-modernist [PM] one.[43] The case for, and the definition of, the first is strong; the latter two are more tentative, especially with respect to the line that supposedly separates them. For its part, the discussion of Ukrainian postmodernism has yielded some serious studies.[44] But in its present (especially political and cultural) setting, and in light of our discussion, the triad of postulated discourses arguably boils down to only two: a more or less conscious and often militant anti-Europeanist discourse (the TR mode) and a Europeanist one that leaves begging the question of the historicist and restorationist nature of contemporary Ukrainian neo-modernism.

Some Preliminary Conclusions

The tension between the European and the anti-European positions or orientations in the Ukrainian cultural process is an ongoing and perhaps even defining part of its character. The political situation at the time of writing (2011) seems to confirm this quite starkly. But this tension is hardly a new development. The 1596 Union of Brest with the Church of Rome and the ensuing massive polemical literature that lasted for the better part of two centuries is a major early example of it, with the Khmel'nyts'kyi uprising and the Mohyla Academy, respectively, as its key political and intellectual codas. The debate following the Union reflected a struggle on the one hand to "Europeanize" the Ukrainian/Ruthenian church, but in effect the whole body politic, and on the other to defend the identity of both in the face of assimilation by a more powerful, more advanced, and putatively more civilized Europe, as Ivan Borets'kyi perceptively saw it in the early seventeenth century. Europe was feared and not without reason. It was, moreover, a real Europe, not a specter or a rhetorical construct. It only happened to have as its primary hypostasis the Polish-Lithuanian Commonwealth. Part of the rhetoric from the Polish perspective is also clear in its disdain for, and fear of, the other side – from Skarga in his polemics to Sienkiewicz in his *Ogniem i Mieczem*, and then (switching genres, but not mode) to such things as the discourse of the Narodowa Demokracja (Endecja), the Polish nationalist movement of the first four decades of the twentieth century, and Jan Gerhard's *Łuny w Bieszczadach* (Glow over the Bieszczady, 1959), his novel about armed conflict between Poles and Ukrainians after the Second World War. And while this paradigmatic chain mixes genres and levels of discourse, it articulates a basic, common perspective on Ukraine and Ukrainians as reflecting an "eastern" or "Asiatic" heart of darkness (a perspective shared by some Ukrainians, including Kulish).

Just under 300 years after the Union of Brest, the attempt by Mykhailo Drahomanov to shift Ukrainian thought and cultural and political values decisively into a European mode is a major and heroic stage in Ukrainian intellectual history; through his followers Franko and Lesia Ukraïnka it was to become a major legacy. But it was not without its constant challengers, from the civilized and articulate populist Borys Hrinchenko to the uncivilized, voluntarist and fascistic Dmytro Dontsov. While the challenges last to this day, a deeper, informed assimilation of Drahomanov's perspective on and valuation of Europe has still not occurred within the mainstream (certainly the curricular mainstream) of contemporary Ukrainian society. It has happened, to be sure, among the Western-leaning intellectuals, but they are hardly a mainstream. Very tellingly, Drahomanov's corpus is as unavailable as it was over 120 years ago when his disciple Pavlyk solemnly promised to collect and publish the works of his (and Franko's) teacher – and the greatest Europeanizer in Ukrainian history, certainly of the modern period. But at least he is known. His early modern counterpart, Meletii Smotryts'kyi, is hardly remembered in the curriculum, or indeed the canon. And the only scholar that treats him with the requisite scholarly thoroughness and sophistication is a Western one.[45]

Unquestionably, the central figure of modern Ukrainian literature and modern Ukrainian nation formation is Taras Shevchenko, whose position on the

Europe/anti-Europe axis is, I think, profoundly and creatively ambiguous. He can be (and certainly has been) placed on the side of the European values of liberty and national self-realization, and commentators of various caliber and ilk have striven to show typological similarities between his world view and basic romantic (and therefore also European) modalities and values, which are there. But a strong case can be made that these do not constitute his central, defining core. His freedom-loving and antityrannical stance, his intellectual proclivity for Enlightenment values (almost all expressed in his Russian-language prose), and his invocation of a whole mass of rationalist, social, and reformist themes (also largely in the prose) are modulated by the fact that the spirit of freedom and of parrhesia (speaking truth to the powerful of this world without fear of consequence, which Foucault considers one of the central legacies of ancient Greece)[46] is directed against an empire that combines the "Asiatic" features of despotism and tyranny with the bureaucratic-rationalist modes and values that stem from Europe. And his ironic comments on the "wise Germans" who supplant the affective with the practical (metaphorically by planting potatoes on what were once battlefields soaked with blood) or scholars who determine where the sun should rise and set also speak to his fundamental position, which argues that, on some levels, especially on the level of prophecy, wisdom is folly.

One need not squabble over proportions. The issue is that there is a fundamental and transcendent (and at times irrational) archetypal, mythical, millenarian, and highly numinous thought that guides Shevchenko's writing, above all his poetry, and his sense of self and his mission, and it does not fit the European, or rather the Europeanist, mode as we have been speaking of it here. One can argue that there are typological features that link Shevchenko to elements of the European tradition – to the mystic Jakob Boehme, for example, as Chyzhevs'kyi has shown, or to Protestantism, as Drahomanov saw it, but the core of the matter is Shevchenko's ability to touch and evoke and to speak to the collective unconscious. This key is both profoundly native (*ridnyi*) and universal, and it is, moreover, innocent of the intellectual, historical, and cultural mediation of Europe. Shevchenko's poetry transcends it. And that is all to the good: it provides a model and animates rootedness and identity. Even when we assert the values of Europe, this aporia should still be in the back of our minds.

Notes

1 See especially the useful, if basically course level, Kevin Wilson and Jan van der Dussen, eds., *History of the Idea of Europe* (London: Routledge, 1995).
2 See my "Ukrainian Studies: Framing the Contexts," *Slavic Review* 54, no. 3 (1995): 674–90 and "The Soviet and Post-Soviet Discourses of Contemporary

Ukraine: Literary Scholarship, the Humanities and the Russian-Ukrainian Interface," in *From Sovietology to Postcoloniality*, ed. Janusz Korek, vol. 32, *Södertörn Academic Studies* (Södertörn: Södertörns högskola, 2007), 61–81.

3 Thus Dmytro Nalyvaiko's voluminous *Ochyma zakhodu: Retseptsiia Ukraïny v zakhidnii Ievropi XI–XVIII st.* (Kyiv: Osnovy, 1998) offers naive apologetics and devotes itself almost entirely to paraphrasing depictions of Ukraine in various Western sources; it pays little if any attention to the underlying cultural and literary structures, premises, biases, and issues. Two short essays with the same name, "Ukraine between East and West," one in Ivan L. Rudnytsky's *Essays in Modern Ukrainian History* (Cambridge, MA: Harvard University Press for the Harvard Ukrainian Research Institute, 1987), 1–9, the other in a collection of essays by Ihor Ševčenko, *Ukraine between East and West* (Edmonton: Canadian Institute of Ukrainian Studies Press, 1996), 1–11, deserve mention. Both provide valuable context and nuance; neither addresses the specific area of literature and literary relations.

4 See Hryhorii Hrabovych [George G. Grabowicz], "Literaturne istoriopysannia ta ioho konteksty," in *Do istoriï ukraïns'koï literatury* (Kyiv: Krytyka, 2003), 591–607.

5 Friedrich Nietzsche, *Zur Genealogie der Moral: Eine Streitschrift, Werke in drei Bänden* (Munich: Hanser), 2: 820.

6 Wilson and Dussen, *The History of the Idea of Europe*, 16–17.

7 Ševčenko, *Ukraine between East and West*, 2.

8 As Ševčenko notes, "while ca. 369 a Greek Church Father called Constantinople the 'presiding city of Europe,'starting with the tenth century and ending with the fifteenth, we have texts that can be cited to show that the Byzantines themselves did not consider their capital to be part of Europe." Ševčenko, *Ukraine between East and West*, 2.

9 In Ukrainian literature the earliest and most articulate claim to this role is made in the "Virshi na zhalosnyi pohreb" (Verses for the Mournful Funeral) of Kasiian Sakovych.

10 See Roger Kean, *Forgotten Power: Byzantium, Bulwark of Christianity* (Ludlow: Thalamus, 2006).

11 See Elizabeth and Michael Jeffries, "The 'Wild Beast from the West': Immediate Literary Reactions in Byzantium to the Second Crusade," in *The Crusades from the Perspective of Byzantium and the Muslim World*, ed. Angeliki E. Laiou and Roy Parviz Moyyahedeh (Washington, DC: Dumbarton Oaks Research Library and Collection, 2001). In this same spirit the Albigensian or Cathar Crusades of 1209–29 were visited by papal and royal decree on the Cathars of Languedoc to exterminate "heretics" – which later led to the first Inquisition. Whether these projects are more representative of Europeanness or of Christianity is a separate question.

12 Kulish discovered the mid-seventeenth-century poetry of Klymentii Zinoviiev, publishing it in the journal *Russkaia beseda* in 1859 and then in *Osnova* 1 (1861).

13 See, for example, Mykhailo Hrushevs'kyi's *History of Ukrainian Literature*, most of which first appeared in the 1920s. *Istoriia ukraïns'koï literatury v shesty tomakh i deviaty knyhakh* (Kyiv: Lybid', 1993–5); see also the heightened interest in the "princely period" of Kyivan Rus' among members of the so-called Prague School. It finds expression, for example, in Oksana Liaturyns'ka's *Kniazha emal'* (Prague: Proboiem, 1941).

14 See Mark Phillipson, "Alteration in Exile: Byron's 'Mazeppa,'" *Nineteenth Century Literature* 58, no. 3 (2003): 291–325.

15 See my "History and Myth of the Cossack Ukraine in Polish and Russian Romantic Literature" (PhD diss., Harvard University, 1975).

16 See, for example, Ryszard Łużny, *Pisarze kręgu Akademii Kijowsko-Mohylańskiej a literatura polska: Z dziejów związków kulturalnych polsko-wschodniosłowiańskich w XVII–XVIII wieku* (Cracow: Nakładem Uniwersytetu Jagiellońskiego, 1966).

17 See Hryhorii Hrabovych, "Semantyka kotliarevshchyny," in *Do istoriï ukraïns'koï literatury*, 291–305.

18 See, e.g., Paul Stock, *The Shelley-Byron Circle and the Idea of Europe* (New York: Palgrave, 2010).

19 See Hrabovych, *Do istoriï ukraïns'koï literatury*, 423–8. Christian Raffensperger's *Reimagining Europe: Kievan Rus' in the Medieval World* (Cambridge, MA: Harvard University Press, 2012), which appeared a year after this essay was written, addresses some of the issues treated here and argues that Kievan Rus' was indeed part of Europe, especially according to the markers or domains the book focuses on: "religion, marriage, culture" (2). One can agree with the dynastic politics component here, although the notion of culture remains somewhat more fraught. The argument of basic common ground with Europe is, to be sure, less problematic in the time frame envisioned (the narrative of this book ends with 1146, i.e., "the disintegration of central control in Rus'," see p. 4). The great bulk of the present essay, however, deals with the periods that follow (the Renaissance and after), when the asymmetries between the cultural frames and literary discourses become much more pronounced.

20 See Oleksandr Bilets'kyi, "Perekladna literatura vizantiis'ko-bolhars'koho pokhodzhennia," in *Zibrannia prats' u piaty tomakh,* vol. 1 (Kyiv: Naukova dumka, 1965), 128–87; I. P. Eremin, "O vizantiiskom vliianii v bolgarskoi i drevnerusskoi literaturakh IX–XII vv.," *Literatura drevnei Rusi* (Moscow: Nauka, 1966), 9–17; and my "Toward a History of Ukrainian Literature," *Harvard Ukrainian Studies* 1, no. 4 (1977): 407–523, here 444–6.

21 Eremin, "O vizantiiskom vliianii," 10.

22 Bilets'kyi, "Perekladna literatura," 130.

23 See Ihor Ševčenko's bleak assessment of this aporia in his "Three Paradoxes of the Cyrillo-Methodian Mission," *Slavic Review* 23, no. 2 (1964): 220–36.

24 In Ukrainian literary studies, both Soviet and post-Soviet, such figures as Paweł z Krosna/Pavlo Rusyn (c. 1470–1517), Iurii Drohobych/Jerzy Drohobycz (1450–94), and especially Stanisław Orzechowski/Stanislav Orikhovs'kyi (1513–66) are frequently claimed for Ukrainian literature without working out the cultural and institutional background. The pattern in Polish scholarship has also been all but exclusively Polonocentric, but the accompanying scholarly contextualization has been much more substantial.

25 See especially Meletii Smotryts'kyi's *Threnos* (1610).

26 See his *Knyzhytsia*; see also my "The Question of Authority in Ivan Vyšens'kyj: A Dialectics of Absence," *Harvard Ukrainian Studies* 12–13 (1988/1989): 781–94.

27 Mykhailo Vozniak, *Pys'mennyts'ka diial'nist' Ivana Borets'koho u Volyni i u L'vovi* (Lviv: Vydavnytstvo L'vivs'koho universytetu, 1954), 26. See also Vozniak, *Istoriia ukraïns'koï literatury*, vol. 2, pt. 1 (Lviv: Prosvita, 1921), 171, cited in Ševčenko, *Ukraine between East and West*, 118 (given here with minor stylistic emendations).

28 See my "Some Further Observations on 'Non-Historical' Nations and 'Incomplete' Literatures: A Reply to Ivan L. Rudnytsky," *Harvard Ukrainian Studies* 5, no. 4 (1981): 369–80.

29 See Daniel Bratkowski, *Świat po części przejrzany* (Cracow, 1697).

30 See my "History and Myth of the Cossack Ukraine."

31 See my "Semantyka kotliarevshchyny."

32 See my "Teoriia ta istoriia: 'horyzont spodivan'' i rannia retseptsiia novoï ukraïns'koï literatury," in *Do istoriï ukraïns'koï literatury*, 46–126, here 108–16.

33 Taras Shevchenko, "Peredmova do nezdiisnenoho vydannia 'Kobzaria,'" in *Povne zibrannja tvoriv u shesty tomax* (Kyiv: Vydavnytstvo Akademiï Nauk URSR, 1964), 6: 312–15.

34 The poem begins, "Nation without direction, without honor and dignity / Without truth in the legacies of wild forefathers, / You who emerged from the mindless courage / Of desperate drunkards and great brigands," and concludes, "Here is your universal mirror. Peer / Into it and see a miserable Asian. / Cease taking pride in your past plunder / And find your way to the family of cultured nations." Panteleimon Kulish, *Zibrannia tvoriv* (Lviv: Prosvita, 1908), 1: 255–6.

35 See, for example, the writings of such authors as Mykhailo Orest and Evhen Malaniuk.

36 See Hryhorii Hrabovych, "Shevchenko, iakoho ne znaiemo," in *Shevchenko, iakoho ne znaiemo: z problematyky symvolichnoï avtobiohrafiï ta suchasnoï retseptsiï poeta* (Kyiv: Krytyka, 2000), 111–13 and passim.

37 In a provocative article Alexander Kiossev has spoken of this as a near-universal self-abasement, even "self-colonization" of Eastern and Southern Europe, and paradigmatically the Balkans, vis-à-vis Western Europe. Alexander Kiossev, "Notes on the Self-Colonizing Cultures," *Scribd*, accessed on 22 September 2013, http://www.scribd.com/doc/43518916/Alexander-Kiossev-Notes-on-the-Self-Colonising-Cultures.

38 This maxim goes back to the principle of *nihil novi nisi commune consensu* (nothing new except by consent) that underlay the Sejm act of 1505 that forbade the king to issue laws without the consent of the nobility.

39 See Svitozor Drahomanov and Ivan L. Rudnytsky, "A Bibliography of Drahomanov's Major Works," in *Mykhaylo Drahomanov: A Symposium and Selected Writings*, vol. 2, no. 1 (3), *Annals of the Ukrainian Academy of Arts and Sciences in the US* (New York: Ukrainian Academy of Arts and Sciences in the US, 1952), 131–40.

40 Including from such scholars as Solomiia Pavlychko, Tamara Hundorova, and Vira Aheieva.

41 It certainly spans a larger time frame than I had earlier assumed. See my "Commentary: Exorcising Ukrainian Modernism," *Harvard Ukrainian Studies* 15, no. 3–4 (1991): 273–83.

42 See my "A Great Literature," in *The Refugee Experience: Ukrainian Displaced Persons after World War II*, ed. Wsevolod W. Isajiw, Yury Boshyk, and Roman Senkus (Edmonton: Canadian Institute of Ukrainian Studies, 1992), 240–68.

43 Volodymyr Ieshkiliev and Iurii Andrukhovych, eds., *Mala ukraïns'ka entsyklopediia aktual'noï literatury, Pleroma*, 3 (Ivano-Frankivs'k: Lileia NV, 1998), 81–2, 91–2, and 108–9.

44 See especially Tamara Hundorova, *Pisliachornobyl's'ka biblioteka: ukraïns'kyi literaturnyi postmodern* (Kyiv: Krytyka, 2005) and Roksana Kharchuk, *Suchasna ukraïns'ka proza: postmodernyi period* (Kyiv: Akademiia, 2008).

45 See David A. Frick's magisterial *Meletij Smotryc'kyj* (Cambridge, MA: Harvard University Press for the Harvard Ukrainian Research Institute, 1995).

46 See Michel Foucault, *Fearless Speech* (Los Angeles, CA: Semiotexte, 2001).

PART ONE

Ukraine in the Common Cultural Space of the European Baroque

Plurilinguism and Identity: Rethinking Ukrainian Literature of the Seventeenth Century

GIOVANNA BROGI BERCOFF

Linguistic pluralism has fueled emotional and politically charged debates not only in our days. It has been an enduring problem for the perception of Ukrainian Medieval and early modern literature and culture as a structure distinct in relation to the neighbouring literatures and cultures, and it still seems to be a major barrier to a consideration of Ukrainian culture and identity as a part of modern European belonging. Diachronic analysis of some of the major literary genres and most important works of the seventeenth century may help us to understand the identity of the premodern literary system of the Ukrainian lands. It may also illuminate this system's complex interrelation with the broad system of European literature and the narrower systems of Polish and Russian literature, the most influential ones in the region at the time.

Research into the relationship between the plurilinguism of Ukrainian literature and its very existence as a coherent system began in the 1960s. The present state of knowledge enables plurilinguism to be considered a matter of fact among educated people in the Ukrainian lands in the seventeenth and eighteenth centuries. Plurilinguism was a common phenomenon in prenational European countries from the late Middle Ages onward. It became particularly widespread among the elites of the *respublica litterarum* after Humanism made the intermingling or parallel use of Latin and vernacular languages normal throughout Europe. Slavic countries participated in this pan-European phenomenon with different degrees of intensity: Dalmatia, Croatia, Bohemia, and Poland may be considered as part of the mainstream of Renaissance and baroque culture and its plurilinguism, while Eastern (Orthodox) countries were only partially affected or cut off. Plurilinguism reached Ukraine, together with other typical products of European Humanism, and there acquired special weight because of the country's geo-historical situation, but it crossed the Russian border only later, in the eighteenth century.

The languages of the Polish borderlands and of the various Ukrainian regions, as well as of the literary works of the period, have become objects of investigation in recent decades. Yet many questions about them remain open or only partially answered. Some of these questions may be formulated as follows: Why did authors choose one language or another, and how was their choice connected to historical and political circumstances or social factors? Since a Polish canon began to be conceptualized as early as in the seventeenth century, is it possible also to sketch a posteriori a literary system forming a coherent structure that, in spite of the different languages used, may be considered a canon of Ukrainian literature of the seventeenth century? Are there criteria that would permit consideration of the works of poets and writers as belonging exclusively or specifically to that postulated canon? Would such a construction imply the deconstruction of another literary canon, just as the construction of a new nation implies a deconstruction of a previously existent political body? The examination of some of the more important works of the late Renaissance and baroque periods suggests that language was an important but not a sufficient criterion of cultural and protonational identification. There were large overlaps between the Ukrainian literature on the one hand, and the Polish and Russian on the other. Authors and works may be seen as carrying various identities – whether viewed through the prism of their self-perceptions, or that of modern scholarship employing the most "objective" criteria possible. However, many markers allow us to place certain works and authors in a central position within a coherent system that may be considered to be a recognizable Ukrainian canon. Like other literary systems, the Ukrainian one participated in a larger European structure of recognized principles and values, as well as in neighbouring systems that interacted at various levels, at different times taking more or less central or peripheral positions. A full analysis of such problems would take the space of a book. Here I shall merely try to consider some significant examples.

Between Religion and History

Some of the most remarkable works by Ukrainian and Belarusian literati in the Polish-Lithuanian Commonwealth in the seventeenth century were written in Polish. They reflected the specificity of the Ukrainian Orthodox revival of Mohyla's time (it occurred in a socium different from that of the neighbouring societies and religious environments), and at the same time adhered to the set of rules of the international *respublica litterarum*. What makes them recognizable as Ukrainian? How do they interact with analogous literary works that issued from neighbours who at the same time were political dominators?

Syl'vestr Kosov's *Paterikon abo żywoty SS. Oycow Pieczarskich* (Patericon, or Lives of the Holy Fathers of the Caves, Kyiv, 1635) and Afanasii Kal'nofois'kyi's *Teraturgēma* (Miracles, Kyiv, 1638), though different in beauty and method, reflect the same kind of erudite genre, historical, ecclesiastical, and encyclopedic character that was cultivated in the Catholic countries in order, on the one hand, to meet the expectations of the Roman Church of the Counter-Reformation and, on the other, to serve the local pride and missionary intent of monastic orders and venerated religious centres.[1] There were various reasons for Kosov's and Kal'nofois'kyi's choice of the Polish language. Polish was the language of education and state in the Commonwealth. Its "cultural pressure"[2] was augmented by social prestige and literary refinement. It also ensured intelligibility and visibility in the social milieus that comprised the Polish establishment and that needed to be convinced of the cultural and sacral dignity of the re-established Orthodox Church and, through it, of the society – ecclesiastical leaders and Cossack notables – that was the bearer of that religious and cultural code. Religious, intellectual, and literary values expressed a protonational consciousness or, perhaps, were even consciously chosen with the intention of fostering it. Most relevant in this regard was Kosov's decision to write a glorification of the Caves Monastery not *ex novo*, but on the foundation on the pre-existent *Kievskii Paterik* (Kyiv Patericon), a Church Slavonic collection of lives of monks probably written in the thirteenth century. This piece of writing was one of the first testimonies of a conscious appropriation of one's own past history by a protonational Ukrainian society, represented, in this case, by the nobility and, mainly, by the ecclesiastical elite. The ecclesiastical character of Kosov's and Kal'nofois'kyi's work was in keeping with the political situation of Ukraine at the time: the lack of a lay political authority representing it as a nation made the Orthodox Church exert the functions of a centripetal force for Cossacks and other strata of the population which, more or less consciously, were the bearers of a proto-Ukrainian identity.[3] Thus, works that had a predominantly religious character as far as their content, imagery, and forms of expression were concerned also contained important signs of articulating the special set of values recognized by the community where the works functioned, independently of the language used.

Kosov's search for historical roots in the sacred sphere of history was functionally similar to the search for ancient (Roman, Sarmatian, Illyrian, Thracian, etc.) forefathers and glorious past deeds in the Renaissance historiography of Poland and other Western Slavic and European countries. This fashion affected the so-called Cossack historiography of the seventeenth and eighteenth centuries as well: in it, lines of political development were drawn from late Kyivan to Galician and, later, Cossack state organizations; dynastic successions were detected (e.g., from Riurik to Gedimin and the Polish kings); and mythical stories were told of a Sarmatian or Khazar ethnogenesis. This historiographical approach was akin to Polish or Western Renaissance history writing, where the "nation" was represented by a dynasty or a political entity, and the nobility by Sarmatian (or Khazar) or ancient or biblical forefathers. Such back-projections onto a mythical past expressed different kinds of social consciousness, but all of them possessed strong markers of a protonational identity.[4] They also testified to Ukraine's strong intellectual and cultural attachment to contemporary late Renaissance and baroque European and Polish standards. In an ideal canon of Ukrainian literature the works of Kosov and Kal'nofois'kyi would take a central position, their linguistic choice notwithstanding. Even though written in Polish, they have not found a place in the Polish literary canon.

Kosov and Kal'nofois'kyi had important followers who wrote about venerated religious centres or miracle-working items or places. This literary genre has been poorly investigated, but such works as Galiatovs'kyi's *Nebo novoie* (The New Heaven, Lviv, 1665) and *Skarbnytsia potrebnaia* (The Necessary Treasure-House, Novhorod-Sivers'kyi, 1676), and Dymytrii Tuptalo's *Runo oroshennoie* (The Bedewed Fleece, Chernihiv, 1683)[5] have recently attracted scholarly attention.

By the 1670s, when these works were written, the Ukrainian political and cultural situation had changed considerably from what it had been at the time of Kosov and Kal'nofois'kyi. There was now in existence a Ukrainian body politic, the Hetmanate, but it gravitated more and more towards the Russian political sphere of influence. The struggle of some of the Hetmanate's prominent Orthodox hierarchs against ecclesiastical submission to the Moscow Patriarchate was doomed to failure. Galiatovs'kyi's writings were generally reflective of Cossack society. The three works about miracles named above were written in *prosta mova*, the Ukrainian literary language of the time, Tuptalo's being the closest to Church Slavonic. However, markers identifying them as part of a Ukrainian canon are not especially evident, in spite of the language used. The evolution of the genre and of the situation of communication brought them closer to other possible canons – the Russian and Church Slavonic. *The Bedewed Fleece*, devoted to the miracles of the Chernihiv icon of the Virgin, was the author's first published work. Its basically Church Slavonic (though still Ruthenized) language indicates that the work was addressed in the first instance to Ukrainian believers, but at the same time to Russians and other Orthodox readers. The work is deeply rooted in the realia of the Chernihiv eparchy through its main subject and through the person of the archbishop Lazar Baranovych, who commissioned it. It is equally rooted in Ukrainian neoscholastic syncretism, and an image of Ukrainian society unambiguously emerges from some of its representations of miracles and personages. No less evident, however, is the intention of both patron and author to incorporate each miraculous event connected with Chernihiv into the framework of an ancient and sacred tradition of universal Orthodox church history. This incorporation would confer sacral prestige and historical mythopoetic gravity upon the Virgin of the Elijah monastery and, thereby, upon Baranovych's eparchy, at the same time including them in a Russian and a pan-Orthodox system of values.

The coexistence of a pan-Orthodox and a local perspective in *The Bedewed Fleece* is coherent with Baranovych's political and ecclesiastical world view, his ambitious program to create an Orthodox-Catholic anti-Ottoman league, and his desire to influence the tsar. The reception history of the *Fleece* suggests analogous conclusions. The *Fleece* had many editions and circulated widely, undergoing progressive "Russianization." Its last edition appeared in the 1750s and was probably connected with Tuptalo's canonization.[6] Through its "situational functionality" both in the local Eastern Slavic and the pan-Orthodox contexts and the later progressive Russianization of its Ukrainian heritage, the work reflects the peculiar situation of the Hetmanate in the time of Samoilovych and Mazepa. Though written in Ruthenian Church Slavonic by the Ukrainian son of a Cossack officer for a Ukrainian bishop and printed by that bishop's printing press, in an ideal canon of Ukrainian literature the *Fleece* would be considered less central than Kosov's earlier achievement, though the latter had been written in Polish.[7]

The reception history of the *Fleece* can serve as a metaphor of the evolution of authors' self-perceptions in a diachronic perspective: after the turmoils of the 1660s and 1670s, in the 1680s and 1690s the Kyivan learned monks could feel secure in a strong and flourishing Hetmanate. Though they were now subordinated to the Moscow patriarchate, they were aware of their cultural superiority with respect to Muscovy, and the tension between religious universalism and regional pride was mostly latent, in spite of the conflicts between the Moscow Patriarchs and representatives of the Kyivan learned tradition. The situation changed radically when, after 1700, the same learned monks lived and worked in Russia and felt that the Petrine reforms had rapidly made their cultural background so obsolete and unwanted that they could not even be published. As we shall see later, in the first years of the eighteenth century a sense of "otherness" dominates the letters and non-official writings of the learned monks. Varlaam Iasyns'kyi's death (1707)[8] is a symbolic date marking the beginning of this sense of extraneousness, which may be considered a further paradigmatic quality of the Ukrainian literary heritage of the seventeenth and eighteenth centuries. Baranovych escaped this experience, but Tuptalo, or Dymytrii Rostovskii as he is more commonly called in the Russian tradition, had to live through all the bitterness of the advancing process of Russianization (or "Malorossianization").

Panegyrical Literature

Panegyrical works comprised a major part of the books printed in Ukraine and were surpassed in number only by works of ecclesiastical and doctrinal literature.[9] Because of their content, as well as their beauty, panegyrics have a significant role to play in the definition of a Ukrainian canon in the time of baroque. Their complicated play with words and images; their division into chapters; their versification, rhetoric and poetic figures; their openness to a syncretism of the arts – all of these features show that these panegyrical works elaborated Polish models and applied the dominant rules of rhetoric and poetics typical of the European baroque. The intermingling of biblical quotations and classical *exempla* connects these works to the pan-European baroque syncretism of Christian and ancient symbolism that had been codified in the Polish-Lithuanian Commonwealth by Maciej Kazimierz Sarbiewski. A definition of the Ukrainianness of these works is not easy, even when they are written in *prosta mova*. The issue of ascribing works (or a whole genre) to one literary canon or another is made complex by the existence of internal differentiation even within a single literary canon. Indeed, according to recent scholarship, Polish language panegyric literature presents strong regional differences even inside the broad literary canon defined as Polish: abundant ornamentation and exceeding length seem to distinguish the Polish panegyrics in the manuscripts of the Lithuanian lands of the Commonwealth from works of the same genre composed in other parts of the realm.[10] Inside the Commonwealth, regional specificity is even more evident in Ukrainian panegyrics, regardless of the language used: images based on heraldic symbols create perceptible connections with the realia of the place and time; printing and engraving methods are typical of Ukrainian typographers; and the syncretism that brings together Christian and ancient symbols is not only constant throughout Ukrainian panegyrical literature but reflects a symbolism specific to Kyivan devotion and mythology.

What makes seventeenth-century panegyrics Ukrainian, rather than Polish or Russian, then? We may agree with the editor of *Stolp tsnot Syl'vestra Kosova* (Pillar of Virtues of Syl'vestr Kosov, Kyiv, 1658) that the specificity of Ukrainian baroque texts lay less in language or formal devices than in their content and orientation in the religious polemics of the time.[11] Among the Christian virtues of the deceased Metropolitan, the author of the *Pillar of Virtues*[12] at first extols his patience and ability to convince others (i.e., with his rhetoric skills), but what is considered most praiseworthy is his broad and up to date culture, grounded in the learning and religiosity at the very heart of the Kyivan tradition. Thanks to the learning he has fostered, Kosov has made his people known among other peoples, thus gaining the highest appreciation for himself, for the "sons of Rus'" (synove Rossiistii) and for the "Rus' country" (Rossiiskaia strana).[13] Even enemies have recognized his merits. Culture and religion are inseparable: the Orthodox *ecclesia* represents the centre of self-identification, but the author compares the authority and excellence of the late Metropolitan to that of emperors and kings (28–9), thus giving a political significance to religious culture. In several places there are reminders of the unity of the land of Kyiv and Galicia (Halitsii krai, 96): ecclesiastical unity matches the political idea of uniting the Ukrainian lands, which (almost) constantly nurtured Ukraine until the end of Mazepa's time. In the final "Lamentation" (Threny) the author stresses the importance of Kosov not just as Metropolitan but also as Exarch of the Patriarch: this title is mentioned in the final parts, thus taking its place in the *conclusio*; the *ornatus* confers upon the passage a particular pathos and rhetoricity. The see occupied by Kosov is called "equal to apostolic" (ravnoapostolskii prestol, 98), and the parallel use of the symbols of Volodymyr and Constantine confers equal dignity upon the Kyivan and the Constantinopolitan sees. The former becomes a "Kyivan New Jerusalem," equal in dignity to the earliest Christian heritage, which it continues.[14] The link to the "apostolic" nature of the Church where Kosov served as Exarch – let us remind the reader also of Stanisław Orzechowski's [Stanislav Orikhovs'kyi's] sixteenth-century narration of the five baptisms of Rus', the first being by St Andrew the Apostle – was fundamental for the reaffirmation of the Constantinopolitan jurisdiction of the Kyivan Orthodox Church, especially at the moment when the fate of Ukraine between Muscovite domination and a possible return to the Commonwealth was at stake. The very fact of recalling the Kyivan Christian foundation myth demonstrates the author's conscious wish to legitimate the past heritage of the Ukrainian lands (Mohyla's restoration of the Church of the Tithes, founded by Volodymyr, had been no less important) and matches Baranovych's almost constant opposition to submission to the Moscow Patriarchate.[15] These features are consistent with the view that Baranovych was possibly the main author of the *Pillar*.

Similar markers of Ukrainian specificity appeared earlier in *Virshi na zhalosnyi pohreb zatsnoho rytsera Petra Konashevycha Sahaidachnoho* (Verses for the Mournful Funeral of the Gallant Knight Petro Konashevych Sahaidachnyi).[16] Sahaidachnyi was the Cossack hetman who died in 1622 in the service of the Polish king after the Battle of Khotyn. This panegyric is a collection of short poems written by (or in the name of) nobles, prominent burghers, and churchmen, and edited by Kasiian Sakovych. The imprint of Polish verse and the frequent antique reminiscences place the poems within the frame of Renaissance culture. The topoi and images match the secular character of the protagonist, whom the verses endow with gigantic moral and civic significance. His virtues are military (skill as chief of the Cossack community, endurance in war), civic (faithfulness to the "homeland" and the sovereign, indefatigable activity), and religious (faultless devotion to the defence of the "holy faith" against "pagan Tatars and Turks"). This ideal image of the perfect "lytsar" (knight) is very similar to that of the Polish "rycerz." Nonetheless, the personality of Sahaidachnyi conveys the main moral and civic ideals of Ukrainian society: he is the pillar of the Cossack host without which Ukraine would not exist (221); he belongs to the "noble seed" of Japheth; and his ancestors arrived as conquerors to Constantinople with the "Rus' monarch Oleh" (za Oleha, ross'koho monarkha) and were baptized with Volodymyr (221). Not merely a warrior, he learned "good Orthodox letters" at the glorious Ostroh school ("it would not be easy to find another similar Zamojski, who could as well wield pen and sword") and engaged his high intellect to intercede with "his lord-king on behalf of our true holy faith" (231). Here too, the unity of Ukraine is recalled: the hetman's immortal glory "will last as long as the Dnipro and the Dnister, rich in fish, do flow" (234). A traditional flair is imparted by details such as the rivers "rich in fish," images hinting at folk tradition (e.g., of "Germans eating white bread with butter" while the Cossack hetman endures privation and practices hard warrior virtues), and in metaphors – well known in chronicles and war accounts – such as that of a victorious battle as a breakfast that the Cossacks serve to the Infidels together with lunch, finally sending them to Pluto's realm for dinner (231). As Greece glorifies Nestor, Achilles, and Pericles, the author continues, Troy glorifies Hector, and Rome glorifies the Curtiuses and Pompeus, so we, too, may be proud of our hetman, who lies in his grave for the defence of the fatherland (234). I will not expand here on the meaning of "oichyzna" (fatherland), but the consciousness of a centuries-old culture sustained by both civic (in this instance, military) and religious values gives evidence of the "Ukrainian" nature of the panegyric, which may thus be seen to contribute to an awareness of a protonational identity existing side by side with (or, indeed, in spite of) a parallel Polish political loyalty. The Greek, Roman, and Trojan parallels used for the glorification of the hetman recollect Ilarion's eleventh-century glorification of Volodymyr: together with the allusions to Oleh's conquests and Volodymyr's baptism they acted as confirmation of the political importance of the Cossacks as defenders of Orthodoxy at a time when stormy negotiations among Orthodox, Roman Catholics, and Uniates were on the agenda.

The panegyrics to Kosov and Sahaidachnyi were written in a strongly Polonized *prosta mova*. In the last decades of the seventeenth century the existence of a splendid princely court around Mazepa and his ambitions to unite Left and Right Bank Ukraine in a centralized, hereditary, autonomous *Het'manshchyna* fostered the appearance of many remarkable panegyrics. They were all extremely long, elaborate, and full of ancient allegories and biblical references. The dominant language of these panegyrics was no longer *prosta Rus'ka mova*, but Polish, frequently alternated or mixed with Latin.

Indeed, Polish remained a language widely used in Ukraine until the eighteenth century, though by then it had acquired new social functions. In the seventeenth century it was an excellent tool for secular communication, but also for Orthodox polemical literature aimed at nobilitating the "true faith" through scholarship and opposing the Polish-speaking adversary. It was even the language of such important texts as confessions of faith and hagiographic poetry. It became the ceremonial language of Mazepa's court.

The existence of a court was fundamental for the development of a cultural and literary system in a protomodern society. The cultural and literary system of Mazepa's day was the products of the court no less than of the Mohyla College. In this system literature was integrated through a set of generally recognized values; religion and tradition, as well as civic, juridical, and war customs had been transmitted through several generations; and the construction of a collective memory reached back to the Middle Ages. This complex of views and cultural conventions began to be consciously perceived as a coherent system of reference for the dominant part of both the lay and the ecclesiastical elites. As an expression of the culture of that period and as part of that system, literature was plurilingual: since the system thought, spoke, learned, and communicated in four languages, it was natural that the literary canon should develop in the same four languages. Even if teaching and cultivating "the sciences in our Slavonic writing,"[17] as Sakovych put it, was considered the highest intellectual achievement and most polemical literature was written in (more or less "slavonicized") *prosta mova*, the use of several languages remained a constant feature of Ukrainian culture and literature until at least the 1720s. Variations in the choice and functions of the language depended on multifarious factors related to the cultural training of each writer (his schooling, his readings, his family ties), but mainly on the communicative situation.

In the time of Mazepa's hetmancy the main language used for laudatory literature at the court of the new potentate was, apparently, Polish. The spoken language of the courtiers was certainly Ukrainian, though. Poets, however, felt themselves to be receivers of the inspiration of the Muses, endowed with the gift of distributing eternal glory to their Maecenas. Such an elevated duty demanded that poets have at their disposal a prestigious language, adequate rhetorical and poetic means, and the whole system of classical mythological references in order to impart glory to the necessary historical narratives. The Polish language was a ready medium for such tasks. Ian Ornovs'kyi and Pylyp Orlyk were the most famous panegyrists in Mazepa's elite, but several other names could be added. Monks trained in Polish Jesuit colleges used Polish with no less ease and mastery than did the courtiers. The most famous such churchman was Stefan Iavors'kyi, the author of long and extremely elaborate panegyrics for the glorification of the hetman and of Metropolitan Iasyns'kyi. Iasyns'kyi himself was trained in Cracow and certainly appreciated panegyrics written in Polish (though, for purposes of communicating with his Orthodox flock, he wrote sermons in *prosta mova*).[18]

Why did Polish gain such functional importance in Ukraine during Mazepa's hetmanship, becoming a semi-official ceremonial language for the Hetmanate? Was this only due to personal tastes and to the Polish training of both lay and ecclesiastical elites? Does the excellence of Polish as a literary means of expression explain the panegyrists' linguistic choice? The unsatisfactory level of investigation does not allow us to have exact ideas about the functional status of the languages used in the Hetmanate, but the facts adduced above suggest the following: during the period of Polish political supremacy the most important panegyrics were written in *prosta mova*. In Mazepa's time, under Muscovite dominance, on the other hand, courtiers preferred Polish. Did the choice of language not reflect, besides personal taste, training and the prestige of Polish, as well as (or mainly?) a desire to differentiate oneself from the politically dominant culture? Even admitting that such a choice may have been unconscious, my hypothesis is supported by the different linguistic situation prevailing in Russia: there Polish lost its strong position as a language of the court after the fall of Sof'ia and Golitsyn, and at Peter's court it soon went out of fashion. Latin, too, had a different status in the Hetmanate than it did in Moscow and Saint Petersburg: until the 1720s knowledge of Latin in Russia was limited to a very tiny elite and to the "emblematic forms" of state propaganda or diplomacy.[19] Thus, linguistic choice may be considered a marker of Ukrainian difference with respect to Moscow at the time of Mazepa's highest glory, though, given the present state of research, this idea must remain a hypothesis.

Let us now consider the panegyrics written for Mazepa from the point of view of their belonging to one literary system or another. They were written in Polish and Latin, in accord with the peculiarities of the "flourishing baroque" of the formerly Eastern parts of the Commonwealth, and adopted the main symbols of classical mythology in combination with biblical quotations and references that were in use in Polish panegyrical literature. The need to laud the hetman and his family or the metropolitan made content extremely important in Ukrainian panegyrics: it is sufficient to see Iavors'kyi's allusions to Maecenas and Virgil and his image of Mazepa on a triumphal chariot, reminiscent of Roman triumphal imagery, to appreciate the extent of the hypertrophic glorification of the Hetmanate – as well as the total dependence of the literary system to which such texts belonged on classical and baroque European models.

The Polish forms and rhetorical schooling notwithstanding, these Polish-Latin panegyrics have not been traditionally included in any Polish literary canon.[20] Only after the 1960s did Polish scholarship show an interest in this kind of literature, carefully locating it, however, in the Ukrainian context or framing it as a carrier of European and Polish culture into Russia.[21]

Quite different has been the approach to seventeenth-century Ukrainian and Belarusian literature in Russian scholarship. Not counting erudite prerevolutionary scholarship, interest in Ukrainian Polish-language texts in Russia dates back to the 1970s, but it gained momentum only after the 1980s. Though recalling the Ukrainian or Belarusian origin and schooling of the authors, Russian scholars tended to adopt a consistently Russian perspective, incorporating the works of Ukrainian baroque poetry into the Russian literary discourse – which is partially correct since the erudite monks wrote a considerable part of their most important works at the Muscovite court. Connections between Ukrainian and Belarusian baroque culture, on the one hand, and the Russian on the other, are very strong, both genetically and typologically. Orthodoxy was a powerful unifying factor, doctrinal disputes between Muscovite Patriarchs and Kyivan monks notwithstanding.

Nonetheless, the question becomes much more complicated if one analyzes single works within this general context. Is it appropriate to consider the panegyrics to Mazepa in a book devoted to Russian baroque literature?[22] One may speculate that the panegyrics were written, in part, to enhance Mazepa's prestige in Moscow. Pylyp Orlyk's *Hyppomenes sarmacki* (The Sarmatian Hippomenes, Kyiv, 1698) is a glorification of Mazepa's nephew Ian Obydovs'kyi as a steward of the tsar. Orlyk's eulogy is very strongly oriented towards the Russian (imperial) horizon, perfectly taking into account the political situation of the real and apparently immutable dependence of the Hetmanate on the tsar.

However, the textual and intertextual connection of the panegyrics devoted to Mazepa to the complex of literary, social, and political markers of the Kyivan tradition is so strong that their inclusion in a Russian literary canon is problematic: they were produced and printed in Ukraine in one of the languages (Polish) that normally circulated in the Hetmanate (but no longer in Russia); they were addressed to the hetman, his court, and the Kyivan ecclesiastical and civic community; and they were based on values that were essential for the Cossack state and its dominant society, but not for the Russian state where they progressively acquired negative significance under the growing pressure of Peter's power. I would add that, in spite of the similarity of baroque stylistic devices and topoi throughout Europe, the Russian and Ukrainian uses of these European devices were not identical. Not only did the language used in the Ukrainian lands have to be Russianized before it could function in the Russian cultural environment, Ukrainians were fond of the ornate, indeed extravagant forms of the "flowery" baroque, while Russians preferred simpler linear forms. The exuberant accumulation of metaphors and allegories in the Ukrainian texts was but one aspect of their considerable difference from Russian poems – a difference observable in the stylistic use of techniques and images, in content and form. The Russian texts were mainly based on simple comparison, anecdotic narrativity, and transparent quotations from the Scriptures or other authorities.[23]

Sermons and Hagiography

The above considerations equally apply to Iavors'kyi's sermon *Vinograd Khristov* (Christ's Vineyard, Chernihiv, 1698): written and printed in Ukraine in *prosta mova* and addressed to the nobles and Cossacks participating in the wedding of Mazepa's nephew (and supposed heir), it hardly belongs in a history of Russian baroque literature – all the more so as nuptial sermons were not foreseen in wedding ceremonies in Russia and remained extraneous to the Russian church until at least the beginning of the eighteenth century.[24] No nuptial sermon is to be found in editions of Simeon Polotskii.

Baroque sermons generally follow a fixed set of rhetorical rules and have therefore been considered uniform and "boring" all over Europe. Recent reassessment shows how differentiated they may be in function and style, as well as in social and historical context. The first "must" for sermons is to be comprehensible to a broad public. Ukrainian preachers wrote predominantly in *prosta mova*. The alternative to this language was Church Slavonic. Let us look briefly at the interplay between language and the situation of communication. It is interesting to observe the difference between Galiatovs'kyi and Antonii Radyvylovs'kyi on the one hand, and Baranovych on the other. As Baranovych wrote sermons for the tsar, their language could not but be Church Slavonic. Virtues and vices, though expressed through selected features of Western baroque origin, were classified according to the needs and mentality of the highest ranks of an already imperial court bound to traditional Orthodox thinking. Galiatovs'kyi and Radyvylovs'kyi wrote sermons for a society where social stratification was much more differentiated and schools existed even for low social strata. In my opinion, the fact that, in spite of the author's (and Simeon Polotskii's) efforts, Baranovych's sermons could not be printed in Moscow indicates how different that society was.[25] Thus, the linguistic choice for sermons is only part of the set of markers that can determine whether a particular work can be plausibly viewed as part of a Ukrainian or Russian canon.

Quite interesting is the case of Baranovych's hagiographic poetry. *Apollo chreściański* (The Christian Apollo, Kyiv, 1670) and *Lutnia Apollinowa* (Apollo's Lute, Kyiv, 1671) are in Polish, follow Polish conventions of versification, and make extremely complex use of Sarbiewski's teachings about conceptist poetry. Regardless of their aesthetic value, of the texts considered here those that sit most comfortably within a canon of Polish literature are Baranovych's verses; indeed, some of them were (sparingly!) included in anthologies of Polish poetry.[26] If we look for markers of a Ukrainian identity in the two collections of Baranovych's Polish poems, the author's ethnic origin and his membership of the highest ranks of the hierarchy of the Kyivan metropolitan jurisdiction are relevant but not sufficient in themselves. *Apollo's Lute* is probably the most marginal collection of poems from a Ukrainian perspective, though even in relation to "canonical" Polish standards Baranovych's hypertrophic conceptism is peculiar: the exceedingly complex works that comprise his religious poetry are reminiscent of the baroque tradition of the Eastern parts of the Rzeczpospolita.

Indeed, it is easier to insert into a Ukrainian canon *The Christian Apollo*, published in another edition with the title *Żywoty świętych* (Lives of the Saints) in the same year. The book has three variants: one has dedicatory verses in Latin and Polish, another has a dedication to Tsar Fedor, and the third has no dedication at all. The composition of the *Lives* is also peculiar; they are more like short eulogies than *vitae*, giving evidence for placing the saint in a particular category (martyr, witness, apostle, or hermit) and singing his or her praises. Though Polish influence is evident at every level (Piotr Skarga is a major source), Surius and other possible Western models are present, and Spanish parallels have been found. Though the use (and abuse) of audacious baroque devices and topoi make the *Lives* the typical fruit of a flourishing European baroque, the work nonetheless presents similarities to the Church Slavonic tradition of "Prologues" – collections of short lives in verse that were used in Orthodox liturgical practice since its Byzantine beginnings.

This simultaneous invocation of two cultural traditions gives an insight into the destination of the book and the author's intentions. Baranovych wanted the book to circulate in the Polish-Lithuanian Commonwealth for the glorification of Orthodox saints, but he also wanted it to circulate at the court of the (culturally Polish-influenced) Tsar Fedor, probably with the aim of furthering his utopian plans for a joint Roman Catholic and Muscovite anti-Osmanic crusade. With this purpose in view he created a special "Kyivan canon," including such saints as Anthony and Theodosius, Volodymyr and his sons, and the Metropolitans Peter, Aleksii, and Ionas; these saints were venerated in Ukraine, but also in Muscovy, at the same time being recognized by Western Counter-Reformation hagiology (they were included in the Bollandists' *Acta Sanctorum*).[27] He was probably also motivated by a desire to see Kyiv remain under the jurisdiction of the Constantinopolitan see, which had consecrated Peter, Aleksii, and (partially) Ionas, and to have recognition of the priority of the Kyivan see with respect to the Muscovite. Addressed to the whole Eastern Slavic *ecclesia*, Baranovych's work had special ties with the Caves Monastery and the cultural sphere of Ukraine, both sacred and political. *Lives* was published when Kyiv was still under Constantinopolitan jurisdiction.

The Baroque Path Comes to a Dead End

The facts presented above indicate that Russian literary criticism, and the idea of a Russian canon that we have adopted as a working tool, are much more inclusive with respect to Ukrainian baroque literature than their Polish counterparts. Much more work is needed to give a correct evaluation of the differentiations and overlappings between Ukrainian and Russian, than between Ukrainian and Polish canons.

Let us try to conceptualize the interrelation of different "belongings" in the last decades of the Ukrainian Hetmanate and of its literary baroque. Authorial self-perceptions and personal feelings, the circulation of texts in contemporary and later societies, and participation in supranational systems must constantly be considered.

In the Hetmanate of the late seventeenth and early eighteenth centuries lines of delimitation and markers of specificity are less evident than previously for a considerable part of the liturgical, doctrinal, or devotional literature. This kind of literature was written in Church Slavonic and addressed to the broad Orthodox community of believers (and rulers) not only in the Eastern Slavic lands but also in such places as Serbia, Moldavia, Romania, and Bulgaria. Emanuel Kozachyns'kyi lived in Serbia, where in the 1730s he organized a Collegium in Sremski Karlovci and bound his celebrity to a school drama on Urosh the Fifth. Eastern Slavic learning influenced South Slavic history writing; the Bulgarian historian Spiridon Savva quoted Dymytrii Rostovskii at the end of the eighteenth century. By that time, however, Kyivan models were circulating in *Slavia Orthodoxa* as part of the Russian-Slavic version of baroque culture and were significant as carriers of Russian imperial anti-Osmanic politics in the Balkans. Ukraine as a separate region had disappeared from the cultural map of Eastern Orthodox countries, and the Russian interpretation of Orthodox Slavic culture engendered an imperial pan-Slavic ideology whose political significance continues to our days.

To be sure, religious Church Slavonic literature did not lose its original Ukrainian markers at all levels. The graphic features and engravings in printed books, elaborations of Western culture and style, three- or fourfold meanings of texts, and philosophical training required for their reception remained in evidence. Baroque literature takes on specific local forms wherever it appears, be it in Serbia, Russia, or Bulgaria.[28] Nonetheless, many of the most valuable works appear as central in a supranational literary canon but peripheral in national canons.

A good example of a work of such transnational impact is Tuptalo's *Zhytiia sviatykh* (Lives of the Saints, Kyiv, 1689–1705). Though fully embedded in Kyivan learning and writing tradition, the main significance of these *Lives* lies in the impact they have to this day in the whole *Slavia Orthodoxa*. What is more, writing for Orthodoxy at large was certainly the author's intention: in the *weltanschauung* of the Cossack's son Tuptalo, belonging to the Ukrainian fatherland did not contradict the highest purpose of serving God, the only true Orthodox faith, and the community of believers. Double "literary belonging" was normal in the seventeenth and eighteenth centuries, just as double identity (and loyalty) was in national self-consciousness. As regards our contemporary need to have conceptual grids for literary interpretation, this state of affairs allows us to look at the same works from several points of view, considering them as part of the evolution of a Polish, Russian, or Church Slavonic literary canon, or of a pan-Orthodox or general European baroque system of literary, mental, social, and communicative paradigms.

History and the biographies of writers offer a precious opportunity to give an outline of the evolution of the literary self-perception and of the reception of a significant corpus of literary works written by two of the protagonists of the period under discussion. In 1700 Stefan Iavors'kyi and Dymytrii Tuptalo were appointed by Peter to two metropolitan sees in the tsardom. The former even became the "place keeper" of the patriarch; in the absence of a patriarch in Moscow he styled himself "exarch," in his own mind probably linking this exarchate to the patriarch of Constantinople, though in the Russian church everybody assumed it to be the Moscow patriarch. Be that as it may, the literary activity of Iavors'kyi and Tuptalo before and after their nominations as metropolitans in Russia may serve as a metonym for the destiny of Ukrainian baroque culture in the eighteenth century.

Tuptalo's homiletic practice was always purely ecclesiastical, and it is difficult to differentiate between its Kyivan and Russian periods other than on the basis of language. However, his efforts to transplant scholastic teaching and theatre to Rostov were frustrated by the ministry of church affairs, which withdrew financial support. The world chronicle he wrote in his last years, intended to transmit to priests and believers a basic knowledge of sacred history, was a blend of church history and biblical exegesis grounded in Roman and Flemish Counter-Reformation erudition, late Byzantine chronicles, and patristic (Eastern and Western) tradition. In spite of Iavors'kyi's efforts, nobody in Moscow or Petersburg was interested in publishing this work. His main work remains the four volumes of the *Lives of the Saints*.

Tuptalo belongs to a Ukrainian literary canon because of his origin, self-consciousness, schooling, the place of printing of his works, the dominance in his works of Western influence, and his linguistic practice (Middle Ukrainian or Church Slavonic).[29] His pan-Orthodox significance, however, gained momentum in diachronic perspective. Veneration of Dymytrii as a saint after his death submerged the Ukrainian (including Polish and Western) "imprint" of his life, education, and literary output, as well as the estrangement he had experienced in Russia; after Peter's time, Russia appropriated him in both literary and spiritual terms. Whether or not this is fair is another question, but it is the case. Furthermore, this shift in reception corresponds to the "deep layers" of Dymytrii's own personality – his mind and soul were oriented towards religious values, while state and nation were feeble concerns in his *weltanschauung*. He died, symbolically enough, in October 1709.

The destiny of Iavors'kyi's literary output has several points in common with that of Tuptalo, though there were profound differences between the character and the intellectual lives of the two men.

In Russia, in his capacity as the most senior prelate of the Russian Church,[30] Iavors'kyi wrote antiheretical tracts, a treatise concerning the Constantinopolitan patriarchal see, and hundreds of sermons. Scholarly attention has focused almost exclusively on the "laudatory sermons" (pokhvalitelnye slova). As a matter of fact these represent only about 10 per cent of his homilies, the others being of purely ecclesiastical character. A comparison of these sermons with those of Iavors'kyi's Ukrainian period, which remain unpublished, has never been undertaken. The manuscript of the latter indicates that the preacher thought of his work essentially in religious terms and as an ecclesiastical duty; even when the religious symbols had a clear political target, the sermons aimed at affirming ecclesiastic law and authority. To assess properly the function of Iavors'kyi's huge homiletic activity and his interest for the relationship of Church and State, we have to consider his deeds and intentions as a complex

structure. I will focus on just one aspect of it: his relationship to the monastery in Nizhyn. Writing sermons for Peter (and being his adviser for church
affairs at least in the early 1700s)[31] was a lucrative deal for the Metropolitan
of Riazan'. However, he did not use the money he earned for his own benefit
or for worldly luxuries, but for building a monastery in Nizhyn as a centre for
monastic learning and a haven for the kind of culture that he represented and
believed to be threatened in Peter's Russia. Significantly enough, he had to
wait years to overcome Peter's refusal to let him go to Ukraine for the consecration of the new monastery church; the evidence suggests that Peter was
conscious of the ideological danger Iavors'kyi and his milieu represented for
him and his plans.

Iavors'kyi's major work, *Kamen' very* (Rock of Faith, Kyiv, 1728) is considered to be the first Church Slavonic theological treatise of the Orthodox
faith. Iavors'kyi made use of the same kind of sources as Tuptalo: Counter-
Reformation theology (with Bellarmino as a main point of reference), Eastern
and Western patristic literature, and, later, Slavo-Byzantine tradition (rather
sparingly, however). The whole was organized according to the system of
Western neoscholastic logical philosophy. The thousand-page volume could
not be printed before his own and Peter's death.

It is interesting to recall what Iavors'kyi *did not* write in Russia. There are
no indications in documents, letters, or literary works of the reasons for his
choices of literary activity, but some explanations may be sought in psychological, social, and other contextual circumstances. Presumably, a major factor
that influenced Iavors'kyi's literary choices in Russia was his high ecclesiastic
rank, which made him feel responsible for the development of church life and
doctrine, as well as moral teaching and the defence of Orthodoxy. Moreover,
he must have felt himself alien in a world dominated by such people as Peter
himself, Menshikov, Petr Tolstoi, and the many personalities of the "new kind"
around the tsar. He opposed Peter's divorce and his new female "company."
For him the only option was to withdraw into his own domain: the church
and religion, and his beloved baroque ecclesiastical erudition. Practical factors
may also have come into play; epistolographic convention notwithstanding,
there must have been a good deal of truth in his famous letter to Dymytrii Tuptalo in which he complained about the many vanities that hindered his erudite
activity. Indeed, he had work enough preparing sermons, caring for the Moscow Academy, resisting the intrigues of the Russian churchmen, monitoring
the construction of the Nizhyn monastery, and trying to place his own men in
ecclesiastical posts. He concentrated on antiheretical writings. This was also
one of the few ways in which it was possible to assert some degree of political
(or, more precisely, ideological) opposition. As a result, he never again wrote

panegyrics in the style of those he had written for Mazepa. Mazepa's court had been a place that inspired him to "weave" panegyrics. He could not have had the same feelings for Peter's lavish and shockingly scandalous court. For his part, Peter preferred other panegyrists: Iosyf Turobois'kyi, Feofan Proko-povych, Havryïl Buzhyns'kyi, and others. Iavors'kyi did not write treatises on poetics or rhetoric, either – he was no longer a teacher, but the highest-ranking hierarch in Russia, and it was no longer within his competence to write text-books. He wrote epitaphs for Iasyns'kyi on his death but they were not pub-lished. The only successful poetic work that he wrote in Russia was the famous Latin elegy he composed to accompany the gift of his remarkable library to the Nizhyn monastery. Thus, his poetic works are addressed to Ukraine, not to the Russian milieu in which he lived.

How do these works fit into the grid that enables us to consider them part of one or more literary canons, and what was the history of their reception? Iavors'kyi's Kyivan works lie at the very centre of a Ukrainian literary system: the content, languages used, addressees and circulation, author's intentions, ideological and political messages, set of images, dimensions of the works, and their appeal to the taste of the "flourishing Baroque" all make the panegyrical works and the nuptial sermon[32] typical of the Ukrainian tradition. Connected by deep intertextual links to the literary culture of the Polish-Lithuanian Com-monwealth, they belong to a Polish canon, too, though in Polish literary his-tory they are considered peripheral. The "most Polish" of Iavors'kyi's works is probably a poem to the Virgin Mary dating back to the years of his educa-tion in Jesuit colleges. The autograph is in a book that he bought in Poland. Unfortunately there is no definitive evidence that it is an original composition rather than a copy of another author's work.[33] On the other hand, it would be problematic to include Iavors'kyi's Polish-language works written in Ukraine in a Russian canon, even though they were written within the boundaries of the growing and increasingly imperial Russian polity.

More ambiguous is the issue of the canon to which Iavors'kyi might be said to belong after his (forced) emigration to Russia. His polemical treatises and sermons written after 1700 may be ascribed to a Russian literary canon; they were written for Russian listeners in the context of the Russian church and state in a Russianized Church Slavonic sometimes adapted to Peter's taste for brev-ity and intelligibility.[34] It is not without significance that the manuscript of these works was prepared by the preacher himself, possibly to be printed in Kyiv. In Russia it was published only in part, and as late as the nineteenth century.[35] Moreover, such sermons could never have been written, nor even conceived of, without Kyivan, Polish, and Western Catholic erudition. The cultural soil from which these sermons grew had been transported rather late, and only in part, to the Russian terrain, and the reception of Metropolitan Stefan's sermons in eighteenth-century Russia was not always enthusiastic – Prokopovych took Iavors'kyi's place in the mind and heart of Peter, and Stefan's detractors were always numerous in both capitals. These "functional" facts place Iavors'kyi's sermons not outside of the Russian literary canon but in a somewhat peripheral position relative to it. A deep appropriation of Iavors'kyi's homiletic heritage as "really Russian" became definitive in the nineteenth century, and by that time the Ukrainianness of the sermons was forgotten, while their Orthodox and imperial components were stressed.

Somewhat analogous is the fate of *Rock of Faith*, though this extraordinary achievement was soon recognized as a cornerstone for both Russian and pan-Orthodox culture and philosophy. The Ukrainianness of this work is even more neglected by scholarship and public opinion; since the end of the eighteenth century the work has functioned as the first monument of "modern" Russian theology and as testimony of Russia's definitive acceptance of Western culture (and hence of her right to be considered a part of Europe). A reassessment of this work, and similar ones like Tuptalo's *Letopisets* (Chronicler, first published in 1784),[36] should acknowledge that the Ukrainian matrix and the Western European and Polish cultural components had a primary role in the conception and fulfilment of Iavors'kyi's masterpiece, though the author's intentions and their realization extended beyond the reach of his cultural roots, and the work belongs to both the Russian and pan-Orthodox literary, philosophical, and cultural systems.

Intriguing is the history of the reception of Iavors'kyi's "farewell" *Elegy to the Books*.[37] Written 1721 in Latin for Ukrainian monks and for an institution that was intended to represent the best of Ukrainian seventeenth-century culture, the poem was soon perceived in Russia as a chef-d'oeuvre of Russian culture: it was published in Latin and translated several times and copied in all the parts of the Empire. According to all the evidence, by the 1720s Latin tradition had begun to function in Russia in cultivated society. The *Elegy*'s lyrical subtlety and intense use of classical references suited the expectations of literati and readers. The sense of the "Ukrainian belonging" of the *Elegy* was completely lost beyond Ukraine itself: one may speak of the *Elegy* as a Russian "bestseller" of the eighteenth century.

The success of the *Elegy* may reflect the beginning of an interest in individual feelings corresponding to the evolution of European literary taste towards "sentiment" and "psychology" at the turn of the seventeenth and eighteenth centuries. There is another group of texts where personal feelings, moods, melancholy, and bitterness are expressed with an intensity very infrequent in premodern Eastern Slavonic literature, especially in Russia proper – the letters that the leading Ukrainian literati and church hierarchs wrote to one another when they lived and worked in Russia.[38] As I wrote some years ago, Tuptalo's and Iavors'kyi's epistolary exchanges are among the most impressive testimonies of their actual way of thinking and feeling.[39] The extant letters, written between 1707 and 1709, testify to a different world than that of their scholarly, homiletic, panegyrical, or doctrinal writings. Irony had a primary role in these letters, while solitude and estrangement glimmer in every line. The peculiar mixed language that already Ternovskii called "foppery" (shchegolstvo)[40] was a sort of linguistic code used among Ukrainian and Belarusian literati who were separated by distance, but united by a common cultural and literary heritage and secret common feelings. Though less sophisticated and complex, a similar plurilingual code had been familiar to Simeon Polotskii and Lazar Baranovych three decades earlier; it remained unknown to the Russian colleagues of the Ruthenian writers. This internal code was a uniquely effective means for expressing ideas and feelings that did not yet have a linguistic code of their own. As an example I quote Tuptalo's letter to the hegumen of the Holy Spirit monastery in Vilnius (28 December 1707):

[...] *Eheu quam levibus pereunt ingentia causis* (Mantuanus). A barziej samego WMM pana **терпенію святому** *compatior*, z większym to przewielebności twojej będzie zbawieniem. *Dulcior est fructus per multa pericula ductus* (Cornel. Gal.). **Егоже Бог любит, наказует** [Hebr. 12: 6] [...] Wielkie są po prawdzie u świątobliwości Waszey ruiny, tylkoż i u nas nie wiem jeżeli mniejsze. [...] W tym chyba jedynym *differimus* między sobą, że nam **бѣда от своих**, a WWM państwu **от чуждых**. Ale *nociva a quocunque exercita non sunt iucunda, nec quemque iuvant* [...] Nie dziw temu, czas jest woienny. *Nervus belli pecunia*.[41]

([...] *Alas, how little causes may destroy great things* [Virgil Mantuanus]! The more *compassion I have* for your Gracious Lordship's **holy sufferance**, the greater the salvation it will bring Your Grace. *Sweeter is the fruit coming from perilous endurance* [Cornelius]. **For whom the Lord loveth he chasteneth** [Heb. 12: 6]. [...] Great are indeed the misfortunes striking Your Holiness, but I wonder whether in our parts they are any less. [...] In one thing alone, perhaps, we *differ*: that to us **evil comes from our own kind,** while to Your Gracious Lordship it comes **from outsiders**. But *nuisance is unpleasant from whatever place it comes, nor is it of help to anyone* [...] No wonder, it's wartime. *C'est l'argent qui fait la guerre.*)

In no other words than this collage of Latin quotations, Polish "discoursing," and Church Slavonic emphasis could Tuptalo express his ironic position towards the grievances of his friend living in Lithuania under Polish rule;

furthermore, Tuptalo's anguish was caused by the oppression coming from the very authority (the tsar and the Russian state) that was, at least theoretically, responsible for defending his ethical and religious traditions.

Another example of playful elegance and intellectual complicity is to be found in Iavors'kyi's letter to a friend who had addressed him as a "sun." Iavors'kyi plays with the concept of irony, which was new to Orthodox tradition and vocabulary: in place of the word lacking in Church Slavonic, the author introduced the Latin term, and then continued with a Latin quotation from Cicero, resuming Church Slavonic after the end of the phrase in a moralizing (though still slightly ironic) way:

Аще бых не ведал, яко сицево именование от любления происходит, непшевал бых быти *ironiam, simili illi, ubi lupus ovium pastor appellatur: o praeclarum ovium custodem lupum.* **Но понеже любве закон.**[42]

(Did I not know that your way of addressing me derives from your friendship, I would speculate *it to be ironical, as where the wolf is called a shepherd: Oh, an excellent protector of sheep, the wolf!* **However, since it is the law of love.)**

Into which of the canons under consideration should these letters be placed? Not intended to be published, they served as personal communication[43] among educated individuals who followed the international rhetorical rules established for epistolography. They are part of a general European humanistic canon where mixed Polish and Latin, or Latin, French, and Flemish were commonly used by such prominent and exemplary literati as Jan Kochanowski or Just Lipsius. The quoted letters belong by all rights to the Polish and the Ruthenian tradition; their place there is secured by the origin and education of the authors, the "internal" circulation foreseen for the letters, the mixed language, the quotations from ancient and modern Latin-language writers and Eastern and Western Church fathers, and the omnipresence of the Bible. In an ideal Ukrainian canon these letters would lie at the very centre.

Would their inclusion in a Russian canon be possible? I would suggest that reasons to include them in the Russian literary system are close to non-existent. Though written in Russia, they expressed a set of values that were universally accepted in their original milieu and homeland, while their attitude towards the Russian society appears negative. Though this marker is not per se sufficient to exclude the letters from Russian literature, it does give a measure of the deep alienation that the authors felt in the milieu where they were obliged to live, deprived of the possibility of expressing the set of values typical of their rank, education, ethical principles, traditional heritage, and personal feelings.

With the end of Mazepa's hetmancy and its culture, Ukrainian literature and the whole system of coexisting languages and expressive codes had apparently arrived at a dead end. The experience of the baroque, however, was not forgotten – it became the latent mainstream for the rebirth of Ukrainian culture and language in the nineteenth and twentieth centuries. The language question evolved in completely new terms and political and cultural sets of rules changed radically, but many connections to the old paradigm remained and still present unsolved issues.

Notes

1 For some Polish examples and their relationship to Roman prototypes, see Giovanna Brogi Bercoff, "O typologii polskiego piśmiennictwa w XVII wieku na przykładzie historiografii erudycynej," in *Królestwo Słowian: Historiografia Renesansu i Baroku w krajach słowiańskich*, ed. G. Brogi Bercoff (Izabelin: Świat literacki, 1999), 156–71.

2 See Antoine Martel, *La langue polonaise dans les pays Ruthènes, Ukraine et Russie Blanche* (Lille: 1938); G. Brogi Bercoff, "Zum literarischen Gebrauch der Mischsprache im ostslavischen Bereich im 17.–18. Jh.," *Ricerche slavistiche* 43 (1996): 183–208; G. Brogi Bercoff, "Plurilinguism in Russia and in the Ruthenian Lands in the Seventeenth and Eighteenth Centuries: The Case of Stefan Javors'kyj," in *Speculum Slaviae Orientalis: Muscovy, Ruthenia and Lithuania in the Late Middle Ages*, ed. Vyacheslav V. Ivanov and Julia Verkholantsev (Moscow: Novoe izdatel'stvo, 2005), 9–20.

3 Among the most important works about these issues are Frank E. Sysyn, *Between Poland and the Ukraine: The Dilemma of Adam Kysil, 1600–1653* (Cambridge, MA: Harvard University Press for the Harvard Ukrainian Research Institute, 1985); Frank E. Sysyn, "The Cultural, Social and Political Context of Ukrainian History-Writing: 1620–1690," *Europa Orientalis* 5 (1986): 297–302; Serhii Plokhy, *The Cossacks and Religion in Early Modern Ukraine* (Oxford: Oxford University Press, 2001), 111–44; Natalia Iakovenko, *Paralel'nyi svit: Doslidzhennia z istoriï uiavlen' ta idei v Ukraïni XVI–XVII st.* (Kyiv: Krytyka, 2002); and M. Drozdowski, *Religia i Kozaczyzna w Rzeczypospolitej w pierwszej połowie XVII wieku* (Warsaw: Wydawnictwo DiG, 2008).

4 See the works cited in note 1 and their bibliographies, and the synthetic but clear account in Serhii Plokhy, *Tsars and Cossacks: A Study in Iconography* (Cambridge, MA: Harvard University Press for Harvard Ukrainian Research Institute, 2002), esp. 10–15. Some tentative comparative remarks are in my "Renesansni istoriohrafichni mify v Ukraini," in *Ukraïna XVII stolittia: Suspil'stvo, filosofiia, kul'tura: Zbirnyk pamiati Valeriï Nichyk*, ed. Larysa Dovha and Natalia Iakovenko (Kyiv: Krytyka, 2005), 421–35.

5 A first, shorter edition may have already existed in 1677 (see Iakym Zapasko and Iaroslav Isaievych, *Pamiatky knyzhkovoho mystetstva: Kataloh starodrukiv, vydanykh na Ukraïni* [Lviv: Vyshcha shkola, 1981–4], I, 93).
6 See G. Brogi Bercoff, "Old and New Narrative: 'Runo Oroshennoe' by Dimitrij Tuptalo, Metropolitan of Rostov," *Starobălgarska literatura* (Iubileen sbornik v chest na 60-godishninata na Krasimir Stanchev i Aleksandŭr Naumov) 41–2 (2009): 359–66. On the canonization of Dymytrii Tuptalo see G. Brogi Bercoff, "La canonizzazione del primo santo del Settecento russo: storia e funzione," in *Liturgia e agiografia tra Roma e Costantinopoli: Atti del I e II seminario di studio, Roma, Grottaferrata 2000–2001*, ed. Krassimir Stantchev and Stefano Parenti (Grottaferrata: Monastero esarchico, 2007), 381–93.
7 The iconography of some editions of the *Fleece* also supports this contention. See Plokhy, *Tsars and Cossacks*, 41–2 and 53.
8 On the crucial significance of 1707 for the political evolution of Mazepa's hetmanate, see T.G. Tairova-Iakovleva, *Ivan Mazepa i Rossiiskaia Imperiia: Istoriia "predatel'stva"* (Moscow and Saint Petersburg: Tsentrpoligraf, Russkaia troika, 2011).
9 According to the catalogue compiled by Iakym Zapasko and Iaroslav Isaievych, panegyrical works are almost 140 in number, followed by polemical works (about 50 items), sermons (28), and hagiographies (19) (*Pamiatky knyzhkovoho mystetstva*, 1981–4). In fact the Zapasko-Isaievych catalogue is not exact in differentiating Ukrainian works from others. The "Ukrainianness" of a considerable number of the panegyrics included is doubtful: they were not only written in Polish, but commissioned by, dedicated to, and destined for circulation among Polish personages. In such cases Ukraine as the place of printing is a feeble marker of belonging to a "national canon," even by premodern standards.
10 See Jakub Niedźwiedź, *Nieśmiertelne teatra sławy: Teoria i praktyka twórczości panegirycznej na Litwie w XVII–XVIII w.* (Kraków: Księgarnia Akademicka, 2003), and the interesting proposal for an "internal comparative approach" in Kwiryna Ziemba, "Projekt komparatystyki wewnętrznej," *Teksty drugie* 91–2 (2005): 72–82. For the declamatory origin of the complex compositions of heraldic panegyrical poetry, see Walter Kroll, *Heraldische Dichtung bei den Slaven* (Wiesbaden: Harrassowitz, 1986), 17 and 107–18.
11 Martin Erdmann, *Heraldische Funeralpanegyrik des ukrainischen Barock: Am Beispiel des "Stolp cnot Syl'vestra Kossova"* (Munich: Sagner, 1999), 15–21.
12 The young Baranovych as the main author probably had numerous colleagues participating in the "construction" of his text (Erdmann, *Heraldische Funeralpanegyrik*, 18–19).
13 These terms appear in all parts of the text. See, for example, the reprint of the text in Erdmann, *Heraldische Funeralpanegyrik*, 10.

14 Erdmann has observed here a reminiscence of Ilarion's *Slovo o zakone i blagodati* (*Heraldische Funeralpanegyrik*, 127).

15 On the "long duration" of the idea of the Constantinopolitan jurisdiction of Kyiv, see Viktor Zhivov, *Iz tserkovnoi istorii vremen Petra Velikogo* (Moscow: Literaturnoe obozrenie, 2004). On Baranovych, see Teresa Chynczewska-Hennel, "Pojednanie polsko-ukraińskie w wierszach Łazarza Baranowicza," in *Kultura staropolska – kultura europejska: Prace ofiarowane Januszowi Tazbirowi w siedemdzięsiątą rocznicę urodzin*, ed. Stanisław Bylina et al. (Warsaw: Semper, 1997), 325–9 and David A. Frick, "Lazar Baranovych, 1680: The Union of Lech and Rus," in *Culture, Nation and Identity: The Ukrainian-Russian Encounter (1600–1945)*, ed. Andreas Kappeler et al. (Edmonton: Canadian Institute of Ukrainian Studies Press, 2003), 19–56.

16 Quotations are from O. Myshanych, ed., *Ukraïns'ka literatura XVII st.* (Kyiv: Naukova dumka, 1987).

17 Myshanych, ed., *Ukraïns'ka literatura XVII st.*, 229. The term "pys'mo slovenske" (Slavonic writing) probably encompassed both *prosta mova* and (Ruthenian) Church Slavonic.

18 A unique autograph of his sermons lies unpublished in the manuscript section of the National Library of Ukraine in Kyiv, awaiting restoration for twenty years. When will the time arrive to have it at least digitized, if not published in a scholarly edition?

19 For the function of Latin in Russia, see G. Brogi Bercoff, "Plurilinguism in Russia and in the Ruthenian Lands," 13–19. On the late emergence of knowledge of the classics in Russia, see M.J. Okenfuss, *The Rise and Fall of Latin Humanism in Early-Modern Russia* (Leiden: Brill, 1995), esp. 93–102. As far as Russian panegyrical literature is concerned, it was certainly influenced most by the Ukrainian examples of Mazepa's time, though Prokopovych and his colleagues probably had Western models in mind as well. See O.A. Derzhavina, ed., *Panegiricheskaia literatura petrovskogo vremeni* (Moscow: Nauka, 1979) and Lidiia Sazonova, *Literaturnaia kul'tura Rossii: Rannee Novoe vremia* (Moskva: Iazyki slavianskikh kul'tur, 2006), esp. 363–425.

20 However, identifying canon with language, Karol Estreicher mentions all the Polish-language publications of this type in his *Bibliografia polska*, 2nd ed. (Kraków: Uniwersytet Jagielloński, 1959).

21 The first path-breaking book on this topic was Ryszard Łużny, *Pisarze kręgu Akademii Kijowsko-mohylańskiej a literatura polska* (Kraków: Uniwersytet Jagielloński, 1966).

22 See Lidiia Sazonova, *Literaturnaia kultura Rossii*, esp. 483–518.

23 Unfortunately, investigation of these matters is just beginning. In addition to the excellent work of Lidiia Sazonova I draw attention to Paola Cotta Ramusino, *Un poeta alla corte degli zar: Karion Istomin e il panegirico imperiale* (Alessandria:

Edizioni dell'Orso, 2002). Cotta Ramusino devotes much attention to the formal differences in literary style between Karion Istomin and Italian prototypes of emblematic literature. See also G. Brogi Bercoff, "Lazar' Baranovich v pol'skoi i tserkovnoslavianskoi ipostasi," in *Verenica liter: K 60-letiiu V.M. Zhivova*, ed. Aleksandr Moldovan (Moscow: Iazyki kul'tury, 2006), 327–40. For example, a comparative analysis of the Ukrainian texts and Simeon Polotskii's sermons (*Obed dushevnyi*, 1681, and *Vecheria dushevnaia*, 1683) is badly needed.

24 G. Brogi Bercoff, "Die Kunst der Variation: zur Barockpredigt in der Ukraine und in Russland," in *Bibel, Liturgie und Frömmigkeit in der Slavia Byzantina: Festgabe für Hans Rothe zum 80. Geburtstag*, ed. Dagmar Christians, Dieter Stern, and Vittorio S. Tomelleri (Munich: Sagner, 2009), 375–89; G. Brogi Bercoff, "Modele teoretyczne i ich aktualizacja w siedemnastowiecznym kaznodziejstwie na przykładzie *Mowy duchownej* Piotra Mohyły," in *Libris satiari nequeo: Oto ksiąg jestem niesyty*, ed. Joanna Partyka and Ariadna Masłowska-Nowak (Warszawa: Instytut Badań Literackich PAN, 2010), 55–62. On the rather late and partial penetration of Ruthenian models into Russia see also Hans Rothe, *Religion und Kultur in den Regionen des Russischen Reiches im 18. Jahrhundert* (Opladen: Westdeutscher Verlag, 1984).

25 Baranovych's *Mech dukhovnyi* (Spiritual Sword) and *Truby sloves propovednykh* (Homiletic Trumpets) were printed in Kyiv in 1666 and 1674 respectively. See G. Brogi Bercoff, "Barokova homiletyka u skhidnoslovians'komu kul'turnomu prostori," in *Contributi italiani al XIV Congresso Internazionale degli Slavisti* (Firenze: Firenze University Press, 2008), 179–200 and the bibliography presented there.

26 See Andrzej Vincenz, ed., *Helikon Sarmacki: Wątki i tematy polskiej poezji barokowej* (Wrocław: Zakład Narodowy im. Ossolińskich, 1989).

27 Having in mind the fostering of the Church Union, some Western Catholic hagiographers considered Rus' saints and metropolitans as belonging to the "universal church" until 1526. See G. Brogi Bercoff, "The Utopia of the Ecclesiastical Union in the 18th Century: J.S. Assemani," in *Filologia e letteratura nei paesi slavi*, ed. G. Brogi Bercoff, J. Jerkov, and E. Sgambati (Rome: Carucci, 1990), 669–79; G. Brogi Bercoff, "The Cyrillo-Methodian Tradition and the Russian Christianism in the Counter-Reformation," in *The Legacy of Saints Cyril and Methodius to Kiev and Moscow*, ed. Anthony-Emil N. Tachiaos (Thessaloniki: Hellenic Association for Slavic Studies, 1992), 521–34; G. Brogi Bercoff, "I Żywoty Świętych di Łazarz Baranowicz," in *Scritti in memoria di Andrzej Litwornia*, ed. A. Ceccherelli et al. (Rome: Accademia Polacca delle Scienze, 2007), 81–97.

28 See Milorad Pavić, *Istorija srpske književnosti baroknog doba (XVII i XVIII vek)* (Beograd: Nolit, 1970), esp. 260–83 and G. Brogi Bercoff, ed., *Il Barocco letterario nei paesi slavi* (Rome: La nuova Italia scientifica, 1996).

29 Significantly enough, however, Tuptalo wrote most of his *Diariusz* in Polish. See
    Gary Marker, "A Saint's Intimate Life: The 'Diariusz' of Dimitrii Rostovskii,"
    in *Everyday Life in Russian History*, ed. Gary Marker et al. (Bloomington, IN:
    Slavica, 2010), 127–44.
30 As mentioned above, he styled himself "Exarch," probably not as a "substitute"
    of the Patriarche of Moscow, but thinking of the Patriarch of Constantinople as
    the highest authority, following the "model" of the Kyivan Metropolitan see. See
    G. Brogi Bercoff, "A Marginal Note on Marginal Notes: The Library of Stefan
    Javorskij," *Palaeoslavica* 10, no. 1 (2002): 11–25; Zhivov, *Iz tserkovnoi istorii*.
31 In Iavors'kyi's notes on the margins of his books there is evidence that he tried to
    be a "guide" for the tsar in canon law (see G. Brogi Bercoff, "A Marginal Note").
32 It is difficult to make judgments about other Kyivan sermons, since they have not
    yet been published, let alone investigated.
33 See my publication and analysis of the text: "Niepublikowany wiersz Stefana
    Jaworskiego?" *Terminus* 2 (2004): 53–64.
34 The paucity of scholarly investigations makes comparison with Iavors'kyi's
    Kyivan sermons difficult.
35 *Propovedi*, I–III (Moscow: Sinodal'naia tipografiia, 1804–5).
36 See Il'ia A. Shliapkin, *Sv. Dimitrii Rostovskii i ego vremia (1651–1709 g.)* (Saint
    Petersburg: Transhel', 1891), 428.
37 For an analysis of the poem see Dmitrii Liburkin, *Russkaia novolatinskaia
    poeziia: Materialy k istorii. XVII–pervaia polovina XVIII veka* (Moscow:
    Rossiiskii gosudarstvennyi gumanitarnyi universitet, 2000), 121–9. According to
    Liburkin the original title was *Possessoris horum librorum luctuosum libris vale*.
38 Marina Feodotova, *Epistoliarnoe nasledie Dmitriia Rostovskogo: Issledovanie i
    materialy* (Moscow: Indrik, 2005), 451–3 and 132–4.
39 "Zum literarischen Gebrauch der Mischsprache im ostslavischen Bereich im
    17.–18. Jh.," *Ricerche slavistiche* XLIII (1996): 183–208.
40 Filipp Ternovskii, "Pis'ma Mitropolita Stefana Iavorskogo," *Trudy Kievskoi
    Dukhovnoi Akademii* 1, no. 4 (1866): 538. Iavors'kyi used mixed language when
    writing to his fellow members of the Synod in order to convince them to vote for
    his Ukrainian candidates (*Opisanie dokumentov i del khraniashchikhsia v arkhive
    Sv. Pravitelstvuiushchago Sinoda* [Saint Petersburg, 1869], I, CCCCLXXIV, N.
    XLVI).
41 Feodotova, *Epistoliarnoe nasledie*, 135, 137–8, 161–2, and 252. In the quotation
    and translation Latin round script indicates Polish, italics indicate Latin, and bold
    type Church Slavonic.
42 Ternovskii, "Pis'ma," 548. The quotation *O praeclarum ovium custodem lupum* is
    from Cicero, but it probably also evoked intertextual associations with the Gospel
    of St John.

43 A special case is the letter Iavors'kyi wrote to his Ukrainian friends in the newly
   founded Holy Synod in December 1721. Among other issues, he recommended
   his protégés for election to the Synod; he then adopted the mixed language of the
   "domestic milieu" as a perfect tool for communication under the circumstances.
   This language might have reflected spoken usage, but it may also have been a
   "private" jargon among people belonging to a similar political and cultural "party"
   (see also note 40 above).

The Image of the Intercession of the Mother of God in Ukraine: East versus West

MICHAEL S. FLIER

There is perhaps no image in the history of the icon on Ukrainian territory that has engendered more ink and remained more elusive than that of the Intercession of the Mother of God.[1] Its murky beginnings in Galicia, its disappearance for a century or more, its re-emergence in the fifteenth century in Eastern and Western variants, and its flourishing in the seventeenth and eighteenth centuries have all been analysed, questioned, discussed, and reviewed without universally accepted conclusions. The purpose of the present study is to examine specific issues as a means of gaining a clearer sense of the origins, development, and influences that have shaped this central representation of Ukrainian iconography.

Specialists are agreed on one fundamental fact: the inspiration for the Intercession narrative is inextricably linked to the Byzantine Church of the Mother of God at Blachernai, a royal commission originally completed outside the walls of Constantinople by Emperor Marcian around 453. Emperor Leo I (r. 457–74) built an adjacent chapel called Hagia Soros ("holy reliquary") to house the robe (*riza*) of Mary, Mother of God, retrieved from Palestine in 473. The cult of the Deposition of the Robe was initiated by Patriarch Sergios (610–38) with its own service and feast day on 2 July to celebrate this remarkable relic.[2]

The church was also renowned for an image of Mary, called Blachernitissa after the church, located in the large basilica, probably in the conch of the main apse.[3] According to tradition, a portable icon of that image, the Oranta (the Virgin with arms raised up in prayer), was brought out to face and repel armies attacking the capital, the Avars and Persians in 626, the Arabs in 717–18, and the Varangian Rus' in 860.[4]

In addition to its protective power, the Blachernitissa image was associated with a regular, "habitual" miracle that brought attention and honour to the Blachernai church.[5] A curtain hid it from public view throughout the course of the week. During the vespers service on Friday evenings, however, the curtain would rise up by itself, revealing the image. It remained lifted until the Ninth Hour (around 3:00 p.m.) on Saturday. The raising and lowering of the curtain occurred on its own; there was no mechanism, manipulation, or magic force involved.[6] The original church complex was destroyed by fire in 1434.

In the tenth century, a certain Nikephoros wrote the *Life of Andrew the Fool*.[7] It was Andrew who was steadfastly praying in the Blachernai Church of the Reliquary at the fourth hour of the evening (around 10:00 p.m.), together with his companion Epiphanios, when he had a vision of the Mother of God entering the nave through the western, or royal, doors, flanked by John the Forerunner, John the Theologian, and a retinue of other holy men dressed in white, some preceding and some following her, singing hymns. When she reached the ambo, she knelt and prayed for a long time. Andrew asked Epiphanios whether he could see the Lady and Mistress of the world and he answered, "Yes, I do, my spiritual father."[8] She apparently entered the sanctuary and prayed for the people in attendance. She ultimately removed her veil, which flashed like lightning, and spread it with her own hands over all in attendance as a sign of protection. The veil remained visible as long as she was present but disappeared once she had left.[9] It is this miraculous vision of her veil or maphorion (Church Slavonic *pokrov*) that is linked so closely with her protective intercession as witnessed by Andrew the Fool, identified as a Scythian in the *Life* but taken by Slavs to be one of them. Recent research suggests that the earliest translation of the *Life of Andrew the Fool* into Church Slavonic was in the eleventh or early twelfth century, with a later Rusian redaction by the early thirteenth century, and a Ukrainian redaction in the early fifteenth century. The abridged redaction in the *Prolog* dates to the early twelfth century.[10]

Although most specialists agree that the Virgin's robe and veil are one and the same relic, because of the different names – *riza* and *pokrov* – there was and still is at times confusion among the faithful that these were separate items, stored together in the Blachernai Reliquary Church in a sealed container along with a portion of the Virgin's belt or girdle (*poias*).[11] With this basic background presented, we can now turn to the iconographic images of the Intercession on Ukrainian territory. They are partly distinct from those on Russian territory in that they are based on Western as well as Eastern traditions.

As a parallel to the Eastern Intercession, the cult of the Virgin of Mercy that arose in the West in the thirteenth century derived its iconography from a vision of the Cistercian monk Caesarius of Heisterbach (ca. 1180–ca. 1240) reported in his *Dialogus Miraculorum* (ca. 1230). The miracles associated with Blachernai in the East resonated with this Western cult as well. Thus the stage was set for aspects of both Eastern and Western traditions of the Protection of the Mother of God to make their way to the East Slavs.

In Ukrainian territory, the Protection of the Mother of God as depicted in icons of the Intercession provided a vital connection for Ukrainian elites to claim their place in the social, political, and religious culture of the imagined community. In his insightful analysis of the historiography of Ukrainian early modern icons of the Intercession of the Mother of God – *Pokrova Bohorodytsi* – Serhii Plokhy cut through the layers of generalized and politicized interpretations by imperial and Soviet historians and art specialists to reveal the religious and social context of the variegated imagery of this icon type in eastern and western Ukraine.[12] The depiction of social unity, with representatives from the ranks of royalty, the church, and leading figures of the community, could be contextually manipulated, now serving to portray the idealized incorporation of Little Russia into the all-Russian imperial project in eastern Ukraine, now presenting the rapprochement of the Ruthenian Uniate polity and Polish authorities in western Ukraine, all under the watchful protection of the Mother of God. Plokhy's readings of various Intercession icons show how ever-present Ukrainian-Russian or Ukrainian-Polish political and social tensions might typically be ignored by adherents of the Ukrainian national cause, who preferred to see portraits of Cossack officers and Ukrainian leaders as bellwethers of Ukrainian independence rather than the co-opted elite of the powers that be, whether Russian or Polish.

The Pokrova iconography offered those elites the possibility of using Eastern and Western approaches to the Protection of the Mother of God to make her definitive intercession on their behalf manifest, incorporating them into the very sacred space created by the icon's composition. The Western sources for Pokrova may be traced through fourteenth-century Poland back to thirteenth-century Italy in the form of the Virgin of Mercy (Madonna della Misericordia), with the Virgin shielding under her mantle the whole world (*Mater Omnium*), members of a specific society grouped by status, or single individuals.[13] If we cite only two examples, from Duccio (ca. 1300) and Piero della Francesca (1462), we see the clear features of the Western compositional model (figures 1, 2) that could exert influence, apparently first detected in Ukrainian territory in late fourteenth–early fifteenth-century frescoes of the Horians'ka rotunda of St Anne near Uzhhorod, but flourishing in the seventeenth and eighteenth centuries as exemplified by the Pokrova icons from Deshky and Savarka (figures 3, 4).[14]

What is notable in the Ukrainian cases is that the figures under protection do not so much cluster around the Virgin and address themselves in prayer uniquely to her, as stand under her protective mantle and gaze out towards the beholder, much more in the manner of the Eastern renditions of Pokrova, as seen in an eighteenth-century Pokrova icon from Sulymivka (figure 5), a much more self-reflexive model than the Western counterparts of the Virgin

1: *Madonna of the Franciscans,* Duccio di Buoninsegna, ca. 1300.

2: *Madonna della Misericordia,* Piero della Francesca, 1462.

of Mercy. These patrons of the Virgin apparently wished to be seen not simply as penitents, pleading for succor, but as proud representatives of the elites of society, the favoured few basking in the glory of their status.

3: *Pokrova*, Deshky, late seventeenth–early eighteenth century.

4: *Pokrova,* Savarka, 1750?

With one striking exception, the Eastern models of Pokrova begin with the fifteenth century, contemporary with the first known church dedicated to the Intercession near the stone fortress of Sutkivtsi in Podillia (1471). The fifteenth-century Pokrova icon from Richytsia is an excellent example (plate 1).

5: *Pokrova*, Sulymivka, 1730–40.

Arrayed against the architectural background of the Blachernai Church in Constantinople, the Mother of God appears on a cloud above the altar, her veil or maphorion held aloft by two angels symbolizing her protection over all in the church. Groupings of prelates in rows on the left and other saints and secular figures on the right stand as witnesses to this miraculous vision, which also features Romanos the Melodist, who is credited with composing hundreds of *kontakia* hymns in honour of Mary, including the Great Akathistos Hymn. Since Romanos died in 556 and St Andrew the Fool in 936, Romanos is better understood here as part of Andrew's vision, an index to the hymns sung by the saints that accompanied Mary into the building during the evening service. St Andrew, who can be seen at the centre right, points out the Virgin to his companion Epiphanios.

If the iconographic sources of the Western model for the Protection of the Virgin are fairly clear, those for the Eastern model of the Intercession are more problematic. In virtually all cases, East Slavic Orthodox iconography proceeds from Byzantine sources. The problem for the Intercession imagery is that there is neither a Byzantine prototype nor a Byzantine feast day commemorating the Intercession. Efforts to claim the contrary have not been convincing.[15]

Received opinion has primarily understood the introduction of the Intercession iconography in East Slavic territory as being firmly connected with Andrei Bogoliubskii's cult of the Mother of God, and the association of his patron saint, Andrew the Fool, with her vision of protection. Around 1158 he built a church dedicated to Mary in Bogoliubovo, his royal compound in the Suzdalian principality south of Vladimir. He is also credited with initiating the feast day in honour of this miraculous vision on 1 October, although the feast day itself is not noted in chronicles until the fourteenth century.[16]

We have no icons of the Intercession in Rus' from this earliest period, but some seventy-five years later, in 1233, we find our first image inscribed as the Intercession, on the western doors of the Suzdal' Cathedral of the Nativity of the Mother of God (figure 6).

The doors comprise part of a set of the so-called Golden Doors, copper portals embossed in gold with representations of various biblical scenes and holy figures, including the Intercession image.

This image features the Mother of God Hagiosoritissa – that is, an interceding type commonly found in depictions of the Deёsis. She is shown with the maphorion suspended in air above her, wondered at by four angels with a vignette of Christ conferring his blessing from on high. There is no direct indication of Andrew the Fool. A century later we see two fully evolved Russian iconographic types, the Suzdalian and the Novgorodian.

The Suzdalian type (plate 2) shows Mary standing on a cloud against a background presumably rendering the interior of the Blachernai Reliquary Chapel. She is dressed in tunic and maphorion, but holds a red maphorion in both hands with angels supporting either end. Andrew the Fool and Epiphanios are at the lower right, a church prelate at lower left. Standing

6: *Intercession*, Suzdal', Cathedral of the Nativity of the Mother of God, western doors, detail, 1233.

on the ambo in the centre of the lower register, scroll in hand, is Romanos the Melodist. Since Mary still holds onto the maphorion, this scene is probably meant to represent the moments just before she spreads the veil over the congregation with the angels ready to assist. Mary is the main focus of attention. As distinct from the image on the Suzdalian door, Christ is nowhere to be seen.

The Novgorodian type (plate 3) also shows Mary Oranta standing on a cloud placed above the sanctuary within the space of an architecturally much more structured three-aisle church with five domes. Two angels hold the maphorion in the space above her. A group of prelates and angels populates the sanctuary, whereas St John the Forerunner and St John the Theologian stand in the nave with other saints on the left, opposite Andrew the Fool, Epiphanios, and two other saints present on the right. The sanctuary doors are represented but Romanos is not. The vignette of Christ above repeats the earlier pattern of the Suzdal' doors.

The earliest extant Suzdalian icon is dated to the 1360s; the earliest Novgorodian icon to 1399. It should be noted that the oldest known Novgorodian church now dedicated to the Intercession is in the city kremlin and dates to 1305. Another, originally constructed in the Zverin Monastery in 1335, was rebuilt in 1399 and had the aforementioned icon as its namesake, but both were produced well before the fifteenth-century Ukrainian example just discussed.

A comparison of the Novgorod and Suzdal' types with the Ukrainian Eastern type of Pokrova reveals certain shared features. The strong architectural composition, the angels holding the maphorion aloft, the Virgin Oranta, and the vignette of Christ above are reminiscent of the Novgorod type; the Virgin holding the maphorion with angels assisting, and the inclusion of Romanos the Melodist, allude to the Suzdal' type. Romanos is found in a composite Novgorod-Suzdal' type, but only in the late fifteenth–early sixteenth centuries from Novgorod. What to make of these relationships? As noted earlier, in the all-Russian imperial narrative, the cult of Pokrov, the feast day, and the iconography were ostensibly created during the late twelfth-century reign of Andrei Bogoliubskii, motivated by the link to his patron saint Andrew the Fool, and then spread to other parts of Rus', including Novgorod and Pskov in the northwest and Ruthenian territories in the southwest.

The problems with this narrative were made abundantly clear in 1995 by Maria Pliukhanova.[17] In brief, virtually all aspects of the early ties between Prince Andrei Bogoliubskii and the Intercession remain open. The famous Church of the Intercession on the Nerl' is not given a name in the earliest chronicle accounts and nothing in the external decoration would indicate a reference to Pokrov although, in truth, that is the case for most of the Intercession churches in the Rusian northeast. There is no contemporary record of the prince or the Vladimir eparchy launching a 1 October feast day. Moreover, it is far from clear that Andrei's patron saint was actually Andrew the Fool: Andrew of Crete or the Apostle Andrew are possible candidates as well. The earliest records definitively linking him with Andrew the Fool are from the seventeenth century, the very time when the cult of Andrei Bogoliubskii was in ascendance to further Muscovite authoritarian claims. He was ultimately canonized only in 1702. In addition, it is not obvious that the image of the Intercession on the Suzdal' Golden Door refers to the vision of St Andrew the Fool (neither St Andrew, Epiphanios, nor any other witnesses are depicted) or whether it is a generalized celebration of her role as intercessor for mankind, as recognized through one of her most famous attributes, her maphorion or veil.[18]

It is with this background in mind that we recognize that Liudmyla Miliaieva three decades earlier also contradicted the scenario set forth by the finely tuned imperial machine.[19] In 1914, during the Russian occupation of eastern Galicia, an old icon was brought to the attention of Kyivan curator Danylo Shcherbakivs'kyi, who identified it as a Pokrova icon of the ancient type (plate 4).

The icon was restored in the 1950s by Nikolai Pertsev of the State Russian Museum in Leningrad.[20] He determined that the icon had been renovated three times: in the fifteenth–sixteenth centuries, in the eighteenth century, and in the nineteenth century.[21] Despite the frankly naive draftsmanship, Pertsev suggested that certain features in the use of colour were reminiscent of the pre-Mongol period.[22] Hermitage paleographer Marina Sotnikova ascribed the older of the two inscriptions to the first half of the thirteenth century.[23] If these datings are accurate, the icon would be contemporary with the Intercession panel on the Suzdal' Golden Doors. Miliaieva dated the icon to the twelfth–thirteenth centuries; most other specialists have opted for the thirteenth–fourteenth centuries.

A 2001 carbon dating of the wooden panel on which the icon is painted has convinced a few specialists that the icon is from the period 985–1015, that is, roughly from the time immediately preceding the official baptism of Rus' (988/989) to the death of Volodimer (1015), some two centuries before the earliest previous attributions.[24] This highly dubious dating may be challenged by recalling that carbon dating refers only to the wood itself and not to the painting covering its surface.

The Galician icon is nonetheless equally remarkable for its iconography. Although the two angels holding the maphorion aloft is a familiar theme, there are many puzzling differences. One presumes that the large deep blue semicircular arch over the Virgin is meant as a ciborium or perhaps the conch of the main apse of the Blachernai church. But contrary to the Novgorodian, Suzdalian, and later Ukrainian traditions, the Virgin Oranta is seated on a throne, not standing on a cloud above. The half-length Christ Emmanuel is depicted on her breast, as though he were actually a medallion, familiar in images of the Virgin of the Sign, which underscore the Incarnation, as seen in the famous twelfth-century example from Novgorod (figure 7).

7: *Virgin of the Sign*, Novgorod, twelfth century.

But more likely, he is meant to be seen as the infant Christ, not seated so much in his mother's lap as carried within the folds of her veil, as shown in the seventeenth-century image of the Virgin of the Sign from Rohatyn (figure 8).

With the enthroned Virgin and Child as the central image, it is clear that this is not the vision of the Mother of God associated with St Andrew the Fool in the Blachernai church, in which she has a completely active role. In Andrew's vision there is neither mention of her sitting nor of the presence of the infant

8: *Virgin of the Sign*, iconostasis, Church of the Holy Spirit, Rohatyn, mid-seventeenth century.

Christ. And yet the billowing veil would seem to allude to it. Likewise, the figure to the right is presumably Andrew the Fool pointing to the Virgin, although he is apparently not dressed in garb typical of a holy fool, that is, in ragged clothing, half-naked. Similarly the identities of the figures next to Andrew on the right and of the two prelates on the left are not clear. These issues need to be addressed to establish a preliminary iconography of the Galician Pokrova.

The enthroned Virgin Oranta with Child is itself an infrequent image; most Orantas are full-length or half-length, as seen in the well-known representations from Kyiv and Iaroslavl' (figures 7, 9, 10).

Previous investigators have pointed to ancient examples, such as those from the Armenian Echmiadzin Gospels of 989 or the Bulgarian Tomić Psalter ca. 1360, understood as models and not direct forebears (Figure 11, plate 5).[25]

9: *Virgin Oranta*, mosaic, Cathedral of Holy Sophia, Kyiv, eleventh century.

These references are relevant insofar as they establish the early existence and use of the image of the seated Oranta with Child. But in what context is that image used? The consistent semantics behind the seated Oranta with Child

10: *Great Panagia*, icon, Iaroslavl', twelfth century.

represent the Divine Incarnation of Christ associated with the text from Luke 1:35, just following the Annunciation to which Mary replies: "'How shall this be, seeing I know not a man?' And the Angel answered and said unto her, 'The Holy Ghost shall come upon thee, and the power of the Highest shall over-shadow thee: therefore also that holy thing which shall be born of thee shall be called the Son of God.'"

11: *Virgin Oranta Seated with Child*, Echmiadzin Gospel, Armenia, 989.

This very text is contained within the Akathistos hymn of the Mother of God, composed by Romanos the Melodist: "The power of the highest shall overshadow then, unto conception for one not experienced in marriage."[26] The effect of the Incarnation as a divine overshadowing can be represented pictorially, as seen in a Serbian psalter from Munich, dated the last quarter of the fourteenth century (figure 12).

Plate 1. *Pokrova*. Richytsia, near Rivne. Fifteenth century.

Plate 2. *Intercession.* Suzdal'. Pokrov Monastery? 1360s.

Plate 3. *Intercession.* Novgorod. Zverin Monastery. 1399.

Plate 4. *Pokrova*. Galicia. Twelfth–thirteenth century? Thirteenth–fourteenth century?

Plate 5. Tomić Psalter. *Virgin Oranta Seated with Child.* (Bulgaria). 1360.

Plate 6. *Akathistos: Conception.* Church of Panagia, Meronas, Amari, Crete. Ca. 1400.

Plate 7. *Pokrova.* Galicia. Detail of Saint Andrew the Fool, Epiphanios (?), and a youth. Twelfth–thirteenth century? Thirteenth–fourteenth century?

Plate 8. Tomić Psalter. *Akathistos: Singing Your Giving Birth.* Bulgaria. 1360.

Plate 9. *Pokrova.* Galicia. Detail of inscriptions. Twelfth–thirteenth century? Thirteenth–fourteenth century?

Plate 10. *Pokrova.* Galicia. Detail of prelate and deacon, and Epiphanios and his servant. Twelfth–thirteenth century? Thirteenth–fourteenth century?

12: *Oranta Seated with Child*, Serbian psalter, Munich, last quarter fourteenth century.

Two handmaidens, or two angels in some versions, hold up a curtain behind the Virgin as an index of the miraculous Incarnation of Christ, symbolically replacing the mandorla found in the Tomić Psalter. Some renderings of Akathistos icons of the Conception show even more striking similarities to the Galician Pokrova in the placement of the curtain and attendant drapery, as seen in two examples from fourteenth-century Crete (figure 13, plate 6).

13: *Akathistos: Conception*, Church of Panagia, Roustika, Rethymnon, Crete, 1390–1.

This link with the Seated Oranta, specifically in the context of the Akathistos hymn cycle dedicated to the Mother of God, permits us to make a deeper connection with the cult of Pokrova and the representations in the Galician icon.

The Akathistos cycle is important here, because excerpts from it are included in the Intercession office. It was the French Byzantinist R.P.D. Lathoud who first suggested that the Pokrova service had two primary Byzantine sources, the Akathistos service for the fifth week of the Great Fast, and the 2 July service for the Deposition of the Robe of the Mother of God in the Blachernai Reliquary.[27] The Deposition and Akathistos services use synonymous phrases for the Virgin that incorporate the word *pokrov* and have the meaning "O protector of the whole world" or "O protector of all mankind": человѣкъквъ покровѣ, покровѣ всѣхъ человѣкъквъ, всемоу мироу покровѣ. The Virgin Blachernitissa, understood as the defender, the protectress, is also known by the Greek ἐπίσκεψις, "an overshadowing for protection," that is, "she who defends or protects."[28]

The connective thread binding the Deposition, the Akathistos, and the Veil with the *Life of Andrew the Fool* also extends to the putative composer of the Akathistos Hymn, Romanos the Melodist, whose feast day falls on 1 October, the same day as that of the Intercession. An illiterate pilgrim from Syria, Romanos had come to Constantinople during the reign of Anastasios I (r. 491–518) and served as a sexton in a local church, before accepting a similar assignment at the Cathedral of Holy Sophia. He spent evenings deep in prayer at the Blachernai Church. Patriarch Euphemios (r. 490–6) soon noticed his piety and devotion to the church and appointed him to be a singer, despite his lack of training. He was ridiculed and despised by the other singers. He went home in dejection, only to have a vision of the Mother of God, who commanded him to eat a scroll she handed to him. Obeying her command, Romanos was possessed of an immediate ability to compose hymns. When his turn came at the evening vigil to sing in honour of the holiday, he opened his mouth and sweetly sang his famous Christmas kontakion "Today a Virgin gives birth to him who is pre-eternal" (Дѣва днесь, Пресꙋщественнаго раждаетъ), celebrating the fruit of the Divine Incarnation. All in attendance marveled at his talent. The patriarch immediately inquired as to the source of his deep wisdom and Romanos revealed his vision of the Mother of God. The embarrassed singers begged his forgiveness and the patriarch instantly ordained him as a deacon. Romanos composed numerous hymns for the great feasts and saints days, the most famous being the Akathistos hymn.[29]

It is the particular presence of Romanos the Melodist in the Ukrainian and Suzdalian types, but *nota bene* not in the early Novgorod types, that might be of value in deciphering the basis for the Galician Intercession icon.

Given the very different earliest images we see for the Intercession on East Slavic territory before the fourteenth century, it is likely that the Slavonic translation of the *Life of Andrew the Fool* generated enough interest in the eleventh–twelfth centuries to stimulate the beginnings of a cult of the Intercession. In the Suzdalian northeast, it generated the Virgin Oranta Blachernitissa praying to Christ, the image ultimately based on the *Life of Andrew the Fool* with Romanos added as the singer of the praises of the Virgin Protectress holding her maphorion.

In the Galician southwest, the scene was primarily devoted to the Protectress Oranta as the Bearer of Christ Incarnate, with Andrew's vision rendered only indirectly through the billowing veil above (plate 7). As such, the imagery for her appears to have been influenced by iconography from the Akathistos tradition, namely, a seated Oranta, often with the medallion of the Christ Child on her breast. The iconographic curtain held behind her by two maidens was easily replaced by her veil held by two angels, with Andrew the Fool pointing to it from below (plate 8). The seated Oranta depicted here is apparently not with a medallion of the Child but with the Child himself contained within the folds of her robes and sitting on her lap. Thus she is more securely interpreted not as St Andrew's vision but as the image in the main apse of the Blachernai Church, with the dark-coloured arc around her representing the triumphal arch of the church itself. The scene then depicts the actual service attended by Andrew the Fool, with the vision of the maphorion alone as a metonymic signal of the Virgin's spiritual presence. As noted in the *Life of Andrew* itself: "As long as the most Holy Mother of God was there the veil was also visible, but when she had withdrawn they could not longer see it. No doubt she had taken it away with her, but her favour she left to those who were there. [Epiphanios saw this through the mediation of the God-bearing father, for he enjoyed freedom of approach and communicated his vision to Epiphanios, acting as mediator for him]."[30]

As for the three persons on the right, the figure pointing is traditionally identified as Andrew the Fool. The nimbus assures us of his sanctity. But the two figures to the right are more problematic: The person next to Andrew, traditionally understood to be Epiphanios, is devoid of the nimbus and is wearing a hat, a strange addition for a youth observing an Orthodox service. A beardless figure standing behind him is wearing a pointed hat. As for the two figures on the left, we see a saintly prelate wearing the *sakkos* of a patriarch standing next to a beardless deacon, identified by the long *orarion* worn over his *sticharion* – a sign of the office.

In his long chapter on the Galician Pokrova icon, Volodymyr Aleksandrovych offers his own explanation of all five figures, in some cases rejecting the assumptions of other scholars. Following Miliaieva's original reading, he accepts the figure pointing to be Andrew the Fool.[31] He identifies the beardless figure in the rounded hat as Epiphanios, and, in a completely new and convincing reading, he interprets the young figure in the pointed hat behind Epiphanios as his servant, the very one mentioned in the *Life of Andrew the*

Fool: "When a night-long doxology was held in the Holy Casket at Blach-ernae blessed Andrew attended, behaving in his usual way. Epiphanios was also present, and with him one of his servants."[32] He takes the prelate on the left, dressed in a *sakkos* (reserved for patriarchs before the fourteenth century) to be St John Chrysostom, author of the regular Divine Liturgy used in the Eastern Orthodox Church. He justifies his appearance as the reflection of a special cult of the saint in the court of Galician prince Danylo Romanovych (r. 1205–64, with interruptions), John Chrysostom apparently being the prince's patron saint.[33] The adjacent figure in his view is a young deacon. Although this portion of the icon is in extremely poor condition, Aleksandrovych asserts that the deacon, whom he understands to be a generalized figure, holds a cup in his right hand, assisting St John in the celebration of the Eucharist. With this read-ing, he rejects outright an earlier identification of the deacon as Romanos the Melodist.[34] Unfortunately, his reasoning in rejecting the deacon as Romanos and accepting the youths as Epiphanios and his servant is illogical. Although he admits that the tradition of Romanos appearing in icons of the Intercession is an old one, he insists that this deacon cannot be Romanos because he lacks the nimbus of a saint. The same stricture does not seem to hold when he iden-tifies the youths next to St Andrew as Epiphanios and his servant, even though Epiphanios is without nimbus as well, despite his saintly status in other icons of the Intercession. To add to the confusion, Aleksandrovych asserts that the author of the icon was consistent in distinguishing such spiritual marking, but that exceptions are found in other icons.[35]

If we allow for the possibility that the icon painter has, in fact, been incon-sistent in representing saintliness – the naive rendering of the images certainly permits such a possibility – then one might be tempted to identify the deacon as Romanos. His feast day is 1 October, after all, coincident with the celebration of the Intercession. And he does appear in the earliest Suzdalian icons of the Intercession. Furthermore, Vasyl' Putsko interprets the item in the right hand of Romanos not as a cup, but as the top of a rolled-up scroll.[36] In point of fact, the typical iconography associated with Romanos the Melodist indicates a book or scroll together with a censer. Nonetheless, the iconographic scroll for Roma-nos is always held in his left hand and is unrolled to reveal the words of his Christmas kondakion. This iconographic deficiency together with the lack of nimbus lead me to agree with Aleksandrovych and analyse the young deacon as a participant in the service attended by Andrew, celebrating the liturgy of St John Chrysostom.

As for the youths next to Andrew, I also agree with Aleksandrovych in see-ing them as Epiphanios and his servant, albeit without nimbuses. And here once again, their hats – a turban-like headgear for Epiphanios, a pointed cap for his servant – may very well be influenced by images of the Akathistos Hymn, in which singers adjacent to the Mother of God in the image of Conception are shown wearing the rounded turban-shaped *skaranikon* (from the mid-twelfth century on) or the pointed *skiadion* (from the fourteenth century on); see plates 7, 8, 10.[37]

The important point here is that even though in this early period the cult and the iconography of the Intercession were not settled either in the north or in the south of Rus', there is a common reference – direct or indirect, through the choice of the seated Oranta – to Romanos the Melodist in both Galician and Suzdalian, but not early Novgorodian, typology. Novgorod appears to provide the more structured architectural background that ultimately resonates in Moscow and later in early modern Ukraine.

In this regard, it is worth recalling that Andrei Bogoliubskii and his kin were southerners by birth and tradition. The connection with the composer of the Akathistos Hymn and its imagery might also tie in with the increased frequency of the performance of the Akathistos service in monasteries in Constantinople and beyond from the twelfth century on and with numerous fresco cycles and psalters in the Balkans referring to the Akathistos Hymn beginning ca. 1300.[38] The influence of such increased dissemination would easily have been felt most keenly in southern Rus'. If valid, such a connection would tend to support the dating of the Galician icon to the thirteenth–fourteenth centuries.

Further evidence of this later dating of the Galician icon comes from philological data, morphological and orthographic. In the late fourteenth century, we find the first traces in southern Rus' of the grammatical gender shift of the word *Pokrov* (masc. sg.) to *Pokrova* (fem. sg.), a sign perhaps that the notion of protection inherent in Mary's head covering was generalized to the Virgin herself as protectress, not simply a bearer of protective attributes but the embodiment of protection itself, *pars pro toto*. This switch provides fertile ground in the fourteenth–fifteenth centuries for developing the cult of the Intercession by dedicating namesake churches and by continuing the tradition of the Eastern type of Intercession against the background of the vision of Andrew the Fool and the hymns of Romanos *or* by accepting the Western model that provides direct juxtaposition of the protected elites under the mantle of the Mother of God without a narrative intermediary (see figures 3, 4). Whether cast as veil or robe, the function of Mary's garment in either tradition remains the same.[39] The culture of early modern Ukraine was clearly expansive enough to incorporate both types through a filter of Western European stylization, and in this capacity the Intercession flourished in the seventeenth and eighteenth centuries.

As for orthography and morphology, one last issue deserves our attention: the two inscriptions on the icon (plate 9). When Miliaieva published her 1965 article, she noted their presence and transcribed both.[40] She read the black one (fifteenth–sixteenth century) as покровъ п꙯рта бца. In actual fact it reads покровъ п꙯ртыа бца – "the Intercession of the most holy Mother of God." Miliaieva read the cinnabar inscription (early thirteenth century) as покровы сть бл. In fact it reads покровъі сть бца. It is curious that she did not comment on the unexpected form покровъі, and that all succeeding writers have ignored it or only noted it in passing without comment.[41] In light of the discussion above concerning the figural references and the dating of the Galician Pokrova icon, it is worth considering what the older inscription might tell us about this controversial Ukrainian artefact.

Ostensibly покровъі looks like a nominative plural of the noun покровъ. In Early Rusian the nominative plural would have been покрови, but with the jer shift and the neutralization of phonemes *i* and *y* to *i* throughout most of East Slavic, the pronunciation of *i* came to depend on the palatalization of the preceding consonant. If soft, the vowel would have been pronounced [i]; if hard, the vowel would have been pronounced [y]. In most Ukrainian dialects, and especially those in Galicia (excluding the Carpathians), the consonant hardened before original *i* in the mid to late thirteenth century, therefore [pokrovy] would have been the likely pronunciation.[42] The possible confusion about whether the Blachernai reliquary contained a robe or mantle (*riza*), a veil or maphorion (*pokrov*), and a belt or girdle (*poias*) may have motivated the appearance of this otherwise inexplicable plural title referring to multiple pieces of Mary's protective wardrobe from Blachernai, all represented in the icon. Attention to the miraculous relics rather than the specific event of the Intercession may help explain why there seems to be no trace of church dedication to the Intercession itself before the late fifteenth century in Ukraine and therefore why Ukraine, unlike Russia, could be open to both Eastern and Western models of the Virgin's protection that come to the fore in the fifteenth century. It is also conceivable that the plural might refer both to the Virgin's headgear and, from the Akathistos and Intercession services, to the Virgin's characterization by Romanos as the protector of all mankind (человѣкwвъ покрове, покрове всѣхъ человѣкwвъ, всемоу мироу покрове), that is, metaphoric as well as metonymic protection.

An alternative explanation would recognize the form покровъі not as a nominative plural masculine noun but rather as a genitive singular form of the reidentified feminine noun покрова. The form покрова instead of покровъ first begins to appear in texts from Ukrainian territory in the late fourteenth century. Such a reading assumes a preceding noun such as праздьникъ or памать "holiday, feast" that was obscured in later overpainting, thus the Feast of the Protection of the most Holy Mother of God.

In either case, the analysis of the Galician Pokrova icon here supports the later dating – thirteenth–fourteenth centuries – and indicates a representation that celebrates the protective powers of the Mother of God through the imagery of the Akathistos hymn of Romanos the Melodist and the veil that inspires the vision of St Andrew the Fool as he attends a late night service in the Blachernai Cathedral with his disciple Epiphanios.

In retrospect, the evolution of the imagery of the Protection of the Mother of God on Ukrainian territory may signal the effects in distinct historical periods of different Eastern and Western waves of influence on the iconographic representation of this significant visual association with Mary. In the period leading up to the late fourteenth century, the protective capacity of Mary and her apparel (maphorion, robe, belt), foregrounded in the life of Andrew the Fool, could be conflated with Mary's representation in the Akathist hymn as protectress of man through the Incarnation, with iconography coming from the Byzantine East and the Caucasus (plate 4). The emergence of specifically Intercession iconography from Suzdal' (plate 2) and later Novgorod (plate 3) may have reinforced the personalization of protection in Mary as Pokrova, resulting in the appearance of church dedications to the Intercession and resultant icons from the fifteenth century on (plate 1). Representations of the Virgin's protection coming from Western Europe through Poland presented an alternative perspective dominated by the Virgin and her protective robe providing shelter to members of the Ukrainian Cossack elite by the eighteenth century, even backgrounding the vision of St Andrew the Fool (figure 5), or leaving it represented only indirectly as an index of the miraculous maphorion (figures 3 and 4). This rich variety of depiction demonstrates Ukraine's significant role as cultural intermediary between East and West among the East Slavs.

Notes

1 See Volodymyr Aleksandrovych, *Pokrov Bohorodytsi: Ukraïns'ka seredn'ovichna ikonohrafiia* (Lviv: Natsional'na Akademiia Nauk Ukraïny, 2010) with its extensive bibliography about the Pokrova icon and related issues (411–36), and his thorough and useful review of the numerous hypotheses about the age and meaning of the icon, esp. 83–181.

2 See Annemarie Weyl Carr, "Threads of Authority: The Virgin Mary's Veil in the Middle Ages," in *Robes and Honor: The Medieval World of Investiture,* ed. Stewart Gordon (New York: Palgrave, 2001), 61–3.

3 Nikodim Kondakov, *Ikonografiia Bogomateri*, 2 vols. (Moscow: Palomnik, 1914–15/1998), 2: 64. See also Cyril Mango, "The Origins of the Blachernae Shrine at Constantinople," in *Radovi XIII. Međunarodnog kongresa za starokršćansku*

arheologiju (Split – Poreč, 25.9–1.10 1994), pt. 2, ed. Nenad Cambi and Emilio Marin (Split: Arheološki muzej, 1998) [= *Vjesnik za arheologiju i historiju Dalmatinsku,* vol. 87–9, supplement], 61–75.

4 The protective role of the Mother of God in the victory of 626 is specifically celebrated in the thirteenth kontakion of the Akathistos hymn sung on the Saturday (Friday evening) of the fifth week of the Great Fast.

5 Kondakov, *Ikonografiia Bogomateri*, 2: 57.

6 Venantius Grumel, "'Le Miracle habituel' de Notre-Dame des Blachernes à Constantinople," *Échos d'Orient* 30 (1931): 129–46, here 145, note 1; Lennart Rydén, "The Vision of the Virgin at Blachernae and the Feast of Pokrov," *Annalecta Bollandiana* 94 (1976): 63–82, here 69–70; Bissera V. Pentcheva, "The Blachernai Responds: The Icon of the 'Usual Miracle,'" chap. 5 in *Icons and Power: The Mother of God in Byzantium* (University Park, PA: Pennsylvania State University, 2006), 145–63.

7 For comment on the dating of the Greek original, see Lennart Rydén, "The Date of the *Life of Andreas Salos*," *Dumbarton Oaks Papers* 32 (1978): 127–55. See the reconstructed Church Slavonic versions along with a textological and philological analysis in Aleksandr Moldovan, ed., *Zhitie Andreia Iurodivogo v slavianskoi pis'mennosti* (Moscow: Azbukovnik, 2000), 16–450; Ernst Hansack, review of *Zhitie Andreia Iurodivogo v slavianskoi pis'mennosti*, by Aleksandr Moldovan, ed., *Russian Linguistics* 26 (2002): 127–32.

8 Moldovan, ed., *Zhitie*, 399.

9 Ibid., 399–400.

10 Ibid., 17, 40, 49, 106.

11 See André Grabar, "Une source d'inspiration de l'iconographie byzantine tardive: Les ceremonies du culte de la Vierge," *Cahiers archéologiques fin de l'Antiquité et Moyen Age* 25 (1976): 147–52; Weyl Carr, "Threads of Authority," 62–6; and John Wortley, "The Marian Relics at Constantinople," *Greek, Roman, and Byzantine Studies* 45 (2005): 171–87. On the Deposition of the Virgin's Robe in Blachernai, celebrated on 2 July, and the Deposition of the Virgin's Belt, celebrated on 31 August, see Sergei Bulgakov, *Nastol'naia kniga dlia sviashchenno-tserkovno-sluzhitelei,* 2nd ed., rev. and exp. (Kharkiv: Tip. Gubernskogo Pravleniia, 1900), 224–5 and 306–7.

12 Serhii Plokhy, *Tsars and Cossacks: A Study in Iconography* (Cambridge, MA: Harvard University Press, 2002).

13 See, especially, Mieczysław Gębarowicz, *Mater Misericordiae – Pokrow – Pokrowa w sztuce i legendzie środkowo-wschodniej Europy* (Wrocław: Zakład narodowy imienia Ossolińskich, 1986).

14 H. Lohvyn, *Ukrainskoe iskusstvo X–XVIII vv.* (Moscow: Izd. Iskusstvo, 1963), 82–5.

15 John Wortley, "Hagia Skepê and Pokrov Bogoroditsi: A Curious Coincidence,"
    Analecta Bollandiana 89 (1971): 149–52; Lennart Rydén, "The Vision of the
    Virgin," 78–82.

16 Kondakov, *Ikonografiia Bogomateri*, 2: 93. It is interesting to note that the
    Novgorodian churches currently dedicated to the Intercession are simply
    called churches of the Holy Mother of God, not the Intercession, in chronicle
    manuscripts dated even as late as the fourteenth–fifteenth centuries; see, for
    example, the index entries for churches of the Intercession in Arsenii Nasonov,
    ed., *Novgorodskaia pervaia letopis' starshego i mladshego izvodov* (Moscow:
    Institut istorii AN SSSR, 1950), 619.

17 Maria Pliukhanova, *Siuzhety i simvoly Moskovskogo tsarstva* (St Petersburg:
    Akropol', 1995), especially 23–62. A recent, thorough accounting of manuscripts,
    church dedications, and the like has yet to yield a definitive date for the creation
    of the holiday dedicated to the Intercession: V. M. Kirillin, "Pokhval'noe slovo
    prazdniku Pokrova Presviatoi Bogorodilsy neizvestnogo drevnerusskogo avtora:
    Osobennosti soderzhaniia, mesto, i vremia sostavleniia," *Drevniaia Rus': Voprosy
    medievistiki* 3, no. 49 (2012): 5–20 and 4, no. 50: 13–27.

18 R.P.D. Lathoud, "Le thème iconographique du 'Pokrov' de la Vierge," *L'art
    byzantine chez les slaves*, 2 vols. (Paris: P. Geuthner, 1932), 2: 302–14.

19 L. S. Miliaeva, "Pamiatnik galitskoi zhivopisi XIII v.," *Sovetskaia arkheologiia* 3
    (1965): 249–58.

20 Nikolai Vasil'evich Pertsev, *Nikolai Vasil'evich Pertsev: Katalog
    restravratsionnnykh rabot* (St Petersburg: Khudozhnik Rossii, 1992), 49–52.

21 Ibid., 50.

22 Ibid., 51–2.

23 Miliaeva, "Pamiatnik," 251–2.

24 Nikolay Kovalyukh et al., "Dating of Ancient Icons from Kiev Art Collections,"
    Radiocarbon 43, no. 2B (2001): 1066–7.

25 For example, Aleksandrovych, *Pokrov Bohorodytsi,* 133, where the author cites a
    reference to Engelina Smirnova's comment on the rare iconography found in the
    late tenth-century Armenian Etchmiadzin gospels and in the old western Ukrainian
    Pokrova icon in *Matenadaran: Sokrovishcha knizhnogo iskusstva v sobraniiakh
    SSSR*, ed. Vigen Kazarian, vol. 1, *Armianskaia rukopisnaia kniga VI–XIV vekov*
    (Moscow: Kniga, 1991), 31.

26 The Slavonic version of the kontakion reads as follows: "Сила вышнего всѣни
    тогда, къ зачѧтиоу браконеискоу снѣи." Cited from Aksiniia Dzhurova,
    Tomichov Psaltir, 2 vols. (Sofia: Kliment Ohridski University Press, 1990), 1: 17.

27 Lathoud, "Le thème iconographique," 302–3.

28 Ibid., 306.

29 *Zhitia sviatykh na russkom iazyke izlozhennye po rukovodstvu Chet'ikh-minei sv. Dimitriia Rostovskogo,* vol. 2, *Mesiats Oktiabr'* (Moscow: Sinodal'naia tipografiia, 1902), 21–5.

30 *The Life of Andrew the Fool,* Lennart Rydén, ed., vol. 2, *Text, Translation and Notes. Appendices,* Studia Byzantina Upsaliensis, no. 4, pt. 2. (Uppsala: Uppsala University, distrib. Almqvist and Wiksell International, 1995), 254–5. It is worth noting here that Christa Belting-Ihm understands Andrew's vision as the result of his staring at a monumental image of the Blacherniotissa type; see *"Sub matris tutela": Untersuchungen zur Vorgeschichte der Schutzmantelmadonna,* Abhandlungen der Heidelberger Akademie der Wissenschaften, Philosophisch-Historische Klasse, 1976, no. 3. (Heidelberg: Carl Winter, 1976), 59–61. The Church Slavonic text reads as follows: да донѣлиже бѣаше тамо ст҃аѧ бц҃а. видиста и та. а понелѣже ѿиде. боле того не видисте. взѧла бо бѫдеть со собою. а бл҃ть оставила есть сѫщимъ тамо, cited from Moldovan, *Zhitie,* 399–400. By analysing this scene as the actual service, I agree with Aleksandrovych in rejecting the notion that it represents instead the "habitual miracle" associated with the Blachernai Cathedral, since that tradition has no association with Andrew's vision; cf. *Pokrov Bohorodytsi,* 90–3.

31 Miliaieva, "Pamiatnyk," 252; Aleksandrovych, *Pokrov Bohorodytsi,* 91, 140.

32 Aleksandrovych, *Pokrov Bohorodytsi,* 149–60. Translation from Rydén, *Life,* 255.

33 Aleksandrovych, *Pokrov Bohorodytsi,* 147–8.

34 Aleksandrovych, *Pokrov Bohorodytsi,* 140–2. Cf. Miliaieva, "Pamiatnyk," 251, note 2; A. Aleksandrov, "Ob ustanovlenii prazdnika Pokrova Presviatoi Bogoroditsy v Russkoi Tserkvi," *Zhurnal Moskovskoi patriarkhii* 10 (1983): 76; and Vasyl' Putsko, "Ukrainskie i belorusskie ikony Pokrova XVII–XVIII vv.: Istoki ikonograficheskoi skhemy," in *Belorusskii sbornik: Stat'i i materialy po istorii i kul'ture Belorusii,* no. 2 (St Petersburg: Russkaia Natsional'naia Biblioteka, 2002), 36.

35 Aleksandrovych, *Pokrov Bohorodytsi,* 140–1, 154. His examples of exceptions include the mid-fourteenth-century Suzdal' Intercession discussed above and the Pokrova *kleimo* from the sixteenth-century icon of the Nativity of Christ with Scenes from the Theotokos Cycle from the Church of the Intercession in Trushevychi.

36 Vasyl' Putsko, "Pro tserkovne maliarstvo Ukraïny XIV st.," *Istoriia relihiï v Ukraïni. Naukovyi shchorichnyk 2004,* bk. 2 (Lviv, 2004), 516.

37 Citation from Neil K. Moran, *Singers in Late Byzantine and Slavonic Painting* (Leiden: E. J. Brill, 1986), 37, 44, 51.

38 Citation from Nancy Patterson Ševčenko, "Icons in the Liturgy," *Dumbarton Oaks Papers* 45 (1991): 56.

39 Lathoud, "Le thème iconographique," 314.
40 Miliaeva, "Pamiatnik," 251.
41 Aleksandrovych, *Pokrov Bohorodytsi*, 117, remarks the form with *y* but makes no attempt to clarify its possible meaning.
42 George Y. Shevelov, *A Historical Phonology of the Ukrainian Language* (Heidelberg: Carl Winter Universitätsverlag, 1979), 380–1.

"Europe" in Seventeenth- and Early Eighteenth-Century Ukrainian Texts: Between Geography and Ambivalent Judgments

NATALIA YAKOVENKO

Thanks to the works of Western humanists and especially the publication of Maciej Miechowski's *Tractatus de duabus Sarmatiis, Asiana et Europiana*,[1] the first book with geographic and ethnographic content to appear in Poland, use of the word "Europe" to denote a single metageographical whole, which was modelled during the Renaissance age, entered the discourse of the elites in the Polish-Lithuanian state between the second quarter and middle of the sixteenth century. However, this innovation did not take root immediately in Ruthenian-language writing, such as chronicles, devotional verse, and religious texts of a hortatory and polemical character. Here, as previously, that which the humanists understood as "Europe" was called the "West," usually appearing in paired contrast to the "Greek" ("our") "East," as, for example, in these lines from a poem dating to the late 1580s–early 1590s:

Горе оным, иже Церков изражают...,
Оставляют Восток и бѣгут на Запад; [...]
Помраченіє ума людей славолюбных
Наносит с Западу устав душогубных; [...]
Кланяємся на Восток, а на Запад плюєм,
Єгда крещеніє святоє приіймуєм.[2]

(Woe betide those who object to the Church...
They abandon the East and flee to the West; [...]
The dimming of minds of glory-loving people
Is brought from the West by the statutes of murderers; [...]
We bow to the East, but spit on the West,
When we accept holy baptism.)

Owing to the dearth of proper sources it is impossible to determine conclusively whether these lines refer to unfamiliarity with "Latin" texts or the conscious preservation of the Orthodox tradition, according to which the entire "Latin" world was identified with the "West." As may be cautiously assumed, one argument in favour of the latter is the fact that the word "Europe" does not even appear in the first Polish-language secular text, which was an entirely new genre for Rus': the lengthy funeral poem *Epicedion* (1585) on the death of Prince Mykhailo Vyshnevets'kyi, which was written by the prince's servant, the Orthodox Volhynian nobleman Zhdan Bilyts'kyi.[3] The author of the poem is already more or less proficient in the use of rhetorical devices and ancient mythology, and his descriptions of battles are modelled on the versified insertions in Maciej Stryjkowski's chronicle. However, unlike Stryjkowski, the only metageographical concept that he uses is "Asian lands" (*Azyjskie kraje*), not "Europe." Because literary convention required placing the renown of the celebrated princely family in some kind of broader context, the author limits himself to making a diffuse declaration about its loud reverberations in all "foreign states" (*państwach cudzych*).[4]

Instead, the concept of "Europe" already appears – probably for the first time – in the next extant work that was written in the secular genre, new to Rus'. This text is the panegyric Προσφώνημα (Address, 1591), written by the pupils of the Lviv brotherhood school in honour of Metropolitan Mykhailo Rahoza (its author is believed to be the teacher of "Slavic" and Greek grammar, Kyrylo Trankvilion Stavrovets'kyi,[5] who, as scholars assume, was a graduate of the Latin cathedral school in Lviv).[6] The poem about Lviv's coat of arms begins thus:

Герб тезоименитаго князя Лва град сей маєт,
Єго же имя *по всей Европіи* российскій род знаєт.

(This city has the coat of arms of the prince of the same name, Lev;
Its name is known in *all of Europe* by the Rossian clan.) (Emphasis added)

In the Greek-language preamble to the congratulatory poem, the metropolitan is called "Ευρώπης άστον" (Europe's star); the same is repeated in the translation: "вси тя, ... *Европія звѣзду*, едино око Россіи, всѣх язик гласы гласуют" (the voices of all tongues call you ... *Europe's star*, sole eye of Rossia).[7]

While the new "spatial orientation" recorded here signalled a change in cultural code, Ruthenian authors of the period gave no interpretation of it in theoretical treatises, nor did they leave even incidental reflections on why and in what types of image the term "Europe" entered the Orthodox discourse, and how this image changed over time. Thus, it is only from oblique statements that researchers can recreate, with greater or lesser reliability, that "composite image" of Europe which, in the perception of Ruthenians during the early modern period, slowly began to accumulate new content until by the turn of the seventeenth century it coincided with the "real" Europe as a geographic entity. Although sources reflect these changes, they do so erratically, unfortunately. Only a scant few mentions dating to before the mid-seventeenth century are extant; these will be examined in the first part of this article. Meanwhile, the second half of the century is represented by a considerable body of texts in which "Europe" is present in the form of references in the margins to works by Western authors. Of inestimable value here are such sources as the many treatises of Ioannikii Galiatovs'kyi, one of the most prolific writers of the Kyiv Mohyla circle during the second half of the seventeenth century. The second part of this article is devoted to a reconstruction of Galiatovs'kyi's conjectural "library," which may offer a detailed picture of the owner's level of familiarity with the geography of Europe. The article concludes with a brief survey of the new content that we encounter in the use of the word "Europe" in the late seventeenth and early eighteenth centuries.

"All of Europe" in the Perceptions of Ruthenians during the First Half of the Seventeenth Century

After the above-mentioned Lviv panegyric of 1591, the second time that we encounter "Europe" is 1598, in the polemical brochure *Отпис на лист ... отца Ипатія* (Reply to a Letter ... of Father Ipatii), published in Ostrih. Here we read that, after capturing Constantinople, the Turks "opened up the gates to all of Europe."[8] The addressee of the brochure, the Uniate metropolitan Ipatii Potii, angrily called the author of this text (known as the Cleric of Ostrih) an "undereducated biting horsefly."[9] However, it is clear that the Cleric, like the author of the Lviv panegyric of 1591, was quite well educated. After all, "all of Europe," to which they were both referring, had migrated onto the pages of Orthodox texts, most likely via the instructional practices of *studia humaniora*. It has not been determined which books were used to teach poetics and rhetoric at Ostrih Academy (where *Отпис* was composed). As regards the Lviv confraternity school, the 1601 catalogue of that institution's library listed twenty Latin books (besides the works of writers of antiquity, there were two unnamed books that should, strictly speaking, be called "grammars"), and among the twenty-five "Liakh" (*лядських*) books is Marcin Bielski's work, *Kronika wszystkiego świata*,[10] from which readers could glean a considerable amount of information about "all of Europe."

Clearly, the metageographical concept of "Europe" must have remained in the Lviv school discourse (the Ostrih school went into decline in the early seventeenth century), but, owing to the dearth of appropriate monuments of scholastic provenance, this can only be an assumption. As well, one cannot exclude the likelihood that the Lviv and Ostrih innovations in the perception and description of space did not penetrate the more conservative city of Kyiv. It is noteworthy that the funeral declamation of the pupils of the Kyiv brotherhood school on Hetman Petro Sahaidachnyi's death, which was composed in 1622 by the school's rector Kasiian Sakovych, does not contain the word "Europe." In these verses, which are embellished with all the features of scholastic rhetoric, the hetman's glory resounds not throughout "all of Europe" (as it does in the Lviv panegyric of 1591), but in "all the Tatar, Turkic lands, and even in northern countries."[11]

As might be expected, the religious polemics of the first third of the seventeenth century are replete with references to Rome and the "Western land" (*Западная сторона*). This "West" is presented not in spatial but in religious terms: it is a metaphor of the threat to "Greek piety." According to the anonymous author of *Perestoroha* (Warning, 1607), for example, the "Western land" is a place where "the pope, leading everyone to obedience to him, curses, torments, kills, dispatches armies ... threatens, shouts, trumpets, constantly wages war, subjecting the small and the great to temptation"; there "arrogance reigns," "pagan philosophy and Aristotle's teachings turn the word of God inside out," and, finally, it is "not Christ's faith but the Antichrist's"[12] that blossoms. We encounter these same accents in the pamphlet *Threnos* (1610), even though it was written by Meletii Smotryts'kyi, who was much better educated than the author of *Perestoroha*: for him the symbolic "Rome" is the "source of misfortune ... a house full of anger," whence "flow so many troubles in every direction," where harlotry has become ensconced, and "even heaven and God" are sold.[13] Finally, even such a moderate and erudite polemicist as the hieromonk of the Kyivan Caves Monastery, Zakharii Kopystens'kyi, who read Baronius, Bellarmino, and Botero, as well as Polish preachers and chroniclers, does not use the word "Europe" in his treatise *Palinodiia* (Palinode, 1621). In this work the West appears as a diffuse, nameless space called the "German lands" (*німецькі краї*), which are contrasted to the "Greek" religious world: "And if we, Ruthenians, go to the German lands for learning, we go in quest not of Latin but of Greek wisdom, taking back as our own that which for a brief period the Greeks entrusted to the Westerners."[14]

Against the background of the above, the intensive introduction of the concept of "all of Europe" in the 1630s into texts written by professors of the Kyiv Mohyla Collegium, whose founder was Metropolitan Petro Mohyla, and, more broadly, by people from Mohyla's milieu, may be likened to a genuine explosion. Thus, the first scholastic panegyric *Εὐχαρισϑήριον* in honour of Mohyla (1632), written by Sofronii Pochas'kyi, a professor of rhetoric, sonorously proclaims in a passage in praise of history,

Познаєт дѣльность славных россійських гетьманов,
Вѣдомості доступить в житю можных панов,
Європу тот, Азію з Афрікою змѣрить,
Которій розум в широких гісторіах ширить.[15]

(He shall know the deeds of the glorious Rossian hetmans,
Learn of the lives of powerful men,
And measure Europe, Asia, and Africa,
Who increases his knowledge in broad histories.)

In the following scholastic declamation in honour of Mohyla (*Mnemosyne*, written in 1633 by an anonymous author) the spatial horizon is even broader; characteristically, the enumeration of its component parts begins with the word "Europe":

Gdyż Europa, Azja i kraj Ameryka
Z płomienistą Łybią Mohyłów wykrzyka.[16]

(Because Europe, Asia, and the land of America,
Together with the fiery Libya shout [the praises of] the Mohylas!)

Finally, in the hagiographic treatise *Τερατουργήμα* (Teraturgēma), written by Afanasii Kal'nofois'kyi in 1638, "Europe" is already being transformed from an abstract, metageographic unit into "one's own" space, to which Rus' also belongs and whose famous places are "known" in Europe. "Rus' begins the history of its people (for very much earlier it staunchly occupied part of Asia and Europe) with three brothers"; the city of Pereiaslav, "founded by Volodymyr the Great beyond the Dnipro River, [is] famous in Europe."[17]

"Europe" would continue to figure as a term with various shades of meaning on the pages of Ukrainian texts throughout the 1630s, in parallel with the transformation of the spatial imaginary that was inspired by professors of the Mohyla Collegium. For example, whereas for pre-Mohyla authors space was divided into four "universal parts, as East, West, North, South,"[18] in the eyes of the Mohyla Academy graduate and later rector of his alma mater, Ioannikii Galiatovs'kyi, space acquired a fundamentally different configuration. For example, Galiatovs'kyi's poem "Pieśń o pokorze" (Song of Humility), which was included in the treatise *Messyjasz prawdziwy Jezus Chrystus* (Jesus Christ, the True Messiah), published in Kyiv in 1672, begins thus:

Nakłoń, o Ewropa, nakłoń uszy swoje,
Usłysz, o Afryka, usłysz pieśni moje...
Przymi Ameryka, przymi wdzięczne słowa,
Bądź Azyja lutni słuchać, bądź gotowa.[19]

(Incline, O Europe, incline your ears.
Hear, O Africa, hear my songs...
Accept, America, accept words of gratitude,
Asia, be ready to listen to the lute, be ready.)

It is difficult to know whence writers of the Kyivan circle drew their information about the European West. Part of Petro Mohyla's immense collection of books (over 3,500 volumes) – the nucleus of the library of the collegium that he founded – perished together with later additions in a fire in 1780, and part of it was dispersed.[20] Hence, contemporary scholars have access only to a handful of lists of titles that we are sure were in circulation in Kyiv before the mid-seventeenth and early eighteenth centuries: a list of books purchased by Petro Mohyla in 1632–3 in Cracow and Warsaw;[21] an inventory of books owned by the hieromonk of the Kyivan Caves Monastery, Afanasii Kal'nofois'kyi;[22] a list of books owned by Dymytrii Tuptalo (Rostovskii);[23] and catalogues of the libraries of Stefan Iavors'kyi and Feofan Prokopovych. Among the books owned by Mohyla and Kal'nofois'kyi there were as yet no geographic atlases, works on geography, or even popular compendia with "universal" content. There were also no atlases in Iavors'kyi's library, which numbered 609 volumes; instead, we find there works that could have provided geographical knowledge indirectly, such as *Historici Summi, Hortulus Historico-Politicus* by Elias Reusner (Reusnerus), *Chronica gestorum in Europa singularium recentiorum* and *De praecipuis Germaniae urbibus pene ducentis* (both without an indication of their authors), as well as a Polish translation, published in 1609 by the Jesuit Mikołaj Łęczycki, of Giovanni Botero's popular book *Delle relationi universali* (Polish title: *Relacje powszechne*),[24] the first section of which consists of descriptions of Europe, Asia, and Africa. Among Dymytrii Tuptalo's books we see a similar array of books containing information on the cities and countries of the West, as well as one atlas – *Delineationes sive tabulae totius orbis*. Finally, Prokopovych's book collection, which, according to its owner, numbered 3,000 volumes[25] as of 1720, contained 41 works with exclusively geographical content, including 14 atlases by Jean Bleau (Blavius), which appeared in various editions between 1620 and 1662; Abraham Ortelius's *Thesaurus geographicus* (1611); Gerhard Mercator's *Atlas minor* (1634); and Sebastian Münster's *Universalis typus orbis terenni* (1650).[26] The most recent work in this list, Johann Beckmann's *Historia orbis terrarium, geographica et civilis*, was published in Leipzig in 1685. Prokopovych could have easily acquired this literature during his final journey to the West in 1694–1702, and thus would have used it in his lectures for the students of Mohyla Academy in 1704–16.

Thus, it would appear that geographical knowledge derived from specialized works was a rather belated phenomenon at the Kyiv Mohyla Collegium. This is not to say that the education offered was worse than anywhere else in East-Central Europe: in Poland's Jesuit colleges, with which the Mohyla Academy's teaching practices were most closely connected, the designation of geography as a separate subject took place only in the first half of the eighteenth century.[27] European geographic nomenclature entered seventeenth-century Ukrainian texts indirectly – by way of books in which it was mentioned one way or another.

Sources of Knowledge about Europe

The materials most helpful for the reconstruction of a list of writings that could have provided indirect knowledge of Europe are the works of Ioannikii Galiatovs'kyi, who diligently abided by the erudite practice of placing references in the margins of his books. We see this practice first in the works of Meletii Smotryts'kyi, Syl'vestr Kosov, and Afanasii Kal'nofois'kyi; by the second half of the seventeenth century it had become ubiquitous.

Ioannikii Galiatovs'kyi (ca. 1625–88) studied at the Kyiv Mohyla Collegium in the 1640s; it is not known where he continued his studies. He returned in 1655 and began teaching at his alma mater, serving as its rector from 1658 to 1663. Then for several years he "wandered" again, as he himself put it. Finally, in 1668, on the invitation of his teacher Lazar Baranovych, he returned to the Hetmanate and in 1669 was consecrated archimandrite of the Ielets'kyi Dormition Monastery in Chernihiv, where he resided until his death.[28] Galiatovs'kyi is a rather mysterious figure because there is no information on his origins, place of birth, or even his real surname: there is no toponym from which his surname could have derived, nor any similar-sounding lexeme.[29] He was, however, one of the most prolific writers of the second half of the seventeenth century, a model of Kyivan scholarship for his contemporaries. Galiatovs'kyi was the author of eighteen theological, hortatory, and polemical works: nine were written in the Middle Ukrainian language and nine in Polish. Some of his works were republished several times, a clear indication that they enjoyed considerable popularity.

It is worth emphasizing that Galiatovs'kyi's Ukrainian-language texts, notwithstanding their rhetorical adeptness, were written in a language close to the vernacular, which suggests a relatively popular audience comprising, above all, future (or practising) priests who could use the homilies, exempla, and miracula cited by the author in their own sermons. On the other hand, it is significant that, even though Galiatovs'kyi is oriented towards the "ordinary" user, he consistently notes in the margins of his works the literature that he has consulted. Does this add authority to his reflections? Does it encourage rereading? Or is the goal essentially didactic: to provide students of homiletics and polemical theology with a reading list? The last of these conjectures is the most probable. After all, the fundamental treatise on moral theology, written by Galiatovs'kyi's contemporary Innokentii Gizel' (*Мир з Богом человѣку*; Man's Peace with God, 1669), which was intended not for the beginner but for the theologian,[30] contains references only to the Bible and the Church Fathers, although in his foreword the author mentions that he drew upon "external teachers." It was, in fact, the probable didactic subtext of Galiatovs'kyi's Ukrainian-language works addressed to a broad public that determined their selection for analysis here. The works under consideration are *Ключ разумѣнія* (The Key of Understanding; Kyiv, 1659 and 1660; Lviv, 1663 and 1665; and in translation into Romanian, Bucharest, 1678);[31] *Небо новое* (The New Heaven; Lviv, 1665 – two editions; a Polish translation, Lviv, 1677; and a translation closely resembling Church Slavonic, Mohilau, 1699); *Месіа правдивий* (The True Messiah; Kyiv, 1669; a Polish translation, Kyiv, 1672); *Скарбница потребная и пожитечная* (A Necessary and Useful Treasury; Novhorod-Siverskyi, 1676); *Грѣхи розмаитіи* (Various Sins; Chernihiv, 1685); *Боги поганскіи* (Pagan Gods; Chernihiv, 1686); and *Душѣ людей умерлых* (The Souls of Dead People; Chernihiv, 1687 – two editions).[32]

In the margins of these works Galiatovs'kyi lists, in addition to references to the Holy Scriptures, Church fathers, and theologians (including such "Latin" figures as Augustine, Lactantius, Origen, Tertullian, Alain de Lille, Albert the Great, Ambrose of Milan, Anselm of Canterbury, and Thomas Aquinas), the abbreviated titles of more than 150 books, many of which are mentioned more than once and in various works, with volumes, chapters, and even specific pages indicated. This practice suggests that Galiatovs'kyi had the majority of the cited books close at hand, that is, they may have been part of his library. Of course, the possibility that he borrowed references from other works cannot be excluded, but such cases are more or less instantly identifiable: they are usually one-time citations rather than detailed references, listing either the author's name alone or the title of a book with no author indicated.

The citations suggest that "Galiatovs'kyi's library" contained the following: twenty works of antiquity (the usual works of Virgil, Ovid, Pliny, Plutarch, and Cicero, a collection of anecdotes by Valerius Maximus, but also Christian texts by Justinian the Philosopher and such writers of Late Antiquity as Boethius, Venanzio Fortunato, and Cassiodorus); seven Byzantine histories (by Eusebius of Caesarea, Zonaras, Nicephorus Callistus, Nicetas Choniates, Sozomenos, Socrates, and Sophronius); as well as three collections of the lives of saints of Byzantine origin (John Moschus, Simeon Metaphrastes, and Stefan Sviatogorets).[33] It is significant that Galiatovs'kyi's cites all Byzantine texts according to their Latin translations: the historians most probably according to the codex *Auctores historiae ecclesiasticae*, which was first published in Basel in 1544 and later reprinted many times both in its entirety and for individual authors, and the hagiographies according to *Historiae seu vitae sanctorum orientalium et occidentalium* by the Carthusian monk Laurentius Surius in a translation by Lodovico Lippomano. (Between 1551 and 1618 this popular codex went through four printings.) The same is true of the writings of the Byzantine Holy Fathers, which Galiatovs'kyi cites according to their Latin translations, as is eminently clear from the Latinisms that he employs. However, the frequency of republications in the sixteenth and seventeenth centuries both in the form of separate works and collections known as *opera omnia* was so significant that it would be unrealistic to attempt to trace which editions he consulted.

A separate linguistic segment is comprised of nineteen Polish authors. Nearly half of these references are in *Mesia pravdyvyi* (The True Messiah, 1660), where Polish books serve as the principal foundation of Galiatovs'kyi's anti-Jewish polemic. Among them are the well-known anti-Semitic pamphlets of Marek Korona (1645) and Sebastian Miczyński (1619), and exempla illustrating "Jewish evildoing" from supplements to the treatises of Sebastian Petricius (1605) and Szymon Sirenius (1613). A brochure written by the Cracow neophyte Michael Judeus (1583) was also used, as well as the remarkable "letter of Rabbi Samuel," which had a long publishing history: it first appeared in Latin (Cologne, 1493, 1499; Nuremberg, 1498), and then in a German translation (Augsburg, 1524) and a Polish one (Cracow, 1538). Finally, two accounts concerning the pseudo-Messiah Sabbatai Tzvi (Zevi), which were published in Poland in 1666, are identified as translations of German news brochures of that period.[34]

In other works by Galiatovs'kyi the largest number of references are to the writings of chroniclers (Marcin Bielski, Alessandro Guagnini, Marcin Kromer, and Maciej Stryjkowski); individual exempla from Piotr Skarga's work *Żywoty*

świętych (Lives of the Saints); the homilies of Piotr Skarga, Szymon Starowolski, and Jakub Wujek; the history of the Częstochowa icon of the Mother of
God by Mikołaj from Wilkowiec (1568); the so-called "peregrination" of
Mikołaj Krzysztof Radziwiłł (it is not clear which edition, the Polish or the
Latin, is meant here);[35] and the Latin-language description of Loreto Cathedral,
which was published in Lyons in 1660 by the Polish Dominican, Justyn Miechowski (Justinus Miechoviensis). In a polemical context, Galiatovs'kyi makes
a single mention of a treatise written by the Jesuit Mikołaj Cichowski, who in
1648 engaged in a public debate about the Filioque with the then rector of the
Kyiv Mohyla Collegium, Innokentii Gizel'.

Finally, among the cited texts published in Poland were three by Ruthenian
Uniates who wrote in Polish and Latin: Iakiv Susha's work on the miracles
wrought by the Kholm Mother of God; Teodozii Borovyk's about the miracles
associated with the icon of the Mother of God in the church in Zhyrovychi; and
a work about a miracle-working icon at a monastery in Myslenychi by its priest
Wojciech Ofiarowicz.

Polish intermediary texts play a surprisingly minor role in providing access
to Western literature. Literally recapitulating page after page of Cesare Baronio's *Annales ecclesiastici a Christo nato ad annum 1198* (according to my
tally, there are nearly 115 references to the *Annales* in Galiatovs'kyi, from
the introduction to the final "apparatus," as he calls it), Galiatovs'kyi uses the
original version of the work, not the abbreviated Polish translation by Piotr
Skarga, and in the foreword to *The True Messiah* he even adds the special
caveat that he used the "complete Latin Baronio" because "in the incomplete
Polish Baronio you will not find everything in full." What does not appear to
be in doubt is Polish mediation with respect to two works written in Italian, a
language that Galiatovs'kyi did not know: Giovanni Botero's *Delle relationi
universali*, mentioned earlier, and Torquato Tasso's epic *Gerusalemme liber-
ata* in Piotr Kochanowski's translation, *Goffred abo Jeruzalem wyzwolona*,
which was published in Cracow in 1618 and 1651. As regards Valerius Maximus, Plutarch, and Joseph Flavius, whose works were also published in Polish
translation, these Latin texts were part of the school curriculum, and Galiatovs'kyi would hardly have needed a translator in order to read them. Polish
mediation is also very unlikely with regard to the use of Roberto Bellarmino's
Compendium doctrinae christianae (Polish translation: 1611) because in Galiatovs'kyi's works we see references to three other works by this distinguished
Jesuit theologian (*Disputationes de controversiis christianae fidei*, *Tractatus de
potestate summi pontificis*, and *De Jezu Christo*). The same may be said of the
works of Justinian and the magnificent medieval collection of homiletic examples known as *Magnum speculum exemplorum*. A textological comparison of

the exempla that Galiatovs'kyi borrowed from it revealed differences from the Polish translation (Szymon Wysocki, 1612, 1621, and 1633 editions).[36]

The rest of the literature that was used by Galiatovs'kyi, that is, about two-thirds of the whole, was by Western authors, especially collections of exempla and miracles, beginning with popular medieval ones. For example, we encounter as many as three references to the works of Gregory of Tours: *Septem libri miraculorum martyrum*, *Libri miraculorum in gloria martyrum*, and *Vitae patrum*. Also actively referenced are *Speculum historiale* by Vincent of Beauvais, *Hortulus reginae* by Wilhelm Meffreth (Meffrethus), *Dormi secure* by John of Werden (Ioannes Verdensis), *Dialogus miraculorum* by Caesar of Heisterbach (Caesarius Heisterbacensis), *Legenda aurea* by Jacopo de Voragine (Iacobus de Voragine), and *Sermones de tempore et sanctis* by Johann Herolt (Ioannes Heroltus Discipulus). There are also frequent references to Latin theologians, ranging from John Duns the Scot and his medieval commentators to authors who were practically Galiatovs'kyi's contemporaries: the Spanish Franciscan Juan de Cartagena (Ioannis de Carthagena), the German Jesuit Adam Kontzen (whom Galiatovs'kyi calls a "wise professor"), the Belgian theologian Jacques Marchant (Iacobus Marchanus), and, finally, the Flemish Jesuit Cornelius a Lapide. Galiatovs'kyi's works contain more than thirty references to this distinguished Jesuit, who is mentioned several times as a "wise theologian" and "church teacher."

It is worthwhile mentioning here that Cornelius was the most popular author among the church intellectuals associated with the Kyiv Mohyla Academy. One of his works was already mentioned in a list of books owned by Afanasii Kal'nofois'kyi,[37] a later compilation of Cornelius's commentaries on the Holy Scriptures was in Stefan Iavors'kyi's library, and among Feofan Prokopovych's books there were as many as three editions published in various years.[38] Giovanna Brogi Bercoff, who studies Cornelius's influence on the sermons of Varlaam Iasyns'kyi, has written a detailed comparison of Dymytrii Tuptalo's *Лimonuc* (Chronicle) with the commentaries of Cornelius. She concludes that, despite certain dogmatic differences, the texts of the Flemish Jesuit were "the most important model and source" of Tuptalo's work.[39] Finally, we also encounter the works of Cornelius during a later period, in eighteenth-century Kyivan monasteries and church libraries.[40]

Among the other literary works in Latin that were used no less actively by Galiatovs'kyi are chronicles and "histories." In contrast to the above-mentioned compendia of exempla, these are mostly the works of humanist authors of the late fifteenth and sixteenth centuries, such as *De origine, gentis et principum sive regum Bavarorum* and *Chronicon insigne Monasterii Hirsaugiensis* by Johann Trithemius, *Rerum Ungaricarum decades quattuor* by Antonio Bonfini

(Antonius Bonfinius), *Historiarum de regno Italiae libri XV* by Carlo Sigonio (Carolus Sigonius), *Commentarii de rebus gestis Alphonsi Regis* by Enea Silvio Piccolomini (Aeneas Sylvius), *Historia Regni Bohemiae* by Jan Skala of Dubravka (Joannes Dubravius), *Vandalia* by Albert Krantz (Albertus Crantius), and others. Finally, a considerable number of examples are taken from sixteenth- and seventeenth-century "encyclopaedias" that contained the most diverse types of information, for example, items on how to recognize demons (*De praestigiis daemonum*) by Johann Weyer (Johannes Vierus), on "inventing things" (*De rerum inventione*) by Vergil Polydore (Vergilius Polidorus), on the content and meaning of names (*Onomasticon propriorum nominum*) by Conrad Gessner (Conradus Gesnerus), and about remarkable and instructional events in people's lives (*Magnum theatrum vitae humanae*) by Theodor Zwinger (Theodor Zwingerus). (It is highly probable that one of the expanded editions of this monumental five-volume work that was reissued in 1631 or 1656 was available to Galiatovs'kyi, who used more than forty instructional exempla from it.) Worth noting are books mentioned in footnotes, which offered readers so-called "scientific curiosities" (*scientia curiosa*) and descriptions of strange natural phenomena and pagan superstitions. In Galiatovs'kyi's works we find references to a much-published work about "Chaldean antiquity," *Berosi sacerdotis Chaldaici antiquitatum* by Giovanni Nanni (Joannes Annius Viterbiensis); *Hieroglyphica seu de sacris Aegyptiorum aliorumque gentium literis commentarii* by Valeriano Pierio (Valerianus Pierius), which was used as a textbook on emblematics in Jesuit colleges; a book about exotic pagan customs, *De theologia gentili et phisiologia christiana sive de origine et progressu idolatriae* by Gerhard Vossius; and a collection of tales about various wonders of nature, *De admirandis rerum naturae* by Simone Maioli (Simon Maiolus) in the re-editions of 1607 and 1691. Other Kyiv Mohyla professors also used Maioli's works: they are cited four times by Afanasii Kal'nofois'kyi,[41] and they are also mentioned in the libraries of Iavors'kyi and Prokopovych.[42]

New Accents in the Perception and Interpretation of Europe

The types of books that were read by Kyivan professors offered adequate firsthand information about Europe. Keen familiarity with its map is attested by the convincing example of Ioannikii Galiatovs'kyi, in whose homiletic exempla there are so many European toponyms that it is hard to keep track of them, as well as by other Ukrainian printed texts of the last third of the seventeenth century and the beginning of the eighteenth. On the whole, these writers were familiar with approximately fifty European macro names that, in turn, are divided into regions and "states" (*панства*). Besides the generalized concepts of "Italy" and the "Wallachian land," Sicily, the "Venetian state," the "Roman land," and the "Florentine state" are also mentioned; in addition to the Habsburg empire and the "German land," we find Bavaria, the "Saxon land," Brandenburg, Prussia, and other place names; along with the word "France" we encounter the political toponyms Burgundy, Flanders, Tarascon, and Brittany; alongside the concept of "Spain" and the "Spanish kingdom" we find Castile, Catalonia, and Aragon. On the whole, "European geography" encompasses territories stretching from Spain, Portugal, Italy, Greece, "Bulgaria," and Serbia in the south to Britain and the Scandinavian countries in the north. As regards cities, the most frequently mentioned (in descending order) are Rome, Venice, Florence, Mainz, Paris, Bologna, Vienna, and London.

Also worth noting are new semantic accents that are recorded for the first time in this period. Particularly striking are those cases where Mohyla graduates present Rus' as an actual part of Europe – its eastern ("Sarmatian") branch. For example, in the redaction of the Hustynia Chronicle, which was written by Mykhailo Losyts'kyi in 1670, we read: "The Wends went from the Black Sea and filled many northern countries in Europe. And now the Rus' live there and others ... There are two Sarmatias: one is the Asian, and the other is our European ... According to the old geographers, our European Sarmatia has borders."[43]

Having entered the orbit of "our world," Europe lost its earlier features of the "Latin West" as the source of threat to the Orthodox faith. Thus, in one of his letters (1679) to Innokentii Gizel', archimandrite of the Kyivan Caves Monastery, Lazar Baranovych, archbishop of Chernihiv, calls Kyiv the "Ruthenian Paris,"[44] that is, a centre of theology and scholarship, while Samiilo Velychko writes that "Rome may be called the mother of all European cities" (*всѣх европейских градов матерію нарещися может*).[45] Another accent that appears with particular clarity in Velychko's monumental work of the early eighteenth century not only highlights the "our-ness" of Europe but also contrasts "our Europe" with "distant countries": "See, now, the free peoples of various tribes and languages in the vicinity, including at that time also the free, noble Sarmatian Cossacko-Ruthenian [people], who since ancient times were renowned for their bravery not only in their own Europe but also in distant Asian countries [...] unknown in part of the European world, the Saracens of ancient earlier times arrived with their many armies in our Europe from the most distant Asian countries."[46]

In parallel fashion, some authors bolster the motif of "we are in Europe" with the topos of *antemurale Christianitatis* (bulwark of Christianity), which was germane to the discourse in the Rzeczpospolita as early as the sixteenth century and came into more intensive use in the final quarter of the seventeenth century as a result of the conflict with the Ottoman Empire. This topos colours references to Europe by accenting "our" special role as defenders of the Christian – European – world. For example, in his 1687 panegyric glorifying Hetman Ivan Samoilovych, Pavlo Baranets'kyi, the "master of grammar" at the Kyiv Mohyla Academy, poses the following rhetorical question:

Who is Europe's first patron?
Let them ask us: no greater one will be found.[47]

A year later another panygyrist, Ivan Ornovs'kyi, a member of Lazar Baranovych's circle, in his short poem "Muza Roxolanska" written in honour of Ivan Mazepa, predicts the following for the hetman:

Za tobą,
świata ruskiego jedyna ozdobo,
Pójdą zwycięstwa i tryumfy w tropy,
Ręka cię w wojszcze posili Europy.[48]

(After you,
Sole ornament of the Ruthenian world,
Victories and triumphs will follow,
Your military hand will strengthen Europe.)

Thus, throughout the 1630s, the Kyiv Mohyla scholarly milieu unquestionably fostered a change in the perception of the European space. The catalyst for the penetration of the metageographical concept of "Europe" into the Ukrainian lexicon and, later, the emergence of a sense of personal affiliation with this "Europe" was the sudden change in educational communications, above all the introduction into Ukrainian teaching practice of textbooks, texts, and pedagogical models from the Latin school of *studia humaniora*. Among other cultural innovations, this change rendered spatial perceptions about "our" place in the world more rational: identification with an amorphous spiritual unity (the "Greek East") was supplanted by clear-cut localization of "our" past and present on the map of Europe. Characteristically, as these innovations were consolidated, the role of Polish cultural mediation in shaping the image of Europe diminished. The study of Ioannikii Galiatovs'kyi's "library" demonstrates that by roughly the second half of the seventeenth century Polish authors had forfeited their role as the chief authorities and sources of information for Kyiv Mohyla professors, and that books published in the West had become the main source of information on Europe.

This reorientation does not mean that the Byzantine cultural space disappeared from view. It continued to coexist with "Europe," as extant sermons for various feast days in the church calendar attest. To date, however, no scholarly research has been done on how the two were interwoven – in what proportions and from what axiological perspectives. It is precisely this kind of analysis that could reveal the nature of the "polymorphism" (Giovanna Brogi Bercoff's term) of the Ukrainian cultural space – that is, its multilayered character, changeability, and susceptibility to external influences,[49] including its interweaving of "Greek" (Eastern) and "Latin" (Western) elements of identity in the consciousness of Ukrainians.

Translated from the Ukrainian by Marta D. Olynyk

Notes

1 Miechowski's book was published in Cracow in 1517, and by the mid-1540s it had been republished five times abroad and reissued four times by Polish print shops, including three Polish-language translations. See *Nowy Korbut: Piśmiennictwo staropolskie*, vol. 2 (Warsaw: Państwowy Instytut Wydawniczy, 1964), 518–19.

2 V. Kolosova, V. Litvinov, et al., comp., *Ukraïns'ka literatura XIV–XVI st.* (Kyiv: Naukova dumka, 1988), 478, 488, 500.

3 The poem was published in Cracow in 1585; the sole extant copy, whose whereabouts are not known today, was reissued in the appendixes to Andrei Storozhenko, *Stefan Batorii i dneprovskie kazaki* (Kyiv: Tip. I. L. Frontskevicha, 1904), 163–220. The author of the poem is anonymous. For speculations on the probable author, see Natalia Iakovenko (Yakovenko), "Shliakhtych 'latyns'kyi' chy 'latynizovanyi'? Notatky na poliakh poemy *Epicedion* (1585 rik)," in *Paralel'nyi svit: Doslidzhennia z istoriï uiavlen' ta idei v Ukraïni XVI–XVII st.* (Kyiv: Krytyka, 2002), 148–53.

4 The poem *Epicedion* as published in Storozhenko, *Stefan Batorii*, 200, 216.

5 Mykhailo Vozniak, *Istoriia ukraïns'koï literatury*, vol. 2, pt. 1 (Lviv: Prosvita, 1921), 77–8.

6 Konstantin Kharlampovich, *Zapadnorusskie pravoslavnye shkoly XVI i nachala XVII veka* (Kazan: Tipo-litografiia Imperatorskago universiteta, 1898), 384.

7 Cited in Volodymyr Shynkaruk, Valeriia Nichyk, and Andrii Sukhov, eds., *Pamiatky brats'kykh shkil na Ukraïni: Kinets' XVI–pochatok XVII st.; Teksty i doslidzhennia* (Kyiv: Naukova dumka, 1988), 170–1 (my emphases here and elsewhere).

8 *Ukraïns'ka literatura XIV–XVI st.*, 274.

9 Hipacy Pociej, *Antirresis abo Apologia przeciwko Krzysztofowi Philaletowi*, ed. J. Byliński and J. Długosz (Wrocław: Wydawn. Uniwersytetu Wrocławskiego, 1997), 240.

10 *Pamiatky brats'kykh shkil na Ukraïni*, 30–3.

11 Volodymyr Krekoten', comp., *Ukraïns'ka literatura XVII st.* (Kyiv: Naukova dumka, 1987), 223.

12 *Ukraïns'ka literatura XVII st.*, 55–6, 58, 66.

13 Rostysław Radyszewśkyj, ed., *Roksolański Parnas: Polskojęzyczna poezja ukraińska od końca XVI do początku XVIII wieku*, pt. 2, *Antologia* (Cracow: DWN, 1998), 79–81.

14 *Pamiatniki polemicheskoi literatury v Zapadnoi Rusi*, pt. 1 (St Petersburg: Tipografiia i litografiia A. Transhelia, 1878), col. 900 (Russkaia istoricheskaia biblioteka, vol. 4).

15 Volodymyr Krekoten' and Mykola Sulyma, comp., *Ukraïns'ka poeziia: Seredyna XVII st.* (Kyiv: Naukova dumka, 1992), 183–4.

16 *Láment dómu knjažát ostrozskich = (Lamentatio des Hauses Ostrog) 1603: Text, Übersetzung, Kommentar, Facsimile: Beiheft zu Die älteste ostslawische Kunstdichtung, 1575–1647*, ed. Hans Rothe (Giessen: W. Schmitz, 1976), 340.

17 *Seventeenth-Century Writings on the Kievan Caves Monastery*, with an introduction by Paulina Lewin, Harvard Library of Early Ukrainian Literature, vol. 4 (Cambridge, MA: Harvard Ukrainian Research Institute, 1987), 128, 255.

18 This is how Meletii Smotryts'kyi describes space in his work *Grammatiki slavenskiia pravilnoe syntagma* (The Correct Syntax of Slavonic Grammar, 1618), repr. ed. (Kyiv: Naukova dumka, 1979).

19 Radyszewśkyj, *Roksolański Parnas*, 275.

20 Iaroslav Isaievych, *Ukraïns'ke knyhovydannia: vytoky, rozvytok, problemy* (Lviv: Instytut ukraïnoznavstva im. I. Krypiakevycha NAN Ukraïny, 2003), 367–8.

21 *Arkhiv Iugo-Zapadnoi Rossii*, vol. 7, pt. 1 (Kyiv: Universitetskaia tipografiia, 1887), 186–9.

22 They are mentioned in Kal'nofois'kyi's undated (ca. 1638–46) last will and testament. See Volodymyr Aleksandrovyč and Bohdan Strumiński, "The Will and Testament of Afanasij Kal'nofojs'kyj," *Harvard Ukrainian Studies* 15, no. 3–4 (1991): 423–4.

23 For an inventory of the late metropolitan's property, which was compiled in 1709, see Il'ia Shliapkin, *Sv. Dimitrii Rostovskii i ego vremia (1651–1709 g.)* (St Petersburg: Tipografiia i khromolitografiia A. Transhel', 1891), supplements, 54–8.

24 For the catalog of Iavors'kyi's library, see Sergei Maslov, *Biblioteka Stefana Iavorskogo* (Kyiv: Tipografiia M. T. Meinandera, 1914). The books referred to are listed in Maslov's catalogue on pages xvi, xxv, xxix, and xxxv respectively.

25 Prokopovych mentions this in a letter to Iakiv Markovych. See Feofan Prokopovych, *Filosofs'ki tvory*, vol. 3 (Kyiv: Naukova dumka, 1981), 206. An appendix to this edition contains a catalogue of Prokopovych's library, where titles abridged in the original manuscript are given in full (378–442).

26 Prokopovych, *Filosofs'ki tvory*, 399–401.

27 Cf. Filip Wolański, "Staropolskie podręczniki i kompendia geograficzne jako źródło wiedzy o świecie w XVIII wieku," in *Staropolskie kompendia wiedzy*, ed. Iwona M. Dacka-Górzyńska and Joanna Partyka (Warsaw: Wydawnictwo DiG, 2009), 195–202.

28 Zoia Khyzhniak, ed., *Kyievo-Mohylians'ka akademiia v imenakh, XVII– XVIII st.* (Kyiv: Vydavnychyi dim "KM Akademiia," 2001), 165–7.

29 The closest in sound is the Moldovan Galats (Latinized: Galatia). However, I have not able to find any suggestion of a connection to Moldova in Galiatovs'kyi's works.

30 Cf. L. Dovha, "Nauka pro pokutu v ukraïns'kykh tekstakh XVII st.," Innokentii Gizel', *Vybrani tvory u 3 tomakh*, comp. Larysa Dovha, vol. 3 (Kyiv: Svichado, 2010), 191.

31 *Kliuch Razumieniia* was also translated into Church Slavonic in 1669 in Russia at the Iversk monastery on Lake Valdai. However, the translation was never published. See Konstantin Kharlampovich, *Malorossiiskoe vliianie na velikorusskuiu tserkovnuiu zhizn'*, vol. 1 (Kazan': M. A. Golubev, 1914), 426.

32 For a more precise survey of publications, see Konstantyn Bida, *Ioanikii Galiatovs'kyi i ioho "Kliuch Razumieniia"* (Rome: Vydavnytstvo Ukraïns'koho katolyts'koho universytetu im. Sv. Klymenta Papy, 1975), xliii–li. Of the above-mentioned editions, I used the 1659 facsimile edition of *Kliuch Razumieniia* (it differs from subsequent editions), which was reprinted in Bida's work; with regard to the remaining works, with the exception of *Mesia pravdyvyi*, I consulted the following republished work: Ioanykii Galiatovs'kyi, *Kliuch rozuminnia*, ed. Inna Chepiha (Kyiv: Naukova dumka, 1985). Finally, I analyzed *Mesia pravdyvyi* on the basis of the original 1669 edition, a copy of which was graciously loaned to me by Valerii Zema.

33 Stefan Sviatogorets (a Bulgarian?) was a fifteenth-century monk living on Mount Athos, who translated into Church Slavonic a list of miracles wrought by the wonder-working icon of the Iversk Mother of God. Galiatovs'kyi recounts these miracles according to the Russian edition of the translation, which was published in 1659 under the title *Kniga glagolemaia rai myslennyi* by the printing house of the Iversk-Valdai monastery after a copy of the Iversk icon was brought there from Mount Athos.

34 See Daniel Clarke Waugh, "News of the False Messiah: Reports on Shabbetai Zevi in Ukraine and Muscovy," *Jewish Social Studies* 41, no. 3–4 (1979): 304–5, 321.

35 The Latin version of Radziwiłł's travel notes, entitled *Hierosolymitana peregrinatio*, was published in Braunsberg (Braniewo) in 1601, and the Polish version (*Peregrynacja abo pielgrzymowanie do Ziemie świętej*) was published five times between 1607 and 1683.

36 S. Shevchenko, "K istorii 'Velikogo Zertsala' v Iugo-Zapadnoi Rusi: 'Velikoe Zertsalo' i sochineniia Ioannikiia Galiatovskogo," *Russkii Filologicheskii Vestnik* 62, no. 3 and 4 (1909): 110–30.

37 Aleksandrovyč, *The Will and Testament of Afanasij Kal'nofojsky*j, 423.

38 Maslov, *Biblioteka Stefana Iavorskogo*, vii; Prokopovych, *Filosofs'ki tvory*, vol. 3, 434.

39 Giovanna Brogi Bercoff, "L'omiletica di Varlaam Jasyns'kyj fra retorica e teologia. Alcuni esempi inediti," *Russica Romana* 8 (2001): 21–4; G. Brogi Bercoff, "The Letopisec of Dimitrij Tuptalo, the Metropolitan of Rostov, in the Context of Western European Culture" (Contributi italiani all'XI Congresso Internazionale degli Slavisti, Bratislava 1993), *Ricerche slavistiche* 39–40, no. 1 (1992–3): 337–50, here 345.

40 Olena Dziuba and Vira Frys, "Biblioteky Ukraïny," in *Istoriia ukraïns'koï kul'tury*, vol. 3, *Ukraïns'ka kul'tura druhoï polovyny XVII–XVIII stolit'* (Kyiv: Naukova dumka, 2003), 815 (library of the Saint Sophia Cathedral), 816 (collection of Tymofii Shcherbats'kyi), 818 (books of St Cyril monastery) and 826 (library of Feofil Krolyk).

41 Kalnofoyskiego Athanasiusa, Τερατουργηµα lubo Cuda, 174, 218, 290. The fourth reference appears in one of the paraneses that Kal'nofois'kyi added to the "Parergon of Miracles" of the Kupiatitsky icon of the Mother of God (321).

42 Maslov, *Biblioteka Stefana Iavorskogo*, xxvi; Prokopovych, *Filosofs'ki tvory*, vol. 3, 396.

43 *Polnoe sobranie russkikh letopisei*, vol. 40, *Gustynskaia letopis'* (St Petersburg: Institut istorii RAN, 2003), 14.

44 *Pis'ma preosviashchennogo Lazaria Baranovicha*, 2nd ed. (Chernihiv: n. p., 1865), 117.

45 Samoil Velichko, *Letopis' sobytii v Iugo-Zapadnoi Rossii v XVII-m veke*, vol. 1 (Kyiv: Izdatel'stvo Vremennoi komissii dlia razbora drevnikh aktov, 1848), 89.

46 Velichko, *Letopis' sobytii v Iugo-Zapadnoi Rossii*, vol. 1, 31; Velichko, *Letopis' sobytii v Iugo-Zapadnoi Rossii*, vol. 3 (Kyiv, 1853), 7.

47 Radyszewśkyj, *Roksolański Parnas*, 323.

48 Radyszewśkyj, *Roksolański Parnas*, 378.

49 Giovanna Brogi Bercoff, "Ruś, Ukraina, Ruthenia, Wielkie Księstwo Litewskie, Rzeczpospolita, Moskwa, Rosja, Europa śrowkowo-Wschodnia: o wielowarstwowości i polifunkcjonalizmie kulturowym," in *Contributi italiani al XIII congresso internazionale degli slavisti*, ed. Alberto Alberti et al. (Pisa: Associazione italiana degli slavisti, 2003), 325–87.

Too Close to "the West"? The Ruthenian Language of the *Instruction* of 1609

MICHAEL MOSER

Early Modern Ruthenians (Ukrainians and Belarusians) in Europe

Within the Slavic Orthodox world, early modern Ruthenian (Ukrainian and Belarusian) culture occupies an exceptional position. In the sixteenth and seventeenth centuries no other Orthodox group was as strongly affected by the European religious Reformation and Counter-Reformation, Renaissance, and baroque culture as were the Ruthenians of the Kingdom of Poland and the Grand Duchy of Lithuania.

For the Ruthenians of the time, the encounter with European culture usually occurred via Polish mediation. As far as language as an integrative element of Ruthenian identity is concerned, the intense encounter with Poles and other Europeans yielded a multitude of new loan concepts and, accordingly, loan words from Western languages. Owing to the spread of early modern information technologies (the art of printing) and the reformation of the educational sphere, the "common" language (*Gemeinsprache* = "prosta(ia) mova"/"prostyi iazyk"),[1] which had gradually emerged in the preceding decades, soon turned out to be more dispersed and refined than ever before. Not least of all, this language served as a powerful instrument for defining oneself and one's own group.

At the same time, the encounter with European culture constituted a challenge and even a threat for Ruthenians. In terms of language, not only was it obvious that by the second half of the sixteenth century increasing numbers of representatives of the Ruthenian elites had adopted the Polish language and culture, but even the high variety of the Ruthenian written language itself had become extremely similar to the Polish language of the Polish elites.

Perceiving this threat, the Ruthenians began to champion the religious and economic rights of "the Ruthenian nation" in the multinational and multilingual settings of the Kingdom of Poland and Grand Duchy of Lithuania. They did so, however, in a language that clearly betrayed Polish cultural predominance.

Perhaps no other document illustrates this better than the *Instruction* and *Lament* of 1609.

The *Instruction* and *Lament*

On 2 January 1609 the Ruthenian burghers of Lviv issued a document entitled *Лѧментъ, албо Мова до Кр Его Мл* (Lament, or a Speech to his Grace the King). This well-known text was integrated into the so-called *Инъструкциѧ* (Instruction, 1609), a certification of authority for the burghers' envoys to the Warsaw Diet. The *Instruction* dates to the time when Lviv had about seventeen thousand to twenty thousand inhabitants, 20 per cent of whom were Ruthenians/Ukrainians.[2] In that document the Ruthenian representatives claimed that "we, the Ruthenian nation of the Greek religion" (*Народ росскй релѣи Кгрецкое*) "voice a controversy with the Polish nation regarding the same liberty, use of trade laws and all kinds of business that have been guaranteed by the Polish Kings of holy memory to Lviv, to us, the Ruthenian [nation] on par with the Polish nation."[3] The spirit of the text is quite well represented by the nine occurrences of the possessive pronoun *нашъ*. The following examples are cited in order of their appearance:

1) Просити Его Кр мл, Абы насъ ведле Процесу релѣи Нашое Кгрецкое / И въ волном Уживаню Процесы̃ 3 Сакраменты. И иншими wбрѧды / В рынку, И въ Улицахъ Уживати волно Заховати рачилъ (1); 2), И дотого Просити, Абы Прешкрипцiѧ На добрахъ Стоѧчих / Наших руских Небыла (1); 3) and 4) Если бы кто z Народу Нашого руского, Хотѣлъ Ново прӥмовати / Мѣсцъкое Право, албо цехи Ѩкиеколвекъ, То wбы непрезъ иншихъ / Нацы̆ Люде̃, Але През самых Старшихъ Наших руских Мещанъ / И Предмещанъ бывалъ Залецанъ (1v); 5) А претожъ Просити Кр Его Мл, Абы ... до ровныхъ волносте̃ хрстиѧнъских Такъ / дховных, ведле Процесу релѣи Нашое Кгрецкое Ѩко И свѣцких, / Уживанѧ Припустити рачилъ (1v); 6) Понеконъдъ су̃д Полскй кривды Нестерпимые выгублѧючи / нас Спотомствы Нашими Намъ Народу рускому Чинѧт, / И Бѣды Неслыханые, Котрими утѧжени Естесмо / Над Ѩрмо Египъскои Неволѣ (2v); 7) То ест Напрод / наветъ, Божницѣ, Напрод / Старожитны̃ Натуралны̃ Народ Нашъ рускй мает свое вѣчум, / И цр̃ковъ Набоженства своего воЛвовъ (3); 8) and 9) У Ксѧндза Фѣрлеѧ референдара Его Кр Мл GD Певномъ / А неимылномъ Часу Приволанѧсѧ Справы тоеи Нашеи / до Суду Кр довѣдовати Бы Тежму едно даровати. / А другое wбецати. Асамым Завше Пилновати (3v); GDстатокъ лепшости вшелѧко̃ Буд вседержителю вруки Его С̃тые / И Пилности Посломъ Нашим<ъ полецае>мъ (4).

Along with "our business" and "our envoys," the burghers mention not only "our real estate" and "our elder Ruthenian burghers and dwellers of the suburbs" (as opposed to "other nations' people") but also less "pragmatic" aspects, such as "our Greek religion" and "our ancestry." Most notably, the document even speaks about "our ancient natural Ruthenian nation." Elsewhere in the *Lament*, the burghers complain that the Ruthenians lack rights "in their own native Ruthenian land, in this very Ruthenian Lviv" (*Чим бы толко Чл҃къ Живъ быти моглъ. Того Неволенъ русинъ / Наприрожоно҃ земли своѐ руско҃ уживати, втомто руском / Лвовѣ* [3]).

The *Instruction* and particularly the *Lament* have often attracted the attention of scholars (a historically contextualized interpretation of the text can be found in Kapral').[4] The entire document was already published in 1904 in Amvrosii Krylovs'kyi's classical study on the Lviv brotherhood.[5] Only the *Lament* was re-edited several times, for instance by Mykhailo Hrushevs'kyi,[6] in the sixth volume of his *Istoriia ukraïns'koï literatury* (History of Ukrainian Literature), which came out only after the breakup of the Soviet Union. Finally, a few years ago, Iaroslav Isaievych published a facsimile of the first page of the *Lament* in his study on the Lviv brotherhood.[7]

In this article I will analyse the language of the *Instruction* and the *Lament* on the basis of a facsimile of the entire manuscript.[8] This approach is necessary because Krylovs'kyi's edition, which was adopted by his successors, is not entirely reliable. As is typical of many older editions of Middle Ruthenian texts, it includes some questionable interpretations. Among others, the following readings should be amended:

[*до Права*] *Ѽкоторое* … [*Конътровертуемо*] (1), not *в которое*,[9] [*Его*] *Кр* [*Мл*] (1), not [*его*] *кор.* [*милости*],[10] *А* [*звласча*] (1) with the conjunction, not *звласча*,[11] *wбы* (1v), not *абы*, *Нанъ* (1v), not *пань*,[12] *увѣжаютъ* (1v), not *убѣжаютъ*,[13] (cf. Polish *uwiedzać* "seduce," *релѣи* (1v), not *релѣе*),[14] *фундыши* (2), not *фундуши*,[15] *Статисѧ* (2v), not *остатися*,[16] *Египъскои* (2v), not *египетъскои*,[17] *Перѐстѧ* (2v, read: *Перейстѧ*), not *перестя*,[18] *Чл҃къ* (3), not *человѣкъ* in the Russian or Church Slavonic appearance,[19] *Горчары* (3) rather than *Гончары*,[20] *зацнѣ҃шого* (3), not *зачнѣйшого*,[21] *Кашталѧне* (3), not *каштеляне*,[22] *Лимѣтации* (3v), not *лимитации*,[23] and *Ксюндза* (3v) rather than *ксяндза*.[24]

In my brief study I will not elaborate on more general views on the early modern Ruthenian or "Middle Ruthenian" language (which in this particular case may be safely called "Middle Ukrainian," too, because Belarusian aspects do not play any role here).[25] The *Instruction* is quite close to a more or less prototypical Middle Ruthenian high-variety language. This idiom, which has often been called "prosta(ia) mova," although contemporaries usually just called it "the Ruthenian language" (that would be "*руски҃ ѧзыкъ*" or "*руски҃ ѧзыкъ*," according to the orthography employed in the *Instruction*), served as a polyfunctional and highly normalized idiom of Ruthenian high culture with virtually all features of a modern standard language except for full-fledged codification (this was, however, a widespread situation in early modern European language communities).[26] From a later (and clearly anachronistic) point of view, this language suffered from at least two "vices": First, records of other varieties of Ruthenian, as in occasional renderings of contemporary oral speech (in short, humoristic plays called *intermediae* or in chronicles and charters), clearly demonstrate that this Ruthenian high variety was quite distant from the language actually spoken by Ruthenian "commoners" (be they Ukrainian or Belarusian). Second, this high-variety Ruthenian language was extremely close to the Polish language of the time.

As I argue elsewhere, the prototypical "prosta mova" differed from Polish only inasmuch as it was written in the Cyrillic alphabet and retained Ruthenian phonology as well as inflectional morphology. Both the vocabulary and the syntactic organization of the texts were, however, virtually identical to Polish models of the time.[27] Below, I will demonstrate that the language of the *Instruction* is characterized by extreme closeness to Polish, which in part even exceeds that of the prototype variety. The relative brevity of the corpus allows for a statistics-based approach. It is precisely statistics that will lead us to a clearer picture of the true relationship between the more or less prototypical "prosta mova" and Polish, two languages that were, beyond any doubt, mutually intelligible almost without any constraint.

Ruthenian and Polish

The most striking feature of the language of the *Instruction* is its extreme closeness to Polish. Below, I offer my own tentative translation of the first lines of the *Instruction* into the Polish language of the time:

Инъструкцил	Instrukc(y)ja[28]
Пленѣпотенцию, То естъ Зуполную моцъ. албо порученство вшелілкое	Plenipotenc(y)ję, To jest zupełną moc, albo poruczeństwo wszelakie
Мы всѣ весполъ еденъ Заедного Народ росскиῖ релѣи Кгрецкое Мещане	My wszy(s)tcy wespół jeden za jednego naród ruski reli(j)i greckiej mieszczanie
И Предмещане, wбога уридовъ И юрисдицыи замковое И мѣсцкое	I przedmieszczanie, obojga urządów i jurysdykc(y)ji zamkowej i miejs(c)kiej
Будучие Люде Лвовилне. Подаемо Посланцом своимъ. (Instruction, fol. 1)	Będące ludzie lwowianie. Podajemy posłańcom swoim.

The exercise of "translating" the entire text of the *Instruction* into Polish reveals the following results: If one transfers the Ruthenian morphemes into Polish simply by changing them according to the strict rules of historical phonology and some other, less regular, developments (e. g., Ruthenian *котрое/Которые* vs Polish *który*), then only a handful of stems (not roots!) are not encountered in the Polish language of the early seventeenth century: *всѣ* (1), *все* (1); *Примити* (1, Pol. *przyjąć*); [*кривды*] *Нестерпимые* (2v); *вѣчум* (3); *набольше* (1v) (Pol. *najwięcej*), [*щось*] *Болшого* (3) along with *цос Болшого* (3) (Pol. *coś większego*); [*Если бы Прокуратор Нехотѣл, албо вмылѧл,*] *И ли*[*сѧ Надражал И Неставал*] (3v); [*пожидовъску.*] *Или* [*По Сараценску*] (1v); *вседержителю* (4) (the form is not Polish; if translated, it is rendered as *wszechdzierżyciel*); [*въ убирѣ*] *Сиѓенническо*м (1v).

As for the first three forms, however, identical roots are found in Polish, too: Regarding *wsz-y(s)tek*, Middle Polish (and in some phrases even Modern Polish) has preserved only unexpanded stem forms of the type *wszech*, *wszego*, *wszemu*, *wszem*, *wszej*, *wszech*, and *wszemi*; moreover, along with the stem *в(е)с-* one also encounters *во вшистко*м (1) in the text. Regarding *Примити*, its imperfective aspectual partner in the text is *примовати* (as in the Polish *przyjmować*), not *примати*. As for the adjective *Сиѓенническо*м, it should be pointed out that it refers to an Orthodox priest. The present passive participle *Нестерпимые*, finally, occurs with *кривды*, which is very likely a Polonism.

Apart from that, it must be noted that one should read [*На*]*кождыˉ* [*рокъ*] (1v) in the text, yet *o* occasionally looks like *a* elsewhere in the manuscript (one would also rather read *фамоти* instead of *фамати*; e. g., see below). Elsewhere, *a* can be clearly read in the same root: *Каждого ремесла* (2), *Каждому вколичныхъ Панствъ НеприѧтеЛеви* (3). The morphemic structure coincides more or less with that of the Polish vocabulary of the time. To give just one example, deverbative nouns occur with the reflexive particle *сѧ,* as in [*А невмылномъ Часу*] *Приволанѧсѧ* [*Справы тоеи Нашеи*] (3v) (cf. Polish *przywołania się*). The syntax is more or less identical with the Polish syntax of the time. This is exemplified by the use of topical *o* + accusative case (*Права Ѽкотрое Пред Его Королевъскою Млстю Конътровертуемо* [1]), comparative *nad* + accusative case (*Утѧжени Естесмо мы Народ Руски, w̃ Народа Полского, Ѧрмомъ над Египъскую Неволю* [3]), the omission of *рѣчъ/rzecz* in *То Сурова И Нехрстиѧнска* (1v) or the use of the Polish-Latin accusativus cum infinitivo in *А зажъ Панове цехМистрове* [...] *цос зацнѣˉшого* [!] *всобѣ НадВ̃оска Вш Кр Мл быти розумѣют* (3). Constructions like these are not necessarily genuinely Polish; they were common in Ruthenian and Polish and partly originated elsewhere. A study of the phraseology and in particular the juridical phraseology would reveal, in all likelihood, full coincidence with the Polish language of the time (see phrases such as

Пленѣпотенцию … Подаемо [1]; *до Права Сжотрое … Конътровертуемо*
[1], *Дла лепшое вѣры Печат При Ложилисмо, И руками Подписали* [1], etc.).
Again, this does not mean that all these elements are genuinely Polish. As is well
known, such phrases often originate in Old and Middle Czech, and in many cases
the Czech loans are in turn loan translations from Latin or German.

As mentioned above, the language of the *Instruction* is very close to the typical high-variety Ruthenian language that was employed in a broad array of literary and non-literary genres around 1700. It is still not clear to which degree this
language might reflect the spoken language of the Ruthenian elites of the time.
It is obvious, however, that the bookish, syntactic organization of such texts was
very remote from the everyday speech even of the elites, and it is even more
obvious that this language was very remote from the idioms spoken by the absolute majority of Ruthenian (Ukrainian and Ruthenian) commoners.[29]

What Remains Ruthenian?

In light of the above-mentioned observations, one might ask now what precisely
remains largely "intact," that is, "truly" Ruthenian in the Ruthenian high variety
around 1600? As I argued earlier,[30] this is 1) the Cyrillic script, 2) the phonological structure of all morphemes, and 3) inflectional morphology. Each of these
aspects deserves to be studied against the background of the *Instruction*.

1. The Cyrillic Script

The Cyrillic script is such an important symbol of Ruthenian identity that in
the *Instruction* even a Latin-written fragment is rendered in Cyrillic according
to Ukrainian rules (as exemplified by the elements in bold print in the first two
lines; *ѣ* means [i], [g] is rendered with *кг*, and the Latin *l* is rendered with a
soft *l'*). Only towards the end does the author render two words in Latin letters:

Анно домѣнѣ, а̄ ӯ пз̄, Електи Сунтъ фамоти, Домѣнѣ
Нѣколаусъ Зарокговски, Ѩнес Валах, Геwргиусъ Раихъ.
Нѣколаусъ Домплах, Станѣслаусъ Клепар етъ Леонасъ
Лѣнднер, Инъ консулес резидентесъ.
    Сенѣwресъ Механѣкорум
Инъ кворум wмнѣумъ кграду примо контуберньи Сарторумъ,
    а̄
Сенѣwресъ сунтъ, Петрусъ, Етъ Стецко.
Итем, субъ, А̄о. 86. Сенѣwрес Сарторум, Андрис, етъ Стецко,
    в̄

Итемъ Инъфериусъ, Ão 1510 Сенѭwpec Сарторумъ,

ᷓ

Андрисъ, етъ Мѣхно

Итемъ Субъ Ão, Мѭлезимо Квѭнъентезимо Сарторумъ

ᷘ

Стецко Кумъ Сенѭwpecъ Андреи Рутенѭ.

Итем, аᷘуᷓчᷓ Мѭхно етъ Матыс, етъ алѭбѭ Локорум.

ᷔ

Итем, Ão аᷘуᷓчᷓ. Іоанъ расъ, Стецко Кампѭамъ.

Субъ имо квовкве Анно сунтъ Церти Консулес, кви hic non

Сунтъ скрипти. (2; emphasis added)

2. Phonological Structure

In general, the Ruthenian phonological structure also remains intact in the *Instruction*. Yet, as always, comparatively recent loans (recent with regard to early modern Ruthenian) should be analysed separately.

2.1. Polish loans

In most cases, it is impossible to establish whether an element common to Ruthenian and Polish is a loan from Polish (or vice versa) because inter-Slavic loans were often adopted according to morphological, not phonological, rules.[31] However, one does find some phonologically marked Polish stems in the *Instruction* (in the following list I treat Bohemisms like Polonisms because I have no doubt that they were adopted into Ruthenian via Polish):

– c < *tj*, *kt'*: *моцъ* (1), *Фбецуем* (1), *wбецати* (3v), *Злецаем* (1), *Залецанъ* (1v), < *полецае* > *мъ* (4: the manuscript is damaged here, yet Krylovs'kyi's reconstruction is perfectly convincing), [*Анъдрѐ*] *бѭлдаговиц* (4: that is, the surname has the Polish reflex, although Polish surnames of the *Mickiewicz* type have the Ruthenian reflex) = 7 word forms;
– $š$ < **3rd palatalization of velars**: *вшелѭкй* (1v), *вшелѭкое* (1), *Вшелѭких* (4x: 1, 2, 3, 3), *вшелѭкие* (1), *вшелѭкого* (2v), *вшелѭко̃* (4), *виистком* (1), *Завше* (3x: 3, 3v, 4) = 13 word forms;
– e < *ъ*: *весполъ/веспол* (4x: 1, 1, 3, 3) *ведле* (6x: 1, 1, 1v, 1v, 2, 3v), *Мѣстечку* (1v), *Городецкй* (1v), *зе* [*Лвова*] (1v), *тераз* (3), *Певномъ* (3v), [*Натом*] *Сѐмѭ* (3v), *НаСѐмѭ* (3v), *Сѐму* (3v), *насѐм* (4v) = 19 word forms;

– *e-*, **not** *o-*: *еденъ* (3x: 1, 1v, 3), *едного* (4x: 1, 1, 1, 3), *Едно* (2x: 2, 3v),
  Еднако (1), *еднак* (2) = 11 word forms;
– *g*, **not** *h*: *Кгрецкое* (3x: 1, 1, 1v) = 3 word forms;
– **metathesis of Polish origin:** *Кролıа* (1v), *Кролевъ* (2x: 1, 1), *Кр* as in [*Его*]
  Кр [*Мл*], *Кр* [*Его Мл*], [*Вш*] *Кр* [*мл*], etc. (22x: 1 [5x], 1v [5x], 2v [2x],
  3v [9x]); along with only one occurrence of the pleophonic form in [*Пред*
  Его] *Королевъскою* [*Млстю*] (1),[32] *Брон* [*Бе̃*] (5x: 2v [4x], 3v), *Брон* [*нас*
  Пастырү добры̃] (3v; along with more occurrences of *Боронıатъ* (1v)
  etc.), *Насамы̃ Прод* (1), *НаПрод* (3x: 2v, 3, 3) = 35 word forms;
– **metathesis of Polish rather than Church Slavic origin:** *Предмещане*
  (1), *Предмещаномъ* (1), *Предмещанъ* (2x: 1v, 4v), *Пред* (3x: 1, 1, 1v),
  Предсıажъ (3v), *презъ* (3x: 1v [3x]), *пренасвıатъшим* (1v), *презыски*
  (1v), *Презысковъ* (2v), *Преложенъствъ* (3, along with *Za переводомъ*
  (1v), *длıа Перестороги* [3v]), *древы* (3, in connection with *Уквıѣчены̃*),
  Потреба (2x: 3v [2x]), *кү Потребѣ* (3v) = 20 word forms;
– **Czech metathesis as used in Polish loans from Czech):** *звласча* (1),
  Власные (1) = 2 word forms;
– **(reflexes of) nasal vowels:** *Понекондъ* (3x: 1, 2v, 3v), *менъжне* (3) = 4
  word forms;
– **Polish vowel contraction:** *Ιана* (1v), [*рады НатоНѣ*]*машъ* (2v; this
  form can barely be regarded as the reflection of a dialectal contraction) = 2
  word forms;
– *e* **instead of** *o* **in** *тежъ,* **пре- (***prze-***) instead of** *про-*: *тежъ* (10x: 1, 1v
  [2x], 2 [3x], 3, 3v [3x]), *претожъ* (1v, along with *Протож* [1]) = 11 word
  forms;
– **reflexes of syllabic liquids:** *Барзо* (2); *мовити* (2x: 1, 1v), *Мова* (3) = 4
  word forms;
– **retained** *dl*: *быдло* (3v) = 1 word form;
– **reflex of** *къй-* **(and reflex of nasal vowel):** *Ксюндза* (3v), *У КсıѐндЗа* (3v)
  = 2 word forms;
– **Polish** *co*: *за цо* (1v), *цос* (2x, 3 [2x]) (along with *што* [1, 2, 3v (2x)]), and
  що [1v], *щос* [3]) = 3 word forms;
– **lack of epenthetic** *l*: *постановене* (2, along with *выгүблıают* [3] etc.) =
  1 word form
– **Polish Latinism and Bohemism** *Костелы* (< *castellum*) (3) = 1 word
  form.
  In sum, we have here 139 indisputable loans from Polish.
  Some slightly less certain loans from Polish are:
– **nouns in** *-ен(ь)ство*: *Набоженства* (3),[33] *порүченство* (of Czech
  origin, see *u* from the back nasal vowel) (1) = 2 word forms

- **a Bohemism in Polish:** *на̄Спроснѣ̃шие* (with *s-*) (1v) = 1 word form.
- **other items that are most likely of Polish origin:** *вбо̃га* (2x: 1, 2), *хорых* (2x: 1, 1v, against the background of Ukrainian *хворий* with preserved *v*), *колвекъ* (4x: 1 [3x], 1v), *Зуполную* (1), *Поневаж* (3x: 1, 1v, 3v), *А зажъ* (3x: 1v, 3 [2x], treated as one word, cf. Polish *azaż*), *поне* (3x: 1, 2v [2]), *Посполитое* (2x: 1, 3v), *Приходнемъ* (2v), *Ѡкрутне* (1v), *Иле* (2), *Пане* (2v), *Пану* (4x: 1 [4x]), *Панове* (4x: 1v [2x], 3 [2x]), *Панов* (2x: 3v [2x]), *Паны* (instr. pl.) (1v), *до Паньствъ* (2v), *Панствъ* (3),[34] *Перѣ̃стꙗ* (despite the pleophony) (2v), *Лечъ* (2x: 2v, 3), *Чти* (loc. sing.) (2), *зацнѣ̃шого* (3), *Учтиве* (1), *Же* (5x: 1, 3 (4x)), *вбы* (1v) = 49 word forms.

Together with these 52 items, a total of 191 are probably of Polish origin.

2.2. Latin loans

The following loans from Latin are used in the text (I exclude ancient loans, such as *жидове* and *костелъ* [the latter has been treated as a Polonism, above, whereas *жидове* is not counted at all]): *Привиле̃* (1v), *Привилѣ̃а* (2x, 1 [2x]), *Привилеиꙗ* (1v), *Привилеиив* (1v), *Привилѣ̃ку* (1v), *декрет* (2v), *декрету* (2x: 1, 3v), *декрета* (2), *Здекретован* (2), *ет[ц]/етц* (4x), *фундованы* (1), *фундованых* (2x, 1 [2x]), *фундацыꙗ* (2), *фундацы̃* (2x: 1, 2), *фундыши* (2), *релѣи* (3x: 1 [2x], 1v), *3 Сакраменты* (1), *з Сакраментамы* (1), *Сакраментом* (instr. sing.) (1v), *Маестатъ* (3), *маестату* (gen. sing.) (3), *юрисдицыи* (2x: 1, 2), *Прокуратор* (3v), *Прокураторовъ* (3v), *Процесу* (2x: 1, 1v), *Процесы* (1), *Процесиꙗх* (1v), *Протестацие* (1v), *Протестацыю* (3v), Гонер (1v), *Ѡнера* (3, *honera* was used along with *onera* in Latin), *Инъ контумацые* (2), *Инъ контумациам* (2), *[Акта] Електовые* (2), *[книгъ] Електовых* (2), *Конътровертуемо* (1), *контроверъсии* (3v), *Евангелика* (3v), *Евангелицких* (3v), *Приформовавии* (1v), *Инъформацыю* (3v), *Инъструкциꙗ* (1), *мунѣмента* (1), *статус каузы* (1), *пропоноват* (1), *Унѣи* (1), *Лꙗвде* (1v), *Прешкрипциꙗ* (1), *Нацы̃* (1v), *Кауциꙗ* (1v), *Копѣю* (1v), *Автентице* (1v), *Акта [Електовые]* (2), *в Канъцелꙗрыи* (3v), *картъ* (2), *Сумы* (2), *Скасовали* (1v), *колациꙗми* (2), *Бестии* (1v), *Адверсаромъ* (2v), *Лꙗментъ* (3), *Натуралны̃* (3), *екземплꙗ* (3), *Пленѣпотенцию* (1), *Сенаторов* (3v), *Сенаторскихъ* (3), *Инстанцые* (3v), *Лимѣтации* (3v), *Паписта* (3v), *мандатом* (3v), *референдара* (3v), *[Неприꙗтелев] Коронных* (3), *Кашталꙗне* (3), Генвар (4) (cf. a Greek stem in *Клеросом*). These items total 88 word forms (*инъ* is counted separately, like all prepositions; in *статус каузы* (1) two word forms are counted).

It is very likely that most of the cited Latinisms entered Ukrainian through Polish. Some of the loans exhibit Polish features that support this view, namely: *j* in *Привиле̃* (1v), *Привиле̃а* (2x, 1 [2x], *Привилеиіа* (1v), *Привилеивв* (1v), *Привиле̃ку* (1v), *релљи* (3x: 1 [2x], 1v), *ы* in *юрисдицыи* (2x: 1, 2), *Нацы̃* (1v), *фундацыіа* (2), фундацы̃ (2x: 1, 2), *Процесы̃* (1) along with *Процесиіах* (1v) etc., *š* < Latin and German *s*: in *фундыши* (2), *Прешкрипциіа* (1), *Каштальіне* (3). Moreover, some Latin loans behave morphologically in the same way as in Middle Polish: *Привиле̃* (nom. sing.) (1v), *Привиле̃а* (nom. pl.) (1v), *Привилеиив* (gen. pl.) (1v), *декрету* (gen. sing.) (2v), *декрета* (nom./acc. pl.) (3), *мунѣмента* (1), *екземплѩ* (3) (acc. pl.), *Паписта* (nom. sing.) (3v), *статус каузы* (1), *Автентице* (1v). As for *Инъ контумацые* (2), *Инстанцыые* (3v), see below.

2.3. Words based on German roots

Most German words (again I exclude ancient loans, such as -*куп*-, *король*-, *лихва*, as well as loan translations, such as *мѣсто*) were probably adopted via Polish, too. In the text the following elements occur: *Завдіачне* (1), *Печат* (1), *Печатю* (1v), *рынок* (1v), *В рынку* (2x: 1 [2x]), *в ринку* (1), *Скриику* (2), *до скринки* (2), *рады* (2v), *ра̃цы* (instr. pl.) (2x: 1v, 3), *На ратүшу* (1v), *Под ратушемъ* (1), *мүсимо* (1), *Примүшаютъ* (1v), *Крамов* (1), *шацүнком* (1), *цехъ* (1v), *С цеху* (1v), *цехове* (2x: 1v, 3), цехи (2x: 1v, 2v), *цеховъ* (2x: 2 [2x]), *цехов* (2v), *в цехах* (3), *цеховою* (1v), *цехмистры* (1v), *цехМистрове* (3), *цехмистровъство* (2), *Побүнтовали* (1v), *решты* [, албо встатокъ] (2v), *шкод* (gen. pl.) (2v), *Жартъ* (2x: 2v [2x]), *в [самом] Мүрѣ* (3, originally from Latin), *наветъ* (3), *Ротмистрѣ* (3), *фортельми* (3v), *ратунку* (3v), *Гетмани* (3), *сіа дожебрати* (3v), *Гроше̃* (3v, originally Latin), *Папежнику* (loc. sing.) (3v), *Гарбаръскую* (3v), *шпетна* (4v).

Some of these 48 loans from German are phonologically marked as Polonisms: *š, ž* < German *s*: *На ратүшу* (1v), *Под ратушемъ* (1), *решты* (2v), *шкод* (2v), *шпетна* (4v), *Гроше̃* (3v), *Жартъ* (2v), *сіа дожебрати* (3v), *Папежнику* (3v); *j* < *dźc*: ра̃цы (1v, 3); *у* after *r*: *рынок* (1v), *В рынку* (1), along with *в ринку* (1); cf. only soft *r'* in *Скринку* (2), *до скринки* (2) as Polish *skrzynka* with *rz* ([ž] < [r']); *ra* < *re, ar* < *er*: *ратунку* (3v), *Гарбаръскую* (3v).

3. Inflectional Morphology

Although Ruthenian inflectional morphology is largely intact, one does find some counterexamples.

3.1. Nouns

3.1.1. Polish Accusative Singular -e.
In the following example, one finds a genuinely Polish inflectional ending of a noun ending in -a: *Справе пропоноват маютъ* (1). The noun apparently reflects the Polish accusative form *spraw-ę* with a denasalized ending. In two other cases, the same ending occurs after [j]: see *Нащо И Протестацие Показуемъ* (1v), along with the intact Ruthenian ending in *Протестацыю Гарбаръскую* (3v); see the Polish form *protestac(y)ję*); *Инстанцые Чинити* (3v); see the Polish form *instanc(y)ję*. These three forms may be regarded as obvious Polonisms. The form *Справе* must be added to our list of clear-cut Polonisms (the other elements have already been counted as non-Ruthenian because of their lexical stem).

3.1.2. Polish Masculinum Personale.
In three fragments the text seems to demonstrate a Ruthenian reflection of the Middle Polish tendency towards the development of the new gender category *masculinum personale*: 1) *В котрых то воͮсках видимо же бывали и сутъ / Гетмани, Ротмистрѣ, Полковники, Сотники, Десѧтники ет[ц]* (3). In this fragment, the form *Гетмани* (Polish *Hetmani*), and even more so the form *Ротмистрѣ*, come into play, although the letter *и* of the ending in *Гетмани* is always problematic in Ukrainian, and the *ѣ* in *Ротмистрѣ*, which certainly renders ['i], could perhaps be explained by the fact that, in accordance with the Polish *rotmistrz* (nom. pl. *rotmistrzy*), *Ротмистр(ь)* may have been adopted as a soft stem altogether. (Ievhen Tymchenko, however, has no entry for *ротмистръ/ ротмистрь* and records *мистръ* only with the hard stem.[35]) The retained *k* in the last three noun stems demonstrates, of course, that they are not treated as *masculina personalia*.

Two other sentences reveal even more likely candidates for this Polish gender category: 2) *А зажъ Панове цехМистрове И ремесницы Львовские / Шевцѣ Кравцѣ, рѣзники, Поворозники, Горчары, етц етц етц / цос зацнѣшого wсобѣ НадВоͮска Вш Кр Мл быти розумѣют* (3); 3) *А того Заживати Намъ Боронѧтъ Панове Полѧцы* (1v). On the one hand, nouns with the nominative plural ending -*ove* come into play; the ending is widely considered to be of Polish origin. On the other, the forms *ремесницы* and *Полѧцы* with the reflex of the second palatalization of velars are of even greater interest. In all likelihood they are motivated by the Polish model and can barely be treated either as Ruthenian archaisms or Church Slavonic elements. As a minimum, I add the two latter forms to the list of definite Polonisms.

3.1.3. Latin Endings. The form *вѣчум* with the Latinized ending (instead of *вѣче*) seems to be a hapax legomenon, and neither historical dictionaries nor the card file of the *Slovnyk ukraïns'koï movy XVI–pershoï polovyny XVII st.* (Dictionary of the Ukrainian Language of the 16th–First Half of the 17th Century, 1994–2010) at the Institute of Ukrainian Studies in Lviv has an entry: *Старожитны̃ Натуралны̃ Народ Нашъ руски̃ маеᴛ свое вѣчум, / И црковъ Набоженства своего воЛвовъ* (3).[36] The use of the Latin ending seems to be a mere idiosyncrasy.

The Latin loan phrase *in contumatiam*, as rendered in Cyrillic script in *Народ руски̃ абы был всужонъ Здекретован, албо / Инъ контумациам здан* (2), stands apart. Elsewhere, the Polish ending is used with the same stem in *Если бы теж Заносили декрета ІАкие, албо Инъ контумацые* (2) (see 3.3.1.1.). The latter forms were counted as Latinisms earlier. Owing to its ending, the word form *вѣчум* must be added to our list of definite Latinisms.

3.2. Verbs

3.2.1. First Person Present Singular Plural -my. This ending, as encountered once in *Понекондъ маемы домы свои дѣдичные в рынку Под ратушемъ* (1), was adopted in all likelihood from Polish. Elsewhere, one finds the endings -*мо* as in *мусимо* (1) along with -*мъ*, as in *Показуемъ* (1v). Because of its ending, the form *маемы* is listed as a Polonism (although the phonological shape of the lexical stem is intact).

3.2.2. естесмы and First Person Singular Plural -смы. Polish *естесмы* occurs once; the ending -*смы* is used five times with the past tense or the conditional mood. These are the relevant fragments: *Поневажъ Естесмы и мы Понекондъ добро речи Посполитое* (3v), *Илесмы змогли до̃ти* (2), *Просити, абысмы ш̃шкод, Презысковъ И Накладовъ / Адверсаромъ Неплатіӑчи. Волни Были* (2v), *Бысмы были И немотное быдло, Альбо вѣцы іакие / Предсіӑжъ до Вш Кр Мл Волатибысмы Мусѣли* (3v), *Просим Справедливости Сто̃е И ратунку, Абысмы доровных / Волносте̃ Знародом Полским Были Припущени* (3v). Along with *Естесмы*, the form *Есте̃смо* occurs three times (1, 2v, 3): here the stem structure is genuinely Polish, too. The genuinely Ruthenian personal ending -*смо* is used once with a past tense form in *Дліӑ лепшое вѣры Печаᴛ При/Ложилисмо, И руками Подписали* (1). These six forms have to be added to the list of Polonisms.

3.2.3. становши. The most plausible interpretation of this form is that it is motivated by the Polish model (*stanowszy* is an irregular form of *stanąć* in

Polish): *И w еден бокъ 3 Народо*м *Полскимъ становши, Завше въ́рне / И менъ́жне вшеля̇ких Неприя̇телев Коронных, И маестату / В*ш *К*р *М*л *громiа̇тъ* (3).

3.3. Adjectives and De-adjectival Forms

3.3.1. Polish Comparative Suffixes. The suffix -*š*- instead of -*i(j)š*- is used in [С] *пренасвя̇тъшим* [*Сакраменто*м] (1v), cf. Polish *przena(j)świętszy*. The Polish form of the comparative suffix -*ejš*- occurs twice in a form of address that is most probably a loan from Polish; see *Наꙗснѣ̃ши̃ Мл̃стивы̃ К*р (3) and *Наꙗснѣ̃ший Мл К*р (3v). Elsewhere, the genuinely Ruthenian *ѣ* appears in *на̃/ Спроснѣ̃шие* (1v), *зацнѣ̃шого* (3), cf. also горѣ̀ (3).[37]

3.3.2. Middle Polish Superlative Prefix на-. Preceding [j], the prefix *на* (instead of *на̃-* [read: *най*], cf. Middle Polish *naj-* along with *na-*) is encountered in *Наꙗснѣ̃ши̃ Мл̃стивы̃ К*р (3) and *Наꙗснѣ̃ший Мл К*р (3v). It occurs once again in a different context in *пренасвя̇тъшим* (1в), cf. *на̃больше* (1v) and *на̃/Спроснѣ̃шие* (1v).

3.3.3. Adverbs Ending in -е. Adverbs ending in -*е* occur often: see *Завдя̇чне* (1), *Ꙗвне* (1v), *Скрите* (1v), *Ѡкру̃тне* (1v), *въ́рне* (2х: 3 [2х]), *менъ́жне* (3), etc. Adverbs ending in -*е* are widely considered to be of Polish origin (which does not apply to adverbs ending in -*ѣ*). As regards the use of *ѣ* and *е*, see 3.3.3.2. Those four word forms that have not been listed for other reasons yet (*Ꙗвне, Скрите, въ́рне* [2х]) will be added to the list.

3.4. Numerals
The ending of the numeral *Чтыре̃* (read: *Чтырей*) in *Чтыре̃ Народо*в *всамо*м *Му̃рѣ Мѣ̇ста Лвова су̃т фу̃ндованы* (3) is obviously adopted from Polish *czterej*. Altogether, the look of the numeral seems to be genuinely Polish. It will be added to the list.

4. General Statistics

The text consists of 1,722 word forms.[38] If one extracts the Latin fragment, consisting of 93 words, a corpus of 1,629 words remains. Altogether, 347 out of 1,629 forms, or 21.3 per cent, are with great probability (non-ancient) loans of Polish (191 + 19 morphological), Latin (88 + 1 morphological), or German (48) origin. If the Latin fragment is included, 440 out of 1,722 forms constitute as much as 25.5 per cent. The following indicator is even more impressive: out of 1,629 word forms (including many frequent prepositions, conjunctions, even the separately counted reflexive particle, etc.), only 11 stem occurrences (0.68 per cent) have no immediate equivalent in Polish that is not identical, apart from the rules of historical phonology (or some other, less regular, changes of the *который/który* type).

Conclusion

The *Instruction* of 1609 (including the *Lament*) clearly attests to the fact that the Ruthenian burghers of Lviv struggled to maintain their separate identity (in fact, a national identity in the prenationalist meaning). On the other hand, the Ruthenian language of the text again demonstrates the tremendous impact that Polish models had on the Ruthenian higher culture of that time. Since the language of the *Instruction* differs only slightly from the prototypical high variant of the Middle Ruthenian language (which tends to avoid such forms as the acc. sing. *справе*), this strong Polish impact was obviously not primarily caused by the fact that the *Instruction* was addressed to the Warsaw Diet and the Polish King but reflects a general trend. Apparently, early modern Ruthenians did not regard the closeness of their language to Polish as problematic as long as the Cyrillic alphabet, the Ruthenian phonological structure of the morphemes, and the Ruthenian system of inflectional morphology were preserved. At the same time, however, it is quite obvious that people who were able to use a language as encountered in the *Instruction* would be able to switch to Polish very quickly.

In the age of nationalism, a language like that of the *Instruction* could not serve as a successful immediate model for the elaboration of a modern, national written language. Language had by then become an even more important symbol of the nation. As a typical *Abstand* language,[39] modern Ruthenian or, as it was renamed, modern Ukrainian (and modern Belarusian) was to be shaped as a language that would become as remote from Polish as it was from Russian.

Notes

1 See Mikhael' Mozer [Michael Moser], "Shcho take 'prosta mova'?" in *Prychynky do istoriï ukraïns'koï movy*, 2nd ed. (Kharkiv: Prapor, 2009), 76–81.

2 Myron Kapral', *Natsional'ni hromady L'vova XVI–XVIII st. (Sotsial'no-pravovi vzaiemyny)* (Lviv: L'vivs'kyi Natsional'nyi Universytet im. I. Franka, L'vivs'ke viddilennia Instytutu ukraïns'koï arkheohrafiï ta dzhereloznavstva im. M. S. Hrushevs'koho NAN Ukraïny, 2003), 249–50.

3 *Instruktsiia ukraïns'koho naselennia mista na seim dlia zakhystu ioho prav i pryvileïv* (hereafter *Instruction*), oryhinal, 2 sichnia 1609, 4 fols., Tsentral'nyi

Derzhavnyi Istorychnyi Arkhiv u L'vovi (Central State Historical Archive in Lviv; hereafter TsDIA [Lviv]), fond 129, list 1, file 421, fol. 1.

4 Kapral', *Natsional'ni hromady L'vova*, 124–7.

5 Amfrosii Krylovskii [Amvrosii Krylovs'kyi], *L'vovskoe stavropigial'noe bratstvo* (Kyiv: Tipografiia Imperatorskago Universiteta Sv. Vladimira, 1904), 35–7 (appendix).

6 Mykhailo Hrushevs'kyi, *Istoriia ukraïns'koï literatury*, vol. 6, *Literaturnyi i kul'turno-natsional'nyi rukh pershoï polovyny XVII st.*, Kyïvs'ka biblioteka davn'oho ukraïns'koho pys'menstva. Studiï, vol. 1 (Kyiv: AT "Oberehy," 1995), 705.

7 Iaroslav Isaievych, *Voluntary Brotherhood: Confraternities of Laymen in Early Modern Ukraine* (Edmonton: Canadian Institute of Ukrainian Studies Press, 2006), 72.

8 I would like to express my sincere gratitude to Professor Roman Shust of Lviv National University who kindly offered me a CD with photographs of the original document. I would also like to thank Professor Frank Sysyn of the Canadian Institute of Ukrainian Studies and the Ukrainian Free University in Munich for several discussions on Middle Ruthenian.

9 Krylovskii, *L'vovskoe stavropigial'noe bratstvo*, 32.

10 Ibid., several times.

11 Ibid., 33.

12 Ibid.

13 Ibid.

14 Ibid., 34.

15 Ibid.

16 Ibid., 35.

17 Ibid.

18 Ibid.

19 Ibid., 36.

20 Ibid.

21 Ibid.

22 Ibid.

23 Ibid., 37.

24 Ibid.

25 As regards my own views on Middle Ruthenian, see my articles: "Ohliad istoriï ukraïns'koï movy seredn'oï doby," in *Prychynky*, 40–54; "Rus'ka (bilorus'ka ta ukraïns'ka) mova seredn'oï doby: zahal'na perspektyva," *Prychynky*, 55–74; "Shcho take 'prosta mova'?" *Prychynky*, 75–111; "Zrazkova 'prosta mova' ta ïï syntaksa," *Prychynky*, 112–31; see also Daniel Bunčić, *Die ruthenische Schriftsprache bei Ivan Uževyč unter besonderer Berücksichtigung der Lexik*

seines Gesprächsbuchs Rozmova/Besĕda; Mit Wörterverzeichnis und Indizes
zu seinem ruthenischen und kirchenslavischen Gesamtwerk, Slavistische
Beiträge, vol. 447 (Munich: Otto Sagner, 2006) and Achim Rabus, *Die Sprache*
ostslavischer geistlicher Gesänge im kulturellen Kontext, Monumenta linguae
slavicae dialecti veteris. Fontes et dissertationes, vol. LII (Freiburg im Breisgau:
Weiher, 2008).

26 See Mozer, "Shcho take 'prosta mova'?"
27 Mozer, "Shcho take 'prosta mova'?"
28 I have slightly modernized the orthography.
29 See Mozer, "Shcho take 'prosta mova'?"
30 Mozer, "Shcho take 'prosta mova'?" and Mozer, "Zrazkova 'prosta mova.'"
31 Michael Moser, "Philologie als Schlüssel zu den nach morphologischen Prinzipien
adaptierten Polonismen im Russischen," *Studia Slavica Academiae Scientiarum*
Hungaricae 52 (festschrift for Prof. István Nyomárkay), 2007: 299–308.
32 This kind of variation of Polonized and non-Polonized forms is all but untypical
for early modern Ruthenian. See Helmut Keipert, "Metaslavismentypen in
ostslavischen Texten des 17. Jh.," in *Wokół języka: Rozprawy i studia poświęcone*
pamięci profesora Mieczysława Szymczaka (Wrocław: Zakład Narodowy im.
Ossolińskich, 1988), 197–210; and Michael Moser, "Einige phonologisch
markierte Metapolonismen in Kyrylo Trankvilion-Stavrovec'kyjs 'Перло
многwцѣнноє,'" in *Bibel, Liturgie und Frömmigkeit in der Slavia byzantina.*
Festgabe für Hans Rothe zum 80. Geburtstag, ed. Dagmar Christians, Dieter
Stern, and Vittorio S. Tomelleri (Munich: Otto Sagner, 2009), 430–47.
33 Confirmed by Oleksandr Mel'nychuk et al., eds., *Etymolohichnyi slovnyk*
ukraïns'koï movy v semy tomakh (Kyiv: Akademiia nauk Ukraïns'koï RSR.
Instytut movoznavstva im. O. O. Potebni, 1982–2012), 4: 11–12.
34   The Polish source of Ukrainian *pan* is confirmed in O. S. Mel'nychuk et al., eds.,
Etymolohichnyi slovnyk ukraïns'koï movy, 4: 272–3.
35 Ievhen Tymchenko, *Materialy do slovnyka pysemnoï ta knyzhnoï ukraïns'koï movy*
XV–XVIII st., 2 vols. (Kyiv: VCP "Litopys-XX," 2002–3).
36 I am grateful to my colleagues in Lviv for allowing me to consult the card file
during my stay in their city in October 2010.
37 Here it should be noted that the scribe distinguishes *ѣ* and *e* quite consistently
(see also 3.3.3.). The *e* in *немотное* (3v) might reflect a Polonized pronunciation;
the fact that the word is used together with a genuinely Polish word in *немотное*
быдло (3v) should be taken into account. The *e* in the root of the stem *мещан-* is
written consistently. Clearly, the burghers of Lviv did not "Ukrainianize" the
e in this loan, whereas all forms with the stems *Мѣст-* and *мѣсц-* reveal the
etymologically correct Ukrainian. See *Мещане* (1), *Предмещане* (1), *Мещаном*
(1), *Предмещаномъ* (1), *Мещанъ* (1v), *Предмещанъ* (1v), *мещан* (4v), *предъ/*

мещан (4v), along with *Мѣста* (3), *Мѣстечку* (1v), *мѣсца* (1v), *мѣсцъки̃*
(1v), *мѣсцкое* (1), *Мѣсцъкое* (1v), *Мѣсцъких* (2v), *мѣсцко̃* (loc. sing. fem.)
(2), and *Намѣстника* (3v). The verb *Ѡбецуем* is a straightforward Polonism,
so the Polish *e* in the root is no surprise. The situation is more confusing with
regard to *лепшости* (4) and *Длѧ лепшое вѣры* (1), along with *длѧ Лѣпшеи
вѣры* (1). The scribe might well have been acquainted with both forms: *lipš*-
with the genuinely Ruthenian reflex (cf. Modern Ukrainian *ліпший*) and *lepš*- in
accordance with Polish *lepszy*. Of all these possible Polonisms, I add only the
three comparative forms to the list of Polonisms.

38 As in other documents (and especially manuscripts), spaces between alphabetic
strings do not necessarily coincide with word boundaries. For merely technical
reasons, I count letter combinations as symbols for numbers as one word form.
Although some numbers in the Latin text are rendered with Cyrillic letters
too, I treat them as Latin words because in all likelihood they were meant to
be pronounced in Latin. Other forms that are questionable with regard to word
counting are treated as follows: the reflexive particle *сѧ* is always counted
separately (because it is mobile: see *Еслисѧ / Где сним покажутъ* [1v]).
The same applies to the mobile endings *смы/смо* and even the particle *бы*:
ПриЛожили смо (1), *Бы смы были* (3v), *Если бы* (1v), *Волати бы смы* (3v),
but *Ѩкобы* (1v) and *Абы* (1v). The pronominal form *му* is counted separately:
Теж му едно даровати […] (3v). The particle *то* is also counted separately:
see *въ том то рụском Лвовѣ* (3). The particle *колвекъ* is also counted as a
separate word form: *што колвекъ* (1). Prepositions are treated as separate forms
not only in *З народом Полским* (1); *с потомствы* (2v) but also in *всѣ веспол
еденъ За едного* (1), *длѧ того* (1v), *зацо за цо* (1v) (all prepositions are clearly
written together) and even *По христиѧнскому* (1) (in this case, the preposition is
written separately). The forms *Протож* (1), *претожъ* (1v) (cf. Polish *przecież*),
and *Азажъ* (3) (cf. Polish *azaż*) are, however, counted as one word (although
А зажъ is obviously written separately), and the same applies not only to *зас*
(3v) (cf. Polish *zaś*) and *И лисѧ … Или сѧ …* (3v) but also to *Насамы̃Прод* (1,
though written together and paralleled by *Напрод* (2v etc.): cf. Polish *naprzód*
and *nasamprzód*). Less problematic is the negative particle, which I always count
separately if it negates a verb, although the particle is usually written together
with the verb. Therefore, I treat *Нехотѧмъ* (3) as *Не хотѧмъ* 2. I am perfectly
aware that in all these cases other approaches are feasible. I should also add that
in general the solutions I propose tend to generate more word forms than others.
Accordingly, the percentages would change as well. However, the general picture
would probably remain the same.

39 Heinz Kloss, "Abstand Languages and Ausbau Languages," *Anthropological
Linguistics* 9 (1967): 29–41.

Ukraine and the General Crisis of the Seventeenth Century: The Khmel'nyts'kyi Uprising among the Early Modern "Revolutions"

FRANK E. SYSYN

Speaking at a gathering in 2005 to honour Theodore Rabb, the noted author of *The Struggle for Stability in Early Modern Europe*, J. H. Elliott commented that when he mentioned the topic of his paper a colleague had responded "Crisis? What crisis?"[1] Elliott's topic was "The General Crisis in Retrospect: A Debate without End." In taking up this theme, he returned to a time in the 1950s and 1960s when the debates among early modern specialists resonated on both sides of the Atlantic, when Marxists and non-Marxists broke lances, and when walls separating national historiographies tumbled as historians rushed to include their evidence and views on the Crisis, which began as European and then extended to global proportions. The Crisis was seen as manifested in the numerous European upheavals of the 1640s and 1650s with the English or Puritan revolution as its centerpiece. Consequently, the question of what brought societies to open conflict and how revolutionary upheavals were before the end of the eighteenth century developed in tandem with the writing on the Crisis. Although the discussions had largely run their course by the 1980s, Elliott was justified in seeing the debate as unending. Fields such as climate studies kept attention on the seventeenth century as a period of climatic turbulence and an ice age in Europe and beyond.[2] The mid-seventeenth century figured prominently in a 1991 monograph on revolution and rebellion by Jack Goldstone, who saw a worldwide population rise of the sixteenth and early seventeenth century in states without technical progress in producing foodstuffs as bringing on the convulsions of the mid-century.[3]

The great debates took place at a time when Ukrainian historians were cut off from the Western intellectual community. Polish economic historians shaped discussions of the European economy, above all of the grain trade and it consequences, but republican Poland-Lithuania did not play a major role in the discussions. A major Russian historian of France, Aleksandra Liublinskaia,

argued for a Marxist class interpretation of the Fronde, but despite her importance in the debate, Russia also played a peripheral role.[4] Indeed Russia only
came to the fore in the works of the Western scholars Robert Crummey and
Chester Dunning that appeared in the late 1990s in response to Goldstone's
book.[5] Ukrainian historians were largely silent during the great debates.[6]
This isolation and the paucity of literature in Western languages explain to a
considerable degree why Ukraine and the Ukrainian revolt were mentioned
in discussions of the Crisis and the seventeenth-century revolts, but were not
extensively analysed by scholars who took part in the discussions.[7] When
Elliott says in his recent article that additional case studies would be desirable for further discussion of the Crisis thesis, he could hardly have a better candidate than Ukraine.[8] Certainly Robert Crummey pointed to this need
in calling the Khmel'nyts'kyi revolt "the most dramatic manifestation of the
'general crisis of the seventeenth century' in the East Slavic, Orthodox lands,"
but maintained that, as a product of the Polish-Lithuanian state, it would have
to be examined separately.[9] In order to conduct this examination, we must first
examine the general discussion and then its treatment of Ukraine and the
Polish-Lithuanian Commonwealth.

The General Crisis and Early Modern Revolutions

The concept of the General Crisis originated in the works of Eric Hobsbawm,
who together with a number of his Marxist colleagues had formed the journal
of "scientific history," *Past and Present*, in 1952.[10] They were influenced by
the Annales school and wished to end the parochialism of British historical
studies. Hobsbawm was interested in the long process of the breakdown of the
feudal order and the birth of capitalism. He identified an economic crisis in
the seventeenth century during which England was the only state in which the
crisis implanted new capitalist forms, thereby undergoing a bourgeois revolution.[11] Like many economic historians, he had a place in his model for Eastern
Europe. The very vibrant school of Polish economic historians of the interwar
and post-war period had provided considerable data for an understanding of
economic ties in early modern Europe and its impact on society.[12] Hobsbawm
saw the Baltic grain trade as strengthening local feudalism in Eastern Europe,
reducing the pool of purchasers of local goods there, and furthering the second
serfdom in these lands.

In focusing on a crisis in the feudal order and class conflict, Hobsbawm
buttressed his case by pointing to the seventeenth century as an age of "social
revolt," of revolutions that some historians had seen as a general "social-
revolutionary crisis."[13] His source for this social-revolutionary crisis was

Soviet history writing by Boris Porshnev, which in turn derived from an indication in Marx.[14] At the same time, Hobsbawm also noted that the concurrence of numerous revolts had been highlighted by Robert Merriman in his *Six Contemporaneous Revolutions*. Merriman sought to establish whether the revolutionaries influenced each other and why one period had so many outbreaks.[15] For non-Marxist historians the numerous upheavals of the 1640s and 1650s posed a question of what brought so many diverse societies to crisis at the same time and how one could categorize the revolts if the designation "social revolt" was not the only category worthy of attention.

In contrast to Hobsbawm, the other major participant of the Crisis debate, Hugh Trevor-Roper, in an essay first published in 1959, saw the Crisis as one of the "country" revolting against expanding courts and bureaucracies, though without long-term success.[16] While he maintained that economic difficulties deepened the Crisis, he saw it above all as "a crisis in the relations between society and State." His thesis was that the Renaissance courts had become too expensive and provoked a backlash by the country, in circles far from modernizing forces and in many ways among groups that were archaic. Trevor-Roper concentrated on the Renaissance states of Western Europe and tried to draw parallels among England, France, and Spain in his discussion of bureaucracies that had outgrown themselves.

The economic and political crises outlined by the two great English historians served as the foci around which historians throughout Europe assembled data, compared upheavals, and explored new avenues for explaining pan-European phenomena such as climatic change and the "Military Revolution."[17] One of the most successful combinations of economic and political data came from the Danish historian, Niels Steensgaard.[18] He saw the state's pressure for taxation in difficult economic times as the cause of the Crisis. These pressures came above all with absolutist states, and he saw the attempt to form such states by the 1650s as a pan-European phenomenon. The states' demand for higher taxes had unleashed the instability in mid-seventeenth century Europe. As Steensgaard put it, "the six contemporaneous revolutions can only be seen as one if we rechristen them 'the six contemporaneous reactions.'"[19]

If Steensgaard was willing to see a commonality across Europe in the 1640s and 1650s, other scholars were more cautious. From the beginning the thesis of a General Crisis had its critics, none more eminent than J. H. Elliott. Elliott's work on Catalonia, a region or land that invites many comparisons with Ukraine, gives his study or vision special significance. In his inaugural lecture at King's College, London in 1968 he dealt with the question of "Revolution and Continuity in Early Modern Europe."[20] He put in question the uniqueness of the mid-seventeenth century revolts that happened to coincide with what economic historians had seen as a downturn by pointing to the 1560s cluster of revolts. He argued that these revolts – despite their massive and violent nature – had occurred in a period of relative prosperity, so they did not attract the attention that the seventeenth-century ones did. He insisted on the diversity of early modern revolts when he discussed what had become widely referred to as "the general revolution."[21] Based on his broad reading of sources, he suggested that many of his colleagues had placed too much emphasis on the social revolt as inherently more important. He argued that his generation's attuning to the cries of the unfortunate had made it somewhat deaf to the cries of the more fortunate for freedom from arbitrary power. It was among them that Elliott saw the makings of successful revolts. He maintained that the popular uprisings could achieve little or nothing without assistance from groups within the ruling class. On another important characteristic of early modern revolts, he maintained that "foreign aid, in fact, seems to have been an indispensable requirement for any revolt, if it were to have a chance of perpetuating itself."[22]

Elliott's greatest contribution to discussion of early modern revolts and societies was his attention to the concept of the patria. The various patriae that he discussed were idealized communities that ranged from cities to whole realms. He demonstrated that these idealized communities signified a heritage of rights and liberties that could be defended against any intrusion, including that of one's own monarch. These patriae were chiefly the preserve of the upper and literate classes who had also imbibed humanist learning. Elliott maintained that the nineteenth-century romantic writers who had ascribed modern national sentiments to early modern revolts had dissuaded later scholars from examining the sentiments about patria that were being ever more articulately expressed in the early modern period. He offered a nuanced discussion of how defence of the patria could in some instances take on the characteristics of a protonational solidarity and how the political nation's attention to its threatened heritage could fuse for short periods with lower orders' antagonism towards the foreign in protonational outbursts. As he put it, "in these circumstances, a revolt originally sparked by religious protest or sectional discontents was capable of gathering support and momentum by combining in a common patriotism the constitutionalism of the privileged classes and the general antipathy to the outsider felt by the population at large."[23] He remarked how transitory such coalitions were and how quickly they evaporated, especially when the upper classes saw social strife endangering their position.

Another of Elliott's useful perceptions was that a society that sought renovation was frequently involved in innovation. His reflection pertained to the increasing discomfort that scholars were showing in labelling the early modern upheavals as revolutions. As historians came closer to the field of comparative history, they also paid more attention to social scientists' discussion of what constituted a revolution. While the initiators of the discussions (Hobsbawm, Merriman) used "revolution" rather freely, those that came later searched for precision in their nomenclature. Following the political scientists they sought to identify what brought a society to revolt or violence. One of the most influential of these discussions surrounded a collection of essays titled *Preconditions of Revolution in Early Modern Europe*, edited by specialists on the eighteenth century, Robert Forster and Jack P. Greene.[24] The topics of the essays ranged from the Netherlands sixteenth-century "revolution" to the eighteenth-century Pugachev Rebellion, with the heaviest concentration on the 1640s in England, the Spanish domains, and France. The editors established a typology of great national revolutions (the Netherlands and England), national revolts with the potential to become revolutions (the Catalan revolt and the Fronde), a large-scale regional rebellion with limited potential to become a revolution (Pugachev), a secessionist coup (Portugal), and urban jacqueries (Sicily and Naples). In summarizing their findings, they maintained that "social tensions born of conflicts over status and authority more than of material stress, weaknesses in political structure, state ambitions, discontent with existing regimes and government policies, elite participation, an alternative ideology capable of uniting dissident elements, an institutional vehicle for opposition activity, and some prospects for success – these appear to have been the major ingredients of the revolutions and revolts treated in this volume and important preconditions of political upheaval in early modern Europe."[25] Yet their emphasis on the differentiation of each upheaval demonstrated that they were merely collecting generally comparable phenomena and not outlining necessary preconditions. In an extensive review of the book, A. Lloyd Moote winnowed down the preconditions of revolt (not revolution) to a discredited regime, alienated elements of the upper orders comprising a socio-economic elite, economic and political stress that threatened their position, some vehicle of protest, and perhaps the concept of a patria.[26] He firmly rejected, however, that a full-fledged revolution was possible before the eighteenth century when societies became forward-looking and stable enough to be the object of revolutions.

By the 1970s the image of the early seventeenth century as a time of crisis was well established and reached the general literature. A generation of historians assimilated the concept from Henry Kamen's *The Iron Century: Social Change in Europe, 1550–1660*.[27] This social history sought to give voice to the lower orders and dispossessed of Europe. Kamen amply wrote about economic history and the second serfdom in Eastern Europe in a manner supportive of the economic argument for a General Crisis. When he came, however, to discuss the topic in section 4, he placed a question mark after the heading "A General

Crisis?" Here he argued for a strict construction, maintaining that "there are only two, distinct, senses in which the concept of a 'General Crisis' can be manageably discussed. The first of these, which we have touched on before, is the notable recession in the European economy, observable in the decade 1610–20 and pronounced after about 1640. The second of these is the series of governmental crises of the decade 1640–50."[28] In his chapter, "The Revolutions of State," he discussed the Khmel'nyts'kyi Uprising under the "Revolution in Eastern Europe" rubric.[29] In his conclusion, "The Response to Political Crisis," he saw the decade of 1640–50 as one of economic crisis and the challenges faced by the states to be war and taxation. He saw the nobility that had undergone a century of diminishing income and power confronting its greatest test. He warned against putting all the revolts in a single mould. He declared that all the revolutions were stillborn and an age of aristocracy followed the Iron Age.

The entire discussion of the Crisis took a major turn in the 1970s when Theodore Rabb published *The Struggle for Stability in Early Modern Europe*. Turning away from the turmoil and revolts of the mid-century and the period that preceded it, Rabb instead focused on the relative stability that came to Europe around 1660. His emphasis was on how the royal governments and the defenders of traditional privileges and autonomies had come to terms. Much of his discussion centred on the creativity in art, science, and learning of the late seventeenth century. In his work he created a prevailing vision for the late seventeenth century that has only recently been challenged by Steve Pincus, who sees far less stability in the late seventeenth century in his examination of the Glorious Revolution.[30]

The interest in early modern revolts developed independently of discussions of the Crisis, which by the 1980s had lost much of their vitality. By the time Perez Zagorin wrote his comparative study of Western European revolutions and rebellions in 1982, he could dismiss both the Hobsbawm and the Trevor-Roper concept of the Crisis.[31] Zagorin's typologies and descriptions, especially of provincial rebellions and the Dutch revolutionary civil war, provided many analogies for Poland-Lithuania and Ukraine, which are not included in his analysis. He saw Western European revolts as falling into five major categories: conspiracy and coup, limited largely to the action of noble and aristocratic elites; urban rebellion, either by plebeian and inferior groups against urban elites and governments or by urban communities against external royal and state authority; agrarian rebellions by peasants and others against landlord and/or state authority; provincial, regional, and separatist rebellion by provincial societies or dependent realms against their monarchical state centre; and kingdom-wide civil war against monarchies based on noble and aristocratic leadership and involving the entire society.[32]

A major study of European revolts in this period is the masterful monograph on political violence in early modern Europe by Yves-Marie Bercé.[33] Here one finds no mention of the Crisis. Unlike Zagorin, Bercé includes the entire European continent in his purview. He especially focuses on peasant revolts. He maintained that "such outbreaks result from the convergence of a feeling of injustice (legal or fiscal) and a source of provocation (the threat or the hope of a change). The provinces that were the richest in privileges gave the signal for revolt: peasant elites and traditional leaders placed themselves at the head of them. The trigger of revolt is not destitution, but injustice – and not objective injustice, but the conviction of it. Political violence arises as a result of opinion, not of an objective situation" and "even peasant revolts do not necessarily break out at the most crushing moments or in the places where status conditions are at their worst."[34] Bercé's work is especially important for his identification of military borders in a chapter entitled "Traditions of Violence," which describes places and groups that figure time and again in the chronicles of insurrection.

Still, the General Crisis theory had far from played its way out by the 1980s. Geoffrey Parker had globalized the theory by his research on weather and famine. Jack Goldstone, who attracted the interest of Russian specialists in the late 1990s, argued that "early modern" agrarian states (including China) had been unable to deal with the consequences of rising population and prices and had been driven to state breakdown. Their incomes were unable to meet their needs. Their elite groups had multiplied too rapidly, leaving many frustrated younger sons. Lack of land and opportunities led to social disorder, especially as cities swelled with the restless.[35] The Goldstone thesis turned attention once again to broad issues of economy and the relation of state to society.

Elliott returned to the question of the General Crisis through analysing how the debate reflected a generation's intellectual and political interests. He described the period of the 1970s as a "bleak era" in which "the revisionists settled down to the systematic deconstruction of everything we thought we knew and understood before their demolition squads appeared on the scene," and "the links, or presumed links, between the economy and politics had been snapped, and what had once been seen as great revolutions were all too easily reduced to the contingency of day to day events."[36] In discussing how subsequent studies could still be employed in rethinking the findings of the Crisis discussion and its age, Elliott pointed to the need to reassess the vitality of republican forms of government and the examination of kings' favourites (Olivares, Richelieu) as goading subjects into revolt so that only the later reassertion of the role of kings could bring stability.[37] As recently as 2008, the *American Historical Review* devoted a forum section to the Crisis, with divided opinions on its usefulness as a concept.[38]

Ukraine in the Discussion of the Crisis and the Contemporaneous Revolutions

What role did Ukraine and the Polish-Lithuanian state play in the debates and discussion? Their mentions were relatively frequent, but their actual weight in the discussions was not great.[39] The peripheral attention to the Ukrainian revolt was perhaps best expressed by the great specialist in Swedish history, Michael Roberts, who maintained that "the case of Sweden may reasonably be held to present features of more than local interest: the country resembled a western European state a good deal more closely than did (for example) the Ukraine; and in 1650 Stockholm looks much nearer to the center of the revolutionary movement than (for instance) Naples or Amsterdam. If we are really determined to bring the Cossacks and the Ironsides within the scope of a single explanation, it does not seem legitimate to leave Sweden out of the reckoning."[40] We may allow Roberts his rhetorical flourish. We could merely answer that seventeenth-century authors saw the Cossacks and Ironsides as part of one world that was shaking. Maiolino Bisaccioni devoted his second-longest essay to the civil war in Poland in his monograph on civil wars first published in Venice in 1653.[41] The longest essay was on England.

Economic historians were most likely to include Ukraine in their discussions, though the paucity of sources on the central Ukrainian heartland of the revolt and the dearth of research on the economy of that region meant their remarks usually referred to Polish and West Ukrainian territories.[42] Hobsbawm's initiation of the discussion illustrated how theories of price rise in agricultural goods until the early seventeenth century, the extension of the second serfdom in Eastern Europe, and the increase of large holdings using corvée labour were seen as bringing about the Ukrainian uprising.[43] He asserted that the growing demand for grain "tempted serf-lords into that headlong expansion of their dominions and intensification of exploitation which led to the Ukrainian revolution, and perhaps to demographic catastrophe."[44] While the degree of serfdom among the inhabitants of the Cossack heartland and the amount of grain exported from the lower Dnipro Basin remain disputed to this day, the impetus to introduce the economic and social relations that prevailed further west into the Dnipro Basin certainly provoked opposition. Generally, Polish historians saw these new economic trends as hastening economic and demographic growth, while some Ukrainian and Soviet historians depicted the "feudal" relations as regressive.[45] Indeed, in the 1920s the Ukrainian Marxist historian Matvii Iavors'kyi saw the Cossack producers as a new capitalist class that had broken through the regressive feudal structures of the Polish economy.[46] More certain is the expansion of the Ukrainian economy as a result of the rapid colonization of central Ukraine in the 1620s–40s.[47] Whatever the aggregate tendencies in Europe, central Ukraine of the mid-seventeenth century was a land of rapidly increasing population and economic production. Only additional research will show whether the bad weather and harvests that affected surrounding areas around 1648 also occurred in Ukraine.

Hobsbawm pointed to the demographic losses unleashed by the revolt and the long series of wars that followed. Certainly the incessant wars that drew in Muscovy-Russia, Sweden, Transylvania, the Crimean Khanate, and the Ottomans in the second half of the seventeenth century caused tremendous loss of life and devastation of whole regions. Despite the losses during the revolt and war, including from plague and pestilence, central Ukraine appears to be a zone of rapidly increasing population that quickly resettled devastated areas. Recent research has shown that even the Jewish communities that sustained great losses in the early phase of the revolt were rapidly re-established in the lands that remained under the Commonwealth's control.[48] Losses in surrounding regions drawn into the conflict, such as the Grand Duchy of Lithuania, were of a more lasting nature. In his discussion of demography Goldstone placed Ukraine as the land of the highest population growth in Europe from 1500 to 1600–50.[49] What is not spelled out in Goldstone's discussion is that despite war and devastation the demographic and economic dynamism continued throughout the century in central Ukraine, though population shifted especially to the Left Bank of the Dnipro.

Much of the interest in the Ukrainian revolt centred on it as a servile or peasant revolt; that is, as a social revolt. Indeed, after the 1930s, Soviet historiography dogmatically insisted that the peasant and antifeudal elements of the uprising predominated and placed it among a large series of Russian and Ukrainian "peasant wars." Hobsbawm, who had drawn his characterization of the period from Porshnev, also looked to Lenin as a major source for what he calls the "Ukrainian revolution of 1648–1654" and a "major servile upheaval."[50] Indeed, in some cases the attention to the peasant or plebeian aspect of the revolt overshadowed its complexities in social constituency. Thus Bercé, though he pointed out Ukraine as a military borderland, designated all the Cossack-led revolts as peasant wars, even though in his short description of the Khmel'nyts'kyi Uprising he dealt with the clash of civilizations (Catholic-Polish and Orthodox-Ukrainian) and the elements of civil war in the revolt.[51] In contrast, Henry Kamen was closer to the mark. He labelled the Khmel'nyts'kyi Uprising a "revolution of state," and when he discussed popular revolts he mentioned the importance of "brigands."[52] He included the Cossacks in this category as the backbone of the Ukrainian popular revolts. Without citing their work, he was agreeing with Ukrainian historians such as Hrushevs'kyi and Lypyns'kyi.[53] He mentioned that peasant revolts lasted until 1649 and that the peasants were suppressed and slaughtered in 1650, that is, after the Zboriv Agreement was enacted and nobles began to return to Ukraine.[54] One may argue that Kamen cut off peasant support for the revolt too soon, especially for the lands where the Cossacks held sway and where peasants still rallied to the Cossack banner when there were attempts to restore the old order. He did, however, make a careful distinction between peasants and the Cossack frontiersmen who were the backbone of the revolt.

Albeit not in analysing the Khmel'nyts'kyi Uprising, the Cossack question did enter the discussions on the General Crisis through writings about Russian Cossacks. This occurred most fully in the late 1990s as Crummey and Dunning sought to examine Crisis theories in a way that would restore the role of the Russian Cossacks, which had been downplayed in Soviet writings. Some of the most interesting discussion of the Cossack issue came in Marc Raeff's analysis of the Pugachev revolt, Forster and Greene's use of his essay in their typology of early modern revolts, and Moote's discussion of their theorizing. In his discussion of the role of the Cossacks in the Pugachev revolt, Marc Raeff maintained that, "like the feudal revolts and rebellions in the name of regional particularism in Western Europe, the Cossacks opposed the tide of rational modernization and institutionalization of political authority. They regarded their relationship to the ruler as a special and a personal one based on their voluntary service obligations; in return they expected the czar's protection of their religion, traditional social organization, and administrative autonomy."[55] Indeed, the Khmel'nyts'kyi Uprising also fits this model, substituting the Polish king for the Russian tsar. In contrast, however, to the Russian Cossack revolts that could only rectify perceived injustices through putting forth a true tsar to replace the unjust and illegitimate present ruler, the Ukrainian Cossack revolts were more similar to the Western European ones in demanding that the monarch and the Commonwealth adhere to agreements with the Cossack Host – which would restore what the Cossacks alleged were traditional rights that had been eroded.

In comparing the Pugachev rebellion to the seventeenth-century European revolts, Raeff saw similarities in that Russia, like France or Spain in an earlier period, was developing an absolutist state. The circumstances of Poland-Lithuania were far different, in that modernization of a certain type in Ukraine was being carried on within the framework of the magnate-controlled economy and political structures. Indeed, if the Polish monarch was to become the dominant force in institutionalizing political authority, the magnates and noble elite would have to be curbed by other forces. Władysław IV did see the Cossacks as an instrument through which he could increase his powers if they could provoke a war against the Ottomans that he would win. Even after the revolt, Khmel'nyts'kyi ostensibly proffered the idea of assisting Władysław's successor John Casimir to rule as other European monarchs did. However much the rulers of the Republic (Rzeczpospolita) might have wished to aggrandize their power, they could not really break from their noble citizens. The social chasm between the noble-based Commonwealth and the peasant-backed Cossacks made such arrangements impossible. At the same time, Khmel'nyts'kyi's victories made it possible for his political ambitions to grow so that he could conceive of breaking with Poland. The victories also made his followers reluctant to return to the old order. Thus, when Forster and Greene saw the Cossacks as a regional elite and an institution similar to the parliamentary bodies and vehicles in the West that were needed for early modern revolts in the Pugachev uprising, they were in fact describing a situation more inherent to the Khmel'nyts'kyi Uprising.[56] Perhaps with good cause Moote rejected this designation for the Cossacks of Pugachev's time and argued that Russia lacked the institutions needed for even a rebellion, not to speak of a revolution of the Western model.[57] It would have been interesting to see if he would have made the same argument for Khmel'nyts'kyi's Cossacks.

One of the major reasons that the Ukrainian revolt was left out of so many of the discussions of the Crisis was that the Polish-Lithuanian state was not developing in the direction of absolutism. The conflict was not one between an extending state with its powers, especially of taxation, and the country/society, but more about landowners' increasing exactions on the Ukrainian frontier population. The nobles' republic, as it was subsequently called, is seen as an anomaly on the European map. The nobility of the seventeenth century resisted forming a large standing army not only as a way to avoid taxes but even more as a way to stop the aggrandizement of royal power. The year 1648 is often seen as the beginning of the Commonwealth's "crisis" from which it never recovered, but the roots of its decline are believed to extend far into its past. The stability that much of the remainder of Europe achieved at the end of the century through absolutist states did not come to the Commonwealth. Robert Frost has persuasively argued that this vision underestimates the powers of the Polish kingship and sees the monarchy as having lost the battle even before 1648.[58] Frost does much to show that the nobles had reason to fear absolutist tendencies. He argues that King John Casimir had squandered chances to expand monarchical powers by concentrating solely on the issue of creating a hereditary monarchy. The struggle to curb the king meant that the Commonwealth's political nation did not bring all the forces it had to bear against the Khmel'nyts'kyi Uprising.

By including the Khmel'nyts'kyi Uprising in the "revolutions of state," Henry Kamen provided the corrective to Merriman's *Six Contemporaneous Revolutions*. For Kamen, the revolts of the 1640s were all crises of the state's inability to handle war and taxation. In commenting on the Ukrainian revolt, he maintained that "in the Slav lands war was the very determinant of politics, and through it the duchy of the Ukraine was born."[59] Essentially, he cast the revolt as having founded a new polity. He took his account only up to 1654 and the Pereiaslav Agreement, which he saw as creating Ukraine and bringing about war between Russia and Poland. In essence, Kamen placed the Ukrainian revolt as an equivalent of the Dutch revolt of the late sixteenth and early seventeenth century, rather than the other revolts of the 1640s – namely, as a revolt that created a new polity.

The Ukrainian Case

How, then, should the revolt be viewed in the context of early modern revolts and discussions of the Crisis of the seventeenth century?[60] What does the discussion on the Crisis and early modern revolts or revolutions offer to the study of the Khmel'nyts'kyi Uprising and how does inclusion of the Khmel'nyts'kyi Uprising enrich the discussion?

The Khmel'nyts'kyi Uprising can be seen as an additional type of "revolution" to the five types identified by Zagorin for Western Europe. Two of his categories, agrarian and urban rebellions, occurred within the framework of the Khmel'nyts'kyi Uprising, but only because they were sparked by the Cossack rebellion. Yet the two broader categories that Zagorin offers are insufficient for describing the Khmel'nyts'kyi Uprising. Certainly, the revolt was not a kingdom-wide civil war against the monarchy based on noble and aristocratic leadership and involving the whole society. There were some early phases when the revolt of the secondary elite might have turned into a pro-monarchical revolt against the magnate groups, but the social war aspects of the revolt and the strength and solidarity of the noble order in the Commonwealth, to which the magnates belonged, made this turn impossible. The revolt was also not fully a provincial revolt against a monarchical state centre, in that it was not led by the provincial elite and the territories of the revolt did not constitute a well-defined province. The essential characteristic that made for a difference in Ukraine was that the revolt was a civil war in a military borderland in which a weak central power supported the newly introduced social order against an armed frontier population. Played out on a territory that also had religious and cultural-historical divergences from the core territories, the frontier military group could, and did, expand its agenda and the areas to which it laid claim. It could not, however, transcend its regional frontier character or its association with Ruthenians and Orthodoxy to extend into the central territories of the state.

Turning to Forster and Greene's categories, it would seem useful to recast their categorization of the Pugachev rebellion to a new category, "a large-scale regional rebellion that developed into a revolution" when we apply it to the Khmel'nyts'kyi Uprising. Obviously the use of "revolution" is a topic fraught with semantic difficulties. But if one looks at the changes in political structures, economic holdings, social relations, and even the dominant myths of the society in Ukraine, one sees radical change in Cossack Ukraine that certainly fulfills the rather minimalist terms of revolution used by Zagorin ("A revolution is any attempt by subordinate groups through the use of violence to bring about (1) a change of government or its policy, (2) a change of regime, (3) a change of society, whether this attempt is justified by reference to past conditions or to an as yet unattained goal")[61] and even the broadened definition of Eugene Kamenka used by Forster and Greene ("any sharp, sudden change or attempted change in the location of political power which involved either the use or the threat of violence and, if successful, expressed itself in the manifest and perhaps radical transformation of the process of government, the accepted foundations of sovereignty or legitimacy, and the conception of the political and/or social order").[62] Within its regional context, the Khmel'nyts'kyi Uprising had fulfilled most of the criteria of the Kamenka definition by Christmas 1648, and despite many setbacks held on throughout the 1650s and beyond.[63]

In many ways, the Khmel'nyts'kyi revolt was similar to the six contemporaneous reactions as Steensgaard defined them. It was a reaction to change that had been brought to Ukraine by the Polish state, mainly in curbing the Cossack Host and stationing a standing army in the Dnipro Basin. But even more it was reaction to the change wrought by the large landowners who had set up virtual statelets in Ukraine. Both the relatively small standing army and the magnates' troops were unable to deal with a Cossack-led revolt that was backed by the Crimean Tatars. The reaction took place in a military borderland that was just on the verge of restructuring and integration into the social and economic structures that prevailed to the west. In this land where the populace was not yet subjugated to full serfdom, the perception of injustice, to use Bercé's insight, was greatest. Not distant Warsaw but the statelets of the magnates weighed as an ever more onerous burden on the frontier population that opposed these changes. Therefore Trevor Roper's court and country conflict might be seen as playing out on a local level. The country was, in a way, reacting against the statelets, the magnates, and their servitors and agents.

The explanation of early modern revolts as being caused by a division in the elite has some relevance to the revolt in the Commonwealth. The revolt would not have occurred if there had not been a division in the elite, with the circle around the king who wanted a Turkish war encouraging Khmel'nyts'kyi and the Cossacks to think that they would take part in a war planned by the king against the Ottomans. Although he was not an Olivares or Richelieu, the Crown Chancellor Jerzy Ossoliński, detested by the masses of nobles whom he viewed as rabble and by those magnates who did not share his power at court, may be seen as a type of favourite who elicited antagonism. But here the antagonism was not that of those who rebelled but rather of those who were to defend the state. The wrangling between the peace party led by Ossoliński and the war party led by Jeremi Wiśniowiecki greatly undermined the Commonwealth's ability to deal with the revolt in its initial phase. The person of the king was crucial to the revolt in that Władysław encouraged the Cossacks to aspire to changing their situation. When they unexpectedly sought to do so through revolt, his unfortunate demise removed him just as he was essential for negotiating a compromise; the elective monarchy was thrown into the cumbersome process of selecting a successor. The most important strength of the revolt was that it facilitated the rise of a Cossack elite that had hitherto been denied elite status by the monopolization of status and power by the nobility. Here Goldstone's demographic factor might be invoked. The Commonwealth sought to limit the Cossacks to six thousand persons, and the magnates sought to replace them with private troops just as the population was exploding and ever more Cossacks' sons wished to retain their fathers' status and not be reduced to peasants.

From the first, the revolt benefited from having an institutional structure in the Zaporozhian Host. This institutional structure allowed the rebels to call in foreign assistance, for the Cossack Host had long-standing contacts with the Tatars and was a recognized entity in foreign affairs. Elliott pointed out that any successful revolt needed to find support from abroad, and the history of the Khmel'nyts'kyi revolt from the start and well past 1654 was the history of a constant search for foreign support that would provide an appropriate arrangement for the Cossack Hetmanate. Initiated by a secondary, not primary elite, the revolt benefited in being able to marshal peasant and urban lower orders against the magnate-noble regime and the existing order. Although the Cossack leaders, especially the nobles among them and those who hoped to come to an accommodation with the Commonwealth, were opposed to the jacquerie elements of the revolt, they were able to ride them out without the split from the revolt that occurred in areas such as Catalonia. At the same time, the rebels could use religious and xenophobic sentiments (anti-Jewish, anti-Catholic, anti-Polish) in raising their standards. Nevertheless, the rebels were geographically confined to the military borderland, where their real constituency resided,

with outreaches to the lands of the Rus', the Orthodox religious and Ruthenian protonational group they adhered to. The attempts to go beyond this base,
to the territories around Cracow in 1651 or during the campaigns of 1656–7,
failed. Here one should pay attention to Lawrence Stone's and John Elliott's
observations on the need to study territories that do not rise in rebellion.[64] In
essence the Polish territories with their thick layer of nobles and their lack
of religious affinity with the Orthodox Cossacks were not fertile grounds for
revolt.

Although no fully established patria led by the upper orders of society
existed on the territory of the revolt, a quasi-Rus' patria had been conceived
of by the Ruthenian nobility and clergy before 1648. Of all Elliott's insights,
his attention to the patria has had the most lasting impact on Ukrainian history
writing, whether through work on the incorporation lands of the Union of Lublin (Kyiv, Volhynia, Bratslav, and Chernihiv) as an incipient Rus' patria before
1648 that foreshadowed the Cossack Hetmanate, or the considerable work on
otchyzna (fatherland) in dealing with the political culture of the Hetmanate
that developed out of the revolt and transformed the political thought of the
Commonwealth.[65] Yet for the Khmel'nyts'kyi Uprising, Elliott's finding on
patria as the object of loyalty of a political nation who could rise in its defence
against an intrusive monarch or state does not have such immediate applica-
bility. Although the Ruthenian Orthodox nobility had complained about the
infringements on its faith and in a general manner cast the Union of Lublin of
1569 as a form of charter for regional rights, it did not evolve a clear conceptualization of Rus' of the Lublin incorporation as its patria and it did not rise up
in revolt in this amorphous patria's defence. In the Ukrainian case, the patria
would fully emerge only after the revolt and as the object of loyalty of the new
elite that was formed by the revolt.

Instead, the Cossacks who rose in revolt usurped the political nation of the
central Ukrainian lands. The Cossacks had first of all a concept of the liberties
of the Host, primarily as guaranteed by the monarch. Only slowly did they conceptually assume responsibility for the territory, and it would be a generation
before they conceived of that land as a patria distinct from their former fatherland (*ojczyzna*), the Polish-Lithuanian Commonwealth. The Cossack revolt
that challenged the old nobility's position as the leaders of Rus' and the Ruthenian faith had links with both the Cossacks' social superiors and their inferi-
ors. The Cossacks were able to attract individuals from the nobility (albeit its
bottom ranks) and the popular masses in a conflict in which the Cossacks were
struggling against innovations of the state in establishing new means to control
the Ukrainian lands and against the magnates who were limiting the Cossacks'
economic and social freedom. Within that context they were able to pose their

struggle as against the Poles (Liakhs) who were cast as national and religious "others" also associated with a social group, the landowning nobility.[66] In discussing national feeling in early modern revolts, Elliott maintained that in the circumstance of foreign rulers, foreign officials, and foreign troops on native soil, one could combine the defence of the patria with the xenophobia of the lower orders, in combinations that he called fragile and transitory. While the violent social war of 1648–9 frightened off many of the Ruthenian privileged elite, the rebels did succeed in portraying the conflict as one of the Ruthenians against the Liakhs. In so doing they were able to "other" their opponents, even though many of them, including the great Prince Jeremi Wiśniowiecki, were fully of Ruthenian stock. Without the ability to cast their opponents as alien, the rebels would not have been as successful in winning any of the segments of the former privileged groups.

Only after the Cossack revolt succeeded did the concept of a new patria emerge in the Cossack Hetmanate, following upon the attempts by Khmel'nyts'kyi to set up a Cossack polity. Within the Commonwealth social cleavages were so great that the two sides were irreconcilable as long as the question of the restitution of the pre-1648 order was demanded by the Polish side. Yet the rebels were able to become more conservative as they shied away from their peasant followers and attracted large numbers of nobles. By the early 1650s the Cossack Hetmanate, a political and social order based on the Cossack Host, had emerged from out of the Polish-Lithuanian Commonwealth. Although it did not hold all the territories that Khmel'nyts'kyi aspired to, and though it needed to accept foreign suzerainty, it proved to be one of the most successful outcomes of early modern revolts and creations of the age of Crisis.

Integrating Ukraine into the discussion of the Crisis and of revolts or revolutions will add the example of a non-primary elite-led revolt that was able to marshal a popular uprising to challenge a European state. In this case the state was a monarchical noble republic. As Elliott has redirected us to rethink the possible vibrancy of republics of the period, we must reconsider the Cossack republic that emerged from the revolt and the noble republic that struggled against it. The military frontier nature of the core territory of the revolt and the newness of economic and social circumstances facilitated the overthrow of the established order. The central role of the Cossacks, whose military structure could be adapted to civil administration and whose ranks could be expanded to take in a large part of the population, provided an institutional basis for replacing the prior structures. The Host's search for contacts with a sovereign gave the revolt an international aspect from its beginning and ultimately involved the Ukrainian rebels in negotiations with numerous surrounding states. Religious differences with the state they rebelled against, antagonism towards elements of the old order, and xenophobia all played a role in strengthening the tenacity of the revolt. The revolt did not bring down the Commonwealth, and by the late 1660s the Commonwealth did win back a large part of the land where the revolt had first succeeded. It did so without accepting absolutism or even fully embracing the introduction of a large regular army. Yet by the 1660s on the land beyond the Dnipro a new polity and society had emerged based on the outcome of the revolt. In the borderland of the Commonwealth and of Europe, the mid-century Crisis had brought about a new social-political entity.

Notes

1 J. H. Elliott, "The General Crisis in Retrospect: A Debate without End," in *Early Modern Europe: From Crisis to Stability*, ed. Philip Benedict and Myron P. Gutman (Newark: University of Delaware Press, 2005), 31. Rabb's book appeared in 1975.

2 Elliott, "The General Crisis," 45 and Geoffrey Parker and Lesley M. Smith, "Introduction," in *The General Crisis of the Seventeenth Century*, ed. Geoffrey Parker and Lesley M. Smith (London: Routledge and Kegan Paul, 1978), 6–9. For a more recent argument on the climatic factor, see Geoffrey Parker, "Crisis and Global Catastrophe: The Global Crisis of the Seventeenth Century Reconsidered," *American Historical Review* 113, no. 4 (2008): 1053–79.

3 Jack A. Goldstone, *Revolution and Rebellion in the Early Modern World* (Berkeley: University of California Press, 1991).

4 Aleksandra Liublinskaia, *French Absolutism: The Crucial Phase, 1620–1629* (Cambridge: Cambridge University Press, 1968). In addition, Boris Porshnev, the specialist in seventeenth-century French history and international affairs, had works available in Western languages. Two discussions appeared after the major debates. Paul Dukes wrote on "Russia and the 'General Crisis' of the Seventeenth Century," *New Zealand Slavonic Journal* 2 (1974): 1–17. Dukes argues that Muscovy was increasingly seen as European in the seventeenth century and that the uprisings in Moscow and other towns in 1648–50 should be considered in the "laboratory" of European revolts. Peter Brown wrote on military issues, including a comparison with Poland-Lithuania. See Peter B. Brown, "Muscovy, Poland, and the Seventeenth Century Crisis," *The Polish Review* 27 (1982): 55–69.

5 Robert O. Crummey, "Muscovy and the 'General Crisis of the Seventeenth Century,'" *Journal of Early Modern History* 2 (1998): 156–80 and Chester Dunning, "Does Jack Goldstone's Model of Early Modern State Crisis Apply to Russia?" *Comparative Studies in Society and History* 39, no. 3 (1997): 572–92.

6 The only exception may be Bohdan Kentschynskyj, as Yaroslav Fedoruk has recently argued. See "Overcoming Historical Stereotypes and Analyzing Ukrainian

Foreign Policy," in Mykhailo Hrushevsky, *History of Ukraine-Rus'*, vol. 9, bk. 2, pt. 2, *The Cossack Age, 1654–1657*, trans. Marta Daria Olynyk, ed. Yaroslav Fedoruk and Frank E. Sysyn with the assistance of Myroslav Yurkevich (Toronto: Canadian Institute of Ukrainian Studies Press, 2010), xxxv. Fedoruk points out that in his Swedish-language works on Charles X's eastern policy Kentschynskyj used the term "Crisis" for 1654–5. He also wrote an article on the "Ukrainian revolution" and the Russian attack on Sweden. Still, despite the terms used, Kentschynskyj did not engage the general theories on the Crisis or bring the Ukrainian "revolution" into the discussion of the revolutions/revolts of the mid-seventeenth century.

  7 On English-language historiography, see Frank E. Sysyn, "English-Language Historiography in the Twentieth Century on the Pereiaslav Agreement," *Russian History* 32, no. 3 (2005): 513–30.

  8 It is interesting that Germany and German historians were largely left out of the initial study of the Crisis. Sheilagh C. Ogilvie, "Germany and the Seventeenth Century Crisis," *The Historical Journal* 35, no. 2 (1992): 421. This article is included in the second edition of Geoffrey Parker and Lesley M. Smith, eds., *The General Crisis of the Seventeenth Century* (London: Routledge, 1997), 57–86.

  9 Crummey, "Muscovy and the 'General Crisis of the Seventeenth Century,'" 177. A recent doctoral dissertation in Sweden has dealt with the Grand Duchy of Lithuania in the context of the discussion of the Crisis: Andrej Kotljarchuk, *In the Shadows of Poland and Russia: The Grand Duchy of Lithuania and Sweden in the European Crisis of the Mid-17th Century*, Södertörn Studies in History 3 (Stockholm: Södertörns högskola, 2006).

10 I am indebted in this discussion and my choice of literature to the incisive discussion of the Crisis by Robert Crummey, "Muscovy and the 'General Crisis of the Seventeenth Century,'" 157–61.

11 "The General Crisis of the European Economy in the 17th Century," *Past and Present* 5 (1954): 33–53 and "The Crisis in the Seventeenth Century–II," *Past and Present* 6 (1954): 44–65. For the former and many other essays, see the volume of reprints from Trevor Aston, ed., *Past and Present, Crisis in Europe 1560–1660* (London: Routledge and Kegan Paul, 1965).

12 Marian Małowist played an especially important role and published in *Past and Present*: "Poland, Russia, and Western Trade," *Past and Present* 13 (1958): 26–41.

13 Eric Hobsbawm, "The General Crisis of the European Economy in the 17th Century," in *Past and Present: Crisis in Europe 1560–1660*, 37.

14 Ibid., 51, note 17.

15 *Six Contemporaneous Revolutions* (Oxford: Clarendon Press, 1938).

16 Hugh Trevor-Roper, "The General Crisis of the Seventeenth Century," in *The Crisis of the Seventeenth Century: Religion, the Reformation, and Social Change* (New York: Harper and Row, ca. 1967), 43–81.

17 Michael Roberts, *Essays in Swedish History* (Minneapolis: University of Minnesota Press, 1967), 56–81 and 195–225; Roberts Geoffrey Parker, *The Military Revolution* (Cambridge: Cambridge University Press, 1988); and Brian M. Downing, *The Military Revolution and Political Change: Origins of Democracy and Autocracy in Early Modern Europe* (Princeton: Princeton University Press, 1992).

18 Niels Steensgaard, "The Seventeenth-Century Crisis," in Parker and Smith, eds., *The General Crisis of the Seventeenth Century*, 26–56.

19 Ibid., 44.

20 John Elliott, "Revolution and Continuity in Early Modern Europe," *Past and Present* 42 (1969): 35–56, reprinted in Parker and Smith, eds., *The General Crisis of the Seventeenth Century*, 110–33. Citations are from the reprint.

21 Ibid., 111.

22 Ibid., 129.

23 Ibid., 126.

24 Robert Forster and Jack P. Greene, *Preconditions of Revolution in Early Modern Europe* (Baltimore, MD: Johns Hopkins Press, 1970).

25 Ibid., 17.

26 The review, "The Preconditions of Revolution in Early Modern Europe: Did They Really Exist?" first published in the *Canadian Journal of History* 8 (1973): 207–34 is reprinted in Parker and Smith, eds., *The General Crisis of the Seventeenth Century*, 134–64. The quoted passage is on p. 155 of the reprint.

27 Henry Kamen, *The Iron Century: Social Change in Europe 1550–1660* (London: Weidenfeld and Nicolson, 1971).

28 Ibid., 309.

29 Ibid., 324–6.

30 The concepts of the mid-century as revolutionary and economically distressed have recently been challenged by Steve Pincus, who has argued for economic growth in England well into the century and has cast the Glorious Revolution as the really revolutionary event of the epoch. Steve Pincus, *1688: The First Modern Revolution* (New Haven, CT: Yale University Press, 2009).

31 Perez Zagorin, *Rebels and Rulers, 1500–1660*, 2 vols. (Cambridge: Cambridge University Press, 1982), 1: 136–9.

32 Ibid., 1: 41.

33 The French original was published in 1980. Yves Marie Bercé, *Revolt and Revolution in Early Modern Europe: An Essay on the History of Political Violence* (Manchester: Manchester University Press, 1987).

34 Ibid., 221.

35 Goldstone, *Revolution and Rebellion*, xxii–iv.

36 Elliott, "The General Crisis," 43.

37 Ibid., 46–7.

38 In addition to the Parker article mentioned in footnote 2, the Forum includes Jonathan Dewald, "Crisis, Chronology, and the Shape of European Social History" (p. 1031–52) and J.B. Shank, "Crisis: A Useful Category of Post-Social Scientific Historical Analysis?" (p. 1090–9), *American Historical Review* 113, no. 4 (2008).

39 One of the more interesting and informed mentions is in Parker and Smith, "Introduction," *The General Crisis of the Seventeenth Century*, 16.

40 Michael Roberts, "Queen Christina and the General Crisis of the Seventeenth Century," in *Crisis in Europe 1560–1660*, ed. Trevor Aston (London: Routledge and Kegan Paul, 1965), 221.

41 "Historia delle guerre civili di Polonia," in *Historia delle guerre civili di questi ultimi tempi*, 2nd ed. (Venice, 1654), 272–397.

42 The work of Jerzy Topolski was especially influential. See his *Narodziny kapitalizmu w Europe XIV–XVII wieku* (Warsaw: Państwowe Wydawnictwo Naukowe, 1965) and *Gospodarka polska a europejska w XVI–XVII wieku* (Poznań: Wydawnictwo Poznańskie, 1977).

43 Eric Hobsbawm, "The General Crisis," 37 and 43–4.

44 Ibid., 48. Here Hobsbawm cites the works of Jan Rutkowski and the Ukrainian émigré Marxist historian Roman Rozdolsky. Interestingly, Hobsbawm asserts that serf-exploiting agriculture did not extend into the Black Sea area until the eighteenth century because of Turkish policies. Here he means Romania and the Balkans (p. 52, note 34).

45 For historiography on this topic, see the bibliographic note and update, Mykhailo Hrushevsky, "Literature on Socioeconomic Conditions and Colonization in Eastern Ukraine in the Fifteenth and Sixteenth Centuries," in *History of Ukraine-Rus'*, vol. 7, *The Cossack Age to 1625*, trans. Bohdan Strumiński, ed. Serhii Plokhy and Frank E. Sysyn with the assistance of Uliana Pasicznyk (Toronto: Canadian Institute of Ukrainian Studies Press, 1999), 440–2.

46 Matvii Iavors'kyi, *Narysy istoriï Ukraïny*, 2 vols. (Adelaide: Knyha, 1986), 1: 65–139.

47 For literature on this topic, see the note and update, Mykhailo Hrushevsky, "Ukrainian Colonization East of the Dnipro: The Left Bank and Sloboda Ukraine," in *History of Ukraine-Rus'*, vol. 8, *The Cossack Age, 1626–1650*, trans. Marta Daria Olynyk, ed. Frank E. Sysyn with the assistance of Myroslav Yurkevich (Edmonton and Toronto: Canadian Institute of Ukrainian Studies Press, 2002), 667–70.

48 See the discussion of demography and renewed Jewish life in the special issue on the Khmel'nyts'kyi Uprising and the Jewish massacres, *Jewish History* 17, no. 2 (2003), especially the articles by Shaul Stampfer, Moshe Rosman, and Frank E. Sysyn.

49 Goldstone, *Revolution and Rebellion*, 344.

156   Frank E. Sysyn

50 In the discussion on "Seventeenth Century Revolutions," held in July 1957 and published in *Past and Present* 25 (1963): 63–72, Hobsbawm declared that "the increasing feudalization [of Eastern Europe] – partly the result of the area's conversion into a dependent economy – produced a major peasant revolt on the frontier of feudal power, in Ukraine" (p. 63). Interestingly, in a 1960 article on seventeenth-century economy, Hobsbawm saw the expansion of the serf-estate economy as leading to the social tensions that brought about the "Ukrainian-Cossack revolution." "The Seventeenth Century in the Development of Capitalism," *Science and Society* 24, no. 2 (1960): 105.

51 Bercé, *Revolt and Revolution*, 161.

52 Kamen, *The Iron Century*, 345. On brigands, see Bercé, *Revolt and Revolution*, 144–8. On Cossacks as brigands or outlaws, see Linda Gordon, *Cossack Rebellions: Social Turmoil in the Sixteenth-Century Ukraine* (Albany: State University of New York Press, 1983).

53 He cites W. E. D. Allen, *Ukraine: A History* (Cambridge: Cambridge University Press, 1940) as his source (p. 447).

54 Kamen, *The Iron Century*, 379.

55 Marc Raeff, "Pugachev's Rebellion," in Forster and Greene, *Preconditions of Revolution*, 190.

56 Forster and Greene, *Preconditions of Revolution*, 14 and 17.

57 "The Preconditions of Revolution in Early Modern Europe: Did They Really Exist?" *The General Crisis of the Seventeenth Century*, 145–7.

58 Robert Frost, "'Initium Calamitatis Regni?' John Casimir and Monarchical Power in Poland-Lithuania, 1648–1668," *European History Quarterly* 16 (1986): 181–207.

59 Kamen, *The Iron Century*, 327.

60 For literature on the Khmel'nyts'kyi Uprising, see the bibliographic note and update, "Scholarly Literature on the Khmelnytsky Era," Hrushevsky, *History of Ukraine-Rus'*, 8: 690–718.

61 Zagorin, *Rebels and Rulers* 1: 17.

62 Forster and Greene, *Preconditions of Revolution*, 1.

63 See my discussion of the Khmel'nyts'kyi Uprising as a revolution, "War der Chmelnyćkyj-Aufstand eine Revolution? Eine Charakteristik der "grossen ukrainischen Revolte" und der Bildung des kosakischen Het'manstaates," *Jahrbücher für Geschichte Osteuropas* 43 (1995): 1–18.

64 Elliott, "The General Crisis in Retrospect: A Debate without End," 44. In the *Past and Present* discussion in 1957, R. F. Leslie commented: "the expansion of the Polish grain trade reached a peak around 1600. But in Poland proper enserfment did not lead to peasant revolt, perhaps because the ranks of the peasantry were split, the richer peasants, though serfs, having a common interest with the lords in

sweating the poorer ones. Only in Ukraine did the revolt break out." "Seventeenth Century Revolutions," 66. The reasons why Polish peasants did not rebel remain an open question. There was the Kostka-Napierski revolt in 1651 in the Zakopane region that was inspired by the Khmel'nyts'kyi Uprising, but it was soon crushed.

65 For literature on the fatherland in the Cossack Hetmanate, see Serhii Plokhy, *The Origins of the Slavic Nations: Premodern Identities in Russia, Ukraine, and Belarus* (Cambridge: Cambridge University Press, 2006). On the Lublin incorporation lands as an incipient Rus' patria see Frank E. Sysyn, "Regionalism and Political Thought in Seventeenth-Century Ukraine: The Nobility's Grievances at the Diet of 1641," *Harvard Ukrainian Studies* 6, no. 2 (1982): 167–90.

66 See Frank E. Sysyn, "Ukrainian-Polish Relations in the Seventeenth Century: The Role of National Consciousness and National Conflict in the Khmelnytsky Movement," in *Poland and Ukraine: Past and Present*, ed. Peter J. Potichnyj (Toronto: Canadian Institute of Ukrainian Studies, 1980), 58–82.

Catherine of Alexandria's Crown of Golden Liberty

NATALIA PYLYPIUK

Is golden liberty a gold more precious than all?
> John Clarke, *Quaestiones aliquot declamatoriae* (1633)[1]

The loyalty of Subjects toward [their] Ruler secures
For them the most important gift among human beings.
I judge that, among all, the most important thing is liberty
To which, when juxtaposed, rank cedes its place.
All creatures that by nature aspire toward freedom
Can attest to my [claim].
Golden liberty: so they call it.
> Kasiian Sakovych, *Verses on the Sorrowful Obsequy for the Illustrious Knight Petro Konashevych-Sahaidachnyi* (1622)[2]

The historian of education Javier Vergara Ciorda maintains that the cultural construct "Europe" is substantiated by "the concept of man – and more concretely the human person – and the idea of liberty in its highest sense [...] as a regulating ethical norm of life, of its rights and responsibilities, of good and justice, of order and authority. These are concepts which, in their continual reiteration, have made up the personality and this most genuine feature of the European identity."[3]

I propose that the nexus between Europe's humanist identity and early modern Ukrainian culture resides in the educational system, which Orthodox confraternities in Ruthenian (i.e., Belarusian and Ukrainian) lands of the Polish-Lithuanian Commonwealth adopted in the 1580s in order to invigorate the church of Rus'. The new schooling gave preference to Slavonic and Greek. But after Petro Mohyla's reforms of 1632, which overtly imitated the

Jesuit model, the Orthodox educational establishment privileged instruction in Latin for most subjects while retaining Slavonic for liturgical and religious purposes. Respectively, Polish and Ruthenian became the ancillary tools for learning these languages.

As in all neo-Latin schools, at the Kyiv Mohyla Collegium and its affiliates, the poetics-rhetoric sequence was subjugated to language acquisition. Mohylanian professors, like the humanist authors they emulated, emphasized the unique role of human speech as a source of culture and upheld that the aim of the poet was to teach, persuade, and impart pleasure. This modification of the Horatian unity was in full agreement with Cicero's teleological perspective on the civilizing power of speech.

Before studying theology, Mohylanian students learned poetics, Ciceronian rhetoric, and Aristotelian philosophy (logic, dialectics, physics, metaphysics, ethics). Thus, unlike their Rus' predecessors, who had little access to the classical legacy, Ruthenians read the "pagan" thinkers of antiquity. Relying on Latin editions, which had been prepared in Western Europe, they learned to appreciate the place of classical rhetoric "in the physically demonstrative social systems that so powerfully institutionalized its doctrines: city-state democracy and its republican redactions, as well as aristocracy."[4]

In this paper I explore the humanist – hence European – identity of early modern Ukrainian culture by focusing on one play, whose text survived in a manual of Ciceronian rhetoric prepared for the year 1703–4. Titled *Declamatio de S. Catharinae Genio* (The Speech of St Catharine's Guardian Spirit), the play elaborates on the "historical" conflict between Catherine of Alexandria, a legendary fourth-century martyr, and the pagan emperor Maxentius.[5] Reiterating countless West European narratives about her martyrdom that raise important questions about individual freedom, religious repression, as well as gender and power, the play also reveals the aspirations of the Mohylanian athenaeum in the age of Ivan Mazepa and suggests that liberty – to borrow Vergara's words – is "a regulating ethical norm of life."

The political dimension of the play is best appreciated from a comparative perspective. With this objective in mind I have selected Hernando de Ávila's *Comedia de Sancta Catharina,* which was performed on 25 November 1596 in Córdoba's Jesuit college,[6] and the Polish *Dialog na uroczystość Świętej Katarzyny panny i męczenniczki* (Dialog on the Feast of St Catherine, Virgin and Martyr) of 1694. Attributed to Jan Paweł Cichoński, the latter was performed on the popular stage, probably in the environs of Cracow.[7] By juxtaposing works written approximately one century apart and at opposite ends of the European continent, I endeavour to flesh out the elements that bring early modern Ukraine closer to Europe and those that relegate it to the periphery.

Catherine of Alexandria's prominence developed only during the late middle ages.[8] Her classical learning made Catherine especially relevant to the intellectual scene of the sixteenth century, at a time when humanists endeavoured to "adapt religious subjects to the form and language of classical theatre." As James Parente explains:

> martyr drama contributed to the moral education of Christian youths as it trained them in rhetoric and public speaking. The plays varied in literary quality from dramatized hagiographical legends with an awkward Plautine frame to serious attempts to establish a pantheon of Christian heroes, reminiscent of, but superior to, the ancients [...] In the religious wars and political upheaval [...] models for the ideal behavior of a persecuted Christian were desperately needed to encourage the members of churches to defend their respective faiths.[9]

Imitating their respective prose sources, which were compiled in the sixteenth century (martyrologies for the English Protestants and Calvinists, hagiographies for the Catholics), martyr dramas offered narratives about miracles – such as "painless tortures, retinues of angels guiding the saints into heaven" – to inculcate the boys with the central virtues of fortitude and constancy, so that they could endure the persecution they might one day experience.[10]

During the Tridentine revival of the cult of saints, the Jesuits transformed martyrs into the "quintessential warrior[s] of the Counter-Reformation." Together with St Eustachius, St Catherine became a favourite character on the Jesuit stage, where she remained popular well into the eighteenth century. Dramaturges emphasized – besides her learning and chastity – Catherine's conversion (an important tool "in areas with a mixed Catholic-Protestant population"), focusing especially on her superhuman strength to endure torture, a quality that derived not from her Christian faith or humility, but from her temerity: "The Catholic Church was less interested in the martyr's imitation of Christ's passion – an exemplum of a passive hero, to be sure – than in the adaptation of classical heroic virtues for ecclesiastical ends." By minimizing the Christological parallel of the martyr's death, Catholic authors instilled the "secular goals of the Church."[11]

Catherine was the patron saint of Córdoba. When the *Comedia de Sancta Catharina* (henceforth, *Comedia*) was performed on her feast day in 1596, the city was also hosting don Francisco de Reynoso, the bishop elect. The play's author, Father de Ávila, who taught grammar, humanities, and moral theology in Córdoba's Jesuit college, dedicated to the incoming hierarch an introductory panegyric, in which Phoebus, Apollo, and his "sisters" offer their music and songs. Similar references to mythology abound in the play's prologue by Cristóbal Mosquera de Figueroa, a courtier, accomplished poet, and friend of de Ávila with whom he collaborated on other projects.

All tragedies were required to have a prologue. Mosquera's text sets out the theoretical principles underlying the play and establishes correspondences between the characters in classical tragedy with those in the Christian composition at hand, explaining that in the play the immortal God, His Son Christ, and Catherine replace the Jupiter, Phaeton, and Titans of antiquity. Mosquera also posits that the disastrous ending of a classical tragedy becomes – through martyrdom – a triumphal apotheosis, inasmuch as death in the Christian view is not the result of *fatum*. The prologue thus prepares the audience for the *Comedia*'s jubilant finale, which comes after a gruesome fifth act.

The first three acts of de Ávila's martyr play were followed by his own burlesque interlude, "*Orfeo y Euridice,*" which weaves the classical myth with local rituals of magic, witchcraft, and divination. This jocose work teaches that such rituals lead to hell while making numerous allusions to the rich picaresque tradition in Spanish literature. The entire, rather elaborate spectacle lasted six hours.[12]

Each of the *Comedia*'s five acts opens with scenes in Latin. Amounting to approximately one-fifth of the play, they involve, for the most part, male characters. The remaining scenes are all in Castillian, polymetrically expressed. In the first act, Magencio (i.e., Maxentius) asks his councillors whether the sacrifices to the gods have been prepared. As he walks to the temple, Catherine intercepts him, demanding a stop to all sacrifices. She begs the emperor to recognize that he is deceiving his subjects, and proposes that kings should be authors of justice, not injustice.

Mesmerized by Catherine's beauty, Magencio has her brought to the palace. As she waits for him, angelic messengers alert her to an imminent disputation with learned men. They place a ring on her finger and a tasseled doctor's cap on her head, thereby visually confirming Catherine as a symbol of both learning and divinely inspired wisdom. Alluding to classical depictions of Pallas Athena, the Greek goddess of wisdom, they also give her the sword and shield of Faith's warriors. When the emperor arrives, Catherine responds to his questions: Her father ruled without exercising force or tyranny, establishing the rules by which Alexandria is still governed. She studies logic, philosophy, rhetoric, and geometry. A Christian, she is married to God whose golden wedding band she wears. Magencio incarcerates her and summons the philosophers of his realm to the *pretorium* for a disputation.

In the second act, the lengthiest of the play, the philosophers are brought to court and instructed on how to proceed. The conversation among the men is entirely in Latin. Faustina, the empress, asks her husband to treat Catherine well. She also tells him about a disturbing dream, which neither he nor his councillors can interpret. Then Catherine is brought in, supported by angels. She discusses with the philosophers the mysteries of the Trinity within a unitary God, as well as the Incarnation. The debate is very academic, and Catherine cites Aristotle, Socrates, and Plato, successfully arguing against polytheism. Most remarkably, she discusses the fine points of theology in the vernacular, not Latin. Acknowledging defeat, the philosophers request to be baptized. This act elicits the wrath of Magencio, who orders their death by burning, as well as the lashing and incarceration of Catherine.

In the third act, Faustina confides to her lady-in-waiting, Delia, her desire to become a Christian. Her lengthy soliloquy is the moving confession of a wife neglected and betrayed by her husband. Both women elegantly praise Catherine's beauty and intelligence. Magencio's general, Porfirio, visits the ladies and the three decide to visit the prisoner. When Catherine discovers that he has not read Christian books, she responds that in the clamor of war, the delicate whisper of God might be inaudible.

In the fourth act, Magencio learns of Faustina's conversion and complains that Bellona, the goddess of war, never humiliated him as did that "skinny little woman" (i.e., Catherine). He begs his wife to recant, but she responds that all humans must observe a law higher than the king's. As Faustina explains, Magencio has the right to govern the country and her body, but he may not govern her faith or her soul. If his inherent cruelty silences her tongue, her soul will appeal to divine mercy. Estronio, a pagan priest, records like an inquisitor the entire conversation. Porfirio begs Magencio to observe the law of faith and love when dealing with the empress, but the emperor repudiates Faustina, removing her royal insignias and condemning her to death. The tragic essence of de Ávila's *Comedia* resides in this conflict between husband and wife. When Porfirio and his soldiers also profess Christianity, Magencio orders their beheading.

In the last act, the emperor is enraged to hear that one of his own councillors and a pagan priest admire the Christians for valuing their convictions more than their lives. Realizing that Catherine is behind the unrest in Alexandria, he orders her tortured at the wheel, which the angels destroy with bolts of lightning. Once again, she refuses to recant, explaining that Christ, her mystical spouse – and not adulterous Mars – is her sovereign lord. Catherine is finally beheaded; milk instead of blood issues forth from her severed head. A choir of angels sings celebratory verses, mentioning her imminent union with the celestial spouse. Holding lit candles, the angels lead a procession, consisting of all those who were martyred before Catherine. Carrying their respective insignias, they advance to the mount where she is buried. This jubilant scene is performed to the accompaniment of organ music and a choir of virgins.

Four moments in the *Comedia* deserve special attention: (1) Catherine's declaration that kings ought to be authors of just laws; (2) her use of Castillian when discussing questions of theology; (3) the elegant discourse of all three female characters, which contrasts with the intemperate tone of Magencio and the priest Estronio; and (4) Faustina's observation that the emperor may not govern her faith or soul, and that even kings must obey a higher law. These are quite remarkable if we note that by the late 1500s Spain had reached the peak of its power and, thanks to the enforcement of Philip II, Catholic ortho-doxy had intensified the Inquisition. Among the latter's activities, there were efforts to make sacred texts "inaccessible to the laity in general but to women in particular, who were deemed to be mentally incapable of understanding [them] and inherently susceptible to diabolical influence."[13] In this period, Crypto-Jews, many of whom lived in Córdoba, continued to be persecuted because they refused to venerate statues and paintings of the Holy Family and the saints. In light of this, father de Ávila's play raises yet unstudied questions about the manner in which its conception and reception were affected by the repressive climate.

The Jesuits came to the Polish-Lithuanian Commonwealth in 1564; they soon established a wide network of schools and recruited native sons to the society. Among the latter, Piotr Skarga (1536–1612) greatly contributed to the revival of the cult of saints with the publication in 1579 of his *Lives of the Saints*. Written in Polish during his tenure as rector of the Vilnius Academy, this monumental work was republished eight times during his lifetime. The *Lives* included a substantial entry about Catherine,[14] a text that contributed to her popularity on the Polish school stage. Extant records show that between 1584 and 1688 at least seven plays were composed for her feast day in various Jesuit institutions.[15] And just as in early modern Spain, Germany, and the Neth-erlands, plays about St Catherine entered the repertoire of the Polish popular stage.

The *Dialog na uroczystość Świętej Katarzyny panny i męczenniczki* (hence-forth, *Dialog*) of 1694 also bears a title in Latin: *Dialogus pro festo Sanctae Catharinae Virginis et Martyris*. Its brief prologue does not address questions of literary theory but merely recalls the suffering of early Christians under pagan tyranny, introduces the main characters, and concludes requesting the audience's devoted attention.

Organized into six brief acts, the *Dialog* was performed with five interludes (*Aulicus* [Courtier], *Błazno* [Fool], *Dziad* [Beggar], *Żyd* [Jew], and *Pedagoga* [Teacher]).[16] As in the Spanish *Comedia*, this play's first act deals with the decree ordering sacrifices, but here it is announced by *Praeco* (town crier), a jocular character who ridicules Maksencyjusz (Maxentius) while asking the town's barmaids to give him vodka (*horileczka*) so that he can toast the emperor's soul, which already belongs to Satan. His humour sharply contrasts with the panegyrical tone of the court official, Marszalek, who praises the emperor.

In the second act, the emperor learns of the resistance mustered by the Christians. He orders them lashed, upon which Katarzyna (Catherine) entreats him to reconsider his decision. In the ensuing debate with the philosophers, the play's only scene conducted partly in prose, the main topics – as expected – include the Trinity and the Incarnation. However, Katarzyna delivers her most important arguments in Latin. The emperor sends the vanquished philosophers to the stake while his servant Charon (the play's sole classical reference) promises diligent execution of his command. Groza (Grimness, an allusion to a fairytale personage) and Tatar (who speaks with a Ukrainian accent) ridicule the learned men. Charon, Groza, and Tatar behave like boors, and when they reappear to arrest the emperor's next victims, they exhibit pleasure at the misfortune of the fallen while claiming that they are merely executing orders. They are also vindictive towards those who earlier held positions of authority. At the end of the second act, Maksencyjusz orders Katarzyna's incarceration, placing his Palatine – "Hetman Porfirius" – in charge of her.

In the third act, which is quite brief, Porfirius and the empress, Cesarzowa, visit the prisoner, who assures them that their conversion will bring them life eternal. The fourth act contrasts the barbarity of the emperor with the gentleness of his wife. Upon learning of her admiration for the Christians, Maksencyjusz grows irate. Calling her a monkey, he disowns Cesarzowa and orders that her breasts be cut off before decapitation. Katarzyna blesses the empress, counseling that her soul should not fear pain in the name of Christ. At this point, Porfirius and his Decurio confess that they also are Christians, for which they are condemned to death. In this act, as in the second, minor characters supporting the actions of the emperor (Groza, Czechaczek [the Executioner], Charon) mock the victims and behave like petty lackeys.

In the fifth act, Katarzyna again rejects the advances of the emperor. Condemned to death, she prays to her heavenly spouse. Groza, growing impatient, commands her to extend her neck, but the beheading is not shown. In the sixth act, a choir of angels proclaims that Katarzyna has reached the eternal kingdom. The archangels Michael, Raphael, Gabriel, and Uriel descend to earth and transport her body to Mt Sinai. They reunite her body with the head and give Katarzyna proper burial. Michael concludes the act, saying farewell to the martyr.

The epilogue provides a summary, emphasizing that Katarzyna suffered her torments patiently, preferring to elicit the wrath of a tyrant than to offend God.

It counsels the audience to avoid the vanities of this world and then, turning to the girls, it exhorts them to preserve their virtue and to love purity. Worth noting here is the fact that in Europe – besides being the patron saint of schools and universities, especially the faculties of theology and philosophy – Catherine of Alexandria was also the patron saint of girls of marrying age.[17] The epilogue concludes with an appeal for donations, so that the troupe could present greater and better plays for the edification of the soul.

As in the *Comedia,* the *Dialog* inculcates the need to endure suffering and the importance of preserving chastity. Devoid of classical references, the latter cultivates a popular audience and consciously relies on the ludic traditions of marketplace theatres to portray a socially stratified society, where lack of education and lower social status go hand in hand. The author uses a language close to the literary standard of the period, and ably introduces lexical and stylistic variations to depict the emotional state of characters. He conjoins moral lessons with comical effects that rely on ethnic stereotypes. His work is concise; the display of erudition is not his objective. Therefore, the use of Latin in key moments of the theological debate begs the question whether censorship measures precluded the use of Polish.

Skarga's *Lives of Saints,* together with his powerful invectives against the Orthodox, had a profound influence on the Ruthenians. The first prominent intellectual response by an Orthodox author was Syl'vestr Kosov's *Patericon,* published in 1635 at the Kyivan Caves Monastery. A nobleman from Vitebsk, Kosov (ca.1600–57) obtained his education in Jesuit schools (Vilnius and Lublin) and then in the famed Zamojski Academy. Written in Polish, his *Patericon* draws attention to native Orthodox holy men in a language accessible to all subjects of the Commonwealth.

Efforts initiated by Metropolitan Mohyla to produce an Orthodox version of the lives of saints did not come to fruition during his lifetime or that of his successor, Kosov. They were resumed under Metropolitan Varlaam Iasyns'kyi, who invited Dymytrii Tuptalo to Kyiv in 1684 and – with the help of Hetman Mazepa – secured the conditions necessary for the conduct of such a project. Born into a Cossack family in Kyiv region, Tuptalo (1651–1709) was educated at the Kyiv Mohyla Collegium where he obtained a solid humanistic education. He served as a preacher in various towns and, with the exception of a brief sojourn in Vilnius and Slutsk, lived most of his life until 1701 in Hetman Ukraine. Unlike Skarga's *Lives,* which were written in Polish rather than Latin, Tuptalo's monumental *Book of the Lives of Saints* (*Knyha zhytii s[via]tykh*) was written in Slavonic instead of the Ukrainian vernacular.

Tuptalo's *Lives* appeared in four parts, published by the Kyivan Caves Monastery in 1689, 1696, 1700, and 1705. Of these the earliest one, which contained an extensive *vita* of Catherine, caused consternation in Russia because it was released without the consent of Moscow. Mazepa, who travelled to Moscow in 1689, included Tuptalo in his retinue and exerted much diplomatic effort to obtain support for the publication of the subsequent volumes. As the American scholar Gary Marker indicates, the next three parts appeared under extremely close scrutiny of the Russian hierarchy.[18]

As Tuptalo admits in a marginal note, his narrative about Catherine relied on the *vita* by Simeon Metaphrastes and the Moscow *Anthologion* of 1660.[19] The latter was a translation prepared for the Russian court by Arsenios the Greek from his native tongue into Slavonic.[20] The basis of his work had been a publication by Agapios Landos of Crete (Venice, 1641), which in turn drew from a Latin version of the Catherinian legend.[21]

Among extant Mohylanian plays, the *Declamatio de S. Catharinae Genio* (henceforth, *Declamatio*) is one of three written entirely in Polish.[22] Its authors were a group of students, well acquainted with both the work of Tuptalo and a Latin redaction of Catherine's life. They also had access to Skarga's *Lives* or their Ruthenian translation, which circulated in manuscript form.[23] However, the *Declamatio*'s exuberant classical allegories and baroque conceits distance it from both Skarga's and Tuptalo's prose, and bring it closer to the poetics of the Spanish *Comedia* and the Jesuit stage in general. Worth noting in this context is the fact that in Hetman Ukraine, one of the influential models for the acceptance of Christianized classical symbols and myths was the monumental work on poetics by Maciej Sarbiewski, a renowned neo-Latin poet, professor at Jesuit institutions (Polotsk, 1618–20; Vilnius, 1627–35), and organizer of the humanist circle at the Vilnius Academy.

The *Declamatio* is the only known martyr drama composed by Mohylanians. It has a markedly secular flavor, which is missing from school plays written in Slavonic for the Easter and Christmas cycles. The fact that its authors gave stage directions, all in Latin, and identified the two female characters as guardian spirits (*Genius Catharinae* and *Genius Augustae*) – thus facilitating their performance by male actors – suggests that the drama was indeed staged. The performance could have taken place on 24 November (a date mentioned in the play) in the presence of fellow students, preceptors, and school patrons. And, given its opening scene, in which Catharina enumerates the qualities she expects in an ideal spouse, the audience of the *Declamatio* might have included daughters of the Cossack nobility and prominent Kyivan burghers, as well as their parents.

The manual that preserved the *Declamatio* is titled *Arbor Tulliana Iasinsciano de caelo*. Prepared by professor Ilarion Iaroshevyts'kyi, it draws on humanist authors of the Renaissance and is devoted mostly to Ciceronian rhetoric. However, it also contains: (1) sample speeches that serve as templates for further exercises; (2) introductions to philosophy, logic, physics, and the standard Jesuit rhetoric by Cypriano Soares (1560); and (3) actual speeches addressed on separate occasions to Hetman Ivan Mazepa.[24] One of the two extant copies of the manual also contains two sections on the "*conceptus*" of St Catherine and one featuring her biography.[25] This suggests that the students composed the *Declamatio* under Iaroshevyts'kyi's tutelage. The date of his manual precludes the possibility that the play was inspired by the imperial cult of St Catherine, which Peter I launched publicly four years later, in 1707.[26] On the contrary – as I shall argue shortly – the *Declamatio* draws a parallel between the tyrannical Maxentius and the Russian tsar while portraying the Alexandrian martyr as an exponent of the political values of the Ukrainian szlachta.

Iaroshevyts'kyi, who died at a comparatively young age in 1704, was a graduate of the Mohylanian collegium. In 1703 he prepared yet another manual, a bipartite construct, devoted to Ciceronian rhetoric and to dialectics, whose title also mentions Metropolitan Iasyns'kyi: *Oriens illustrissimus Iasincianae Cynthiae Tulliano caelo.*[27] Recently, scholars have attributed to Iaroshevyts'kyi yet another manual, *Cedrus Apollini pharetrati Rossiaco Orpheo*, which comprises the poetics and rhetoric sequence of 1702–3.[28] This manual contains a remarkable neo-Latin poem, modelled in part on Virgil's *Aeneid*. Titled *Carmina Heroica*, it celebrates Mazepa's campaigns of 1695–8 and his capture of Turkish fortresses along the Dnipro, including Kizikerman. The Italian scholar Giovanna Siedina convincingly argues that this panegyric discourse endeavours to inscribe native history into European *Latinitas* and to acknowledge Mazepa's contribution to the *antemurale Christianitatis*.[29]

The date of the earlier manual suggests that Iaroshevyts'kyi also authored the morality play for Holy Week, titled "Pre-eternal Wisdom ... Performed in 1703 by the Noble Youth of Rus' at the Kyiv Mohyla Collegium."[30] The theme of this Slavonic work is congruent with the project, initiated in the 1690s, which through visual and textual means endeavoured to portray Mazepa and Iasyns'kyi as protectors and benefactors of wisdom's abode, that is, the collegium and St Sophia, the cathedral church of Kyivan Rus'.[31] It thus appears that the choice of topic for the *Declamatio* was deliberate. As a symbol of wisdom and learning, Catherine's character complemented this project. Moreover, it was logical for students of rhetoric – the art of persuasion – to select a "historical" personage known for her skills in this discipline.

The authors of the *Declamatio* did not prepare a prologue or an epilogue, which suggests that their immediate concern was not the explication of the genre at hand or direct engagement with the audience. Yet, contrary to what the play's title suggests, their composition is much more than a school recitation, delivered as an exercise in elocution. Consisting of ten brief acts, called *inductiones*, it can be easily considered a drama.[32]

Overtly displaying erudition, in language similar to the Polish panegyrics by Pylyp Orlyk, Ivan Ornovs'kyi, and especially Stefan Iavors'kyi, the *Declamatio* is written for the most part in hendecasyllables. It also includes speeches composed in Sapphic stanzas, some of which are quite moving, have a pleasant rhythm, and offer images reminiscent of Jan Kochanowski's poetry. Consider, for example, the opening monologue, in which *Amor Terrestris* (Earthly Love) seeks to awaken Catherina from her deep sleep:

1. Co za przyczyna, powiedz kto na niebie,
   Naco ciężky sen, ku iakiey potrzebie,

   Że zdewinkował delikatne ciało,
      By wstac nie miało?
   [...]
25. Czy nie Lucyna tak cię wkołysala, –
    Zwolawszy Muzy zagrac roskazala

    Ku odpocznieniu wdzięcznemi głosy,
    Czesząc twe włosy?
29. Kto widział kiedy takowe pieszczoty
    Długo przesypiac, a nie miec roboty?

    Co to za roskosz, że w połdnia samego
    Wżywasz snu tego?
33. Podobno Neptun z swemi Syrenami
    Wpoył słodkiemi ciebie kanarami,

    Albo słuch pieniem swym napełnił sporo,
       Przesliczna coro!
37. Lecz bys z Meduzą urody nie zbyła,

    Same bogynie w czymes uprzedzila
    A y mądrosci sen długy zaszkodzi,
    Czyste rwiąc łodzi? (R5: 246)[33]

Tell [me], whosoever is in heaven, for what reason,
for what purpose is this heavy sleep; why was it necessary
to fetter [this] fragile body,
      to prevent it from waking?
[...]
Was it not Lucyna who rocked you to sleep,
calling upon the Muses and ordering them to play,
to relax you with graceful voices,
      while combing your hair?
Who ever saw such tender indulgence
to oversleep for so long, while having nothing to do;
What a luxury that at midday
      you still enjoy your dreaming?
Probably Neptune with his Sirens
satiated you with the sweet melodies of canaries,
filling up your ears with songs,
      O beautiful girl!
But would that you not lose your beauty as did Medusa,
you who have excelled the goddesses;
a long sleep will harm your wisdom,
      and your chastity might be interrupted by life.

By situating the first *inductio* in an idyllic setting and commencing with Earthly Love's address, the authors creatively interpreted Tuptalo's narrative, which starts with an account of Catharina's background and her family's insistence that she marry. At Earthly Love's recommendation that she surrender her youth to a prominent suitor, Catherina finds it "odd" that "love out of love [should] impose burdens" (*Dziwno ... Miłosc z miłosci ciężary nakłada* [R5: 247, verses 95–6]). She is more fascinated by her vision of a Lady, "clothed with the sun" and "crowned with twelve stars," who speaks at length about "freedom" *(o swobodzie)* and wishes to lead the girl out of the "labyrinth of idolatry" into her own garden (R5: 248, verses 117–22).

The Lady in Catharina's vision is a reference to the Woman of the Apocalypse of Revelations 12:1–2, an image that Mohylanians employed to represent the Theotokos as bearer of wisdom.[34] Consider, for example, her portrayal in a painting that commemorated a disputation on peripatetic logic, which was held in honour of Iasyns'kyi, probably during his installation in 1691 as Metropolitan of Kyiv, Halych, and all Rus'.[35] Another visual text of the period depicts the Woman of the Apocalypse being lifted into the heavens on "the wings" of Mazepa's coat of arms.[36] The garden to which the Lady invites Catherine is an allusion to Mohylanian manuals of poetics, rhetoric, and dialectics, which were dedicated to the Theotokos and whose titles often comprised horticultural metaphors.

Still drawing on Tuptalo's narrative, the first *inductio* also shows Catharina turning to a hermit (*Eremita*) to explain her disturbing dream. She addresses him as a servant of Jove and asks whether it was Apollo, Titan, or Mars who sought to frighten her at midnight by waking her with refulgent light:

167 Padam ci do nog, sługo Jowiszowy,	I bow to you, O servant of Jove;
Proszę pokornie, powiedz mi sen owy	I beg you humbly to tell me about the dream
Ktory widziałam iakoby naiawy,	that I saw as if it were real;
Powiedz mi prawie!	tell me!
171 Czy to Apollo na mnie zagniewany,	Is Apollo angry at me,
Czyli sam Tytan uflorysowany	or embellished Titan himself
Twarz płomienistą mnie prezentował,	showing me his blazing face,
Przez sen turbował?	[and] disturbing me in my sleep?
175 W samey połnocy wszystką mię oswiecił,	At very midnight lighting up everything,
Albo Mars srogy ognie swoie wzniecił,	or was it fierce Mars who started his fires
By mię prestraszył w połnocney godzinie	to frighten me at midnight
Przy ciemney minie.	with his dark face.
(R5: 249–50)	

Besides thus alluding to the rituals of divination associated with the feast of St Catherine, the first act also introduces Catharina on her own, as a young girl, torn apart between sensuality and mystical vision.

The hermit, who speaks like a Kyivan monk well versed in classical mythology and the poetic tastes of the Ukrainian szlachta,[37] blames Juno for turning the days into nights, and warns that her son, Vulcan, forges chains for those who surrender into his and Juno's "service" (*poddanstwo*):

203 Moia powinnosc rospowiedzic tobie,	My duty is to tell you,
Zwłaszcza w takowey będącey żalobie,	especially since you are in such a woeful state,
Co by to bylo, czymes przestraszona:	what it could have been, what exactly frightened you:
Znac to Junona,	Know that it is Juno
207 Ktora dni w nocy często wariiuie,	who turns days into nights, [and]
Wulkan zayste tam kaydany kuie	Vulcan who forges chains
Na tych, ktorzy się im w poddanstwo daią,	for those who become their subjects
Y snu uznaią. (R5: 250–1)	and experience dreams.

Worth recalling here is that, in an ancient Greek tragedy, it was Vulcan who chained Prometheus – one of the Titans – in punishment for stealing fire from the gods and giving it to the mortals. Evidently, the *Declamatio* draws on the same tradition that led Mosquera in his prologue to draw a parallel between the Christian heroine and the Titans.

Upon her conversion, the hermit gives Catharina an image of the Theotokos, promising that her beloved will soon appear. Then, *Cantus Angelicus* (Angelic Song) warns that Bellona and Mars are already opening the gates of war because they thirst for the blood of Catharina, who is now in the "service of God" (*Bogu na służbę* [R5: 252, verses 257–74]). Here *Cantus Angelicus* uses the neutral noun *służba* when referring to "service." Let us recall that earlier the hermit used the politically charged lexeme *poddanstwo* when he warned Catharina that those who "surrender into [Vulcan's and Juno's] *service*" will be enchained.

Foreshadowing the disputation, *Cantus Angelicus* indicates that Pallas Athena has endowed Catharina with wisdom, whereas Apollo, the Muses, and Cicero have gifted her with eloquence. Neither Vulcan nor Charon will break her constancy. Catharina will also excel in her arguments, attaining victory through wisdom; then her chaste virtue will open the gates to heaven (R5: 253, verses 268–88). The first *inductio* concludes – as it began – on the theme of love. Now, however, it is *Amor Caelestis* (Celestial Love) who sends her a ring to confirm her mystical nuptials. Given that Catharina's vision involved a representation associated with the Theotokos as bearer of wisdom, I posit that her mystical spouse is a hypostasis of divine wisdom.

Catharina's first encounter with the emperor, who is called Caesar throughout the play, takes place in the second *inductio*. She proclaims that his heroic glory in war is now masked by the rising stench and smoke of animal sacrifices. The emperor's priests (*Sacerdotes*) treat him as a valiant hero, who in the army of Bellona vanquishes enemies throughout all regions (R5: 256, verses 370–3). Charity, Faith, and Hope assist Catharina in the discussion with Caesar and his senators. The impetuous girl hurls insults at her interlocutors, calling them brainless (R5: 259, verse 343). In an overtly sexist manner one of the senators comments that she was endowed with beauty so as not to fall into the darkness of anguish. Caesar, visibly disturbed by the attack on his majesty, calls Catharina a poisonous and slanderous beast and orders her incarceration.

After she is led away in chains, Caesar dictates an appeal, to which he "adds" his signature and state seal on 20 November. In this official document, titled *Diploma,* the emperor summons all the young people educated by Wise Pallas and all doctors of philosophy to come on 24 November to the city of Alexandria, which is famous for its scholarship. They are to participate in a disputation with a wise and beautiful lady who has insulted the gods. The document acknowledges that it is especially difficult to suffer such insults because they come from a woman. Interestingly, in the *Diploma* Caesar styles himself as the "Illustrious and Invincible Maxentius, Hereditary Landlord of Great and Little Egypt and the Most Powerful Caesar of All Alexandria, Most benevolent Son of the God Hermes" (*Nayiasnieyszy y niezwyciężony Maxentiusz, Wielkego y Malego Aegyptu Dziedzic y cały Alexandryey Cesarz naypotężnieyszy, syn nayżyczliwszy Ermigera boga* [R5: 261]). This surprising title, which has no parallel in any of the Catherine plays I have read, appears to be a parody of the Russian tsar's official title, as it appears on the title page of Tuptalo's *Book of the Lives of Saints*: "Most Illustrious, Most Sovereign and Most Pious, our Great Lords Tsars and Great Princes Ivan Alekseevich, Peter Alekseevich: of All Great and Little and White Rossia Autocrats, and of many States and Lands, Eastern and Western and Northern Heirs, Hereditary Landlords and Legatees, and Lords and Possessors."[38] I posit that in the *Declamatio,* Caesar is an allegory of Peter I. And, inasmuch as the noun "diploma" denotes a document issued by an educational institution, and philosophical disputations were the norm at the Mohylanian collegium, it is plausible that the play's authors introduced this scene in ludic self-reference.

The famous disputation takes place in the third *inductio* and is much shorter than the one in the Spanish *Comedia.* Catharina's critique of the pagan gods marshals a humanist understanding of the role of speech: the gods are mute statues, incapable of discourse. To support her argument, she cites Homer, thereby adhering to Tuptalo's narrative. She also mentions the Sybil's prediction of the birth of Christ, a point that appears in the *vitae* by Skarga and Tuptalo. Once Catharina marshals evidence drawn from the "opponents' side," the pagan philosophers concede her victory. She then predicts that they will be baptized by fire and their own blood. Unlike her Spanish and Polish counterparts, the Mohylanian Catharina does not broach the nature of the Trinity. She addresses the concept of the Incarnation only indirectly when mentioning that the Christian God is a speaking God.

In the fourth *inductio,* one of the senators counsels the despondent emperor, who fears the dissolution of the state through Catharina's betrayal of the gods, to offer her the crown and the throne. As expected, she rejects these. In the fifth *inductio* the emperor's wife, Augusta, ponders who will be a true friend to her in old age and expresses the desire to see Catharina. At this point Porfirius Palatinus, the emperor's official, makes an appearance, and the empress requests his help; both visit the prisoner. Catharina – addressing him as "illustrious hetman of the armies" (*hetmanie woysk sławny* [R5: 279, verse 910]) – reassures Porfirius that in heaven his name will be inscribed in the book of eternal life, and not on perishable pyramids or marble columns (R5: 279, verses 911–13). This *inductio* concludes with the conversion of Porfirius and his soldiers. The hetman's confession of faith adheres to Orthodox dogma about the procession of the Holy Spirit (R5: 279, verses 936–40).

Let us recall that in the Polish *Dialog,* Porfirius was also called a hetman. But Catharina's epithet, "illustrious," evokes references to hetmans of the Zaporozhian army. Her mention of columns and pyramids is even more tantalizing because it brings to mind the constructs erected in Moscow for the 30 September 1696 celebration of the capturing of Azov, which had taken place in July of that year, and in which Mazepa – together with his Cossack army – had played a significant role. According to an official account published in 1697, besides triumphal gates, there were columns with carved reliefs of Hercules, carrying a rod and a green branch, and of Mars, holding a sabre and shield. At the top of the columns, there were signs, which respectively read: "By the prowess of Hercules" and "By the prowess of Mars." Then, on each side of the triumphal gates, there was a pyramid – the one praising "valorous seamen," the other lauding "the most valorous soldiers." Julius Caesar's aphorism "He came, he saw, he conquered" appeared on three different cartouches. Before the entrance to one of the gates there hung a trellis, woven in gold and inscribed with the words, "The Victory of Tsar Constantine over the impious Tsar Maxentius the Roman."[39] Thus, official ceremonies cast victorious Peter I both as Caesar and as the first Christian Emperor, and allegorized the defeated Turks in the figure of Constantine's pagan predecessor.

The historian Gregory Freeze states that one week after the celebrations, the "Dutch deserter Jakob Jansen, whose betrayal had dearly cost the first Azov campaign, was broken on the wheel and then beheaded before a huge crowd."[40] The published account of 1697 refers to Jansen as "Iakushka," without identifying his last name, and mentions that during the solemn procession he had been paraded – costumed as a Turk – with the instruments of his torture.[41] Jansen's gruesome execution was very similar to the fate that the legendary Catherine met at the hands of Maxentius.

The authors of the *Declamatio* may have been responding to the published account of the celebrations in Moscow, and subtly proposing that – contrary to official propaganda – Peter I was akin to the tyrannical Maxentius. In literary history this is not the first instance when the martyr's story is used to allude to recent political turmoil and religious repression. Consider, for example, the *Life of Saint Katherine of Alexandria* by the Augustinian friar John Capgrave (1393–1484), in which the church's persecution of John Wyclif's followers is implicitly criticized.[42]

In the sixth *inductio* Celestial Love and a group of angels announce to Catharina that soon she will be inducted among the heroes and crowned with the laurel of immortality. In the seventh the emperor complains that he cannot handle all the betrayals around him. His senators recommend the cruelest punishments for Catharina. When she is brought to him, Caesar marvels at her appearance because it does not reveal the marks of punishment. Reacting to his accusation, the guards protest that they did not feed her, and Catharina begs the emperor not to unleash his ire at the innocent men. She has been receiving nourishment from a dove (i.e., the Holy Spirit) sent by her heavenly beloved, who has also prepared for her a "crown of golden liberty!" (*złotey wolnosci mnie zgotował wieniec!* [R5: 284, verse 1068]). Caesar offers the imperial crown in exchange for her submission to the gods. Hearing her rejection, his advisor recommends the torture wheel, but the angels destroy it.

The trope "golden liberty" in Catharina's speech is drawn from the vocabulary of the szlachta's political system in the Polish-Lithuanian Commonwealth. This system recognized, among other things, a mutually binding contract between the monarch and his noble subjects, equal legal rights for all nobles, religious freedom, and the right to form confederations in the pursuit of common political goals. Throughout the seventeenth century, szlachta ideology informed the aspirations of the Cossacks, who – in exchange for military service – expected rights and privileges from the Polish monarchs. During Mazepa's hetmancy this program gained special currency.[43]

The szlachta's aristocratic republïcanism found reinforcement in European neo-Latin manuals of rhetoric whenever drills and theme writing exercises included a question drawn from classical antiquity: *aurea libertas auro pretiosior omni?*[44] Interestingly, an oratorical exercise on the topic *libertas auro pretiosior* (liberty is a gold more precious) appears in a Mohylanian manual, titled *Lyra variis praeceptorum chordis*, which was prepared in 1696, seven years before Iaroshevyts'kyi's students composed the *Declamatio*.[45] In Ukrainian literature, the earliest and most famous application of such an exercise is found in Kasiian Sakovych's *Verses on the Sorrowful Obsequy for the Illustrious Knight Petro Konashevych-Sahaidachnyi, Hetman of His Royal Grace's Zaporozhian Host*. Composed in Ruthenian, the verses were publicly performed by Sakovych's students at the school of Kyiv's Confraternity of the Theophany on 28 April (8 May) 1622, during a solemn ceremony commemorating the recently deceased hetman, who had been mortally wounded in the service of Sigismund III at the Battle of Khotyn. The initial oration in Sakovych's *Verses* marshals the trope of "golden liberty" to discuss a cardinal social transaction, namely the exchange of service for corporate or individual rights and privileges. Declaring that the desire for freedom is an innate faculty, he posits that liberty is the only true reward for the loyalty (*virnost'*) of subjects (*poddanykh*). In Sakovych's Ruthenian, the etymology of "subjects" is closely related to the concept of "service" (*poddanstwo*), which the hermit mentions in the *Declamatio*'s first *inductio*. In his oration, Sakovych warns that the discontent among the king's Orthodox subjects will lead to civil war.[46]

In the eighth *inductio*, the emperor's wife, Augusta, calls him unworthy of Caesar's title, because he is a tyrant. The enraged Maxentius orders that her breasts be cut off, as well as other horrific tortures. Augusta pronounces a moving prayer, and Caesar has her removed beyond the city's walls. In the next *inductio* she is decapitated. After giving her proper burial, Porfirius and his soldiers reiterate their faith. Upon witnessing this, the emperor commands them to prepare for their own beheading. In the last *inductio,* Maxentius, surrounded by his senators, again fails to persuade Catharina. Rejecting him, she turns to the Creator in prayer, asking her mystical spouse to lend her his hand. Her last words are addressed to the emperor's soldier (*ad militem*), requesting that the execution be carried out promptly, so that she can soon admire the celestial palaces. Unlike its Spanish and Polish predecessors, the Mohylanian play does not end in jubilation.

The *Declamatio* demonstrates the lasting impact that the *studia humanitatis* had on early modern Ukrainian culture. The scholarly precondition for the play's existence was Tuptalo's creation of a native redaction of *vitae,* sanctioned by the Orthodox Church. However, the play's deployment of

Christianized classical symbols, intellectualization of the Christian legacy, references to God as a speaking entity, and adaptation of the "golden liberty" trope bear the imprint of humanistic rhetoric, as well as the political aspirations of the Ukrainian nobility. The play closely conforms to the tradition of martyr dramas established by the Tridentine revival: Catharina exhibits temerity, fortitude, and constancy. She comprehends that there will be no earthly recompense for her intellectual victory or chastity. And like a warrior for the faith, she accepts martyrdom, defiantly rejecting the advances of a male predator and tyrannical ruler.

The *Declamatio* was composed in the same year that Mazepa's close allies, Mykhailo Myklashevs'kyi and Opanas Pokors'kyi – respectively the colonel and secretary of the Starodub regiment – were conducting secret negotiations in the hope of striking a triune Confederation of Poland, Lithuania, and Ukraine. At the negotiations, Myklashevs'kyi stated that Ukraine seeks to enjoy the same freedoms (*vol'nosty*) as those flourishing in the Polish Crown and the Lithuanian Duchy, and that "it would be unseemly for Ukraine to continue under the Muscovite yoke" (*dalii Ukraïni pod iarmom moskovskym ne podobno.*)[47]

This concurrence leads me to speculate whether the *Declamatio* does not represent something more than a veiled rejection of Petrine propaganda and a critique of the displays of power that took place in Moscow after the capturing of Azov. In depicting Catharina's temerity and preference for the "crown of golden liberty" over Caesar's imperial crown, it appears that Iaroshevyts'kyi's students are promoting the secular goals of the Kyivan church and the political aspirations of Mazepa's entourage. Also, their portrayal of Catharina's ethical choices and her subsequent martyrdom appears to be an attempt to inculcate the audience with the central virtues of fortitude and constancy in expectation of an imminent war. If my suppositions are correct, the authors of the *Declamatio* had fully grasped the purpose of martyr dramas in humanist Europe.

The *Declamatio* also brings to the fore those elements of early-modern Ukrainian culture that relegate it to the periphery of Europe. In addition to the delayed adoption of humanistic schooling, the play illustrates the unresolved language question. By mid-seventeenth century, West European and Polish neo-Latin schools introduced the teaching of native vernacular languages and literatures. The linguistic reorientation of the humanistic curriculum had been a gradual process that responded to the challenges posed by court and merchant schools, both of which were oriented to the present and the vernacular rather than Latin and the "classical past." Court schools, moreover, upheld a theory of style that emphasized "bringing pleasure" over teaching and persuading.[48]

Spanish monarchs munificently supported the vernacular theatre. And, in the attempt to transform a socially heterogeneous public into a homogeneous entity that would identify with the values of the nobility, they used spectacle – in its many forms – as a tool for political and social propaganda. Catering to the expectations of the masses, the Spanish national theatre offered much action, a variety of verse forms, and marvellous special effects while upholding such concepts as the defence of the monarchy, the safeguard of honour as the raison d'être of the individual and social life, and the constant reaffirmation of love as universal justification.[49]

The collaboration between the humanist de Ávila and the courtier Mosquera is a good example of the effect that competing theories of style had on Spanish culture. On the day of Córdoba's patron saint, the college was compelled to entertain the town audience in Castillian. Latin still performs a role in de Ávila's *Comedia*, but it constitutes no more than 20 per cent of his play. Its use may have been prompted by the visit of the new diocesan Ordinary, as well as the desire to demonstrate the students' proficiency in the universal language of the church and of scholarship. In true humanist fashion, the Jesuit professor Christianizes classical symbols. And, while carefully avoiding the political concepts of the national theatre, he also freely employs its strategies for spectacular entertainment. Most importantly, de Ávila is cognizant of Spanish literary traditions.

Like the kings of Spain, Polish monarchs supported vernacular plays in their court theatre, whose actors also performed Italian opera and commedia dell'arte, and welcomed Italian, French, and German companies. By the early seventeenth century, this led to the development of thriving itinerant troupes, which worked independently from the court and performed in Polish on a variety of topics, not only religious. In early modern Ukraine there was no institution analogous to the Spanish or Polish royal court that would promote vernacular theatre. Students of the Mohylanian collegium and other schools did form itinerant companies, but these were strictly seasonal and their repertoire was limited to comic interludes and plays based on biblical motifs. Moreover, their texts reveal significant regional variations of language, which is not surprising because the grammar of Ukrainian, unlike Slavonic, was never codified in this period. It should be recalled here that the Polish *Dialog*, albeit written for the popular stage, uses the literary standard of the period.

The construct of a society that had vertically integrated in defence of the Rus' religion, the Kyiv Mohyla Collegium was the sole institution meeting the educational needs of Orthodox Christians before they would proceed to universities or other schools in Poland and Europe. The Orthodox nobility and Cossack elite did not establish an alternative educational model, which would challenge the humanistic theory of style promoted at the collegium, until 1776. Consequently, when the reading of selected vernacular texts became an accepted practice in the *trivium,* Mohylanian professors turned to an accessible source, the most readily available part of the Polish repertoire.[50] From the very inception of Mohyla's school, Polish had been the ancillary tool for learning Latin and enjoyed more opportunities for practical application in everyday life. Thus it remained the language of literary and social prestige within the school's milieu long after Ukrainian lands came under Russian jurisdiction.

In 1691, the poet Ioan Velychkovs'kyi addressed this situation by presenting Iasyns'kyi, his former professor of poetics and newly installed metropolitan, a collection of *carmina curiosa* in the "natural tongue." His introductory remarks defended the need to initiate a tradition of poetry in the native vernacular, but his words fell on deaf ears and the metropolitan never published the collection.[51] Neo-Latin manuals prepared at the collegium continued to accord prestige to texts endowed with the authority of "antiquity." And, as a manual of poetics compiled in 1733 concedes, among Slavic authors, only Polish poets had achieved the stature of antique writers.[52] This circumstance might explain why the authors of the *Declamatio* are not cognizant of Kasiian Sakovych's verses, where the trope of "golden liberty" plays a key role.

Hetman Mazepa's court supported an ensemble of musicians, but did not house a theatre that would offer performances in Ukrainian or any other vernacular. Perhaps this would have been an unrealizable proposition for a man, who – in the service of the tsar – frequently engaged in military campaigns not of his own volition. Thus, the function of communicating Mazepa's political aspirations fell to the schoolmen whose institution benefited so much from his generosity. Many among them were members of the szlachta to whom it made perfect sense to transform a European stage heroine into a warrior for golden liberty.

Notes

1 *"aurea libertas auro pretiosior omni?"* Cited according to Foster Watson, *The English Grammar Schools to 1660: Their Curriculum and Practice* (London: Frank Cass and Co Ltd, 1968), 465–6.

2 *"Вѣрность Подданих против Пану то справует,/ Же им, што найболшого єст в людех, дарует./ Найбольшую реч межи всѣми сужу вольность,/ Которой в стосованню уступуєт годность./ Того ми посвѣдчити могуть всѣ створеня,/ Которыи з натури прагнуть свобоженя./ Золотая вольность – так еи називають."* Cited according to Hans Rothe, ed., *Die älteste ostslawische Kunstdichtung 1575–1647*, vol. 2 (Giessen: W. Schmitz Verlag, 1976), 219. Translation mine.

3 Javier Vergara, "The History of Europe and its Constituent Countries: Considerations in Favour of the New Europe," *Journal of Social Science Education* 6, no. 1 (2007): 16.

4 John Bender and David E. Wellbery, "Rhetoricality: On the Modernist Return of Rhetoric," in *The Ends of Rhetoric: History, Theory, Practice*, ed. Bender and Wellbery (Stanford: Stanford University Press, 1990), 7.

5 Volodymyr Riezanov, *Drama ukraïns'ka: Starovynnyi teatr ukraïns'kyi*, vypusk 5 (Kyiv: UAN, 1928), 245–92.

6 Cayo González Gutiérrez, ed., *Comedia de Santa Catalina. Comedia Tanisdorus. Teatro clásico del siglo XVI* (Gijón: 2003), 7–230.

7 Julian Lewański, ed., *Dramaty Staropolskie: Antologia.* VI (Warsaw: PIW, 1959), 137–73.

8 For the history of narratives about St Catherine, see Riezanov, *Drama ukraïns'ka*, 5, 88–100, and Gary Marker, *Imperial Saint: The Cult of St. Catherine and the Dawn of Female Rule in Russia* (DeKalb: Northern Illinois University, 2007), 29–54.

9 James A. Parente, Jr, *Religious Drama and the Humanist Tradition* (Leiden: E. J. Brill, 1987), 186.

10 Ibid., 187.

11 Ibid., 187–8.

12 Julio Alonso Asenjo, "Teoría y práctica de la Comedia, Tragedia o Tragicomedia de Sancta Catharina (inédita) del P. Hernando de Ávila," *TeatrEsco*, online PDF, http://parnaseo.uv.es/Ars/teatresco/Revista/Catharina.htm.

13 Alison Weber, "Counter-Reformation Misogyny," in *The Counter-Reformation,* ed. David Martin Luebke (Oxford: Blackwell, 1999), 153.

14 Piotr Skarga, *Żywoty Świętych Starego i Nowego Zakonu*, vol. 4 (Cracow: W. Ks. Jezuitow, 1936), 318–25.

15 Vladimir Rezanov [Volodymyr Riezanov], *K istorii russkoi dramy: Ekskurs v oblast' teatra iezuitov* (Nizhyn, 1910), 385; Jan Okoń, *Dramat i teatr szkolny: Sceny Jezuickie XVII Wieku* (Warsaw: PAN, 1970), 362, 368, and 575; Kazimierz Władysław Wójcicki, *Teatr Starożytny w Polsce*, vol. 2 (Warsaw: G. Senewald, 1841), 239–45. I was not able to access any Polish Jesuit play for this exercise.

16 These interludes were not accessible to me.

17 Vestiges of rituals practiced on St Catherine's day can still be seen in France (e.g., *catherinettes*), Germany, and Spain. In early twentieth-century Ukraine, on 7 December (24 November, Old Style) girls would bring into the house cherry branches from the orchard and force them to bloom by the New Year. They would also organize traditional *vechornytsi* (without dancing, because of Advent), to which young men were invited. For details, see Mykola Babak, *Narodna ikona seredn'oï Naddniprianshchyny 18–20 st. v konteksti selians'koho*

kul'turnoho prostoru (Kyiv: Knyha, 2009), 440–1. Consider also the now almost extinct tradition of *katarzynki* in Poland, which involved rituals of divination for bachelors, as opposed to the rituals, known as *andrzejki,* performed by young women.

18 Marker, *Imperial Saint,* 108.

19 I thank Professor Daria Syroyid (Lviv) for giving me a digital copy of the 1689 publication.

20 According to Marker, the 1660 *Anthologion* helped transform Catherine of Alexandria from a saint privately venerated by the women of Russia's imperial household into an icon with public visibility, 86–9.

21 Riezanov, *Drama ukraïns'ka,* 5, 84–5.

22 Paulina Lewin, "Drama and Theatre at Ukrainian Schools in the Seventeenth and Eighteenth Centuries: The Bible as Inspiration of Images, Meanings, Style, and Stage Productions," *Harvard Ukrainian Studies* 8, no. 1–2 (1984): 98.

23 Riezanov, *Drama ukraïns'ka,* 5, 94.

24 Iaroslava Stratii, V.D. Lytvynov and V.A. Andrushko, compilers, *Opisanie kursov filosofii i ritoriki professorov Kievo-Mogilianskoi Akademii* (Kyiv: Naukova dumka, 1982), 52–4.

25 Riezanov, *Drama ukraïns'ka,* 5, 242.

26 In 1707 Peter I privately married his mistress, who in 1711 was to become an official persona, as the sovereign Tsaritsa Ekaterina Alekseevna, and around whom the first Russian imperial cult of St Catherine was soon constructed (Marker, 126–44). Born Marta Elena Skowrońska, the woman assumed the name Catherine soon after beginning her relationship with Peter I. Her earliest documented signature as Ekaterina Alekseevna dates from 6 October 1705. See Arkhimandrit Varlaam, *Russkii arkhiv* 1, no. 2 (1874): 569.

27 Stratii et al., *Opisanie,* 50–2.

28 Ibid., 49–50.

29 Giovanna Siedina, "Un poema epico neolatino su Ivan Mazepa," *Studi Slavistici* 4 (2007): 85–115.

30 Natalia Pylypiuk, "Mudrist' Predvichna (1703) – drama-moralite dlia arystokrativ," *Kyïvs'ka akademiia,* vypusk 10 (2012): 11–30.

31 Natalia Pylypiuk, "The Face of Wisdom in the Age of Mazepa," in *Mazepa and his Time: History, Culture, Literature, Political Thought,* ed. Giovanna Siedina (Alessandria: Edizioni Dell'Orso, 2004), 367–400.

32 Riezanov, *Drama ukraïns'ka,* 5, 86–8.

33 This in-text citation and all subsequent ones refer to volume 5 of Riezanov's collection. My translation (here and subsequently) offers a prose rendering of each stanza, rather than a poetic, verse-by-verse equivalence. I thank Dr Wacław Osadnik (University of Alberta) for his assistance.

180   Natalia Pylypiuk

34 For other biblical allusions in the play, see Lewin, "Drama and Theatre at Ukrainian Schools in the Seventeenth and Eighteenth Centuries," 120.

35 Pylypiuk, "The Face of Wisdom in the Age of Mazepa."

36 See Ivan Reklyns'kyi's engraving in Ioan Maksymovych's *Bohorodytse Divo* (Chernihiv, 1707). Cf. Pylypiuk, "The Face of Wisdom," Figure 9.

37 Marker (126–44) indicates that Dymytrii Tuptalo's redaction of Catherine's *vita* served as a template for Tsarevna Natal'ia Alekseevna's play about the martyr, *Komediia sv. Ekateriny*, which was performed at the private theatre she established in 1707. Extant excerpts of the prose speeches by the hermit (*Starets* in the Tsarevna's play) do not contain any reference to classical mythology. See O.A. Derzhavina et al., eds., *P'esy stolichnykh i provintsial'nykh teatrov pervoi poloviny XVIII v.* (Moscow: Nauka, 1975), 158–9.

38 *"Presvîtlîishikh Derzhavnishikh i Bl[a]goch[es]tivîshikh, Velikikh G[osu]d[a]rei n[a]shikh Ts[a]rei i Velikikh Kn[ia]zei, IOANNA ALEKSÎEVICHA, PETRA ALEKSÎEVICHA,: vseia Velikîia y Maly[ia] i Bîlyia Rossïy Samoderzhtsev, i mnogikh G[osu]d[a]rstv i Zemel', Vostochnykh i Zapadnikh y Sîvernykh, O[t]chichei i Dîdichei i Naslîdnikov i G[osu]d[a]rei i Obladatelei."*

39 Vasilii Ruban, ed., *Pokhod boiarina i bolshago polku voevody Alekseia Semenovicha Sheina k Azovu ... s podrobnym opisaniem vsekh voennykh i torzhestvennykh proizshestvii* (St Petersburg: 1773),179–82. This anonymous account, which was probably produced by one of the emperor's offices, was originally published in 1697.

40 Gregory L. Freeze, *Russia: A History* (Oxford University Press, 2009), 104.

41 Ruban, *Pokhod boiarina*, 192.

42 Karen A. Winstead, *John Capgrave's Fifteenth Century* (Philadelphia: University of Pennsylvania Press, 2007), 79–82.

43 Natalia Yakovenko, *Narys istoriï Ukraïny z naidavnishykh chasiv do kintsia XVIII stolittia*, 2nd ed. (Kyiv: Krytyka, 2005), 404–8.

44 See note 1, above.

45 See Vitalii Masliuk, *Latynomovni poetyky i rytoryky XVII–pershoï polovyny XVIII st. ta ïkh rol' u rozvytku teoriï literatury na Ukraïni* (Kyiv: Naukova dumka, 1983), 204.

46 See note 2, above. Also see: Natalia Pylypiuk, "Golden Liberty: Kasiian Sakovych's Understanding of Rhetoric and Preparation for the Civic Life," in *States, Societies, Cultures: East and West. Essays in Honor of Jaroslaw Pelenski*, ed. Janusz Duzinkiewicz et al. (New York: Ross Publishing Inc, 2004), 885–920.

47 Serhii Pavlenko, compiler, *Doba het'mana Mazepy v dokumentakh*, vol. 1 (Kyiv: Kyievo-Mohylians'ka Akademiia, 2008), 266: points 1 and 4 of document no. 295.

48 Natalia Pylypiuk, "Kyïvs'ki poetyky i renesansni teoriï mystetstva," in
    Ievropeis'ke vidrodzhennia ta ukraïns'ka literatura XIV–XVIII st., ed. Oleksa
    Myshanych (Kyiv: Naukova dumka, 1993), 75–109.
49 José Antonio Maravall, *La cultura del Barroco* (Barcelona: Editorial Ariel, 1975),
    497–520.
50 Władysław Korotaj, "Dynamika rozwoju piśmiennictwa polskiego od połowy
    XVI do końca XVII wieku," in *Wiek XVII – Kontrreformacja – Barok. Prace
    z historii kultury*, ed. Janusz Pelc (Wrocław: Instytut Badań Literackich PAN,
    1970), 274–90.
51 Natalia Pylypiuk, "Poetry as Milk: A Seventeenth-Century Metaphor and its
    Pedagogical Context," in "Early-Modern Ukraine," ed. Dushan Bednarsky, Zenon
    E. Kohut, and Frank E. Sysyn, special issue, *Journal of Ukrainian Studies* 17, no.
    1–2 (1992): 189–203.
52 Ryszard Łużny, *Pisarze Kręgu Akademii Kijowsko-Mohylańskiej a literatura
    polska: Z Dziejów Związków Kulturalnych Polsko – Wschodniosłowiańskich w
    XVII–XVIII w.* (Cracow: Uniwersytet Jagielloński, 1966), 100.

The Wisdom of Virtue: Iosyp Turobois'kyi's Praise of Ioasaf Krokovs'kyi

GIOVANNA SIEDINA

Neo-Latin poetry featured in the manuals of poetics that were written and used at the Kyiv Mohyla Collegium has been studied insufficiently.[1] This is a pity because the poetical models proposed by the authors of these manuals and teachers of poetics are an important resource for reconstructing the cultural, ideological, and political discourse of the Kyivan intellectual elite in the second half of the seventeenth century and the first half of the eighteenth. For over a century the Kyiv Mohyla Collegium was the main institution of higher learning in Ukraine. Its courses of poetics and rhetoric, together with the prose and poetic texts they offered to students, can tell us much about the way in which, through Latin language and literature, the Ukrainian intellectual elite assimilated the values of the European culture that had its roots in humanism and the Renaissance. These sources also reveal the distinctive manner in which European cultural values were adapted to Ukraine's religious and cultural history and traditions. Thus, the importance of studying these texts for the history of Ukrainian literature and culture is self-evident.

Panegyric poetry is one of the principal genres of Mohylanian poetics. In fact, since the main goal of poetry at the time was to contribute to the education of pious men and loyal subjects, the best way to achieve this was to represent exemplary human actions that would constitute models worthy of emulation. The didactic function of praise was all the more effective when the characters being praised were familiar to students – a circumstance that favoured the latter's identification with the former. For Mohylanian teachers and professors – the religious and intellectual elite of the time – poetry was also a privileged space for expressing, in addition to linguistic and moral-theological teachings, views whose ideological nature and political import could not escape an attentive hermeneutic reading of the text.

I shall discuss these didactic and ideological aspects by analysing a long and complex poem dedicated to Ioasaf Krokovs'kyi in 1699, when he was archimandrite of the Kyivan Caves Monastery. Despite his elevation to three prominent Orthodox ecclesiastical posts in the Hetmanate (rector of the Kyiv Mohyla Collegium, archimandrite of the Kyivan Caves Monastery, and metropolitan), Krokovs'kyi's life and literary output have attracted little scholarly attention.[2] The same may be said of the poetry that has Krokovs'kyi as its object and dedicatee. Indeed, although some Latin poems devoted to him have been published in Ukrainian translation,[3] the absence of both the original texts and any commentary, contextualization, or analysis of these panegyrics renders their publication ineffective and inadequate for creating a broader picture of the history of Ukrainian literature and does not elucidate its ties with Latin and neo-Latin European literature.

Born circa 1648, Ioasaf Krokovs'kyi studied at the Kyiv Mohyla Collegium and then continued his studies abroad, at the Academy of St Athanasius in Rome. After returning to his homeland, in 1683 he became a monk of the Kyivan Pustynno-Mykolaïvs'kyi monastery and was then appointed its hegumen in 1688. Shortly afterwards he was elected to the post of chief administrator of the Bohoiavleniia Monastery. After having taught poetics, rhetoric, and philosophy[4] at the Kyiv Mohyla Collegium, where he had also served as prefect, he became its rector in 1693–7 (in 1693, while serving as hegumen of the Kyivan Pustynno-Mykolaïvs'kyi monastery, he was ordained hegumen of the Kyivan Brats'kyi monastery). In the academic year 1689–90 he introduced a four-year course of theology,[5] and in 1697 he was appointed archimandrite of the Kyivan Caves Monastery. In 1693–4 Krokovs'kyi headed an important delegation to Moscow on behalf of Hetman Ivan Mazepa and Metropolitan Varlaam Iasyns'kyi to petition the tsar to grant the Kyiv Mohyla Collegium material support and recognition of its status as an academy. The mission was a success, and the delegation obtained two tsarist charters. The first of these documents confirmed the properties of the Bohoiavleniia Monastery, while the second granted permission to teach philosophy and theology, the right to self-government and immunity from civil and military authorities, and the right to accept Orthodox students from areas of Ukraine under Polish rule.[6] Because of the high esteem enjoyed by Hetman Mazepa and Metropolitan Iasyns'kyi,[7] after the death of the latter in 1707 Krokovs'kyi was appointed metropolitan of Kyiv. In October 1708 he met with Mazepa's personal staff in connection with the hetman's poor health. After Mazepa's defection to the Swedes, Krokovs'kyi was summoned to Hlukhiv where, together with the archbishop of Chernihiv and Novhorod-Sivers'kyi and the bishop of Pereiaslav, he issued an anathema against Mazepa, thus remaining firmly loyal to Tsar Peter I. In 1718 Krokovs'kyi was summoned to St Petersburg for questioning in connection with his involvement in the rebellion allegedly fomented by Peter's son, Tsarevich Aleksei. He was stopped en route and taken to the Arkhangel'sk Monastery in Tver', where he died on 1 July under murky circumstances.

Efforts to start filling in the "black hole" in scholarly analyses of Krokovs'kyi's connection to the written word were launched by Gary Marker.
Marker, who analysed Krokovs'kyi's akathist to St Barbara (1698) and his
introduction, addressed to the tsar, in the 1702 edition of the *Paterik*, points
out the rhetorical strategies that Krokovs'kyi employs to convey his message.
In the first text, Krokovs'kyi places subtle stress on the particular role and
pre-eminence of the clergy in preserving Kyiv's sacred heritage. In the second
text, all the while celebrating Peter's victories at Kazikermen and Azov, Krokovs'kyi, through his message of peace and love, implicitly invites the tsar
to desist from embarking on new offensive wars. This idea is also conveyed
in visual terms by the engraved frontispiece and the accompanying verses.
Indeed, in the engraving Peter is represented as victorious but with no weapons, riding with open arms in a sort of prayer position, as if "transposing the
divine love of the Theotokos and Christ child from Heaven to Earth."[8] Marker's findings are consonant with the themes and implied message of the poem
that I analyse below.

Moreover, the central theme of the poem, Krokovs'kyi's virtue and his being
inspired by wisdom, reveals the author's intention to insert the archimandrite
and future metropolitan into what Natalia Pylypiuk defines as a "project, initiated in the 1690s, which – through visual and textual means – endeavored
to portray Mazepa and Iasyns'kyi as protectors and benefactors of Wisdom's
abode, i.e., the collegium and St. Sophia, the cathedral church of Kyivan
Rus'."[9] Considering that Krokovs'kyi was then archimandrite of the Kyivan
Caves Monastery, I would add that this central institution of Orthodoxy in the
Hetmanate, as well as its protectress, the Mother of God, was included in this
project.[10]

The poem is found in fols. 21v–25v of the 1699 manual of poetics *Hymettus extra Atticam*,[11] which the specialized literature has deemed to be anony-
mously written and has wrongly dated to 1718–19.[12] The course was actually
published in 1699 (as we read on fol. 2v), and it was taught in the 1699–1700
academic year. This date is fully compatible with other extant information
about the author, who, as I discovered by deciphering the griphus at the end
of the poem analysed in the present study, was Iosyp Turobois'kyi.[13] It is an
irony of fate that, while Turobois'kyi remained almost unknown in Ukrainian
literature, he steadily entered the history of Russian culture for his celebratory
works in honour of Peter I. Indeed, like many Mohylanian clerics of the late
seventeenth and early eighteenth centuries, after completing his studies and
teaching poetics and rhetoric at the Kyiv Mohyla Collegium,[14] in April 1701
he left for Moscow to contribute to the development of education there, on
orders from the tsar. He became a teacher of rhetoric and philosophy (1701–3)

and first prefect (1703–5) of the Slavic-Greek-Latin Academy; in 1708 he was appointed archimandrite of the Simonov monastery in Moscow; and in 1711, according to Smirnov, he moved to the Novospasskii Monastery.[15]

Throughout his brilliant career Turobois'kyi combined his formidable skills as a teacher and organizer with his talents for writing and orating, which were duly expressed in the celebration of Peter I's victories. For example, he organized the solemn celebration of the Russian tsar's victorious return from Livonia, for which he wrote the scenario and greetings. Published in 1704 under the title *Preslavnoe torzhestvo svoboditelia Livonii i Ingermanliandii* (The Glorious Celebration of the Liberator of Livonia and Ingermanland), it contained two prefaces, one addressed to the tsar and the other to the reader. The latter featured a description of the triumphal arch that was erected at the Slavic-Greek-Latin Academy to honour Russia's victory. Already in this work Turobois'kyi reveals his mastery of rhetorical devices as he explains to the Russian reader the reasons for using allegorical characters from pagan mythology and history instead of Biblical and Christian ones. The argument that this was a new kind of "civic praise … established in all political, not barbarian nations, so that praiseworthy and respectable virtue may grow"[16] is quite persuasive, as it links Russia's rise as a European power with the adoption of *Latinitas*, which had its roots in classical culture.

Turobois'kyi also wrote the description of the triumphal arch erected near the Slavic-Greek-Latin Academy on the occasion of the victory at Poltava (*Politiko-lepnaia ἀποθέωσις dostokhvalnyia khrabrosti vserossiiskogo gerkulesa presvetleishago*) [Political Apotheosis of the Praiseworthy Bravery of the Most Illustrious Hercules], Moscow, 1709), in which, according to *Slovar' russkogo iazyka XVIII veka* (Dictionary of the Russian Language of the Eighteenth Century), the word "apotheosis" appears for the first time in a Russian printed text and is explained by Turobois'kyi in the preface to the reader.[17] Panegyrics to Peter I were also included in school plays written at the Slavic-Greek-Latin Academy, in whose composition Turobois'kyi took part. Without a doubt, the roots of his widely recognized mastery in mythologizing Russian history and autocracy by skillfully exploiting the rhetoric arsenal of baroque poetics[18] may be traced back to his Kyivan period, concerning which available sources provide scanty factual data:[19] after studying at the Kyiv Mohyla Collegium in the 1690s, he became a teacher of lower grammatical classes and poetics in 1699–1700 and of rhetoric in 1700–1. Departing for Moscow in April 1701, he left behind two courses in manuscript: rhetoric and philosophy. These manuals, together with his poetics course, seem to be the only extant materials that can help reveal more about Turobois'kyi's ideological outlook and his relationship with Krokovs'kyi.[20]

The poem is presented as an example of *silva*, succinctly characterized by the author as "an epic poem that briefly treats a true or feigned story, someone's praise or blame and similar themes."[21] While it certainly belongs to the *genus demonstrativum*, the poem is not easily classifiable in that it displays features of a panegyric poem, a *carmen gratulatorium*, and a *carmen genethliacum*.[22]

The poem consists of 263 lines and can be roughly divided into three parts. It is constructed in the form of a dialogue between the poet, on the one side, and Apollo and four of the Muses, on the other. The rhetorical device of placing the poet's praise into the mouths of the gods makes it authoritative and persuasive. I will concentrate on those sections that constitute the ideological core of the poem, summarizing the rest.

In the title the poet defines himself as "Entheus poeta,"[23] thus hinting at a Platonic conception of the poet as someone who is inspired by a *furor divinus* and, at the same time, as one who is a passive agent of the Muses.[24] Indeed, running through the poem is a theatrical movement between earth and sky, the human and the divine.

The poem opens with the image of the poet seized by poetic inspiration and taken into the ether, from where he is transported to the summit of Parnassus by the winged horse Pegasus. From the very outset a contrast is drawn between the might of the gods and the seeming weakness of the poet; the latter may be viewed as a *topos modestiae* or an implied *recusatio* designed to underscore the difference between the moral stature of the addressee and the humbleness of the addresser. Indeed, in the first part, words denoting fear, trepidation, and even terror recur frequently: *pavor* and *timor* appear three times each; the verb *metuere* and the same root substantive *metus*, as well as the verb *terrere* appear twice; and, finally, the adjective *tremulus* is used.

The magnificence of the gods and all that pertains to them is described by means of a series of powerful metaphors and similes underscoring the incommensurable gap that exists between them and humans. Thus, resorting to a litotes, the author describes the power of Pegasus's flight as even stronger than the triple trail of a lightning bolt. The image of light is dominant and is expressed by the frequent use of such words as *fulgor* (four times), *lux* (three times), *lumina* (five times), and the verb *radiare* (twice). As will become clear below, the images and metaphors used in reference to Krokovs'kyi belong to the one semantic field, which creates a powerful association and hints at his belonging to a superior world because of his many virtues.

When the poet, astride Pegasus, approaches Mount Parnassus, the sight of it terrifies him, and after he is borne to its summit, the extreme brightness of the eternal fires and his fear of this unfamiliar sacred place make him faint. A seemingly divine voice then speaks to the poet and heartens him, enjoining him to let go of his excessive fear, for he is being transported to his homeland, the seat of the poets:

47   Sic ubi repebam subito vox aethere lapsa:
        Heus, inquit, propriam metuis Patriam quid Vates?
        Quid nimirum terrent Parnassi Regna Poëtam?
50   **Hic** Liber pater **hic** magnus quoque regnat Apollo,
        Musarum Patria **hic**, divis habitata Camaenis:
        Parce metu Vates, nimio quoque parce timori,
        Sedibus ast divûm Venerandis sumito Curam:
        Haec mens est superum labor ille fuitque caballi.
55   Vix dicta audivi divino haec ore putabam:
        Cesserat ergo timor nimij **cessere** pavores,
        Reddita suntque sibi sensim mens palpebrae et artus.
        Sed medio rutilae **lucis fulgore** statutus
        Causam scire volo quae tanti **luminis** esset
60   Omnesque in partes mea **lumina** circumduxi.
        Ecce sacer chorus frontem redimitus adoreis
        Gramine ridenti residens, **fulgentior** astris,
        Quae **radiant** caelo medijs in nocte tenebris,
        Quantum nempe decet **fulgere** Deumque Deasque,
65   Cuius **fulgore** is vertex **radiabat** amaeno
        Hunc ego cognovi propiusque accedere visum:
        En sacros vultus video quoque pronus adoro
        Intentosque suo reperi invigilare labori.

(47   And thus, as I was crawling, suddenly a voice dropped from the ether
        Hey, it said, why, O poet, do you fear your homeland?
        How is it that the kingdoms of the Parnassus frighten the poet?
50   Here reigns the father Bacchus, here reigns too the great Apollo,
        Here is the home of the Muses inhabited by the divine Camenae:
        do not be afraid, O poet, refrain too from your excessive fear,
        On the contrary, take care of the venerable seats of the gods:
        This is the mind of the gods, while that was the work of the horse.
55   As soon as I heard these words, I thought they came from the divine mouth:
        therefore dread vanished, the excessive fears faded away,
        Little by little my mind, my eyelids, and my limbs were restored to themselves.
        But as I am placed in the midst of the red-lit radiance
        I want to know the cause of so great a light

60   And to all parts I turned my eyes.
      Here is the sacred chorus, the forehead wreathed with glory
      sitting on the cheerful grass, brighter than the stars
      that shine in the sky amidst the darkness of the night,
      exactly to the degree it is fitting for the God and Goddesses to shine,
65   of whose agreeable brilliance shone that celestial rod.
      And I recognized this and it seemed to come closer:
      Behold! I see the sacred faces and prone I adore them
      I found them intently watching over their work.)

The convincing force of the narrator's voice is reinforced by the use of anapho-ras (*Hic liber Pater hic magnus quoque regnat Apollo,* / *Musarum Patria hic*), and in the following line, *Parce metu Vates, nimio quoque parce timori*, through the device of synonymy to express the concept of fear (through *metus* and *timor*). Line 56 features a parallel in the statement *Cesserat ergo timor nimij cessere pavores*, created by the repetition of the verb *cedere*: fear is expressed here by a third synonym, *pavor*. Once his intellect, sight, and movement are restored to him, the poet, no longer afraid, is curious to understand the origin of the bright light that he sees all around him. Finally, he realizes that this brilliance comes from the chorus of the nine Muses. Here, once more, the met-aphor of light is skillfully couched in different terms; in eight lines we have nine words indicating light, whose variation is effected through *adnominatio* and polyptotons: *fulgore* (twice), *fulgentior, fulgere*; *lucis*; *luminis, lumina*; *radient*, and *radiabat*.

The ensuing depiction of Apollo and the Muses is divided in two parts: in the first part (lines 69–78) each personage is intent upon gathering a different plant or flower, while in the second (lines 80–9) each is depicted performing his or her own art or science with its corresponding attributes and instruments. The individual descriptions seem to echo the famous poem "Nomina musa-rum," the authorship of which is controversial, but they are equally present in Ambrose Calepinus's famous multilingual dictionary, from which our author may have drawn them. However, he varies them creatively, and the frequent enjambments add movement to this scene, conveying an atmosphere of joy-ful cooperation among the sisters. The only "exception," one might say, is the depiction of Melpomene, the Muse of tragic poetry, who is said to recite not tragic but sweet, elegiac verses ("Melpomene suaves elegos [non tragica] promit").

Once Apollo and the chorus of Muses have tuned their instruments, the poet sees them setting off for a destination unknown to him. Their departure gives him the courage to speak and to try to stop them, and his heartfelt request that they reveal where they are headed is effectively rendered by the *amplificatio verborum* of their designation and by the subsequent chiasmus: they are called "Pimpleae Vates placidae, mitis sorores Parnassi, Vigiles Divae laticisque biformis," an allusion to their being poets, sisters, and goddesses. The poet resorts to *amplificatio sententiarum* in his request for information on what kind of feats they are going to celebrate, and thus what kind of genre of song they will sing, whether *genethliacum, epithalamium*, or other types of encomiastic poetry: *panegyric, epinicion, gratulatio*, or *elogia*. These lines can also be viewed as poetry about poetry, in which the poet calls attention both to the predominance of the *genus demonstrativum* and to his own practical embodiment of the prescriptions that he gives his students: in fact, in lines 95–8 of this same manual Turobois'kyi exemplifies the *exordium per interrogationem* of the encomiastic, or panegyrical, poem.

At the same time, the insistence on the celebration of military feats in the series of questions contained in lines 100–4, which are characterized by the use of adjectives that markedly contrast with those reserved for the Muses and other genres of poetry, is meant to emphasize not the glory that military victories bring their architects but, rather, the misery, cruelty, and sorrow that war brings. This distinction is underlined by the locutions *trucem arenam* (savage place of contest), *cruore madentes lusus* (amusements dripping with blood), *spicula duri ferri conspersa cruore* (the points of the hard sword covered with blood), and by the image of the scaly Mars: there is no true and lasting glory in military actions, the author seems to imply. In contrast, childbirth, evoked by Hymenaeus, is a joyous occurrence, and the celebration of other historical events and characters, as well as church dignitaries, hinted at in lines 105–8, carries a neutral connotation:

92 Ast mihi iam sensus animosque audacia fandi
    Restituit. Supplex ergo tum talia dixi:
    Phaebe pater nobis spes unica, Vos quoque posco
95 **Pimpleae vates placidae, mitisque sorores**
    Parnassi, vigiles divae laticisque biformis
    Dicite quo celeres cursus gradusve veloces
    Figitis? An **Lucina** deûm partusque reducunt?
    An **hymeneus** laetis revocat succendere thedas
100 Ignibus? **autve trucem scuamati Martis arenam**
    Bellonaeque cruore madentes visere lusus
    Complacuit? Ferri cecinisse ve spicula duri
    Hostili victorum acie conspersa cruore?
    Vincentumve comas lauro coronare placebit?

105   Aut ubi praecelsi sedem fixere senatus
Regnorumve decus placuit celebrare Coronis?
Caesareosve paludatus,[25] mitrasve celebres?
Tempora praesuleis aut insignita tiaris?

(92   And the courage to speak now restored my senses and
my mind. Then, suppliant, I said these things:
"Father Apollo, our sole hope, and you too, O gentle poetesses
95   of Pimpla, and meek sisters of the Parnassus, vigilant
sisters of the two-formed water, I ask:
Tell [me], whither do you direct your quick movements or your swift steps?
Perhaps Lucina and the births of the gods lead you back?
Perhaps Hymenaeus calls you back to light the torches with joyful
100   fires? Or it pleased you to see the savage place of contest of the scaly Mars
and Bellona's amusements dripping with blood?
Or it pleased you to have sung the points of the hard sword
covered with blood by the hostile army of the winners?
Or it will please you to deck with laurel garlands the heads of the winners?
105   Or it pleased you to celebrate with crowns where highest senates fixed
The seat or glory of the kingdoms?
Or Caesar's generals, or the famous mitres?
Or the temples of the prelates bestowed with tiaras?)

The central part of the poem (lines 115–232) features congratulations on the occasion of Krokovs'kyi's birthday. The fact that the praise is placed in the mouth of Apollo and four of the nine Muses (Clio, the Muse of history; Calliope, the Muse of epic poetry; Urania, the Muse of astronomy; and Polyhymnia, the Muse of sacred poetry, sacred hymns, and eloquence) is highly significant. The choice of these particular Muses is deliberate, as we will see shortly.

In Apollo's speech we find the established features of the genre: the goddess Lucina, who presides over birth and glorious, noble ancestry, and Krokovs'kyi's virtue, which leads him to great achievements. The insistence on moral virtue (the word "virtue" appears ten times in lines 117–24) as Ioasaf's highest quality anticipates the opposition between acts of peace and the cultivation of human and divine sciences on the one hand, and the art of war on the other.

Indeed, virtue is said to have bound itself to Krokovs'kyi since birth. In order to illustrate the physical and moral stages of his growth, as well as his advancement in learning and religious doctrine, the poet, through the voice of Apollo, resorts to a Roman metaphor. At first, virtue binds him with a golden amulet (*aurea bulla*), which in Rome was hung around the neck of winners and noble children, and later, freeborn children. The "tutelage" of the young Ioasaf is subsequently taken over by Pallas and Apollo; once the amulet is removed from his young neck,[26] the former weaves with her sacred thumb the *toga praetexta*, that is, the outer garment of Roman freeborn children, which seems to indicate a sort of infusion of wisdom into him. Apollo adorns his head with ribbons of laurel and so does Hermes – just reward for Krokovs'kyi's cultivation of poetry and oratory, as well as for his protection of the liberal arts in his role as rector of the Kyiv Mohyla Collegium. After reaching adulthood and having donned the free *toga*, Ioasaf is shown as excelling in virtue, knowledge of letters, the doctrine of sacred things, and spiritual wisdom (*sophia*). Apollo emphasizes that, even though Krokovs'kyi is a religious dignitary, he has never abandoned his love for literature; indeed, he is inflamed by it to a degree never demonstrated by Maecenas or Alexander the Macedonian (the Great).[27] Thus, the wisdom of which Ioasaf is a bearer reflects, at least partly, that tendency of Renaissance philosophy which associated speculative wisdom with moral virtue and civic action.[28] In Turobois'kyi's depiction, Krokovs'kyi seems to be the "perfect" incarnation of the humanistic "transformation of wisdom from contemplation to action, from a body of knowledge to a collection of ethical precepts, from a virtue of the intellect to a perfection of the will."[29]

Moreover, the virtue that Turobois'kyi attributes to Krokovs'kyi, especially in lines 125–36, seems to mirror the Erasmian definition of wisdom as *virtus cum eruditione liberali coniuncta*, which Eugene Rice defines as "one idea of wisdom peculiarly characteristic of the Renaissance."[30] This idea of wisdom as a combination of virtue and learning is a profoundly Christian conception: indeed, on the one hand, *sapientia* is conceived as knowledge of a God whose central attribute and very nature is virtue, and as an active imitation of Christ. On the other, *eruditio* is learning conceived as a moral process whose function is to hold "true opinions" about things and "to know what is good and what is bad in order that we may virtuously follow the good and flee the bad ... Wisdom unites the ethical insights of learning with the practice of virtue."[31] Although the conceptualization of wisdom elaborated by the Mohylanian cultural elite requires further study, it seems plausible that the celebration of Krokovs'kyi, in this and other poems that I have analysed,[32] inserts itself into the above-mentioned project discussed by Natalia Pylypiuk.

In order to celebrate Ioasaf in a fitting way, Apollo uses a *topos* that is recurrent in Mohylanian poetics: the Greek Parnassus is abandoned in favour of a Mohylanian Parnassus. This makes the point that one's own literary achievements are not at all inferior to those of the ancient classics, while asserting one's active participation in the wider stream of European culture:

109   Hoc ubi prolatum sincero corde patebat
110   Divis, en subito dignati sistere gradum.
       Pieridum princeps hinc sacro fatus ab ore:
       Quid mea deposcis vates actusque viasque?
       Ignorasve diem sacram illuxisse Iosaphi [sic]
       Natalem, magni Rossorum Luminis inquam?
115   Cuius sic unas spectesve[33] genusve Lucina
       Nobilem spectavit generoso sanguine natum;
       Nec nasci fuerat satis, ipsa ast **Virtus** ad alta
       Prognatum esse videns voluit sibi[34] nectere **bullam**.
       Iamque puer magnae subito rudimenta ferebat
120   Indolis, ac parvo regulabat corpore **virtus**.
       Mox ubi **bulla** rudi demissa est aurea collo
       Praetextam Pallas sacrato pollice nevit
       Ac ego lauratis decoravi tempora vittis,
       Hermes facundo posuit quoque vertice laurus.
125   Haec ubi deposita est, **toga** iam quoque **libera** sumpta
       Creverat ac **virtus** juvenis crescentibus annis,
       Inde sophum lauro rutile [sic!] ambivere corollae,
       Abdidit alma decus superumque scientia rerum.
       Nec licuit tantum saecli lattere [sic] tenebris
130   Lumina quin ferre[35] vel religionis ab umbris
       Aut huic conferret celsâ **virtute** decorem;
       Contulit et verae pietati iuncta venustas
       Doctrinae, Sophia atque supernarum arbitra rerum,
       Post classes rossis doctè se tradita rostris
135   Nec modo desistit literarum ast flagrat amore
       Qualis Maecenas fuerat nusquam Macedoque.
       Hunc igitur nostrâ celebrem quo dignius oda,
       Linquo Parnassum patrium sed pegma reposco
       Plausurusque sibi dulci modulamine vocis
140   Annosa laurus sincerè votaque porto.

(109   When what I had said with a sincere heart was manifest to
110   The gods, behold, at once they deigned to halt their steps.
       Then the prince of the Pierids spoke from his sacred mouth:
       "Why, O poet, do you ask about my things and my acts and my ways?
       Or do you ignore that Ioasaf's sacred birthday has risen bright,
       I mean, [the birthday] of the great light of the Ruthenians?
115   Of him thus Lucina watched the unique appearance or the descent,
       the noble born of generous blood;

nor had being born been enough, but virtue herself, seeing that he
was born to accomplish lofty deeds, wanted to attach a [golden] amulet to
him.
And already as a child at once he brought the rudiments of a great
120   innate character, and virtue governed his little body.
As soon as the golden amulet was taken off the young neck,
Pallas wove with her sacred thumb the *toga praetexta*,
and I adorned his temples with bands of laurel;
Hermes too placed laurel on [his] eloquent head
125   when this was taken off, and the free toga was now taken up.
As the years grew, so also grew the young man's virtue;
thence the red garlands circled the wise man with laurel,
The propitious knowledge of the gods removed [Ioasaf's] gaze from the
things' beauty.
And it was not permitted that such a great man lie hidden in the darkness of
the world
130   without carrying the lights of religion out of the shades
or bestowing beauty on religion with his high virtue;
[to this] contributed also the doctrine's beauty united to true piety,
and wisdom, arbiter of the things of the gods,
having skillfully handed herself over after the armies to Rus' speaker's
platforms,
135   and he not only does not give up his love of letters but is inflamed by it
as never Maecenas and the Macedonian had done.
Therefore, in order to celebrate him more appropriately with our ode,
I abandon my ancestral Parnassus, but I demand a pulpit,
and to applaud him[36] with a sweet harmony of the voice
140   from an old time I sincerely bring a laurel and vows.)

Clio, the protectress of history, is the first Muse to speak. Her presence is probably meant to remind readers that Krokovs'kyi was a historian; indeed, according to ancient and contemporary chronicles, in those very years the dedicatee was compiling the *Litopysets'* (1685–1712), an account of events of Ukrainian Rus' and world history. Clio is also called upon to set Ioasaf's merits against a historical and mythological background, and both her presence and her discourse implicitly state that Krokovs'kyi has gone down in history. Echoing Apollo's speech, she declares that Ioasaf's qualities and virtue lead from the summit of the Parnassus to the ancestral roof that belongs to her. To illustrate this, the poet places into Clio's mouth a series of comparisons with historical and mythological characters chosen for their outstanding exemplification of each virtue. This list exemplifies *copia verborum*, the lexical abundance

used to illustrate the variety of ways in which one basic idea may be expressed
in Latin:

142   Clio post roseo renidens haec protulit ore:
       Nostros Aoniae cultor si noscere calles
       Est animus: ducunt virtus meritusque[37] Iosaphi
145   Vertice Parnassi misso sub tegmen avitum,
       Nempe meum mandare aptus quoque tempora fastis
       Magnorum: superat questum Virtutibus Abbas
       Tum factis. Ceciditque sibi frux carius ultro
       Iustus Aristides, Themis, gravesque Catones,
150   Antonij pietas, sors atque Polycratis ipsa,
       Magnus Alexander famâ tum nomine celso,
       Herculis invictum robur, durique labores,
       Pompeius constans, magni clementia Titti [sic!].
       Sobrius ac Zenon, Sapientia sacri Solonis,
155   Religioque Numae, quid plura loquar? Virtutis
       Nobile praecelsae dicas hunc esse theatrum,
       Quo capiant cuncti vitae rudimenta decorae.
       Hic igitur longum magno quo crescat in aevum
       Nomine, serta fero roseis implexa corollis
160   Magnaque longevis referam sua nomina fastis

(142   Then the shining Clio uttered these things with her rose-coloured mouth:
       "O worshipper of Eonia, if you wish to know our
       paths, Ioasaf's virtue and merits lead us,
145   having left the summit of Parnassus, under the ancestral roof
       that is mine; being apt also to entrust the times to the annals
       of great people, the abbot overcomes complaints with his virtues and works.
       And at once it became clear that he matched such beloved and honest men
       As the just Aristides, Themis, and the grave Catos,
150   Anthony's pietas, and the very fate of Polycrates,
       the great Alexander, whose name was then high in fame,
       Hercules's invincible strength, [his] hard labors,
       the constant Pompey, the clemency of the great Titus.
       And the sober Zeno, the wisdom of blessed Solon,
155   and Numa's devotion, what else [should I] say?[38] You could
       say that this is the noble theater of exceptionally high virtue,
       So that all may learn the first notions of an honorable life.
       Therefore, in order that this may grow for a long time with
       a great name, I bear wreaths entwined with small roseate garlands
160   And I will refer their great names to great age registers [calendars].)

Justice, the first virtue, is represented by the Athenian statesman Aristides, Themis (goddess of justice), and the two Catos (Cato the Younger and Cato the Elder). The virtue of *pietas* is personified by a certain Antonius, probably Marcus Antonius the orator, grandfather of the famous general and triumvir, Mark Anthony; as for Polycrates, the reason behind his choice may reside in his prosperity as well as in the fact that, though a tyrant, he was an enlightened one.[39] Hard work is aptly represented by Hercules and his labors; the other virtues that Ioasaf possesses are epitomized by historical characters from Roman and Greek history: Pompey for constancy; Emperor Titus for clemency; Zeno of Citium, the founder of the Stoic school of philosophy, for sobriety; Solon for wisdom (*sapientia*); and Numa Pompilius, the second Roman king, for religious devotion. Lastly, Ioasaf's seat is said to be the theatre of the highest virtue, where everyone can learn the basic rudiments of an honourable life.

Then it is Calliope's turn to speak. Even though she is the protectress of epic poetry, she is shown with the tools of a sculptor, and she states that she creates marble monuments. However, the crux of her speech is a series of questions devised to amplify the concept that epic poetry is meant not only to celebrate glorious military feats of the past (as epitomized by Homer's *Iliad*, Lucan's *Pharsalia* [*Bellum civile*], and Statius's *Thebaid*) but also those personalities who have gained renown through their moral and spiritual merits. This assertion, by calling attention to Turobois'kyi's poetry, attests to his understanding of the perfect hero and, more generally, of the heroic theme. This expansion of the topic of epic poetry, which considers all activities involving the intellect as noble and no less worthy of being celebrated than military feats on the battlefield, reflects the Renaissance approach to the *heroicum carmen* – designed to surpass the celebration of *res gestae regumque ducumque et tristia bella*, as Horace defined the topic of the heroic poem.

That a moral victory is superior to a military one is also underscored by the matching, through polyptotons, of words with the root of *victoria*, such as *vincere, victor, victrix*: in lines 183 and 187 we find the words *victrix* and *virtus* and *vincerit* and *virtus*, which, with the aid of alliteration, create a powerful association between virtue and the victory over one's senses and passions that virtue is able to grant.

Moreover, in lines 184–6 Calliope declares that only those who are able to rein in their soul (i.e., only those who cultivate virtue) are able to achieve military victories. Since the personage who is celebrated for cultivating virtue here is the archimandrite of the most important Orthodox monastery in the Hetmanate, it is implied that victory comes from God:

161   Vix sacro Clio finivit ab ore loquelas
      Scalpriger interea chalibem marmorque subornat
      Calliopè, nostramque movent miracula mentem.

Quo tandem properet seu quos heroas amico
165   Carmine contendat celebrare ac marmore duro
Nec latuit divam mens nostra attonita vatem
Subridensque sacro nobis haec ore locuta:
Quid tandem nostros vates miraris ad actus?
Quid dubiumve movent scalprumque silexque?
170   Haeccine sola putas scuamato credita Marti?
Nervum clara aut tantum nota acta referre
Quos Bellona sua victores aegide fecit
Aut quos Iliace celebrat victoria Troiae,
Bellaque Pharsaliae, celebris vel diruta Thebeis?
175   Credita non tantum saxo mea scalpra fatigat
Gloria Archivorum, aut victor post bella Gradivus,
Famae vivacis pernotos ire nepotes
Altum sollicitans multo gravate cothurno;
Gestit et innocuus sua victor saxa iugali
180   Refrenare, quibus solido det nomina seclo.
Nec melius saevus victores ensis adaptat
Sero laudandos post praelia crede nepoti
Quam victrix proprij virtus firmissima sensus.
Non qui devictis dominatur gentibus, at qui
185   Frenati felix animi moderatur habenas
Carpaciam molem in sua mandat lucra revinci.
Vincerit[40] effrenos natu Krokovia virtus,
Cum sensus, animos libitu pro rite gubernans,
Praefixam valeant haud quo transcendere metam,
190   Marmora dura fero scalpro scindenda profundè:
Altius aeternae teneant quo stigmata famae.
Krokovi faciamque orbi fluitare verendum
Nomen marmoribus, laudum non absque trophaeis.
Protulit innocuae posuitque silentia linguae.

(161   As soon as Clio finished her speech from the sacred mouth,
meanwhile Calliope, as a chiseler, prepares the arrow point and
the marble, and wonders move our mind.
The place, at last, to which the divine prophetess hastens or the heroes
165   she strives to celebrate with [her] dear song and with the hard marble
did not escape notice by our astonished mind,
and, smiling, she uttered these things with her sacred mouth:
"Why, finally, O poet, do you look with admiration at our acts?
Or which doubt do the chisel and the flint excite?

170   Do you think only these things are to be entrusted to scaly Mars?
        That the bowstring [should] report only illustrious and famous deeds,
        The men whom Bellona made winners with her shield,
        or those whom the victory of Troy celebrates in Greek,
        And the wars of Pharsalia, or the destruction of renowned Thebes?
175   Not only the glory of the Achaeans, entrusted to me, wearies my chisel
        with stone, or Mars, victor after the wars,
        who incites the renowned descendants of long-lived fame to advance
        into the deep sea, with the burden of a heavy cothurnus;
        the innocent victor as well is eager to curb his own stones for
180   his wife, with which he may give names to a solid age.
        Neither, believe me, the savage sword prepares winners, whom
        after battles tardily their descendant will have to praise better[41]
        than the steadiest virtue, winner of one's own senses.
        Not he who rules over subdued peoples but he who happy governs
185   the reins of a curbed soul, commands that the huge Carpathian
        mass be conquered for his gain.
        Krokovian virtue will have won those born unbridled
        by leading the senses and the souls according to his will in a right way
        so that they may not step over the set goal.
190   I carry marbles hard to be deeply torn with the chisel:
        So that they may preserve higher the marks of an eternal fame.
        And I will make Krokovs'kyi's revered name flow with marbles
        in the world, not without trophies of praises.'
        Thus she spake and imposed silence on her harmless tongue.)

The emphasis in Calliope's words on the superiority of moral victories over military ones is not perfunctory, considering the year in which the poem was written, 1699. Indeed, in three years preceding, 1695–8, there had been a massive deployment of Russian and Ukrainian Cossack troops, led by Hetman Ivan Mazepa, to conquer the fortresses of Kizikermen and Azov. The siege of the two fortresses, particularly Azov, resulted in a multitude of victims. Moreover, the participation of Ukrainian Cossack forces in Russia's campaigns against Turkey and the Crimea were practically a constant feature of Mazepa's hetmancy. In addition, memories of the period known as the Ruin, which plunged Ukraine into a spiral of internecine strife, violence, and growing decline for nearly thirty years (1657–87), were still fresh. Thus, the constant, almost daily, experience of armed conflict is certainly at the root of the implicit desire for peace contained in lines 161–94.

However, the central idea, expressed in lines 184–6, is that military victories are also brought about by virtue; a similar idea is expressed by Turobois'kyi in his 1700 manual of rhetoric *Cornucopiae artis oratoriae*,[42] in a sermon on *sapientia* entitled *Oratio in laudem Sapientiae*. The central concept of the oration is expressed in the Ciceronian sentence on which it is based: *Sapientia nihil est praestantius* (Nothing is more excellent than wisdom). In the main section of this work Turobois'kyi, arguing that while earthly riches and power are perishable since they are dispensed by a fickle fate, declares, *Sola sapientia extra fortunae luxum tuta capessitur* (Only prudent wisdom is seized eagerly without the luxury of luck), and reinforces his thoughts on the immortality of man's spiritual and intellectual achievements in these two famous lines: *Vivitur ingenio, caetera mortis erunt* (Genius lives on, all else will belong to death; *Elegiae in Maecenatem*, Appendix Virgiliana, I, line 38) and *Ingenio stat sine morte decus* (Time cannot wither talents' well earned-fame; Propertius, *Elegies* III, 2, line 26). Moreover, the author asserts, only wisdom generates military victories that are stable and whose outcome is long lasting, and he summarizes this idea in the following statement, which differs slightly from what had been said in lines 184–6: *Sola eruditae Palladis opera Carpaciam molem in sua mandat lucra revinci* (Only the work of the learned Pallas commands that the huge Carpathian mass be conquered to its own gain).[43] In this statement on the impossibility of achieving steady victories without wisdom one may also read an implicit desire for peace, for only peace allows for the cultivation of wisdom. Krokovs'kyi's opinion on this topic is subsequently reinforced by his appeal to peace contained in his introduction to the 1702 edition of the Kyivan Caves Patericon. As Marker has pointed out, through the skillful use of allegories, biblical quotations, and the visual narrative offered to him by an engraving he commissioned for this edition, Krokovs'kyi celebrates Peter as the victor over the infidel Ottomans, while also entreating him to desist from embarking on new offensive wars.[44]

Urania's speech, as is to be expected, is centred around astronomical mythology. She also admits to having abandoned Parnassus in order to rush to Ioasaf's seat; having tired of the habitual vision of the known skies, she now enjoys the pleasures of Ioasaf's home, whose splendor eclipses the bright sky. It is made clear that Krokovs'kyi's abode is the Kyivan Caves Monastery. The consecration of this new centre of the Muses is decreed by Phoebus himself, who has established his seat here, in the very spot where the blazing gem of the consecrated Varlaam (Iasyns'kyi) had shone.[45] However, the female governor of the skies is the Christian protectress, the Virgin of the Caves, called *inclyta moderatrix caeli*. This characterization exemplifies the coexistence in the poetry of this period of pagan and Christian protectors, as well as the reaffirmation of the supremacy of Christian patrons. The founders of the Kyivan Caves Monastery, Antonii and Feodosii, are likened to the two stars Phosphorus (morning star) and Hesperus (evening star), which in reality are the planet Venus in its morning and evening guises. Krokovs'kyi is then depicted as taking part in a kind of sanctification or assumption to the heavens; the remains of the monks buried in the monastery caves are likened to the stars of Ioasaf's vault (metonymically compared to the celestial vault by the appellation *Astrisonus*).

The fact that the poet dwells upon the Virgin Mary calls attention both to her function as protectress of the Kyivan Caves Monastery (formally known as the Monastery of the Dormition of the Mother of God in Kyiv) and to what Florovskii defines as Krokovs'kyi's theological mindset, which he would have acquired during his stay in Rome. In it, the central place is occupied by veneration of the Virgin Mary conceived without original sin.[46] However, as Florovskii also states, among the Kyivan religious elite of the time the devotion to Marianism and the cult of the Immaculate Conception of the Virgin Mary was an established fact. Moreover, devotion to the Virgin Mary as the supreme Christian protectress and inspirer of poetry is reflected in Mohylanian poetics, in which she is the dedicatee of a number of prefatory poems:[47]

195 Vranie tandem cordis sic fatur ab imo:
Si tibi Thespiadis Vates cognoscere gressus
Est mens? Me Ioasaph scito in tentoria ferri.
Hactenus excelsum semper speculabar Olimpum,
Sydera quo vergant, remeet quo colle per axem
200 Queis Phaebus fessosve caballos abluat undis,
Fulgida queis Hecate nocturnis surgit ab oris,
Aut ubi consurgit roseo de, aurora, cubili,
Titan auratos demum fert unde capillos.
Ast haec iam nostris speculatio non placet oclis,
205 Nativum specto dum summi pegma Krokowi,
Quod caelum proprio superat fulgore serenum.
Hic sua supremo deposta cubilia Phaebo
Ignea quo Barlaae sacrati gemma reluxit.
Splendida perpetuam hoc defixit Trivia sedem
210 Virgo Peczarei Moderatrix Inclyta Caeli
Phosphorus hoc renidet sacer ac Antonius Arae.
Rossius hoc fulget Theodosius Hesperus alter.
Quotquot Peczareis decumbunt Corpora Criptis
Quid nisi sunt stellae Ioasaphi tegmine captae,
215 Non secus ac celsa Astrisoni aula haec continet astra.
Haec igitur longis speculer quo pegmata seclis
Faustaque de visis semper sibi[48] ut omina reddam,
Haec mens, hic animus Parnassi haec causa relicti.

(195   Finally, Urania thus speaks from the depth of her heart:
        "If you, O poet, intend to know the steps of the
        Thespiad, may you know, O Ioasaf, that I am brought into the tents.[49]
        Till now I always watched the lofty Olympus,
        whither the stars be directed, by which hill comes Phoebus back
200   through the sky or with which waves he washes the tired horses,
        from which night shores rises the gleaming Hecate,
        or where the dawn springs up from her rose-coloured bed,
        At last, from where Titan brings his golden hair.
        But our eyes now do not like this watching,
205   while I look at the native pulpit of the supreme Krokovs'kyi
        Which, with its own splendor, surpasses the clear sky.
        Here the supreme Phoebus has set up his own dens,
        Through whom the sparkling gem of the consecrated Varlaam shone out.
        This pulpit the splendid Trivia fixed as a perpetual seat,
210   The Virgin, illustrious governess of the Caves' sky,
        For this shines the sacred morning star and Anthony of the altar.
        For this the Rus'ian Feodosii shines like another Hesperus.
        However many bodies lie down in the Caves' crypts,
        What are they but stars captured from Ioasaf's vault,
215   No differently from how Jupiter's lofty hall contains these stars.
        Therefore, in order that I look at these pulpits throughout the long ages,
        and in order for me always to return auspicious omens for him,
        This is the intention, this is the feeling, this is the reason for having left
        Parnassus.)

Finally, Polyhymnia is shown gesturing while she speaks; indeed, her speech is full of movement. Since she is the one who closes the Muses' discourse, her words contain encouragements and entreaties to the poet to sing the supreme name of Ioasaf. In her words, the sanctification process is carried further: Apollo/Phoebus runs towards the vault of his father Zeus/Jupiter, desiring that the high name of Ioasaf be carried beyond both beds of the sun (*solis utrumque cubile ultra*). This expression is used to indicate the two cardinal points, east and west, and, by extension, the whole earth, and thus Ioasaf's name, should be carried beyond the earth to the sky. By showing that the pagan gods and goddesses pay homage and offer assistance to Ioasaf, this image is meant to emphasize the superiority of Christianity. The use of hyperbolic images and style is suggested by the poetics of the baroque, which viewed it as a powerful way of mythologizing one's history and creating a fantastic one wherein the names of heroes and characters of pagan mythology should express the extraordinary merits of the celebrated character, astonishing the reader:

219   Conticet Vranie: loquitur Polymnia gestu:
220   Neque morare Deas cunctae nam currimus illuc
       Auratum Ioasaphi ubi magni pegma resedit
       Dicturae laudes suaves cantusque daturae
       Inclyta lauratis ornantes tecta coronis.
       Haec mandat **virtus** Ioasaphi, haec cura camaenis,
225   Hic animus Phaebo currenti ad tegmina patris
       Quo per tesqua rotet sublimis laurea Pindi
       Dignandum nomen, vel solis utrumque cubile
       Vltra praeproperis ducat venerable [*sic*][50] cothurnis.
       I sequere, et gressus nostros comitare poëta
230   Te decet excelsum nomen celebrare Parentis,
       Linquere nec Musas, nec magnum credito vatem:
       Scilicet hac causa his te Pegasus intulit oris.

(219   Urania is silent: Polyhymnia speaks with gestures:
220   "And do not keep the goddesses, in fact we all run thither,
       Where the golden pulpit of the great Ioasaf resides,
       to tell charming praises and to sing chants
       Adorning the illustrious roofs with laurel garlands.
       This Ioasaf's virtue commands, this is the concern of the Muse
225   This desires Phoebus, who runs toward his father's roofs,
       so that through the deserts Pindus's sublime laurel
       may rotate the esteemed name, or may lead it, venerable,
       beyond both beds of the sun with his swiftiest *cothurni*.
       Go, follow, and accompany our steps, O poet.
230   It befits you to celebrate the eminent name of the parent
       and not to abandon the muses, and not to believe the poet great:
       Certainly for this reason Pegasus brought you onto these shores.)

Once the Muses have finished speaking, the poet finds himself unable to do anything. In the last part of the poem (lines 233–63), just like at the beginning, the poet declares that he is frightened and now unable to fill with his praise the void left behind by the Muses. This *topos modestiae* is allegorically expressed by the *sertus incultus* (unrefined wrath) that he would only be able to weave with his own strength and then by his own *rudior Musa* (rather rude Muse), which is said to characterize his poetic output. Finally, following the advice of

Apollo and the Muses, he decides to present Ioasaf, protector of the Mother of the Caves, with the few works that he has dedicated to the Virgin Mary.[51] In conclusion, Turobois'kyi expresses the wish for Krokovs'kyi, archimandrite of the Kyivan Caves Monastery, to introduce a new golden age dedicated to "our powerful Goddess" (*Diva potens nostra*), the "celebrated Muse" (*Celebrata Camaena*), which, in light of the above, can only refer to the Mother of God.

The analysis of Turobois'kyi's poem dedicated to Krokovs'kyi helps shed some much-needed light on the ideological discourse of the Kyiv Mohylanian elite at the turn of the seventeenth century. It was a time when the Kyiv Mohyla Collegium flourished thanks to the generous protection of Hetman Mazepa and Metropolitan Iasyns'kyi's intelligent and far-sighted policy of strengthening the Ukrainian Church. During this period the Collegium was granted implicit official status as an academy and confirmation of its prerogatives and privileges. After some delay, its curriculum mostly caught up to similar academies in Poland-Lithuania and Western Europe, and its finest students were sent both to the West and the East: to the former, to pursue their studies in Western European schools and academies, and to the latter, to contribute to educational and cultural development in the Russian capital. Ioasaf Krokovs'kyi, former rector of the Kyiv Mohyla Collegium, who acceded to the second-most-important post in the Orthodox Church in the Hetmanate after the metropolitan, is depicted as the perfect incarnation, in his *sancta eruditio*, of the Renaissance ideal of wisdom, particularly in its Erasmian articulation. This portrayal is a tacit assertion of Ukraine's full-fledged assimilation of and participation in contemporary European culture. At the same time, Turbois'kyi, who in his poetic celebration of Krokovs'kyi as a model of virtue availed himself masterfully of the lexical and rhetorical arsenal of the cultural language of contemporary Europe, sought to make a contribution to the project that endeavoured to portray the key institutions of Ukrainian Orthodoxy and their representatives as Wisdom's abode. My next project will be to study other literary works devoted to Krokovs'kyi in order to determine whether their representation of the future Metropolitan of Kyiv, Halych, and all Rus' (1708–18) provides further evidence of my hypothesis.

Notes

1   The bulk of this poetry is still in manuscript form, as are the manuals of poetics
    in which it appeared. I have analysed and translated into English or Italian some
    poetic compositions mainly, but not exclusively, of the *genus demonstrativum*
    type, in several articles: Giovanna Siedina, "Neo-Latin Poetry in the Kyivan
    Poetics: Ukraine in the European *Latinitas*," in *Ukraine's Re-Integration into*

Europe: A Historical, Historiographical and Politically Urgent Issue, ed. Giovanna Brogi Bercoff and Giulia Lami (Alessandria: Edizioni Dell'Orso, 2005), 197–226; "Il retaggio di Orazio nella poesia neolatina delle poetiche kieviane: alcuni modi della sua ricezione," in *Kiev e Leopoli: il "testo" culturale*, ed. Maria Grazia Bartolini and Giovanna Brogi Bercoff (Florence: Firenze University Press, 2007), 11–36; "Un poema epico neolatino su Ivan Mazepa," *Studi Slavistici* 4, no. 1 (2007): 85–115; "Bellica virtus: le celebrazione di Ivan Mazepa nelle poetiche kieviane. Spunti di riflessione," in *Nel mondo degli Slavi: Incontri e dialoghi tra culture; Studi in onore di Giovanna Brogi Bercoff*, ed. M.G. Di Salvo, G. Moracci, and G. Siedina (Florence: Firenze University Press, 2008), 2: 571–81; "The Poetic Laboratory of the Kyiv Mohylanian Poetics: Some Practical Illustrations," *Studi Slavistici* 8, no. 1 (2012): 41–60. For a brief overview of other studies on this topic, see Siedina, "Poetic Laboratory."

2 Gary Marker, "Love One's Enemies: Ioasaf Krokovs'kyi's Advice to Peter in 1702," *Harvard Ukrainian Studies* 29, no. 1–4 (2007): 193–223, here 194.

3 I refer to three panegyrics, the first of which is "Iter laureatum" by H. Vyshnevskyi, published in part in *Antolohiia ukraïns'koï poeziï* (Kyiv: Dnipro, 1984), 1: 228–36. The other two panegyrics, "Insigne honorum … solium" and "Monumentum perennis gloriae" by Ivan Narol's'kyi, dedicated to Krokovs'kyi's ascension to the Metropolitan See (1708), have been published in the anthology Valerii Shevchuk and Vasyl' Iaremenko, comp., *Slovo mnohotsinne: Khrestomatiia ukraïns'koï literatury, stvorenoï riznymy movamy v epokhu Renesansu (druha polovyna XV–XVI stolittia ta v epokhu Baroko (kinets' XVI–XVIII stolittia)*, vol. 3, *Literatura vysokoho Baroko (1632–1709 rik)* (Kyiv: Vyd-vo "Akonit," 2006), 781–3. The first of Narol's'kyi's poems was first published in 1982, in the anthology *Apollonova liutnia: Kyïvs'ki poety XVII–XVIII st.* (Kyiv: Vyd-vo TSK LKSMU "Molod'," 1982), 144–5. For an analysis of these two panegyrics, see Giovanna Siedina, "O felice Rus', rallegrati! I panegirici per l'ascesa al soglio metropolitano di Joasaf Krokovs'kyj," in *Linee di confine: Separazioni e processi di integrazione nello spazio culturale slavo*, ed. Giovanna Moracci and Alberto Alberti (Florence: Firenze University Press, 2013), 121–45.

4 As far as I know, his poetics course has not been preserved, while his manual of rhetoric is extant in manuscript form. See Viacheslav Briukhovets'kyi, *Kyievo-Mohylians'ka akademiia v imenakh XVII–XVIII st.: Entsyklopedychne vydannia* (Kyiv: Vydavnychyi dim "KM Academiia," 2001), 298.

5 Theology was probably taught earlier at the Kyiv Mohyla Collegium as part of the philosophy course, but it did not enjoy independent status. See Nikolai Petrov, "Kievskaia Akademiia vo vtoroi polovine XVII veka," *Trudy Kievskoi dukhovnoi akademii* 3, no. 9 (1895): 46–8. Petrov emphasizes the innovative character of Thomistic theology as taught by Krokovs'kyi. Besides this fundamental

recognition, during his rectorship Krokovs'kyi also "initiated several reforms, including the practice of appointing a permanent accountant to balance income and expenditures." See Alexander Sydorenko, *The Kievan Academy in the Seventeenth Century* (Ottawa: University of Ottawa Press, 1977), 61.

6 See the provisions of the tsarist charter dated 11 January 1694 in Petrov, "Kievskaia Akademiia," 51. As for the permission to teach philosophy and theology – implicit recognition of the Kyiv Mohyla Collegium's status as an academy – the tsarist charter simply acknowledged an already existing situation. (Official tsarist recognition of its status as an academy came only in 1701.)

7 Krokovs'kyi was Iasyns'kyi's closest collaborator in the last years of the Kyivan metropolitan's life. See Viktor Askochenskii, *Kiev s drevneishim ego uchilishchem Akademieiu* (Kyiv: V. Univ. tip., 1856), 2: 5–6. For a detailed description of Krokovs'kyi's praiseworthy activities for the benefit of the Kyiv Mohyla Collegium and the Ukrainian Church, see Stepan Golubev, *Kievskaia Akademiia v kontse XVII i v nachale XVIII stoletii* (Kyiv: Tip. I.I. Gorbukova, 1901), 6–8, 19, 53–8, 69–70.

8 Marker, "Love One's Enemies," 212.

9 See Natalia Pylypiuk, "Catherine of Alexandria's Crown of Golden Liberty" in the present volume and her article, "The Face of Wisdom in the Age of Mazepa," in *Mazepa and His Time: History, Culture, Literature, Political Thought*, ed. Giovanna Siedina (Alessandria: Edizioni Dell'Orso 2004), 367–400.

10 See Sergei Averintsev, "K uiasneniiu smysla nadpisi nad konkhoi tsentral'noi apsidy Sofii Kievskoi," in *Drevnerusskoe iskusstvo i khudozhestvennaia kul'tura domongol'skoi Rusi* (Moscow: Nauka, 1972), 25–49. Averintsev does a fascinating job of reconstructing the evolution of the concept of σοφία in Greek and Judeo-Christian culture and dwells at length on the sophiological interpretation of the Virgin Mary.

11 Its full title reads: *Hymettus extra Atticam duplici tramite neovatibus scandendus, seu Poesis bipartita tum ligatae tum solutae orationis praeceptionibus instructa Roxolanaeque iuventuti in Collegio Kijovo Mohil [sic] proposita anno quo Turca ab deleto pax nata gubernat in orbe hIC DoMInans terrIs Cara feraXque VIret.* The manuscript is stored at the Manuscript Institute (IR) of the National Library of Ukraine in Kyiv (NBU) under call number 315 П / 122.

12 See, e.g., Ryszard Łużny, *Pisarze kręgu Akademii Kijowsko-Mohylańskiej a literatura Polska: Z dziejów związków kulturalnych polsko-wschodniosłowiańskich w XVII–XVIII w.* (Cracow: Uniwersytet Jagielloński, 1966), 83; Vitalii Masliuk, *Latynomovni poetyky i rytoryky XVII–pershoï polovyny XVIII st. ta ïkh rol'u rozvytku teoriï literatury na Ukraïni* (Kyiv: Naukova dumka, 1983), 56.

13 A griphus is a riddle in which the letters forming the name of a person or object are described indirectly, through objects that are similar to them in shape. For

example, the letter O can be likened to the sun or a globe, the letter C to the moon, the letter I to a column, and so on. By guessing the letters that are hidden behind the objects described in the griphus and by arranging them correctly, one decodes the ciphered name.

14 Turobois'kyi's manuals of rhetoric and philosophy (courses he did not teach because he was already in Moscow) are extant in manuscript form. See Briukhovets'kyi, *Kyievo-Mohylians'ka Akademiia v imenakh*, 548–9.

15 See Sergei Smirnov, *Istoriia Moskovskoi Slaviano-Greko-Latinskoi Akademii* (Moscow: V. Got'e, 1855), 205. According to another scholar, in 1710 Turobois'kyi left for Kyiv, where he died. See Konstantin Kharlampovich, *Malorossiiskoe vlianie na velikorusskuiu tserkovnuiu zhizn'* (Kazan': Izd. Knizhnago magazina M. A. Golubeva, 1914), 1: 570–4.

16 V. Grebeniuk and O. Derzhavina, *Panegiricheskaia literatura petrovskogo vremeni* (Moscow: Nauka, 1979), 21.

17 Grebeniuk and Derzhavina, *Panegiricheskaia literatura*, 63–6. See Irina Hmelevskikh, "Dve knigi o rimskikh drevnostiakh Bartoli-Bellori i ikh perevody na russkii iazyk iz biblioteki Petra Velikogo," *Cahiers du monde russe* 51, no. 1 (2010): 101–20, here 115–16; Petr Morozov, *Istoriia russkogo teatra* (St Petersburg: Tip. V. Demakova, 1889), 1: 326.

18 See L. Chernaia, "Obraz Petra I v panegirikakh Iosifa Turoboiskogo," *Poltavskaia bitva i ee mezhdunarodnoe znachenie: Tezisy dokladov iubileinoi mezhdunarodnoi nauchnoi konferentsii* (Moscow: Ministerstvo kul'tury Rossiiskoi Federatsii, 2009).

19 Askochenskii, *Kiev s drevneishim ego uchilishchem*, 1: 314, dwells only briefly on Turobois'kyi's Moscow period. Petrov, *Kievskaia Akademiia*, 3: 56, merely states that Turobois'kyi taught rhetoric in 1701.

20 For a description of them, see Nikolai Petrov, *Opisanie rukopisnykh sobranii, nakhodiashchikhsia v gorode Kieve* (Moscow: Universitetskaia tipografiia, 1891), no. 240 (p. 279) and no. 154 (p. 247), respectively. Turobois'kyi's manual of rhetoric (*Cornucopiae artis oratoriae*) contains models of orations dedicated to Krokovs'kyi and Mazepa. As far as I have been able to determine, there is no surviving correspondence between Krokovs'kyi and Turobois'kyi.

21 The attribution of *silvae* to epic poetry in this and other Mohylanian manuals seems to reflect a certain blurring of the boundaries between epics and the poetry of praise with its roots in the Renaissance didactic theory of art. See O. B. Hardison, *The Enduring Monument: A Study of the Idea of Praise in Renaissance Literary Theory and Practice* (Chapel Hill: University of North Carolina Press, 1962), esp. 43–67 and 71–2. All genres traditionally ascribed to *sylvae/silvae*, notwithstanding their different themes and forms, contained the element of praise. For their treatment, see J.C. Scaliger, *Poetices libri septem* (Lugduni: Apud

Antonium Vincentium, MDLXI, 1561), bk. III, chap. C and subsequent chapters. The fact that the genres attributed to *sylvae* contain the element of praise is also highlighted in some Mohylanian manuals. See, e.g., *Cunae Bethleemicae* (1687), the manuscript of which is held NBU, IR, call number 499 П / 1729. See also Jakub Niedźwiedź, *Nieśmiertelne teatra sławy: Teoria i praktyka twórczości panegirycznej na Litwie w XVII–XVIII w.* (Cracow: Księg. Akademicka, 2003), 63–4, 174–5.

22 Although the poet states that his poem was written for the archimandrite's birthday, it cannot be totally ascribed to the *carmen genthliacum* because the latter was generally written in honour of a newborn.

23 The full title is: "Entheus Poeta ad natales Illustrissimi ac R[everendissimi] in Christo Patris Ioasaphi Krokowski Magni magnae Lavrae Peczariensis Archimandritae Patris ac Patroni sui clientissimi Ferias, tributarias Operis Primitias consecrans, Anno quo Fortunna [sic] maneas preclarus posco Iosaphe" (Inspired Poet for the Birthday of the Most Illustrious and Most Revered Father in Christ Ioasaf Krokowski, Great Archimandrite of the Great Cave Monastery, Father and Patron of His Most Protected [Client], Consecrating the Festive Days, Tributary First-Offerings of the Work, in the Year in Which I Ask, O Ioasaf, that You Remain Splendid in Fortune).

24 For a useful overview of the theory of poetic divine frenzy from Plato to the premodern age, see Ernst Robert Curtius, *European Literature and the Latin Middle Ages*, trans. W. R. Trask (London: Routledge and Kegan Paul, 1979), 474–5.

25 The correct word is "paludatos."

26 See Propertius, *Elegies*, IV, 1, 131–2.

27 The author is probably referring to Krokovs'kyi's supervision and editing of different religious texts in his position as archimandrite of the Kyivan Caves Monastery, as well as to his 1698 Akathist to St Barbara (Marker, "Love One's Enemies," 201–5). These writing and publishing activities are part of Krokovs'kyi's efforts to take the light of religion out of the shadows in line 130.

28 See Eugene F. Rice, Jr., *The Renaissance Idea of Wisdom* (Cambridge, MA: Harvard University Press, 1958), esp. 149–77.

29 Ibid., 149.

30 Ibid., 213–14.

31 Ibid., 161.

32 Siedina, "O felice Rus', rallegrati!"

33 The correct word is probably "species."

34 The author uses "sibi" instead of "ei."

35 From the metrical point of view, "ferret" would be correct here.

36 Here too the author uses "sibi" instead of "ei."

37 Should be "merita."

38 In other words, "Why should I say more?"

39 Known as the tyrant of Samos (538–522 BC), Polycrates built an aqueduct, a large temple of Hera, and a palace on this Greek island. In 522 he celebrated an uncommon double festival in honour of the god Apollo of Delos and Delphi. Under his rule Samos attracted sculptors, scientists, and poets, one of whom was Anacreon.

40 The correct word is "vicerit."

41 What is meant here is that the sword does not produce more victors than virtue.

42 The full title is *Cornucopiae artis oratoriae omni genio eloquentiae fructu ad genium et ingenium gentis Roxolanae accomodo. Fecundae in Kijovo Mohilaeani Athaenei promptuario neo Rhetori oblatae anno quo faecunda Virgo Puritatis fructum generi humano salutiferum proposuit. 1700.* The manuscript is stored at NBU, IR, call number ДС/ p 240.

43 Most likely, the phrase "Carpacia moles" allegorically signifies a fortress or an enemy who is difficult to conquer or subdue.

44 Marker, "Love One's Enemies," 208–21.

45 The poet is hinting at the fact that Iasyns'kyi, who was one of Krokovs'kyi's teachers, had also been archimandrite of the Kyivan Caves Monastery before him.

46 In *Puti russkogo bogosloviia* (Paris: YMCA Press, 1983), Georges Florovsky states that it was precisely during Krokovs'kyi's rectorship that students' congregations known as *Sodalitas marianae* arose. Their members devoted their lives to the Virgin Mary and her Immaculate Conception, and had to swear an oath to profess (and defend against heretics) the doctrine that "Mary is not only without actual mortal or venial sin, but also without original sin." On students' congregations at the Kyiv Mohyla Collegium, including the Marian ones founded during Krokovs'kyi's rectorship, see Petrov, "Kievskaia Akademiia," 580–2.

47 For an analysis of these poems, see Dzh. S'iedina [Giovanna Siedina], "Novolatyns'ki virshovani prysviaty ta peredmovy do Kyievo-Mohylians'kykh poetyk," in *Studien zu Sprache, Literatur und Kultur bei den Slaven: Gedenkschrift für George Y. Shevelov aus Anlass seines 100. Geburtstages und 10. Todestages*, ed. Andrii Danylenko and Serhii Vakulenko (Munich: Otto Sagner, 2012), 341–70.

48 Again, this word should probably have been "ei."

49 This image may allude to Krokovs'kyi's family coat of arms, which featured a tent.

50 Probable misspelling of "venerabile."

51 I have not seen any poetic works dedicated to the Virgin Mary attributed to Turobois'kyi, except for the prefatory poem in his manual cited above.

PART TWO

Recovering Europe: Ukraine's Romanticisms and Modernisms

Ukrainian Prose from the 1800s to the 1860s: In Quest of a European Modernity

MARKO PAVLYSHYN

"Modernity" in this inquiry is the configuration of economic, social, and cultural circumstances ascendant in the west of Europe from the Enlightenment onward – and, in time, practically everywhere else.[1] Two features of modernity are relevant to this discussion: first, among educated people, a widespread commitment to secular humanism imagined as the fruit of human reason and thus valid in all cultures; and, second, a belief that the nation is the largest natural unit of human organization and one that should express itself through a unique national culture and, usually, a sovereign nation state.

Scholars have noted the role of literature in shaping both of these dimensions of modernity,[2] but the special function in this process of literary prose has commanded less attention. In modernity the efficient transmission of meaning and, accordingly, intelligibility and transparency became prime discursive virtues, facilitating the connection, essential in modernity, between communication and action. In an ideal situation this connection would be enacted in venues for the expression and discussion of socially and politically pressing matters (parliament, press, and salon) that were labelled by Habermas and others as the "public sphere." Here the consensus would be built that, in turn, would legitimate action, state and private, in the public interest. The vehicle for such communication in the public sphere could only be prose.

For most of its history prose has been regarded as a "neutral" and "natural" means of deploying language – in contrast to poetry, which is wrought and aesthetically charged. Rhetoric and more recent work of the formalists and the narratologists have alerted us to the fact that the neutrality and naturalness of prose, especially literary prose, are but relative: that prose "deforms" everyday language as poetry does.[3] On the other hand, it has also been recognized that the signifying practices characteristic of most prose do, indeed, "attempt to establish ... an effect of neutrality of subject position" by means of "strategies that appear 'natural.'"[4] The connection of prose to modernity was well observed by Benedetto Croce, who held that "literature" (in its modern, post-1760s, sense)[5] is a body of writing in which the aesthetic and emotive immediacy of poetry is balanced by the functional, civilizing, and communicative quality of prose.[6]

Modern European nation building owes an obvious historical debt to poetry with its well-attested ability to generate and generalize myths of identity and to fill the idea of nation with emotional content. Yet prose is no less important to the national project. Possession of a functioning, communicative prose signals a link to the rationality and efficiency of the modern that helps establish a nation as a participant in the international community of similarly modern nations. Prose is an essential part of the Crocean compound of prose and poetry that constitutes the civilized modern (and therefore, by definition, European) literature that can serve as a symbol of a nation, command the respect of its members, and provide generous content to a national education.

The imperative of a practicable prose was seldom articulated by Ukrainian literati of the early nineteenth century – such figures as Ivan Kotliarevs'kyi, Petro Hulak-Artemovs'kyi, Ievhen Hrebinka, and members of the group often referred to as the Kharkiv Romantic School, including Izmail Sreznevskii, Amvrosii Metlyns'kyi, and Mykola Kostomarov. Encouraged by the Europe-wide Herderian enthusiasm for the creativity of ordinary people, many of these writers focused their attention on folklore, especially the folksong and historical song, often seeking to emulate its "spirit" in their own works. Insofar as they did reflect upon the situation of the infant Ukrainian literature, they often invested disproportionate effort into their polemics against the dominance in the Ukrainian writing of their time of the powerful burlesque verse tradition engendered by Kotliarevs'kyi's *Eneïda*. Likewise, historians of modern Ukrainian letters have paid scant attention to role of prose in the genesis of a Ukrainian literature that could claim to be modern and European. The purpose of the following is to reflect on the contribution to a literature with these attributes by a selection of writers conventionally celebrated as its pioneers.

In the Ukrainian lands within the Russian Empire, to which the present observations are limited, obstacles in the path of the development of a modern Ukrainian prose were many. Educated Ukrainians inhabited two cultures, a Russian and a Ukrainian one, but were socialized into associating the former with prestige, high culture, and high social status, and the latter with an absence of prestige, informal folk culture, and the peasantry. Several activists, including at different times in their careers Kostomarov, Sreznevskii, and Danylo Mordovtsev, were dubious as to whether a modern high-culture project for Ukrainians was feasible or even desirable. Some treated what little prose there was as part not of a modern but an antiquarian project. Hryhorii Kvitka-Osnovianenko's stories, for example, were framed as nostalgic endeavours to record the fading charms of a doomed patriarchal and rustic lifestyle, not as steps along the path towards a modern form of communication. Unsurprisingly, given this context, which we would recognize as colonial and marked by a dominance of the imperial Russian culture so complete as to be regarded as natural, many activists of the national movement failed to identify the promise of modern prose when at last, in the works of Marko Vovchok, it appeared. Finally, the implicit cultural impediments to the development of Ukrainian cultural connections to European modernity became explicit in 1863 when the Valuev circular forbade the publication in Ukrainian of any non-fictional writing and especially any writing intended to further the education of ordinary people, permitting the publication only of belles-lettres.

Scholars have observed that members of the Ukrainian gentry writing in the early nineteenth century, whether in Russian or Ukrainian, conceived of their work as an informal provincial supplement to the mainstream literature generated in St Petersburg and Moscow and disseminated to the rest of the empire by the metropolitan journals.[7] Their writings (and their dramatic works) catered to a demand for the reflection of their local identities and ethos, including nostalgic affection for the patriarchal old-world practices of the Cossack-derived social elite and, not infrequently, a sentimental attachment to the culture of the peasants upon whose exploitation their lifestyle depended. These mild affirmations of cultural distinctiveness within an overarching ideological context of empire loyalty were often self-deprecating and self-ironic, as was the case in Hryhorii Kvitka-Osnovianenko's "Suplika do pana Izdatelia" (Petition to Mr Publisher, 1833): "Not everything should be for the Russians: maybe we too need, you know, to have an idea of something ... not the whole lot, but a bit ... while in your opinion we're just ... compared to you, what are we?"[8]

Such informality and lack of pretension to a notable place at the table of "serious" metropolitan culture, and therefore to participation in the communicative sphere of European modernity, marked even the work conventionally considered the starting point of modern Ukrainian literature, Ivan Kotliarevs'kyi's *Eneïda*, his travesty on Virgil's *Aeneid*. When the first parts of the comic epic were published in 1798, they appeared without the author's knowledge or consent. Evidently, the author had been satisfied for the masterpiece to circulate in manuscript and did not seek broader publication for it. *Eneïda* made a crucial – and modern – contribution to a national symbolic system by bridging, for the first time, the gap between the historical heritage of the Cossacks and the contemporary lifestyles of Ukrainian gentry and peasants, thus invoking a trans-class image of the Ukrainian nation.[9] What is not generally recognized is that Kotliarevs'kyi also produced a respectable model for modern Ukrainian prose. His comedy *Natalka Poltavka,* imbued with the individualism and egalitarianism of the Enlightenment in its sentimentalist redaction, also commented on the linguistic situation in early nineteenth-century Ukraine. The untutored peasant girl Natalka is able to articulate coherently, in her own language, the tenets of a universalist humanism, while the official Voznyi, her unsuccessful suitor, comically mixes modern Russian with the old bookish language influenced by Church Slavonic. The possession of "elite" linguistic resources, therefore, does not a priori enable one to talk sense, while the language of ordinary folk has the resources to produce the stylistically neutral, transparent, intelligible discourse that is necessary and sufficient to express thoughts and feelings about the human condition. Vasyl' Chaplenko noted that the speech of Natalka and other characters from the lower social orders reflects Kotliarevs'kyi's realization, not widely shared by his contemporaries, that vernacular Ukrainian was neither intrinsically coarse nor especially gentle; rather, it was "neutral."[10]

Natalka Poltavka, first performed in 1819 but not published until 1838, though popular on the stage to this day, is unlikely to have greatly influenced the Romantic discussion of the Ukrainian language and its literary potential. This discussion drew its arguments mainly from observations based on folk poetry and the historical folk epic, the *duma*. Izmail Sreznevskii, a reader of Johann Gottfried Herder,[11] spared no superlatives early in his career in extolling the virtues of vernacular Ukrainian:

> At present, it seems, there remains no person to whom, and no purpose for which, one would need to demonstrate that Ukrainian (or, as others prefer to call it, Little Russian) is a language, and not a dialect of Russian or Polish, as some used to argue; and many are convinced that it is one of the richest of the Slavic tongues, yielding nothing, for example, to the Bohemian in abundance of words and expressions, the Polish in vividness, or the Serbian in mellifluousness; though yet unrefined, it may already compete with the learned languages in its syntactic elasticity and profusion. It is a language that is poetic, musical and colorful.[12]

Romantic respect for the folk genius and the language that bore it was reflected in the folkloric collections of Nikolai Tsertelev and Mykhailo Maksymovych, and in the integration of folkloric themes and motifs into the poetry of Levko Borovykovs'kyi, Amvrosii Metlyns'kyi, Mykola Kostomarov, Mykhailo Petrenko, and others. Yet the real status of Ukrainian in the Russian Empire of the first half of the nineteenth century was well symbolized by the publishing conventions of the time. In the typical almanac or anthology only the folkloric (or, occasionally, literary) texts appeared in Ukrainian. The rest was in Russian: title, publication information, permission of the censor, introduction, commentary, and scholarly apparatus. Furthermore, as if to emphasize the non-normative status of the language of the common people, many such publications contained the compilers' reflections, in Russian, on the form that a future standard Ukrainian orthography might take. Thus, the Ukrainian text was offered to readers as an object of scholarly or antiquarian interest, a thing to be studied and perhaps enjoyed, but by no means itself a vehicle for scholarship or critical discussion. The framework of public ratiocination and judgment within which these texts were to be used was imperial and constructed out of the language of empire. While bringing to light the distinctive cultural identity of the Ukrainian lands, it reinforced rather than challenged the Empire's power gradients and cultural hierarchies.

Calls by Ukrainian literati for a dignified literature sensitively representing thought and emotion more often than not were contradicted by the actual literary output of those same writers. In 1827 Petro Hulak-Artemovs'kyi published his translation of Goethe's poem "Der Fischer" in the Moscow journal *Vestnik Evropy*. The editor explained in a lengthy note that "out of curiosity [the author] decided to *see* whether it is possible to convey in the Little Russian language feelings that are tender, noble, and elevated, and that do not force the reader or listener to laugh, as does Kotliarevs'kyi's *Eneïda* and other verses written with the same aim" (emphasis in the original).[13] But mostly Hulak-Artemovs'kyi showed no wish to abstain from "forcing the reader or listener to laugh," systematically resorting to a "low style" characterized by colloquialism, barbarism, and the syntactical marks of conversational speech, all of which were in evidence in his imitations of three of Horace's odes.[14] In another context Hulak-Artemovs'kyi naturalized Horace as "po-nashomu *Haras'ko*, a po-moskovs'kii, lybon', Horatsii" (*Haras'ko* in our language, and Horace in Russian; emphasis in the original).[15] Even the translation of "Der Fischer," while not directly parodic or burlesque, was replete with exclamations, questions, and verbal forms such as "smyk," "t'okhk," "stuk," "hul'k," and "khliup" that are characteristic of vivid and dynamic, but highly informal diction.[16] Hulak's Ukrainian, characterized by the exaggeration and excessive use of a few features of conversational speech, took on the quality of a caricature of the voice of the common people. It became a medium not for the articulation of a new solidarity between the educated classes and "the people" but for the accentuation of the differences between them: "playing the artless peasant" in fact reinforced a regional *gentry* identity. By contrast, Hulak-Artemovs'kyi's translation of Milton into Russian affected a laboured high style full of archaisms, abstract nouns, and poeticisms; it was an attempt – perhaps not a very convincing one – to assert membership of the prestige world of Russian-language metropolitan culture. Nothing could more clearly convey what was, in the author's mind, the division of labour between the two languages. In a situation where writing in Ukrainian appeared to enforce a highly mannered linguistic performance that included playing the fool and assuming a peasant persona, it is scarcely surprising that the common-sense neutrality of prose confronted Ukrainian writers with special difficulties. The verse fabulist Ievhen Hrebinka, remarked one historian of the Ukrainian literary language, "did not dare" (*ne navazhyvsia*) to write prose.[17]

It was against this background that in the 1830s Hryhorii Kvitka-Osnovianenko produced the first sizeable body of Ukrainian-language fictional prose (although, like all of his contemporaries, he wrote most of his literary output and letters in Russian). As early as 1834, the ethnographer and historian Osyp Bodians'kyi lauded Kvitka-Osnovianenko as the pioneer of this genre in Ukrainian literature: "All praise to Mr Hryts'ko, who was the first so courageously and so colourfully to plunge upon his rampant steed into the domain of the narrative genre that today is so universally beloved."[18] Ever since, many historians of literature have greeted Kvitka, perhaps not quite deservedly, as the progenitor of "serious" Ukrainian prose.[19]

Kvitka was a country gentleman dedicated to the monarchy. While abhorring cruelty to peasants, he did not condemn serfdom per se and fluctuated between caricature and idealization in his depiction of the lower social orders. His attitude to things Ukrainian evolved from irony to sympathy: students of his life sometimes see him, the significantly older contemporary of the Kharkiv Romantics, as catching up in his middle age with the younger men's Romantic preoccupations. His early Russian-language "Malorossiiskie anekdoty" (Ukrainian Anecdotes, 1822) were self-deprecating comments on, sometimes, the collective folly of his countrymen, and sometimes their appealing generosity and lack of guile. His earliest use of Ukrainian-language prose came in three Russian-language plays featuring the character Shel'menko, a speaker of Ukrainian and, as his name suggests, a scoundrel.[20] Like most of Kvitka's comedies, these plays satirized general human foibles and corruption in the lower reaches of the government service. (Characters of higher official rank were reserved for deus ex machina appearances at the end to restore justice, punish the guilty, and assure the viewer that the tsarist system was not beyond repair.) Anchored in the burlesque tradition, Shel'menko's diction is part of the plays' repertoire of comic effects. Shel'menko switches from an archaic learned language (sometimes biblical, sometimes the "chancellery language … of the Lithuanian statute")[21] to a vernacular laden with folklorisms. Invariably, he follows the tag "pysano bo iest'" (for it is written) not with a quotation from scripture but with a folk proverb. The joke rests in the supposed incongruity between literate culture and the culture of the ordinary people. Kvitka repeatedly invoked this difference, but – unlike his predecessor Kotliarevs'kyi – never pointed to the possibility of eliminating it in a functional literary language based on common speech.

Kvitka defended, in print and correspondence, the rights of the Ukrainian language to cultural development. "We should shame and silence those who harbour the extraordinary view that one should not write in the language spoken by 10 million," he wrote to Maksymovych,[22] later returning repeatedly to this democratic topos.[23] He lauded the beauties of Ukrainian, asserting them to be untranslatable,[24] claimed for the Ukrainian language an antiquity greater than that of the Russian,[25] and even suggested that Russian translations of Ukrainian works in metropolitan journals be grouped with translations from indisputably foreign literatures like the French and the German.[26] Yet these were rhetorical flourishes: Kvitka was well aware that, even if Ukrainian possessed an array of qualities "just like those of a proper language,"[27] it was far from being a "proper language" if a proper language is a standard literary language that meets all the demands – communicative, aesthetic, and symbolic – that a modern society places upon it. That being the case, Kvitka, like Hulak-Artemovs'kyi before him, felt obliged to justify some of his Ukrainian prose as a kind of experiment to demonstrate the expressive capacities of Ukrainian. He had composed the sentimental story "Marusia," he claimed, to settle a wager with another Ukrainian writer who considered Ukrainian unsuited to "serious and moving" writing. "I wrote 'Marusia' and proved that it is possible to be emotionally touched by the Ukrainian language," he wrote with the satisfaction of a researcher discrediting a fallacious theory. But the awkwardness and strangeness of the very idea of writing seriously in Ukrainian were made clear in the sentence immediately following: "The local people (*zdeshnye*) suggested that I publish it, and, insuring myself against the mockery of Russian journalists, I wrote 'The Soldier's Portrait.'"[28] On the one hand, Kvitka expressed confidence in the approbation of his local (gentry) readership. On the other, he anticipated that a work challenging the burlesque stereotype of Ukrainian writing would itself be an object of derision. Accordingly, he produced as an antidote a story that fully met these stereotypical expectations. "Saldats'kyi patret: Latyns'ka pobrekhen'ka, po-nashomu rozkazana" (The Soldier's Portrait: A Latin Fable, Told in Our Language) would reward renewed investigation with the toolkit of postcolonial criticism, so revealing it is of the play of cultural power in a Ukrainian provincial setting – of the force, both open and unobtrusive, of the imperial culture and its representatives, and the subversions and resistances resorted to by the locals. Of relevance to this discussion, however, is Kvitka's readiness to reinforce the association between the Ukrainian language and literary barbarism and tomfoolery, eloquently announced in the title itself. The term "patret" confronts the reader at once with the unstandardized status of the Ukrainian language. Neither the standard Russian "portret," nor the archaic Ukrainian "parsuna," "patret" comes across as a distorted (because misheard?) and therefore uneducated borrowing from the Russian, attesting to the absence in Ukrainian of even the most elementary high-culture vocabulary. The parodic content of the story is directly announced: it is to be the paraphrase of a "Latin fable." Fable is rendered by "pobrekhen'ka," a word that, though derived from "brekhnia" (falsehood), has the form of a diminutive and therefore presents the fiction-as-untruth as an object of familiarity and affection, entirely to be toler-ated in the local cultural environment.[29] Finally, this charming falsehood is to be narrated "po-nashomu" – "in our language." The use of this adverb (and not another based on one of the conventional names then in use for the Ukrainian language – "po-ukraïns'komu" or "po-malorosiis'komu") was highly character-istic of Ukrainian writing at the time. In "The Soldier's Portrait" it announces the prenational, purely local group consciousness that Kvitka ascribes to his narrator. This comically limited self-awareness is demarcated from the cosmo-politanism attributed to the implied author "himself." The latter is figured as possessing the sophisticated cultural tools, acquired through a classical educa-tion, that are needed to perform the transformations of which travesty consists.

"Marusia," likewise, notwithstanding Kvitka's pride in its difference from the burlesque mainstream of Ukrainian writing, is less remote from "The Sol-dier's Portrait" than the author insisted. Its effect is based on the exaggerated use of selected emotion-inducing elements of language: not barbarisms but extended descriptions of feelings, moralizing speeches in the spirit of Enlight-enment Christian piety, and the accumulation of diminutives as markers of gentleness. Neither of Kvitka's modes, the parodic or the sentimental, con-tributed to modernizing Ukrainian prose. This was not because Kvitka's world view reflected an antimodern ideology – even though it is true that his anach-ronistic pastoral idealization of the peasantry was not far removed from conde-scension or, as one fierce critic put it, "typically Enlightenment disregard and even scorn."[30] Such social distance between the implied author and the implied audience was especially evident in a work intended to be read or listened to by peasants, *Lysty do liubeznykh zemliakiv* (Letters to My Beloved Compatriots, 1839), a text notable for its condescending tone and its staunch advocacy of the social status quo. Rather, Kvitka's prose failed to point in the direction of modernity because it did not seek to be a neutral, transparent medium for the transmission of content. Not the stories told or the characters represented were the main subject matter of Kvitka's prose, but the telling itself. Furthermore, in his apologias for the literary use of Ukrainian Kvitka often made the claim that what can be expressed in Ukrainian cannot adequately be rendered in another language. This language contained "beauties inexpressible in any [other] language";[31] the author proclaimed himself unable to compel his characters to speak "in the commonly used language" (*obshchim iazykom*);[32] Russian and Ukrainian were languages so very different in the experiences and mentalities that they reflected that what is well expressed in the one sounds dry in the other.[33] (In fact, all of Kvitka's stories that were written in Ukrainian were also published in Russian, mostly in his own translation. Paradoxically, the translator of "The Soldier's Portrait," the linguist Vladimir Dal', adduced the alleged untranslatability of the Ukrainian language as one of the arguments justifying its use in literature.)[34] Such claims about the unique ability of the Ukrainian language to express Ukrainian experience were intended as arguments in favour of its literary development. Unintentionally, however, they also lent weight to the idea that the Ukrainian identity was so distinctive as to be incommunicable and the Ukrainian social and cultural milieu so intensely local as to be bereft of universal interest and irrelevant to the broader public.[35] If entry into European modernity meant entry into a widening sphere of public ratiocination, then the prose of Kvitka-Osnovianenko offered no such pathway.

Nowhere were the ties binding Kvitka's Ukrainian prose to a non-modern experience of the world more evident than in his correspondence. Practically all of his surviving letters, many of them to the editors of the Moscow and St Petersburg journals that published his work, were in Russian – the stylistically neutral Russian that was Kvitka's default medium for the transaction of practicalities and the discussion of literary matters. He also wrote three letters to Shevchenko, all of them in Ukrainian, and all in the parodic manner inherited from Kotliarevs'kyi's *Eneïda*. They are saturated with barbarisms, and the persona that Kvitka devised for himself as the author of the letters is improbably folksy and naive. True to the tradition of burlesque corporeality, this persona describes the effect of reading Shevchenko's *Kobzar* (The Minstrel, 1840) in physiological terms: "And later on, when we began to read the poems, well! May you hate me if I'm lying: the very hair on my head, not that there's much left of it, stood on end, and there was a tingling next to my heart, and everything went green before my eyes."[36] Kvitka's letters to Shevchenko might be viewed as set-piece demonstrations of the author's reluctance, despite his exhortations elsewhere to the contrary, to use the Ukrainian language in normal prose and therefore to involve it in the transparent exchanges of ideas that are among the hallmarks of European modernity.

Shevchenko's poetry made a transformative contribution to the conception of Ukraine as a modern nation: it crystallized a symbolic system that clearly demarcated the national self from the Other, and it identified landscapes, histories, and destinies that became symbolic of the nation. As far as prose was concerned, Shevchenko wrote most of his fictional and autobiographical works in Russian, but in his letters, practically alone among his contemporaries, he adhered in general to the principle of writing to each of his addressees in what he considered to be their native language: in Ukrainian to Lazarevs'kyi, Lyzohub, Kulish, Bodians'kyi, and Maksymovych, and in Russian to Varvara Repnina, Aksakov, and the Tolstois. These letters thus reflect the view, characteristic of the political phase of national movements, that ethnic and cultural identities do, or should, overlap, and that a marker of any such modern (national) identity is, or should be, a national language.[37]

Historians of the Ukrainian literary language acknowledge Panteleimon Kulish for introducing Ukrainian into genres essential for the advancement of modernity, including literary and cultural criticism and polemics, scholarly prose, and the novel. In his famous epilogue to his own Russian translation of *Chorna rada* (The Black Council, 1857), his historical novel set in the Cossack period, Kulish set out his reasons for putting up with the difficulties of writing a complex text in a literary language still in formation: he was intent upon "the development of the South-Russian language to the high level of historical narration."[38] *Chorna rada* was, indeed, a significant step towards the ideal of prose as a transparent vehicle for content. The narrative itself, as well and the novel's historical and historiosophical reflections, were presented in a relatively neutral style free of the mannerisms of a Kvitka-Osnovianenko. Even the dialogue, which offered temptations to indulge in the exaggerated "imitation" of colourful "Cossack" language, was restrained and dignified.

And yet, in Kulish's critical and publicist prose there remained a residue of rustic barbarism. Such features were entrenched in his "Lysty z khutora" (Farmstead Letters), where they accompanied an antiurban, anticentralist, and antimodern ethos that was offered to the reader as common sense. Paradoxically, Kulish's critique of Kotliarevs'kyi in one of the letters, a prelude to his praise of Shevchenko, was formulated using precisely the vulgar low style it professed to combat: "[Kotliarevs'kyi came into] our simple house ... and started spouting nonsense about some Aeneas or other ... Really! He would have done better not to versify like that at all! ... He's a city toff dressed up to look like one of us."[39] For all its avowed earthy folksiness, this prose style did not, in fact, resemble the speech of ordinary people even as recorded by Kulish himself in his *Zapiski o Iuzhnoi Rusi* (Notes Concerning Southern Rus', 1856). Typical of the authentic material published in *Zapiski* was the oral autobiography of Arkhyp Nikonenko, a performer of *dumy*. Nikonenko's account of his life was marked by words borrowed from Russian, but was otherwise stylistically neutral.[40]

Also unlike the idiom of ordinary people, though in a different way, was the Ukrainian prose of Marko Vovchok – which, nevertheless, was so unlike the mannered Ukrainian prose that preceded it that contemporaries greeted it as the unmediated voice of the peasantry. Marko Vovchok was a native speaker not of Ukrainian but of Russian. She learnt Ukrainian in the course of the folkloric and ethnographic research that she conducted in the early 1850s with her husband Opanas Markovych. Her Ukrainian writing belonged to the beginning of her literary career, when she wrote a number of short stories that Kulish published in 1857 as *Narodni opovidannia* (Peasant Tales). For most of her life she was a writer of Russian prose and a translator into Russian, mainly from the French. *Narodni opovidannia* engendered a great deal of discussion as a powerful statement against serfdom: Vovchok's peasant narrators, most of them women, presented emotionally understated but morally and politically unambiguous accounts of serfdom as a social and legal system that mercilessly exploited peasants' labour, denied their rights as autonomous human beings, and delivered peasant women to their male owners as powerless objects of sexual predation. It has recently been noticed that Vovchok's works engaged in feminist advocacy as much as they opposed serfdom.[41] A fresh reading of Vovchok would reveal her interest in the psychological impact of trauma, physical and sexual abuse, bullying, and in the physical and social consequences of depression.

As a writer of Ukrainian prose and as a practising ethnographer, Vovchok was convinced of the linguistic authority of her peasant informants. She gathered ethnographic and linguistic data in market places, compiled vocabularies, and looked for words used by ordinary people as bases for abstract terms or names for modern phenomena.[42] Yet Kulish's claim that Vovchok's literary works were "pure ethnography" was valid only as a metaphor. It is true, as students of Vovchok's work have repeatedly pointed out, that her Ukrainian prose is rich in grammatical features that frequently occur in folksongs – diminutives and postnominal epithets in particular.[43] But Marko Vovchok organized these elements into a new prose that was carefully crafted, and one of the main effects that she successfully produced through her craft was that of artless naturalness. Similarly, despite adopting some motifs from folktales, as elaborately documented by Soviet-era scholars,[44] Marko Vovchok's stories are more dissimilar than similar to the real folk tales that she and Markovych recorded.[45] The folk tales were rich in fantastic situations, generally lacked recognizable connections to the social realities of contemporary peasant life, and did not thematize the role of the storyteller – in contrast to the essential structural features of *Narodni opovidannia*.

Marko Vovchok's achievement lay less in her persuasive mimesis of the peasant voice, for which her contemporaries unanimously praised her, than in the neutrality of narrative tone that she imparted to her folk narrators. Her *Narodni opovidannia* drew attention not to the collection's language or style but to the events narrated and states of affairs revealed. She employed folk markers in moderation and almost always remained cognizant of the rhetorical virtue of *aptum* – the appropriateness of style to the subject matter.[46]

The use of first-person peasant narrators enabled Marko Vovchok to sidestep the problem of plausibly representing characters belonging to social classes that did not typically use Ukrainian. Kvitka had resorted to the naturalism of having his characters speak the language characteristic of their class, resulting in what were effectively bilingual and even trilingual texts. He had exploited the consequent contrasts and incongruities for comic effect. Marko Vovchok was able to put into Ukrainian the direct speech of characters belonging to the gentry because, within the world of her stories, the dialogue of the upper classes, like everything else, was reported by a peasant narrator with a consistent linguistic repertoire. This unity of diction projected the possibility of a single literary language transcending sociolects – that is to say, the standard language of a nation comprising different social classes.

Marko Vovchok's success in producing a natural and transparent prose facilitated the concentration of readers' attention on the issues she raised in the works, which were examples of *littérature engagée* very much in the spirit of her times. Her works in Ukrainian were apprehended by the intellectuals of the left and right as contributions to the great debate on serfdom, the major public issue in the Russian Empire in the years preceding 1861. Marko Vovchok was able to use Ukrainian to communicate about matters of public interest as though this were unproblematic – as though Ukrainian were already a literary language. Perhaps that is one of the things that Shevchenko meant when he famously advised Turgenev that the best model from which to learn Ukrainian was the prose of Marko Vovchok.[47]

Neutrality and naturalness characterized Marko Vovchok's letters as well as her fiction. From 1857 onward she wrote to her husband Markovych in Ukrainian, with no instance of the self-parodic code switching that was typical, for example, of Kulish. The letters show no evidence that their author believed that writing in Ukrainian limited the emotional or intellectual scope of what she could say. Among Vovchok's contemporaries perhaps only Vasyl' Bilozers'kyi, the publisher of the periodical *Osnova*, grasped the nature of the innovation that her prose represented. Inviting her to send letters to the journal from abroad, he wrote, "Describe everything you see, hear and think in your own way and in our language. That would serve as an example and as worthwhile instruction. We would learn from you that in our language it is possible to write and speak clearly and intelligently about everything in the world."[48] In the event, a few years later Marko Vovchok did write her "Letters from Paris" – most of them in Russian, but some in Ukrainian. The Ukrainian letters confronted her with a challenge, but only a technical one: how to find the right Ukrainian words to name the phenomena encountered in one of the capitals of European modernity. For Vovchok the more general question of whether one could or should write journalistic reports about Paris in Ukrainian, or allow such modern subject matter to remain the preserve of Russian, had been settled.

Historians of the Ukrainian literary language have remarked how quickly Marko Vovchok's prose came to be emulated – by the authors who published in *Osnova*, by Oleksandr Konys'kyi and Iurii Fed'kovych, as well as the young Ivan Nechui-Levyts'kyi and Panas Myrnyi.[49] Generally this influence is seen as the legitimation and domestication of a natural, plain style understood to be imitative of the diction of ordinary people. There is partial truth in this claim, but the more substantive accomplishment of Marko Vovchok in Ukrainian literature lies in her practical demonstration of the possibility of using the Ukrainian language, and developing it on the basis of its existing resources, "to write and speak clearly and intelligently about everything in the world" – that is to say, as an unrestricted medium for transmitting the full range of messages that need to be communicated in modernity.

Notes

1 Among the many definitions and descriptions of modernity, those of relevance to this study include S. N. Eisenstadt, "The Civilizational Dimension of Modernity: Modernity as a Distinct Civilization," in *Comparative Civilizations and Multiple Modernities* (Leiden: Brill, 2003), 493–518, and the essays gathered in *The Benefit of Broad Horizons: Intellectual and Institutional Preconditions for a Global Social Science: Festschrift for Björn Wittrock on the Occasion of His 65th Birthday*, ed. Hans Joas and Barbro Klein (Boston: Brill, 2010).

2 See, e.g., Ernest Gellner, *Nations and Nationalism* (Oxford: Blackwell, 1983), 32–8; Anthony D. Smith, *National Identity* (London: Penguin, 1991), 61 and 84; and Allen Carey-Webb, *Making Subject(s): Literature and the Emergence of National Identity* (New York: Garland, 1998).

3 Gary Saul Morson and Caryl Emerson, *Mikhail Bakhtin: Creation of a Prosaics* (Stanford, CA: Stanford University Press, 1990), 19.

4 Wlad Godzich and Jeffrey Kittay, *The Emergence of Prose: An Essay in Prosaics* (Minneapolis: University of Minnesota Press, 1987), 110.

5 René Wellek, "Literature and Its Cognates," in *Dictionary of the History of Ideas: Studies of Selected Pivotal Ideas*, ed. Philip P. Wiener (New York: Charles Scribner's Sons, 1973), 3: 81–8, here 82.

6 Benedetto Croce, *Poetry and Literature: An Introduction to Its Criticism and History*, trans. Giovanni Gullace (Carbondale: Southern Illinois University Press, 1981), 41.

7 Ahapii Pylypovych Shamrai, ed., *Kharkivs'ka shkola romantykiv*, 3 vols. (Kharkiv: Derzhavne vydavnytstvo Ukraïny, 1930), 1: 113; George G. Grabowicz, "Subversion and Self-Assertion: The Role of *Kotliarevshchyna* in Russian-Ukrainian Literary Relations," in *History of the Literary Cultures of East-Central Europe: Junctures and Disjunctures in the 19th and 20th Centuries*, ed. Marcel Cornis-Pope and John Neubauer (Amsterdam: John Benjamins, 2004–6), 1: 401–9; and Oleksandr Borzenko, "Provintsiinyi chytach i stanovlennia novoï ukraïns'koï literatury," *Dyvoslovo* 2001, no. 2 (February): 15–16.

8 H[ryhorii] F[edorovych] Kvitka-Osnovianenko, *Zibrannia tvoriv u semy tomakh* (Kyiv: Naukova dumka, 1978–81), 7: 113.

9 Marko Pavlyshyn, "The Rhetoric and Politics of Kotliarevsky's *Eneida*," *Journal of Ukrainian Studies* 10, no. 1 (1985): 9–24.

10 Chaplenko, *Ukraïns'ka literaturna mova: Ïï vynyknennia i rozvytok* (New York: Ukraïns'kyi tekhnichnyi instytut u N'iu Iorku, 1955), 54.

11 See Sreznevskii's letters to his mother, quoted in Shamrai, *Kharkivs'ka shkola*, 1: 199 and 1: 202.

12 Sreznevskii, letter to Ivan Snegirev, 7 August 1834 (Shamrai, *Kharkivs'ka shkola*, 1: 235). Srezvenvskii's panegyric is reminiscent of the praise that William Jones, the discoverer of Sanskrit for European scholarship, lavished upon that language: "The Sanscrit language, whatever be its antiquity, is of a wonderful structure; more perfect than the Greek, more copious than the Latin, and more exquisitely refined than either." Sir William Jones, *Discourses Delivered Before the Asiatic Society: And Miscellaneous Papers, on the Religion, Poetry, Literature, etc., of the Nations of India* (London: Charles S. Arnold, 1824), 28.

13 Iarema Aizenshtok, annotation to Petro Hulak-Artemovs'kyi, "Rybalka (malorosiis'ka balada)," in *Tvory*, ed. Iarema Aizenshtok (Kyiv: Dnipro, 1964), 244. Aizenshtok quotes the editorial text in Ukrainian translation.

14 "XIV oda Horatsiia, kn. II," "IX oda Horatsiia, kn. II," and "XXXIV oda Horatsiia, kn. I." All three were dated 1832, but published in 1896, 1888, and 1882 respectively. The tone of the first two lines of the first of these is typical of these works as a whole:
    Ой час би, Грицьку, нам, ой, час пошануваться:
    Не все ж нам, братіку, не все парубкувать.
    (Really, Hryts'ko, its time for us, you know, it's time to take it easy: / We can't carry on like bachelors the whole time, mate.) Hulak-Artemovs'kyi, *Tvory*, 80.

15 Petro Hulak-Artemovs'kyi, "Deshcho pro toho Haras'ka," *Tvory*, 60–1, here 60.

16 Hulak-Artemovs'kyi, "Rybalka," *Tvory*, 71–2.

17 Vitalii Rusanivs'kyi, *Istoriia ukraïns'koï literaturnoï movy* (Kyiv: ArtEk, 2002), 164.

18 *Uchenye zapiski Moskovskogo universiteta* 6, no. 5 (1834): 307, quoted in O. I. Honchar, *Hryhorii Kvitka-Osnovianenko: Seminarii* (Kyiv: Vyshcha shkola, 1974), 21.

19 See, e.g., Chaplenko, *Ukraïns'ka literaturna mova*, 72.

20 "Dvorianskie vybory, chast' vtoraia, ili vybor ispravnika" (1830), "Shel'menko – volostnoi pisar'" (1831), and "Shel'menko – denshchik" (1840).

21 Rusanivs'kyi, *Istoriia ukraïns'koï literaturnoï movy*, 159.

22 Kvitka-Osnovianenko, *Zibrannia tvoriv*, 7: 228.

23 Ibid., 7: 259, 323.

24 Ibid., 7: 228.

25 Letter to Andrei Kraevskii, quoted in Shamrai, *Kharkivs'ka shkola*, 1: 8–9.

26 Kvitka-Osnovianenko, *Zibrannia tvoriv*, 7: 323.

27 Ibid., 7: 228.

28 Kvitka-Osnovianenko, letter to Petr Pletnev of 15 March 1839, *Zibrannia tvoriv*, 7: 215. Kvitka makes very similar claims in a letter to Mikhail Pogodin (7: 206) and a slightly later letter to Pletnev (7: 217).

29 The story is the expansion of the Latin tag "ne sutor ultra crepidam" (let the shoemaker not [judge] higher than the shoes).

30 Dmytro Čyževs'kyj, *A History of Ukrainian Literature*, 2nd ed. (New York: Ukrainian Academy of Arts and Sciences in the United States; Englewood, Colorado: Ukrainian Academic Press, 1997), 422.

31 Letter to Kraevskii of 28 December 1841, *Zibrannia tvoriv*, 7: 338.

32 Letter to Pletnev, 8 February 1839, *Zibrannia tvoriv*, 7: 215.

33 Letter to Pletnev, 15 March 1839, *Zibrannia tvoriv*, 7: 216.

34 See Dal's introductory remarks to the publication of his translation in *Sovremennik*. Kvitka-Osnovianenko, *Zibrannia tvoriv*, 3: 453.

35 The untranslatability of culture is a topos that runs through the history of the discussion of translation and its potential. For a recent instance see José María Rodríguez García, "Introduction: Literary into Cultural Translation," *Diacritics* 34, no. 3–4 (2004): 2–30, esp. 24–5.

36 Letter to Shevchenko, 23 October 1840, *Zibrannia tvoriv*, 7: 266–8, here 266.

37 Miroslav Hroch, "The Social Interpretation of Linguistic Demands in European National Movements," in *Comparative Studies in Modern European History: Nation, Nationalism, Social Change* (Aldershot: Ashgate, 2007), 67–96, here 68–9.

38 Ralph Lindheim and George S.N. Luckyj, eds., *Towards an Intellectual History of Ukraine: An Anthology of Ukrainian Thought from 1710 to 1995* (Toronto: University of Toronto Press and the Shevchenko Scientific Society, Inc., 1996), 105–21, here 120.

39 Panteleimon Kulish, *Tvory v dvokh tomakh* (Kyiv: Dnipro, 1989), 2: 257.

40 "Rasskazy Arkhipa Nikonenka o sebe samom," *Zapiski o iuzhnoi Rusi*, ed. Panteleimon Kulish, vol. 1 (St Petersburg: Kulish, 1856), 8–14.

41 Vira Aheieva, "Cholovichyi psevdonim i zhinocha nezalezhnist'," in *Try doli: Marko Vovchok v ukraïns'kii, rosiis'kii ta frantsuz'kii literaturi*, ed. Vira Aheieva (Kyiv: Fakt, 2002), 101–13.

42 Evgenii Brandis, *Marko Vovchok* (Moscow: Molodaia gvardiia, 1968) and, especially, O. I. Dei, *Fol'klorni zapysy Marka Vovchka ta Opanasa Markovycha* (Kyiv: Naukova dumka, 1983).

43 Chaplenko, *Ukraïns'ka literaturna mova*, 127.

44 In the collection *Marko Vovchok: Statti i doslidzhennia* (Kyiv: Naukova dumka, 1985), see the essays: M. Ie. Syvachenko, "Do temy: Marko Vovchok i narodna kazka," 239–81 and O. I. Dei, "Narodna balada pro sestru ta brativ-rozbiinykiv i ïï opratsiuvannia Markom Vovchkom," 282–310.

45 O. I. Dei, *Fol'klorni zapysy Marka Vovchka ta Opanasa Markovycha*.

46 In some slightly later works, such as "Diak" (The Cantor, 1859–60), however, possibly under the influence of critics' enthusiasm for what they saw as the ethnographic veracity of *Narodni opovidannia*, Vovchok succumbed to the temptation of multiplying proverbs and other folkloric items to the point of mannerism.

47 Ivan Turgenev, "Spohady pro Shevchenka" [1876], *Spohady pro Tarasa Shevchenka* (Kyiv: Dnipro, 1982), 334–6.

48 Quoted in M. D. Bernshtein, *Zhurnal "Osnova" i ukraïns'kyi literaturnyi protses kintsia 50-kh–60-kh rokiv XIX st.* (Kyiv: Vydavnytstvo AN URSR, 1959), 32.

49 Chaplenko, *Ukraïns'ka literaturna mova*, 129 and, in assent with him, Rusanivs'kyi, *Istoriia ukraïns'koï literaturnoï movy*, 235.

A Ticket to Europe: Collections of Ukrainian Folk Songs and Their Russian Reviewers, 1820s–1830s

EDYTA M. BOJANOWSKA

Since the early nineteenth century, dealing with Ukrainian folk songs has meant entering a highly politicized terrain. It is commonly stressed that in the century's early decades, assertions of Ukrainian identity were fully compatible with an imperial Russian identity. While this is largely true, debates about Ukrainian folk songs at that time showed this compatibility's limits and how it came to unravel by mid-century. The topic was used to marshal or deny Ukraine's nationalist claims by focusing on what George Grabowicz has called the "right to life" question of Ukrainian language and literature.[1] Beyond negotiating Ukraine's place within imperial culture, Ukraine's folklorists – who, incidentally, included Russians – challenged the incipient Russocentric model of this culture. Folk songs became an arena for a national rivalry in which Ukraine's cultural "right-to-lifers," so to speak, managed to put the discourse of Russian cultural hegemony on the defensive. They did so by promoting a Herderian folkloric nationalism that gave them an advantage over the Russians.

Johann Gottfried Herder (1744–1803) made folk traditions central to Europe's romantic world view by integrating them into his comprehensive philosophy of cultural nationalism. Herder held that a nation was an organic community united by shared culture, history, and language. For him, a nation was rooted in the common people (*Volk*), and – unlike for Hegel – it led a completely separate existence from that of the state. Herder recommended abandoning Enlightenment universalism for indigenous specificity. Only by developing distinctly national cultures could nations contribute to what Herder called *Humanität*, that is, the fullest realization of humanity's spiritual faculties. The epidemic of forgeries of ancient folk relics, such as James Macpherson's celebrated *Poems of Ossian* (1752–65) or Václav Hanka's *Rukopis královédvorský* (The Manuscript of the Queen's Court), signalled the importance of folk antiquity for modern nationalizing cultures. Folk songs that survived among the common people, which Herder called "the archives of a nationality" and "imprints of [its] soul," provided evidence that such grassroots creativity continued into the modern era.[2] A nation that was unable to establish the antiquity of its "spirit" had its cultural credentials questioned. Herder's own collection, *Volkslieder* (Folk Songs, 1778–9), later renamed *Stimmen der Völker in Liedern* (The Voices of People in Songs, 1807), included songs of the Slavs, for whom Herder predicted a cultural revival. It also featured several Cossack songs.[3] In Herder's schema, Ukraine was poised to become the "new Greece" of an inclusive Slavic "nation" extending from the north of Russia to the Black Sea and encompassing parts of Poland and Hungary.[4]

The Russians' troubles in producing a reputable folk song collection, made all the clearer by the successes of their counterparts in Ukraine, may well have contributed to their cooling towards Herder and their eventual embrace of a Hegelian, state-focused conception of nationality. Yet to underrate the nationalist significance of folk traditions in the 1820s and 1830s is to adopt, anachronistically, this later, Hegelian perspective on the hierarchy of national assets that would become the dominant Russian position. I propose to discuss more synchronically the early nineteenth-century collections of Ukrainian folk songs and their reception in the Russian press, and to do so in the context of pan-European Herderianism.

Herder's ideas were widely popular not only in Russia but also in Ukraine, thanks in large part to the activities of the Kharkiv romantics in the 1810s and 1820s. Up to the 1840s, Herderian nationalism had a profound impact on Russian culture, not least through the mediation of other thinkers who were popular in Russia, such as Schiller, Schelling, the Schlegel brothers, Goethe, and Fichte, as well as such minor figures as Sismondi and Mme de Staël. In 1829 Nikolai Grech published an abridged Russian translation of Herder's magisterial *Ideen zur Philosophie der Geschichte der Menschheit* (Ideas for a Philosophy of the History of Humanity, 1784–91), which had also been known in Russia through the French translation by Edgar Quinet. In Ukraine, Kharkiv University was an important centre of Herderian thought, so it is no coincidence that many figures mentioned in this article were its graduates.[5]

Russian folk song collecting began in the late eighteenth century but developed into a sustained romantic fashion from the 1830s onward.[6] Just as a truly national literature was the goal of writers, so a comprehensive scholarly edition of Russian folk songs became the goal of folklore enthusiasts. Despite the great demand for such a publication, countless complaints about its absence, and plans for its creation, the first three decades failed to produce a collection of Russian folk songs considered worthy of the nation.[7] The first significant, if not particularly good, nineteenth-century publication appeared only in 1838 (I.P. Sakharov, *Pesni russkogo naroda* [The Songs of the Russian People]). The first volumes of Petr Kireevskii's *Pesni, sobrannye P.V. Kireevskim* (Songs Collected by P.V. Kireevsky) were published in 1860–74; others appeared only in the Soviet period (1911–29).[8]

Major studies of Russian ethnography by Aleksandr Pypin and Mark Azadovskii begrudgingly concede the importance of Ukraine's folklore collectors. However, these studies' evolutionary narratives of Russia's growing national awareness are structured to obscure this fact. Pypin briefly notes the disproportionate share of Ukrainians among the first "Russian" Slavists, and admits that Mykhailo Maksymovych's Ukrainian collection surpassed Sakharov's later efforts by far.[9] Azadovskii confronts this issue more directly:

> In Russian folklore studies, as in Russian literature, the importance of Ukrainian folklorists was great. At a time when Ukrainian literature and scholarship had already produced such publications as the collections by Tsertelev, Maksymovych, Sreznevskii, among others, Russian literature in its folk investigations was mainly using eighteenth-century editions ... and the few early nineteenth-century publications, poor and scattered by comparison. In this way, the Ukrainian folklorists unwittingly (*nevol'no*) influenced Russian society in this direction, providing at the same time concrete examples and models.[10]

This admission is made cursorily, however, in the middle of Azadovskii's chapter on Ukrainian, not Russian, folklorism. For Azadovskii, the influence of Ukrainians on a culture as "major" as Russian can only be "unwitting" and accidental – a notion that David Saunders has since put to rest.[11]

As Azadovskii's comments make clear, the successes of other Slavs in producing rich, literarily useful folk song collections made a similar Russian publication an especially urgent task. In the 1820s, journals such as *Vestnik Evropy* (The Herald of Europe), *Moskovskii telegraf* (The Moscow Telegraph), *Moskovskii vestnik* (The Moscow Herald), and *Teleskop* (The Telescope) apprised the Russian public of other Slavs' folkloric research.[12] Among the pioneers of folk song collecting in East Slavic lands was a Pole, Zorian Dołęga-Chodakowski (real name: Adam Czarnocki, 1784–1825) who regarded Ukrainian folk songs as the pinnacle of Slavic folklore. The five thousand songs that he collected between 1813 and 1817, which were never separately published, remain the biggest collection of Slavic folk songs recorded by a single person.[13] Mykhailo Maksymovych, who came into possession of a part of Chodakowski's collection, published some of them in 1834; a bigger selection appeared in print only in the 1970s, after Chodakowski's long-lost transcripts were rediscovered.[14]

Prince Nikolai Tsertelev (1790–1869), a Russian of Georgian origin who lived for many years in Ukraine and studied at Kharkiv University, published the first important nineteenth-century collection of Ukrainian songs. His 1819 volume focused on the epic *dumy*, or historical songs, which in Tsertelev's view movingly expressed the "poetic genius of the people" and showed their "dialect" as "capable of poetry no less than other languages."[15] For Tsertelev, however, the songs were but crumbling antiquities: "These are unsightly ruins that witness the beauty of the crumbled edifice! ... A dying echo of the harmony that once resounded on the banks of the Dnieper!"[16] Such collector-antiquarians claimed to be merely smoothing the pillow of the dying nations and preserving their traces for posterity.

The antiquarian approach, however, was soon replaced by a romantic aesthetic that led folk heritage out of the graveyard and onto the centre stage of the so-called nationalist "revivals." In Europe, the activities of Sir Walter Scott (*The Minstrelsy of the Scottish Border*, 1802–3) and the Grimm brothers (*Kinder- und Hausmärchen* [Children's and Household Tales], 1812), all popular in the Slavic world, facilitated this transition. In Russia, the theoretical articles of Kazimierz Brodziński, a Polish romantic and a Herderian who inspired Petr Viazemskii to coin the Russian term for "nationality" ("*narodnost'* "),[17] facilitated a reappraisal of the Slavic folk heritage. In 1826 *Vestnik Evropy* translated an article in which Brodziński proposed a road to a nationally conscious romantic literature that would lead through Slavic folk traditions. He prophesied the dawn of a new Slavic civilization in a manner that recalls Herder: "The time will come when from the [Slavic folk songs], as once from the Greek rhapsodes, the creative mind of the Slav will compose its own *Iliad* or its own *Odyssey*."[18] The Ukrainians and the Serbs, who in Brodziński's view possessed the richest folk traditions, were most likely to accomplish this task (he claimed that few Polish songs had survived and never mentioned Russian ones).

A year later *Vestnik Evropy* published a letter by Prince Tsertelev to the Ukrainian ethnographer, botanist, linguist, and historian Mykhailo Maksymovych (1804–73), also a Herderian. Tsertelev's letter had accompanied a delivery of thirty-two songs for Maksymovych's upcoming collection. Echoing Brodziński, Tsertelev posited folk poetry as the antidote to foreign imitation. He complained that Russians were unique among enlightened Europeans in ignoring folk culture, a fact that he found particularly vexing in light of the foreigners' interest in Russian folk traditions. He mentioned František Čelakovský's 1813 Czech publication that included Russian and Ukrainian songs. "Aren't the Russian litterateurs ashamed?" Tsertelev exclaimed.[19]

Such patriotic gripes and international rivalries were quite common among nineteenth-century folklorists.[20]

Other Russians who were chagrined by the lack of a proper collection of Russian songs soon found Maksymovych's success galling. Stepan Shevyrev, a Slavophile-leaning ideologue of Official Nationality and a future professor of Russian literature at Moscow University, wrote: "Our philologists ought to see any such publication as a reproach to their own inactivity. Why don't we rush to collect Russian songs, so dear to our hearts, which the old generation may soon carry away with them forever?"[21] Indeed, Maksymovych's 1827 volume of *Malorossiiskie pesni* (Little Russian Songs) gained instant acclaim as an important scholarly publication and captivated the literary world. Pushkin admitted to "stealing" from it when writing "Poltava."[22] Nikolai Gogol' and the Polish writers of the "Ukrainian school" used it as a literary resource. It earned praise from Mickiewicz and Šafárik. A good indicator of the Ukrainian intelligentsia's enthusiasm for Maksymovych's collection is Kostomarov's claim that he had memorized it.[23] The collection was extensively reviewed and excerpted in Russian journals. In the preface, which was reprinted in *Vestnik Evropy*, Maksymovych acknowledged his debt to the Polish and Russian pioneers of Ukrainian folklore: Brodziński, Dołęga-Chodakowski, and Tsertelev.[24] The Polish scholar Stefan Kozak treats this preface as Ukraine's first manifesto of romantic ideology.[25]

Maksymovych attempts in the preface to combine the imperial Russian and local southwestern identities, an amalgam that Faith Hillis has called "the Little Russian idea."[26] Yet this amalgam cracks under the pressure of Maksymovych's Ukrainian particularism. On the one hand, he hopes that his collection will prove useful for "our literature," by which he means imperial Russian literature of which Ukrainian literature is a part. On the other, he affirms Ukraine's separate historical experience and cultural identity. Maksymovych is tellingly silent about Ukrainians' consanguinity with Russians. His proto-Ukrainians include Slavs, "other Europeans, and to an even greater extent, it would seem, Asians."[27] Maksymovych notes that, like Russian songs, Ukrainian ones use the tonic system. With Polish songs they share "frequent rhyme, or at least euphony, and sonorous and frequent diminutives that produce softness and harmony, in which they are superior to the Russian songs."[28] The Ukrainian songs' "Polish" features thus account for their superiority over the Russian songs. However, Maksymovych considers the Ukrainian language as closer than either Russian or Polish to other Slavic languages, thus suggesting that it is the most Slavic of the three.[29]

Contrasts between Russian and Ukrainian folk songs, such as the one that Tsertelev draws in his public letter to Maksymovych, would become a common, if politically sensitive, feature of Ukrainian folkloric manifestos. For Tsertelev, such contrasts signalled disjunctive national paradigms, as each tradition conveyed "the spirit of its nation" (*dukh svoei natsii*). While, in Tsertelev's view, Russian folk songs excelled in descriptive poetry and painted powerful images, the Ukrainian ones took the lead in lyricism and displayed powerful feelings.

Tsertelev did not privilege one tradition over the other, though he walked a fine line when contrasting the "coarse and savage customs" depicted in the Russian songs to the ideals of fame, love, and freedom found in the Ukrainian ones.[30] Maksymovych, by contrast, when copying the device in his *Little Russian Songs*, presented the Ukrainian songs and national traits as unequivocally more attractive. Maksymovych's version became the most influential iteration of this contrastive rhetorical device. In his view, Russian songs

> express a spirit submissive to its fate that readily surrenders itself to its decrees. A Russian is not accustomed to taking an active part in the vicissitudes of life, which is why he has befriended nature and likes to paint it, often making it more beautiful than it actually is. Only in this can his soul freely express itself. He does not seek to capture in song the circumstances of actual life, but, on the contrary, seeks to separate himself from all that exists, and, having covered his ears with his hands, seems to want to lose himself in the sound. This is why Russian songs are distinguished by deep melancholy (*unylost'*), a desperate forgetfulness, a certain spaciousness and flowing elongation (*razdol'e i plavnaia protiazhennost'*).[31]

In the Ukrainian songs, by contrast,

> there is less of such luxuriousness and elongation. Being an expression of the spirit's struggle with fate, they are distinguished by flights of passion, concise firmness, and emotional power, and equally well by naturalness of expression. Instead of forgetfulness and melancholy (*unylost'*), we see in them discontent and anguish (*toska*); there is more activity in them ... Prince Tsertelev was right to notice that Russian [songs] have better descriptive poetry ... while in the Little Russian songs we find the dramatic rendition of a subject. Their power stems largely from the laconicism of their language.[32]

Maksymovych's message was clear: Russian songs reflect the Russian spirit, which is submissive, unfree, and despondent, while Ukrainian songs reflect the Ukrainian spirit, which is defiant, freedom-loving, and active.

This message was not lost on the nationalistically minded Russians associated with *Moskovskii vestnik*, which was owned by the historian Mikhail

Pogodin. Though Stepan Shevyrev reviewed Maksymovych's work very favourably in *Vestnik*, he "disagree[d], or rather, [did] not understand on what basis the author, when speaking about the differences between Russian and Little Russian songs, conclude[d] that the former ones express[ed] 'a spirit submissive to its fate,' that 'a Russian is not accustomed to taking an active part in the vicissitudes of life, and having befriended nature, does not seek to capture in his songs the circumstances of active life.'"[33]

To counter Maksymovych, Shevyrev points to Russian brigand songs about exploits (*razboinich'i*), which "often give full rein to a forceful imagination." Shevyrev does, on the other hand, agree with Maksymovych's characterization of Ukrainian songs, though in stating this, Shevyrev diminishes their attractiveness. Rhetorically, his praise of Ukrainian songs resembles Mark Antony's praise of Brutus as an "honorable man" in Shakespeare's tragedy. Shevyrev agrees that the Ukrainian songs mainly express anguish (*toska*): "It gives them a certain monotonousness, while in the Russian songs, in our opinion, it is not possible to determine one feeling that would be expressed in all of them."[34] According to Shevyrev, Russian songs contain irony, fantasy, and natural gaiety, while the Ukrainian ones apparently lack wit and humour.

In short, Shevyrev revalorizes Maksymovych's comparison to cast the Russian people and its folk songs as superior. *Moskovskii vestnik* considered it so important to prove Maksymovych wrong and Shevyrev right that throughout 1827–8 it continued to publish Russian folk songs of the brigand variety or ones that expressed "anguish," which was sometimes announced explicitly in the titles.[35] The polemic's other consequence was that Maksymovych refrained from overt comparisons between Russian and Ukrainian songs in his subsequent publications. This polemic demonstrates the degree to which collecting, publishing, and discussing folklore became nationalistically charged activities in the late 1820s. Folk songs, as Ahapii Shamrai put it, were "an ideological fact."[36]

The 1830s saw the ascendancy of the governmentally sanctioned ideology of Official Nationality. Formulated by Tsar Nicholas I's Minister of National Education, Count Sergei Uvarov, the ideology was based on a tripartite slogan of "Orthodoxy, Autocracy, and Nationality" and represented a statist version of Russian nationalism. In the aftermath of the Polish November Uprising of 1830–1, championship of Russian national interests within this official framework involved a promotion of Ukrainian culture that was to counteract irredentist Polish nationalism. Research into Ukrainian history and language was now obliged to stress the Ukrainians' antagonism towards the Poles and their relatedness to the Russians. As Johannes Remy has shown, Ukrainian and Ukrainophile intellectuals found ways to exploit the cover of Official Nationality for their own purposes – their "lip service to all-Russian nationality" notwithstanding. Ironically, as a result of their efforts, the conceptual foundation of the Ukrainian nation was, in Remy's words, "far more advanced" in 1855, the year of Nicholas I's death, than it had been at the beginning of his reign in 1825.[37]

In 1833, another Russian enthusiast of Ukrainian folklore, a graduate of the Kharkiv University and a Herderian, Izmail Sreznevskii (1812–80), contributed to these efforts through a multivolume miscellany titled *Zaporozhskaia starina* (Zaporozhian Antiquity, 1833–8). Its first volume included mostly historical songs, many of which were later found to be inauthentic. Sreznevskii structured the miscellany as a kind of "memory project," to use Taras Koznarsky's phrase, aimed at telling a history of Cossack Ukraine.[38] Sreznevskii did not deploy the Russian-Ukrainian contrast, but, as Remy argues, he promoted an "exclusive concept of Ukrainian national identity" by using "Ukrainian" and "Russian" as mutually exclusive concepts and by expunging "Russians" from his historical narrative until the Cossack wars of the mid-seventeenth century. Remy also reminds us that, although Sreznevskii changed his mind later, he was among the first to predict that the Ukrainian language should and would become the literary language of Ukraine.[39]

The Minister of National Education, Uvarov, took note of the Ukrainian ferment and reportedly asked Nikolai Gogol' to review Sreznevskii's, Tsertelev's, and Maksymovych's publications.[40] Gogol' acceded to this request with his 1834 article "On Little Russian Songs" ("O malorossiiskikh pesniakh"). However, instead of reviewing the collections, he offered his own poetic paean to the songs. Gogol's venue was an official governmental journal, *Zhurnal Ministerstva narodnogo prosveshcheniia* (The Journal of the Ministry of National Education). Gogol's collaboration with this journal was meant to prove him worthy of promoting Official Nationality from a professorial lectern in Kyiv (he was then applying for a post there). He therefore dutifully gave Ukraine a metonymic designation that safely nestled it within the imperial state: "that flowering part of Russia."[41] This verbal tag played a role similar to that of the obligatory invocations of Marxism-Leninism in the Soviet period, and Gogol' deployed it in his writings on Ukrainian history.[42] To offer another example, *Severnaia pchela* (The Northern Bee) proclaimed that Sreznevskii's *Zaporozhian Antiquity* cheered the lovers of "the fatherland's legends" and acquainted readers with "the most poetic borderland (*krai*) of the Russian Empire."[43] Such formulations affirmed the region's belonging to the Russian Empire as much as they evinced the Russian public's justifiable anxiety that these folkloric projects might be feeding local separatism. In later years Russian censors explicitly invoked the risk of separatism when banning publications of Ukrainian folk songs.[44]

Like his predecessors, Gogol' contrasted the Russian and Ukrainian traditions to the advantage of the latter, basically corroborating Maksymovych's conclusions: "Russian melancholy (*zaunyvnaia*) music expresses, as M. Maksymovych rightly observed, a forgetting of life: it strives to depart from it and muffle daily cares and worries. But in Little Russian songs music merges with life: its sounds are so vivid that they seem to speak … and each word of this striking speech penetrates the soul."[45] Like Maksymovych, Gogol' emphasized the dramatism of Ukrainian songs that, he believed, demonstrated the Ukrainians' active past and strong national spirit.

Thus, despite Shevyrev's protests, Maksymovych's rubrics of Ukrainian and Russian national traits proved influential. Osyp Bodians'kyi copied Maksymovych almost verbatim, if without attribution, in his 1835 review of Slovak songs. Like Gogol', he fully endorsed Maksymovych's claims about the melancholy, self-forgetfulness, and passivity that distinguish the songs of Northern Rus'. In the Southern songs, by contrast, Bodians'kyi found anguish, strong passions, daring, and bold activity.[46] Bodians'kyi additionally speculated about the causes of these contrasts. He grounded the unglamorous qualities of the Northern songs in the inhospitable northern climate and the anemic habitat, both of which condemned the North's gloomy inhabitants to mere subsistence. Their political apathy deprived their songs of dramatic movement. The Southerners, according to Bodians'kyi, lived an active and passionate life. They exercised political agency and were blessed by mild climate and bounteous nature. This is as explicit a catalogue of national differences as can be. Not mincing words, Bodians'kyi further claimed that no Slavic tribes were more dissimilar than the Northern and Southern Rus'ians, their common designation as "russy" being a misnomer rooted in outsiders' onomastic ignorance.[47] This nationally angled dichotomy of the historic North and South of Rus' recalls Gogol's earlier article, "Vzgliad na sostavleniie Malorossii" ("A Glance at the Making of Little Russia," 1834). Both texts also attempt to include Ukrainian history within European, rather than Russian, history by claiming that the Cossacks saved Europe from the Mongols.[48] At least since Karamzin, this had been a standard assertion of Russian historiography.

Amvrosii Metlyns'kyi in 1839 followed Bodians'kyi in investing climactic conditions with explanatory power regarding the question of national divisions, especially when it came to language. For Metlyns'kyi, cold Northern weather caused tense facial movement and narrow openings between lips, which in turn made the Russian sounds tense and diphthongized. The free-flowing, soft, and melodious sounds of the Ukrainian language, by contrast, were the product of a warmer clime.[49]

The most popular journal of the time, *Biblioteka dlia chteniia* (The Library for Reading), sarcastically quipped: "the author seems to be saying that *we* don't keep our mouth open when we pronounce words, that we're afraid lest the sounds freeze in our mouths. In the south … where each winter the temperature falls only to twenty-four degrees below freezing, no more – in the south it's all different. There, nature allows one to keep one's mouth open year round."[50] The author was likely the journal's Polish owner, Józef Sękowski, who was a vocal opponent of Ukrainian culture's "right to life." He cut down Met-lyns'kyi's outlandish linguistic nationalism by noting that the so-called Little Russian language had no stable orthography or vocabulary, hence was not really a language at all, but merely a dialect. The richness of a language, *Biblioteka* contended elsewhere, depends not on nature, but on the richness of ideas that can be expressed in that language.[51] The journal also denigrated Ukrainian history while reviewing Sreznevskii's *Zaporozhian Antiquity*: "the author wishes to recreate the chronicles of a people that does not possess them."[52]

However, *Biblioteka dlia chteniia* rained not only on the Ukrainian folk parade but on the Russian one as well. Though it welcomed with curt and official-sounding praises Sakharov's *Songs of the Russian People*, it derided many minor Russian collectors' lack of professionalism.[53] Sękowski's polemic with Bodians'kyi, who promoted Šafárik's Slavophile theories, crystallized the Polish critic's position: "A primitive song is not yet poetry, but the babbling of an infant."[54] Thus fundamentally opposed to romantic folklorism, *Biblioteka* greeted politely, but through outdated and condescending formulas, Sreznevskii's and Maksymovych's 1834 volumes, calling them monuments of "provincial" linguistic culture (*slovesnost'*), which was on the verge of extinction.[55]

The publication, in the same year, of Kvitka-Osnovianenko's *Malorossi-iskie povesti* (Little Russian Tales) showed that at least for some this extinction might not come soon enough. Kvitka proved that the Ukrainian language could be used for modern literature and serious subjects. While *Biblioteka dlia chteniia* dismissed this important counterevidence to its own claims in a perfunctory review,[56] the paper with the next highest circulation, *Severnaia pchela*, featured an interesting debate about Kvitka. Though enthusiastic, the initial review nonetheless asserted, through an economy-of-scale argument, the uselessness of resurrecting the Ukrainian language: since all educated Ukrainian society speaks Russian, to write in Ukrainian means to narrow one's readership base.[57] Vladimir Dal', the famous Russian lexicographer who grew up in the predominantly Ukrainian town of Luhansk in Novorossiia Province and wrote under the pseudonym of Vladimir Luganskii, begged to differ. Should the Ukrainian language be "resurrected"? Dal's answer was an emphatic "yes." He claimed that instead of the Ukrainians switching to Russian, the Russians should become bilingual. How can one possibly consider superfluous, Dal' asked, a language in which "hundreds of thousands of people speak, especially when this language is a related, brotherly language, derived from the same root as the Russian?"[58] Quite likely, Kvitka's own later famous comment about the absurdity of suppressing a language "in which ten million people speak" in fact takes its cue from Dal' – while correcting Dal's statistics and omitting the notion of the linguistic similarity between Ukrainian and Russian.[59]

Sękowski's protestations notwithstanding, by the mid-1830s, the activities of Eastern European Slavists convinced most Russians that their culture had something to gain from a Slavic turn. Ukrainians or Ukrainophilic Russians propagated these ideas and published their own collections; literary works in Russian on Ukrainian folkloric themes, such as those of Narezhnyi or Gogol', were scoring top marks in *narodnost'*. Meanwhile, virtually all Russian literary commentators up to the early 1830s – Somov, Viazemskii, Bestuzhev, Venevitinov, Kiukhel'beker – stressed the unnational character of Russian literature and warned that Western Europeans were unlikely to recognize as original a literature that imitated Western literary models. All Europe fervently embraced a Herder-inspired romanticism that used folk sources in pursuit of national "local color." Such nationally stylized literature was a ticket to the European club of cultural nations. And Russians – no less than any others – badly wanted this ticket.

In the absence of a well-researched, articulated, and theorized body of work about Russian folklore in the 1830s, the conspicuous success of the popularizers of Ukraine's folklore suggested a tempting solution. Why not claim these Ukrainian – indeed, any Slavic – cultural resources as one's own? The journal that propagated this solution was Nikolai Nadezhdin's *Teleskop* (1831–6). Nadezhdin's seminal article "Evropeizm i narodnost'" ("Europeanism and Nationality") proposed to reorient Russia from Westernization, which had failed to produce a national culture, to Slavicization. This would be accomplished by importing elements of other Slavic languages into Russian, by absorbing the fruits of East European Slavists' ethnographic research, and by legitimizing the Russian empire's claims to the cultural activity of its "own" Slavs. At times, Nadezhdin sounds eerily rapacious: "The work of Šafárik, Kopitar, Hanka, Kollár and other great Slavists will be ours, will be for us!"[60] In Nadezhdin's schema this exercise would not constitute imitation because Slavic cultures cannot properly be regarded as "foreign" to the Russians. Moreover, clearly attuned to the Slavs beyond rather than within Russia's borders, Nadezhdin assures his readers that all Slavs love the Russian Empire and need only a cue to gladly "open up to us all their treasures."[61]

In fact, the program of imitating other Slavs as a method of nationalizing Russia was itself an imitation of other Slavs. When interest in Polish literature peaked in the late 1820s, the Russian press looked with a keen eye on the Poles' appropriation of the folkloric resources of their Ukrainian and Lithuanian rim.[62] To illustrate his program, Nadezhdin framed his article with quotes from Hryhorii Skovoroda (1722–94), whom he introduced as both a "Ukrainian philosopher" (*ukrainskii filosof*) and a "Russian sage" (*russkii mudrets*). Indeed, scarcely a year before, the Russification of Skovoroda was launched on the pages of Nadezhdin's *Teleskop* by a Russophile author of Moldovan origin, Alexander Haşedeu.[63] Incidentally, "Europeanism and Nationality" puts in a useful context Nadezhdin's subsequent decision to publish Petr Chaadaev's notorious "Philosophical Letter," for which the journal was shut down and Nadezhdin exiled. Chaadaev's incendiary assertion that Russia contributed nothing to world civilization seemed less grim if the sun of Slavic spring was about to warm back to life Chaadaev's insensate Russian colossus.

Teleskop proved a hospitable shore for a Ukrainian Slavist born in the Hungarian region of the Habsburg Empire, Iurii Venelin, who considered the Russian Empire a natural home for all Slavs. This agenda underpinned his review of Maksymovych's *Ukrainskie narodnye pesni* (Ukrainian Folk Songs) of 1834. In it, Venelin hijacked Maksymovych's contrastive device from the 1827 edition to send the opposite message: to propound what I would call a yin and yang model of Russo-Ukrainian relations. This model unites Northerners and Southerners (Venelin's *Severiane* and *Iuzhane*) in a robust and powerful all-Russian nation. Moreover, Venelin flips Maksymovych's privileging of the "Southerners" that so upset Shevyrev. Venelin's Northerners now appear active, resolute, extroverted, and curious to roam the world. The Southerners, according to Venelin (who identifies himself as one) are provincial homebodies, quiet and introverted, and accept their fate passively. The Northern Russians are clever in politics; the Southern Russians excel in the humanities. The Southerners are great at making plans; the Northerners at realizing them. "The heart of the Russian nation is in the south," Venelin writes, "while its head in the north."[64] He argues that these two aspects of the "Russian" nationality complement each other to form a superior national alloy. This pronouncement anticipates, and is conceivably a source of, Gogol's own famous statement about the mutual compatibility of the Russian and Ukrainian parts of his soul, an idea that Kostomarov later developed in his theory of two Russian nationalities.[65]

However, the 1834 edition of Maksymovych that Venelin was ostensibly reviewing charts a rather different course. By contrast to Venelin's yin and yang theory of Russo-Ukrainian relations, Maksymovych forged ahead with his championship of a separate Ukrainian identity. The intensification of this direction was marked in the title. The 1827 title *Little Russian Songs* (*Malorossiiskie pesni*) was now replaced with *Ukrainian Folk Songs* (*Ukrainskie narodnye pesni*) – "Ukrainian" having a more nationalistic resonance connected with the Cossack heritage.[66] Already this title change indicated how the "Little Russian idea" of merging local Ukrainian identity with loyalty to the imperial state could easily morph into a separatist sentiment.[67] Maksymovych remained focused on "Ukrainian poetry" (italicized in the preface) and "Ukrainian language," shunning any overtures about their inclusion in larger cultural categories. Adopting Sreznevskii's model, he provided a narrative of Ukrainian history through the historical précis that accompanied the chronologically arranged sections. At the time when discussions of Khmel'nyts'kyi commonly served to reaffirm the happy confluence of two fraternal nations, Maksymovych laconically noted the hetman's *personal* surrender to the Russian tsar, eschewing any suggestion that this was indicative of the people's will or any popular attitudes. He suggested that the entire Kyivan period may in fact belong to Ukrainian, rather than Russian history – an idea that his colleague Gogol' also explored in his historical research.[68] Maksymovych made *Slovo o polku Igoreve* (The Lay of the Igor Host), epigraphs from which headed many of his chapters, basically a work of old Ukrainian literature, noting its similarities to Ukrainian folk songs and *dumy*. He labelled the historic Ukrainian lands "the South-Rus', or simply Rus' land, i.e., Ukraine" (*Iuzhno-Russkuiu ili prosto Rus'kuiu* [sic] *zemliu*, t. e. *Ukrainu*; emphasis in the original). This formulation locates the Rus' identity firmly in the south, its original and continuing locus.[69] Maksymovych's overall message was that Ukraine had an exclusive and historic proprietary claim on the cultural Rus' identity – a conviction that underpinned his later impassioned polemics with an ideologue of Russian imperial nationalism, the historian Mikhail Pogodin.[70] This message implicitly countered the idea, widely popularized in the official Russian discourse, of Ukraine's union with Russia as its "return" to the pristine Russian spirit, from which it had been wrested by historical vicissitudes.

Gone were the risky contrasts between the Ukrainian and Russian national spirit that captured everyone's attention in 1827. But Maksymovych affirmed them more subtly by crediting the Russian authority, Petr Kireevskii, as his source of information about the Russian songs. Neither could he resist the snide comment that while some nations pour the memory of important historical events into medals, others pour them into songs.[71] This comment was a clear put-down of the Russians, since an archaeological find of old Russian medals was widely discussed that year in the Russian press. Inert metal versus living song: one veiled dichotomy that signalled national differences thus slipped into this new edition. All in all, it is unsurprising why Gogol', who contributed from his own extensive collection to Maksymovych's 1834 volume, would discuss its publication as an act of national significance for Ukraine. He looked in Petersburg for an artist, obligatorily a Ukrainian, who could design a book cover with a "national" appearance.[72]

The cultural activity surrounding collections of Ukrainian folklore in the 1820s and 1830s corroborates Roman Szporluk's contention that a distinction between political and cultural nationalism is a false dichotomy. Nationalism, according to Szporluk, is "political *ab initio* – even when those engaged in nationalist activities denied any political intent or meaning, or insisted that their sole object was a scholarly understanding of political culture, folklore, or local history ... 'National awakeners,' questioning by virtue of their endeavours established power structures, power relations, and the values upholding them, are quite obviously engaged in what is at least an inherently political undertaking."[73] Ukraine's folklorists attempted to renegotiate the empire's value system by divorcing cultural capital from geopolitical might. As Herder had taught them, nations were organic entities, so folk songs mattered more than armies. They tried to remake the empire into a more inclusive and egalitarian cultural space, testing its openness to a separate Ukrainian identity.

In the Herder-inspired pan-European hierarchy of cultural values, to which until the 1840s Russians, too, subscribed, a nation demonstrated its legitimacy through the folklore-derived pedigree of its "spirit." The activities of Ukraine's folklorists thus asserted Ukraine's separate identity not only vis-à-vis the imperial centre, but also on a European stage well peopled by other Slavs. Through these activities, Ukraine was writing its own ticket to Europe. Romantic nationalism provided a route where Russia's mediation would not be necessary, just as Europe's contemporaneous recognition of Poles, Serbs, or Greeks as nations did not require in this framework the mediation of the states to which they belonged.

This was a prospect that many Russian intellectuals found alarming. Vissarion Belinskii's hostile attacks in the 1840s on the emergent modern Ukrainian literature focused precisely on cutting off Ukraine's unmediated route to Europe. This undertaking was conceivable only if one rejected the Herderian philosophy of nationalism and adopted the Hegelian one. In Andrea Rutherford's apt phrase, Belinskii believed that Ukraine could access European civilization only by "riding Russia's coattails."[74] This view was a reversal of Nadezhdin's position, voiced only a few years prior, that Russia could in effect access European civilization only by riding the coattails of Ukrainians and other Slavs. The public discourse surrounding the collections of Ukrainian folk songs facilitated an impression that Ukrainians had an important cultural ingredient that Russia lacked. Nadezhdin's solution was to appropriate this ingredient as Russia's own; Belinskii's solution was to proclaim it worthless.

We should appreciate the fact that the Ukrainian folkloric project was a team effort by people of various ethnic backgrounds. Among the collectors, theorists, and philologists were not only Ukrainians, like Maksymovych and Bodians'kyi, but also Russians who grew up or lived in Ukraine, like Sreznevskii, Dal', or the Russified Georgian Tsertelev, and Poles, like Dołęga-Chodakowski or Brodziński. The idea of a Ukrainian *Volksgeist* was infectious. Moreover, the entire Slavic revival that helped reorient Russia's own culture towards the path of nationally conscious art was accomplished through Russia's centripetal relations with its own peripheries and with the larger Slavic world in the early decades of the nineteenth century. It is commonly accepted that the construction of a modern national identity in Russia was the consequence not of an "awakening" to self-awareness but of the careful cultivation of a European fashion that travelled to Russia from the West. But it merits emphasis that this fashion was reformatted for Russian consumption in its near and distant Slavic backyard. Viazemskii coined the very term *narodnost'* while reading Brodziński in Warsaw. Ukrainians or Ukrainophiles were the ones who popularized in Russia a Slavicized romantic literature based on Ukrainian folk material, often by importing Polish models.[75] As a folkloric "Mecca" for both Poles and Russians, Ukraine helped reorient their cultures towards romanticism.[76]

Towards the end of the 1820s, when the Russians' relative inactivity in folk song collecting acquired the air of a national disgrace, the Ukrainians and Ukrainophiles stepped in as advocates for action and as purveyors of models. But their activities centred on Ukrainian, not Russian, folkloric materials and their pronouncements had a complex agenda. On the one hand, they presented their work, somewhat formulaically, as contributing to the glory of the all-Russian fatherland. On the other hand, they used comparisons between Russian and Ukrainian folk traditions as springboards for drawing *national* distinctions. Maksymovych's discourse on Ukrainian folklore proved particularly influential in this regard. The comparative model of national differences that he cemented was widely copied and debated. As the polemics I have examined show, nineteenth-century discussions of folk heritage transcended mere philological interest to become a proxy for debates about nationhood.

Towards mid-century, with Herderianism on the wane, the Russians' admiration for Ukrainian folk traditions gave way to a denigration of them as primitive. When Gogol' insisted on singing Ukrainian songs at his name day party in 1850, accompanied by some of the Ukrainian folklorists discussed in this article, his Russian friends were aghast. Sergei Aksakov described this event in a letter using a dismissive Russian ethnonym for Ukrainians, "khokhly":

Three *khokhly* were just charming – sang even without accompaniment – and Gogol' read to me some interminable *dumy* of some *khokhlatskii* Homer: he recited and the remaining *khokhly* gesticulated and whooped ... Khomiakov, Solov'ev, and I feasted our eyes on this display of nationality, but without much sympathy. One could sense disdain in Solov'ev's smile, in Khomiakov's laughter – good-natured mockery. And I simply felt absurd and funny looking at them, as if they were Chuvash or Cheremis natives ... and nothing more. Bodians'kyi was splendidly frenzied, and Maksymovych melted away like a milk-and-honey lollipop, or the Tatar *klevo-sakhar.*[77]

No longer a ticket to Europe, Ukrainian folk songs were thus redefined as a ticket to Oriental "barbarity."

The Soviet era of officially declared "friendship of the peoples" did not erase such tensions, which resurged in the tumultuous post-Soviet era. In June of 2000, a well-known Ukrainian composer, Ihor Bilozir, died as a result of a beating by Russian-speaking thugs who objected to his singing of Ukrainian songs in a cafe. This violent act sparked angry demonstrations by Ukrainians who demanded a derussification of Ukraine. The mayor of Lviv introduced a temporary ban on all Russian music in public places.[78] Since many Russians grew concerned over the constitutionality of this ban (but not the Ukrainian composer's death), the event was widely reported in the Russian media. Even in present times, public expressions of Ukrainian identity continue to rely on the unifying force of Ukrainian folk songs. During protests at Maidan Square in Kyiv in 2013–14, sparked by President Yanukovych's reneging on his promise to reorient Ukraine towards European institutions, it was with a moving Ukrainian folk lament that the protesters mourned their comrades gunned down by Yanukovych's snipers.[79] As these episodes show, folkloric nationalism retains its explosive power in Russo-Ukrainian relations to this day.

Notes

1 George Grabowicz, "Ukrainian-Russian Literary Relations in the Nineteenth Century: A Formulation of the Problem," in *Ukraine and Russia in Their Historical Encounter*, ed. Peter J. Potichnyj et al. (Edmonton: Canadian Institute of Ukrainian Studies, 1992), 227.

2 Quoted in William Wilson, "Herder, Folklore, and Romantic Nationalism," *Folk Groups and Folklore Genres: A Reader*, ed. Elliott Oring (Logan, Utah: Utah State University Press, 1989), 26.

3 Sviatoslav Hordynsky, "Ukrainian Romanticism and Its Relation to the Western World," *The Ukrainian Review* 32, no. 4 (1984): 49.

4 Johann Gottfried Herder, "Journal meiner Reise im Jahr 1769," in *J.G. Herder on Social and Political Culture*, trans. and ed. F.M. Barnard (Cambridge, England: Cambridge Univ. Press, 1969), 90.

5 Ahapii Shamrai, *Kharkivs'ka shkola romantykiv*, vol. 1 (Kharkiv: Derzhavne vydavnytstvo Ukraïny, 1930).

6 Small eighteenth-century collections – all of which included Ukrainian material – no longer appealed to a romantic. These included Mikhail Chulkov, *Sobranie raznykh pesen* (1773–4); Nikolai L'vov and Ivan Prach, *Sobranie narodnykh russkikh pesen s ikh golosami* (1790); and Kirsha Danilov, *Drevnie russkie stikhotvoreniia* (1804). Danilov was a Cossack from around Kyiv and Prach was a Czech.

7 Mark Azadovskii, *Istoriia russkoi fol'kloristiki*, vol. 1 (Moscow: Gosud. uchebno-pedagogicheskoe izd-vo, 1958), 328.

8 Azadovskii, 342.

9 Aleksandr Pypin, *Istoriia russkoi etnografii*, vols. 1 and 3 (St Petersburg: Stasiulevich, 1890 and 1891), 1: 375 and 3: 25–6.

10 Azadovskii, 288.

11 David Saunders, *The Ukrainian Impact on Russian Culture, 1750–1850* (Edmonton: Canadian Institute of Ukrainian Studies, 1985).

12 See, for example, "O serbskikh narodnykh pesniakh" (about Vuk Karadžić's collection), *Vestnik Evropy* 112 (1820): 112–29; Dołęga-Chodakowski's Ukrainian songs in *Vestnik Evropy* 7 (1829): 244–50; "O prostonarodnykh pesniakh," *Vestnik Evropy* 11 (1827): 191–201 (reprinted from *Kalendarz Lwowski*). For a bibliography of relevant articles from *Moskovskii telegraf*, see Azadovskii, 235–7. See also an article about West and South Slavic songs in *Moskovskii vestnik* 2 (1827) and Iurii Venelin, "O kharaktere narodnykh pesen u slavian zadunaiskikh" *Teleskop* 27 (1835): 1–33, 149–83, 275–326. In addition, journals printed travelogues about other Slavic lands and accounts of other Slavs' customs, history, and contemporary literature.

13 Włodzimierz Mokry, "Wkład Zoriana Dołęgi-Chodakowskiego w życie naukowe i literackie Ukrainy i Rosji," in *Polacy w życiu kulturalnym Rosji*, ed. Ryszard Łużny (Wrocław: Zakład Narodowy im. Ossolińskich, 1986), 23.

14 *Ukraïns'ki pisni v zapysakh Zoriana Dolenhy-Khodakovs'koho* (Kyiv: Naukova dumka, 1974).

15 Nikolai Tsertelev, *Opyt sobraniia starinnykh malorossiiskikh pesen* (St Petersburg: Tip. Karla Kraiia, 1819), 2–3. For a reprint of Tsertelev's introduction, see *Istoriia ukraïns'koï literaturnoï krytyky ta literaturoznavstva: Khrestomatiia*, vol. 1, ed. Pavlo Fedchenko (Kyiv: Lybid', 1996), 56–62.

16 Tsertelev, *Opyt*, 4–5. Prior to Maksymovych, such funereal rhetoric was standard; see I. Kulzhinskii, "Nekotorye zamechaniia kasatel'no istorii i kharaktera Malorosiiskoi poezii," *Ukrainskii zhurnal* 5, no. 1 (1825): 50.

17 Azadovskii, 192.

18 Kazimierz Brodziński, "O narodnykh pesniakh Slavian," *Vestnik Evropy* 13 (1826): 48 (reprinted from *Dziennik Warszawski* [Warsaw Daily]).

19 Nikolai Tsertelev, "O narodnykh stikhotvoreniiakh (Pis'mo Maksimovichu),"
  Vestnik Evropy 12 (1827): 271.

20 David L. Cooper, *Creating the Nation: Identity and Aesthetics in Early Nineteenth-
  century Russia and Bohemia* (DeKalb: Northern Illinois University Press, 2010),
  89–107.

21 Stepan Shevyrev, rev. of *Malorossiiskie pesni* (1827) by M. Maksymovych, *Moskovskii
  vestnik* 6 (1827): 310. See a similar complaint in *Severnaia pchela* 123 (1827): 1.

22 Lazar Chereiskii, *Pushkin i ego okruzhenie* (Leningrad: "Nauka," 1988), 247.

23 Stefan Kozak, "Mychajło Maksymowicz – prekursor romantyzmu na Ukrainie,"
  Kozak, *Z dziejów Ukrainy: religia, kultura, myśl społeczna* (Warsaw: Wyd.
  Uniwersytetu Warszawskiego, 2006), 110.

24 *Vestnik Evropy* 15 (August, 1827): 184–200. For reprints of a few songs and
  Maksymovych's comments on the Ukrainian language, see *Moskovskii telegraf*
  2 (1827): 314–19, 419–20 and 3 (1827): 316–17. In an implicit polemic with
  Maksymovych's view of Ukrainian as a language, *Telegraf* printed in the very
  next volume the classification of a unitary Slavic language's "dialects" by the
  Bohemian philologist Josef Dobrovský from which Ukrainian and Belarusian were
  conspicuously missing, apparently subsumed under the "Russian dialect." See "O
  razdelenii slovenskogo iazyka na narechia," Mikhail Pogodin, trans., *Moskovskii
  telegraf* 4 (1827): 177–8.

25 Kozak, "Mychajło Maksymowicz," 111.

26 Faith Hillis, *Children of Rus': Right-Bank Ukraine and the Invention of a Russian
  Nation* (Ithaca: Cornell University Press, 2013), 12–15.

27 Mykhailo Maksymovych, *Malorossiiskie pesni* (Moscow, 1827), quoted from the
  facsimile edition *Ukraïns'ki pisni, vydani M. Maksymovychem* (Kyiv: Vyd. Akad.
  nauk URSR, 1962), 8. Cited in the facsimile pagination.

28 Maksymovych, *Malorossiiskie pesni*, 16–17.

29 Ibid., 39.

30 Tsertelev, "O narodnykh stikhotvoreniiakh," 276.

31 Maksymovych, *Malorossiiskie pesni*, 17–18.

32 Ibid., 19.

33 Shevyrev, rev. of *Malorossiiskie pesni*, 315.

34 Ibid.

35 The eleventh issue of *Moskovskii vestnik* (1828), for example, printed "Russian
  songs, as it happens, anguished ones" (Russkie pesni, kak raz tosklivye). In
  Moskovskii vestnik, see also "Russkaia razboinich'ia pesnia," 10 (1828): 119–23;
  6 (1827): 331–9; 18 (1828): 108–10.

36 Shamrai, *Kharkivs'ka shkola*, 10.

37 Johannes Remy, "Government Promotion of Ukrainian Studies: The Careers of
  Izmail Sreznevskii, Osyp Bodians'kyi and Amvrosyi Metlyns'kyi, 1825–1855," in

Defining Self: Essays on Emergent Identities in Russia, Seventeenth to Nineteenth Centuries, ed. Michael Branch (Helsinki: Finnish Literature Society, 2009), 267, 254.

38 Izmail Sreznevskii, *Zaporozhskaia starina*, pt. 1 (Kharkiv: Universitetskaia tip., 1833); Taras Koznarsky, "Izmail Sreznevsky's 'Zaporozhian Antiquity' as a Memory Project," *Eighteenth-Century Studies* 35, no. 1 (2001): 92–100. Maksymovych welcomed Sreznevsky's volume in *Molva* 6 (1834): 92–4.

39 Remy, "Government Promotion of Ukrainian Studies," 255–7, 263; Izmail Sreznevskii, "Vzgliad na pamiatniki ukrainskoi narodnoi slovesnosti" (1834), *Istoriia ukraïns'koi literaturnoï krytyky*, 67–8.

40 Nikolai Gogol', *Polnoe sobranie sochinenii* (Moscow: Izd. Akad. nauk SSSR, 1937–52), 8:760.

41 Gogol', *Polnoe sobranie sochinenii*, 8:91.

42 On Gogol's complex engagement with Ukrainian history, see Edyta Bojanowska, *Nikolai Gogol: Between Ukrainian and Russian Nationalism* (Cambridge, MA: Harvard University Press, 2007), 89–169.

43 Rev. of *Zaporozhskaia starina*, *Severnaia pchela* 66 (1834): 261, 263.

44 Aleksandr Kotliarevskii to Mykhailo Maksymovych, letter, 7 December 1868, cited in Boris Kirdan (Borys Kyrdan), *Sobirateli narodnoi poezii* (Moscow: Izd-vo "Nauka," 1974), 10.

45 Gogol', *Polnoe sobranie sochinenii*, 8:96.

46 Osyp Bodians'kyi, rev. of *Narodnié zpievanki cili pisne swetské w uhrah* (1834–35), by Ján Kollár, *Moskovskii nabliudatel'* 4 (1835): 581–4, 589–92. See also Remy, "Government Promotion of Ukrainian Studies," 259–60.

47 Bodians'kyi, rev. of *Narodnié zpievanki*, 584–5.

48 Bodians'kyi, rev. of *Narodnié zpievanki*, 589; for a discussion of Gogol's article see Bojanowska, *Nikolai Gogol'*, 122–43. Bodians'kyi championed Slavs as ancient Europeans in his report on Šafárik's rejection of the Scythian hypothesis, which treated Slavs as migrants from Asia (Osyp Bodians'kyi, "Mysli o drevnosti Slavian v Evrope," *Moskovskii nabliudatel'* 8 [1836]: 48–84).

49 A. Metlyns'kyi [pseud. Amvrosii Mohyla], *Dumky i pisni ta shche de-shcho* (Kharkiv: Univ. tipografiia, 1839), 6–7.

50 Rev. of *Dumky i pisni ta shche de-shcho* by A. Metlyns'kyi [pseud. Amvrosii Mohyla] (1839), *Biblioteka dlia chteniia* 34 (1839): 27–8.

51 Rev. of *O narodnoi poezii slavianskikh plemen* by Osyp Bodians'kyi (1837), *Biblioteka dlia chteniia* 23 (1837): 15.

52 Rev. of *Zaporozhskaia starina*, pt. 2, by I. Sreznevskii (1838), *Biblioteka dlia chteniia* 30 (1838).

53 See reviews of Sakharov in *Biblioteka dlia chteniia* 28 (1838) and 30 (1838); for examples of dismissive reviews of minor Russian collections, see the "Literaturnaia kritika" sections of *Biblioteka dlia chteniia* 5 (1834) or 23 (1837).

54 Rev. of *O narodnoi poezii*, *Biblioteka dlia chteniia*, 15–16. The journal derided Slavomania in a review of Iurii Venelin's *O kharaktere narodnykh pesen u slavian zadunaiskikh*, noting that Venelin made the Biblical Adam into a Bulgarian (16 [1836]).

55 Rev. of *Zaporozhskaia starina* by Izmail Sreznevskii (1833), *Biblioteka dlia chteniia* 2 (1834): 15; rev. of *Ukrainskie narodnye pesni*, by Mykhailo Maksymovych (1834), *Biblioteka dlia chteniia* 5 (1834).

56 Rev. of *Malorossiiskie povesti*, by Hryhorii Kvitka-Osnovianenko (1834), *Biblioteka dlia chteniia* 7 (1834).

57 Rev. of *Malorossiiskie povesti*, by H. Kvitka-Osnovianenko (1834), *Severnaia pchela* 248 (1834): 2.

58 Vladimir Luganskii [pseud. of Vladimir Dal'], rev. of *Malorossiiskie povesti*, by H. Kvitka-Osnovianenko (1834), *Severnaia pchela* 17 (1835): 2.

59 Hryhorii Kvitka-Osnovianenko, *Zibrannia tvoriv u semy tomakh* (Kyiv: Naukova dumka, 1978–81), 7:228. Dal' himself may have been inspired by Iurii Venelin, who in 1834 estimated that the "southern Russian" dialect was spoken by twenty million people, including those living outside of the Russian borders; Iurii Venelin, rev. of *Ukrainskie narodnye pesni*, by Mykhailo Maksymovych (1834), *Teleskop* 22 (1834): 566.

60 Nikolai Nadezhdin, "Evropeizm i narodnost', v otnoshenii k russkoi slovesnosti," in *Literaturnaia kritika: Estetika* (Moscow: Khudozh. lit., 1972): 436–7. The article originally appeared in *Teleskop* 31 (1836): 5–60, 203–64.

61 Nadezhdin, *Literaturnaia kritika*, 436.

62 See, e.g., the translation of Franciszek Dmochowski's 1825 article "Uwagi nad teraźniejszym stanem, duchem i dążnością poezji polskiej," *Moskovskii telegraf* 4 (1826): 183–96, 265–79. On Polish collectors who used Ukrainian songs for a Polish nationalist agenda see Włodzimierz Mokry, "Folklor i jego rola w działalności 'Ruskiej Trójcy,'" *Studia Polono-Slavica-Orientalia* 7 (1981): 141–3.

63 Mokry, "Folklor i jego rola," 444; Alexander Mihailovic, "Pietist Nationalism and the Russian Rediscovery of Skovoroda," *Journal of Ukrainian Studies* 22, no. 1–2 (1997): 75–86.

64 Iurii Venelin, rev. of *Ukrainskie narodnye pesni*, by Mykhailo Maksymovych (1834), *Teleskop* 22 (1834): 572. In addition, Venelin begins to reconceptualize the Ukrainian nation by including within it Ukrainians from outside of the Russian Empire; see Venelin, rev. of Maksymovych, 566 and his "O kharaktere narodnykh pesen u slavian zadunaiskikh," *Teleskop* 27 (1834): 167.

65 Mykola Kostomarov, "Two Russian Nationalities," in *Toward an Intellectual History of Ukraine: An Anthology of Ukrainian Thought from 1710 to 1995*, ed. Ralph Lindheim and George S.N. Luckyj (Toronto: University of Toronto Press, 1996), 122–45; on the complex circumstances of Gogol's statement, see Edyta

Bojanowska, "Nikolai Vasilievich Gogol, 1809–1852," in *Russia's People of Empire: Life Stories from Eurasia, 1500 to the Present*, ed. Stephen Norris and Willard Sunderland (Bloomington, IN: Indiana University Press, 2012), 159–67.

66 Unobtrusively, deep inside the book, Maksymovych obliquely addresses the change in title. He explains that Little Russia is the region of Ukraine that after 1764 united with Russia, while the songs in the current volume come from the autonomous Ukraine from beyond the Dnieper; M. Maksymovych, *Ukrainskie narodnye pesni* (Moscow: Universitetskaia tip., 1834), 120.

67 On "the Little Russian idea" see Hillis, *Children of Rus'*, 12–15.

68 Bojanowska, *Nikolai Gogol*, 143–55.

69 Maksymovych, *Ukrainskie narodnye pesni*, 84, 68, 67.

70 See Maksymovych's letters to Pogodin in Maksymovych, *Sobranie sochinenii*, vol. 3, pt. 1, 188–311. After Pogodin accused Maksymovych of excessive allegiance to Ukraine, Maksymovych proudly accepted the charge in a letter of 1857: "It is natural that I am a 'sincere Little Russian' now as before and will be one until I die: I am not from the Varangian people [i.e., a Russian], but from the Little Russian one. And I love Little Russia, I love its people's language, songs, and history […] That I love our first capital Kyiv more than you is also natural, since feeling both an all-Russian (obshcherusskaia) and the closest, Little Russian, love, I love it also as the native land of my own kin" (*Sobranie sochinenii*, vol. 3, pt. 1, 250). For a selection of Pogodin's letters to Maksymovych see Mikhail Pogodin, *Pis'ma M.P. Pogodina k M.A. Maksimovichu* (St Petersburg: Tip. Imp. akademii nauk, 1882).

71 Maksymovych, *Ukrainskie narodnye pesni*, 4.

72 Gogol', *Polnoe sobranie sochinenii*, 10:249, 301–2; his phrase was "natsional'naia vin'etka."

73 Roman Szporluk, *Russia, Ukraine, and the Breakup of the Soviet Union* (Stanford, Calif.: Hoover Institution Press, 2000), 367.

74 Andrea Rutherford, "Vissarion Belinskii and the Ukrainian National Question," *The Russian Review* 54, no. 4 (1995): 512; see also Bojanowska, *Nikolai Gogol*, 309–12.

75 The works of Orest Somov and Nikolai Gogol' serve as good examples. In proving that folk songs were useful for creative literary practice, Maksymovych appended to his *Little Russian Songs* of 1827 Hulak-Artemovs'kyi's Ukrainian translation or, more precisely, paraphrase of Mickiewicz's ballad "Pan Twardowski," which was republished that year in two other Russian journals; see Stefan Kozak, *Polacy i Ukraińcy: W kręgu myśli i kultury pogranicza* (Warsaw: Wyd. Uniwersytetu Warszawskiego, 2005), 71–2. Sreznevskii's 1834 *Zaporozhian Antiquity* featured, along with an epigraph from Kotliarevs'kyi's burlesque *Aeneid*, one from

Mickiewicz's *Forefathers' Eve*, pt. 2 (*Dziady*, 1823) – but none from a Russian source. See also Shamrai, *Kharkivs'ka shkola*, vol. 1.

76 Kozak, *Polacy i Ukraińcy*, 67–8; M. Janion and M. Żmigrodzka call Ukraine "the most mythogenetic region of Polish romanticism" (cited in Kozak, *Polacy i Ukraińcy*, 116).

77 Sergei Aksakov to Ivan Aksakov, letter, 20 March 1850, quoted in *N. V. Gogol'*, *Materialy i issledovaniia*, ed. V. Gippius, vol. 1 (Moscow: Izd. Akad. nauk SSSR, 1936), 217.

78 *The Ukrainian Weekly* 23 (2000): 9, and 27 (2000): 1, 3, 4. I am grateful to Giorgio DiMauro, who was in Russia at the time, for bringing this story to my attention.

79 See "An Old Ukrainian Folk Song Takes on a New Meaning in the Current Crisis," accessed on 19 February 2015, http://www.pri.org/stories/2014-04-16/old-ukrainian-folk-song-takes-new-meaning-current-crisis, or "'Plyve kacha' – A Ukrainian Folk Song Mourning the Dead of Maidan Square," accessed on 19 February 2015, https://makingmulticulturalmusic.wordpress.com/2014/04/19/plyve-kacha-a-ukranian-folk-song-mourning-the-dead-of-maidan-square/. The singing of this folk lament was also captured in Sergei Loznitsa's documentary *Maidan* (Atoms & Void, 2014).

Discovering "Little Russia": Victor Tissot and Ukraine's Image in the West in the 1880s

GIULIA LAMI

The Swiss writer Victor Tissot (1844–1917) was a popular French author of the belle époque.[1] He moved to France after attending university in Germany. Like many talented foreigners, he chose Paris as his new home because of the opportunities it offered for finding work in the literary and journalistic world. Tissot came into the public eye quite early, in 1875, thanks to his book polemically entitled *Voyage au pays des milliards*, which described his journey to postunification Germany. The title refers to the billions of francs paid by France in keeping with the terms of the Treaty of Frankfurt, which concluded the Franco-Prussian War of 1870–1. *Voyage au pays des milliards* encountered unprecedented success in France (fifty-five editions were published between 1875 and the end of the century) because of its critical assessment of the consequences of the Franco-Prussian War for the fate of Europe. Tissot was identified as a Frenchman because of his literary choice always to speak in the first person about the deceptions and grievances suffered by France and its citizens.

He was recognized at once by the public as an excellent travel writer (*écrivain voyageur*), and he began writing a series of travel books claiming to offer an accurate picture of the countries he had visited. In the 1870s and 1880s he devoted a series of books to Germany, Austria-Hungary, and Russia. Marked by a brilliant journalistic style, they presented a multitude of geographical, political, and cultural facts as *prima manu* materials. Tissot's books suited the tastes of the members of the general public, who were fascinated by foreign countries but were still not accustomed to travelling abroad: in this sense he indulged the reading public's widespread thirst for knowledge that he was able to satisfy in many different ways.

In addition to writing books claiming to offer a historical and political evaluation of the countries he visited, including those that were devoted to the above-mentioned countries, Tissot was the author of more popular works that blended adventure, geography, and science. He translated or adapted European novels into the French language, contributed to anthologies of French and Swiss literature, and wrote novels with an exotic flavor. He was also the editor of the literary supplement to *Le Figaro* from 1891 to 1893 and the director of publications for Hachette. Last but not least, he promoted and sometimes served as the editor of such popular magazines as *L'Écho de la semaine*, *Mon Dimanche*, and *Lectures pour tous*.

Tissot never forgot his native land. Convinced that Switzerland could be developed as a tourist destination, in 1888 he wrote *La Suisse inconnue*,[2] in which he suggested interesting itineraries for foreigners in the hope of attracting visitors even from the United States. He purchased a large property in the district of Gruyère (canton of Fribourg), where he built the Hôtel des Bains. Opened in 1884, it was sold after a few years of operation. At the end of his life he decided to bequeath his estate to the town of Bulle (Gruyère), with the aim of creating a museum and a library. These are still functioning to the present day. Since his books became bestsellers, it is important to analyse what kind of information he offered his readers and what images of the countries he visited were promoted in his books.

Tissot's contemporaries, of course, had other sources of knowledge about foreign lands, including novels and essays written in French or translated from English and German, the daily press, and periodical publications that flourished in France during the last quarter of the nineteenth century. One of the latter was *La Revue des Deux Mondes*, founded in 1830, which monitored international developments during the nineteenth century, including in Eastern and Central Europe. Tissot's personal library, now part of the Musée gruérien in Bulle, contains a large collection of books about Russia, a testament to the writer's lifelong interest in the country.[3]

Tissot combined his claims to being a serious writer with his attempts to be brilliant and "honest," as he was fond of repeating, in recounting what he saw during his travels. It cannot be denied that he was able to cobble together a unique picture based on geographical and historical data and bolstered by opinions and conversations to which he was privy during his train journeys and in restaurants, thus giving the impression that he was always in touch with the surrounding reality.

Tissot was harshly criticized for his hostile attitude towards Germany, which frustrated his pretensions to be an honest commentator. One of his most scathing critics was Henry James, whose review of one of two sequels to *Voyage au pays des milliards* was published in 1877 in the *Nation*. James wrote: "The popularity of his volumes makes them worth noticing, however, with the reflection that it seems a pity that the perusal of this ingenious but essentially vulgar vituperation should appear to the French reader the best way of arriving at that knowledge of the reality of things beyond the Rhine in which they have confessed themselves deficient."[4]

Tissot continued to write about Germany, a subject that had been the key to his success, issuing new books containing old material and adapting them to the tastes of his public. These included *Les Prussiens en Allemagne* (1876), *Voyage aux pays annexés* (1876), *La Société et les moeurs allemandes* (trans. Dr. Johannes Scherr, 1877), *La Police secrète prussienne* (1880), *L'Allemagne amoureuse* (1884), *Les curiosités de l'Allemagne du Nord* (1885), and *Les curiosités de l'Allemagne du Sud* (1886).

His last volume on Germany, published in 1916, was entitled *L'Allemagne casquée: Voyage au pays des milliards*: once again, it was a re-edition of his first book featuring some new materials. Like his earlier publications, it enjoyed success, even though one might argue that after forty years the reading public was very familiar with Tissot's arguments. Evidently his anti-German sentiment – teutophobia, to use the term coined by Henry James – was shared by many of his contemporaries.

Tissot is often described as a biased writer of dubious value, and not simply because he was the author of tendentious books on German topics. His *Voyage au pays des Tziganes: la Hongrie inconnue* (1880)[5] displeased Hungarians, who did not appreciate seeing their country labelled as "the land of the Gypsies."[6] In reality, Tissot was paying homage in this work to the romantic enthusiasm for the exotic sound of the Roma-inspired music with which Hungary was identified in the second half of the nineteenth century. In his opinion, Gypsies were the personification of freedom and the symbol of the vast magnificence of the Great Hungarian Plain, the *Puszta*, just as the Zaporozhian Cossacks were regarded as the symbol of the mighty steppes and thus the most significant image for defining Ukraine.

In the late 1870s Tissot resolved to devote some books to the lands of Austria-Hungary because they were "new and lovely countries" both to him and France. The results of these efforts were *Vienne et la vie viennoise* (1878) and *Voyage au pays des Tziganes* (1880), and he planned to continue with books about Galicia and Bohemia. These were never written, probably because he turned his attention to Russia.

In 1880 he co-wrote, with Constant Améro, a curious novel entitled *La Russie rouge: Roman contemporain*, which explored the problem of nihilism in the region bordering the Neva River. This novel was promptly followed by *La Vie en Sibérie, aventures de trois fugitifs*, also co-written with Améro, and published in 1881.[7] In the meantime, he decided to visit Russia and write. a report on his journey, which took place between the fall of 1880 and early spring of 1881. His return to France coincided with the assassination of Tsar Alexander II of Russia, at which time his Parisian editor, Edouard Dentu, asked Tissot to turn his notes into a "quick" book on Russia. The result was *Russes et Allemands*, a work featuring (once again) old material from his previous books on Germany, in which the main focus was on the possible alliance between Russian nihilism and German socialism. The book was translated into English because, according to a review published in the *New York Times*, "it touches upon some points in Russian life that have not been much discussed in England such as the 'Fathers of Nihilism,' the 'Education of Women in Russia,' the 'Russian Universities,' the 'Decline in Manners,' 'New Germany and New Russia,' the 'Germans in Russia,' 'German Socialism and the Moral Condition of Berlin,' and the internal conditions of Russia itself."[8]

Finally, in 1882 Tissot published a travelogue of his trip to Russia entitled *La Russie et les Russes: indiscrétions de voyage*, in which he illustrated things that he claimed to have seen while travelling "by train, by boat, by *kibitka* and *tarantass*, in the Ukrainian steppes, in the catacombs of Kyiv, in Moscow's prisons, in ignoble Saint Petersburg slums, on the miserable sleds of the icy Gulf of Finland."[9]

It is worth taking a closer look at *Russia and Russians*, the first part of which, *La Petite-Russie* – "Little Russia," as he called Ukraine – is devoted to his journey from Lviv (Léopol) to Kyiv (Kiew). The book had a convoluted history, as it was partially re-edited and appeared under different titles and in various languages (but not in English): the Italian edition, titled *L'Ucraina: Kiew*, was published in the late nineteenth century and distributed to many Italian public libraries. It needs to be borne in mind that in France at the beginning of the 1880s knowledge about Ukraine was scarce: Ukrainian subject matter had been touched on only occasionally, and then only in connection with Polish or Russian history.[10] The earliest articles devoted to Ukrainian folklore or poetry, usually defined as Ruthenian or Little Russian, had appeared only a few years before Tissot's journey to Eastern Europe. This makes Tissot's book an interesting and rich source worthy of analysis, notwithstanding the limitations of his cultural perspective. Unlike his French contemporaries Anatole Leroy-Beaulieu, Émile Durand, or Alfred Rambaud, who also wrote about Ukraine and Russia, he was not a scholar but a popularizer. Still, the quantity of information that he offered was very considerable in relation to what was then available, and his work is revealing of the period's cultural perceptions of Ukraine and Russia. His double identity as a Swiss and a Frenchman gave him a unique opportunity to combine love for tradition with praise of modernity, the former embodied for him by his native land, the latter by the city where he chose to live: Paris, the European metropolis par excellence.

Tissot begins his narrative in Lviv, during an official visit of the Austrian emperor.[11] Tissot recognizes the distinctiveness of Ukraine: he speaks of the Ruthenian language and notes the continuity between the Ruthenian and the Little Russian populations of the two empires. Lviv he considers to be partly a Ukrainian city, noting its difference from Kyiv, which he calls "the mother of all Russian [read: Rus'] cities." He observes that, though ruled by Austria, Lviv possesses a Ukrainian character that derives from the Ruthenian population of the surrounding lands. To give his journey geographical perspective, he claims to have followed the imperial procession to Bukovyna, stopping en route to visit the famous Rabbi of Sadagora (Sadhora) and a convent of dissident Russian nuns – most likely Greek Catholic – who fled to Austria after the reign of Nicholas I. Tissot was accredited as a "journalist," and he was conscious of the importance of this role, commenting, "We were treated as ambassadors of this new, democratic, justly feared power: public opinion."[12]

He appreciates the image of Galician society huddled around the emperor, ranging from members of the high aristocracy to traditionally-dressed Ruthenian (Ukrainian) peasants. The denizens of city hall, the casino, and the great houses, along with the crowds flooding the streets – everyone came out to see the Austrian monarch. Tissot immerses himself in this atmosphere of festivity, satisfying his taste for beauty and folklore. He finds Lviv enchanting: the citadel is "magnificent," as are the elegant white houses engulfed in greenery, the slender bell towers of Latin churches, and the bulbous domes of Greek Catholic ones.

The prospect of leaving this relatively happy and free region to head towards Tsarist Russia sparks feelings of anxiety fueled by nightmarish stories about the Russian border and its strict customs control. Tissot confesses his worries: he must not carry newspapers, books, manuscripts, a swordstick that could be considered a weapon, red chemises, or scarves with too much red that might be seen as a sign of revolutionary involvement.

Eventually, the writer crosses the Russian border unmolested, much to his surprise and relief. He reaches Russia by train, passing through the Ukrainian town of Brody, where he sees a large group of Galician Jews whom he describes with a mixture of astonishment and contempt, par for the course for Western travellers encountering a type of Jew who was very different from the more or less assimilated Israelite to whom they were accustomed. The black kaftans, the curly hair, and darker skin all gave the impression that the traveller was encountering an absolutely different "race."

Tissot's attitude may be qualified as anti-Semitic; his brand of anti-Semitism was widespread among his contemporaries, as many travel accounts attest.[13] It was also connected to social bias: he describes quite neutrally some Jews whom he spots in the centre of Lviv during the emperor's visit – but they are well-dressed merchants. He has words of praise only for young Jewish girls, whose eyes are described as being full of "Eastern lasciviousness."[14] This stereotype of the *belle juive*, likewise, was widespread among Western travellers. The Jews whom Tissot meets on the train are described as a kind of Isaac Laquedem – the legendary Wandering Jew – always in search of gain or profit. This judgment is reinforced by the depiction of Jewish money changers at the Brody railway station: their profiles are described in a way that turns them into birds of prey.

Here, for the first time, Tissot observes that the Jew is the middleman in the service of the Polish noble: he is not only a merchant but also a banker who plays an indispensable economic function. He calls Brody an "insignificant town, without a past and without a future," so the question of what to do here is inevitable. The Jews might answer: trade in "contraband and [make] a lot of children."[15] He claims that everywhere in Galicia and Poland the number of Jews is increasing because they are the Chinese of the West, and they marry very young, in contrast to French Israelites. (The Jews of France are always called "Israelites," not "Jews.")

Tissot's first impression upon entering the Russian Empire is that there is no sign of human presence in the severe and sad landscape. This is a curious remark, considering that the territories traversed by Tissot were populated by significant numbers of Jews, Poles, and "Little Russians" or "Cossacks." The "emptiness" of this space is, of course, a stereotype invoked by Tissot in order to reinforce the idea that the Russian Empire, with its Eastern expanses, is not comparable to other European countries. Thus, reflecting on the character of these vast territories, he expresses the opinion that on the other side of the Ural Mountains, at the very extremity of the Russian Empire, on the routes leading to India and China, there is a need for expansion and a feverish desire to generate progress: there the Cossack saber encounters the English bayonet. The possibility of Russo-British confrontation was a major concern at the time, when no one could foresee the Russo-Japanese War and the defeat of Russia by the young Japanese state. In Tissot's time, the Russian Empire was a young and vigorous state with immense military potential: this idea was, of course, the fruit of Russia's victory over Napoleon, and it remained mostly unchallenged in Europe's diplomatic and military circles until the First World War.

Tissot develops his argument by resorting to the literary device of a casual conversation with a travel companion. Through a well-constructed interplay of questions and answers he offers an assessment of the situation of the church in the Russian Empire. The church is reliant on the state; priests play a weak role in society and exploit the pastoral needs of their flocks in order to earn money

for their own subsistence. He briefly speaks about the lack of religious freedom, explaining that Jews do not have the right to build their temples freely.
In his view, the large number of Jews gathering in Berdychiv for the Sabbath
is ample proof of this.

Tissot describes Berdychiv as the "Russian and Polish Jerusalem." He wants
to spend some time there because it seems to be "curious and unexplored,"[16]
but it disappoints him deeply: "What a horrible town Berditschew is!" It is
dirty, abandoned, and ruined, "like all small, Russified Polish towns."[17] Except
for a few shops, churches, and small Ruthenian peasant markets, it does not
offer anything pleasing to the traveller's eye. It has no cafes, restaurants, or
places to meet; it is a town devoid of "pleasure and joy."[18] The only place of
interest is the theatre, where a Romanian troupe is performing two works of
"Jewish vaudeville": *The Recruits* and *Matches* by Abraham Goldfaden.

Tissot describes his visit to the Jewish theatre in Berdychiv, pointing out
that it has a proper stage and a curtain, hard, cheap seats, and more expensive
ones covered in red fabric. There are many men wearing full beards but "no
long caftans, no skullcaps." The audience is comprised mainly of assimilated,
secular Jews, although many appear to be poor. Some Russian officers with
their wives or companions are also present.[19]

Tissot attempts to explain the situation of the Jews in the Russian Empire.
Oppressed by the authorities and confined to the southwestern part of the Russian Empire, Jews have been hindered in their development and are thus similar to their thirteenth-century ancestors, the Jews of medieval Europe. The
Jews, he adds, are divided into many sects, among them the Hassids who follow the Talmud and reject progress. Jews who want to emancipate themselves,
like the characters in Eliza Orzeszkowa's novel *Meir Ezofowicz* (which Tissot
translated into French in 1888 as *Meyer et Isaac: Moeurs juives*) are forced to
cut their ties with their community. He also emphasizes that young Jews who
abandon the old traditions are easily co-opted into the revolutionary movement, where they are accepted as equals. In his opinion, the hostility between
the local population and the Jews is due to the particular role played by Jews
in that still backward economy. He relates usury to anti-Semitism and is convinced that the development of rural banks is the best way to end a conflict that
is not religious but socioeconomic.[20]

Tissot devotes many pages of his book to the topic of Jews. He was conscious of the influence he could exert on public opinion; hence the ambiguity
of his treatment of Jewish life deserves attention. While Tissot was a relatively
keen observer and reasonably well-informed reporter, he shared the negative
attitudes towards Jews that were characteristic of many authors of travelogues
or journalists of the time.[21] For example, in his opinion, Ukrainians seem to be

more "European" than the non-integrated majority of Jews living in Galicia and Little Russia. A proper contextualization of Tissot's views on Jews and Jewish life in Galicia and the Russian Empire would require engagement with the large body of research into European nineteenth-century attitudes towards Jews; here it suffices to say that Tissot was not unaware of the difficult situation, legal and cultural, of people of the Mosaic faith in those lands. He understood that the social functions performed by Jews largely depended on the structure of the societies in which they lived. He attributed what he saw as a lack of will on the part of East European Jews to emancipate themselves from traditional communitarian duties and habits to a mentality that was different from that of their French or Swiss counterparts, whom he knew better. The Western author saw the emancipated Jew as the only Israelite with whom it was possible to interact on an equal basis. Thus, his descriptions of the Jews of Lviv or the Jews who watched Goldfaden's plays in the Berdychiv theatre are more moderate than his depictions of Jews in general.[22]

Leaving Berdychiv, Tissot introduces the reader to the land of the steppes, a fertile and beautiful country where the Cossack, free as a bird, once rode his small, black horse, his only masters the wind and the thunder.[23] A subject that appealed to Tissot's public was the lifestyle of the gentry, and here Tissot, referring to Turgenev and Gogol', describes his stay in a beautiful country manor near the Ukrainian town of Fastiv. He calls this residence a "castle,"[24] noting that in Great Russia there are no "castles" in the Western sense of the word because "the lords have never been the defenders or protectors of their vassals"; thus, this Ukrainian residence can be described as an elegant and beautiful "villa."[25] About his host, identified as M.X., Tissot says that he was once the owner of a million hectares of land.

The excursion to the "castle" leads to a detailed discussion of the steppe.[26] Tissot touches on a number of topics, such as the fertility of the black earth and the development of agriculture, which he attributes to the investments of wealthy landowners who among other innovations have introduced the cultivation of sugar beet. He describes the life of shepherds and their sheepdogs, and writes about wolves, the slaughtering of livestock, the processing and sale of mutton and sheepskin, milking, and the production of cheese. The result is a vivid image of Ukraine as a land situated halfway between tradition and progress.

Tissot writes about mowing and harvesting and labour migrants arriving from Great Russia and the Carpathian Mountains. He imagines them gathering around a fire in the evening, singing songs, telling stories, and playing the *bandura*. He is especially sympathetic to the Little Russian, who is spiritually lively, sensitive, and a lover of freedom. The status of women in Little Russia is markedly different than in Great Russia, as folksongs reveal. The Little Russian is not interested in the physical aspect of women: what is most important is moral beauty.

Tissot sees the Little Russian as the intrepid horseman of the steppe, a male descending from an ancient warlike race, a Scythian whose blood is purer than that of the Great Russian. Thanks to his chaperone, who is evidently a Little Russian, he gathers much information about the regular Cossacks and the Zaporozhians. Here literary tradition, Gogol' above all, is mingled with some historical facts pertaining mostly to the seventeenth-century Cossack rebellion. According to the writer, the Cossacks were forced to revolt because Polish nobles did not recognize their national and religious rights. Images of the killing of Jews, priests, and Poles are conveyed without commentary and with a certain literary glee.

The description of the writer's first dinner at the villa is truly picturesque.[27] There are about thirty guests, including petty noblemen of the steppe, boys from respectable Warsaw families (great hunters and philanderers), Kyivites, various types of estate managers, travelling merchants, businessmen, neighbours, and an old retired soldier whom everyone calls "Your Excellency." The arrival of a new guest is never a surprise because the house is open day and night. Life at the villa is totally unrestricted, the hospitality frank and cordial, and more people mean more fun and games. The guests travel by carriage or on horseback to picnic lunches, where they drink champagne, take part in discussions, play, and laugh – a far cry from Tissot's experiences in Berdychiv.

In between a tea party and a sumptuous dinner attended by guests from surrounding estates, as well as Poland, Russia, and all of Europe, Tissot and his Little Russian chaperone pay a visit to some peasants who favourably impress the writer. The chaperone explains the more interesting features of the peasants' way of life. Tissot admires their clean, modest cottages, their hospitality and humour, and their stories, particularly tales of vampires. These reflect the southern imagination of the Little Russians, who believe in ghosts, fairies, water-sprites, and sorcerers. Tissot presents his reader with a fine portrait of Shevchenko, recounting his life and the persecution to which he was subjected, and recognizing the importance of his poetry. The source of Tissot's information may have been Émile Durand's article in the *Revue des Deux Mondes*.[28]

Most of the topics raised by Tissot appeared, at one time or another, on the pages of *Revue des Deux Mondes*, which published articles by Anatole Leroy-Beaulieu on the political life of the Russian Empire, as well as articles by Alfred Rambaud on Russian and Ukrainian literature, such as "L'Ukraine et ses chansons historiques" (1875), "Le Poète national de la Petite-Russie: Tarass Grigoriévitch Chevtchenko" by Émile Durand (1876), and "Dans la steppe:

Notes de voyage" (1884) by Eugène-Melchior de Vogüé, whose literary portraits of Turgenev, Tolstoi, Dostoevskii, and Gogol' were also published in the
eminent French journal. Also worth mentioning are "Le Faust polonais" by Leopold von Sacher-Masoch (1874) and "Un romancier galicien, Sacher-Masoch,
sa vie et ses oeuvres" by Th. Benzon (1875). In his *Vienne et la vie viennoise*
(1878) Tissot describes his visit to Sacher-Masoch in Bruck-an-der-Mur, offering a considerable number of details about his life and literary activities.

Tissot's writings responded to the French cultivated public's interest in Eastern and Central Europe, and he did much to reinforce it. It is entirely probable
that Tissot read those same articles on the pages of the *Revue des Deux Mondes*,
sometimes finding useful material for his historical and literary frescos. Much
of his information, however, including what he knew about the language of
the Ukrainians, appears to have come from direct personal contacts with his
hosts and chaperones. This detail might explain the combination of some acute
and precise remarks with banal errors of transliteration and interpretation. Tissot had a strong appreciation for the Ruthenian language and was well read,
but he was scarcely a philologist. He writes that the term "Ruthenian" (which
was current in the Hapsburg Empire) can be applied to the modern Ukrainian
language, the chancellery language of medieval Kyivan Rus', the Lviv exper-
iments with a "Slavonicizing" (morphological) orthography and lexicography,
and even to Church Slavonic. On the one hand, he explains that the Ruthenian
language is more harmonious, expressive, and full of imagery than either Russian or Polish. On the other, he somewhat puzzlingly locates the Ruthenian
language between Polish and Czech.[29] In a footnote he asserts that the written
Polish language was created between the tenth and fifteenth centuries by writers of genius, such as Kochanowski and Gernicki (*sic*), who were of Ruthenian
origin and combined words from their native language with Polish ones.[30]

Tissot makes an interesting comparison between the histories of the Ukrainian
and French languages. The Ruthenian language, as he calls Ukrainian, is
the *Langue d'oc* of Poland, "the purest of all Slavic idioms." Ruthenian, he
claims, was spoken at the Jagiellonian court, and the first Polish codices were
published in that language because, as long as Kyiv was the capital of Rus'
(following the conventions of the time Tissot refers to it as the capital of Russia, although it was Medieval Kyivan Rus'), poets and preachers preferred
to use the Ruthenian language. Tissot also knew that the central Ukrainian
lands were part of the Polish-Lithuanian Commonwealth. Thus, by including
both the Ukrainian written vernacular (*prosta mova*) and Church Slavonic into
the "Polish" cultural space, he could maintain that the first written language
in the Polish Commonwealth was "Ruthenian." After the capital was transferred to Moscow, Tissot claims, the Russian language became fashionable and

Ruthenian was gradually abandoned. Scholars and writers adopted the idiom of the ruling people, and Little Russian was confined to the southern provinces, where it is still the national language and even a vibrant one, despite the Russians' efforts to eradicate it.[31]

At least this last consideration corresponded quite well to the linguistic and social situation of Ukraine under Russian rule in Tissot's time. In another footnote Tissot reminds readers that the Ruthenian language is banned in schools and that until recently it was strictly forbidden to publish books or brochures in that language,[32] clarifying that now, in order to rally to Russia the three million Ruthenians (or Little Russians) living under Austrian rule, the St Petersburg government has softened its harsh stance towards Ruthenian literature. In a later footnote he writes that the Ruthenians form a unique nationality of seventeen million people, fourteen million of whom live in the Russian Empire and three million in Galicia, Bukovyna, and Hungary. Pan-Slavism calls for the union of those separated brothers, and in the event of a war between Austria and Russia it is probable that the Ruthenians living in the Hapsburg Empire will rise up and make common cause with the Russian liberators.

Thus, even though Tissot and his companion speak critically about Russian policies, highlighting the specificity of Ruthenians, nevertheless he is convinced that the empire's stance on the Slavs' unity is well grounded, notwithstanding the differences that exist among the Slavs in general and specifically between Great Russia and Little Russia. The idea of Slavic unity was widespread at the time and accepted by Tissot.

Tissot's travelogue is similar to those of his contemporaries and contains plenty of ideas deriving from the vision of Eastern Europe typical of the ages of European Enlightenment and romanticism: progress and tradition are two apparently contradictory terms that may well define the lens Tissot used to observe the countries he visited. He is in favour of progress, which should be a gradual, inexorable process of modernization, secularization, and liberalization, but he appreciates the traditional way of life as expressed in customs, virtues, folklore, and "local color." We have to consider that Tissot, who lived and wrote in France and became a French intellectual, never renounced his Swiss origins, which he treasured throughout his life. He bequeathed his estate to the municipality of Bulle (Gruyère) for the purpose of building a library and a museum devoted to the culture of this district – in order to preserve and promote the Swiss cultural heritage. This respect for the culture of ordinary people accompanied him during his journeys not only in foreign countries but also in his homeland.[33]

It is worth noting that Tissot explored many problems that he was not able to elaborate upon adequately because in many cases he simply did not grasp the complexity of a given situation; attracted by the folkloric aspect of what he was seeing, he did not make great efforts to reach a better understanding of things. When he left his place of residence for Kyiv, his opinions were already formed. According to him, Little Russia was mainly shaped by the steppe, and Kyiv was already a Russian town. But what did the word "Russian" mean? We discover that Kyiv, "the mother of all Russian cities," has a markedly Eastern flavour. Hence the nature of the city, positioned halfway between East and West, reflects much ambiguity. Tissot describes Kyiv with a tourist's eye for churches, monasteries, and parks. He spends a day at the university in the company of a man called Michel Pétrovitch, who recounts the history of the revolutionary movement from 1860 to the 1880s, describing its theory and practice. His conclusion, shared by Tissot, is that the common people do not participate in this movement, which recruits its membership among the bourgeoisie.

Tissot is shocked by the poverty-stricken and sad appearance of students: their bohemian life is obscure, harsh, and miserable, a painful contrast to the gay life of French students. According to him, herein lies one of the reasons behind the successes of the nihilist movement. The influence of German idealist philosophers and French socialists is not counterbalanced by such activities as sport or dancing, and this fact, together with a chronic lack of food, creates a base for the pathological development of the personality. This interpretation of nihilism, arising from the poverty of the student population, contradicts Tissot's earlier statement about the bourgeois origin of the nihilists. Tissot even offers statistics on the social composition of the student body: only 2 per cent of all students are of peasant origin, while 98 per cent belong to the middle or upper classes.

Tissot is clearly searching for an explanation for the assassination of Alexander II and is confused about what he sees and what he has read in the press; he thus conflates several disjointed pieces of information and does not elaborate further. This conflation presents the limit of his self-proclaimed "scientific approach" to problems. On the other hand, he wants to illustrate the real life of Kyiv. Together with Mr De Molinari, consular agent of France and son of the eminent economist of the *Journal des Débats*, he takes part in the work of a local fire brigade, visits the "commercial and Jewish city of Podol" and a local factory. In the latter, he admires the general work conditions; in his opinion, there is no trace of nihilism among the workers, whose conditions are far better than those of their counterparts in other European countries, including France.

He acknowledges that the Russian worker is provided free lodgings, like a soldier, and receives low-cost food and health care. In the Russian Empire, he argues, there is no proletariat because the worker is still a peasant who owns a little house and a piece of land and wants to save money to send it home.

Tissot disputes the notion that drunkenness is widespread; on the contrary, he asserts that peasants and workers only drink on Sundays, because they do not like to waste money and because taverns are scarce, considering the size of the country.

It is worth noting that the author of a comment on *Russia and Russians* published in the conservative *Revue des Deux Mondes* criticizes Tissot for his excessive "democratic faith." The critic emphasizes that for Tissot "everything comes from the people, everything is done by it." He disputes Tissot's choice of the word "Russians" in his title and argues it would have been more appropriate to refer to "the Russian people" – *le peuple russe* – since the author grants importance only to the virtues of the peasant and the worker, excluding other classes of Russian society.[34] A modern reader, in contrast to the nineteenth-century reviewer, would be unlikely to define as "populist" Tissot's fondness for everyday life, including the life of the lower classes. That Tissot had some positivist inclinations is evidenced by his belief in progress, his anti-clericalism, and his interest in economic and social questions, but he was first of all a typical bourgeois whose enlightened opinions went hand in hand with a refusal of revolutionary ideas and practices.

Tissot devotes much attention to Kyiv's landmarks; he is drawn to monasteries and churches because he is well aware of the interest they can elicit among his readers. He describes, Baedeker style, his visit to the Golden Gate, the Cathedral of Saint Sophia, and the churches of Saint Michael and Saint Andrew, commenting on the beauty of their architecture and interiors. He dedicates an entire chapter to the Kyivan Caves Monastery, which he calls a "religious city." He describes the printing house, the painting workshop, the refectory with its kitchens, shops purveying religious objects, the convent hotel, the restaurant, and the teahouse managed by the resident monks.

During his travels Tissot avoids making comparisons with the Western way of life in order to offer a fresh account of the reality he sees. In the chapter about the "religious city" we find no references to Western churches or monasteries, only a certain degree of scepticism that betrays his secular attitudes. He is amazed by the Caves Monastery and reports a number of stories and legends about Orthodox saints and their relics. He observes the crowds of people gathering inside the monastery walls and remarks upon the most curious figures he sees there, blending direct observation with anecdotes.[35]

For Tissot Kyiv, like all of Little Russia, is special. It is a charming city, "full of Eastern, Asian scents." In this Eastern quality that so appeals to Tissot we detect an echo of the idea of Eastern Europe that, as Larry Wolff observes, was created by the Enlightenment "through a sort of demi-Orientalism that projected the otherness of the Orient onto lands that were indisputably European, characterizing them by a paradoxical combination of resemblance and difference from an implicitly Western sense of civilized Europe."[36] For Tissot, the "Orient does not begin in Galicia but in Kyiv." But for him "Asian" also means "fairytale-like": Kyiv produces a kind of enchantment that stems from its difference from other cities.

Tissot is filled with nostalgia as he takes a final look at Kyiv, seen from the train on which he is heading for Moscow. Quoting Balzac, who had lived in Kyiv and married a Little Russian, he rhapsodizes, "This picture of a bright Kyiv, dazzling, as beautiful as we imagine a city to be in an Eastern tale, made the bleak solitude into which we entered all the more painful and sad in my eyes."[37] The "bleak solitude" to which Tissot refers characterizes the road to Moscow, to Great Russia. The description of the latter is less original than Tissot's descriptions of Galicia or Little Russia, probably because he was more reliant on various literary sources that he consulted before embarking on his journey. He focuses on monuments, recalls some points of Russian history, citing mainly Rambaud,[38] and emphasizes the monotony and sadness of the landscape he observes from the windows of the train.

The most interesting part in this section of his travelogue concerns the everyday life of Muscovites as they visit markets, shops, restaurants, and nightclubs. Searching for the picturesque and the strange, Tissot visits prisons, shelters, lowly taverns, cemeteries, abattoirs, and orphanages, without neglecting to pause at the finest restaurants and *cafés-chantants*, judging their merits by European standards. These transitions from high society to the underworld (and vice versa) sometimes take place over a very short period of time, bringing to the fore an indifference to social ills that seems brutal to the modern sensibility. When writing of Great Russia, Tissot undertakes comparisons with European standards of living somewhat more frequently than in his descriptions of Ukraine. This style may reflect his view of Great Russia as a "real" political entity, an Empire, while Little Russia is merely a "province": the latter's value lies in its regional specificity, its folklore, the beauty of its countryside, and its hint of oriental exoticism. As was usual in Western perceptions of Eastern Europe at the time, Tissot saw Little Russia through the eyes of the imperial culture. Little Russia was charming but not a "value in itself." On the other hand, Tissot unquestionably preferred Galicia and Little Russia to Great Russia. Galicia is part of the Hapsburg Empire and one of the "new and lovely countries" he wants to describe in order to emphasize the difference between Austria-Hungary and Germany, thus continuing the polemics of *Voyage au Pays des Milliards* against Prussia and the Prussian-centred unification of Germany.

The charm of the ceremonies that were organized in Lviv for Franz Joseph's visit delighted Tissot because they offered the image of a state with many loyal subjects, notwithstanding the differences between its ethnic and social groups. In contrast, Little Russia is seen as an underdeveloped country. The depressing quality of Berdychiv is a negative consequence of "Russification." Little Russia is part of the Russian Empire and shares some common features with Great Russia, but it has a different story, a different language, different customs, and a different ethos, as attested by the stories and songs of peasants and Cossacks. The pages devoted to Shevchenko demonstrate the writer's interest in Ukrainian poetry, seen as an original phenomenon in the context of the imperial culture. Tissot seems to understand that the grim outlook for the teaching, use, and development of the Ukrainian language is a result of Russian policies towards Little Russia. At the same time, he considers the "two" Russias as bound by a common destiny.

We have to take into account the political background of Tissot's arguments about Russia: it was his view that after the Berlin Congress (1878) the "League of the Three Emperors" no longer existed, and thus the Russian alliance was "en disponibilité" – at France's disposal. Tissot foresaw a future anti-German alliance consisting of Russia, France, and Great Britain. From this standpoint, therefore, Russia was a great state crucial to providing a counterbalance to Germany's power on the continent because, unfortunately, Austria-Hungary already seemed incapable of opposing the influence of the new and mighty German Empire.[39] Tissot hypothesizes that Russia may be the key to changing the European status quo: in his opinion, this change depends on Russia's attitude to Europe. "Let's wait for this people to come of age," Tissot declares with prophetic pathos, reflecting on the inner strength of the Slavic race that, he believes, is dormant but awaiting insemination by an Idea. "If there is barbarity, it is a vigorous barbarity that someday will contribute to the development of mankind,"[40] he asserts, reshaping the old theme of a Young Russia that stands before an Old Europe – a theme invoked by many Western commentators speculating about Europe's future.[41] Russia, according to Tissot, still has a "fresh energy" that, if disciplined, could help reinvigorate the continent.

Tissot is convinced that Great Russia is not yet European because there is an abyss between its elites and its people, but some forms of progress are beginning to affirm themselves, notwithstanding the continuous challenge posed by the revolutionary minority. After the traumatic death of Alexander II Tissot does not exclude the possibility of a revolution in Russia, but believes a gradual liberalization of autocratic rule to be more likely. Little Russia will participate in this general movement together with Great Russia; both are midway between tradition and modernity.

According to my reading of Tissot's oeuvre, it was precisely because he was a Swiss that he held the traditions of all the peoples of Europe in great esteem, appreciating their loyalty to ancestors and their capacity to preserve the best of their histories without renouncing modernity. In particular, he admired their sense of the past, military virtues, and courage. The Swiss, in his opinion, is a man of freedom, perpetually struggling to preserve that freedom.[42] The Cossack is equally a man of freedom, and something of this independent spirit is still alive in Ukraine. For this reason, Ukraine is very different from Russia, even though the paths of the two countries are intertwined and they both participate in a common future. This future, for Tissot, is undoubtedly European. The Slavic countries in general, and the Russian Empire in particular, he thought, had the potential to contribute to Europe's further development. In harbouring this expectation Tissot was not alone among his contemporaries, many of whom believed in a full Europeanization of the Russian Empire. At the same time, like many others, he was aware of the possibility of a revolution caused by the social distortions resulting from rapid and unbalanced modernization. It transpired that the revolutions of 1905 and 1917, when they did come, had consequences that were the opposite of Tissot's hopes: they once again increased Russia's distance from Europe.

Notes

1 Serge Rossier in collaboration with François Rime, "Victor Tissot (1844–1917): un homme d'affaires littéraires," *Cahiers du Musée gruérien* 7 (2009): 31–48; Alain Bosson, "Victor Tissot, auteur à succès dans le Paris de la Belle Epoque," *Cahiers du Musée gruérien* 7 (2009): 49–54; Giulia Lami, *L'Europe centrale et orientale au 19. siècle d'après les voyages du romancier et journaliste suisse Victor Tissot* (Paris: Champion, 2013).

2 Victor Tissot, *Unknown Switzerland*, trans. Mrs Wilson (New York: J. Pott & Co, 1889).

3 On the shelves of this library I discovered the following descriptions of journeys through Russia and historical or geographical studies of that country: Éd. André, *Un mois en Russie: Notes de voyage d'un membre du jury à l'Exposition internationale d'horticulture de Saint-Pétersbourg* (Paris: Victor Masson et fils, 1870); P. Artamof, *La Russie historique, monumentale et pittoresque*, 2 vols. (Paris: Lahure, 1862–5); O. Audouard, *Les nuits Russes* (Paris: Dentu, 1876); H. Barry, *La Russie contemporaine* (Paris: Libr. G. Ballière, 1873); G. Bonvalot, *Du Caucase aux Indes* (Paris: Plon; Nourrit, 1889); J. Boucher de Perthes, *Voyage en Russie et retour par la Lithuanie, la Pologne, la Silésie, la Saxe et le duché de Nassau, séjour à Wisebade, en 1856* (Paris: Treuttel et Würtz, 1859); R. Calmon [Calmon-Maison], *Trois semaines à Moscou: Mai-juin 1883* (Paris: C. Lévy, 1883); J. Carol [pseudonym of Gérard Gabriel Laffaille], *Colonisation*

russe: Les deux routes du Caucase, note d'un touriste (Paris: Hachette, 1899);
Ed. Cotteau, *De Paris au Japon à travers la Sibérie* (Paris: Hachette, 1888); G.
Damaze de Raymond, *Tableau historique, géographique, militaire et moral de
l'Empire de Russie* (Paris: Le Normant, 1812); E. de Bagreeff-Speranski, *Les îles
de la Neva à St.-Pétersbourg* (Bruxelles: Schnée, 1858); A. de Custine, *La Russie*
(Paris: Amyot, 1855); A. de Démidoff, *La Crimée* (Paris: E. Bourdin, 1855); L.
de Fontenay, *Voyage agricole en Russie* (Paris: A. Goin, 1878); G. de Molinari,
Lettres sur la Russie (Paris: Dentu, 1877); L. de Soudak, *Voyage en Crimée* (Paris:
C. Lévy, 1892); K. de Wolski, *La Russie juive* (Paris: A. Savine, 1887); T. Gautier,
Voyage en Russie (Paris: Charpentier, 1875); L. Godard, *Pétersbourg et Moscou.
Souvenirs du Couronnement d'un Tsar* (Paris: Dentu, 1858); W. Hepworth Dixon,
La Russie libre (Paris: Hachette, 1873); A. Koechlin-Schwartz, *Un touriste
au Caucase: Volga, Caspienne, Caucase* (Paris: J. Hetzel, 1881); J.C. Kohl,
Petersburg in Bildern und Skizzen (Dresden: Arnoldische Buchhandlung, 1841);
P. Labbé, *Un bagne russe* (Paris: Hachette, 1903); F. Lacroix, *Les mystères de la
Russie* (Paris: Pagnerre, 1845); H. Lankenau and L. Oelsnik, *Das heutige Russland*
(Leipzig: Spamer, 1876); L. Léger, *Le monde slave; voyages et littérature* (Paris:
Didier, 1873); L. Léouzon Le Duc, *La Russie contemporaine* (Paris: Hachette
1854); L. Léouzon Le Duc, *La Baltique* (Paris: Hachette, 1855); L. Léouzon Le
Duc, *L'Ours du Nord. Russie, Esthonie, Hogland* (Paris: Dreyfous, 1879); A.
Leroy-Beaulieu, *L'Empire des Tsars et les Russes* (Paris: Hachette, 1881); A.
Lestrelin, *Les Paysans russes* (Paris: E. Dentu, 1861); D. Mackenzie Wallace,
La Russie (Paris: George Decaux; Maurice Dreyfous, 1877); X. Marmier, *Lettres
sur la Russie* (Paris: Garnier frères, 1851); X. Marmier, *Du Danube au Caucase*
(Paris: Garnier frères, 1854); X. Marmier, *Un été au bord de la Baltique et de la
mer du Nord* (Paris: Hachette, 1856); J.B. May, *Saint Pétersbourg et la Russie
en 1829* (Paris: Levasseur, 1850); F. Meyer von Waldeck, *Russland* (Leipzig,
1884); A. Meylan, *À travers les Russies* (Paris: Fischbacher, 1880); A. Poorten,
Un coin perdu de la Russie (Paris: Ghio, 1883); C. Rabot, *À travers la Russie
boréale* (Paris: Hachette, 1894); L. Richtie, *La Russie: Voyage pittoresque de
Saint-Pétersbourg à Moscou* (Paris: L. Janet, 1840); C. Sibille, *À travers la Russie*
(Paris: Delagrave, 1892); A. Silvestre, *La Russie* (Paris: E. Testard, 1892); N.
Tsakni, *La Russie sectaire* (Paris: Librairie Plon, 1888); M. Vachon, *La Russie au
soleil* (Paris: Victor Havard, 1886); *Esquisses Russes par un Russe* (Wurzbourg:
Kressner, 1900); *Religion et mœurs des Russes: Anecdotes recueillis par le Comte
Joseph de Maistre et le P. Grivel, S. J.* (Paris: Leroux, 1879); [I. Golovine], *Voyage
au Pays des Roubles par un militaire français* (Paris: Arnaud et Labat, 1877).

4 Henry James, review of *Voyage aux pays annexés,* by Victor Tissot, *Nation,* 17
   May 1877. See *Literary Criticism: French Writers, Other European Writers,
   Prefaces to the New York Edition* (New York: Literary Classics of the United

States, 1984), 857–60. (James stated erroneously that the book was published by the New York-based publisher F. W. Christern.)

5 Victor Tissot, *Unknown Hungary* (London: Richard Bentley and Son, 1881).

6 Rose Bohuss, *Victor Tissot* (Debrecen: Varosi Neomda, 1935); Cathèrine Horel, *De l'exotisme à la modernité: Un siècle de voyage français en Hongrie (1818–1920)* (Budapest: ELTE Jelenkori Egyetemes Történeti Tanszék, 2004).

7 This book was published numerous times under different titles, including *Aventures de trois fugitifs en Sibérie*; *Les Fugitifs en Sibérie*; *Les Trois fugitifs*, and was translated into English, Italian, German, and Swedish. See *Exiles: A Russian Story* (Philadelphia: T. B. Peterson and brothers, 1881); *Adventures of Three Fugitives in Siberia* (London: Remington and Co., 1883).

8 Review of *Russians and Germans*, by Victor Tissot, *New York Times*, 4 July 1882.

9 See the foreword in Victor Tissot, *Russes et Allemands*, 4th ed. (Paris: E. Dentu, 1881). Tissot oscillated between common French and German transliterations when referring to toponyms. Here, for instance, Kyiv is "Kiew." In my text I use the contemporary English toponyms.

10 Michel Cadot, ed., *L'Ukraine et la France au XIXe siècle* (Paris: Université Sorbonne Nouvelle, 1987).

11 The visit took place in September 1880. See D. L. Unowsky, *The Pomp and Politics of Patriotism: Imperial Celebrations in Habsburg Austria, 1848–1916* (West Lafayette, IN: Purdue University Press, 2005), 64–71.

12 Victor Tissot, *La Russie et les Russes*, 8th ed. (Paris: E. Dentu, 1882), 2.

13 Jean Louis Kummer, "Les voyageurs français en Autriche au XIXe siècle" (PhD diss., Université de Paris IV- Sorbonne, 2007), http://www.theses.paris-sorbonne.fr/kummer/paris4/2007/kummer/html/index-frames.html; Horel, *De l'exotisme à la modernité*. For discussion of Italian travelers, see Giulia Lami, "Viaggiatori Italiani in Russia tra '800 e '900: Opinioni, ambienti, immagini alla scoperta d'un mondo diverso," in *Geografie private: I resoconti di viaggio come lettura del territorio*, ed. Elisa Bianchi (Milan: Unicopli, 1985), 285–301.

14 Tissot, *Russie et les Russes*, 4.

15 Ibid., 14.

16 Ibid., 51.

17 Ibid., 66–7. "Cet aspect de malpropreté, d'abandon et de ruine se retrouve dans presque toutes les petites villes polonaises russifiées."

18 Ibid., 75.

19 Ibid., 77.

20 Ibid., 105.

21 See note 13. Even Th. Bentzon, "Un romancier galicien, Sacher-Masoch, sa vie et ses oeuvres," *Revue des Deux Mondes*, 15 December 1875, 816–37, observes on p. 817 that Jews are described by von Sacher-Masoch in contemptuous terms

that are hardly ameliorated by his ritual expressions of pity for the oppression and persecution they have suffered.

22 For the Jewish population in the Pale of Settlement see Martin Gilbert, *The Routledge Atlas of Jewish History*, 6th ed. (London: Routledge, 2003). On the Jews in the Russian Empire see Salo W. Baron, *The Russian Jews under Tsars and Soviets*, 2nd ed. (New York: Macmillan, 1976); John D. Klier, *Russia Gathers her Jews: The Origins of the "Jewish Question" in Russia: 1772–1825* (DeKalb: Northern Illinois University Press, 1986); Erich Haberer, *Jews and Revolution in Nineteenth-Century Russia* (Cambridge: Cambridge University Press, 1995); Brian Horowitz, *Empire Jews: Jewish Nationalism and Acculturation in 19th- and early 20th-Century Russia* (Bloomington: Slavica, 2009); and Eugene M. Avrutin, *Jews and the Imperial state: Identification Politics in Tsarist Russia* (Ithaca: Cornell University Press, 2010). On the Jews in Poland and Eastern Europe see Daniel Tollet, *Histoire des juifs en Pologne: du XVI siècle à nos jours* (Paris: PUF, 1992) and *Dalla condanna del giudaismo all'odio per l'ebreo: storia del passaggio dall'intolleranza religiosa alla persecuzione politica e sociale*, ed. and trans. Giulia Lami (Milan: C. Marinotti, 2002).

23 Tissot, *Russie et les Russes*, 133.

24 Ibid., 184.

25 Ibid.

26 Ibid., chap. 11.

27 Ibid., 191–2.

28 É. Durand, "Le Poète national de la Petite-Russie. Tarass Grigoriévitch Chevtchenko," *Revue des Deux Mondes*, 15 June 1876.

29 Tissot, *Russie et les Russes*, 207.

30 Ibid., note 2. The author to whom Tissot refers is probably Łukasz Górnicki.

31 Ibid., 208.

32 Ibid., note 1.

33 See Victor Tissot, "In the Gruyère," in *Unknown Switzerland* (New York: James Pott and Co., 1900), 335–71.

34 Review of *La Russie et les Russes*, by Victor Tissot, *Revue des Deux Mondes*, 53 (1882), *Bulletin bibliographique*.

35 Some biographical elements indicate that Tissot, who was born into the Catholic faith, may have been a Freemason, but I did not find any evidence of this.

36 Larry Wolff, *The Idea of Galicia: History and Fantasy in Habsburg Political Culture* (Stanford: Stanford University Press, 2010), 48.

37 Tissot, *Russie et les Russes*, 333.

38 Alfred Rambaud, *Histoire de la Russie: depuis les origines jusqu'à l'année 1877* (Paris: Librairie Hachette, 1878).

39 At one time Tissot considered Austria-Hungary as a potential ally in a future
    "revanche." See Olivier Chaline, "L'Autriche-Hongrie, une alliée pour la
    revanche? Ou les espoirs de Victor Tissot (1878)," in *Regards sur l'indomptable
    Europe du Centre Est du XVIIIe Siècle à nos jours*, ed. Jerzy Kłoczowski, Daniel
    Beauvois, and Yves-Marie Hilaire (Villeneuve-d'Ascq: Revue du Nord, 1996),
    179–86.
40 Tissot, *Russes et Allemands*, 4th ed. (Paris: E. Dentu, 1881), xiv.
41 Dieter Groh, *Russland und das Selbstverständnis Europas: Ein Beitrag
    zur europäischen Geschichte* (Neuwied: Luchterhand, 1961) and Giulia
    Lami, "Russia in the Eyes of Italy between the XIX and the XX century," in
    National Stereotypes: Correct Images and Distorted Images, ed. Bianca Valota
    (Alessandria: Edizioni dell'Orso, 2007), 27–37.
42 "Le Suisse qui vit dans ses montagnes, le Bédouin qui vit dans le désert, et
    l'Hongrois qui vit dans sa puszta sont des hommes de liberté. Consultez l'histoire
    de ces trois peuples; ils ont soutenu une lutte continuelle pour le maintien de leur
    indépendance." See Victor Tissot, *Voyage au pays des Tziganes (La Hongrie
    inconnue)* (Paris: Dentu, 1880), 230–1.

Traditional or Modern, Nativist or Foreign, Ukrainian or European: The Roots of Ivan Nechui-Levyts'kyi's Antimodernism

MAXIM TARNAWSKY

Ivan Nechui-Levyts'kyi is a major figure in Ukrainian realism and a notorious critic of modernism. Many postindependence Ukrainian critics – most notably the late Solomiia Pavlychko, whose work on Ukrainian modernism has had a profound influence on the current generation of critics – equate Ukrainian modernism with a turn towards European cultural paradigms. In this context, it would be easy to assume that Nechui's antimodernist sentiments derive from a nativist, anti-European cultural orientation. But Nechui pays homage to European cultural values, and the sources of his antimodernist position are sooner domestic than foreign. The aesthetic values that dominated Ukrainian literature in the populist and realist era grew out of a fundamental orientation on the cultural, social, and political centrality of the lower classes, the carriers of Ukrainian national identity. But aside from the distinct national identity, these values were no less European than the modernist aesthetic that took their place. Nechui's antimodernist stance in not directed against Europe per se, but against the appropriation by Ukrainian literature of a recent European aesthetic that has an anachronistic relationship, in his view, to the Ukrainian cultural environment of his time. An examination of one his short late works, the satiric story "Bez puttia" (Going Nowhere; the title might also be translated as "Pointless"), allows us to explore the peculiarities of this antimodernist stance and, in particular, suggests a possible antecedent for his satiric attack on decadent modernist writing.

The core element in all of Ivan Nechui-Levyts'kyi's writing is Ukrainian identity. The bulk of his writing is a forceful assertion of its existence, character, and dignity. For the most part, this identity is conceived in national terms. Nechui writes about people who are culturally Ukrainian. But his Ukrainians come in a variety of flavors, including members of other nations that are Ukrainian by dint of their presence in Ukraine. Thus, for Nechui, Ukrainian identity is both national and geographical. Nechui's Ukrainians are differentiated by an assortment of qualities, among them ethnic origin, social rank, urban or rural status, education, gender, wealth, occupation, and other factors, including purely cultural ones. Nechui's satire is often focused on such differentiating qualities. Foreignness, however, is generally a negative characteristic for Nechui and not subject to satiric treatment. Many of Nechui's villains are depicted as foreigners, that is, as Russians and Poles living in Ukraine. Their villainy usually lies in their ability to denationalize Ukrainians by inducing them to abandon their national identity. Jews, too, are sometimes portrayed as villains – in this case, their villainy is economic exploitation. Foreigners of nationalities other than these three occur very rarely in Nechui's works. Some Greeks and Armenians appear in minor roles, but these nationalities, like Russians, Poles, and Jews, are not really perceived as completely foreign: they are part of the Ukrainian landscape. The Europe that is beyond Ukraine (more precisely, beyond the area settled by Ukrainians) is almost completely absent from Nechui's fictional works as a subject, as a location, or as a source of characters. In an early chapter of his novel *Khmary* (The Clouds) there are two French sisters, the marquises de Pourverser, whose father moved to St Petersburg from Provence in search of good fortune. They are the grey eminences of the Kyiv Institute for Noble Maidens where their chief virtues are pretentiousness and speaking French. Their flavor is far more Russian than European. A little further in the same chapter Nechui presents the entertainment at the trendy Kyiv restaurant, *Le Chateau*. It consists of Tyrolean yodellers, whose singing is compared to the sound of Swiss cows, and a German balloonist, whose gas-filled contraption springs a leak. Both incidents are meant to highlight the foolishness and poor taste of the lowbrow high-society public that favours this establishment and fails to recognize that Swiss folklore is no better than the local variety and foreign technology is no guarantee of success. However, a satiric depiction of Ukrainian socialites who favour all things European, no matter how silly, is not indicative of any particular view of Europe on the part of the author.

In his non-belletristic writing, Nechui mentions Europe somewhat more often and in a positive context. In his autobiographical writing, Europe is the essential source of his literary inspiration – he mentions reading the works of classic European authors (Cervantes, Dante, Chateaubriand, Eugène Sue, and Sir Walter Scott) during his seminary years in Kyiv and the influence this had on his development as a writer.[1] In his notorious essays on the development of contemporary literature,[2] European literary standards and ideas (particularly Hippolyte Taine's *race, milieu et moment*) are the benchmark by which Nechui measures progress. Of course, in these writings, Europe is meant to be the positive cultural model that counterbalances the negative model that he sees in Russian culture. Even if the motive for praising Europe has some anti-Russian origin, it is clear that Nechui's view of European civilization is genuinely positive. The antimodernist and antidecadent sentiments he expresses are clearly not an outgrowth of the kind of suspicion or disdain for "Western" values that sometimes characterize East European nativists. So where do these sentiments come from?

Nechui's satiric story, "Going Nowhere" was published in 1900 in the *Literaturno-naukovyi visnyk*, which was still published in Lviv at that time. The story had a subtitle, "Opovidannia po dekadents'komu" (A Story in the Decadent Manner). The plot concerns the romantic relationship between two young Kyivites, Nastusia Samusivna and Pavlus' Malynka; both are the offspring of wealthy families whose fortunes have largely disappeared through a profligate lifestyle.

The story is composed of five sections that somewhat resemble the acts of a play. Act 1 is non-theatrical – it is all scene setting and background. Act 2 depicts the two young lovers engaged in rhetorical lovemaking, expressing their love for each other in a series of ever more colourful, pretentious, ephemeral, abstruse, and confusing metaphors and allusions. Act 3 finds Nastusia in conflict with her father and her aunts, who do not approve of Pavlus'; a sensitive young woman, she is deeply distressed by what she perceives as their boorishness and bullying. Act 4 depicts the culmination of Nastusia's and Pavlus's love in a first kiss, which takes place in the Solomenka district of Kyiv, then a largely working-class neighbourhood characterized by the recently built railroad lines and train station. The young lovers, however, see the industrial landscape as nothing less than idyllic, or at least poetic: they compare the space beneath a railroad trestle to the setting of Offenbach's mock heroic "Orpheus in the Underworld," the show that premiered in Paris in 1858 and made the cancan famous. Act 5 is pure comic denouement. The young lovers flee to Kyiv's Bald Mountain, where they tumble down the hill towards the river in the snow. Peasants heading to market pick them up at the base of the hill and deliver them to a mental asylum, where white-coated doctors allow the lovers to indulge their fantasies and can do little to bring the young couple back to any semblance of reality.

As is often the case with Nechui's satire, the target of his derision is left quite vague. Here, as in most of his satiric works, Nechui is taking aim at human foibles rather than at any specific social or cultural phenomenon. This strategy is perhaps best shown by Nechui's most famous satiric creations, the two devoutly antagonistic village hags Baba Paraska and Baba Palazhka, who do nothing to undermine Nechui's or the reader's affection for the simple customs of the

Ukrainian village, despite the satire. A similar narrowing of satirical focus is seen in Nechui's religious characters, particularly rural parish priests. Despite two generations of Soviet critical nonsense about his anticlerical satires, Nechui shows no general disrespect for religion or for the clergy. In his satiric portraits Nechui does indeed consistently deflate the pretensions of the rich, the powerful, the educated, and the upper class, but this is hardly a consistent social program or a philosophical view: it is the traditional matter of most satire. But when socially motivated satire turns into aesthetic parody, the situation becomes more complex. There is no "traditional matter" for aesthetic parody; the only way to poke fun at an aesthetic phenomenon is to lampoon the specific features that are associated with it. In the case of Nechui's antimodernist writing, identifying the aesthetic phenomenon that he is debunking is not such a simple task. The specific targets of his aesthetic scorn are not clearly identified.

The beginning of the story offers a good example. It opens with an extended description of the two principals, Nastusia and Pavlus'. The description is built on a series of qualities that both of the young lovers share, one of them having too much of an attribute and the other having even more. These qualities are then undermined with seemingly contradictory or inconsistent examples or details. The descriptions of the qualities themselves are also composed of incompatible elements. Thus Pavlus' is beautiful, and Nastusia is, if anything, even more beautiful – but her beauty has the youthful quality of being unwashed. And she's a little pale and seems tired and somewhat withered. They were both brought up in wealth, but her father is out of money – and his father has also squandered his wealth. They both spend time in the fashionable and sophisticated cities of Europe, but they do so in a manner resembling gypsies travelling with their tents. Their sleeping habits are a reversal of what is customary. Nastusia actually sleeps at night, the narrator says, but she goes to bed only just before dawn. Pavlus', however, has reversed night and day and in contrast to the sophistication of his dissolute lifestyle, the narrator compares his sleeping habits to those of owls and bats. Nastusia is deemed to be an intelligent girl, but one without any sense in her head. Pavlus' is not without good sense – but his head just seems to let it leak out. In both cases, the images are those of poorly made barrels. Throughout the description, there is a consistent juxtaposition of European urban sophistication with rural provinciality. The money that spills from the pockets of the two rich brats in European capitals resembles the flour that spills from a sack on a wagon rolling along a lumpy and cratered road. Eventually, in the fourth paragraph, Nechui reveals the key image: "Ioho vsi zvaly bozhevil'nym; ïï – navisnoiu" (7: 295; Everyone called him insane, and her crazy). This is the direction in which the story will move: insanity. The final scene will present the young lovers at the Kyrylivs'kyi

Psychiatric Hospital still raving about their extraordinary love for each other and mistaking an indulgent and patronizing doctor first for Buddha and then for an imprisoned criminal.

In this stream of humorous imagery it is easy to discern a satiric motive. It is far more difficult, however, to identify its particular mode and target. Nechui had ridiculed the financial immaturity and wastefulness of upper-class characters in a number of previous works, so these aspects of his satire are readily understood in the context of his familiar outlook on social questions. However, unlike some of his other efforts at social satire – for example, the novel *Neodnakovymy stezhkamy* (Along Different Paths) – this story ("Going Nowhere") does not contain a sympathetic character through whose eyes the irresponsible behaviour is perceived and through whose sensibility the satiric judgment is reflected. Andrian Hukovych is such a touchstone in *Neodnakovymy stezhkamy*. The reader's judgment of the silly behaviour of Andrian's wife and daughter is confirmed (and moderated, too) by the grief Andrian himself endures in trying to accommodate their spending while still maintaining financial solvency. There is no such character in "Going Nowhere." Pavlus's and Nastusia's fathers are no better than their children, even if Petro Samus' has a sober estimate of his daughter's foolishness and her boyfriend's dissipation. Nastusia's two aunts, Mania and Sofa, may be well intentioned, but they are silly old biddies. So the only perspective available to the reader is one of exclusionary othering, where the satiric victims are presented as those against whom the reader can measure his or her own identity. If that were all there were to the story, what we would have is a simple case of crazy spendthrifts presented as crazy spendthrifts, hardly a formula for effective satire.

"Going Nowhere," however, has larger ambitions. The subtitle, "A Story in the Decadent Manner," signals parody. While the target of the parody is not made explicit, the set of possible candidates for this honour is neither infinite nor completely unknowable. The text is saturated with pretentious comparisons and allusions that are atypical of Nechui's own style. The young lovers are compared to mythological gods. The narrative emphasizes their imagination and inventiveness as opposed to their lack of diligence and studiousness. The language of the protagonists is deliberately elevated and poetical, full of metaphors, rhetorical flourish, and extravagant imagery. Along with the subtitle, these are clear signs that Nechui has embarked on the path of aesthetic parody – he is lampooning a literary style. Specifically, he is ridiculing literary modernism, with its pretentious abandonment of socially relevant themes and simple "objective" aesthetic principles, in favour of esoteric intellectual and philosophical concerns and complex, sophisticated, artistic methods. As with any parody, the success of the enterprise depends on many factors, not least of which is the reader's ability to recognize the parody in the text and that same reader's sensibility regarding the object of the parodic lampoon. Ivan Franko offers an instructive example. In 1900, the same year that Nechui published "Going Nowhere," Franko published his own antimodernist poetic declaration as the foreword to his poem "Lisova idyliia" (Forest Idyll). In it, he derided Mykola Voronyi's appeal for submissions to an almanac by suggesting the modernist poet and compiler was only interested in works that came without a long list of features that included the most important qualities of literature. Today, Franko's witty parody is more often seen as a symptom of his own limited appreciation of the manifold dimensions of literary texts than as an effective comic riposte to modernism; the same occurs with Nechui's considerably less witty story. It is unlikely that many readers will respond sympathetically to Nechui's humour. Modernism is one of the sacred cows of literary good taste and a parody of it based on the old-fashioned aesthetics of realism is out of step with twenty-first-century tastes and values. Moreover, Nechui's text suffers from a problem that Franko's does not. The immediate target of Franko's parody is well known: it is the public call for submissions to the almanac *Z nad khmar i dolyn* (From Above Clouds and Valleys), which Voronyi eventually published in 1903. Familiarity with the parodied text allows the reader to appreciate the parodist's skill, wit, and intention, even if the reader does not necessarily share the parodist's judgment. But what is being parodied in Nechui's "Going Nowhere"?

Among Nechui's available papers and correspondence, there is nothing that identifies the original target of this lampoon. Critics who have written about Nechui have not commented on this question and therefore we are left to our own deductions and speculations. The story itself does not provide any obvious hints. Shortly after the story appeared in *Literaturno-naukovyi visnyk* Nechui discussed it in a letter to Nataliia Kobryns'ka, written, it seems, in answer to her question about a particular word used in the story. After a few remarks on vocabulary, Nechui turns to the story as a whole:

> My story, "Going Nowhere," is a parody of decadence and symbolism in literature, [qualities] that do not find any favor with me. At the same time this is a satire on the folly and disorder in some families that nowadays are in evidence here and there among us, and on some of our contemporary Kyivites. I must confess that all the petty oddities that you will find in the story are collected and copied directly from experience, no matter how strange they may seem, except, perhaps, the very end, or conclusion, which is constructed and combined as the outgrowth of all the foregoing, although even here there is a great deal that I actually saw with my own eyes in my life (10: 367).[3]

Nechui then turns to a discussion of Ibsen, expressing agreement with Kobryns'ka's judgment of Nora in Ibsen's *A Doll's House* as a weak, insufficiently motivated character, a product of the author's (Ibsen's) diluting his usual realism with elements of symbolism. From there he goes on to express his views on symbolism in literature:

> But this symbolism in poetry is not at all to my liking. We Ukrainians and Russians are altogether averse to these riddles in art and poetry. In my view, these symbols only spoil and cripple works that are otherwise beautiful in themselves. A fellow goes and cooks up such a storm of words that you're left goggling like a cow staring at a new gate, because it doesn't recognize its master's home … This symbolism is not going to take root among us. I am certain of this. In Europe it was popular in the middle ages. The *Roman de la Rose* by Guillaume de Lorris [Nechui has Jean de Lorris] a symbolist work in verse, was first published in the thirteenth century! And it was reprinted for 300 years! Up until the sixteenth century. And the ladies in Boccaccio's *Decameron* are also symbolic. And in England, Dryden wrote poems about a symbolic "white hind" and a black deer [in John Dryden's *The Hind and the Panther* (1687) it is not a deer, but a panther that is black], that is, about the conflict between Protestants and Catholics. In Europe, symbolism in poetry is not something new – it is ancient. Perhaps because of this it is understood by the public there and can be rejuvenated. For us, it is just a curiosity and that's all (10: 368).

These remarks to Kobryns'ka, made not long after the composition of the story, are only partially helpful in analysing the work. Symbolism is an important concept, but Nechui's use of this term is not particularly illuminating. His notion of symbolist writing is appropriate in the context of early twentieth-century East European writing. It is less obvious how this concept relates medieval West European religious writing to Ibsen's plays, except in the very basic sense that like medieval religious writing, early twentieth-century writing is also characterized by elements that are distinctly not realist in their stylistic and intellectual essence. Nechui finds fault with Ibsen only insofar as this usually realistic author abandons these familiar principles in favour of something more modern and less grounded in materialist and rational ideas.

By underscoring once again a commitment to realist principles in literature, the comments in the letter to Kobryns'ka do not add anything particularly new to our understanding of "Going Nowhere" or the identity of its satiric targets. A few points, however, deserve attention. Nechui does not cast blame on West European writers for employing symbolist techniques. He allows them to continue in the direction dictated by their own traditions, arguing only that

Ukrainian and Russian literature, grounded in a different aesthetic history, should not move in that direction. While this position favours a non-European course of cultural development for Ukraine, it is not an anti-European argument. Indeed, Nechui is using Europe as the touchstone against which aesthetic achievement is measured. Ukrainian aesthetic traditions are assessed against those in Western Europe but that does not mean that Ukrainian writers should immediately adopt them. Another significant point in this letter is Nechui's and Kobryns'ka's focus on Ibsen in discussing the influence of symbolism. This is not an obvious and inevitable choice. Modernist ideas appeared in dramatic works as well as in other genres, but drama was not the primary venue for their introduction. Perhaps Nechui's association of "Going Nowhere" with modernist theatre reveals a specific concern that helps to explain the satiric intent. Finally, there may be a hidden allusiveness in the titles of the symbolic works that Nechui mentions, particularly the *Roman de la Rose*. But these hints and allusions, if that is what they are, are much too subtle to offer convincing evidence that Nechui is thinking about a specific modernist play.

Another of Nechui's texts that relates to "Going Nowhere" is the essay entitled "Ukrains'ka dekadentshchyna" (Ukrainian Decadence). This essay was not published in Nechui's lifetime; it first appeared in the ten-volume collection of his works in 1968. The collection's editors suggest that the existing text can be dated to 1911 on the basis of the publication dates of the works cited in the essay. In the essay itself, Nechui mentions that he had earlier written the story "Going Nowhere" and offers the essay as a further effort to show the genesis and beginnings of decadence in literature (10: 188). This language is much too opaque to establish any direct connection between the composition of the story and the essay, and the ideas and examples in the latter might be more closely linked with Nechui's thinking in 1911 than in 1900. In any event, the essay is divided into three large sections. The first examines the general features of decadence as a phenomenon and traces its development in Western Europe. Nechui mentions and indeed follows the ideas of Max Nordau,[4] presenting much of the rising tide of modernist art as a product of mental degeneration. Individual writers such as Guy de Maupassant, Baudelaire, Nietzsche, and Oscar Wilde he simply calls lunatics. In section two Nechui turns to Ukrainian literature and describes a number of authors who mix realist and decadent elements in their works. Among them are Ol'ha Kobylians'ka, Nataliia Kobryns'ka, Oleksii Pliushch, and Hnat Khotkevych. While variously condemning particular works and aesthetic features, on the whole Nechui takes a mildly critical view of these authors, in whom he certainly still sees positive traits. He then drifts off into a discussion of his favourite hobby horse, the contamination of the Ukrainian language with West Ukrainian dialectal forms.

In the essay's disproportionately lengthy third section he focuses squarely on the negative qualities of decadent writing. The key culprits here are Volodymyr Vynnychenko and Oleksander Oles'. Nechui references Vynnychenko's third collection of short stories, which, he says, appeared "this year." No doubt, he is referring to Vynnychenko's *Tretia knyzhka opovidan'* (Third Book of Stories), which appeared in Kyiv in 1910. In any event, the stories he discusses – "Moment" (The Moment), "Zina," "Shchos' bil'she za nas" (Something Greater Than We), "Kuplia" (The Purchase), "Rabyni spravzhn'oho" (Slaves to Reality) – are all from Vynnychenko's second period of creativity, after 1905. Surprisingly, Nechui praises the author for many aspects of these stories, comparing the character types of Vynnychenko's protagonists to the troubled romantic heroes of the Young Germany movement of the mid-nineteenth century. It is mostly the plays of Volodymyr Vynnychenko's that come in for direct criticism. Nechui condemns *Shchabli zhyttia* (The Levels of Life) and *Chorna pantera i bilyi vedmid'* (The Black Panther and The White Bear) for what he sees as an exclusive and pathological focus on sexuality. So, too, in the poetry of Oleksander Oles' Nechui finds an excessive concentration on the "dramas of the heart," that is, on the relationships between men and women. Nechui ties these trends in Vynnychenko and Oles' to Western European writers, particularly Guy de Maupassant, but he also finds them in Russian literature, especially in the works of Leonid Andreev.

As the foregoing illustrates, Nechui's essay "Ukrainian Decadence" offers little evidence to illuminate the nature or identity of the satiric target in "Going Nowhere." The essay, written considerably later than the story, associates decadent writing with sexuality or pornography, which Nechui sees as an undesirable subject for Ukrainian literature. Nechui finds these decadent tendencies among Western writers, but he similarly finds them among Russian and Ukrainian writers and he very clearly does not see decadent tendencies as a pernicious defect transferred from a spoiled West to an otherwise innocent and healthy East. Nechui's antidecadent views are not anti-Western. Whatever the object of his satire may be, it is not Europe. There are no clues that might help identify the satiric antecedent for "Going Nowhere" in his essay on decadent literature; they must be sought in the story itself.

In searching for a possible satiric target in this story, the first matters for consideration are the language and national character of the parody. Judging by the specifically Ukrainian setting, the characters' veneration of West European comforts and pleasures, and the absence of satiric foreign allusions or references, it seems likely that the parody is targeted at a work or works of Ukrainian literature. Since Nechui's story was published in 1900, the universe of possible targets is limited – there was not very much modernist writing in

Ukrainian before the turn of the century. Among Ukrainian modernists, only a few had significant publications before 1900. Ol'ha Kobylians'ka had released *Liudyna* (A Person) and *Tsarivna* (A Princess). Mykhailo Kotsiubyns'kyi's earliest works appeared in the 1890s but they still mostly reflected a realist aesthetic. Feminist writers like Nataliia Kobryns'ka and Liubov Ianovs'ka were active before 1900 but their writings did not reflect modernist values. Volodymyr Vynnychenko's works did not appear until the new century. The popular ethnographic theatre was in full swing, but it certainly could not provoke an antimodernist reaction. There was, however, one writer whose innovative ideas in both theme and aesthetics might have elicited a reaction from Nechui. Her name was Lesia Ukraïnka.

In 1896, Lesia Ukraïnka broke her exclusive attachment to lyric poetry and wrote her first play, which she entitled *Blakytna troianda* (The Azure Rose). Despite her best efforts, it took some time to have the play staged. Eventually it appeared in Kyiv on 17 August 1899 in a production by the theatre company of Marko Kropyvnyts'kyi, as a benefit for a popular actress named Ratmirova. The performance attracted a sizable audience and very poor reviews.[5]

The plot of *Blakytna troianda* presents love and insanity in an inseparable combination. Roman Weretelnyk offers a summary of the play:

> Orest Hruich, a young writer, is in love with Liubov Hoshchyns'ka, a young woman whose artistic ambitions no one takes seriously. Liubov initially resists Orest's overtures, fearing to become trapped in marriage. Eventually, however, because of her great need to be loved, Liubov succumbs to Orest's protestations of love and agrees to marry him. Their intended union is complicated by everyone's (especially Orest's mother's) belief that Liubov suffers from a hereditary mental illness. They fear that Liubov, like her mother before her, will go mad and will ruin Orest in the process. After professing her love for Orest, Liubov does go mad, but not for the reasons everyone expects. Rather, her action represents a voluntary descent into madness as a viable alternative to her predicament. Liubov leaves for the Crimea to recover, only to be followed there in a year's time by Orest and his mother, who have decided that he cannot live without her. Faced with no option this time, Liubov commits suicide.[6]

The statement that Liubov's descent into madness is voluntary, it should be noted, is not directly supported by the text of the drama, although it certainly represents a possible interpretation of the events. Contemporary feminist critics including Solomiia Pavlychko, Vira Aheieva, Nila Zborovs'ka, Tamara Hundorova, and Lesia Dems'ka-Budzuliak[7] have taken their cue from Weretelnyk's path-breaking work and analyse the play in the context of late nineteenth-century views of feminine hysteria, a condition Lesia Ukraïnka personally experienced and for which she underwent treatment. They have demonstrated that the play needs to be seen in the context of the early development of feminist ideas and of psychoanalysis. These two fields of developing research did not necessarily fit well with each other at the end of the nineteenth century, and this disharmony provoked Lesia Ukraïnka and other feminist writers to examine the specifics of women's psychology in a peculiarly fatalistic spirit. Lidiia Zelins'ka explains: "this is a play about hysteria, which has been replaced in the plot by the idea of hereditary insanity."[8]

The considerable insight that these literary critics have applied to the play makes it far more interesting and comprehensible but it does nothing to reduce the play's obvious faults. Feminist critics from Weretelnyk to Zelins'ka invariably present apologias for this play, but they also admit, for the most part, its theatrical, intellectual, and literary weakness. The ideas and issues of the play are not clearly focused, the dialogue is stilted and disconnected, and the construction is static and overburdened. These faults reflect features characteristic of all of Lesia Ukraïnka's dramas; most significantly, however, they arise from her inexperience in treating complex intellectual and emotional issues in this genre. *Blakytna troianda* was her very first drama. In later works she would find a more appropriate discourse to present her intellectual designs, and she would reduce the psychoanalytical analyses – particularly autobiographical ones – to their cognitive components. That is, she would embody the conflicts presented in her plays as an intellectual discourse channeled through a rational argument rather than an emotional psychodrama presented as the personal feelings of a protagonist. In this play, however, there is ample justification for the viewer or critic who fails to discern the innovative approach to female psychology and perceives instead confusing, disconnected, and pretentious conversations about the inevitability of insanity when emotions are aroused. This was, in fact, the response to the play when it was first staged.[9] In his important essay about *Blakytna troianda*, Petro Rulin recounts the various reviews that appeared following its premier performance: they were merciless.[10] Of course, some of the critical venom was inappropriate, but, as Rulin himself points out, the abundance of flaws justified the harsh response to the 1899 production and then again to the 1907 production at the Lysenko school.

There is no direct evidence that Nechui actually knew Lesia Ukraïnka's play. In terms of chronological possibilities, there is just enough time between the August 1899 staging of *Blakytna troianda* and the publication of "Going Nowhere" in late 1900 to make it feasible for Nechui's work to have been influenced by knowledge of the play. Indeed, the text of the play was read at meetings in the home of Mykhailo Staryts'kyi in 1897, in which Nechui sometimes participated, so he might have been familiar with the text even earlier. It is not my argument that Nechui's "Going Nowhere" is a direct parody of Lesia Ukraïnka's play. My point is that Lesia Ukraïnka's play could have been part of the modernist wave of materials to which Nechui was reacting. The five-act dramatic structure of Nechui's story and the pretentious language of his protagonists offer small but tangible evidence to support such an argument. Most important, however, is the strange subject itself – love and insanity. Nechui's parodic presentation of a young couple whose love is quite literally depicted as insanity does not ring any particular bells of recognition in the modernist canon, whether Ukrainian or generally European. Moreover, the subject is not particularly associated with modernist themes. It is the particular combination of passionate love and insanity, understood as a metaphorical substitute for hysteria, that makes Ukraïnka's text stand out as a possible target of Nechui's parody. The fact that her drama presents this combination very ineffectively, in an illogical and unconvincing manner that would have seemed outright silly to the eminently rationalist sensibilities of Ivan Nechui-Levyts'kyi, adds more weight to the possibility of a link.

What is most important about the prospect of such a connection, however, is that Nechui's aesthetic parody may have a real antecedent. In today's climate of literary criticism in Ukraine, where recovering works and ideas forbidden under the Soviet regime has a natural attraction, the historical conflict between realism and modernism in Ukrainian literature is mostly one-sided: all the trump cards are in the hands of the modernists and the aesthetic position of the realists – Franko is a good example – is scarcely given serious credit. If Nechui's parody of modernist, decadent aesthetics can be shown to have a real target (*Blakytna troianda*), though a very weak one not really representative of the principal direction and best practices of modernist sensibilities, then the dialogue between realism and modernism in Ukraine acquires new meaning and new life. In particular, this dialogue, it turns out, need not be understood as a nativist rejection of foreign-inspired modern ideas. Such an ideological understanding of cultural developments in Ukraine has been and continues to be a popular and simplistic explanation for the recurring pattern of resistance to avant-garde cultural developments. In a climate of perceived national cultural underdevelopment and discrimination, there is a strong temptation to see avant-garde aesthetics and their accompanying universalist themes as solutions to two persistent problems: the stagnation of aesthetic forms and the myopic isolation of a narrowly focused national culture. Supporters of modernism today and at the beginning of the twentieth century – Lesia Ukraïnka, for example – assume that those who accept Western avant-garde ideas choose hope and future cultural development while those that reject these avant-garde ideas are xenophobic opponents of any change. In the current discourse about European values in contemporary

Ukrainian culture, this dualistic division between nativists and westernizers has been used to discredit and condemn a wide range of writers on the presumption that their rejection of specific, popular Western aesthetic ideas is necessarily a rejection of universal human and cultural values.

Whether applied to today's conservative authors, such as Valerii Shevchuk, or to the conservative authors of an earlier period, such as Nechui, this dualism produces two different streams of Ukrainian cultural development. Modernism with its Western influences and putative universalism acquires a "natural" status as the proper channel for the development of Ukrainian culture, while nativist opponents of the modern are ascribed the role of outsiders, foreigners in the unquestionably European landscape of Ukraine's literature. Just beneath the surface of such a judgment is a comparison to Russian culture, assumed to be the natural counterpart to European culture and thus the presumed model for the nativist sensibility. Ukrainian writers, both of the present and of one hundred years ago, are thus polarized into two groups, an aesthetically progressive modernist vanguard and an obscurantist retrograde opposition. This need not be the only way to see the issue.

Nechui's conservative aesthetics were not very receptive to modernist innovations, but Nechui was not merely antagonistic to everything that was new and different. He was reacting to actual texts – Ukrainian texts, moreover – and asserting a real aesthetic judgment that was not merely a rejection of the new sensibilities. Nechui's jibe at Ukrainian modernism is, like most of his satire, specific in its target and limited in the scope of its application. By spoofing Lesia Ukraïnka, Nechui is establishing her place in the same artistic and national space that he himself occupies. What might seem a rejection of the strange and the foreign was likely an amicable jibe at the absurd and familiar. Nechui's lampoon of Lesia, love, and insanity is, like all of his work, a contribution to Ukrainian writing, to the establishment of a shared, common, national cultural environment. But this Ukrainian cultural space is no less European for being nationally specific and aesthetically antimodernist.

Notes

1 For example, in his "Zhyttiepys' Ivana Levyts'koho (Nechuia) napysana nym samym" (10:14). All references to Nechui's texts are indicated by volume and page number and refer to I. S. Nechui-Levyts'kyi, *Zibrannia tvoriv u desiaty tomakh* (Kyiv: Naukova dumka, 1965–8).

2 "S'ohochasne literaturne priamuvannia" (also known as "Nepotribnist' velykorus'koi literatury dlia Ukrainy i dlia slovianshchyny") and "Ukrainstvo na literaturnykh pozvakh z Moskovshchynoiu."

3 Letter to Nataliia Kobryns'ka, 13 September 1900 (Old Style).

4 Max Nordau (1849–1923) wrote conservative social criticism that emphasized the pathological degeneration of society, particularly as it is revealed in decadent art. His written works include *The Conventional Lies of Our Civilisation* (1883) and *Degeneration* (1892).

5 Iurii Mezhenko, "Khronolohiia artystychnoi diial'nosti M. L. Kropyvnyts'koho (Materialy do biohrafii)," in *Marko Lukych Kropyvnyts'kyi: Zbirnyk stattei, spohadiv, i materialiv* (Kyiv: Mystetstvo, 1955), 471; and Petro Rulin, "Persha drama Lesi Ukraïnky," in Lesia Ukraïnka, *Tvory v 12 tomakh* (New York: Tyshchenko and Bilous, 1954), 5: 12.

6 Roman Weretelnyk, "A Feminist Reading of Lesia Ukraïnka's Dramas," (PhD Diss., University of Ottawa, 1989), 36–7.

7 For general evaluations of Lesia Ukraïnka, including specific references to this play, see: Solomiia Pavlychko, *Dyskurs modernizmu v ukraïns'kii literaturi* (Kyiv: Lybid', 1999), 243–6; Vira Aheieva, *Poetesa zlamu stolit': Tvorchist' Lesi Ukraïnky v postmodernii interpretatsiï* (Kyiv: Lybid', 1999), 91–112; Nila Zborovs'ka, *Moia Lesia Ukraïnka: Eseï* (Ternopil': Dzhura, 2002), 112–22; Tamara Hundorova, *ProIavlennia slova: Dyskursiia rann'oho ukraïns'koho modernizmu. Postmoderna interpretatsiia* (Lviv: Tsentr humanitarnykh doslidzhen', 1997), 244; Lesia Dems'ka-Budzuliak, "Kryza zhinochoï identychnosti v konteksti 'novoï ievropeis'koï dramy,'" *Lesia Ukraïnka i suchasnist'* (Luts'k: Volyns'ka oblasna drukania, 2006), 3: 136–49.

8 "'Blakytna troianda' Lesi Ukraïnky: Problema dyskursu i metodu," *Lesia Ukraïnka i suchasnist': Zbirnyk naukovykh prats'* (Luts'k: Volyns'kyi natsional'nyi universytet im. Lesi Ukraïnky, 2007), Tom IV, kn 1, 69, accessed 24 April 2012, http://www.nbuv.gov.ua/portal/Soc_Gum/Lukrsuch/2007_4_1/R1/ Zelinska.pdf.

9 See the accounts presented in Oleh Babyshkin, *Dramaturhiia Lesi Ukraïnky* (Kyiv: Derzhavne vydavnytstvo obrazotvorchoho mystetstva i muzychnoï literatury, 1963), 26–31; Abram Hozenpud, *Poetychnyi teatr: Dramatychni tvory Lesi Ukraïnky* (Kyiv: Mystetstvo, 1947), 26–9; and Petro Rulin, "Persha drama Lesi Ukraïnky," 5: 7–28.

10 Rulin, "Persha drama Lesi Ukraïnky."

Rewriting Johann Wolfgang Goethe in the Poetry of Western Ukrainian Modernism

STEFAN SIMONEK

This paper is devoted to the artistic devices that the Western Ukrainian poets of the modernist group Moloda Muza (Young Muse) used in order to come to terms with the famous (or infamous?) Western canon outlined by the American scholar Harold Bloom in 1994. At the end of his seminal study Bloom offers several lists of the major literary texts of Europe and America from the fourteenth century onward, which, in his view, comprise the Western canon mentioned in the title of his book. Unfortunately, this canon completely ignores the existence of any literature written in the Ukrainian language. (I hesitate to use the term "Ukrainian literature" at this point because, in addition to several nineteenth-century Russian writers, Bloom mentions Nikolai Gogol', who may also be considered a Ukrainian author writing in Russian.)[1] Since the appendices in Bloom's book do not include such prominent Ukrainian writers as Taras Shevchenko, Ivan Franko, or Lesia Ukraïnka, it is hardly surprising that he also omits the Ukrainian poets Vasyl' Pachovs'kyi, Petro Karmans'kyi, and Bohdan Lepkyi, who, along with others, were members of Moloda Muza, a group of poets who have been described as second- or even third-rate by some major experts in the field of Ukrainian studies. In December 1991, for example, *Harvard Ukrainian Studies* published a number of essays on Ukrainian modernism, in which Danylo Husar Struk[2] and George Grabowicz[3] stated that there was a significant lack of talent among the poets of Moloda Muza.

However, this supposed lack of literary talent clearly did not prevent poets[4] like Lepkyi or Karmans'kyi from coming into contact with those modernist notions that were circulating in Europe around 1900 and that had already been introduced into Western Ukrainian literature by none other than Ivan Franko in his 1896 collection *Ziviale lystia* (Withered Leaves).[5] The poets of Moloda Muza reacted to these aesthetic trends in European culture in a twofold manner, combining their longing to become a genuine part of this

European culture, which Mykola Voronyi in 1901 compared to a distant and fascinating blue sky,[6] with their negative response to it and to the Western canon – which, nevertheless, they articulated by means of the central elements of this very canon.

The positive reception of Europe by Western Ukrainian modernism was clearly visible in both the programmatic and the poetical works of Moloda Muza. In November 1907 the Lviv daily *Dilo* (The Deed) published the group's manifesto, which was signed by Ostap Luts'kyi and featured a number of influential names from several European literatures, including Friedrich Nietzsche, Henrik Ibsen, Maurice Maeterlinck, and Charles Baudelaire.[7] These names, which are regularly encountered in the modernist manifestos of various Slavic literatures, demonstrate the orientation of Slavic modernism towards the culture of Western Europe. The poets of Moloda Muza constantly strove to emphasize this European dimension: they introduced modernist poetic motifs, such as autumn or falling leaves; Petro Karmans'kyi used a motto from Lorenzo Stecchetti to open his collection *Plyvem po mori t'my* (We Sail on the Sea of Darkness, 1909);[8] and Meletii Kichura gave his 1913 collection of poems a non-Ukrainian title.[9] Without a doubt, these literary strategies were meant to emphasize the manifold cultural ties between Western Ukrainian literature around the turn of the century and European modernism, and to place into the foreground the fact that poets like Vasyl' Pachovs'kyi or the even less well known Stepan Charnets'kyi should not be regarded as merely Ukrainian writers but also as European ones.

Unfortunately, in the final analysis all the textual strategies that the members of Moloda Muza adopted, often in a mechanical and superficial way,[10] did not move Western Ukrainian modernism closer to the gates of the Western canon. Indeed, these gates remained closed both to Moloda Muza and to Ukrainian literature in general.[11] In order to cope with this unfortunate situation, writers like Karmans'kyi or Lepkyi in the second phase of their literary careers formulated a kind of negative polemical reaction to the broad values of European culture, which generally refused to accept Ukrainian literature as one of its genuine components. From a methodological point of view, however, this negative response is perhaps more interesting than the various European aspirations of Western Ukrainian writers, since to a significant extent the literary strategies that the Ukrainian poets employed in reaction to their exclusion from the Western canon are reminiscent of the interpretations offered by postcolonial studies during the last decades of the twentieth century.

In order to analyse these reactions by the Moloda Muza poets, it makes sense to take postcolonial elements from different methodological traditions and combine them in a new way. In doing so, it is possible to interpret the re-evaluation of the canon of German culture that Petro Karmans'kyi and Bohdan Lepkyi (together with Pachovs'kyi, perhaps the most gifted poets of Moloda Muza) published during the First World War or shortly after it ended. Karmans'kyi and Lepkyi responded to the literary canon by creating their own variations on Goethe's poems "Erlkönig" (The Erlking) and "Mignon," which can be interpreted with the help of Harold Bloom as a deliberate misreading of a typically strong poet like Goethe by typically second-rate writers[12] or as a way of writing back to the dominant foreign culture, as envisaged by Bill Ashcroft, Gareth Griffiths, and Helen Tiffin in their influential book *The Empire Writes Back*.[13] Gayatri Spivak's seminal essay "Can the Subaltern Speak?"[14] and Tamara Hundorova's compelling interpretation of resentment[15] also provide possible answers to this question, since all the innovative methodological concepts mentioned earlier seek to demonstrate how individuals at the margins of a culture attempt to acquire their own voice and put forward their own notions of cultural values as opposed to the dominant ideas represented by a given cultural centre. Lepkyi and Karmans'kyi sought to be heard even from their subaltern cultural position. They wrote back to the Western canon in a resentful manner, turning upside down the canon represented by well-known poems like Goethe's "Erlking" or his "Mignon," and provoking it by means of a radical re-estimation of Goethe's famous masterpieces. Clearly, these poems had provoked a feeling of resentment towards what was apprehended as Goethe's sheer and seemingly unattainable formal perfection.

Lepkyi's and Karmans'kyi's rewriting of the German classic should be linked to the First World War, which, owing to the extreme brutality of the Austro-Hungarian army on the Eastern front in Galicia, seemed to bring about an apocalyptic breakdown of traditional values and civilization. (In some of his literary sketches Marko Cheremshyna, a Western Ukrainian modernist prose writer who obtained his doctorate at the University of Vienna, depicted the atrocities perpetrated by this army.) The classical texts of German literature, with which the Galician modernist poets had probably been acquainted since their schooldays,[16] could no longer lay claim to their traditional position as symbols of universal cultural values, but in a radical manner were now being rewritten and devalued in the face of this general breakdown of civilization. The Ukrainian poems that are based on Goethe's two famous works and that are presented in this essay demonstrate this connection between war and the re-evaluation of the classics in a most distinctive way.

I will begin with Petro Karmans'kyi, who published his first collection of poetry, *Z teky samoubiitsia* (From the Briefcase of a Suicide) in 1899 and, thanks to his later collections *Bludni ohni* (Will-o'-the-Wisp, 1907) and *We Sail on the Sea of Darkness* (1909), became one of the most prominent writers of Western Ukrainian modernism. All of Karmans'kyi's early collections are characterized by the author's wish to be a participant in European modernism and to emphasize that desire in his poems, which are full of second-hand modernist metaphors borrowed from other European literatures. In 1917 he published a collection of poems entitled *Al fresco*, which begins with the following motto from the nineteenth-century Austrian national poet Franz Grillparzer:

Gar viele sind meinem Gedichte geneigt;	(Many readers like my poem;
Nur daß, wie es geht beim Lesen,	Unfortunately, as is often the case with reading,
Ich bloß diejenigen überzeugt,	I have managed to convince only those
Die früher bereits es gewesen.[17]	Who were already convinced at the start.)

Both the motto and the title of the collection clearly demonstrate Karmans'kyi's interest in German and Italian literature. This collection also contains the author's rewriting of Goethe's "Erlking" entitled "Ukraïns'ka balada" (A Ukrainian Ballad; see Appendix 1). In his version Karmans'kyi quotes the first line of "Erlking": "Wer reitet so spät durch Nacht und Wind" (Who is riding so late through the night, when the wind is blowing), making it unmistakably clear that his poem is based on Goethe's ballad. However, the Ukrainian poet changes the overall structure of the ballad by turning its eight four-line stanzas into five six-line stanzas. The title "Ukrainian Ballad" indicates that the new text has a distinctly national function; the postcolonial textual strategy of rewriting a prestigious text is realized here by means of a poetical occupation where the "Erlking" becomes "our own" Ukrainian text outside the realm of the Western canon, a Ukrainian ballad that is no longer German.

Tamara Hundorova regards postcolonial melancholic resentment first of all as a consequence of conflict between the weak and the strong.[18] Her focus is on the main Ukrainian postmodernist writers of the end of the twentieth century, especially Yuri Andrukhovych from Western Ukraine and Serhiy Zhadan from the easternmost Ukrainian region of Luhans'k. Poets like Lepkyi and Karmans'kyi, by contrast, represent a kind of second-hand Western Ukrainian modernism from the very beginning of the twentieth century. The "complex of ideas of Europe and Europeanness"[19] which, according to Hundorova, postcolonial resentment evokes in a postmodernist context, however, was already an outstanding aesthetic challenge for the Western Ukrainian modernist writers. The theory of resentment, as Hundorova notes, was developed in the modernist era[20]; Western Ukrainian modernist poets were forced to play the part of outsiders in the overall European artistic environment around the turn of the century, in part due to their visible lack of talent. It is not inappropriate, then, to use the term "resentment" to describe the way in which poets like Petro Karmans'kyi and Bohdan Lepkyi rearranged poetic masterpieces of Western European literature for their own purposes.[21]

Whereas a postcolonial state of mind, according to Hundorova, is characterized by a deliberate separation of the self from the "Great West,"[22] the modernist Western Ukrainian poets reacted to the challenge of the Western canon by modifying and restructuring some of its central works. In doing so, Karmans'kyi as well as Lepkyi modified the seeming universality of Goethe's classic poems by adding Ukrainian elements. At first sight these may seem to reduce the overall aesthetic value of these poetical works; on the other hand, the changes made by Karmans'kyi and Lepkyi can also be interpreted as an effort to come to terms with the Western canon from outside that canon.

In Karmans'kyi's "Ukraïns'ka balada" Goethe's dialogues between the father, the son, and the malevolent forces of the cruel Erlking are replaced (as already suggested by the title) by a dialogic reflection on the mournful lot and passivity of the Ukrainian people, and concluded by a satirical and pathetic note typical of the entire *Al fresco* collection. Whereas in Goethe's ballad the focus is on the individual, the Ukrainian poet expands this focus in a simple, rhetorical manner, so that in his text the son no longer expresses his fear of the Erlking but tries to establish contact with the people. This altered focus becomes clear especially in the second stanza:

Тату, я хочу жаль перелити	(Father, I'd like to pour compassion
В грудь міліонів скорбних і бідних;	Into the breast of the millions who suffer;
Хочу до серця люд мій тулити,	I'd like to press my people close to my heart,
Кров'ю кормити ближніх і рідних.	And to feed my near and dear ones with my own blood.)

For Karmans'kyi, therefore, writing back in the sense of Ashcroft, Griffiths, and Tiffin is represented by an overall semantic shift and radical change of context, which turns one of the most prestigious poems of German literature into mere textual background for a political accusation concerning the deplorable state of Ukrainian society at that time. Consequently, the one who dies at the end of the ballad is no longer the son in his father's arms but the heart of the poet, who is able to raise his voice, not for his own sake, but in the universal name of the whole community. The simultaneous, albeit contradictory, semantic processes in Karmans'kyi's poem – expanding the authority of the lyrical subject while shrinking the overall poetic pretensions of the text to a strictly national Ukrainian issue – may be interpreted as a way in which a subaltern literature located outside the Western canon can speak, although in an altered manner.

The poems of Bohdan Lepkyi also offer a brilliant example of writing back to the Western canon by means of a basic re-evaluation of one of its masterpieces, also written by Goethe. Regarded as one of the more gifted second-rate writers of Moloda Muza, Lepkyi published the poetry collections *Osin'* (Autumn) and *Lystky padut'* (The Leaves are Falling), both of which allude to European modernism through their titles, as well as a number of prose works, including a four-volume novel about Hetman Mazepa. He was also a literary scholar and translator into Ukrainian and Polish.[23] Among Lepkyi's poems is a text that presents the intercultural constellation of Karmans'kyi's "Ukrainian Ballad" – a famous German poem rewritten by a Ukrainian writer who acts against the Western canon – in an even more significant way (see Appendix 2). While Karmans'kyi transformed Goethe's "Erlking" within a specifically Ukrainian national context, Lepkyi used (or rather misused in the sense of Bloom's notion of "misreading") Goethe's "Mignon," a poem on the same artistic level as "Erlking," to write back to the canon. For this purpose, Lepkyi emphasizes the difference between "them" (interpreted as the cultural values endorsed by the canon) and "us" (interpreted as cultural values neglected or even negated by the canon) in a more significant manner than Karmans'kyi. The latter's "Ukrainian Ballad," the title of his version of the "Erlking," offers only an indirect challenge to the pre-eminence of aesthetic values represented by German classical literature, which by means of the new title is integrated into an altered Ukrainian cultural setting. Lepkyi makes this basic opposition even more evident by confronting the original Mignon with a reshaped version of this figure, which in the title of Lepkyi's poem ("Nash Min'ion") becomes "our Mignon" and is thus shifted from its original position in German literature and its traditions into an entirely new milieu. Although Lepkyi wrote "Our Mignon" in April 1920 in the German town of Wetzlar, where he was working for the Ukrainian Military and Sanitary Commission (*Ukrainische Militär- und Sanitärkommission*),[24] the poem, regardless of the place in Germany where he wrote it, replaces the longing for Italy traditionally linked with Goethe's "Mignon" with a dramatic description of the cruelties and destructiveness of war. To some extent, this significant deviation from the German text perpetuates the attempts of Western Ukrainian poets to step out of the shadows of Goethe in general and of his poem "Mignon" in particular.

The search for literary emancipation in Western Ukraine began in the nineteenth century with the publication of Osyp-Iurii Fed'kovych's German poems, which were written to some extent under the influence of "Mignon,"[25] and continued with Petro Karmans'kyi who, even before his fellow modernist Bohdan Lepkyi, published in his 1909 collection *We Sail on the Sea of Darkness* a Ukrainian poem with the German title "Kennst du das Land ..." (Do You Know the Land ...; see Appendix 3). Although the title of this poem cites the first line of Goethe's "Mignon," this work may be read as a precursor to Lepkyi's poem, since in a polemical way it shifts the longing for Italy as evoked by Goethe's poem to a land where, instead of lemon trees in full blossom, we find the eternal darkness of bondage (*vichna t'ma nevoli*) – which, incidentally, is a negative metaphor that was already used by Franko to characterize his native Galicia because of its backwardness and lack of modernity.[26]

If we compare Karmans'kyi's "Ukrainian Ballad" and Lepkyi's rewriting of "Mignon," we see that Lepkyi's ballad is much closer to its German counterpart and uses Goethe's poetic motifs in a much more distinct way. Moreover, through these manifold intertextual connections Lepkyi's poem has a much greater polemical thrust against Goethe's "Mignon" than Karmans'kyi's ballad against the "Erlking." Lepkyi's text in no way confirms the original "Mignon" but uses the German poem in order to pass judgment, in light of the ravages of war, upon Goethe's idealistic aesthetics as a symbol for the entire European cultural system.[27] While Karmans'kyi borrows from the "Erlking" the dialogue between father and son and the son's repetitive appeal to his father, Lepkyi expands his "Mignon" from three to five stanzas but retains Goethe's overall stanza structure, and at the beginning of each stanza inserts the equivalent of Goethe's questions, "Kennst du das Land (das Haus, den Berg)?" [Do you know the land (the house, the mountain)?]. Like Goethe, Lepkyi repeats this question in the fifth line of each stanza, and follows with an exclamation corresponding to Goethe's "Dahin! Dahin / Möcht ich mit dir, o mein Geliebter, ziehn!" (Thither! Thither / Would I go with you, O my beloved!). This exclamation, however, is not varied in each stanza, as in Goethe's poem, but remains unchanged in all five stanzas. Even though Lepkyi adheres closely to Goethe's text throughout his ballad, it is not his intention to confirm the German original. On the contrary, by keeping Goethe's poem always in sight, Lepkyi is able to deal with it in the most polemical way and to write back to the positions of the Western canon, responding to the destruction of the European values and cultural ideals that this canon has been thought to represent. Because Lepkyi's poem preserves and emphasizes its link with Goethe's poem, the sharp contrast between a land where lemon trees (and oranges, laurel, and myrtle) are in full bloom and a land that is full of hunger, disease, and violence becomes even more obvious and demarks the precarious position from which the subaltern is allowed to speak – less with its own voice than with the voice of the Other, misplaced, borrowed, and transformed by resentment.

The apocalyptic images of destruction link Lepkyi's text to such works as Georg Trakl's poem "*Grodek*" or the early stories of the Croatian writer Miroslav Krleža, which depict the horrors of the First World War in an expressionist manner. They are repeated also in the third and fourth stanzas of "Our Mignon," where we find a destroyed and profaned church and a teacher tortured to death. In the fifth and last stanzas of his poem Lepkyi uses the image of a military unit without bread, bullets, and boots. This last image continues the list of images of a land laid waste by war that appear in the earlier stanzas. At the same time, it offers the reader a notion of the bedraggled soldier who is nevertheless driven ideologically to fight "the enemy." The entire text makes it clear that Lepkyi rejects the universalist pretensions of the German classic and replaces them with completely different claims. This strategy may also be linked with the phenomenon of resentment, which can take the form of the deliberate reduction of the semantic complexity of a rewritten text (in this case, Goethe's two poems). The three poems by Karmans'kyi and Lepkyi discussed above ("Ukrainian Ballad," "Kennst du das Land …," and "Our Mignon") are characterized by a significant loss of aesthetic qualities in comparison to the German texts to which they refer. In contrast to Goethe's "Erlking," Karmans'kyi's "Ukrainian Ballad" lacks the epic moment that is essential to the literary genre of the ballad and there is no plot. In the final analysis, therefore, "Ukrainian Ballad" is not a ballad at all. As for the two variations on Goethe's "Mignon" written by Karmans'kyi and Lepkyi, both Ukrainian poets ignore the fact that Goethe's three-stanza poem by no means represents a naive glorification of a universal state of harmony, and that the meaning of the text becomes increasingly enigmatic and ambiguous from stanza to stanza. (This aesthetic quality of the poem is linked to the fact that the text was originally part of Goethe's novel *Wilhelm Meisters Lehrjahre* [Wilhelm Meister's Apprenticeship] and makes intertextual allusions that readers can hardly understand without some knowledge of the novel. Such knowledge is not common among readers today and presumably was not in Galician schools in the Habsburg Empire.) Both Lepkyi's "Our Mignon" and Karmans'kyi's "Kennst du das Land …" write back solely to the traditional image of harmony and joy in Goethe's poem in an often banal way and ignore the fact that the original poem, at least in the second and third stanzas, also contains dark and ambivalent poetic motifs, such as the question that appears in the second stanza: "Was hat man dir, du armes Kind, getan?" (What have they done to you, you poor child?). Resentment as an aesthetic quality, therefore, in the case of Karmans'kyi and Lepkyi, also takes the form of a deliberate reduction of the complexity and ambiguity of the original lyrical text in order to overcome what is apprehended as its unattainable and painful perfection.

In light of the postcolonial methodological approaches that invoke subalternity (Spivak), rewriting (Ashcroft, Griffiths, Tiffin), and resentment (Hundorova), there may be a certain logical consistency to the fact that polemical rewritings of Goethe's "Erlking" and "Mignon" are found only in the works of Karmans'kyi and Lepkyi. As mentioned earlier, these two poets are widely regarded as second-rate writers, who are not unjustifiably ignored by the Western canon, as is Bohdan-Ihor Antonych,[28] but simply because they have no right to be included in the canon because of their lack of genuine poetic talent. As a consequence, Karmans'kyi's "Ukrainian Ballad" is certainly no hidden poetic masterpiece awaiting its justly deserved fundamental re-evaluation. But perhaps it was this very fundamental distance from the Western canon that made it possible for the Western Ukrainian poets of Moloda Muza with their imitation of European modernism to challenge the canon from the outside; to turn a popular English proverb on its head, if you can't join them, beat them. Ultimately, it was their inability to become a full-fledged and equal part of the European literary canon (in other words, to join it) that inspired the poets of Moloda Muza to challenge this canon radically from the position of genuine outsiders. The way that Karmans'kyi and Lepkyi rearranged the cultural values represented by Goethe's "Erlking" and "Mignon" in their deliberate rewriting of the German classic writer also confirms Marko Pavlyshyn's perceptive statement that translating culture is by no means an innocent process,[29] since the participants in this game shift cultural elements between contexts that, as far as their embodiment of cultural power is concerned, are hardly ever equal. This notion of an essential inequality between the participants of the Western canon (such as Goethe) and the minor Ukrainian modernist poets outside it (such as Karmans'kyi and Lepkyi) is interpreted by Hundorova in her essay on Ukrainian occidentalism as a "reshaping of one's own national identity, which in its turn results in a cleavage and struggle within it in quest of a Western identity."[30] The way in which the two Ukrainian writers considered here reshaped the works of Goethe demonstrates the literary result of such a search for national identity: Karmans'kyi and Lepkyi selected two well-known poems by Goethe, reshaped them by adding their own (specifically Ukrainian) concerns, and by means of this repositioned the poems outside the Western canon. "Ukraïns'ka balada" and "Nash Min'ion" reflect the highly ambivalent, divided position Hundorova describes as a "cleavage": in their new shape Goethe's poems are hardly equipped to open the gates of Bloom's Western canon from outside; rather, they wander in the no man's land between those gates and the fields of Ukrainian literature.

Appendices

Appendix 1

Петро Карманський:
Українська балада (1917)

Johann Wolfgang Goethe:
Erlkönig

Wer reitet so spät durch Nacht und Wind?
                                    Goethe

Тату, тут тісно! Дух мій в задумі,
В грудях жевріє вічна геєна.
Виллю все горе в пламенній думі,
Най заридає Бог і вселенна.
    Господь з тобою! Клята година
    Пісню збудила. Бідна дитина ...

Тату, я хочу жаль перелити
В грудь міліонів скорбних і бідних;
Хочу до серця люд мій тулити,
Кров'ю кормити ближніх і рідних.
    Най їх. На нарід впала глухота,
    В жилах герольдів підлість ілота.

Тату, несила в пропасть дивитись,
Очі заходять кров'ю і тьмою.
Хочу огненним сонцем займитись,
Біль їм спалити смутком, любов'ю.
    Цить, моя перло! Скажуть лукаво:
    «Гордий! І звідки в тебе се право?»

Тату, не можу здавити мови,
Всякі змагання наші даремні.
В грудях бездонна прірва любови,
Рветься зі серця визов: нікчемні!
    Пробі, мій сину! Браття почують,
    Скажуть, ти Юда. І вкамінують.

Даром. Поетів смуток не чує.
Нарід в розпуці гине під плотом,
П'яний меценас в коршмі торгує
Людом, як власним пасеним
    скотом, –

Wer reitet so spät durch Nacht und Wind?
Es ist der Vater mit seinem Kind;
Er hat den Knaben wohl in dem Arm,
Er faßt ihn sicher, er hält ihn warm.

Mein Sohn, was birgst du so bang dein
    Gesicht? –
Siehst, Vater, du den Erlkönig nicht?
Den Erlenkönig mit Kron und Schweif? –
Mein Sohn, es ist ein Nebelstreif.

„Du liebes Kind, komm, geh mit mir!
Gar schöne Spiele spiel ich mit dir,
Manch bunte Blumen sind an dem Strand,
Meine Mutter hat manch gülden
    Gewand."

Mein Vater, mein Vater, und hörest du nicht,
Was Erlenkönig mir leise verspricht? –
Sei ruhig, bleibe ruhig, mein Kind;
In dürren Blättern säuselt der Wind.

„Willst, feiner Knabe, du mit mir gehn?
Meine Töchter sollen dich warten schön;
Meine Töchter führen den nächtlichen
    Reihn,
Und wiegen und tanzen und singen dich ein."

Mein Vater, mein Vater, und siehst du
    nicht dort
Erlkönigs Töchter am düstern Ort? –
Mein Sohn, mein Sohn, ich seh es genau;
Es scheinen die alten Weiden so grau.

Серце поета з болю вмирає
І на могилах з вітром ридає.[31]

„Ich liebe dich, mich reizt deine schöne
    Gestalt;
Und bist du nicht willig, so brauch ich
    Gewalt." –
Mein Vater, mein Vater, jetzt faßt er mich
    an!
Erlkönig hat mir ein Leids getan! –

Dem Vater grauset's, er reitet geschwind,
Er hält in den Armen das ächzende Kind,
Erreicht den Hof mit Müh und Not;
In seinen Armen das Kind war tot.[32]

Appendix 2

Богдан Лепкий:
Наш Міньйон (1920)

Чи знаєш край, де кров, як море,
    ллється,
Куди не глянь – стоїть при гробі гріб.
Дитина, ніби квіт, нім розів'ється,
Змарніє з зимна, голоду, хворіб, –
Чи знаєш край цей?
       О, туди, туди
Хотіла б я з тобою, милий, йти!

Чи знаєш дім? Давно в нім не палиться
Огонь в печі; посеред білих стін
Данво ніхто не плаче й не сміється.
Як гріб, німий стоїть у полі він.
Чи знаєш дім цей?
       О, туди, туди
Хотіла б я з тобою, милий, йти!

Чи знаєш храм? Сторощені ікони,
Осквернений, сплюгавлений престіл.
Мовчить дзвіниця, бо забрали дзвони,
А з бані хрест упав у траву, на діл.
Чи знаєш храм цей?
       О, туди, туди
Хотіла б я з тобою, милий, йти!

Johann Wolfgang Goethe:
Mignon

Kennst du das Land, wo die Zitronen
    blühn,
Im dunklen Laub die Gold-Orangen glühn,
Ein sanfter Wind vom blauen Himmel weht,
Die Myrte still und hoch der Lorbeer steht?
Kennst du es wohl?
       Dahin! Dahin
Möcht ich mit dir, o mein Geliebter, ziehn.

Kennst du das Haus? Auf Säulen ruht sein
    Dach,
Es glänzt der Saal, es schimmert das
    Gemach,
Und Marmorbilder stehn und sehn mich an:
Was hat man dir, du armes Kind, getan?
Kennst du es wohl?
       Dahin! Dahin
Möcht ich mit dir, o mein Beschützer, ziehn.

Kennst du den Berg und seinen Wolkensteg?
Das Maultier sucht im Nebel seinen Weg;
In Höhlen wohnt der Drachen alte Brut;
Es stürzt der Fels und über ihn die Flut –
Kennst du ihn wohl?
       Dahin! Dahin
Geht unser Weg! O Vater, laß uns ziehn![33]

Чи знаєш школу? Діти, пташенята,
Тиняються попід чужі плоти,
Бо школа ворогом тепер зайнята,
А вчительку замучили кати.
Чи знаєш школу?
                    О, туди, туди
Хотіла б я з тобою, милий, йти!

Чи знаєш полк? В рушницях куль
     немає,
Немає хліба, одягу, чобіт.
Та що йому? Він край обороняє
Від ворогів, а ворогом – весь світ.
Чи знаєш полк цей?
                    О, туди, туди
Хотіла б я з тобою, милий, йти![34]

Appendix 3

Петро Карманський:
Kennst du das Land ... (1909)

Чи знаєте ви край, де вічна тьма неволі,
Вергла на скорбний люд полуду сліпоти?
Де з міліонів хат глядить опир недолі
І бє трівожний зойк: Куди і як іти?
Чи знаєте ви сей, забутий сьвітом край?

Чи знаєте ви край, де сьміх ураз з журбою
Виводять на гробах одчаяний танець?
Де свьтло є гріхом, невіжа чеснотою
Й ніхто не зна', хто він й хто його отець?
Чи знаєте ви сей, забутий богом край?

Чи знаєте ви край, де сонічко з промінєм
Крадеть ся лиш хильцем, немов би зі страхом?
Де зависна товпа пророків бє камінєм
І гидит всїх богів діявольським сьміхом?
Чи знаєте ви сей, окутий тьмою край?

Чи знаєте ви край, де все каляють брудом
Ненависти, вражди і насьмішливих слів?
Де всякий блиск краси придержують під спудом,
Де всякий висший клич стрічає встеклий гнїв?
Чи знаєте ви сей пропащий, бідний край?

Чи знаєте ви край, де мов страшна лявіна
Товче в народню грудь несказаний одчай?
Де всякий сьмілий взрив се тільки морська піна?
Чи знаєте ви сей, проклятий богом край?
Ох, се моя, моя спотворена країна![35]

Notes

1 Harold Bloom, *The Western Canon: The Books and School of the Ages* (New York: Riverhead, 1994), 545.

2 Danylo Husar Struk, "The Journal *Svit*: A Barometer of Modernism," *Harvard Ukrainian Studies* 15 (1991): 256.

3 George Grabowicz, "Commentary: Exorcising Ukrainian Modernism," *Harvard Ukrainian Studies* 15 (1991): 277, 281.

4 Aside from the question of the aesthetic value of Moloda Muza poetry, it is also possible to consider the writers of this group as "minor poets." According to T.S. Eliot (*On Poetry and Poets* [New York: Octagon Books, 1975], 40), minor poetry is a kind of poetry that is read only in literary anthologies. This notion is particularly apt in the light of the reintegration of this group of modernist writers into Ukrainian literature during the last decades of the twentieth century, a process that was propelled, to a significant extent, by means of anthologies. See, e.g., Volodymyr Luchuk, ed., *Moloda Muza: Antolohiia zakhidnoukraïns'koï poeziï pochatku XX stolittia* (Kyiv: Molod', 1989) and Mykola Il'nyts'kyi, ed., *Rozsypani perly: Poety "Molodoï Muzy"* (Kyiv: Dnipro, 1991).

5 However, this process of intercultural mediation initiated by Franko did not embrace the aesthetics of modernism as a whole. In his 1896 collection Franko deliberately used several important images and poetic devices characteristic of French symbolism (Charles Baudelaire, Paul Verlaine) and Polish modernism (Kazimierz Przerwa-Tetmajer), treating these primarily as means of introducing innovations into (Western) Ukrainian literature. At the same time, Franko rejected the allegedly modernist view of the poet as standing outside society, which is why he felt obliged to add a foreword to his collection. We cannot find here (or in other modernist manifestos in Slavic literatures ca. 1900) praise for the emancipation

of art from social or national frameworks; instead, there is a warning to readers not to act like the lyrical hero of the collection. Franko thus ultimately accepted modernism only in a limited way and continued to ridicule the image of the modernist poet (as represented by Paul Verlaine) in his works, as, e.g., in the short story "Odi profanum vulgus" (1899). See Tamara Hundorova, *Franko – ne kameniar* (Melbourne: Monash University, 1996), 100–4; Stefan Simonek, *Ivan Franko und die "Moloda Muza": Motive in der westukrainischen Lyrik der Moderne* (Cologne: Böhlau, 1997), 86–152.

6 "One would wish for works containing at least a touch of philosophy and showing at least a fragment of the fascinating blue sky whose unattainable beauty for centuries has beckoned to us." Mykola Voronyi, "Ukraïns'kyi al'manakh," *Literaturno-naukovyi visnyk* IV–XVI (1901): 14. See also Solomiia Pavlychko, *Dyskurs modernizmu v ukraïns'kii literaturi*, 2nd ed. (Kyiv: Lybid', 1999), 105, in which the author critiques the traditional populist language of Voronyi's short poetical modernist manifesto: "The language of Voronyi's manifesto, its rhetoric, is no more than the old well-known and tired language of populism. 'Modernism' at this juncture proved to be an unformed desire – more a dream than a real endeavour."

7 See, e.g., the way Luts'kyi emphasizes the role of Friedrich Nietzsche as an important forerunner of modernism: "Nietzsche, who for a philosopher had been popularized to an extraordinary degree, sent his *Zarathustra* into the broad fold of contemporary world society." Ostap Luts'kyi, "Moloda Muza," *Dilo*, 18 November 1907, 1.

8 "Triste colui che santamente dorme / ne'l vacuo letto e de'suoi canti il fiore / crescer non sa co'l sangue de'l suo core" (Sad is he who sleeps peacefully in the empty bed and does not know how to make the flower of his poetry grow with the blood of his heart). Petro Karmans'kyi, *Plyvem po mori t'my* (Lviv: Naukove Tovarystvo im. Shevchenka, 1909), 2.

9 Meletii Kichura, *Tempi passati* (Kolomyia: Nakladom avtora, 1913). Kichura's collection also includes a cycle of poems with the non-Ukrainian title "Semper idem" (p. 33).

10 It should be mentioned here that Tamara Hundorova emphasizes the eclectic and heterogeneous character of the poetic motifs in early modernist Ukrainian literature, which was by no means a closed and homogeneous literary system, but in its search for a broader European context always remained open to external literary input. See her article, "Artykuliatsiia modernists'koho dyskursu v poeziï 'molodomuzivtsiv,'" *Slavia Orientalis* 43 (1994): 503.

11 This situation, as the editors of this book suggested in a valuable comment, reflects not so much the artistic shortcomings of the members of Moloda Muza as the unfamiliarity of Western canon makers in general, and of Harold Bloom in particular, with cultures that – to them – remain peripheral and invisible.

12 Harold Bloom, *A Map of Misreading* (Oxford: Oxford University Press, 1980).

13 It goes without saying that postcolonial theory as presented in *The Empire Writes Back* must be radically reshaped in order to apply it to Eastern European literatures; in the introduction to their book Ashcroft, Griffiths, and Tiffin define the term "post-colonial literatures" as "writing by those people formerly colonized by Britain"; a page later they list the literatures of African countries, Australia, Bangladesh, Canada, India, and New Zealand. The only European country mentioned in this extensive list of postcolonial literatures is Malta. See Bill Ashcroft, Gareth Griffiths, and Helen Tiffin, *The Empire Writes Back: Theory and Practice in Post-colonial Literatures* (London; New York: Routledge, 1989), 1–2.

14 Gayatri Spivak's well-known concept of a female colonial subject in search of a genuine possibility to speak must also be reshaped in order to use it in a new Eastern European context, since Spivak (at least at the end of the first version of her essay) makes it clear that the subaltern as female can neither speak nor be heard nor read. See Gayatri Chakravorty Spivak, "Can the Subaltern Speak?" in *Colonial Discourse and Post-colonial Theory: A Reader*, ed. Patrick Williams and Laura Chrisman, 2nd ed. (New York: Harvester Wheatsheaf, 1996), 104. The Western Ukrainian poets of Moloda Muza were certainly able to speak in a metaphorical way, albeit only in a seemingly deformed and insignificant manner, which ultimately did not allow their works to become part of the Western literary canon.

15 Hundorova takes the concept of resentment from Nietzsche's influential essay "Genealogie der Moral" and in a modified way shifts it toward contemporary Eastern European literatures and especially to Ukrainian postmodern literature. At the end of her essay she writes: "In this sequence the sense of *ressentiment* (rancour and discontent) is one of the components of the evolution of a postcolonial identity." Tamara Hundorova, "Postkolonial'nyi melankholiinyi *ressentiment*," in *Ievropeis'ka melankholiia: Dyskurs ukraïns'koho oktsydentalizmu*, ed. Tamara Hundorova (Kyiv: Stylos, 2008), 116.

16 In fact, Goethe's ballad had played an important role in the development of the Ukrainian language in Galicia already during the first half of the nineteenth century. Michael Moser mentions a Ukrainian translation of Goethe's poem by Iosyf Levyts'kyi, which was published in Przemyśl in 1838, and quotes the first and last stanzas of Levyts'kyi's translation. See Michael Moser, "Die sprachliche Erneuerung der galizischen Ukrainer zwischen 1772 und 1848/1849 im mitteleuropäischen Kontext," in *Comparative Cultural Studies in Central Europe*, ed. Ivo Pospíšil and Michael Moser (Brno: Masarykova univerzita v Brně, 2004), 90.

17 Petro Karmans'kyi, *Poeziï* (Kyiv: Ukraïns'kyi pys'mennyk, 1992), 156.

18 Hundorova, "Postkolonial'nyi melankholiinyi *ressentiment*," 103.

298   Stefan Simonek

19 Ibid., 104.
20 Ibid., 105.
21 According to Hundorova, in the Ukrainian self-consciousness the notions of becoming European and of becoming modern were conflated. Hundorova, "Postkolonial'nyi melankholiinyi *ressentiment*," 107.
22 Ibid., 111.
23 See Mykola Syvits'kyi, *Bohdan Lepkyi: Zhyttia i tvorchist'* (Kyiv: Dnipro, 1993).
24 Rolf Göbner, "Ukrainische Emigrationsschriftsteller und -wissenschaftler im Deutschland der Weimarer Republik: Eine Bestandsaufnahme," in *Polen unter Nachbarn: Polonistische und komparatistische Beiträge zu Literatur und Sprache*, ed. Hans Rothe and Peter Thiergen (Cologne: Böhlau, 1998), 402–3.
25 See also Stefan Simonek, "Anmerkungen zur Mehrsprachigkeit der ukrainischen Literatur (19. bis 21. Jahrhundert)," in *Die Ukraine: Prozesse der Nationsbildung*, ed. Andreas Kappeler (Cologne: Böhlau, 2011), 116–17.
26 See, e.g., the end of one of Franko's German-language satirical essays, in which he portrays Galicia as a region where the biblical Genesis stopped on the third day: "Ein vierter Tag ist bis jetzt in Galizien noch nicht angebrochen." Ivan Franko, "Die galizische Schöpfungsgeschichte," *Die Zeit*, 13 April 1901, 18.
27 Discussing the intertextual ties between the Goethe and Lepkyi poems, Renate Lachmann states rather peremptorily that any intertextual relationship between the two texts makes a reference outside these texts impossible in principle. Renate Lachmann, *Gedächtnis und Literatur: Intertextualität in der russischen Moderne* (Frankfurt am Main: Suhrkamp, 1990), 85. This opinion may very well be valid for literatures within the Western canon. In the case of Karmans'kyi's and Lepkyi's poems, however, the references to Goethe's "Erlking" and "Mignon" serve as additional legitimation for the specific national and social aims of the two Ukrainian poets. Pure interaction between literary texts (as Lachmann seems to suggest) without any regard to non-aesthetic problems beyond this interaction seems to be possible only for those literatures that are part of the master narrative of European culture, and the example of the two Ukrainian poems mentioned above clearly demonstrates the difference in relation to this point.
28 See also Bloom's emphasis on the function of artistic values for the Western canon in general: "Nothing is so essential to the Western Canon as its principles of selectivity, which are elitist only to the extent that they are founded upon severely artistic criteria." Bloom, *Western Canon*, 22.
29 Marko Pavlyshyn, "Perekladaiuchy kul'turu," *Krytyka* (Kyiv) 11, no.1 (2007): 16–18, here 16.
30 Tamara Hundorova, "Melankholiia po dorozi v Rym, abo dyskurs ukraïns'koho oktsydentalizmu," in *Ievropeis'ka melankholiia: Dyskurs ukraïns'koho oktsydentalizmu*, ed. Tamara Hundorova (Kyiv: Stylos, 2008), 6.

31 Karmans'kyi, *Poeziï*, 158–9.
32 Johann Wolfgang Goethe, *Gedichte* (Stuttgart: Reclam, 1992), 76–7.
33 Ibid., 88.
34 Bohdan Lepkyi, *Poeziï* (Kyiv: Radians'kyi pys'mennyk, 1990), 303–4.
35 Karmans'kyi, *Plyvem po mori t'my*, 11.

Ivan Franko in Vienna: Towards Conflicting Concepts of Modernity

YAROSLAV HRYTSAK

In the spirit of Petrarch's rhetorical question, "Is all of history anything but the praise of Rome?,," one may claim that most contemporary theories of nationalism are nothing but discussions of and with Ernest Gellner.[1] The gist of his theory – which makes it both so attractive and a target of criticism – is his emphasis on the intrinsic relationship between nationalism and modernity. Gellner saw nationalism as a by-product of the greatest event in world history; namely, the transition from agricultural to industrial society, and this particular by-product simultaneously facilitated this transition. According to Benedict Anderson, Gellner's theory presents "industrialism as a piece of machinery that needed the oil of nationalism to function."[2]

Gellner's theory, powerful and suggestive as it is, has several obvious limitations. The first one is referred to as "a curse of rurality," the reason being that virulent nationalism frequently emerges in regions that have had virtually no (or very little) industrialization.[3] The second limitation concerns Gellner's disregard of intellectuals. In his view, nationalist "thinkers did not really make much difference. If one of them had fallen, others would have stepped into his place ... Their precise doctrines are hardly worth analyzing."[4]

Nowhere else are the weaknesses of his theory as evident as in the case of "non-state" or "non-historical" peoples. According to Gellner, in order to make former peasants fit to work in factories and other modern facilities, one has to provide them with an education. And the only agency that is able to do this on a mass scale is the state. How does this proposition relate to peasants of a "non-state" people ("Ruritanians," in Gellner's words) whose language is different from the language of the "state" people (of the "Empire of Megalomania")? To answer this question, Gellner suggests that the "nationalizing" of Ruritanians is the work of Ruritanian intellectuals who in the modern world cannot successfully compete with Megalomanian intellectuals and, as a result, start to build a nation of (and for) their own.[5] However, this explanation contradicts two aspects of Gellner's main argument: his view that intellectuals have no role to play in nation-building, and his dismissal of the idea that intellectuals may be motivated by vested interests.

In his final years Gellner tried to adjust his theory in response to his critics. Among other things, he acknowledged the role of intellectuals – the impact, not so much of what they write or declare, but of how they perceive reality and, consequently, how they build their activity. Gellner believed that their perception could be reduced to two concepts of knowledge: atomistic/individualistic and organic/collective. He sought to map these two concepts both historically and geographically, and what resulted was a broad spectrum of cases contained between two opposite poles. One pole was represented by the case of the English in early modern times: "The English were at their most individualist when they were also the most traditional ... Other nations had to do violence to their traditional nature so as to become modern: the English only needed to be true to themselves."[6] The opposite pole was represented by the nineteenth-century Habsburg Empire: "There are less blessed parts of the world where this is not so, where the confrontation of atomists and organicists does capture much of the emotional charge, the underlying inspiration of real, concrete political life, where this profound philosophical opposition meshes in with the alliances and hatreds of daily and political life. This was nowhere more so perhaps than in a dynastic empire which ended in 1918, was located in the Danube valley, and controlled extensive areas outside it."[7]

This dichotomy was reflected in a difference between the elites, mostly but not exclusively imperial, that confronted the "big problems" of modernity and thus acquired international recognition, and those of "small nations" striving to build their national cultures – in other words, between Megalomanian and Ruritanian intellectuals. No matter how much Gellner revised his views, his position on the latter remained unchanged: "They could do better when in control of their own closed unit than when competing in the cosmopolitan center."[8]

These points of Gellner's theory have a direct relevance to the biography of Ivan Franko. Franko was born and lived in Habsburg Galicia, which was the epitome of a traditional world and strongly resembled Gellner's Ruritania.[9] And insofar as Franko's activities were very focused on building Ukrainian national culture, he was a typical "Ruritanian" intellectual. Taking cues both from Gellner and his critics, I intend to probe deeper in this discussion, using as a test case Franko's encounters with the political and intellectual milieus of imperial Vienna, which stands at the centre of Gellner's Megalomania.

The starting point of my interpretation is the acceptance of Eastern Europe as an entity with particular characteristics. There are various definitions of this region. The one that best fits the issue under discussion here is Eastern Europe as a normal but "second-hand" Europe:[10] normal, in the sense that all modern cultural phenomena and ideologies – the Renaissance and Reformation, the scientific revolution, Marxism, nationalism, liberalism – found fertile ground and large numbers of adherents here; and "second-hand" because most of these cultural phenomena and ideologies were not generated here but were imported from "the West." As a result, more often than not they had very little, if any, affinity with the historical circumstances in which they originally emerged. In other words, Marxism developed here largely without a proletariat, which did not exist in the local, predominantly agrarian, world; nationalism acted in the name of peasants whose identities were fragmented and in flux, and who were difficult to mobilize along national lines; and liberals strove to gain influence where the middle class, civil society, and the public space were weak and underdeveloped.

The dissemination of modern ideologies under such circumstances can be compared to breeding penguins in the Sahara or growing bananas in Siberia. Neither of these is impossible, but both require special technologies and other forms of support. Nation states had sufficient resources at their disposal, and the farther eastward one went the more the state acted as the main agency of modernization.[11] In the case of "non-state" peoples, who typically lacked such prerequisites, this role was played by the modern phenomenon of literature, which served as an ersatz politics.[12]

The latter tendency is richly exemplified in the life and works of Ivan Franko. In his understanding, literature was meant to be "a toiler in the field of progress," and its aim was "to represent the world not as it is but as it is supposed to be." Thus, early on in his literary career, from the mid-1870s to the mid-1880s, he created a whole world of Ukrainian peasants, workers, women, Jews, and representatives of other modern Ukrainian communities. More importantly, this image of modern Ukrainian communities was blended with the leftist ("radical") culture of which Franko was both a central symbol and a leading creator. Both the image and the culture proved to be very attractive to a new, secular generation of local intellectuals who emerged in the 1870s and 1880s. The rise of the intelligentsia, with Franko as a key figure, was a crucial factor in the victory of Ukrainian identity that vied with other – Polish, Russian, Ruthenian – nationalisms striving for control over this territory.[13]

These main points are illustrated in my biography of the young Franko, which covers a thirty-year period from 1856 to 1886.[14] It offers a new perspective that emerges from criticism of theories of nationalism. Students of nationalism are often blamed for presenting a restricted scholarly agenda by failing to locate national identity within a range of possible types of collective identity.[15] Correspondingly, Franko's was not a case of rivalry between one nationalism and another (Ukrainian versus Polish and Russian) or of nationalism(s) versus empires *only*; it was also a story about various modern projects versus traditional society. In the local Eastern European population, this traditional society was embodied in Ruthenia (Rus'), a conservative utopia of East Christian civilization.[16] It is my contention that by the late nineteenth century Ruthenia was nowhere else as radically "unmade" as in Galicia. Given the important geopolitical status of this region,[17] the victory of Ukrainian identity had much wider repercussions: to a large extent, it made an impact on the new political map of Eastern Europe by helping to put Ukraine on it.

As mentioned earlier, Franko was an epitome of this victory. Perhaps nothing illustrates his views better than the caricature that he designed for the Ukrainian satirical journal *Dzerkalo* (The Mirror). The cartoon shows a locomotive running on full steam and emblazoned with the word *Postupus* (a jocular version of the Ukrainian word for progress). Two bulls are trying to stop it by butting their heads against it. One of the bulls resembles Austrian minister Gyula Andrássy, while the other looks like Chancellor Otto von Bismarck of Germany. This struggle between the train and bulls is observed by a couple of peasants, one of whom says to the other: "Ni, Semene, tsii pari ne pereperty tsiu paru" (a pun: "No, Semen, this pair [*para*] cannot triumph over this steam [*para*]").[18]

This caricature reflects all the main elements of Franko's world view: his belief in unlimited progress; his condemnation of "reactionary forces" that seek to impede it; and his reliance on the "people" (*narod*), who are both the main arbiters and principal beneficiaries of the historical process. Franko thought of himself and his colleagues as locomotive drivers called upon to pave the way for progress and to help the people to understand their historical role. Franko's way of thinking was not particularly original; on the contrary, it was rather typical of Eastern European intellectuals. For example, a locomotive was depicted in a logotype that appeared in the Warsaw weekly, *Przegląd Tygodniowy* (Weekly Review), whose founding in 1866 marked the birth of Polish Positivism. The weekly laid special emphasis on the use of steam power and railways as prerequisites for the rebirth of the Polish nation.[19] After returning from his lengthy exile in 1857, Ukraine's national poet, Taras Shevchenko, prayed for the soul of the inventor of the steam engine.[20] Writing about the steamboat and the draught power of steam, he declared that this "young child, growing not by the day but by the hour, will soon devour all knouts, thrones and crowns, with diplomats and landowners for dessert; playfully, like a schoolboy with a lollipop."[21]

Whereas Shevchenko commented only once on this question, Franko developed his views on technological progress into a consistent and well-thought-out program. One biographer of Franko calls the poetization of technology one of the features of his work that sets it apart from the rest of nineteenth-century Ukrainian literature.[22] In Franko's estimation, the "invention of steam-powered machines, telegraphs, phonographs, microphones, electric machines, etc., was perhaps more revolutionary for the world than the bloody French Revolution itself."[23]

Ironically, even though the Ukrainian project in Galicia was a very modern one, it arrived "third-hand," as Westernization via the East, that is, through the Ukrainian lands of the Russian Empire. Franko and his milieu acted under the influence, and sometimes the direct guidance, of Mykhailo Drahomanov and the Kyiv Hromada, whose members, it was said, carried Taras Shevchenko's *Kobzar* in one pocket and Karl Marx's *Das Kapital* in the other.[24] At the beginning of the 1890s Franko moved for a time to Vienna, which was becoming a centre of alternative modernity. Fin-de-siècle Vienna was full of a new and very different type of modernist who, according to Peter Gay, "hated modernity – they hated, in other words, the rule of the machine, the vulgarity of bourgeois society, the pretensions of parvenus, the waning of community."[25] This movement was international, but with a visible German twist. As Gay remarks, "the historian of Modernist culture who does not know German culture does not know Modernist culture."[26]

Franko had many encounters with Viennese fin-de-siècle culture and politics. He arrived in Vienna in October 1892 to do his doctorate under the supervision of Vatroslav Jagić, professor of Slavic studies at the University of Vienna. Franko's correspondence on the eve of his arrival reveals his ambivalence towards the whole idea of doing his doctorate in Vienna. Although he wrote that he "would like to be in Vienna very much," he admitted that he had planned his stay in Vienna not so much of his own free will but, rather, under pressure from his wife and colleagues, who had literally "pushed" him there. Franko did not have a high opinion of either the Habsburg Empire or its capital. His image of Vienna was dominated by his view of the city as unnatural and decadent, in contrast to the natural and "progressive" culture of Galician toilers, above all, the peasants.[27] It would appear that pragmatic considerations prevailed: Franko realized that a doctorate obtained in Vienna could open the way to a professorial appointment at Lviv University, which would provide him and his growing family financial security – a luxury that he would never be able to enjoy as a writer dependent solely on his craft.

At the University of Vienna Franko attended Jagić's seminar and intensively worked on his dissertation. According to Kyrylo Studyns'kyi, who attended the same seminar, Franko became a sensation there. He forced his professor to change his views on the Ukrainian question. Until his encounters with Franko,

Jagić had refused to distinguish Ukrainians from Russians (or, according to the terminology of the time, Little Russians from Great Russians). On many occasions Jagić told his Ruthenian-Ukrainian students from Galicia: "You have to prove your [national] distinctiveness through works of scholarship." So Franko brought him one study after another and succeeded in convincing him that Ukrainians had a right to an independent life among the Slavic nations.[28]

Franko successfully defended his dissertation in the summer of 1893. Two years later he applied for the position of professor at Lviv University, but he was rejected because of his reputation as a socialist and atheist. Jagić was among those who had recommended and supported Franko's candidacy, and he regretted that Franko did not obtain a position despite his outstanding academic record.[29] Even though Jagić did not share Franko's political ideas, he considered him "the wisest of all living Little Russians."[30] Franko himself was not in despair over this failure. His academic title allowed him to run as a candidate in elections to the Galician and Austrian parliaments, and he viewed his doctorate as a means of boosting his political career.[31] He ran for office twice, in 1896 and 1897, but failed to gain a seat. Franko experienced first-hand what was meant by "Galician elections" in the Habsburg Empire: electoral fraud and legal abuses.

However, some of Franko's other Vienna-related plans proved very successful. On 11 October 1892, shortly after arriving in Vienna, he wrote to his wife: "I am enrolling at the university not only [to obtain] the title of doctor but also for an opportunity to meet learned people; their acquaintance could be more useful to me than the doctoral title itself."[32] Franko's impressive list of Vienna acquaintances included Victor Adler, leader of the Austrian social democrats; Hermann Bahr, a prominent ideologue of Viennese modernism; Tomáš Masaryk, the future president of Czechoslovakia; and, purportedly, Theodor Herzl,[33] as well as many other important representatives of fin-de-siècle Vienna.

By the time Franko came to Vienna, he was an accomplished and successful writer widely published in four languages (Ukrainian, Polish, German, and Russian) in Lviv, Kyiv, St Petersburg, and Warsaw. He was active in political affairs and was the founding leader of the first Ukrainian political party, the Ruthenian-Ukrainian Radical Party, whose platform combined the defence of local peasants' interests with leftist ideology. Even though Franko's political activities led to persecution and arrests, they also served to make him a household name both in and outside of Galicia. In any case, upon arriving in Vienna, Franko saw that his reputation had preceded him; it is difficult to imagine that he would have gone unnoticed.

Nevertheless, to a large extent Franko owed his personal success in Vienna to specific political circumstances. He had tried, unsuccessfully, to establish contacts with various Viennese periodicals in the 1880s.[34] But by the early 1890s the situation had changed. During that decade, Galicia became very topical in Viennese public life. This topicality was the result, above all, of mass migration of Galician Jews to the capital of the Habsburg Empire. Galician Jews, known as "Galizianer," were very visible in Vienna, with their long black garments, fox fur hats, sidelocks, and their habit of gathering in large groups. Their appearance gave rise to anti-Semitic stereotypes and sentiments. Franko's publications on the emigration of Galician Jews sparked public interest: his lengthy article on this topic, which originally appeared in the social-democratic newspaper *Arbeiterzeitung*, was later republished – albeit in a highly distorted form and with an accompanying commentary – by the anti-Semitic *Volkszeitung*.[35]

The second, and more important, reason why Galician issues became so topical in Vienna was the appointment of Kasimir Badeni, former viceroy of Galicia, to the post of prime minister of the Austro-Hungarian Empire. In order to secure a majority in parliament, Badeni struck an alliance with Polish and Czech deputies. The price of this alliance was the introduction of Czech as the state language in the Czech lands. In his politics Badeni championed the cultural and political rights of Slavs against German aggression, a stance that provoked outrage among German-speaking officials in Bohemia and Moravia and German nationalists throughout the empire. Badeni's conservative politics also came under harsh criticism from Austrian social democrats. According to Marko Cheremshyna, then a student at Vienna University, "all of Vienna boiled with rage and threw thunderbolts at Badeni, the Poles, and the Czechs. Wolf and Schönerer in their pan-German circles, Adler, Pernerstorfer and Schuhmeier in their working-class ones, and even Lueger in his Christian Socialist circles kept organizing one meeting after another. All of them criticized the Galician 'noble economy,' exposed the horrendous results of the nobility's domination over our people, and called for the resignation of the government and the brutal Badeni from his position of prime minister."[36] Franko had firsthand experience of Badeni's policies in Galicia: it was Badeni who was personally responsible for ensuring that Franko failed to obtain a position at Lviv University and for the numerous abuses that Franko suffered as a candidate during the 1897 parliamentary elections.

In Vienna Franko enjoyed a reputation as "the best expert on Galician conditions"[37] and as "a master storyteller."[38] Among the Viennese periodicals that invited Franko to work with them, the most influential was the weekly *Die Zeit*, which not only wielded significant influence on public opinion in both Vienna and the Habsburg monarchy at large but also grasped the importance of Galician issues. Isidor Singer, one of the weekly's two editors, complained

to Franko in a letter that the Viennese press did not pay any heed to Galicia
whatsoever. In his opinion, Viennese periodicals, which were "writing all the
time about cruelties against the Armenians or Chinese, were yet to reveal those
horrors that are going on in Galicia." This situation was all the more deplorable
because "the center of our domestic politics now lies in Galicia, and this is
exactly where I would like to shift our readers' interests."[39]

Die Zeit invited Franko to write regular contributions on Galician issues. His
cooperation with this influential weekly was a crucial element of his encounter with Viennese public life. It made some impact on Vienna politics, but
not in the sense that Franko's articles in this periodical led to Badeni's resignation, as one historian has written.[40] In fact, Franko's impact was not that
profound, and Badeni resigned because of internal conflicts within Austrian
political circles.[41] But Franko's publications did have a certain impact. Ievhen
Olesnyts'kyi wrote in his memoirs that Franko's article on the Galician elections made a bigger impression in Vienna than all the speeches and statements
of Ruthenian-Ukrainian deputies in the parliament.[42]

Among Franko's numerous publications that appeared in *Die Zeit*, at least
three deserve special mention. Two of them, the short stories "Svyns'ka kon-
stytutsiia" (The Swinish Constitution) and "Istoriia odnoï konfistkaty" (The
Story of a Certain Confiscation), both republished in several European and
North American journals, were devoted to the same topic, namely, the abuses
of constitutional rights by the Habsburg authorities. His most important publication, the one that put Franko in the centre of an international scandal, was
his article "Ein Dichter des Verrates" (A Poet of Treason, 1897). In this article
Franko sought to expose the double standards of the members of the Polish
ruling elite who complained against German domination in the Habsburg monarchy, yet had no qualms about oppressing Ruthenians in Galicia. Franko saw
the sources of this hypocrisy in the spiritual impact of Adam Mickiewicz, the
Polish poet and national prophet, on Polish society. In Franko's interpretation,
Mickiewicz's poems provided justification for any measures that served Polish
national interests. The article was written in the context of events that were
then taking place in Vienna, such as the most recent attack on Badeni and
his "Polish policies." Unfortunately, the impact of Franko's article went far
beyond his intentions. It appeared at the very moment when the Polish national
elite in the Russian Empire was seeking permission to build a monument to
Mickiewicz in Warsaw. Franko's article, translated and published in Polish
and Russian, was considered a political denunciation to the Russian imperial
authorities. That article nearly cost Franko his life: a Polish nationalist fired a
revolver at Franko as he and his children were leaving their house for a walk;
luckily, the assailant missed. Franko escaped unharmed, but the article cost

him his position. He was fired from the Lviv-based Polish liberal newspaper *Kurjer Lwowski*, which provided his main source of income and where he had worked for ten years (1887–97). The attempt on Franko's life was one of the first cases of political terrorism in Galicia. It symbolized the shift in local public life to the kind of bellicose politics that was unfolding in Vienna. In any event, the consequences of this incident pursued Franko to Vienna.

Another of Franko's triumphs in the Habsburg capital was a speech that he delivered at a public meeting organized by Viennese social democrats in December 1896. The gathering focused on Galicia, and Franko was the keynote speaker. Judging from the generous praise and references to it in the press, his speech was a resounding success. The next day Franko dined with Singer and Adler, the latter a close friend of Franko's. After returning to Lviv, Franko praised Adler's intellect and erudition, and expressed his satisfaction at having gained access to the leading journals and newspapers of Vienna.[43]

Franko profited greatly from his Viennese connections in the worlds of academia and politics. However, his success in belles-lettres, the main field of his ambitions, was much more modest. The road to literary success in Vienna was predicated on success on the stage. As Stefan Zweig wrote in his memoirs, it was every writer's dream to see his play staged in a Viennese theatre. This was the lifelong ambition of Theodor Herzl, for one, when he came to Vienna. Before Franko arrived in Vienna, he had had some success in the world of theatre. His play *Ukradene shchastia* (Stolen Happiness) was staged in Lviv, where it enjoyed an enthusiastic response from Polish and Ukrainian critics alike. During his stay in Vienna he completed the novel *Dlia domashn'oho vohnyshcha* (For the Home Hearth), which recounts the story of an officer's wife who, unbeknownst to her husband, runs a brothel. Choosing a topic based on real events was practically a guarantee of literary success. Franko then tried to turn his novel into a play and submit it to the Volkstheater for consideration. Emma Adler, Victor Adler's wife, urged him to abandon this idea because, as she believed, mounting a production at the Volkstheater was impossible without some sort of patronage. She suggested he try his luck in some of Vienna's less prestigious theatres.[44] We do not know whether Franko followed her advice. What we do know for certain is that none of Franko's works were ever staged in Vienna.

After his failure with *For the Home Hearth*, Franko tried to publish another novel, *Boa Constrictor*, in *Die Zeit*. Judging by the number of translations of this novel, *Boa Constrictor* was the work that brought Franko the widest international recognition. The Polish translator Feliks Daszyński wrote to Franko, "after reading your *Boa* [*Constrictor*], I shivered as though from fever. Show me a man who loves the people more than you! I will say that you are the only one."[45] In order for the journal to publish his novel, Franko needed to get a favourable review from Hermann Bahr, who was responsible for the literature section of the journal. According to Singer, Bahr liked the novel. In the end, however, he refused to publish it under the pretext that it was too long; the Viennese public had little interest in lengthy texts.[46]

Two years later, in the midst of the scandal surrounding "A Poet of Treason," Franko quarreled with Bahr over aesthetic principles. On 10 June 1897 Bahr wrote to Franko about the latter's judgment of Mickiewicz: "I think it is nonsense to draw conclusions about an author's intentions from any aesthetic work. Would I be a 'poet of lesbian love' if I wrote about lesbian relations once or a hundred times? You must understand that what may seem aesthetically satisfying to one person might be morally repugnant to another. 'Treason' is a problem of great aesthetic attractiveness. One could dedicate one's entire life to it without becoming a traitor as a result."[47]

Bahr's disagreement with Franko reflected a profound clash of principles. It marked a watershed between political engagement and political disengagement in literature. The latter paradigm became dominant in fin-de-siècle Vienna. In 1893 Emma Adler asked Franko to write a short novel for an anthology of works that she was compiling for "proletarian children." She emphasized the following: "No tendency should be evident: when it comes to a work of literature, one can do without it altogether."[48] Views similar to those expressed by Bahr and Emma Adler were shared in the Ruthenian-Ukrainian Radical Party by the "young radicals," a group of students in Vienna who were in opposition to "older radicals" like Franko. They considered the views of the older radicals to be naive and even ridiculous.[49] Among other things, they suggested that Franko publish fewer ethnographic materials in the journal that he was editing and instead issue more works by Ibsen, Maeterlinck, and "other modernists."[50]

Franko did not heed this advice. On the contrary, after returning from Vienna he spent some time engaging in acrimonious discussions with younger Ruthenian-Ukrainian poets who tried to write without any political tendency and to create art for art's sake. Franko used – and sometimes abused – his new position as editor (1898–1904) of the established and prestigious journal *Literaturno-naukovyi vistnyk* (Literary and Scholarly Herald) in order to marginalize this new generation. To that effect, he published an interview with Lev Tolstoi in which the Russian novelist claimed not to understand why young artists might wish to emulate Baudelaire, Wagner, or Ibsen: "These were parasites that lived at the expense of people who resolutely did not need them."[51]

Nevertheless, Franko himself could not resist the charms of modernism. The impact of the modernist aesthetic is especially evident in his collection of poetry *Ziviale lystia* (Withered Leaves, 1896). This collection is regarded by many as Franko's finest creation. Vasyl' Shchurat, a younger poet who boarded with Franko in Vienna, wrote a review of this collection in which he called Franko a "Ukrainian decadent." What Shchurat had meant as a compliment, Franko took as a personal offence and penned the following poetic response:

Який я декадент? Я син народа,
Що вгору йде, хоч був запертий в льох.
Мій поклик: праця, щастя і свобода,
Я є мужик, пролог, не епілог.[52]

(What kind of decadent am I? I am a son of the people
That, once locked inside a vault, now strives upward.
My motto is work, happiness, and freedom,
 I am a peasant – the prologue, not the epilogue.)

Ukrainian Franko specialists, both Soviet and non-Soviet, have frequently quoted this stanza with approbation. Those four lines reveal clearly and unequivocally Franko's understanding of modernity as a movement "forward and upward," that is, as human progress that leads to national and social emancipation. Still, in this controversy between Franko and Shchurat it seems that the latter, not the former, was right. In his book about Franko Stefan Simonek persuasively demonstrates that Franko was torn between his position as a public leader and his literary talent. Citing numerous examples, Simonek reveals a close similarity between Franko's poetic images and topics and the writings of leading European modernists, including Paul Verlaine, Valerii Briusov, Stéphane Mallarmé, Oscar Wilde, and others. Simonek treats Franko as a "bashful modernist" and calls for a new reading of Franko – not as a herald of socialist realism but as a critical and interesting writer from the periphery of the Habsburg monarchy.[53]

The Ukrainian literary scholar Ihor Mykhailyn suggests another provocative metaphor. Comparing the aesthetic principles espoused by Franko and Freud, he calls Franko a man of the nineteenth century and Freud a man of the twentieth.[54] However, this metaphor captures only part of Franko's complex and complicated personality, as some undeniable features of his works and activities place him firmly in the twentieth-century context, even though Franko was loath to acknowledge them openly. Apart from his poetry, his embrace of the twentieth century is evident in the evolution of his political views, which is most pronounced in two crucial developments. The first is the change in Franko's perception of the Ukrainian nation. Until the late 1890s Franko shared the views of Ukrainian populists, who equated the Ukrainian nation exclusively with the peasantry. In 1899 Franko left the Ruthenian-Ukrainian Radical Party and joined the centrist Ukrainian National-Democratic Party, justifying his change of party affiliation by his understanding of the building blocks of the Ukrainian nation: apart from peasants, he now conceded, the nation also comprised teachers, priests, and even gendarmes.[55]

The other crucial shift occurred in his attitude to Ukraine's political independence. The idea of independence for Ukraine was introduced by the "young radicals" of Vienna, and initially Franko resolutely resisted and criticized it. By the mid-1890s, however, his position had changed dramatically, and Franko became a vehement supporter of independence. What matters in the context of the present discussion is not his shift per se but the arguments he used to justify it. According to his understanding, the level of social progress in Ukraine did not open much space for Ukrainian political independence. But these circumstances did not really matter all that much, Franko concluded. It was enough that Ukrainians should desire political independence, and once this became an object of their political will, nothing and nobody could stop them. Strong will alone was a sufficient prerequisite for realizing this political ideal. Strong will would lead the Ukrainian people "out of the realms of the possible" and "ignite the hearts of mass circles of people, lead them to the highest sacrifices, increasing their powers in the most horrendous torments and sufferings."[56]

Franko's argumentation here is of a purely voluntaristic character and has very little in common with his previous rational and positivist way of thinking. Another of his works serves as an illustration of his radical ideological evolution. In an essay entitled "At the Turn of the Century" Franko presents an imaginary discussion among three young people on New Year's Eve 1901. Sitting at a festive table, they discuss the legacy of the nineteenth century and what the twentieth century will bring. The discussion focuses on a single issue: social progress and its cost. One of the discussants states the following:

And in the service of the great cause that is the rebirth and consolidation of a nation, we should not fear taking into account a modicum of national exclusivity, one-sidedness, or chauvinism, if you will. Fear not; when national needs are assuaged, and the national hunger sated, the nation will reject the chauvinistic meal, wisdom will triumph over passion, inclusive human and common traits over what divides and differentiates. Therefore, my dears, just as I am not frightened by the momentary blossoming of militarism in the late nineteenth century, I am not inclined to wring my hands over the growth of various national separatisms, tribal and racial chauvinisms. All of these are fruits of the organic growth of modern communities – even *Flegeljahre* of sorts, I'll allow – but nevertheless, they are signs of growth, certainly not decline, or decadence.[57]

In this essay Franko does not reveal his own position. Nevertheless, these words are true to the spirit of his other writings of the time, and they are radically opposed to the main principle that had been proclaimed by Drahomanov and had served as a moral imperative for Franko and his generation, namely, "Clean work requires clean hands." To a certain extent, with this new stance Franko sounded like a herald of the integral Ukrainian nationalism of the 1920s, 1930s, and 1940s. The chief ideologue of that nationalism, Dmytro Dontsov, derived his inspiration from irrational and voluntaristic theories and castigated Drahomanov and his followers, including Franko, for their detrimental influence on Ukrainian political thought. Still, Dontsov and his adherents were not initially aware of Franko's later writings. Upon "discovering" them in the 1930s, they instantly turned Franko into their ideological precursor. Most interestingly, as proof they quoted the above-cited fragment from "At the Turn of the Century." [58]

What does this have to do with the Vienna episodes in Franko's life? The answer to this question may be found in Carl Schorske's famous book on fin-de-siècle Vienna, in which the author shows that after the demise of the Viennese liberal culture of the nineteenth century new trends emerged that were both more aggressive and more creative: pan-German nationalism, Christian socialism, and Zionism. Paradoxically, they provided both Hitler and his future victims with ready-made political models.[59] Borrowing this point, one may risk the generalization that Franko's evolution in his later years opened the way to two extremist and mutually exclusive trends, Ukrainian integral nationalism and Ukrainian communism. Ukrainian leftists and rightists have developed a quaint political tradition of fist fights at Franko's grave and at monuments erected to him. The first such incident occurred in 1926, ten years after his death, and the most recent several years ago near the Franko monument in Lviv, opposite the university that now bears his name. The two opposing sides were harking back to different aspects of Franko's life and works and to his different understandings of modernity before and after his stay in Vienna.

One should not overestimate the role that Franko's Viennese period played in his evolution. After all, Vienna was only one of many places in his intellectual geography. Still, no biography of Franko can or should be written without taking into account his experience in Vienna. Franko's stay in the Austrian capital provoked a powerful psychological crisis that lasted through the final two decades of his life – a crisis that had a strong impact on his works and, indirectly, on the radical transformation of Ukrainian intellectual and political life by the turn of the twentieth century. As Franko's case amply demonstrates, instead of talking about the confrontation of these two rival concepts of modernity, we should be discussing their definite, albeit highly ambivalent, coexistence. This ambivalence marked Ukraine throughout the twentieth century and it persists to this day.[60]

Notes

1 For Gellner's views on nationalism, see Ernest Gellner, *Nations and Nationalism* (Ithaca, NY: Cornell University Press, 1983); Gellner, *Encounters with Nationalism* (Oxford: Blackwell, 1994). On Gellner, see John A. Hall, ed., *The State of the Nation: Ernest Gellner and the Theory of Nationalism* (Cambridge: Cambridge University Press, 1998).
2 Interview with Benedict Anderson, "We Study Empires as We Do Dinosaurs: Nations, Nationalism, and Empire in a Critical Perspective," *Ab Imperio* 3 (2003): 64–5.
3 Tom Nairn, "The Curse of Rurality: Limits of Modernization Theory," in *The State of the Nation: Ernest Gellner and the Theory of Nationalism*, ed. John A. Hall, (Cambridge: Cambridge University Press, 1998), 107–34.
4 Gellner, *Nations and Nationalism,* 124.
5 Ibid., 58–62.
6 Ernest Gellner, *Language and Solitude: Wittgenstein, Malinowski and the Habsburg Dilemma* (Cambridge: Cambridge University Press, 1998), 9.
7 Ibid., 10.
8 Ibid., 12.
9 When formulating the image of Ruritania, Gellner most probably had in mind the Ruthenian population of Slovakia and neighboring Galicia. See Chris Hann, "Nationalism and Civil Society in Central Europe: From Ruritania to the Carpathian Euroregion," *The State of the Nation,* 244.
10 I have borrowed this definition from Gale Stokes, *Three Eras of Political Change in Eastern Europe* (New York, Oxford: Oxford University Press, 1997). See esp. his essay, "Eastern Europe's Defining Fault Lines," in *Three Eras of Political Change,* 7–22.
11 Alexander Gerschenkron, *Economic Backwardness in Historical Perspective: A Book of Essays* (Cambridge, MA: Belknap Press, 1962), 5–30.
12 See George G. Grabowicz, "Province to Nation: Nineteenth-Century Ukrainian Literature as a Paradigm of the National Revival," *Canadian Review of Studies in Nationalism* 16, no. 1–2 (1989): 117–32.
13 See John-Paul Himka, "The Construction of Nationality in Galician Rus': Icarian Flights in Almost All Directions," in *Intellectuals and Articulation of the Nation*, ed. Ronald G. Suny and Michael D. Kennedy (Ann Arbor, MI: University of Michigan Press, 1999), 109–64. See also Yaroslav Hrytsak, "Icarian Flights in Almost All Directions Reconsidered," *Journal of Ukrainian Studies* 35–36 (2010–1): 81–90.

314   Yaroslav Hrytsak

14 Iaroslav Hrytsak, *Prorok u svoïi vitchyzni: Ivan Franko i ioho spil'nota* (Kyiv: Krytyka, 2004). The English translation will be published by the Canadian Institute of Ukrainian Studies.

15 See Shmuel N. Eisenstadt and Wolfgang Schluchter, "Introduction: Paths to Early Modernities – A Comparative View," *Daedalus* 127, no. 3 (1998): 1–18, here 14.

16 This interpretation is put forward by Anna Veronika Wendland, *Die Russophilen in Galizien: Ukrainische Konservative zwischen Österreich und Rußland 1848–1915* (Vienna: Verlag der Österreichischen Akademie der Wissenschaften, 2001).

17 See Klaus Bachmann, *Ein Herd der Feindschaft gegen Rußland: Galizien als Krisenherd in den Beziehungen der Donaumonarchie mit Rußland (1907–1914)* (Vienna and Munich: Oldenbourg Verlag, 2001).

18 Ivan Franko, *Zibrannia tvoriv u piatdesiaty tomakh* (Kyiv: Naukova dumka, 1976–86), 41: 445.

19 Stanislaus A. Blejwas, *Realism in Polish Politics: Warsaw Positivism and National Survival in Nineteenth Century Poland* (New Haven, CT: Yale Concilium on International and Area Studies; Columbus, Ohio: Distributed by Slavica Publishers, 1984), 78.

20 Taras Shevchenko, *Povne zibrannia tvoriv u dvanadtsiaty tomakh*, vol. 5 (Kyiv: Naukova dumka, 2003), 12, 320.

21 Shevchenko, *Povne zibrannia tvoriv*, 5: 86–7.

22 Oleksii Dei, *Ivan Franko i narodna tvorchist'* (Kyiv: Derzhavne vydavnytstvo khudozhn'oï literatury, 1955), 91.

23 Franko, *Zibrannia tvoriv*, 48:111.

24 Roman Serbyn and Tetiana Sliudykova, comp., *Serhii Podolyns'kyi: Lysty ta dokumenty* (Kyiv: Tsentral'nyi derzhavnyi istorychnyi arkhiv Ukraïny, 2002), 345.

25 Peter Gay, *Freud, Jews, and Other Germans: Masters and Victims in Modernist Culture* (New York: Oxford University Press, 1978), 22.

26 Ibid., 27.

27 Leonid Rudnytzky, "The Image of Austria in the Works of Ivan Franko," in *Nationbuilding and the Politics of Nationalism: Essays on Austrian Galicia*, ed. Andrei S. Markovits and Frank E. Sysyn (Cambridge, MA: Harvard Ukrainian Research Institute, 1982), 239–54; Stefan Simonek, *Ivan Franko und die "Moloda Muza": Motive in der westukrainischen Lyrik der Moderne* (Köln: Böhlau, 1997).

28 Studyns'kyi recounted this story in his unpublished memoirs held in the Central State Historical Archive in Lviv (Tsentral'nyi Derzhavnyi Istorychnyi Arkhiv u L'vovi), f. 362, op. 1, od. zb. 11 (Studyns'kyi's account, pp. 12–13).

29 Cited in Marian Jakobiec, "Iwan Franko i Vatroslav Jagić," *Slavia Orientalis* 8, no. 2–3 (1959): 72.

30 *Dokumenty k istorii slavianovedeniia v Rossii: 1855–1912* (Moscow and Leningrad: Izdatel'stvo Akademii Nauk SSSR, 1948), 328.

31 Franko, *Zibrannia tvoriv*, 49: 338.

32 Ibid., 49: 354.

33 In his memoirs Vasyl Shchurat claimed that Herzl met Franko and the two had a long discussion that revealed the similarity of their views. There are, however, serious doubts as to whether this meeting took place. See, e.g., Israel Kleiner, *From Nationalism to Universalism: Vladimir (Ze'ev) Jabotinsky and the Ukrainian Question* (Edmonton: Canadian Institute of Ukrainian Studies Press, 2000), 165; Roman Mnich, "Ivan Franko und Theodor Herzl: Über eine nicht stattgefundene Begegnung in Wien im Winter 1893," *Wiener Slavistisches Jahrbuch* 55 (2009): 235–41.

34 Ivan Franko, *Beiträge zur Geschichte und Kultur der Ukraine: Ausgewählte deutsche Schriften des revolutionären Demokraten 1882–1915*, ed. E. Winter and P. Kirchner (Berlin: Akademie-Verlag, 1963), 449.

35 Franko, *Zibrannia tvoriv*, 49: 363.

36 Marko Cheremshyna, "Frahment moïkh spomyniv pro Ivana Franka," in *Spohady pro Ivana Franka*, ed. Mykhailo Hnatiuk (Lviv: Kameniar, 1998), 282.

37 Franko, *Beiträge*, 458.

38 Ibid., 460.

39 Ibid., 455–6.

40 Adam Hnidj, "Ivan Franko: A Poet of Betrayal. Causes and Consequences," *The Ukrainian Quarterly* 48, no. 1 (1992): 43.

41 For a detailed discussion, see Waldemar Lazuga, *"Rządy polskie" w Austrii: Gabinet Kazimierza hr. Badeniego 1895–1897* (Poznań: Uniwersytet im. Adama Mickiewicza, 1991).

42 Ievhen Olesnyts'kyi, *Storinky z moho zhyttia*, vol. 2, *1890–1897* (Lviv: Vydavnycha spilka "Dilo," 1935), 120.

43 Cheremshyna, "Frahment," 283.

44 Franko, *Beiträge*, 452–3.

45 Quoted in Hryhorii Verves, *Ivan Franko i pytannia ukraïns'ko-pol's'kykh literaturno-hromads'kykh vzaiemyn 70–90-kh rokiv XIX st.* (Kyiv: Vydavnytstvo Akademiï nauk URSR, 1957), 127.

46 Franko, *Beiträge,* 456.

47 Ibid., 470.

48 Ibid., 451–2.

49 See Iaroslav Hrytsak, "Molodi radykaly u suspil'no-politychnomu zhytti Halychyny," *Zapysky NTSh* 222 (1991): 71–100.

50 Franko, *Zibrannia tvoriv*, 50: 44.

51 M. M., "Lev Tolstoi pro dekandentyzm," *Literaturno-naukovyi vistnyk* 10, no. 4 (1900): 129–30.

52 Franko, *Zibrannia tvoriv,* 2:186.

53 Simonek, *Ivan Franko*, 76.

54 Ihor Mykhailyn, "Ivan Franko i Zygmund Froid: pytannia estetyky," in *Ivan Franko – pys'mennyk, myslytel', hromadianyn: Materialy Mizhnarodnoï naukovoï konferentsiï (Lviv, 25–27 veresnia 1996)*, ed. Larysa Bondar et al. (Lviv: Svit, 1998), 311–12.

55 Franko, *Zibrannia tvoriv*, 50: 148.

56 Ibid., 45: 284.

57 Ibid., 45: 291.

58 Mykhailo Mukhyn, "I. Franko iak krytyk politychnykh pohliadiv M. Drahomanova," in *Zbirnyk Ukraïns'koho Naukovoho Instytutu v Amerytsi*, ed. Oleh Kandyba (Saint Paul, MN: Ukrainian Scientific Institute in America, 1939), 76–106.

59 Carl E. Schorske, *Fin-de-siècle Vienna: Politics and Culture* (New York: Vintage Books, 1981), 119.

60 See Iaroslav Hrytsak, "Istoriia dvokh mist: L'viv i Donets'k u porivnial'nii perspektyvi," in *L'viv-Donets'k: Sotsial'ni identychnosti v suchasnii Ukraïni*, ed. Iaroslav Hrytsak, Andrii Portnov, and Viktor Susak (Kyiv: Krytyka, 2008), 27–60.

PART THREE

Ukrainian Visions of Europe from Imperial to Post-Soviet Times

Institutionalizing "Europe": Imperial High Culture and the Ukrainian Intelligentsia from Gogol' to Khvyl'ovyi

OLEH S. ILNYTZKYJ

This paper is a historical overview – necessarily schematic owing to space limitations – of the discursive uses of "Europe" by the Ukrainian intelligentsia from the early nineteenth century to the modernist period, here represented by the journal *Ukraïns'ka khata* (Ukrainian House, 1909–14). The premise is that the concept of "Europe" helped Ukrainian intellectuals in the Russian Empire implement an institutional and structural transformation of their own cultural production and consumption, progressively turning these from auxiliary elements in an imperial or "all-Russian" (i.e., all-East Slavic) system into an autonomous "national" institution. This development began to undermine the broad social consensus among the multi-ethnic imperial intelligentsia that had favoured an "all-Russian" identity, putting a strain on the principle of unified cultural institutions and ultimately becoming a factor in the empire's demise and the rise of a modern Ukraine. Towards the end of the nineteenth century an emergent Ukrainian institution was already competing with the very imperial ("Russian") culture to which Ukrainian intellectuals had earlier keenly contributed.

"Europe" versus Empire

At the beginning of the nineteenth century the Ukrainian cultural elites, as members of the imperial intelligentsia, betrayed the first signs of trying to formulate an alternative "national" culture by challenging a nascent cultural norm in the empire, that is, the idea of an "all-Russian" "nation" that was being fostered by the state (e.g., by means of the policy of "Official Nationality") and growing increasingly popular among important segments of the educated class. Instead of rallying around a unified East Slavic "Russian" "nation," some Ukrainians showed a marked tendency to privilege Ukraine (*Malorossiia*) in their historical, ethnographic, and, later, literary and linguistic pursuits, even as they remained nearly perfect political subjects of the tsar.[1] This fledgling effort to disavow a single shared cultural identity for Ukrainians and Great Russians would soon be fortified by imagining Ukraine as part of "Europe," that is, a society of "nations" possessing unique cultures rather than as a constituent of a single East Slavic nation within the empire. Although quite low-key at first, "Europe" turned out to be a productive model for Ukrainians in that it helped disrupt trends gaining momentum among their Great Russian colleagues, who, through the mediation of the empire, were formulating their own modern nationality on the proposition of East Slavic convergence and homogeneity; in other words, the idea that Great Russians and Little Russians (Ukrainians) were a single entity, an all-Rus' ("Russian") people. For those who accepted this latter paradigm, cultural production by Ukrainians was logically a com-plementary element in a grand "Russian culture," not a separate category des-tined to develop in its own right. This "all-Russian" paradigm struggled to present and maintain the multi-ethnic imperial sphere as coherently "national" and "Russian." The Ukrainian development, on the other hand, highlighted the East Slavic part of the empire as a culturally and historically diverse space with a diverging rather than converging ethnic/national dynamic. Thus, ironi-cally, at the beginning of the nineteenth century the relatively well-integrated multi-ethnic imperial intellectual class (*obshchestvo*), its members united by the common cultural life they led in the capitals, was also unwittingly laying the foundations for two different East Slavic nations.

The earliest Ukrainian defiance of the empire's homogenizing tendencies manifested itself in attempts to differentiate Ukrainian culture and history from other East Slavic phenomena, specifically the Great Russian. This tendency would be most clearly expressed later by Mykola Kostomarov in his article "Two Rus' Nationalities" (1861), which insisted on the separateness of Rus-sians and Ukrainians.[2] However, this effort at differentiation, limited as it was to making distinctions between East Slavs, still left itself open to being treated by imperial society as nothing more than an affirmation of "tribal" manifesta-tions within "all-Russian" culture. From the Great Russian point of view, there was little linguistic impediment to assimilating Ukrainian-produced cultural artefacts as simply "Russian," since most were printed in the capitals and were in Russian, the language of intellectual exchange. The few Ukrainian-language publications were easily explained as reflecting one dialectal manifestation of a single "Russian" language.

The apparent availability of Ukrainian cultural production for "all-Russian" cultural purposes became more problematic, however, when "Europe" came to play an increasingly prominent role in Ukrainian differentiation practices.

"Europe" made it possible to envisage Ukrainian culture not only as something unto itself but also as a category structurally comparable to other "European" cultures. In other words, rather than being aligned with Great Russia in the East Slavic world, Ukraine was aligned with Europe. This mode of thinking initiated a process that, in effect, helped to redefine Ukrainian cultural production: it was not "all-Russian" but "European." Rather than regarding Ukrainian culture as a donor culture supporting shared imperial cultural institutions, for example, "(Russian) literature" and "(Russian) language," it was possible to conceive of completely separate and parallel Ukrainian institutions. Ukraine's "otherness" would thus gradually come to be articulated not just as an intramural, East Slavic "difference" from Great Russia but also as a "European" quality that made Ukraine a candidate for "European" nationhood.

Great Russian reaction to this slow "Europeanization," underwritten by some of the most productive and outstanding Ukrainians within the imperial intelligentsia, was initially met with ironic condescension. Increasingly, however, this attitude turned into anxiety as it became clearer that, should Ukrainian cultural activity become institutionalized independently from the Great Russian, the single, unified "Russian" (that is, "all-Russian") identity and culture would be jeopardized. By 1863, for example, Mikhail Katkov expressed his angst in these words: "Ukraine has never had a distinctive history, has never been a separate state, the Ukrainian people are a purely Russian people, an indigenous Russian people, *an essential part of the Russian people, without which the Russian people cannot go on being what they are*" (emphasis added).[3] By 1911 Petr Struve was betraying outright panic: "Should the intelligentsia['s] 'Ukrainian' idea ... strike the national soil and set it on fire ... [the result will be] a gigantic and unprecedented schism of the Russian nation, which, such is my deepest conviction, will result in a veritable disaster for the state and for the people. All our 'borderland' problems will pale into mere bagatelles compared to such a prospect of bifurcation and – should the 'Belarusians' follow the 'Ukrainians,' [this will lead to] the 'trifurcation' of *Russian culture*" (emphasis added).[4] Struve clearly recognized that the Ukrainian intelligentsia, by then visibly in the embrace of a "European" rather than an "imperial" ideology, was eroding Ukraine's indispensable place within the "Russian" cultural identity. Katkov and Struve understood "Russianness" to be threatened by a zero-sum process: the rise of the Ukrainian nationality would destroy the "all-Russian."

"Europe," as an emergent interpretative framework for imagining an autonomous Ukrainian culture, also raised the level of national consciousness among Ukrainian imperial intellectuals. As they increasingly acquired "European" perspectives on themselves, they evolved from being a class within the imperial community, modestly espousing "differences" from Great Russians, to a separate nationality. These writers, historians, ethnographers, and literary critics gradually transformed themselves from supportive actors in an imperial project to independent, self-conscious leaders of a sovereign Ukrainian cultural institution. To all intents and purposes this evolution reached an irreversible phase during the 1920s, best epitomized by Mykola Khvyl'ovyi's demand that Ukrainian culture move "away from Moscow"; predictably, this slogan was accompanied by a call to embrace "Europe."[5] Thereafter, "Europe" became a common and self-evident idea in the intelligentsia's cultural discourse.

To summarize: before Ukrainian intellectuals "discovered" "Europe," their discourse was limited to drawing distinctions between Ukrainian culture and history and the Great Russian. They were tied to an East Slavic setting and upheld the imperial state culture as the common ground of all intellectuals in the Russian Empire. This manner of articulating cultural difference dominated discourse for a long time and was only infrequently punctuated by references to "Europe." It was only when Ukrainian culture came to be promoted more fully in terms of its "Europeanism" that the "imperial" East Slavic foundations began to be undermined, and common cultural production and consumption with the Russians were gradually abandoned in the name of creating an autonomous, European-style "high" culture.

The relinquishment of the imperial context was a drawn-out affair. However, even in the first half of the nineteenth century a few Ukrainian voices anticipated the paradigm shift towards "Europe." In modelling cultural activity in this new way, they began whittling away at the power of imperial discourse to keep Ukrainians in its service. By bringing in "Europe," these voices began enunciating a different modality of self and culture – one that was more clearly aligned with a European sense of nationhood.

The sections that follow describe some of the milestones in this process.

Nikolai Gogol'

In keeping with the earliest phase of the Ukrainian movement, Nikolai Gogol' (Mykola Hohol', 1809–52) was among those Ukrainians in the empire who staged Ukraine and its history, society, and culture primarily as something different from the Great Russian. To simplify, his oeuvre presents a contrast between Ukrainians and Great Russians, an antithesis that was never to the latter's advantage.[6] A professional imperial writer if there ever was one, Gogol' forged a career by appeasing the state while playing to the "national" interests of both Ukrainians and Russians through his choice of themes, subjects, and settings. In the imperial debate about the nature of the "Russian" nationality, he always accentuated Ukrainian cultural uniqueness and historical separateness.

He drew sharp distinctions between the southern (Ukrainian) and the northern (Russian) Rus', as well as between the two national temperaments. In *Taras Bul'ba*, for example, Gogol' has the Cossacks identifying with (southern) Rus', and the hero of the eponymous novel dreams of the Ukrainian/Rus' land giving birth to "its own tsar."[7] Asked by a member of imperial polite society in December 1844 (i.e., at the peak of his career) to explain what kind of "soul" he had – a Ukrainian or Russian one – Gogol' diplomatically declined to take advantage of such a fine opportunity to declare himself a Russian unambiguously, pleading confusion on the nationality issue but emphasizing, as he always did, the distinctiveness and high worth of the separate Russian and Ukrainian natures.[8] This was years after Vissarion Belinskii proclaimed Gogol' a Russian writer largely because of his Russian themes and because, ostensibly, Ukrainians were a stateless, unhistorical "Russian" tribe who could not possibly create their own literature and were undeserving of their own history.[9]

"Europe" is an obvious aspect of Gogol's life, given that he spent more than a decade living there; it is also a notable, but relatively modest, subject in his work.[10] In his oeuvre, "Europe *and* Ukraine," as a theme, is particularly problematic. Gogol' draws some not overly positive analogies between "Europe" – Italy and Rome – and the life of old-world Ukrainian landowners.[11] Both are backward; yet both Italy and Ukraine are deemed highly livable places, whereas "Europe" in general is simply for sightseeing.

In his 1832 essay, "A Glance at the Making of Little Russia," he calls the Cossack nation (*narod*) in Ukraine (*Ukraïna*) "one of the most remarkable phenomena of European history."[12] This nation's origins are mixed: by virtue of its faith and location it "belongs to Europe," but by virtue of the manner of its life and dress it is "completely Asian." This nation unites two opposite poles: "European caution" and "Asian insouciance."[13] Gogol' narrates his minihistory of Ukraine within the terminological framework of *Rossiia*, a concept close to the notion of "East Slavdom": he recognizes distinct "northern," "middle," and "southern" principalities. The "north" is, moreover, referred to as "Great (*Velikaia*) *Rossiia*." *Rossiia* is also a place in the "west" that comes under the control of the "Lithuanians." Of all these geographical points in *Rossiia*, Gogol's full attention is devoted to "Southern *Rossiia*" and his main argument appears to be this: "And so, southern *Rossiia*, under the powerful patronage of the Lithuanian princes, completely separated from the northern [*Rossiia*]. All connections between them were severed; two *states* came into being, each called by the same name – Rus'" (emphasis added).[14]

"Europe" makes a cameo appearance in *Taras Bul'ba*. In the 1835 edition Gogol' describes how the Cossacks combine Asiatic and European tactics in battle[15] and speaks of them as creatures of "Europe's semi-nomadic East."[16] In the 1842 redaction that same sentence is altered slightly. Ukraine becomes a "semi-nomadic corner of Europe," but one that is important for defending the rest of Europe from "Mongolian," "non-Christian" "predators."[17] In chapter 11, it is Poland's turn to be characterized as "an almost semi-Asiatic corner of Europe," but the narrator attributes this opinion to European "counts and barons" who snootily consider "Muscovy and Ukraine" to be located "already" in "Asia," something that the narrator denies, at least tacitly, by the tone of his text.[18]

These fleeting references indicate that Gogol' conceived of Ukraine as a European periphery, her defensive outpost, but beyond that Ukraine's cultural status in Europe was not elaborated. As a structure, *Rossiia* (East Slavdom) plays a more significant role than Europe. In *Taras Bul'ba* the Ukrainian Cossack nation comes into being through identification with Kyivan Rus' (not Russia). East Slavdom is the space in which Ukrainian-Russian differentiation plays out, a key concern for Gogol'. He chooses to be meticulous when making national distinctions in Eastern Europe: "Poland," "Muscovy," and "Ukraine" are all clearly identified by name. He uses *Moskoviia* (instead of *Rossiia*) to denote Russia as a separate East Slavic political entity, and when he denotes Ukraine by the historically accurate term *Rossiia*, he fastidiously underscores that Ukraine is "the original southern *Rossiia*,"[19] lest there be any confusion with *Moskoviia*, which, by inference, must be the not-so-original northern *Rossiia*.[20] On the basis of this distinction we may conclude that, discursively, Gogol' remained largely locked within the imperial East Slavic world and primarily focused on Ukrainian-Russian differences, without making any major contribution to visualizing Ukraine as a part of cultural "Europe." His own creativity was firmly rooted in shared imperial culture.

Hryhorii Kvitka-Osnovianenko

Gogol's much older contemporary, Hryhorii Kvitka-Osnovianenko (1778–1843), was also a prominent member of the imperial literary class. He made frequent appearances in the periodicals of the capitals and saw both his Russian- and Ukrainian-language works published in Moscow and St Petersburg. While Gogol', like the majority of Ukrainians of his time, pursued his Russian-Ukrainian differentiation practices by restricting himself to the lingua franca of the empire, Kvitka-Osnovianenko, as his literary career progressed, increasingly turned towards experimenting with Ukrainian. The cumulative effect of this trend (also evident among other writers) was that Ukrainian / Great Russian "difference" began to acquire a linguistic dimension, in addition to the historical and ethnographic markers favoured by Gogol'. Conceptually, the Ukrainian language began to evolve from a "dialect" of Russian (the preferred vision of Great Russians) into a separate entity. In turn, Ukrainian-language "writing" in the empire began acquiring the features of a "literature." The emerging efforts to institutionalize Ukrainian literary production as something discrete from general imperial literature also raised the relevance of "Europe" as a countervailing example. One of the more interesting collocations of "Ukrainian Literature" and "Europe" occurs in Kvitka-Osnovianenko's letter to Andrei Kraevskii, editor of *Otechestvennye zapiski* (Notes of the Fatherland), in 1841: "Once again about Little Russian literature: It is developing and will live. Journals (I am not talking about yours) will not eradicate it from the face of the earth; it will overcome opponents and intimidators, [and] in the course of the year something will be published. You can come to its assistance. Give it legal protection in your journal among surveys of *other* literatures ... Moreover, count our literature among *foreign* ones and do not include surveys of our books among Russian (*rossiiskie*) ones; create a *separate* section among Germans, Frenchmen, etc." (emphasis added).[21]

It is noteworthy that Kvitka-Osnovianenko writes to Kraevskii as one member of the imperial literary establishment to another (*Otechestvennye zapiski* published his work). Yet he is not limited to this identification, asserting himself also as a spokesman for "our" literature and books as separate "European" institutions. The French and Germans represent a "national" Europe; their separate languages and literatures serve as templates for Ukrainians. Kvitka-Osnovianenko continues to remain a participant of imperial cultural institutions (the press, publishing houses), but the imperial parameters are no longer as delimiting for him as they were for Gogol'. There is a sense, in fact, that the empire should be institutionally diversified (not just thematically, as was the case at the time), and should create formal opportunities for a Ukrainian culture instead of fostering a single "all-Russian" one, with its hegemonic linguistic and literary ambitions. In this instance, Ukrainian culture is represented not just as different from the imperial (*rossiiskie*) but actually "foreign" to it – in the sense that it is now seen to be on an equal footing (structurally, of course, not quantitatively or qualitatively) with "European" literatures and therefore beyond the imperial bounds of the Russian-Ukrainian binary. Kvitka-Osnovianenko's model already has the potential for changing the organizational structure of culture in the empire. But, as his words also reveal, imperial society resisted any alternative institutionalized "national" culture and, moreover, threatened to "eradicate" it.

Taras Shevchenko

Another rare instance of invoking "Europe" to define Ukrainian literature was Shevchenko's unpublished foreword to the second, unrealized edition of the

Kobzar (1847). Amidst a call to invigorate Ukrainian publishing (by emulating Poles, Czechs, Serbs, Bulgarians, Macedonians as well as Russians)[22]
and a complaint about self-centred Russian notions of Slavic literary unity,
Shevchenko also said the following: "Ignore the Russians. Let them write in
their own language and we [will write] in ours. They have a nation and language, and we have a nation and language."[23]

As is apparent, the national "difference" between Ukrainians and Russians
is still a major preoccupation. But, as in Kvitka-Osnovianenko's case, this concern gives rise to an effort to institutionalize that difference through cultural
practices, such as publishing. Shevchenko triumphs over the singular focus
on Great Russians by situating the Ukrainian cultural discourse in a broader
context, that is, the West Slavic, South Slavic, and the European. The purpose
is to summon into existence a separate nation, language, and literature along an
East-West axis rather than only a North-South one.

What stands out in this short piece is the invocation of Europe in the
guise of two Scottish writers: Walter Scott and Robert Burns. The contrast
between their language choices (English and Scots, respectively) serves as
an analogy for the linguistic split in Ukrainian society (Russian/Ukrainian,
Gogol'/Shevchenko). Shevchenko's foreword endeavours to heal this divide
on "national" (Ukrainian-language) foundations that explicitly include
the common people as potential consumers of culture. Shevchenko, to put
it figuratively, rejected Walter Scott and Gogol' as models for national literature, although he recognized both as representative of their respective
nations. In urging a move away from Russian-language Ukrainian writing,
something both Shevchenko and Kvitka-Osnovianenko continued to practice,
Shevchenko was in effect breaking up the unified, elite linguistic space of the
multi-ethnic imperial intelligentsia and creating a new one for Ukrainian intellectuals that would linguistically bind them within their own separate system
and, by extension, to the common people. A new literature and a new reading
public were being projected on the basis of a European model of nation building rather than an imperial one.

Panteleimon Kulish

Modelling oneself on Europe in light of the empire's "all-Russian" pressures was not an easy task. This was well illustrated by Panteleimon Kulish
(1819–97) in his 1857 article, "On the Relationship of Little Russian Literature to the All-Russian [all-Rus'ian],"[24] which, as the title attests, shifts rhetorically back to the empire and formulates cultural difference primarily in
Russian-Ukrainian (North-South) binary terms, thereby recapitulating some

of Gogol's thinking. In its own way, however, this essay also marks a radical evolution of the notion that the East Slavs are distinct nationalities within a common empire. Kulish asks that "the flight of the Rus' spirit" not be restricted to "the bounds of the ancient Muscovite state"[25] but be allowed for Ukraine as well. In promoting this view, Kulish was making a cautious foray into cultural policy making.

He prepared the ground for his argument with a series of obsequious remarks and disavowals of political separatism (e.g., he criticizes Mazepa) and by rejecting one-sided patriotism or fanaticism, the Ukrainian kind in particular but the Great Russian, gently, as well. Kulish portrays his fellow Ukrainians as loyal subjects of the crown who are committed to the "common good," a single state, and shared civic life. As evidence, he cites Gogol', who "accomplished a feat more patriotic than the people who in their own books praise only northern Rus' and avoid the southern."[26]

This excessive show of imperial loyalism serves Kulish as the staging ground from which to plead for recognition of the cultural distinctions between the southern and northern Rus'. Acknowledgment of this fact by the Russian side, he said, would bring benefits to the entire Rus' people (*russkii narod*), that is, the East Slavs. Thus, Kulish's discourse simultaneously asserts integration into the imperial political space and internal cultural differentiation within it. The pursuit of separate cultural paths (a different language and literature, and by extension, a different nationality) serves the interests of the empire, he argues.

Although Kulish's careful tone and strong defence of the state had a tactical purpose, it was also an effect of the constraints he still felt after the 1847 arrest of the Cyril and Methodius Brotherhood, of which he was a member and in connection with which he was sentenced to a brief term in exile. The extent to which Kulish adapts to the political realities is evident in the fact that when he writes about Taras Shevchenko, he chooses not to mention the poet by name because Shevchenko was just completing a much harsher, ten-year exile for related reasons.

Kulish portrays himself not only as a faithful subject but explicitly positions himself as "a Rus' writer of our time," a person who actively participates in the "renowned literary milieu"[27] – that is, imperial high culture. However, he does not stop there. He also describes himself as a writer who works both "here" and "there" – in imperial culture and Ukrainian culture, the latter now identified as a separate space. Kulish also refers to a category he calls the "South Rus'ian educated society,"[28] from whose vantage point he attempts to explain to the rest of the imperial public why he would risk writing a novel (*Chorna rada* [The Black Council]) in "a language unknown in northern *Rossiia* and not very common among the south Rus' [that is, Ukrainian] reading public."[29]

Kulish describes how Ukrainian educated society – symbolically represented by Gogol', Kvitka-Osnovianenko, and Shevchenko – helped evolve the
unique Ukrainian nationality. He argued that his own novel and literature in
the Ukrainian vernacular in general grew out of Ukrainian society's maturing
needs. Specifically, it was the Ukrainian intelligentsia that had come of age[30]
to such a point of national self-consciousness that it was no longer prepared
to listen to the voice of its people in "translation" (viz., as Gogol' had mediated it); it needed the actual Ukrainian language itself. Truth be told, he said,
the Russian language had been proving itself inadequate for quite some time,
as evidenced by the fact that "not a single Little Russian poet – among them
Gogol' – was satisfied with his work in the northern Rus' language."[31] Declaring the new generation of Ukrainian intellectuals to be "Gogol's heirs in [the
evolution of Ukrainian] self-consciousness,"[32] Kulish sought to carve out a
place for Ukrainian language and literature next to the "all-Russian," insisting
that such inclusion would not be to the latter's detriment. He continued to position Ukrainian literature in the imperial context, but as a separate institution for
the expression of the Ukrainian spirit.

Although Kulish was a highly refined intellectual in the best European tradition and has earned a deserved reputation as a Europeanizer of Ukrainian
culture, his article maintained the separateness of Ukrainian culture in close
institutional alignment with imperial culture. It contained only two explicit
mentions of Europe and one indirect allusion. The first of these was an invocation of seventeenth-century Ukrainian churchmen, who brought their "own
language" to the "North" and introduced it into the "then-Russian literature
as a sophisticated tongue that had mastered pan-European sciences and was
able to express scientific and abstract concepts."[33] In a sense, this established
the "European" pedigree of the Ukrainian intelligentsia as a separate class and
extended its historical roots. In the second instance Kulish makes a case for the
uniqueness of Shevchenko, rather surprisingly, by underscoring his remote-
ness from the Europeanized literary diction that characterized most imperial
writers. Finally, a footnote in the article declares, "The names of Shakespeare,
Byron, and Walter Scott link the English and the Scots, scattered throughout
the world, into a single nation. The name of Gogol' is equally dear to a Great
Russian and a Little Russian. Russian literature since the time of Gogol' has
become even more kindred for Little Russians: in it, they have seen themselves
in the present and the past. On the other hand, the Great Russians, through the
agency of Gogol's works, have, as if again, discovered, fallen in love with, and
embraced Little Russia with their soul."[34]

If Shevchenko had given preference to Burns as a symbol of Scottish nationality over Walter Scott and had used him symbolically to sharpen the linguistic

differences between the English and the Scots (and, by extension, the Russians and Ukrainians), Kulish did the opposite. He invoked Walter Scott and Gogol' in an effort to mitigate the sense of difference, to allay Russian anxieties, and only then did he proceed to plead for Ukrainian linguistic separateness within an overarching common imperial context. However, in contrast to his observations about the English and the Scots, he never went so far as to call Ukrainians and Russians a "single nation."

Mykhailo Drahomanov

The views of Mykhailo Drahomanov (1841–95) on Ukrainian culture and literature were dynamic and fluid. Seeking balance between the Russian Empire and Europe, Drahomanov evinced a clear preference for the latter, but also a pragmatic acknowledgment of the former. In one of his most important articles on these topics, "Russian, Great Russian, Ukrainian, and Galician Literature (1873–4), Drahomanov discusses Ukrainian cultural development as a process of "differentiation" and "decentralization,"[35] a movement away from the common imperial (*rosiis'ka*) sphere. Summarizing this position again in 1876, this time in Russian, he stated:

> [In the above-mentioned article] it was pointed out that in *Rossiia* [the Russian Empire] there does indeed exist an all-Russian literature (*rossyjska* [the word appears in the text in Polish]), which is not at all a synonym for Great Russian or Muscovite [literature]; it is not diametrically opposed to Russian or Little Russian [literatures], [it is] a literature of the aristocratic-bureaucratic pan-imperial society, a common product of eighteenth-century state history and culture ... alongside which, after Gogol', there develops a national Great Russian literature ... but even earlier still – a Ukrainian national literature.[36]

Drahomanov acknowledged that Ukrainian society in Galicia and in the Russian Empire continued to vacillate between a pan-imperial literature, one based on the Russian language, and a separate Ukrainian-language institution.[37] He defended the positive ideological and Europeanizing role that aristocratic Russian-language literature had on Ukrainian society,[38] an institution, he maintained, through which European ideas reached the Ukrainian intelligentsia and transformed it into a national factor.[39] "We Ukrainians found our nation and our very national language only because we passed through the European school; in this respect, the imperial (*rosiis'ka*) literature and the power of the Russian state were most beneficial."[40] He accepts that the "differentiation of culture and literature in Russia (*Rossiia*) into Great Russian and Little Russian cannot but continue."[41]

Drahomanov portrays the pan-imperial literary category as the common "high" inheritance and product of the state's multi-ethnic elite; it stands in opposition to the "national" literatures (Ukrainian and Great Russian), which are oriented towards serving the interests of the people in a language they comprehend, a function for which the imperial Russian-language literature is ill-suited.

Like his predecessors and contemporaries, Drahomanov was an active participant in imperial life – at least until his involuntary emigration in 1876 – and, like Kulish, wrote simultaneously as a Ukrainian writer and as an imperial insider. Yet he clearly saw Ukrainian culture as a separate institution, one that he was prepared to promote and defend against discrimination.[42] Through his publishing activity and Ukrainian-language writing he helped turn Ukrainian culture, an entity of structurally "low" standing in the empire, into an institution of intellectuals. Ultimately, his ambition was to see Ukrainian literature as being on par with the imperial: as a literature that addressed universal issues and problems. While the empire may have remained a frequent point of reference for him, he framed cultural and national issues within a broad and comparative European context, with Europe itself ultimately becoming, by force of circumstances, the site of his scholarly and political activity. He invokes Europe both to criticize the empire and to defend national cultures within it. Ultimately, Drahomanov foresaw that Ukrainian culture would wean itself off the empire; that the empire would stop functioning as an intermediary between Ukraine and Europe. In 1891 he wrote:

> I will allow myself to say that, since the moment I entered public service either as a teacher or as a writer, I never missed an opportunity to tell younger people in Ukraine that they cannot consider themselves educated until they learn at least two or three Western European languages in order to read the most important things. I have often said, orally and in print, that Ukrainian literature will not stand firmly on its own legs until Ukrainian writers receive universal, learned ideas and feelings directly from Western Europe rather than through Petersburg or Moscow, through Russian literature, as is happening even at present.[43]

Ivan Nechui-Levyts'kyi

Although not in the same intellectual league as Drahomanov, Ivan Nechui-Levyts'kyi (1838–1918), a populist and a prolific realist writer, also chronicled the collapse of the common and overlapping culture of the Russian and Ukrainian elites. In 1878 he wrote that at one time Ukraine and Great Russia were able to share a culture (specifically, a literature); however, conditions had changed so fundamentally as to make this no longer feasible.[44] "We need our own Ukrainian literature," he declared. Significantly, he developed his argument in relation not only to East Slavic cultural history (starting with Kyivan Rus') but also to Europe and European literatures, to which he makes frequent reference. Europe, in fact, is the very embodiment of "nationality." Ukrainian literature, beginning with the nineteenth century, is seen as the first advocate of this principle in the Russian Empire, pre-empting Great Russian literary efforts in this respect. For Nechui-Levyts'kyi, it is Europe that sets the standard for vernacular literatures, an axiom, he says, that the empire has not yet completely grasped. For this very reason, Ukrainian writers must only write in Ukrainian. Nechui-Levyts'kyi argues that "each European literature expresses the character of its nation," and he sees Ukrainian literature doing the same. The Ukrainian nation is different not only from other Slavic nations but European ones as well.[45] Differentiation is now taking place along both a European axis and an imperial one.

Ukrainian culture is one of many diverse cultures in Europe, but, according to Nechui-Levyts'kyi, Great Russia is an obstacle to Ukraine's full cultural integration into the European system. "Right now, Moscow is limiting the development of Ukrainian literature … We are falling behind in our development not only in relationship to Europe but even the West Slavs, even Bulgaria, where, as is apparent now, the Turks have not forbidden the Bulgarians to establish primary and secondary schools." Like those before him, Nechui-Levyts'kyi demands legal rights for Ukrainian culture and its separate institutionalization.[46]

Ukraïns'ka khata

Ukrainian intellectuals broke out of their self-imposed imperial parameters most decisively in the modernist journal *Ukraïns'ka khata* (Ukrainian House), published in Kyiv from 1909 to 1914. From a literary point of view, this journal was a virtual *Who's Who* of Ukrainian writers, publishing works not only of current "stars" but also providing a platform for those who would define Ukrainian literature in the coming decades. Among the contributors to *Ukraïns'ka khata* were Hryhorii Chuprynka, Mykola Filians'kyi, Mykhailo Iats'kiv, Petro Karmans'kyi, Hnat Khotkevych, Ol'ha Kobylians'ka, Bohdan Lepkyi, Iakiv Mamontov, Oleksander Oles', Maksym Ryl's'kyi, Mykhailo (Mykhail') Semenko, Volodymyr Svidzins'kyi, Pavlo Tychyna, and Mykola Voronyi.

In a very real sense, modernism was the intelligentsia's first collective break with the empire. Although these writers were dissimilar in outlook, style, and talent, they shared a commitment to a strictly Ukrainian literary institution and agreed on the necessity of separating Ukrainian cultural production and consumption from the imperial mainstream. In one form or another, all these writers espoused a "European" orientation.

In addition to being a major literary journal, *Ukraïns'ka khata* devoted considerable attention to sociocultural and political analysis. In these efforts it showed itself to be an implacable foe of the so-called Ukrainophile movement (*ukraïnofil'stvo*), that is, the moderate, conciliatory faction of Ukrainian society that continued to engage the imperial system in the hope of winning concessions for Ukrainian culture. It says a good deal about the journal that Dmytro Dontsov, who would establish his nationalist credentials a little later, was among its contributors. One of his articles, "Götterdämmerung ukraïnofil'stva" (Twilight of the Gods of Ukrainophilism), is a gleeful savouring of the reversal suffered by this Ukrainian camp in 1914, when Pavel Miliukov and the liberal Kadet Party rejected autonomy and federalism as principles for the empire. Dontsov saw this as a deserved rebuff on the part of the empire to an embarrassing Ukrainian predisposition dating back to Drahomanov.[47] The downfall of Ukrainophilism was, he wrote, a "rehabilitation of Ukrainians as a nation."[48] Not unexpectedly, his article drew on European political analogies to make its point. The names of France's Louis XVI and Honoré Mirabeau appeared and, of course, there was the obvious German, and Wagnerian, symbolism of the title.

Andrii Tovkachevs'kyi

One of the brightest analytical minds in *Ukraïns'ka khata* was a man virtually unknown today, Andrii Tovkachevs'kyi (1885–1965). In his articles – and especially in his polemics with Petr Struve, who, to repeat, strongly advocated the preservation of an "all-Russian" culture – he revealed just how far Ukrainian intellectuals had drifted from their imperial colleagues. He showed not the slightest solidarity with Struve. Whatever sense of commonality may have existed among this lettered class was by now spent. Tovkachevs'kyi characterized Struve's prescription for Ukrainians – continued participation in the empire and in "all-Russian" culture – as a formula for turning *khokhly* into *katsapy* (derogatory terms for Ukrainians and Russians, respectively). His exact phrase read *okatsaplivanie khokhlov*.[49] This ironic exploitation of the Russian language for humorous effect seemed to signal its demotion as a medium of Ukrainian culture. If Russian had effectively served as the "native" literary language for the Ukrainian intelligentsia, the modernists clearly demonstrated that this practice was nearing an end.

Not only was the Ukrainian intelligentsia no longer an ally in the construction of an imperial culture, it also represented itself as a stumbling block to the creation of an "all-Russian" nation. According to Tovkachevs'kyi, "The fact that intellectuals stand at the head of the nation is completely natural. From this [we can] conclude that a 'Russian nation' [as imagined by P. Struve] not only does not exist, but cannot come into existence now … This is the great merit of the intelligentsia … If there were no [Ukrainian] intelligentsia, popular thought, in its search for new spiritual values, perhaps would have moved in the direction of borrowing from Great Russian culture and assimilated, but now it has an alternative solution that is more appropriate for the essence of the nation."[50]

The modernists clearly defined themselves as leaders of a Ukrainian nation rather than as participants in an imperial culture, to which they were creating a rival. They categorically dismissed the notion that Ukrainian and Russian cultures could be in some way complementary and form a greater whole in the empire. To allow for the latter would make Ukrainian culture merely a "free supplement to Great Russian culture."[51] This pithy formulation captures what was perhaps the central, historically important concern of the modernist movement: its resolve not to play a supporting role in imperial culture. The idea that they, the members of the Ukrainian intelligentsia, were somehow fated to regard the high imperial culture as their own was countered with this argument: "The Ukrainian intelligentsia will make full use of Great Russian culture, but it will remain the intelligentsia of its own nation, it will not become 'Russian.'"[52] The goal was to create a high Ukrainian culture that would be analogous to the European and autonomous from the imperial. "We Ukrainians desire to be a nation, everything [that is, all forms of culture] must be our own."[53] From this sentiment it followed that the historical period of "sharing" a culture had ended. The imperial culture would be respected and used as required, but Ukrainian culture would be developed to perform all social functions, from the lowest to the highest. In this way, the modernists opened a front not only against imperial culture but also against Ukrainophilism. The latter was now seen as an exponent of "low" (ethnographic, regional) culture and a carrier of a debilitating mindset dubbed "Little Russianness," both of which the modernists were determined to sweep away as the immature manifestations of a Ukrainianness that was acquired under the conditions of empire.

While the modernists were obviously different from the generation of Gogol', Maksymovych, Kostomarov, and Bodians'kyi, they readily incorporated their predecessors into their new vision, much as Kulish had recognized Gogol' as his forerunner in the process of nationalizing Ukrainian cultural production. The continuing institutionalization of Ukrainian cultural practices now sought to recoup all earlier Ukrainian *imperial* cultural capital that was previously reserved for "all-Russian" "national" purposes. As a result, the emerging Ukrainian national canon included prominent imperial Ukrainian scholars, musicians, painters, and, of course, writers. Tovkachevs'kyi expressed it this way: "Ukrainians need to announce to the world: Hohol' [Gogol'] is our writer, [Oleksander] Potebnia, [Volodymyr] Antonovych, [Mykola] Kostomarov, [Dmytro] Bahalii are our scholars; [Volodymyr] Borovykovs'kyi, [Mykola] Pymonenko, [Serhii] Vasyl'kivs'kyi and others – all of them emerged from the Ukrainian nation and intuitively brought into their creativity the national Ukrainian spirit."[54]

The European contextualization of Ukrainian culture also helped to usher in the discourse of assimilation and denationalization in ways not seen previously in the Ukrainian literary and cultural discourse of the nineteenth century. Gogol', for instance, had criticized his fellow Ukrainians because they tried to pass themselves off as Great Russians in St Petersburg by adding the suffix *-ov* to their names (see his "Starosvetskie pomeshchiki" [Old-World Landowners]). From this we may deduce that Gogol' did not perceive his own Russian-language activity as falling under the concept of "assimilation." There seems to have been a difference between socialization and acculturation to the empire, on the one hand, and representation of oneself as a Great Russian, on the other. By the modernist period such fine distinctions were no longer valid. Now, taking the side of the state and its elite culture was a sign of national assimilation. Tovkachevs'kyi declared: "The desire for a higher level of culture should not necessarily go hand in hand with assimilation. The Great Russian intelligentsia, as is well known, always followed the Western European [intelligentsia] and always tried to achieve a level of Western European culture, but nevertheless never became German or French ... [The desire for a higher level of culture ought to be] fulfilled within the framework of the nation."[55]

Ukraïns'ka khata also offered a reassessment and a nuanced reading of the "all-Russian" intelligentsia as a class.[56] On the positive side, it recognized the exceptional role it played in the civic and cultural life of the empire, especially its struggle against autocracy, for which it often paid a heavy price. On the other hand, this "all-Russian" group was weakly connected to, and poorly acquainted with, provincial life and its peoples. In effect it functioned as a centralized estate within a centralized state, only rarely sympathizing with national, local movements, like the Ukrainian. The indifference of its members to local, national cultures in the empire was contrasted with the outlook of their counterparts in Europe: "Let us recall the attitude in Western Europe toward all kinds of historical monuments, where they are treated as national treasures. Here among us there is nothing analogous because everything is foreign to the all-Russian intelligentsia."[57] The lesson the modernists drew from this distinc-tion was that Ukraine must have its own cultural institutions ("our own press, our own institutions, our own Enlightenment societies [*prosvity*]")[58] and a cor-responding Ukrainian intelligentsia that would support them.

The Europeanization of Ukrainian culture raised a new set of issues in the early twentieth century. In the sociopolitical realm, for example, observers like Dontsov noted in 1913 that Europe was becoming less indifferent towards, and less ignorant of, Ukraine than it had been in the past. Given this, he mused on how Ukrainians should *not* inform Europe about themselves.[59] Current efforts, he said, were not likely to "stir interest" "among foreigners" because they appealed to Europe's "heart," that is, they tried to rouse "feelings" of injus-tice in European public opinion. He argued that Ukrainians should not play on Europe's sympathies to gain recognition because this was a tactic that had helped neither the Poles nor the Finns. It was important, he wrote, to demon-strate that Ukraine served the political interests of Europe, namely, the interests of European democracy.[60]

The more strictly cultural questions at this time concerned the degree to which Europe ought to serve as a model for the Ukrainian intelligentsia. *Ukraïns'ka khata* betrayed anxiety about the potential loss of a distinct "national" physiognomy in light of Ukrainian literature's increasing adoption of European modernist trends. Mykola Ievshan, a major literary critic in the journal, waxed ironic at what he considered manifestations of false "Western European" pretensions among some Ukrainian writers, who attempted to con-vey a higher, more European, image of Ukrainian writings by "erasing" the national character as they did, for example, when they translated poetry into Polish. He saw a dangerous tendency to "demean Ukrainian poetic thought" as such and replace it with "all kinds of foreign [that is, European] detritus, which is called a higher aristocratic form of culture."[61] It would appear that, as the intelligentsia grew relatively secure vis-à-vis imperial culture, some of its members began to sound the alarm about uncritically embracing Euro-pean avant-garde fashions (Nechui-Levyts'kyi was one of them).[62] This issue, in fact, would lead to a rapid differentiation within the modernists' ranks as some turned towards "Europe" as an international and cosmopolitan phenom-enon worthy of Ukrainian emulation, while others sought to defend strictly "national" cultural interests against undue European encroachment.

Conclusion

The history of Ukrainian cultural production and consumption in the Russian Empire shows that in the early phases of this process the intelligentsia was primarily concerned with establishing Ukrainian historical and ethnographic' distinctiveness within a Russophone East Slavic space, but without seriously challenging the legitimacy of the imperial state. The intellectuals imagined themselves in relationship to the crown while affirming their difference from Great Russians. For a long period of time "Europe" as a model for "national" development was a largely latent but surprisingly resilient idea in combating "all-Russianness." Once the elites began reframing the concept of nation and national culture with the benefit of "Europe," they initiated a new stage in their imperial existence, anticipating the establishment of institutions of cultural production and consumption that would be separate from those of the empire.

It would be wrong to understand the developments portrayed here teleologically; "Europe" was, rather, an ideological discourse that developed and sustained itself under unequal power relationships and influenced Ukrainian members of imperial society in different ways. It is safe to say, however, that the "European" model saw remarkable growth and vitality over the course of the nineteenth century, and it is now the standard model among Ukrainian cultural elites, although not necessarily among politicians or the broad masses of society.

Notes

1 This section summarizes themes that I have explored in more detail in earlier papers. Previously, my emphasis was on the "all-Russian" idea and the concept of "imperial culture"; here, I pursue a more systematic examination of the idea of "Europe." See Oleh S. Ilnytzkyj, "Modeling Culture in the Empire: Ukrainian Modernism and the Death of the All-Russian Idea," in *Culture, Nation and Identity: The Russian-Ukrainian Encounter (1600–1945)*, ed. Andreas Kappeler et al. (Edmonton: Canadian Institute of Ukrainian Studies, 2003), 298–324 and Oleh S. Ilnytzkyj, "'Imperial Culture' and Russian-Ukrainian Unity Myths," in *Ukraine, the EU and Russia: History, Culture and International Relations*, ed. Stephen Velychenko (London: Palgrave Macmillan, 2007), 52–69.
2 Nikolai Kostomarov, "Dve russkiia narodnosti," *Osnova* 3 (1861): 33–80.
3 Quoted in David Saunders, "Mikhail Katkov and Mykola Kostomarov: A Note on Petr A. Valuev's Anti-Ukrainian Edict of 1863," *Harvard Ukrainian Studies* 17, no. 3–4 (1993): 372.
4 Quoted in Richard Pipes, *Struve: Liberal on the Right, 1905–1944* (Cambridge, MA: Harvard University Press, 1980), 211–12. For the original, see Petr Struve, "Obshcherusskaia kul'tura i ukrainskii partikuliarizm," *Russkaia mysl'* 1 (1912): 85.
5 Oleh S. Ilnytzkyj, "The Modernist Ideology and Mykola Khvyl'ovyi," *Harvard Ukrainian Studies* 15, no. 3–4 (1991): 257–62; 284–7; Myroslav Shkandrij,

Modernists, Marxists and the Nation: The Ukrainian Literary Discussion of the 1920s (Edmonton: Canadian Institute of Ukrainian Studies, 1992).

6 For an excellent examination of Gogol's Ukrainian aspects and his contrasting attitudes toward Russia, see Edyta M. Bojanowska, *Nikolai Gogol: Between Ukrainian and Russian Nationalism* (Cambridge, MA: Harvard University Press, 2007). I expressed my view of the book in my article "The Nationalism of Nikolai Gogol': Betwixt and Between?" *Canadian Slavonic Papers* 49, no. 3–4 (September–December, 2007): 349–68.

7 For additional details, see my article, "Is Gogol's 1842 Version of *Taras Bul'ba* Really 'Russified'?" in "Confronting the Past: Ukraine and Its History: A Festschrift in Honour of John-Paul Himka on the Occasion of His Sixtieth Birthday," ed. Andrew Colin Gow, Roman Senkus, and Serhy Yekelchyk, *Journal of Ukrainian Studies* 35–6 (2010–1): 51–68.

8 I am, of course, referring to the correspondence between Gogol' and Aleksandra Smirnova-Rosset. For my reading of this episode in Gogol's life, see "Cultural Indeterminacy in the Russian Empire: Nikolai Gogol' as a Ukrainian Post-Colonial Writer," in *A World of Slavic Literatures: Essays in Comparative Slavic Studies in Honor of Edward Mozejko*, ed. Paul Duncan Morris (Bloomington, IN: Slavica, 2002), 153–71.

9 This comes across very clearly in Belinskii's review of Mykola Markevych's *History of Little Russia*. Vissarion Belinskii, "Istoriia Malorossii Nikolaia Markevicha" [1843], *Sobranie sochinenii*, 9 vols. (Moscow: Khudozhestvennaia literatura, 1979), vol. 5, http://az.lib.ru/b/belinskij_w_g/text_2720.shtml.

10 Robert A. Maguire, *Exploring Gogol* (Stanford, CA: Stanford University Press, 1994), 116–18; Sara Dickinson, *Breaking Ground: Travel and National Culture in Russia from Peter I to the Era of Pushkin* (Amsterdam; New York: Rodopi, 2006), 192–9; Mikhail Vaiskopf and Rita Dzhuliani, eds., *Gogol' i Italiia* (Moscow: Rossiiskii gosudarstvennyi gumanitarnyi universitet, 2004).

11 For the text of Gogol's letter about Italy to his Ukrainian school friend Oleksandr Danylevs'kyi, dated 15 April 1837, see N. V. Gogol', *Polnoe sobranie sochinenii*, 14 vols. (Moscow: Izdatel'stvo AN SSSR, 1937–52), 11: 94.

12 Gogol', "Vzgliad na sostavlenie Malorossii," *Polnoe sobranie sochinenii*, 8: 46.

13 Gogol', *Polnoe sobranie sochinenii*, 8: 49.

14 Ibid., 8: 44.

15 Gogol', *Taras Bul'ba. Redaktsiia "Mirgoroda" 1835 g.*, *Polnoe sobranie sochinenii*, 2: 279–355, here 2: 320.

16 Ibid., 2: 283.

17 Gogol', *Taras Bul'ba*, *Polnoe sobranie sochinenii*, 2: 39–197, here 2: 46.

18 Ibid., 2: 160.

19 Ibid., 2: 46.

20 On use of the term *Rossiia*, see Mikhail Maksimovich [Mykhailo Maksymovych], "Ob upotreblenii nazvanii "Rossiia" i "Malorossiia" v Zapadnoi Rusi," in *Vybrani Tvory* (Kyiv: Lybid', 2004), 342–5. On the terminology used to designate Ukraine, see also Zenon Kohut, "The Development of a Little Russian Identity and Ukrainian Nationbuilding," *Harvard Ukrainian Studies* 10, no. 3–4 (1986): 562, 564.

21 Petro Tymoshenko, *Khrestomatiia materialiv z istoriï ukraïns'koï literaturnoï movy* (Kyiv: Radians'ka shkola, 1959), 187.

22 Taras Shevchenko, "Peredmova do nezdiisnenoho vydannia 'Kobzaria,'" *Zibrannia tvoriv*, 6 vols. (Kyiv: Naukova dumka, 2003), 5: 207.

23 Ibid., 5: 208.

24 Panteleimon Kulish, "Ob otnoshenii malorossiiskoi slovesnosti k obshcherusskoi. Epilog k 'Chernoi Rade,'" *Tvory v dvokh tomakh* (Kyiv: Dnipro, 1989), 2: 458–76.

25 Ibid., 2: 473.

26 Ibid., 2: 464.

27 Ibid., 2: 458.

28 Ibid., 2: 462.

29 Ibid., 2: 458.

30 Ibid., 2: 467.

31 Ibid., 2: 474.

32 Ibid., 2: 463.

33 Ibid., 2: 459.

34 Ibid., 2: 465.

35 Mykhailo Drahomanov, "Literatura rosiis'ka, velykorus'ka, ukraïns'ka i halyts'ka," *Literaturno-publitsystychni pratsi u dvokh tomakh* (Kyiv: Naukova dumka, 1970), 1: 80–220, esp. 131.

36 Mykhailo Drahomanov, "Po voprosu o malorusskoi literature," *Literaturno-publitsystychni pratsi*, 1: 369; see also 1: 98–142.

37 Ibid., 1: 80–1.

38 Ibid., 1: 109.

39 Ibid., 1: 110–1.

40 Ibid., 1: 111–12.

41 Ibid., 1: 131.

42 Ibid., 1: 352.

43 Mykhailo Drahomanov, "Chudats'ki dumky pro ukraïns'ku natsional'nu spravu," *Vybrane* (Kyiv: Lybid', 1991), 461–558, esp. 479.

44 Ivan Nechui-Levyts'kyi, "S'ohochasne literaturne priamuvannia," Part I, *Pravda* 2 (1878), 1–41 and Part II, *Literaturnyi zbirnyk: V dopovenenie XIII richnyka chasopysy "Pravda"* (Lviv: 1884), 195–231. See also his work, written under the pseudonym I. Bashtovyi, *Ukraïnstvo na literaturnykh pozvakh z Moskovshchynoiu* (Lviv: Dilo, 1891). For recent editions of these works, see Ivan

Nechui-Levyts'kyi, *Ukraïnstvo na literaturnykh pozvakh z Moskovshchynoiu: Kul'turolohichni traktaty*, ed. Mykhailo Chornopys'kyi (Lviv: Kameniar, 1998). Quotations from this publication follow the online edition at http://sites.utoronto. ca/elul/Nechui/Ukrainstvo/index.html.

45 Nechui-Levyts'kyi, *Ukraïnstvo na literaturnykh pozvakh z Moskovshchynoiu*, http://sites.utoronto.ca/elul/Nechui/Ukrainstvo/ukrainstvo05.Nepotribnist-1.html.

46 Nechui-Levyts'kyi, *Ukraïnstvo na literaturnykh pozvakh z Moskovshchynoiu*, http://sites.utoronto.ca/elul/Nechui/Ukrainstvo/ukrainstvo06.Nepotribnist-2.html.

47 D. D. [Dmytro Dontsov], "Götterdämmerung ukraïnofil'stva," *Ukraïns'ka khata* 3–4 (1914): 278–83, esp. 279. See also Andrii Tovkachevs'kyi's review of Dontsov's *Moderne moskvofil'stvo* in *Ukraïns'ka khata* 1 (1913): 78–9.

48 [Dontsov], "Götterdämmerung ukraïnofil'stva," 278.

49 Andrii Tovkachevs'kyi, "Potsilunok Iudy ukraïns'komu narodovi," *Ukraïns'ka khata* 3–4 (1912): 209.

50 A. Tovkachevs'kyi, "Budynok na pisku, abo 'sobiraniie Rusi' Petrom Struve," *Ukraïns'ka khata* 2 (1912): 120 and 122.

51 Tovkachevs'kyi, "Potsilunok Iudy," 203.

52 Tovkachevs'kyi, "Budynok na pisku," *Ukraïns'ka khata* 3–4 (1912): 230.

53 Ibid., 235.

54 *Ukraïns'ka khata* 2 (1912): 125.

55 *Ukraïns'ka khata* 3–4 (1912): 229–30.

56 K., "Obshcherus'ka intelihentsiia na Ukraïni," *Ukraïns'ka khata* 9 (1909): 489–97 and 10 (1909): 540–52. The author is probably Vsevolod Kryzhanovs'kyi. See O. I. Dei, *Slovnyk ukraïns'kykh psevdonimiv* (Kyiv: Naukova dumka, 1969), 184.

57 *Ukraïns'ka khata* 9 (1909): 496.

58 *Ukraïns'ka khata* 10 (1909): 540.

59 Dm. D-v. [Dmytro Dontsov], "Iak ne povynno informuvaty pro nas Evropu?" *Ukraïns'ka khata* 11 (1913): 701–5.

60 Ibid., 702–3.

61 Mykola Ievshan, "Elehantni zhesty zakhidno-ievropeis'koï shkoly," *Ukraïns'ka khata* 4 (1911): 256–61, esp. 257.

62 For details see Oleh S. Ilnytzkyj, *Ukrainian Futurism, 1914–1930: An Historical and Critical Study* (Cambridge, MA: Harvard Ukrainian Research Institute, 1997), 10–27.

The Train to Europe: Berlin as a Topos of Modernity in Ukrainian Literature of the 1920s

TAMARA HUNDOROVA

Modernity in the Literary Discussion of 1925–1928

London, Paris, Berlin, and Vienna were cultural megalopolises at different times in the course of the twentieth century and symbolized distinct variants of European modernity. Berlin, slowly recovering after Germany's defeat in the First World War, achieved the status of a cultural capital in the 1920s. It became the 1920s prototype of the modern European city. Its image – acute angled, demented, polyphonic, bourgeois, and corrupt – was captured by the expressionist paintings and grotesque caricatures of George Grosz, creator of an image of Berlin that reverberated in Fritz Lang's futurist film *Metropolis*, released in that city in 1926. The documentary *Berlin: Die Sinfonie der Großstadt* (Berlin: Symphony of a Metropolis, 1927), which reported on one day in the life of the capital, enjoyed broad popularity. In 1929 Alfred Döblin's novel *Berlin Alexanderplatz* was published. It depicted the tawdry life of an insignificant man amidst the dynamism of the metropolis. The year 1939 saw the publication of Christopher Isherwood's novel *Farewell to Berlin*, in which the city figured as the capital of modern homosexual culture. Thus Berlin took its place alongside the Dublin of James Joyce's *Ulysses* (1922) and the New York of John Dos Passos's *Manhattan Transfer* (1925) among the urban topoi of modernity.

By 1920 the population of Berlin had reached 3.8 million and the city had become the largest industrial centre in Europe. It continued to be a focus of the socialist and workers' movements, and after the Treaty of Rapallo (1922) political, economic, and cultural ties between Germany and the USSR grew in intensity. Visits to Berlin by Soviet writers were a feature of the period; they took on the character of cultural missions representing the Soviet Union.

Ukraine, too, experienced deep changes in the 1920s. In 1925–8 a vigorous debate took place on the pages of literary and cultural journals. Known as the

"Literary Discussion," the polemics polarized the Ukrainian literary sphere. On one side of the debate were advocates of a new socialist culture characterized by works of high aesthetic merit and oriented towards classical and Western European traditions. The key spokesman of this view was the prose writer Mykola Khvyl'ovyi, master of the art of the polemical pamphlet and inspirer of the literary grouping Vil'na Akademiia Proletars'koï Literatury (Free Academy of Proletarian Art) or Vaplite. Khvyl'ovyi's adversaries claimed closer adherence to Communist Party orthodoxy and emphasized the function of literature and the arts in transforming society.[1] The Literary Discussion raised numerous fundamental questions: on the nature of modernity and the cultural orientations most likely to advance it in Ukraine, on the new art, on the turn towards mass culture under the auspices of the "Red Enlightenment" and the Proletkult, on the dependence of Ukrainian culture upon the Russian, and on the influence of ideology upon culture. Mykola Khvyl'ovyi advocated following the path of Western humanist culture and emulating Western artistic forms and models of development. In doing so he turned away from the traditional populist model of Ukrainian culture, insisting that Ukrainian literature modernize itself by appropriating the achievements of Western culture. These he saw as resulting from a particular conjuncture of cultural and anthropological factors that he labelled "psychological Europe." For Khvyl'ovyi the opposite of "psychological Europe" was "Prosvita," a concept that he based on the name of a nineteenth-century Ukrainian movement for the cultural advancement of ordinary people. In Khvyl'ovyi's usage Prosvita symbolized lowbrow provincial culture on the one hand, and an orientation towards the low-grade mass art promoted by the Proletkult movement on the other. The Discussion, which began as a polemic concerning literature, soon acquired a political dimension (Joseph Stalin himself intervened in it). It ended in political denunciations and the forced self-abolition of Vaplite, one of the most important literary organizations of the period and one in which Khvyl'ovyi played a leading role.

The Literary Discussion unfolded in the context of the idea of the demise of Western culture that the German thinker Oswald Spengler (who called this culture "Faustian") had advanced in his *Decline of the West* (1918, 1922). The publication of the second volume of this work in 1922 gave rise to wide-ranging discussions in Soviet Russia,[2] where it also reignited interest in Nikolai Danilevskii's *Rossiia i Evropa* (Russia and Europe, 1869). Spengler's ideas and elements of Danilevskii's theories played a role in the development of Khvyl'ovyi's concept of a "psychological Europe," which was of considerable importance for the theory of modernity that emerged in Ukraine in the 1920s. Khvyl'ovyi formulated two of his key arguments using the Spenglerian idea of the decline of Western (European) culture as his starting point. First, according to the Ukrainian writer, the West having descended into decay and inertia, its rejuvenation would commence in Asia. This renascence would come about under the banners of a new proletarian culture advancing from the East – from a new province of Europe, of which Khvyl'ovyi considered Ukraine to be a part. Spengler, in setting up his opposition between province and world-city, had given priority to the province, regarding it as the culturally productive element of the two. For him the city and its civilization embodied the collapse of the organic spirit in culture. Khvyl'ovyi, announcing a new phase of cultural history, dubbed it the "Asiatic Renaissance." He compared himself to the activists of the eighteenth-century "Sturm und Drang" movement who saw in antiquity and the Renaissance models for the rejuvenation of their own German culture. "Dialectics instructs us to be torchbearers for the light of Asia," he asserted, "while orientating ourselves toward the grandiose achievements of the European past."[3]

Second, according to Khvyl'ovyi, the new Renaissance could not draw inspiration from the bourgeois art of the contemporary West – of France, for example. (He called Romain Rolland, Henri Barbusse, and Georges Duhamel "epigones of the bourgeois cycle.")[4] Khvyl'ovyi also rejected the aspect of Western culture that he associated with "German clumsiness": it had shaped Ivan Franko, the doyen of Western Ukrainian intellectuals of an earlier generation, but was comical and outdated in an epoch of modernity with its frenetic tempos and rhythms. In a letter to the critic Mykola Zerov Khvyl'ovyi celebrated "the nation that only now, in the twentieth century, has decided to regenerate itself and whose spirit – *and this is important*! – if it resembles anything at all, resembles that of the Romanic peoples" (emphasis in the original).[5] The "spirit of the Romanic peoples," which Khvyl'ovyi associated with the new art, was suitable for the foundations of a new proletarian culture, the creation of a social class – the proletariat; the Romanic, or Romanesque, style represented a symbiosis of the culture of the Roman West and the Byzantine East and embodied the civilizing potential of Christianity as it spread over the lands of the Germanic tribes. At the same time Khvyl'ovyi praised the Faustian spirit of Western culture that Spengler believed to be grounded in a "culture of the will." Khvyl'ovyi directly associated it with a metahistorical psychological phenomenon, the "civic person," which he saw as the product of many centuries and the common property of all social classes.[6] Thus Khvyl'ovyi entered the historiosophical discussion about the nature of Western culture. The anticolonial import of his position was clear: he sought the uncoupling of Ukrainian culture from the Russian, as his slogan, "Away from Moscow!," proclaimed.

By the beginning of 1928 the Literary Discussion was practically over, and the ideas of Europeanism and modernity had acquired a distinctly political coloration. But it was precisely in 1928 and 1929 that Valerian Pidmohyl'nyi, Viktor Domontovych, and Iurii Ianovs'kyi published novels that echoed the recent debates about the Ukrainian path to modernity and Europe. These developments were in no small measure due to the authors' direct personal acquaintance with Western Europe, acquired through journeys to Germany and, above all, Berlin. The experience of Berlin intensified the theme of urbanism in the Ukrainian authors' works while also fuelling their polemical reception of Western culture. Even devotees of "psychological Europe" were forced to modify their visions as they encountered Western culture first-hand, articulating their desire not only to identify themselves with it but also to underscore its differences from the culture of Ukraine. Oleksandr Dovzhenko, for example, who spent some years in Berlin as an official in the Soviet consulate, reached the conclusion that while European culture was not without interest, it was in Ukraine that a new cultural essence was coming into being. "Capitalist Europe," he claimed in 1926, "has nothing but artistic technique behind it, while behind us there is a social revolution."[7]

The object of my analysis, then, is the topos of Berlin that appears to Ukrainian writers of the 1920s as a place of different modernities.

Berlin and Vienna: Types of Modernity

Travelling to the West was a common activity among Ukrainian literati of the 1920s. In 1928 the journal *Hart* (The Tempering) reported that "Comrades Volodymyr Koriak, Ivan Le, Arkadii Liubchenko, Oleksandr Kopylenko, Valerian Polishchuk and Valerian Pidmohyl'nyi have already left for Berlin [...] Of the Kharkivites, Serhii Pylypenko and Mykhail' Semenko have yet to depart. All of them are headed for Western Europe."[8] The trip was to embrace Paris, Berlin, and Prague. Mykola Khvyl'ovyi had visited Germany and Austria somewhat earlier – between December 1927 and March 1928. In December 1928, in the prologue to the first issue of the almanac *Literaturnyi iarmarok* (Literary Fair), Khvyl'ovyi made reference to "our distinguished tourists Arkadii Liubchenko and Valerian Pidmohyl'nyi, as well as Oleksandr Kopylenko" who "send us their warmest greetings from that self-same Berlin and hint broadly at some kind of travel notes of theirs."[9] Khvyl'ovyi himself had written to Zerov in May 1925 as he prepared to travel to Germany, "I am laying the ground for my trip abroad. Europe, by the way, is unlikely to impress me: not having seen it, I hate it already and imagine it as a dull little grey blot."[10] In another letter to Zerov of the same year Khvyl'ovyi revealed the grounds for this antipathy towards Europe: the Europe "with which we are madly in love" was, above all, an ideal metahistorical image of a cultural metropolis generated out of a contrast to the Ukrainian provincial culture born of the tradition of populism.[11] For Khvyl'ovyi the personification of populist cultural provincialism was a character in a story by Volodymyr Vynnychenko, "The Entrepreneur Harkun-Zadunais'kyi" (1903), whom Khvyl'ovyi depicted as the antithesis of the Western cultural type: "Isn't it the case that we are forced with unspeakable pain to drag out the shameful figure of Harkun and to place it, if only for the sake of contrast, alongside the Europe with which we are madly in love?"[12]

Khvyl'ovyi's arrival in Europe changed these perceptions. The romantic ideal of Europe was displaced by a Europe materialized and real. In December 1927 Khvyl'ovyi wrote to Arkadii Liubchenko that "Europe wants to have them [members of Vaplite] here for two or three months. There are things here that are worth seeing. Berlin, where I have been for a few days now, proves this."[13] Khvyl'ovyi also recommended that his colleagues prepare an itinerary for their trip and soon wrote from Vienna that "Germany is definitely a place worth visiting."[14]

These remarks were in keeping with the contrast that later, having returned from the West, he would draw between Vienna and Berlin in his prologue to *Literaturnyi iarmarok*. In the 1920s the two cities embodied different versions of modernity and were often regarded as complementing one another.[15] As Frank Trommler asserts, "Vienna between 1900 and 1945 was constantly mentioned as the other pole of German culture, the serene and history-laden antidote to the center of power and progress to the north."[16] Berlin connoted the new urban modernity with its increasingly frenetic life, industrialization, burgeoning mass culture, and brutal energy, while Vienna was associated with the comforts of the Old World and embodied the melancholy sedateness of the fin de siècle. Robert Musil would invoke this opposition in his novel *Der Mann ohne Eigenschaften* (The Man Without Qualities, 1931–2) by counterposing Habsburg Austria to Wilhelminian Germany. Khvyl'ovyi contrasted the two European cities to demonstrate the difference between the new urban sensibility of Berlin and its Viennese counterpart that brought to his mind the Alps, the Danube, city parks, the Prater, and seductive images of Viennese women. For Khvyl'ovyi Vienna was a cheerful, playful city, while Berlin presented itself to him through the prism not of the urban culture that in fact was evolving there in the 1920s but of stolid Prussian architecture. Khvyl'ovyi used images of Berlin and Vienna when writing of the various cultural styles, both modern and traditional, in the Kharkiv of his day. He inscribed his city into the cultural landscape of the West when he associated Kharkiv's dynamic constructivism with Vienna and its classicism with Berlin. Furthermore, the European cities served to shape the model of modern national culture he wanted to develop: "The Southern Railways

Building (next to the railway station) is forbidding Berlin, while the Industry Building is beautiful faraway Vienna," he observed.[17] The remark rejected the modern classicist style of the Southern Railways offices, built in 1912–14 to the plans of Oleksandr Dmitriiev, and welcomed the constructivist skyscraper of the Industry Building that had just been completed in 1928.

This contraposition was not accidental. There was something akin to tenderness in Khvyl'ovyi's attitude to Vienna, despite his view that Vienna was "nevertheless a province, compared to Berlin."[18] It was the festive Vienna fair with its "motley crowd of cheerful, good-natured people," the Prater fairground, carousels, fantastic horses, Gypsies, and all kinds of "proletarian entertainments" that Khvyl'ovyi – and, he thought, Ukrainians generally – found culturally engaging: "it is, if you like, the 'Sorochyntsi' invention of our tragic countryman, Nikolai Vasil'evich Hohol'."

Weighing up Vienna and Berlin, Khvyl'ovyi gave his preference to Vienna, choosing the Vienna fair as a topos that expressed modernity in terms of human leisure, entertainment, and communication, not of the market and trade. This view was symptomatic of the way in which Ukrainian writers of the first part of the twentieth century apprehended modern Europe. In 1927 the critic and philosopher Volodymyr Iurynets', analysing Khvyl'ovyi's works, remarked that the latter "had no understanding of the 'essence' of the present-day city or of its real poetry. For him the city was not a centre of work, but a pretext for Romantic dreams."[19] In Iurynets's opinion, this reflected the general immaturity of the Ukrainian intelligentsia, which "in reality lives by the 'village,' though it has made sermonizing about the 'city' and 'urbanism' the mission of its life."[20] In fact, however, Khvyl'ovyi's preference for fairground Vienna after his journey to the cultural capitals of Europe was a preference for a particular kind of modernity – humane, anti-urbanist, and close to nature – that echoed Spengler's disdain for technology.

Berlin as Cityscape: The Essayistic Reception

The main tasks set by the Communist Party for Ukrainian writers travelling to Berlin at the end of the 1920s were social critique of the bourgeois West and representation of the Land of the Soviets. What was expected of them was the setting up of oppositions between socialist ideas and bourgeois realities. Accordingly, Soviet Ukrainian writers projected two images of Berlin: one as a socially alien bourgeois city, the other as the proletarian city of "those who build and invent, those who make possible great radio exhibitions, those who organize demonstrations and shoot from barricades."[21] There was also criticism of the so-called "bourgeois nationalist émigrés" who lived in Berlin, notably in the cycle "Vyshnevi usmishky zakordonni" (Vyshnia's Smiles from Abroad) by Ostap Vyshnia, who spent a few months in a sanatorium near Berlin.

In his reflections on the nation Lenin had advanced the notion that in every national culture there are elements that are democratic and socialist, and others that are bourgeois.[22] Adopting this concept of two cultures, the Soviet Ukrainian writers who travelled to Berlin represented it as a socially split city. All of them – avant-gardists, modernists, and populists alike – concentrated their attention in the first instance on the ideologically alien nature of Berlin as a "bourgeois" city. But they also managed to see facets of Berlin that fell outside this general frame and they revealed in their writing other aspects of the life of the large modern European city that Berlin had become in the 1920s. In June 1928 Ostap Vyshnia wrote with irony that, "having arrived in a large European city our compatriot endeavors at the earliest opportunity to observe the disintegration of the bourgeoisie [...] So please understand us, travelers in foreign lands that we are: we are very keen to see the final moments, the last agonies, the death throes of the class enemy."[23]

In his collection *Rozkol Evropy* (The Division of Europe, 1925), the avant-gardist Valerian Polishchuk called Germany the "country of the policeman's boot," but at the same time reported the existence of two Berlins: a daytime Berlin, "heavy and official," "grim and dark grey,"[24] and a Berlin of the night, "glittering with electric suns reflected from the asphalt, flooded with the breathless stream of advertising lights."[25] Advertisements, movie theatres, movement ("the trains of the city railway and the underground, trams, buses and cars are in constant motion; and only after midnight, when all of this stops, do the ancient horse-drawn carriages come creeping out"), asphalt glittering like black parquetry and reflecting the street lamps "like ice at night-time" – all this comes together for him to create a very favourable image of Berlin life. Yet another side of Berlin represents bourgeois modernity and mass culture: Polishchuk remarks on "bourgeois movies with virtuous queens and tender maidens that give themselves up for free to officer heroes."[26] The city looks decadent, and Polishchuk mentions as attributes of this decadence imitations of popular American shows, prostitution, homosexuality, the chauvinism of fascist sport, and student corporations.[27] Mykola Khvyl'ovyi for his part remarked on the absence of ideology evident in Berlin that, he believed, signalled an undermining of Western culture. Observing the Berlin revues with their jazz bands and foxtrots and detecting in them a new Western theatrical genre, he remarked that such revues had transformed the theatre of the West into a "cozy hideaway for the pathological heroes of a George Grosz."[28]

Another traveller to Berlin was the editor of the journal *Chervonyi shliakh* (The Red Path) Ievhen Cherniak, whose view of the West was more sympathetic. In his travel essay "Lysty z dorohy" (Letters from a Journey) of November 1928 he pictured the topography of German culture as monolithic, with cultural centres located close to one another: "there is no sense of that awful yearning to escape from the village or town to the city, to the big cultural center."[29] Such homogeneity was a characteristic trait of the German variant of Western culture, Cherniak thought, implicitly contrasting it to the clash of city and country that were among the themes favoured by Ukrainian writers of the 1920s, in particular Valerian Pidmohyl'nyi in his novel *Misto* (The City, 1928). Another feature of German culture for Cherniak, and one that he remarked upon repeatedly, was the moderation of the German bourgeois: the German bourgeois "does not go to extremes, unlike his French counterpart. As a cynic he is moderate, and his improprieties, too, are moderate – in a word, he indulges in debauchery but at the same time wants to remain the respectable father of his family."[30]

Observing the social, cultural, and anthropological features of Germany, Cherniak described this foreign land with undisguised curiosity. Taken together, details like the mirror-clean Berlin asphalt, the many motorcars, the shopping, the businesslike tone of the city, the cafes "in which the Berliner spends most of his life," the advertising that "impresses with its colossal magnitude, raucousness and wit," the movie theatres (he calls them "temples of art") that are "swathed from their very entrances with luxurious carpets and tropical flowers that remind one of the orangery in an old gentry estate"[31] – all of this creates for him the image of a polyphonic and sublime urban space. But just as the Berlin described by Cherniak possesses the traits of a soft-spoken and attractive bourgeois modernity, there is at the same time another Berlin that expresses a modernity that is eccentric. In particular it is the nocturnal Berlin that becomes a topos of excess. Cherniak, like his compatriots, was particularly drawn to this Berlin of the night, site of the city's "private life." It was at night that, as the narrator confesses, "together with the writer Kh. [obviously, Khvyl'ovyi] we set off to get to know Berlin" or, more precisely, the Berlin of the "nocturnal stock exchange of prostitutes, cocaine and morphine users and other pathological folk."[32] All in all, notwithstanding their attention to political events and their reportages on workers' lives and their demonstrations, the Ukrainian literati were attracted to the private life of the city. Cherniak wrote of Berlin's nightlife at the casino, where the public is entertained by an "effeminate man or manlike woman"; the heavily made-up beauties behind bars that sell alcohol and immediately help drink it; the cocottes and exotic solo dancers; the inevitable jazz band; and above all the so-called "plastic arts" of sixteen-year-old girls. Cherniak's interest in Berlin's bohemian life did not go unremarked in official circles and, as Viktor Petrov reported, "in 1932 Ievhen Cherniak was expelled from the Party and subsequently arrested for his book of impressions of his trip abroad."[33]

Oleksandr Kopylenko created an almost expressionist image of Berlin in his essay "Dva Berliny" (Two Berlins), published in *Literaturnyi iarmarok* in February 1929. This image emphasized the dual nature of the city hidden beneath its "tranquil, vegetative middle-class existence."[34] Kopylenko notes the unreality of this "modern panopticon of capitalism" where "colossal over-consumption" exists hand in hand with "incredible advertising," shop windows exercise a hypnotic effect, and female mannequins in the finest attire contemplate people through their "dead eyes."[35] What makes Berlin a "demented city," according to Kopylenko, is the resemblance of its denizens to characters in an operetta and the fact that their world is a domain of imitation. The living and the dead are inseparable in this modern city, where "the dead eyes of mannequins neither see nor understand how much they are envied by the living eyes of impoverished German women who stare at the diverse articles of clothing draped over dead forms made of papier-mâché."[36] As Kopylenko ironically notes, the artificial nature of European culture is metaphorically expressed by the beggar who masks his naked body with a shirtfront in the same way as he masks his unemployment by selling matches, pins, and other commodities. The doubly masked nature of the city is reflected in the hypocrisy that compels "a man with a hungry glint in his eyes" to wear a "collar, pressed trousers and a jacket that promises before your very eyes to disintegrate into rags."[37] This duality is a sign of the artificiality of Berlin, where the external attributes of prosperity have the quality of stage sets and where the beggar has the vitrine of a jeweler's shop for a backdrop.

In Kopylenko's interpretation Berlin is an agglomeration of the dead and the living, the artificial and the natural; it exists between artificially inflamed demand and excessive supply. The city is hallucinogenic: it is created by "explosions of lights, paints, and colors, curving flashes and the blaze of electric waterfalls."[38] All of the Ukrainians writing about Berlin mention the special delight that they derive from the streets and automobiles. Thus cars "glide along the asphalt," or a car speeds "along pure, shining ice, its shadow racing in pursuit, reflected in the depths of a road surface that is transparent as glass."[39] Beer halls and cafes with their quarts of beer, the music of their jazz bands, and their foxtrot melodies that "spill out in hysterical, hoarse wails like those of sirens"[40] supplement this image of the modern European city.

In general, Berlin is for Kopylenko the antithesis of naturalness. It is a place where appearance and essence do not coincide. He misses no opportunity to underscore the difference between the urban and the rural, so important in Ukrainian culture at the time: over Berlin, "somewhere above," he

observes a "scarcely perceptible full moon and a sky of no use to anyone
[...] In the glare of electricity and amidst the battle of the advertisements
these indispensable accessories of the rural landscape seem here to be a sort
of anachronism."[41]

These and other travel notes from Berlin shaped the image of the city and
of urban culture for many Ukrainian writers, while also confirming for them
Spengler's contention that Western culture lacks organicity and that its demise
has commenced in the cities. In addition, these essays introduced the new
chronotope of the trip abroad into the structure of the Ukrainian urban novel.
The trip to Europe became an important trope in many Ukrainian novels and
stories of the 1920s, helping expand the field of ambivalence of Ukrainian
prose, where observation of the symptoms of Western urban modernity, and
their transposition to Ukrainian soil, went hand in hand with a rejection of what
were regarded as the bourgeois attributes of Western culture. These latter were
conceived of in the spirit of George Grosz's caricatures of his "pathological
heroes," to which reference was made in Viktor Domontovych's *Divchyna z
vedmedykom* (Girl with a Teddy-Bear, 1928), the essays of Valerian Polishchuk, Vynnychenko's *Soniachna mashyna* (The Solar Machine, 1928), and
Khvyl'ovyi's pamphlet *"Zolote cherevo" iak vykhid z repertuarnoho tupyka*
(*The Golden Belly* as a Way Out of the Repertoire's Dead End). There emerged
also the parodic travel account of the journey to the West, which, as Mykhailo
Mohylians'kyi ironically pointed out, included "in the first place an acquaintance with 'dubious institutions,' visits to which in recent years have marked the
beginning of familiarity with European culture for some Ukrainian authors."[42]
Likewise Maik Iohansen in his ironic novel *Podorozh uchenoho doktora Leonardo i ioho maibutn'oï kokhanky prekrasnoï Al'chesty u slobozhans'ku Shvaitsariiu* (Journey of the Learned Doctor Leonardo and His Future Beloved the
Beauteous Alcestis to the Switzerland of Slobozhanshchyna), the first part of
which was published in 1928, regretted that some Ukrainian travellers "only
know how to tell us about the bathroom furnishings in German hotels, the
lunches that can be had in Paris, the dress code of lackeys in London and the
voracity of bed-bugs in the hotels of Spain."[43]

Berlin as a Model City: Its Reception in Literature

Nonetheless, for many writers, the Futurists in particular, Berlin personified
technological modernity itself – the locus where the past joined battle with the
future. These are the terms in which Mykhail' Semenko spoke of Berlin upon
his return from a trip to Europe in the poem "Alt Berlin," where the "dark
cellars, slums and crumbling houses" of old Berlin are contrasted to the new

image of the "giant octopus." Berlin "hums, rid of its museified ruins, it clatters, thunders and stinks of gasoline":

Тисячолітній alt-Берлін, підрівняний, підстрижений, під-
перезаний широкими просторами сучасних будівель
                              вулиць, –
місто-велетень змітає і зрівнює, підпирається монументальними
палацами, Домами, брамами, міліонними пам'ятниками, –
чи не є вже й вони зараз мертвим минулим, що лише
давить землю, – історичним музеєм
перед життєрадісним світлом майбутнього.[44]

(Thousand-year-old alt-Berlin, leveled out, trimmed, gird-
ed with broad expanses of streets full of modern
                              buildings,
the giant city sweeps away and levels out, it leans on immense
palaces, cathedrals, gates, millions of monuments,
are not even they already the dead past that only
chokes the earth, a historical museum
in front of the vital light of the future.)

It is important to note that, in describing Berlin, Ukrainian writers involved themselves in the discussion over "psychological Europe." On the one hand they enthused over the urbanized and dynamic Berlin that symbolized modern Europe, on the other they could not desist from contrasting Western culture and Ukrainian tradition. A paradox arose: while in theory they appealed to the Faustian spirit of Europe, Ukrainian writers voiced a conviction about the otherness and even foreignness of the contemporary West for Ukraine. In other words, going to the West, Ukrainian writers yearned to see their ideals manifested there, but when confronted with the actual realities of modern technological and urban European civilization they found themselves preferring the naturalness and rusticity that for them were the dominant features of Ukrainian national culture.

The travels of Ukrainian writers to the West familiarized them with different variants of modernity represented in the Europe of their day by various cultural metropolises, above all Berlin and Vienna. At the same time their encounter with the West activated their quest for their own modernity – a modernity appropriate to the social, national, and ideological coordinates of their time and place, and to their own national traditions. This exploration is exemplified in Mykhailo Mohylians'kyi's novel *Chest'* (Honour), written in 1929 but not published until 1990, which entered into a discussion with authors who had reported on their trips to Europe. The novel relates the story of a main character, the surgeon Dmytro Kalin, who departs for an extended period of scientific training in Berlin but is constantly homesick for Kyiv. The novel ironically idealizes the "native land" and venerates naturalness as opposed to European urbanism and technology. In the protagonist's mind the natural, not the urbanistic, features of Berlin awaken associations with Kyiv, causing him nostalgically to reflect that "in Kyiv you walk out of Great Pidval'na Street onto Volodymyrs'ka, you look to the right, and your eye dashes out to the fields:

O Fields, O ye Fields,
You are our native land!"[45]

The petit bourgeois European Berlin, the narrator points out in *Chest'*, is alien to Kalin. In the end, he can find something of his own only in the Berlin Tiergarten, or perhaps, as the protagonist puts it, it was "just a hint at something of 'his own.'"[46] In Berlin "for a long time he could find nothing of his own, nothing individual. The city was altogether deliberate, invented, rich in bourgeois comforts and bourgeois vulgarity [...] rather fussy and unpleasantly raucous."[47] It is no coincidence that Kalin's prevalent mood becomes "exultation at the thought that he would be returning home."[48]

It is worth noting that 1928 and 1929 saw an extensive discussion on the theme of the city that was ignited by the appearance of Valerian Pidmohyl'nyi's novel *Misto*.[49] Berlin impressions added substance to the discussion of Ukrainian urbanism and its social content. Mohylians'kyi, in particular, was critical of Pidmohyl'nyi's novel because, as he saw it, it failed to raise social issues and because it contained no "Kyiv, no modern Kyiv, a city with a capital letter, just as it contains no real contraposition of city and village."[50]

The idea of the novel *Chest'* corresponded to the stance that Mohylians'kyi adopted in the discussion of 1925–8 on "Europe" and "Prosvita." While accepting the topicality of the contraposition, he claimed that Khvyl'ovyi "was far from suggesting that one should borrow or appropriate in bulk everything 'European.'"[51] At the same time Mohylians'kyi subjected Ukrainian populism to moderate critique, in many respects agreeing with Khvyl'ovyi's. Similar moderation is to be observed in *Chest'*, where the author undertakes a revision of the European chronotope, notably that of Berlin, contrasting it to the romantic organicism of semirustic Kyiv.

A character from Domontovych's novel *Divchyna z vedmedykom*, Ipolit Varets'kyi, is also sent on a mission to Berlin, where the final part of the novel is set.[52] This ending, unexpected and artificial, can be explained as a commentary on the trips of Ukrainian writers abroad. The plot is as follows: Varets'kyi, a Soviet engineer, falls in love with Zyna, a nymphet with a teddy bear. In protest against bourgeois marriage, Zyna, who symbolizes the spirit of unfettered modern behaviour, has a liaison with a yard keeper and vanishes from view, departing for Germany. Varets'kyi, too, goes abroad. In a fancy cafe-restaurant where "all Berlin" is gathered, he witnesses a quarrel between a highly paid red-haired prostitute and a typical German bourgeois, and the prostitute's subsequent suicide. Upon returning home Varets'kyi learns that the prostitute was Zyna.

From the very beginning, Domontovych stresses the alienation of his character from Berlin: "I am a stranger here and I am indifferent. I observe"; "I dislike this restaurant romance, as I dislike much else in today's Berlin."[53] The description of the cafe-restaurant contains details familiar from Ukrainian writers' depictions of Berlin:[54] noise, jazz band music, made-up women, the odor of perfumes, grimacing tuxedoes, and "those many faceless men whom George Grosz paints in frock-coats with collars and ties but with no heads."[55]

The author's choice of an ending in Berlin may have been random, but it can be seen as polemical, in that it is an instance of the play with implausibility to which the novel refers: "Zyna yearned to displace from love everything that was merely similar to love but was not love itself and, disregarding the plausible, sought to attain the outermost limits of the implausible. And then she became helplessly entangled in the implausible, and it destroyed her."[56] "Implausibility," which can be achieved through the suspension of contingencies and bourgeois prejudices, emerges as one of the novel's main ideas. True love, however, is achieved neither in Kyiv, where it is merely part of a novel about production, industrialization, and the life of engineers, nor in Berlin, where it becomes an episode in a melodramatic bourgeois novel. It seems that Domontovych used the Berlin text as a deus ex machina in order to suggest that Zyna's extravagance and playfulness, which in the novel signify the essence of modernity itself, are well suited to the perverse modern West but alien to Ukrainian patriarchal culture.

Thus Domontovych, whose 1920s contributions to the genres of the romantic novel and the fictionalized biography raised the ire not only of proletarian critics but of Khvyl'ovyi himself, introduced into Soviet Ukraine – provocatively – a genre popular in the West: melodrama. Yet Domontovych's novel of romance also entailed a dimension of cultural philosophy and intervened in the discussion of Ukrainian modernity. Central to this dimension of the novel was Machiavelli's text *Il Principe* (The Prince), which plays a role both in the novel's Berlin episode and in an event narrated as occurring in Kyiv. The idea that connects them is that of "clement cruelty," presented in Domontovych's novel as an embodiment of a new ethics. Varets'kyi, who has bought a folio of Machiavelli's *Il Principe* in Berlin, identifies himself in a dream with the innocent Messire Rimino who was assassinated by the syphilitic Cesare Borgia in the name of clement cruelty. The Kyiv episode concerns Mykola Buts'kyi, who murders his beloved wife to set her free from the suffering caused by poverty and unemployment in an act also analogous to Borgia's clement cruelty. Such acts appear in Domontovych's novel as markers of a new age in which "love, mercy, and cruelty … are relative concepts."[57] Thus Domontovych, a writer oriented towards the West, uses the mask of melodrama to discuss the capacity of Ukrainian culture to accept the idea of the "implausible" that, like "clement cruelty,"[58] underscores the relative nature of the visible and real that is the key to Western modernity.

In his conception of modernity Domontovych implicitly opposes Khvyl'ovyi's thesis of an "Asiatic Renaissance." Domontovych brings modern Berlin, Renaissance Florence, and the Kyiv of the 1920s together into a metahistorical reality. He sees European modernity as a form of consciousness that transcends historical epochs, not as a continuous unfolding of a will to life, as proposed by Khvyl'ovyi. In the end, for his conception of Europe he turns not to the Faust-like public personality that Khvyl'ovyi favours, nor to a Nietzschean vitalism inspired by "a spirit of joy and cult of earthly beauty,"[59] but to Machiavellian voluntarism.

Berlin: Reactive and Constructive Receptions

Domontovych was the pseudonym that the philologist Viktor Petrov adopted as a writer. As Petrov he had earlier introduced Ukrainian intellectuals to his "reactive" approach concerning the question of Europe. In 1926 he published in the journal *Zhyttia i revoliutsiia* (Life and Revolution) an article analysing the Western journey of Panteleimon Kulish. For many writers of the 1920s Kulish, the author of Ukraine's first historical novel in the spirit of Walter Scott, the translator of Shakespeare, and an energetic cultural activist, was an embodiment of a Western orientation in Ukrainian letters. Khvyl'ovyi, for example, thought that "as far as the ideal of a revolutionary and a citizen is concerned, one can find none greater than Pan'ko Kulish. He alone, I think, shines like a beacon from the darkness of the Ukrainian past. He alone can be regarded as a real European, as a person approximating the type of the Western intellectual […] Kulish was, in essence, the ideologue of a strong 'third estate.'"[60] Analysing Kulish's journey to Europe, Petrov (Domontovych) argued that Kulish's Westernizing tendencies were not as active or as absolute as they seemed to Khvyl'ovyi, and that his attitude to the "third estate" was problematic. Kulish's journey was driven neither by touristic nor aesthetic motives but by his interest in social themes. Petrov pointed out that Kulish was deeply interested in the contrast between the wild Ukrainian villages of Volyn' and the civilization of Berlin. But at the same time he experienced a strong sense of disappointment with members of the European middle classes, whom he called "arithmetic people," and their "petty loathsome bourgeois existence."[61] Thus, Kulish's journey to Europe and, in particular, Berlin, according to Petrov, intensified his commitment to anti-urbanistic, rural, and populist ideals. "The journey abroad is a kind of reagent" for Kulish, Petrov claimed; "in Ukraine Kulish felt himself to be a European, a city person [...] But here, among Europeans, amidst the bustle and roar of the great cities he realized that he was a *khutorianyn* [a farmsteader], a man in love with the village."[62]

Petrov's article about Kulish's European journey sheds light on the reception of the West that we encounter among Ukrainian writers of the 1920s and that I term "reactive." Having seen the real West, they found there neither a "psychological Europe," nor the Faustian spirit that they hoped would characterize a future Ukraine. They present themselves as Westerners mostly at home, in Ukraine; in the West they are farmsteaders.

It should be noted that the *reactive* reception coexists with its *constructive* counterpart. Ukrainian authors borrow the urbanist attributes of Berlin and superimpose them over Ukrainian realities, or they make references to Berlin as a megalopolis of contemporary modernity without naming it. This strategy is especially noticeable when Berlin figures as an empty sign, a symbol. Valerian Pidmohyl'nyi, one the writers who went abroad in 1928, had in the same year (even before his journey) published his novel *Misto,* which, as Khvyl'ovyi noted, "even the Germans found interesting."[63] A second edition followed in 1929. Since the novel was written before Pidmohyl'nyi's trip to Europe, it contains no reference to any Berlin experiences. Indeed, Pidmohyl'nyi left no memoirs or notes about his visit to Berlin at all. Perhaps one of the reasons for this was the fact that in 1923 he had been obliged to offer excuses for the publication of his works in the émigré publishing house "Nova Ukraïna" (New Ukraine), based in Prague and Berlin. What is certain is that Pidmohyl'nyi wrote nothing about his journey to Berlin in 1928, but did write about his trip to Moscow in 1929.[64]

From the very beginning the critics were divided in their assessment of *Misto,* and in the middle of 1929 Mykhailo Mohylians'kyi criticized it sharply in his article "Ni sela, ni mista" (Neither City Nor Village). Yet the new edition of the novel in 1929 after Pidmohyl'nyi's return from abroad confirmed that the author had held to his views, and that some of his reactions to Kyiv as a modern city, the "insatiable city"[65] that must be both hated and loved, could only have been intensified by his impressions of Berlin. The same is true of the erotically charged atmosphere of a modern city that Pidmohyl'nyi conjured up in his descriptions of Kyiv.

Berlin is also a shadowy presence in Iurii Ianovs'kyi's expressionist novel *Maister korablia* (Ship's Master, 1928). Like many other Ukrainian writers, Ianovs'kyi had not been to Berlin, but he could not omit mentioning it, and introduced it elliptically in connection with the travel of one of his female characters, the ballet dancer Taiakh, to Europe. Taiakh, who symbolizes the erotic and passionate East, writes from Genoa and Milano to a friend in Ukraine of meeting a man, an Italian, who personifies for her, in almost Spenglerian terms, the ancient ideal of beauty. The next point in Taiakh's travels was to have been Berlin. But this part of the journey never appears in the novel, delineating a vacuum that is by no means accidental given the role of fragmentation and montage in the novel's structure. An Italian (Renaissance) ideal is thus asserted in the novel, but that of Berlin remains an unrealized possibility – a background before which unfolds an image of Ukrainian life.

Nonetheless, there is a perceptible German trace in the novel, impregnated as it is with Nietzsche's neo-romantic symbolism. *Maister korablia* appeals to the image of modern Europe that Nietzsche had seen in the combination of ancient myth and the Berlin text.

Conclusions

The reception of the Berlin text in Ukrainian literature at the end of the 1920s, after the visits of several authors to Berlin, was part of the debate concerning Europeanism and urbanism in Ukrainian culture. Travel essays about the journey to Berlin become a pre-text for the development of urban imagery in the works of Ukrainian authors. In the novel *Dveri v den'* (A Door into the Daytime, 1929), for example, Geo Shkurupii creates the ironic and expressionist image of a jazz band, as though translating it from Berlin into a Kharkiv beer hall: "The jazz band, set swinging by the astringent sounds of saxophones, cymbals and drum, executed passionate contortions as it loomed in a corner of the hall, obscured by clouds of cigarette smoke. Afflicted with fever, it trembled and shook. Afflicted with gout, it tottered on its feeble, thin legs, its catlike wailing and mewing penetrating through to the bustling life of the street."[66]

A key figure in discussions concerning the new urbanism was Volodymyr Vynnychenko, who lived in Berlin in the 1920s and set the action of his *Soniachna mashyna* (1921–4) in Berlin as well. Soviet Ukrainian critics of the 1920s criticized this futurological novel for its lack of urban atmosphere and its depiction of Berlin as somewhat rural.[67] In fact, however, the novel was overtly expressionistic and structured to produce a grotesque defamiliarization of bourgeois Berlin as a monster city. Vynnychenko uses the technique of montage to insert snippets of the modern city into the novel and has recourse in his descriptions to the visual images of Berlin created by the expressionists and Dadaists: there are "well-like streets" (*kolodiazi-vulytsi*) where "a rabid wind races, wild-maned, overheated, all lather and sweat"; where the sky is "yellow-grey, sulfurous, its eyes ghastly, dilated, feral";[68] and where "in the cafes and restaurants at the bottom of immeasurably deep streets, in the damp corners of bars steam rises from hot, sweaty clumps of human bodies."[69] The Berlin of Vynnychenko, on the one hand, is expressionistic and resonates with Lang's *Metropolis*, shot four years after Vynnychenko's novel was completed. On the other hand, the writer counterposes a stone-dead Berlin to the kingdom of "the Great Mother": nature, the sun, grass, sexual instincts, and a newly invented magic elixir, solar bread. This opposition of the urban and the rustic became an unconscious template for subsequent Ukrainian writers. It was applied in different ways, however: adherents to the reactive reception employed Vynnychenko's template to trump the civilization of the West with the organicism and simplicity of rustic Ukraine, whereas representatives of a more imitative reception strove to reimagine the Ukrainian city along Western urbanist lines, but were insufficiently versed in urban culture to do so effectively, as Iurynets' pointed out in his critique of Khvyl'ovyi.

The reception of Berlin throughout the 1920s was directly connected to the overarching situation in Ukrainian culture. Mykola Khvyl'ovyi advocated catching up with Europe and adopting the Western "ideal of the civic person." Mykola Zerov spoke of Europe as a "school of culture" and a "symbol of cultural tradition" that could help raise the level of the arts in Ukraine. Looking to Europe, Ukrainian writers hoped to find a connection to the source of Western modernity. In whatever way, Europe existed in the ideas and consciousness of the Ukrainian cultural elite as an ideal metacultural and metasocial category. The travels of Ukrainian writers abroad played a significant role in rendering this category more precise. Their impressions of Berlin as a Western cultural metropolis helped sharpen their cultural and psychological image of Europe. Europe presented itself to them in two perspectives – one "civilizational," the other "cultural" – and many Ukrainian authors apprehended the civilizational, technological image of modern Berlin as alien. Nonetheless, the desire for a natural, semirural environment that some Ukrainian writers found congenial and hoped to rediscover in Berlin did not translate into a socialization of the rustic image of Ukrainian culture that had been traditional for nineteenth-century populists and was now associated with "Prosvita." One might rather say that the encounter with Europe reinforced the inclination of Ukrainian writers to seek a national and cultural identity of their own. In this quest they simultaneously experienced their closeness to and yet difference from the West. Their images of different Berlins laid out a broad, dynamic, and multi-faceted paradigm supporting multidirectional cultural quests for ideas of self and other. Charged with exporting the socialist idea to the West, Ukrainian authors laboured under ideological constraints. Yet they were able to use the experience of their westward journeys to subvert the ideologized notions of what was "one's own" and what was "alien" in the Ukrainian literature of the 1920s, and to erect a protective shield against the monologism of the Soviet literature of the 1930s.

Notes

1 For an account of the Literary Discussion see Myroslaw Shkandrij, *Modernists, Marxists and the Nation: The Literary Discussion in Ukraine During the 1920s* (Edmonton: Canadian Institute of Ukrainian Studies, 1992).

2 See, for example, the collection *Osval'd Shpengler i zakat Evropy* (Moscow: Bereg, 1922).

3 Mykola Khvyl'ovyi, "Ukraïna chy Malorosiia?" in *Tvory u dvokh tomakh* (Kyiv: Dnipro, 1991), 2: 576–621, here 619. On the orientalist dimensions of Khvyl'ovyi's theory see Tamara Hundorova, "Melankholiia po dorozi v Rym, abo Dyskurs ukraïns'koho oktsydentalizmu," in *Ievropeis'ka melankholiia: Dyskurs ukraïns'koho oktsydentalizmu*, ed. Tamara Hundorova (Kyiv: Stylos, 2008), 13–18.

4 Khvyl'ovyi, "Lysty do Mykoly Zerova," *Tvory u dvokh tomakh* 2: 840–81, here 865.

5 Ibid.

6 Khvyl'ovyi, "Dumky proty techiï," *Tvory u dvokh tomakh*, 2: 444–514, here 467.

7 Oleksandr Dovzhenko, "Do problemy obrazotvorchoho mystetstva," in *Vaplitians'kyi zbirnyk*, ed. Iurii Luts'kyi [G. S. N. Luckyj], 2nd ed. (Oakville, Ontario: Mosaic Press, 1977), 173.

8 H.D., "Nashi pys'mennyky za kordonom," *Hart* 12 (1928): 97.

9 Mykola Khvyl'ovyi, "Proloh do knyhy sto trydtsiat' pershoï," *Tvory u dvokh tomakh*, 2: 697–703, here 699–700.

10 Mykola Khvyl'ovyi, "Lysty do Mykoly Zerova," *Tvory u dvokh tomakh*, 2: 855.

11 Ibid., 861.

12 Ibid.

13 Mykola Khvyl'ovyi, "Lysty do Arkadiia Liubchenka," *Tvory u dvokh tomakh*, 2: 882–4, here 882.

14 Ibid., 884.

358   Tamara Hundorova

15 See Julius Bab and Willy Handl, *Wien und Berlin: Vergleichende Kulturgeschichte der beiden deutschen Hauptstädte* (Berlin: Deutsche Buch-Gemeinschaft, 1926).

16 Frank Trommler, "Berlin and Vienna: Reassessing Their Relationship in German Culture," *German Politics and Society* 23, no. 74 (2005): 11.

17 Mykola Khvyl'ovyi. "Proloh do knyhy sto trydtsiat" pershoï,' *Tvory u dvokh tomakh*, 2: 700.

18 Ibid.

19 Volodymyr Iurynets', "M. Khvyl'ovyi iak prozaïk," in Khvyl'ovyi, *Tvory v piat'okh tomakh* (New York: Smoloskyp, 1986), 5: 415–38, here 436.

20 Ibid.

21 Valerian Polishchuk, "V kraïni politseis'koho chobota," in *Rozkol Evropy: Khudozhn'o-sotsial'ni ta pobutovi narysy* (Kharkiv: Knyhospilka, 1925), 18.

22 V.I. Lenin, "Critical Reflections on the National Question" [1913], *Collected Works*, vol. 20 (Moscow: Progress Publishers, 1972), esp. "National Culture," 23–6. See also Peter Kenez, "Lenin's Concept of Culture," *History of European Ideas* 11 (1989): 359–63.

23 Ostap Vyshnia. "Rozklad burzhuaziï," in *Tvory v semy tomakh* (Kyiv: Derzhavne vydavnytstvo khudozhn'oï literatury, 1963–4), 4: 213.

24 Valerian Polishchuk, "V kraïni politseis'koho chobota," 12–3.

25 Ibid., 13.

26 Ibid.

27 Ibid., 15.

28 Mykola Khvyl'ovyi. "'Zolote cherevo' iak vykhid iz repertuarnoho tupyka," *Tvory u dvokh tomakh*, 2: 625.

29 Ievhen Cherniak, "Lysty z dorohy (Nimechchyna)," *Zhyttia i revoliutsiia* 11 (1928): 154.

30 Ibid., 160.

31 Ibid., 164.

32 Ibid., 167.

33 Viktor Petrov, "Ukraïns'ki kul'turni diiachi URSR – zhertvy bol'shevyts'koho teroru," *Mystets'ka storinka*, http://storinka-m.kiev.ua/article.php?id=264 (accessed on 5 October 2011).

34 Ol[eksandr] Kopylenko. "Dva Berliny (Uryvky vrazhen')," *Literaturnyi iarmarok* 3, no. 133 (1929): 204.

35 Ibid., 206.

36 Ibid.

37 Ibid., 213.

38 Ibid., 205.

39 Ibid., 208.

40 Ibid., 211.

41 Ibid., 215.

42 Mykhailo Mohylians'kyi, "Chest': Roman patetychno-ironichnyi," *Vitchyzna* 1 (1990): 121.

43 Maik Iohansen, "Podorozh uchenoho doktora Leonardo i ioho maibutn'oï kokhanky prekrasnoï Al'chesty u zlobozhans'ku Shvaitsariiu," in *Vybrani tvory*, 2nd rev. ed. (Kyiv: Smoloskyp, 2009), 392–3.

44 Mykhail' Semenko, "Alt-Berlin," *Chervonyi shliakh* 4–6 (1929): 5.

45 Mohylians'kyi, *Chest'*, 127.

46 Ibid.

47 Ibid.

48 Ibid., 128.

49 See V. Mel'nyk, "Na perekhresti mista i sela," *Slovo i chas* 11 (1990): 23–33.

50 M. Mohylians'kyi, "Ni mista, ni sela: z pryvodu romanu V. Pidmohyl'noho 'Misto,'" *Chervonyi shliakh* 5–6 (1929): 274.

51 See Natalia Shumylo, "'Zhyttia liuds'ke – khram, a ne morh!' Pro roman Mykhaila Mohylians'koho," *Vitchyzna* 1 (1990): 88.

52 One of Ostap Vyshnia's short stories in the cycle "Vyshnevi usmishky zakordonni," "Iak pereïkhaty mytnytsiu" (How to Pass Through Customs), mentions a teddy bear souvenir bought in Berlin: "I'm traversing the vast distance from Berlin to Kharkiv, and I don't have the right to take a bear with me?! [...] So what am I supposed to do – travel just like that, without a bear to play with? What sort of trip is that?" (Vyshnia, *Tvory v semy tomakh*, 4: 239). One can conjecture that this passage might have been the source for the connection between Berlin and the girl with a teddy bear in Domontovych's novel.

53 Viktor Domontovych, *Divchyna z vedmedykom* (Kyiv: Krytyka, 2000), 171–2.

54 See, especially, Vyshnia's "Rozklad burzhuaziï" (Disintegration of the Bourgeoisie): "In Berlin, for example, at practically each step on practically every street you'll see either a dance café or a dance bar or a dance restaurant, where the bourgeoisie dances to the tones of a jazz band day and night, their bodies, fat and thin, interwoven with one another" (Vyshnia, *Tvory v semy tomakh*, 4: 213).

55 Domontovych, *Divchyna z vedmedykom*, 173.

56 Ibid., 177.

57 Ibid., 163.

58 Ibid.

59 Ibid.

60 Mykola Khvyl'ovyi, "Dumky proty techiï," *Tvory u dvokh tomakh*, 2: 473.

61 Viktor Petrov, "Khutorianstvo i Evropa (Lysty Kulisha z-za kordonu r[oku] 1858," *Zhyttia i revoliutsiia* 7 (1926): 74.

62 Ibid., 78.

63 Mykola Khvyl'ovyi, "Proloh do knyhy sto trydtsiat' pershoï," *Tvory u dvokh tomakh*, 2: 700.

64 "Iednannia radians'kykh literatur: pys'mennyky pro podorozh do Moskvy," *Proletars'ka pravda*, 28 February 1929, 5.

65 Valerian Pidmohyl'nyi, *Misto* (Kyiv: Molod', 1989), 40.

66 Geo Shkurupii, "Dveri v den'," in *Dveri v den'* (Kyiv: Radians'kyi pys'mennyk, 1968), 21.

67 Oleksandr Bilets'kyi, in particular, noted the farmstead-like ambience of Vynnychenko's Berlin. Bilets'kyi, "*Soniachna mashyna* V. Vynnychenka," *Krytyka* 2 (1928): 31–43.

68 Volodymyr Vynnychenko, *Soniachna mashyna* (Kyiv: Dnipro, 1989), 187.

69 Ibid., 217.

Between Cultural Memory and Trauma: An Interpretation of Mykola Khvyl'ovyi's "My Being"

ALEXANDER KRATOCHVIL

There is necessity for remembering the horror, but of course there's necessity for remembering it in a manner in which it can be digested, in a manner in which the memory is not destructive. The act of writing the book, in a way, is a way of confronting it and making it possible to remember.[1]

The title of this article with its two juxtaposed terms, memory and trauma, indicates a certain tension. It is the tension between two different states of mind that may be involved in remembering the past. Memory is a selective process, a conscious recollection of past events and their meaningful construction into a narrative. Trauma, on the other hand, implies the impossibility of conscious recall of a traumatizing event and the inability to integrate that event into a meaningful order. To simplify, one could say that trauma begins where memory ends. This boundary is the setting of Khvyl'ovyi's famous story; it is a place where the literary exploration and representation of the "horror" of traumatic experience and its impacts takes place, much in the way that the epigraph from Toni Morrison suggests. I shall explore Khvyl'ovyi's story as a case study of the capacity of literature to handle the tension between memory and trauma, between representation of the unspeakable and the construction of a meaningful narrative.

In Mykola Khvyl'ovyi's story "Ia (Romantyka)" (My Being),[2] first published in 1924 in a collection of short stories titled *Osin'* (Autumn), the narrator, a member of the Cheka, tells us about events in a small town during the short period of rule by a revolutionary Bolshevik tribunal of which he is a member. It is the time of the so-called Civil War with governments changing and power shifting between Bolsheviks, the Ukrainian National Republic, monarchists (Vrangel' and Denikin), and anarchists (Makhno). The action takes place in

Central or Eastern Ukraine. In the course of the narration the reader is confronted with the characters' different reactions to the violent circumstances and
cruelties of War Communism. This multiperspective focus is presented and
commented upon by the first-person narrator, whose own action in this violent
situation is at the centre of the story. The cruelty of warfare is echoed by his
inner struggles and the turmoil in his psyche. His tragedy culminates when he
shoots his own mother in the name of the ideals of the revolution.

   The killing of the mother can be interpreted as a symbolic turning point in
the self-awareness of individuals and society during the war or its aftermath.
It may mean the loss of pre-war certainties and the coming of an entirely new
organization of social and individual life. The First World War and the revolutions that followed constituted such a turning point; they were also an experience common to most of Europe. The war and revolutions across Europe have
been described as inserting a "gap" into history: "The sense of a gap in history
that the war engendered became a commonplace in imaginative literature of
the post-war years. Poets and novelists rendered it in images of a radical emptiness – a chasm, or an abyss, or an edge – or in images of fragmentation and
ruin, all expressing a fracture in time and space that separated the present from
the past."[3]

   Separation from the past was felt as a collapse of values. The link to concepts of pre-war identity was destroyed. That is why European writers of the
1920s often spoke of the lost generation of the war. In his work on novels about
the First World War Samuel Hynes states: "A generation of innocent young
men, their heads full of high abstractions like Honour, Glory and England,
went off to war to make the world safe for democracy. They were slaughtered in stupid battles planned by stupid generals. Those who survived were
shocked, disillusioned and embittered by their war experiences."[4] The members of that generation (including, often, the writers themselves) were highly
sceptical and had no more illusions about the romantic ideals they fought for.
In Erich Maria Remarque's novel *Im Westen nichts Neues* (All Quiet on the
Western Front, 1929) the narrator complains of the loss of cultural memory on
a grand scale: "How senseless is everything that can ever be written, done, or
thought, when such things are possible. It must be all lies and of no account
when the culture of a thousand years could not prevent this stream of blood
being poured out."[5] One could quote many passages from European literature
of the 1920s that give voice to similar viewpoints. Consequently, writers often
looked for alternative approaches to life. Studies of literature about the First
World War frequently examine the ways in which authors sought to integrate
the experience of war into new sociocultural frames. Such studies, exemplified
especially by work on German and British First World War literature, often

focus upon the ideological aspects of literary texts – conservative, nationalist, communist, democratic, pacifist, and even utopian – and their implications for cultural memory. Such works try to make sense, at least to a certain extent, of the apparently senseless and traumatizing events of war and revolution by integrating them into what Paul Fussel calls a "modern memory."[6] Telling examples of such "ideological" interpretations, in addition to *All Quiet on the Western Front*, are Ernst Jünger's very different "modern memory project" *In Stahlgewittern* (The Storm of Steel, 1920), or, in the Soviet context, Aleksandr Serafimovich's *Zheleznyi potok* (The Iron Flood, 1924), Isaac Babel's *Konarmiia* (Red Cavalry, 1926), and, last but not least, such Ukrainian prose works as Iurii Ianovs'kyi's *Vershnyky* (The Riders, 1935) or Khvyl'ovyi's "My Being."

Literature about warfare can be read in the context of "modern memory," but it is, as well, a literary processing of traumatizing events and their effects upon individuals and societies. "Modern memory," based as it was on a privileged concept of the Self, on rationality and totalizing metanarratives, deconstructed itself through its internal contradictions. These emerged particularly in the context of the mechanized slaughter of the First World War and its traumatizing impact. The imagination of such writers as Jünger responded to this by attempting to reconstruct the assumptions of "modern memory" in texts that are often described as "modernist." Notwithstanding Jünger's attempts to keep to the assumptions of modernity, his texts show considerable instability and evoke a sense of absurdity that persistently undermines his attempts to interpret the war through the prism of a "classical modern memory." John King notes that "*In Stahlgewittern* was intended to be a 'monumental history' with [Jünger] himself as heroic subject but failed to contain the deconstructive energy of the war."[7]

These prose works undermine ideological paradigms and are more frameless in cultural terms than readings of them generally concede. Jünger's writings about the First World War reflect his experiences over years of combat service at the front line. Writing against this background of intense personal war experience, he suggests a new approach to inner life, a new "Being." In the preface to the 1929 English edition of *The Storm of Steel*, Jünger stated that "time only strengthens my conviction that it was a good and strenuous life, and that the war, for all its destructiveness, was an incomparable schooling of the heart."[8] Here Jünger points to the problematic impact of war on the human psyche. Recently published studies of Jünger's writing on the First World War show that his prose reconstructed the war as a phantasmagorical, retrospective, and self-determined adventure, but that at the same time its traumatizing elements, captured in detailed realistic descriptions, reveal the inhumanity and mechanization of war slaughter. Jünger's prose combines the trauma perspective with phantasmagorical and stunning symbolic encoding – offering a special mode of insight and perception that undermines plain ideological interpretations.[9]

Similar phenomena are to be found in Khvyl'ovyi's stories about war. If we assume that war experiences have traumatizing – serious and disturbing – impacts on self-awareness and world perception, we can read this kind of prose as an attempt to represent the unrepresentable of the narrator's experience. The narrators of such stories reveal their distrust of reality through unconventional rhetoric and fragmented plot sequences; they break up coherent narrative, introduce cyclical forms of narration, and use expressive and unusual metaphors. This rhetoric constitutes a literary mode that questions a cultural memory seriously damaged by traumatic experience. Literature, the literary imagination, and the mimesis of memory that it is able to generate contribute a great deal to the representation of the otherwise unrepresentable. Such a mimesis of memory or, more precisely, mimesis of reconstructing memory through narration we find in Khvyl'ovyi's story "My Being."

Before analysing "My Being" as a trauma narrative I shall outline some conceptual considerations regarding the study of literary accounts of trauma. The investigation of trauma commenced at the end of the nineteenth century in the work of, among others, Jean-Martin Charcot, Josef Breuer, and especially Sigmund Freud, who created trauma as a concept of mind. This concept captures the fragmentation of understanding and the disorientation that followed the First World War as a discourse about the "other side" of modernity. That discourse has inspired writers of fiction no less than scientists. The problem of how to remember and narrate in literature a painful and even horrible past has been crucial throughout the twentieth century (and continues to be so in the twenty-first). Trauma studies, especially those concerning the Holocaust, point to the problematic nature of literary accounts of traumatizing events.[10] In trauma studies there is no consensus on how one might evaluate the literary representation of trauma because there is a strong sense that direct testimony is the only appropriate mode of trauma narration. Theodor Adorno's dictum that "to write poetry after Auschwitz is barbaric" is symptomatic of the suspicion with which literary accounts of traumatic events and human catastrophes have been viewed. Literary texts are sometimes suspected of diminishing and trivializing traumatic events. Yet, while Adorno's dictum was often seen to place a ban on literary representation of the Holocaust, Adorno himself later conceded that "it is now virtually in art alone that suffering can still find its own voices, consolation, without immediately being betrayed by it."[11]

Critics of literary and even non-fictional accounts have argued that fictional devices such as the construction of chronology, characterization, or a directive narrative voice interfere with testimony and, furthermore, that such literary testimonies as Aleksandr Solzhenitsyn's *Arkhipelag GULAG* (The Gulag Archipelago, 1973) or Andrei Siniavskii's *Golos iz khora* (A Voice From the Chorus, 1976) rationalize or reinterpret traumatic events after the fact, philosophizing about death, for example, or universalizing personal experience. The crucial difference between testimony and literary narration, as Lawrence Langer points out, is that witnesses of trauma experience do not feel a sense of agency analogous to that of an author who is in control of a narrative: "Writing about Holocaust *literature*, or even written memoirs [...] challenge[s] the imagination through the mediation of a text, raising issues of style and form and tone and figurative language that [...] can deflect our attention from the 'dreadful familiarity' of the event itself" (emphasis in the original).[12] Other critiques point to the fact that trauma survivors' experience resists normal chronological narration and normal modes of artistic representation: traumatized individuals live in durational or cyclical rather than chronological time, continuing to experience the horrors of the past through internal shifts back in time and space instead of perceiving the past as differentiated from the present.

Such observations about trauma narration made in the context of social science and psychology provide important suggestions for investigations into literary narratives. I use the term "trauma experience" here as a category whose meaning resembles the one it has in psychology. Trauma experiences destabilize our sense of reality and challenge the model of our world perception. Literary texts may internalize the uncertainties of traumatic experience through a refusal of sense-making narration. Traumatic narration may embody many obstacles to communicating such experience through formal devices: silence, simultaneous knowledge and denial, dissociation of personality, break-up of time and space relations, resistance, and repression. These devices reflect a growing awareness of the effects of historical cataclysms on the individual psyche.

Telling examples of such writing may be found in the works of Mykola Khvyl'ovyi and other Ukrainian writers of the 1920s who put war, revolution, and their consequences at the centre of their oeuvre.[13] In "My Being" the killing of the mother should be read as a symbolic representation, not as the account of a real event, as has on occasion been the case in the past (and sometimes still happens). According to George Grabowicz's interpretation of the story the narrator is split into different roles or masks. These masks – the Lenin-like inhuman ideologist Dr. Tahabat; the so-called "degenerate," a sadistic guard of the revolution; and the humane but weak-willed Andriusha – participate in the narrator's inner struggle, his own inner revolutionary tribunal. Grabowicz considers that "in 'Ia (Romantyka)' role and role playing are revealed as internal psychic processes, and the whole is indeed recast as a psychodrama."[14]

The reading of the text as a psychodrama opens the way to different interpretations, one of them being the reading of the story as a trauma narrative where the plot is a projection of the inner dissociation of the narrator – as evident, for example, in the following fragment, in which the members of the revolutionary tribunal are to sign a death warrant, but one of them has doubts:

> But Andriy strides nervously back and forth, trying to speak up. I know what he is thinking about: he wants to say that this isn't honest, that communists don't do such things, that this is an orgy, etc., etc.
>
> Ah, what a strange person he is, this communist Andriy! But when Dr. Tahabat threw the empty bottle on the velvet rug and signed his name very legibly under the verdict:
>
> "to be shot"
>
> all of a sudden I was seized by despair. This man, with a wide forehead and white bald skull, with his cold reasoning and a stone in place of his heart – he was my lord whom I could not escape. He was my animal instinct. And I, the chairman of the black tribunal of communism – I was a puppet in his hands, obeying the desires of the fierce animal.
>
> "But where is the solution?"
>
> – Where is the solution? – I could see no solution. (121)

Another actor with a role in the psychodrama is the narrator's mother, a highly symbolic and multifunctional figure in the narrator's inner world who at one point is even idealized as an archetype: Mary the Mother.

"My Being" not only constitutes a psychologically interesting depiction of the dissociation of a personality but also manifests a symbolic mode of narration that has opened the way for different interpretations of the story over the decades since its publication. From the perspective of an inquiry into trauma narration, literary symbolism functions as a pointer to the unspeakable of trauma. The literary symbol, in pointing beyond itself, is an ideal vehicle for the communication of trauma. It links the specific to the general, the individual experience to cultural and aesthetic knowledge.

From a post-structuralist viewpoint symbolic knowledge is neither about words nor about things but about the memory of words and things, about its own archaeology, as Foucault might have put it. It is knowledge about knowledge. Ronald Granofsky states in his study of contemporary British, American, and Canadian trauma novels that this knowledge is "a meta-encyclopaedia of symbolism" and "an effective and appropriate literary mode to deal with collective trauma."[15] He stresses the connection between an emotional (rather than rational) response to experience, on the one hand, and the utility of literary symbolism in dealing with that response, on the other.

The symbolic mode of trauma narration points to the link between individual experience and cultural memory. It also supports the development of an experimental narrative when new information resists assimilation into memory. This process corresponds with the dissociation of the personality illustrated in the passage quoted above. The following illustrates even more clearly the representation of schizophrenia through symbolic encoding:

> So I, confused, assure myself that this isn't true, that there is no mother in front of me, that this is nothing more than a phantom.
>
> – Phantom? and I jump up again.
>
> No, this is just what is wrong! Here, in this silent room, my mother is not a phantom, but a part of my own criminal being which was set free by me. Here in this dark corner, on the edge of the city, I hide a part of my soul away from the guillotine.
>
> And then I, like an animal in a wild fit, close my eyes and, like a male animal in the springtime, choking, I whisper:
>
> "Who cares about the details of my inner experiences?"
>
> I am a real communist. Who dares to say otherwise? Don't I have the right to rest for a while?
>
> The votive lamp in front of the Virgin's icon burns dimly. In front of it my worried mother stands like a statue. But I stop thinking. My head is caressed by a peaceful, blue dream. (125)

The reader gets a sense of the traumatizing process that is taking place in the psyche of the narrator. If at the beginning of the story the Virgin Mary was a prophet of a better world ("Out of the distant mist, out of the quiet lakes of untouchable communism ... the Virgin Mary is walking"), in the course of the narration this mother seems to become a phantom or a ghost, something that the narrator's mind can no longer grasp. The phantom or ghost as a metaphor for traumatic reenactment is, by curious coincidence, a figure of speech not uncommon in reflections upon trauma, whether in literature (e.g., in Toni Morrison's *Beloved* [1987], Kurt Vonnegut's *Slaughterhouse Five* [1969], or Isabel Allende's *The House of the Spirits* [1982]) or in scholarly texts.[16]

Like the phantom, the metaphorical representation of something as existing, yet haunting, is an expressive symbolic encoding that alludes to romantic iconology: communism is a "blue dream," while the commune is an imagined place far away beyond the mountains, that is to say, in another world. There are other evocations of standard romantic symbols in "My Being." The colour blue, in particular, refers to the blue flower, a central symbol in romanticism (and in Khvyl'ovyi's stories until the mid-1920s).[17] The blue flower stands for desire, love, and metaphysical intuition. There is a connection with the religious symbols of the Virgin Mary: she is not only the prophet of the commune, the personification of a better time (communism) and place (commune), but also a source of confidence, reliability, and safety. When the mother turns into a phantom or ghost, the dream of a better future becomes a nightmare and "the soul lies under the guillotine."

In the centre of this trauma narration is a search for identity in a modernist sense. It is no accident that "My Being" carries a dedication to Mykhailo Kotsiubyns'kyi's story "Tsvit iabluni" (Apple Blossom, 1902), a story about the dissociated psyche of a writer watching his young daughter die and recording his dissociation through stream-of-consciousness writing. This dedication, alluding to what Renate Lachmann might have called a "memory of the literary,"[18] places Khvyl'ovyi's text into an intertextual relationship with an earlier self-reflective quest for a modern(ist) metanarrative. In this context Khvyl'ovyi's narrator tries to get to the bottom of the metanarrative of "communism." He challenges it with a critical mind because it has turned into a nightmare – but he cannot dismiss it.

The narrator's stream of consciousness places the reader in the middle of a narration that wanders among the shifting levels of the narrator's self and marks his efforts to establish anew an order for himself and the world surrounding him, to close the gap in his modern memory. But the individual trauma of the first-person narrator has a social dimension as well. The narrator's "masks" (Dr. Tahabat, Andriusha, the "degenerate") can be read as projections of society. According to Kai Erikson, the damaged collective organism of a traumatized society can be described in the same way as the damaged body of an individual;[19] "trauma is never simply one's own," states Cathy Caruth.[20]

I have a whole mob of nuns behind my back! Yes, I have to hurry: the cellars are full up.

I turn around, determined and ready to say the inexorable:

"Shoot them!" ...

but as I turn around, I see – just before my eyes – my mother, my suffering mother, with her eyes of the Virgin Mary.

I jumped aside in consternation: what is this? Hallucination? I jumped aside in consternation and shouted:

"You?"

Out of the crowd I can hear the sorrowful:

"My son! My rebellious son!"

I feel that I am going to faint any minute. I feel dizzy, I grabbed the back of the chair and stooped toward the ground.

But at this moment a wave of laughter burst toward the ceiling and disappeared. This is Dr. Tahabat.

– "Mama?!" Oh, you lousy bastard! "You want pee-pee? Mama?!"

I took hold of myself and grabbed my gun.

"The hell with you!" – and I jumped at the doctor.

But he looked at me calmly and said:

"Steady, steady, you traitor to communism! Why don't you do with your 'mom' (and he distinctly said 'mom') what you did with the others?"

I turned around silently. (133)

While individual trauma occurs as a deep invasive impact upon the psyche, "collective trauma can be defined as blow to the basic structures of social life that destroys the bonds between people and damages the sense of communality."[21] So the narrator's trauma affects not only his inner world but also his relations to the outer world. The narrator feels highly vulnerable and realizes that the outer world, too, is no longer an effective source of protection for him. He will lose his mother and his revolutionary "brothers in arms," Dr. Tahabat and Andriusha. He is in danger of losing the structuring confidence of his "Being."

In the passage above we have the breakthrough of the traumatic event. The defining characteristic of a traumatic event is its capacity to provoke fear, helplessness, or horror in response to the threat of injury or death. This breakthrough is overwhelming, alien, and destructive. The trauma narration reaches its climax. The narrator becomes aware of the dilemma of his traumatic experience: he is caught between, on the one hand, pressure to complete the process of knowing about the catastrophic outcome of his revolutionary "blue" dream, which has turned into a nightmare and, on the other, the powerlessness and fear that prevent him from doing so.

... I was stupefied. Pale, almost dead, I stood in front of the crowd of nuns, confused and derided. (I could see myself in the huge mirror hanging in front of me.)

... Yes! – they have finally gotten hold of the other part of my soul!

I shall never hide myself again like a criminal in the suburbs of the city! I have only one right left:

– *not to say anything to anybody about how "My Being" was split in two.* (133; emphasis in the original)

After the disintegration of the narrator's personality ("how 'My Being' was split in two"), the trauma narration reveals the problem of retelling and re-experiencing traumatic events. The leftovers of a meaningful world are destroyed, and the narrator suffers from an inability to engage in traumatic re-en-actment ("not to say anything to anybody"). The distorted Self even refuses to save the mother for fear of continually re-experiencing his trauma (through the disintegration of his revolutionary trust and therefore of his self-confidence). Trauma narratives in general reveal the tension of renarrating and thus re-experiencing traumatic events. We find this in Khvyl'ovyi's story as well:

> – I, the chairman of the black tribunal of communism, was carrying out the duties entrusted to me by the revolution.
> … Was it my fault, then, that the image of my mother did not leave me that night, not for one moment?
> Was it my fault? (135)

The narrator tries to come to terms with the devastating experience that has destroyed his "blue" romantic dream and put into question his personal safety and mental health.

We are guided through the narrative by the disorientation and conflicts of the narrator's traumatized mind. His mind is explored through affective and unconscious associations, and so it comes as no surprise that the way to re-establish order and the narrative of the distant blue commune beyond the mountains is to blow this mind out with a bullet, symbolically encoded in the killing of his mother, Maria. Let us quote the relevant passage in extenso:

> But what is this, a hallucination? All of a sudden I heard a voice. Is it the voice of my mother?
> And again I know that I am a contemptible person, and there is an unpleasant feeling inside my breast. And I did not want to cry, but just to shed my tears, as in my childhood, on somebody's warm chest.
> Then I burst out:
> "Am I going to have her shot?
> What is this: reality or a dream?"
> But this was reality: true reality of life – fierce and ravenous, like a pack of hungry wolves. This was reality without solution, inescapable like death itself.
> … But maybe this is a mistake?
> Maybe I should not do it? [...]
> I hold my gun in my hand, but my hand grows weak, and I have a feeling that I will start crying soon, as in my childhood, on somebody's warm chest. I want to shout:

– Mother! Come here, I tell you! I have to kill you.

And my brain is being sliced by the sorrowful voice. I can hear again my mother say that I (her rebellious son) have tired myself out completely. [...]

The flowers became brighter. Storm was approaching. The enemy attacked. The insurgents are retreating.

... Then I, not knowing what I was doing, seized by a strange fit of happiness, put my arm around my mother's neck and pressed her head to my chest. Then I brought my gun to her temple and pulled the trigger.

She leaned on me like a cut stalk of grain. I put her on the ground and looked around in consternation. (141–5)

The quotation shows the impact of trauma on the structure of the narration. The narrator reflects on his state of mind ("I know that I am a contemptible person"); the reiteration of the traumatizing event ("'Am I going to have her shot? What is this: reality or a dream?' But this was reality: true reality") is manifested in the repetition of the motifs of the mother and of her killing. The vocabulary changes from detailed description ("put my arm around my mother's neck and pressed her head to my chest. Then I brought my gun to her temple and pulled the trigger") to expressions that evoke a blurred mind, fuzzy perceptions, and the loss of memory.

The killing of the mother presents the strongest symbol of a world thrown out of joint by warfare. The effects are traumatized individuals and societies. Stories about them across Europe often portray madness as the ultimate sanity in a mad world. In "My Being" trauma is not directly negated; the narration reproduces the effects of trauma in order to take the individual, or a collective, beyond them. Literary accounts of trauma are able to call for the investigation of the human consequences of sociocultural constellations and historical events and their impact on interactions between the public and private sphere, the political and the psychological, and on the process of constructing identities and building memories.

In exploring connections between individual and collective trauma, literature has an advantage over social science and history in that it can develop experimental narratives of how trauma affects individuals and collectives. In this way trauma narrative is a significant mode of representing the past, the identity, and the memory of a collective. Such media as literature and film play an important role in this process of memory building. They not only problematize and undermine existing historical narratives and political frames but construct a European sphere of transnational and transcultural memory.

At a time of competing and even mutually contradictory interpretations of memories in Central and Eastern Europe, trauma narratives offer a complementary "Europeanness," transforming loss into cultural memory – not memory as a European metamemory of "memorialization," but rather a memory that narrates the traumatized and repressed experiences of what have been called the European "Bloodlands."[22] Reflection upon, and recognition of, traumatic events enriches collective memory and amplifies the notion of a "European identity" in whose construction trauma narratives can play an important part.

Notes

1 Danielle Taylor-Guthrie, ed., *Conversations with Toni Morrison* (Jackson, MS: University Press of Mississippi, 1994), 247–8.
2 The title "Ia (Romantyka)" might be translated as "I (A Romantic Tale)." In the following, the title adopted in the published English translation will be used: Mykola Khvyl'ovyi, "My Being," trans. George Tarnawsky, in *Modern Ukrainian Short Stories*, ed. George S. N. Luckyj (Littleton, CO: Ukrainian Academic Press, 1973), 115–45. Page numbers in parentheses refer to the text of this edition.
3 Samuel Lynn Hynes, *A War Imagined: The First World War and English Culture* (New York: Atheneum, 1991), xi.
4 Ibid., x.
5 Erich Maria Remarque, *All Quiet on the Western Front*, trans. A. W. Wheen (London: G. P. Putnam's Sons, 1929), 286–7.
6 Paul Fussel, *The Great War and Modern Memory* (New York: Oxford University Press, 1975); Astrid Erll, *Gedächtnisromane: Literatur über den Ersten Weltkrieg als Medium englischer und deutscher Erinnerungskulturen in den 1920er Jahren* (Trier: Wissenschaftlicher Verlag Trier, 2003) contains an extensive bibliography on this topic.
7 John Edward Joseph King, "Writing and Rewriting the First World War: Ernst Jünger and the Crisis of the Conservative Imagination, 1914–25" (PhD diss., Oxford, 1999), 2.
8 Ernst Jünger, *The Storm of Steel* (London: Chatto and Windus, 1929), xii.
9 See, for example, Klaus Gauger, *Krieger, Arbeiter, Waldgänger, Anarch: Das kriegerische Frühwerk Ernst Jüngers* (Frankfurt am Main: Lang, 1997) and Michael Gnädinger, *Zwischen Trauma und Traum: Ernst Jüngers Frühwerk* (Frankfurt am Main: Lang, 2003).
10 See Shoshana Felman and Dori Laub, *Testimony: Crises of Witnessing in Literature, Psychoanalysis and History* (New York: Routledge, 1991).
11 Theodor W. Adorno, "Commitment," in *Aesthetics and Politics*, ed. Ronald Taylor (New York: Verso, 1980), 177–95, here 188.
12 Lawrence Langer, *Testimonies: The Ruins of Memory* (New Haven, CT: Yale University Press, 1993), xii–xiii.

13 Other stories by Khvyl'ovyi involving traumatized memories include *Povist'pro santoriinu zonu* (Novel about the Sanatorium Zone, 1924) and "Redaktor Kark" ("Editor Kark," 1923).

14 George Grabowicz, "Symbolic Autobiography in the Prose of Mykola Khvyl'ovyi (Some Preliminary Observations)," in *Cultures and Nations of Central and Eastern Europe: Essays in Honor of Roman Szporluk*, ed. Zvi Gitelman et al. (Cambridge, MA: Harvard Ukrainian Research Institute, 2000), 173.

15 Ronald Granofsky, *The Trauma Novel: Contemporary Symbolic Depictions of Collective Disaster* (New York: Lang, 1995), 6.

16 See, for example, Manfred Weinberg, "Trauma – Geschichte, Gespenst, Literatur und Gedächtnis," in *Trauma: Zwischen Psychoanalyse und kulturellem Deutungsmuster*, ed. Elisabeth Brönfen, Birgit R. Erdle and Sigrid Weigel (Cologne: Böhlau, 1999), 173–207.

17 The title of Khvy'lovyi's first book of short stories was *Syni etiudy* (Blue Etudes, 1923).

18 See Renate Lachmann, *Gedächtnis und Literatur: Intertextualität in der russischen Moderne* (Frankfurt am Main: Suhrkamp, 1990).

19 Kai Erikson, "Notes on Trauma and Community," in *Trauma: Explorations in Memory*, ed. Cathy Caruth (Baltimore, MD: Johns Hopkins University Press, 1995), 188.

20 Cathy Caruth, *Unclaimed Experience: Trauma, Narrative, and History* (Baltimore, MD: Johns Hopkins University Press, 1996), 24; see also 15.

21 Valentina Adami, *Trauma Studies and Literature: Martin Amis's Time's Arrow as Trauma Fiction* (New York: Lang, 2008), 15.

22 Timothy Snyder, *Bloodlands: Europe between Hitler and Stalin* (New York: Basic Books, 2010).

Literaturnyi iarmarok: Mediation between Nativist Tradition and Western Culture

HALYNA HRYN

In late 1928 a new periodical appeared on the literary scene in Kharkiv. Sporting a brightly coloured constructivist cover of Anatol' Petryts'kyi's design, it declared itself an unaligned monthly almanac, a forum where literary wares of all artistic currents would be displayed and sampled. The name chosen was *Literaturnyi iarmarok* (Literary Fair), an image laden with local, national, and metaphoric meaning: it drew on the carefree ambience of Gogol's *Sorochinskaia iarmarka* (Sorochyntsi Fair, 1832), set in the neighbouring Poltava region, and of native son Kvitka-Osnovianenko's *Saldats'kyi patret* (The Soldier's Portrait, 1833). Instead of editorials the first issue featured commentaries called *intermedia*, in which characters such as Herring in a Barrel (*Oseledets' Vbochtsi*), Gypsy with a Whip (*Tsyhan z batizhkom*), Golden Rooster with a Blue Cape Draped over His Shoulder (*Zolotyi pivnyk u synii svyttsi naopashky*), and the melancholic Little Grey Demon Zanuda (*Siryi chortyk Zanuda*; literally, "whiner") offered opinions on the literary works and on events of the day. It was the brainchild of Mykola Khvyl'ovyi and Maik Iohansen and the new mouthpiece of the reorganized literary group known formerly as VAPLITE (*Vil'na Akademiia Proletars'koï Literatury* – Free Academy of Proletarian Literature).[1]

The rival radical avant-garde journal *Nova Generatsiia* (New Generation, 1927–30) responded with jeers: "one can safely say that such 'Little Russianness' was long gone even in 1918," qualifying a return to local idiom as unpardonable provincialism.[2] The comment impels us to examine the particular quality of *Literaturnyi iarmarok*'s Westernizing modernism – its mediation between nativist tradition and European high culture – because a serious conversation with the European canon was at the very centre of this almanac's mission and because it was here that many of the first truly mature Ukrainian modernist works were published. The term "nativism," for the purposes of this study, is defined in contrast to the abstraction of the avant-garde and is not intended to signify any of the political connotations of exclusivity that the term has come to embrace. Rather, it is seen as a manipulation of local, folkloric, and traditional realia and discourses to draw on a wellspring of internal cultural resources as a creative exercise.

In the time between December 1928 and February 1930 twelve issues (or rather, "books") of the almanac appeared, some with considerable delay. Individual artists were commissioned to create a "carousel" for each issue and to sketch drawings in the margins. An anonymous editorial board took credit for the first two books; subsequent issues had individual "editors," each with his own "autobiography written by a good friend." There were no articles on current affairs or editorials as such. Every book contained a prologue, epilogue, circulars, and announcements; a calendar to commemorate a literary or historical figure; a special plate "From the Album of the Artist" to showcase a page from a specific artist's sketchbook (usually from the creator of that month's carousel); miniature drawings and graffiti-type slogans running up the margins (sometimes stamped in coloured ink on an unrelated page of text); advertisements of new releases by other publishers; and commentaries called *intermedia* to introduce and link the literary works. Books 7 and 9–11 dispensed with *intermedia* in exchange for equally fictitious "letters" between writers, and in the final volume a single prologue, signed by Khvyl'ovyi, announced the suspension of publication.

The range of literature and art presented on the pages of *Literaturnyi iarmarok* shows a remarkable integration with international literary and art movements. Western trends had begun to make serious inroads into Ukraine during the relatively liberalized atmosphere following the 1905 revolution in the Russian Empire. Of major significance was the steady drawing together of Russian imperial culture with that of Western Europe – the growing dialogue of organizations such as the art nouveau World of Art (*Mir iskusstva*), as well as the more radical avant-garde of Davyd Burliuk, Kazimir Malevich, and Alexandra Exter, with their counterparts in Paris and Munich. There had also been the earlier introduction of William Morris's arts-and-crafts ideas in the 1890s and the establishing of contacts with the Bloomsbury group and later the Vorticists in England.[3] Indeed, one could digress here to say that this was one of those rare moments when cultural influence flowed not just *from* Europe but *to* Europe: Diaghilev's *Ballets Russes* performed regularly in Paris between 1909 and 1929 (bringing together Stravinsky, Nijinsky, Balanchine, and Prokofiev with Picasso, Léger, and Matisse in equal creative collaboration and truly changing the course of European dance); and the focus on textile design among the Russian Empire's avant-garde not only played a vital role in shifting attitudes to applied and decorative arts worldwide but contributed significantly, perhaps even decisively, to the emergence of abstract painting. This cultural ferment was richly reflected in the journals of the empire, and it had a very direct impact on the formation of the Ukrainian literary generation of the first third of the twentieth century.[4] Ukrainians were involved in these processes on every level. For those who wanted it, "Europe" was already part of their artistic consciousness.

In light of these facts, we may legitimately question whether all those slogans of the 1925–8 Literary Discussion – down with *Prosvita*! We want to learn from Europe! (which, frankly, sound so pathetic in some interpretations) – can be taken at face value. On the surface Prosvita, a prerevolutionary literacy society whose name evoked associations of cultural backwardness, was being cast in contrast to Europe as a source of artistic education. More likely, however, these were not the cries of ignorant neophytes but rather part of a coded internal political discussion that had everything to do with a power struggle in a police state and far less with either the Prosvita society or with Europe. The conditional nature of "Europe" is revealed in Khvyl'ovyi's pamphlet *Ukraïna chy Malorosiia* (Ukraine or Little Russia, 1926), where the following argument is presented: VAPLITE's goal is to create a national European literature, and the model is Germany of the late eighteenth century – the Sturm und Drang generation of writers who, by invoking creative genius and an intense romantic aesthetic, rebelled against the dominant French Classicism and made a breakthrough to lay the foundations for modern German literature.[5] But in rejecting French Classicism, the Sturm und Drang writers turned to their own version of "Europe" (according to Khvyl'ovyi) – Shakespeare's England – for their model of a national literature: "This was a movement, as we know, not against France but against the tastes of the French court. The Classicist period of German art decisively resolved this question once and for all with *The Sorrows of Young Werther* and *The Robbers*. This does not at all mean that young people of the time were nationalistically inclined; quite the contrary, Goethe and Schiller, as we know, were cosmopolitans … And yet the original source was still England – 'Europe' for Germany of the time … and Goethe went to Shakespeare."[6] Thus the entire arsenal of intellectual constructs employed by Khvyl'ovyi throughout the Literary Discussion was deployed to stimulate this creative endeavour: there is Urbino, the birthplace of Raphael, from which the Renaissance was launched; there is Mt Olympus and Mt Helicon, where elite writers can pursue their craft undeterred by political contingencies; there is the whole range of cyclical theories (Vico, Danilevskii, Spengler), buttressed by the Marxist deterministic march of history, which were to demonstrate that this outcome is inevitable; and there is even the wild energy of the Scythians, the Eastern conquistadors, borrowed from the Russian Silver Age. All these resources were summoned to create the combustive creative energy necessary to shatter the gridlock of political dogma and small-minded thinking.[7]

Such was the goal, but would there be a specific aesthetic? Certainly, some degree of romantic inspirational fervor was to be part of the mix, but more important was a commitment to intellectual sophistication – a familiarity with the European canon of "great books" to the extent possible. Beyond that, VAPLITE (the Free Academy of Proletarian Literature, after all, is what they called themselves) gave free rein to its writers. Thus one can assume the aesthetic theories of "romantic vitaism" and "active romanticism" to be essentially false arguments. "Romantic vitaism" was a rallying call for creative geniuses to enact a breakthrough in the manner of Sturm und Drang; in the case of "active romanticism," VAPLITE appears to have simply been forced into a defensive position by the ascendant party-sponsored organization VUSPP (*Vseukraïns'ka Spilka Proletars'kykh Pys'mennykiv* – All-Ukrainian Association of Proletarian Writers, the Ukrainian incarnation of Russian "on-guardism"), which was promulgating an aggressive program of monumental realism.

The very name *Literaturnyi iarmarok* chosen for the new periodical was a form of épatage directed at both Marxism and the avant-garde. By 1928 VAPLITE had lost its right to speak publicly through its own journal and was only allowed an almanac. In response to this muzzling they invoked nativist tradition and, choosing *Literary Fair* as the title of their almanac, turned to a concept quintessentially local, as the Kharkiv-Poltava region was renowned for its fairs. Hand in hand with the colourful palette exploited so well by Gogol' and Kvitka-Osnovianenko in their descriptions of these fairs came another deeply archetypal feature: Ukrainian folk humour that had served as the wellspring from which Kotliarevs'kyi's *Eneïda* (The Aeneid, 1798) and subsequently Gogol's Ukrainian tales originated. As George Grabowicz notes in his article on the subject: "It is already apparent that at that first stage *kotliarevshchyna* determines the identity and consciousness of Ukrainian literature; it is the first thesis. If we accept the proposition that literature is a subset of the cultural process and that the phenomenon of nativism, as an inevitable response to the realia of political history and colonial status, characterizes in large measure Ukrainian culture of the 19th and 20th centuries, then *kotliarevshchyna* stands before us as a deep archetype."[8]

Similarly, the dissident Ievhen Sverstiuk, in his insightful samizdat essay "Ivan Kotliarevs'kyi smiiet'sia" (Ivan Kotliarevs'kyi is Laughing) draws attention to both the subversive and the regenerative functions of Kotliarevs'kyi's *Eneïda* for the Ukrainian polity of the late eighteenth century: "The *Eneida* marked one of the most typical arteries of our literature – the ambivalent humor that further rises to satirical comprehension and a spiritual victory over the coarse and powerful forces that stand over and against the Ukrainian people."[9] The theory of laughter has received extended treatment in Mikhail Bakhtin's inquiry into carnival. Basing his analysis on popular rituals and spectacles of the Middle Ages that inform the writing of Rabelais (*The Life of Gargantua and Pantagruel*, 1532–64), Bakhtin sees carnival as an alternative reality created in opposition to the deadly seriousness of official celebrations of Church feast days. As social and cultural hierarchies are suspended, a special kind of communication takes place during carnival time, impossible in everyday life – a special, carnivalesque, marketplace style of expression.[10]

Yet although *Literaturnyi iarmarok* reifies carnival's and *kotliarevshchyna*'s key functions – subversion and regeneration through laughter – it strips away many of the genre's expressive modes: coarseness, bawdiness, countrybumpkin naiveté, retaining only pure wit. It is *not* burlesque. In a kind of intuitive pre-emptive strike Khvyl'ovyi reminds us: "Don't let's get lost in 'Pantagruelisms' – give us 'storm and stress'! Our epoch remains, despite everything, the great epoch of renaissance, which opens the doors to that spring air running towards us like a light joyful breeze from Asia."[11]

The subversive aspects of *Literaturnyi iarmarok*'s laughter were not lost on the party functionaries. A conference on Marxist criticism held in late December 1928 to discuss the publications of that year left the following minutes:

> Comrade *Ie. Kasianenko*: ... The situation of our critics is rendered extremely complicated because of a recent habit of our authors: they a priori write in such a way that the critic doesn't know from which side to approach a given work. We have a series of such works; let's say, *Narodnyi Malakhii* [People's Malachi], where the main character is a paranoiac. The next work in chronological order is *Fal'shyva Mel'pomena* [False Melpomene], where the characters are overly talkative Petlurites ...
>
> The most recent literary phenomenon is *Literaturnyi iarmarok*. The critic needs to think hard how to criticize it, given that one is forced to criticize a clown [*blazen'*]. In the intermedias of *Literaturnyi iarmarok* we have before us a clown rather than a responsible entity; how do you criticize it, how do you approach it? We must react negatively to phenomena such as *Literaturnyi iarmarok*, and to react with no less erudition [*kvalifikatsiieiu*] than the respective authors. (*Skrypnyk*: That's right!) This is an especially difficult task.[12]

Here one is reminded that the *blazen'* figure has as an antecedent the mythological archetype of the trickster, of which the *Till Eulenspiegel* incarnation is perhaps the most famous Western European example.[13] The trickster deceives, subverts, and "holds up a mirror" to the faces of the powerful of his world.

However, it is not only the trickster that is shared with Europe. The essence of *Literaturnyi iarmarok*'s subversive discourse is to be found in its *intermedia*; indeed the *intermedia* genre defines the artistic and organizational form of the almanac. *Intermedia*'s origins lie in Western Europe of the late Middle Ages in the farces performed by itinerant entertainers, along with clowning, jugglery, singing, dancing mimicry, and burlesque (French *soties*, German *Fastnachtspiele*, Italian *inframessi*, *kluchtspelen* in the Netherlands). In time they became a part of church drama as comic interludes between the serious acts of morality plays, and as such appeared in the Polish-Lithuanian Commonwealth as in the rest of Europe. Through the Polish educational system they became popular in seventeenth- and eighteenth-century Ukraine, particularly in the Ukrainian puppet theatre known as *vertep*. The *intermedia* are thus a product of diverse traditions: Western medieval drama, seventeenth- and eighteenth-century Ukrainian baroque school plays, native carnival, and folklore. Their range is geographical (Western Europe, Poland, local) and temporal (traditional idiom, the Middle Ages, baroque, the 1920s); and for the specific purposes of *Literaturnyi iarmarok* the *intermedia* are an artful juxtaposition of the high and the low.

The practice of framing stories with intermediary commentary is not only a well-established trope in storytelling but also has a long history in Western literary culture (and not only), beginning with Boccaccio's *Decameron,* Chaucer's *Canterbury Tales*, and even in some measure the *Scheherezade*. (It cannot escape notice that Gogol's narrator of his Ukrainian tales Rudyi Pan'ko is of the same tradition.) In the case of *Literaturnyi iarmarok*, however, we can posit another direct, highly literary source – the German writer E.T.A. Hoffmann, who had such a profound effect on Khvyl'ovyi and an entire generation of early Soviet writers.[14] Hoffmann's *Die Serapionsbrüder* (Serapion Brothers, 1819–21) is a four-volume collection of his tales, many previously published but now set into a framework of discussions held by the Serapion Society, a group that met at stated intervals when one or more of the "brothers" would relate a tale. The discussions that precede and follow each tale delve deeply into issues of literature and art, examining how each story embodies the "Serapiontic principle," the brothers' specific philosophy of art that entails entering a creative trance.

Iurii Bezkhutryi's close reading of Khvyl'ovyi's programmatic work *Arabesky* (Arabesques, 1924, 1927), a de facto exploration into the nature of creativity, has shed much light on Khvyl'ovyi's creative universe (one in which the image of *iarmarok* was already firmly embedded at the time *Arabesky* was written).[15] The work contains frequent allusions to Hoffmann's text – the images of the "fire" of intuition, creativity, or fantasy (*ohon' svoieï intuïtsiï, ohnetsvit moieï fantaziï*); the visitations by authors-mentors (Sterne, Gogol, Dickens, Hoffmann, and Swift); and many others.[16] Khvyl'ovyi not only embraces the Serapiontic principle for his own writing, but also seems to be responding to a general reception of German romanticism and its characteristic device of employing cultural symbols in literary works at once seriously and ironically. For example, Ludwig Tieck's three-volume *Phantasus* (1812–17), invoked by Hoffmann as the literary model for the frame of *Die Serapions-brüder*, contains a scene in which the young artists raise toasts, each to their favourite author, and through the course of the evening go through a semimystical transformation to take on a physical resemblance to their mentors: Ernst resembles Goethe, Lothar – Shakespeare, and Friedrich – Novalis.[17]

Although the register shifts from solemnity to humour, *Literaturnyi iarmarok*'s *intermedia* present similar scenes: Hoffmann appears in a cloud of pink mist and, assuming an oratorical pose, introduces Mykola Bazhan's *Hofmanova nich* (Hoffmann's Night); Balzac previews Oles' Dosvitnii's *Sirko* as an incisive social satire; Jean Arp sees Flemish motifs à la Rubens in Senchenko's *Chervonohrads'ki portrety* (Chervonohrad Portraits) (cf. paintings by Peter Paul Rubens and Jan Brueghel the Elder, both titled *Flemish Fair*); Anatole France praises Ivanov's *Nich i den'* (Night and Day); and the "full list of collaborators of *Literaturnyi iarmarok*" includes Mykola Hoffmann and Teodor Amadei Bazhan, Walt Polishchuk and Valerian Whitman, Lev Panch and Petro Tolstoi, Maik Cervantes and Miguel Iohansen, Henrik Kulish and Mykola Ibsen, Mykola Pil'niachok and Borys Khvyl'ovyi, Adam Shevchenko and Taras Mickiewicz.[18]

The prologue-*intermedia*-epilogue formula was adopted as the basic structure of the journal's editorials where the already-mentioned burlesque cast of Gypsy, Rooster, and Demon is joined by Averröes, the renowned Spanish commentator of Aristotle; the characters of Kvitka-Osnovianenko's play *Svatannia na Honcharivtsi* (Matchmaking at Honcharivka, 1836); the mystery futurist poet Edvard Strikha and his love Zozé; and many others. Series of philosophical dialogues are conducted: in the first one alone, Goethe is in discussion with Bazhan, Ianovs'kyi, and Khvyl'ovyi, while Joseph Conrad converses with Kulyk on racial issues. The text makes mention of Winckelmann, Fichte, Hegel, and Napoleon; Galileo, Bacon, Newton, and Leonardo da Vinci; Hafiz, Nietzsche, and Meredith; Montaigne and Descartes; and Goethe's *Faust* (1808, 1831) and *West-östlicher Divan* (West-Eastern Divan, 1814–19). Languages used include Ukrainian, German, French, Greek, and Latin.[19]

These writings were a highly creative intrusion into the deadly serious tone that had come to dominate literary life. Their functions are manifold: on the one hand they spoof and subvert, on the other they aim to raise the discussion of cultural issues, profoundly important to their authors, to a level beyond the reach of their detractors. Their seemingly naive characters turn out to be quite familiar with Swift, Beaumarchais, Figaro, Dziga Vertov's camera-eye, the concepts of revolution and Thermidor, the importance of satire for a free society, and coercion and betrayal. Employing a kind of Aesopian language, they were accessible only to those who knew the "code," – Ukrainian history, literature, and culture as a facet of European intellectual thought – a circle that by definition excluded most of the censors and party-minded critics who were charged with ensuring that *Literaturnyi iarmarok* did not stray from the party line. In other words, they were a mystification into which the reader could be initiated, but that initiation entailed sustained intellectual effort.[20] The melding of native with foreign, and humour with erudition, is used to camouflage deeper and more disturbing political realities, as the following glance at several of the *intermedia* in the first volume illustrates.

The Little Grey Demon is moping ("in the manner of Hamlet") and wants to shoot himself.[21] He is the sceptic, perhaps one of those sceptical (or rather desperately depressed) about the rosy future of Soviet society. He is also Khvyl'ovyi, as a close reading of Khvyl'ovyi's *Arabesky* shows. The Gypsy tells him to go ahead and shoot himself and not to depress anyone else. The Gypsy has a whip, a sign of authority, and is not particularly witty ("not being, unfortunately, a witty person, he nonetheless terribly loves to joke"; one might guess him to be a VUSPP representative).[22] He tries to sell his wares cheaply, but nobody seems interested in buying.[23] The Golden Rooster, his aide-de-camp, sports the blue-and-yellow colours of the Ukrainian nationalist persuasion, but also has some less than attractive characteristics: he is servile before the Gypsy when necessary and abuses the Little Grey Demon when he can get away with it ("The Golden Rooster with a Blue Cape Draped over His Shoulder hops around after his patron on one leg, occasionally running up ahead and looking into the Gypsy's eyes").[24] In other *intermedia* the Golden Rooster collects rumors and runs to inform the Gypsy of them; during the "Green Mare" debate he crows three times,[25] reminding the reader of the cock-crow that followed Peter's betrayal of Christ and introducing the context of treason.

The Little Grey Demon continues to mope, then cry, and then finally scream hysterically. The Golden Rooster intervenes: "(*He aims to kick him with his foot and, arching his neck, crows victoriously*). 'Cock-a-doodle-doo!'" The Grey Demon composes himself and the following dialogue ensues:

GYPSY: (*to the demon*). So what is it you call me, Zanuda? Say it again!
GREY DEMON: (*sighing*). I don't call you anything, sir. That's what people call you. It's they that are saying that you're no different than Figaro.

GYPSY: (*going deep into thought*). "Figaro"... Are you talking about that Figaro who's a very jolly fellow?

GREY DEMON: (*sighing*). I'm talking about the Figaro that's Beaumarchais. I'm talking, if you'll forgive my words, about somewhere around the Great French Revolution, when they say a Swift was needed, but instead, unfortunately, a Beaumarchais was born.

GYPSY: (*flicking his whip and thinking*). So it looks like you're against my profession? Too bad! I could have sold you a really good mare ... Too bad![26]

The theme of the sold-out revolution pervades much of Khvyl'ovyi's writing, thus it is no surprise to see it resurface in the *intermedia*. Jonathan Swift, the great social satirist, was clearly preferable to Pierre-Augustin Caron de Beaumarchais, author of the well-known comedies adapted to opera *Le Barbier de Séville* (The Barber of Seville, 1775) and *Le Mariage de Figaro* (The Marriage of Figaro, 1784). Beaumarchais, renowned but not respected for his life of intrigue and speculation, had, by and large, displayed an uncritical, complacent attitude towards the prevailing social order, whichever it might be. When faced with a Thermidor, it is a satirist rather than an entertainer that a revolution needs. The analogy to the contemporary Ukrainian situation was obvious, down to the philistine's love of operetta.

The question of discovering the true identity of the *intermedia* characters is faced when the editors parody the obligatory Boshevik ritual of self-criticism (*samokrytyka*):

On the day's agenda, that is, that of the *intemedia*-fair, stand questions acute and vital for today ...

. . . .

However, in order to maintain a link with yesterday and also pay tribute to our severe age of self-criticism, we ought to, you know, take stock of the experience of "the past" and the effect of Issue no. 131 of our [literary] fair ...[27]

Two new *intermedia* characters come forward to take up the task of unmasking: The Grey Hat (*Syva shapka*) and The Glasses (*Okuliary*), but their plodding ruminations lead nowhere. As the narrator comments, the *iarmarok* is a kaleidoscope of colourful, teeming multitudes:

At any rate the camera-eye was absent. We are forced to convey reality with outmoded primitive verbal and – this we stress – non-objective means ... And really, how can you capture the fair's bright-coloured crowds, struck dumb by the multitude of mixed feelings emanating from the *intermedia* performed by the

Gypsy, the Demon Zanuda, the Rooster, and the *Iarmarkom*! How can you grasp the incomparable Reshetylivka hat, pushed back and to the side, or the European horn-rimmed glasses on someone's "classic Ukrainian" nose![28]

The fair roars, the hawker women shout, the carousel organs howl, horses neigh, cows moo, etc. (see *Fair at Sorochyntsi*). In the middle of the sky stands a hot sun and energetically hurls its rays into the motley fair crowd.[29]

It is through this *iarmarok* ambience that we see the lineage of the *intermedia* characters from Gogol' most clearly, even though only one of the three main figures has an equivalent in *Sorochinskaia iarmarka* – the horse-trading Gypsy who wants to purchase a mare from Solopii Cherevik, the same mare that, in an absurd twist, Cherevik is later accused of stealing.[30] This mare, with its proclivity to disappear and reappear when convenient, together with the phantom red cape with demonic powers (*krasnaia svitka*, as opposed to the blue one on the Golden Rooster), form the kernel of images from which *Literaturnyi iarmarok*'s own Green Mare (*Zelena Kobyla*) is created.

A deeper discussion of cultural and societal ills ensues in the second volume, where the mock "Green Mare" debate is presented. Various known personalities step up to the podium in search of the mare's true identity: is it the native nag of the popular saying in which something unattainable is the "dream of a skewbald mare" ("the skewbald mare of our Zaporozhian ancestors, whose dream, albeit in different historical circumstances, has become by now a classic")? Is it Alexander the Great's stallion Bucephalus? Is it the nationalists' Trojan horse? Is it Mohammed's winged mare al-Buraq? Is it a Canadian bison with hump removed ("because our Green Mare, too, is unquestionably humpbacked. Who wouldn't be, with this kind of life!")?[31] Or is it, in fact, Rosinante, with the immortal Knight of the Sad Countenance (Don Quixote) perched on its crooked back? The knight has now armed himself with a Montblanc pen instead of a sword and had even Ukrainianized his beloved Dulcinea, but then realized his mistake and, searching for synthesis, made her European again:

Poor Knight: he didn't find his synthesis, and his Dulcinea – is nothing more than a market hag. The knight is in a desperate state, and someone must do something about the Green Mare to get him out of this hopeless dead end … Otherwise the knight will die … And we don't want his death. He can still be useful, after all, he's not a bad person and it's not his fault that circumstances have made him so unnecessary … I end with this appeal – do something about the Green Mare, if nothing else, it can still come in handy as a beast of burden or something.[32]

The directness of the passage is striking, for it captures the desperate state of the Ukrainian writers precisely. The idealized Dulcinea (the Ukrainian idea?) has turned out to be a market hag (revolution turned over to the petty speculators?), and the state, having no real need of intellectuals (Don Quixotes) or their literary wares (the Green Mare), may still be willing to use them as beasts of burden. The symbols are mutable but the overall message is unmistakable – it is a feature of the *Literaturnyi iarmarok* discourse to insert such profoundly painful revelations in moments of general hilarity.

At one point we hear of the Green Mare running around the Tiergarten in Berlin, threatening Western civilization. By Book 8, we catch up with her in Paris at the trial of the resurrected Edvard Strikha's love Zozé (Kost' Burevii was the editor of that issue).[33] Ultimately we are brought full circle, to the roots of modern Ukrainian literature, as the trial investigates the mythological Camilla immortalized in Kotliarevs'kyi's *Eneïda*:

Тут ще наїзниця скакала
І військо немале вела;
Собою всіх людей лякала
І все мов помелом мела.
Це звалась діва-цар Камила
До пупа жінка, там – кобила.
Кобилячу всю мала стать:
Чотири ноги, хвіст з прикладом,
Хвостом моргала, била задом,
Могла і говорить, і ржать.[34]

And then there was the rider prancing,
Leading an army not too small;
She frightened all with her appearance,
Swept all before her as with a broom.
This was the virgin-tsar Camilla:
To the navel woman, and horseflesh thither.
Her sex was pure mare, end to end:
Four legs, a tail with cover;
She winked with tail, with rump she pounded,
She could both speak and neigh.

Despite the reality that Europe was still a fortress to be taken by the new Ukrainian literature, *Literaturnyi iarmarok* editors eagerly engaged in a game of juggling with artefacts of Western civilization, using them as building blocks – or perhaps glittering pieces of glass – for a mosaic that was being created on native soil. The sheer joy of erudition was matched by a skill at mystification that was a deliberate challenge not only to state censorship – as a simple advertisement for a just-published edition of Aristophanes' *Lysystrata* demonstrates. If "mystification" operates on the principle that those who cannot keep up are shut out, then readers are rarely sure whether or not they are among them – there are degrees of "initiation," and even the faithful are often thrown "curveballs."[35]

First of all, esteemed reader, do not hurry and, if only for a moment, direct your attention to the comedy of Aristophanes, which we are here discussing. You, no doubt, already know this Athenian author of *tragic drama*, having read his brilliant poems: *Faust, Kobzar, Prometheus*, but it will be a great surprise for you to discover that in addition to this, he also wrote comedies, being, quite justifiably, a precursor of not only Ivan Kotliarevs'kyi, but the *Roman* Molière and the *Frenchman* Plautus. He, this Greek Aristophanes, was a true *trickster*, and you, Ukrainian reader, eager, as you have said many times, to have a good laugh, will have the emotional satisfaction … A striking resemblance! *as Prof. O.I. Bilets'kyi says*. Whether you enter the theater of Aristophanes or the theater of Kurbas, in the first few minutes *you will be completely bewildered*: instead of people – some kind of fantastical figures, crude caricatures, capricious images, which glitter on an unsteady, also fantastical background, which may be at intervals either land, or aerial expanses, or hell: they talk, sing, dance, argue, bark, chirp, and oink. You are stunned, deafened, confused. A chorus appears on the stage in the form of frogs, wasps, birds, and even clouds.[36] … Human conversation is joined by cries of animals, unidentifiable noises, strange sound imitations: ooh-ah, ooh-ah, bom-bax, bom-balo-bax, berekekoax, koax, epopo-popo-poponi![37] – In other words, from Aristophanes' kingdom *you are flown, without transfers, straight to the republic of Literaturnyi iarmarok*, and, lighting your fragrant pipe, you …[38]

As they linked one literary work to another, the *intermedia* provided a forum for the exchange of ideas, an opportunity for artistic cross-pollination, experimentation with genre, camaraderie, and mutual support. They were laboratories, an intermedial space melding belles-lettres with editorial genres, creating out of each volume of *Literaturnyi iarmarok*, and indeed of all twelve volumes as a unit, a self-contained independent work of art.

In his introduction to the reader, Khvyl'ovyi pauses on the etymology of *iarmarok*:

Of course, "iarmarok" comes from the German or, more accurately, from the language of Berlin … and, of course, "iarmarok" strikes an unpleasant chord for our finely tuned ear. But do you really not see that this word underwent ... a brilliant metamorphosis? And that it happened precisely when this word was transferred to us and to the Viennese? Can you really not see that for us, "iarmarok" is a huge red splotch (blinding!) against a blue background, that it's a colourful crowd of happy, good-natured people, that it is, if you please – the "Sorochyntsi" invention of our tragic countryman Nikolai Vasil'ievich Hohol'.[39]

When *Jahrmarkt* arrives in the environs of Kharkiv and Poltava and falls into our (Gogol's) hands it becomes transcendent, something that is our own. A similar metamorphosis, also indigenous, occurs in Vienna, where *Jahrmarkt* is transformed into the fairgrounds of the Prater: "Is the '*iarmarok*' not the 'Prater' for the Viennese, is it not the carousels, the fantastical ponies, gypsies, and thousands of other proletarian amusements?"[40]

Europe, therefore, is no longer Panteleimon Kulish's "mirror" in which one's own miserable "Asiatic" countenance is reflected: Europe is there to be used as artistic material. In the one short year of its existence (1928–9), *Literaturnyi iarmarok* captures the moment ten years after the revolution when, buttressed by institutional support (albeit circumscribed by strict politically determined limits), Ukrainian literary modernism truly comes into its own. Through the interface of literary works, illustrations, and inventive discourse enabling a discussion that bypassed the censors, it embraces the "national" as a creative rather than a historical exercise. Its editors were quite aware that they had created something new and original, born of their modernist focus on the craft of writing and their sustained self-referentiality. The almanac becomes a force field in which authors "bounce off" each other's work, creating something akin to a common text, and also a kind of "hypertext" where everything read is constantly recontextualized. It posits a new role for the reader, the ever-present addressee of the *intermedia*, introducing a far richer experience for those who can rise to the challenge. The entire enterprise, however, rests on an intimate familiarity with European culture in both content and form. The almanac appropriates Western cultural heritage to reinvent it in striking new forms.

Notes

1 *Literaturnyi iarmarok: Al'manakh-misiachynyk*, no. 1–12 (December 1928–November 1929). The classic studies of Ukrainian literary organizations of the 1920s are Myroslav Shkandrij, *Modernists, Marxists, and the Nation* (Edmonton: Canadian Institute of Ukrainian Studies, 1992) and George S. N. Luckyj, *Literary Politics in the Soviet Ukraine, 1917–1934* (New York: Columbia University Press, 1956).

2 *Nova Generatsiia*, 1929, no. 2 (February): 63. For an in-depth study of this group, see Oleh S. Ilnytzkyj, *Ukrainian Futurism, 1914–1930: A Historical and Critical Study* (Cambridge, MA: Distributed by Harvard University Press for the Ukrainian Research Institute, Harvard University, 1997).
3 See Rosalind P. Blakesley and Susan E. Reid, eds., *Russian Art and the West: A Century of Dialogue in Painting, Architecture, and the Decorative Arts* (DeKalb, IL: Northern Illinois University Press, 2007), esp. the essays by Charlotte Douglas and Elizabeth Kridl Velkenier. See also Lynn Garafola and Nancy Van Norman Baer, eds., *The Ballets Russes and Its World* (New Haven, CT: Yale University Press, 1999).
4 For a discussion of Alexandra Exter's impact on the artistic milieu of Kyiv, esp. the new generation of theatre designers that would include Anatol' Petryts'kyi and Vadym Meller, see Myroslava M. Mudrak, *The New Generation and Artistic Modernism in the Ukraine* (Ann Arbor: UMI Research Press, 1986).
5 For a discussion of Khvyl'ovyi's renaissance conception, see Halyna Hryn, "The Executed Renaissance Paradigm Revisited," *Harvard Ukrainian Studies* 27 (2004–5): 67–96.
6 Mykola Khvyl'ovyi, *Tvory u dvokh tomakh*, ed. M. H. Zhulyns'kyi and P. I. Maidanchenko (Kyiv: Dnipro, 1990), 2: 619–20. This and the following translations are mine.
7 Hryn, "Executed Renaissance." For an extended study of the Ukrainian Literary Discussion and Khvyl'ovyi's role, see Shkandrij, *Modernists, Marxists and the Nation*; also Luckyj, *Literary Politics*. For an English-language translation of Khvyl'ovyi's essays (but without the seminal *Ukraïna chy Malorosiia*, see Mykola Khvyl'ovyi, *The Cultural Renaissance in Ukraine: Polemical Pamphlets, 1925–1926*, trans. Myroslav Shkandrij (Edmonton: Canadian Institute of Ukrainian Studies, 1986).
8 George G. Grabowicz, "Between Subversion and Self-Assertion: The Role of *Kotliarevshchyna* in Russian-Ukrainian Literary Relations," in *Culture, Nation and Identity: The Ukrainian-Russian Encounter, 1600–1945*, ed. Andreas Kappeler et al. (Edmonton: Canadian Institute of Ukrainian Studies Press, 2003), 226.
9 Ievhen Sverstiuk, *Clandestine Essays,* trans. George S. N. Luckyj (Littleton, CO: Ukrainian Academic Press for the Harvard Ukrainian Research Institute, 1976), 88.
10 See Mikhail Bakhtin, *Rabelais and His World*, trans. Hélène Iswolsky (Bloomington, IN: Indiana University Press, 1984), esp. 9–11.
11 Khvyl'ovyi, *Tvory u dvokh tomakh*, 2: 621.
12 "Pro marksysts'ku krytyku i robotu zhurnalu 'Krytyka': Stenhorama Ahitpropnarady pry TsK KP(b)U 28 hrudnia 1928," *Krytyka*, 1929, no. 2 (February): 103–4.

388 Halyna Hryn

13 See Lewis Hyde, *Trickster Makes This World: Mischief, Myth and Art* (New York: Farrar, Straus and Giroux, 1998); and Paul Oppenheimer, ed. and trans., *Till Eulenspiegel: His Adventures* (New York: Routledge, 2001).
14 Cf. the Russian literary group Serapionovy Brat'ia (see Lev Lunts, "Why We Are the Serapion Brothers" and "Go West!" in *The Serapion Brothers: A Critical Anthology*, ed. Gary Kern and Christopher Collins [Ann Arbor: Ardis, 1975], 133–6 and 147–57). The name derives from the brotherhood described in Hoffmann's collection, but also from the name of Hoffmann's own close circle of friends, who purportedly served as a model for his literary creation. Mykola Bazhan's long poem *Nich Hofmana* describes Hoffmann and his Serapion circle on a night out.
15 Iurii Bezkhutryi, *Khvyl'ovyi: Problemy interpretatsiï* (Kharkiv: Folio, 2003); see pp. 56–8 for a discussion of the textual relationship between *Arabesky* and *Die Serapionsbrüder*. Khvyl'ovyi's conclusion ("moïm Arabeskam – *finis*" [it's *finis* for my Arabesques]) contains two invocations of Theodor, both Hoffmann's middle name and the name of the host of the Serapion brotherhood's meetings in *Die Serapionsbrüder* (see Bezkhutryi, 57).
16 Khvyl'ovyi, *Tvory u dvokh tomakh*, 1: 311, 317–8. See also *Serapionovy brat'ia: E.T.A Gofman, "Serapionovy brat'ia"; "Serapionovy brat'ia v Petrograde": Antologiia*, ed. A. A. Gugnin, Biblioteka studenta slovesnika (Moscow: Vysshaia shkola, 1994), esp. references to "ognennaia fantaziia poetov" (the fiery imagination of poets), 54 and 62. Cf. E.T.A. Hoffmann, *Die Serapions-Brüder: Gesammelte Erzählungen und Märchen*, 5th ed., Winkler Weltliteratur Dünndruck Ausgabe (Munich: Artemis und Winkler, 1995), 19 ("von einer feurigen Fantasie" [of a fiery imagination]) and 26 ("mit der feurigsten Fantasie begabte Dichter" [poets endowed with the fieriest of imaginations]).
17 *Serapionovy brat'ia*, 22–4. See also Hilda Meldrum Brown, *E.T.A. Hoffmann and the Serapiontic Principle: Critique and Creativity* (Rochester, NY: Camden House, 2006).
18 See *Literaturnyi iarmarok*, no. 1 (December 1928): 42–3 [Hoffmann and Bazhan]; 76 [Balzac and Dosvitnii]; 77, 110 [Arp and Senchenko]; 199–200 [Anatole France and Ivanov]; *Literaturnyi iarmarok*, no. 2 (January 1929): 203–4 [list of contributors].
19 See "Pershyi diialoh," *Literaturnyi iarmarok*, no. 5 (April 1929): 121–6.
20 For an insightful discussion of various strategies of literary mystification, see Jean-François Jeandillou, *Esthétique de la mystification: Tactique et stratégie littéraires* (Paris: Les Éditions de minuit, 1994).
21 See "Intermediia patosu," *Literaturnyi iarmarok*, no. 1 (December 1928): 198–201.
22 "Persha intermediia," *Literaturnyi iarmarok*, no. 1 (December 1928): 42.
23 "Dramatychnyi etiud," *Literaturnyi iarmarok*, no. 1 (December 1928): 138.

24 Ibid.
25 "Zamist' intermediï," *Literaturnyi iarmarok*, no. 1 (December 1928): 74–5; and "Dysput – 'Zelena Kobyla,'" *Literaturnyi iarmarok*, no. 2 (January 1929): 251–2.
26 "Intermediia patosu," *Literaturnyi iarmarok*, no. 1 (December 1928): 201.
27 "Intermediia odnoho iz 697," *Literaturnyi iarmarok*, no. 2 (January 1929): 121.
28 Ibid., 122.
29 "Dramatychnyi etiud," *Literaturnyi iarmarok*, no. 1 (December 1928): 138.
30 N.V. Gogol', "Sorochinskaia iarmarka," in *Sobranie sochinenii v deviati tomakh* (Moscow: Russkaia kniga, 1994), 1: 33.
31 "Dysput – 'Zelena Kobyla,'" *Literatunyi iarmarok*, no. 2 (January 1929): 238–55.
32 Ibid., 239.
33 In 1927 Kost' Burevii had presented himself as the futurist poet Edvard Strikha and was published to favourable reviews in *Nova Generatsiia*. When the hoax was discovered, the journal published an obituary informing readers of his untimely death, but Strikha re-emerged on the pages of *Avangard* and *Literaturnyi iarmarok*. See George Y. Shevelov, "Edvard Strikha: The History of a Literary Mystification," *The American Slavic and East European Review* 14, no. 1 (1955): 93–107.
34 "Moment kul'minatsiinoho napruzhennia," *Literaturnyi iarmarok*, no. 8 (July 1929): 121–33, esp. 132.
35 Jeandillou, *Esthétique de la mystification*, 8–20.
36 Cf. Aristophanes' *The Frogs* (405 BC), *The Wasps* (422 BC), *The Birds* (414 BC), and *The Clouds* (423 BC).
37 Cf. Aristophanes' best-known onomatopoeic chorus, "Co-ax, co-ax, co-ax, Brekekekek, co-ax."
38 "Aristofan 'Lisistrata,'" *Literaturnyi iarmarok*, no. 2 (January 1929): 135; likely authorship Maik Iohansen (all italics mine).
39 "Do knyhy sto trydtsiat' pershoï," *Literaturnyi iarmarok*, no. 1 (December 1928): 5–6.
40 Ibid., 6.

The Poetry of the Sixtiers and Europe: Between Culture and Politics

OXANA PACHLOVSKA

The Sixtiers Today: *Status quaestionis*

In the twenty years of Ukraine's independence Ukrainian literary scholarship has faced the need to reassess in the light of new criteria practically the whole history of Ukrainian literature. The task has proved complex. De-Sovietization of the Ukrainian literary canon could be no more than a general statement of direction. What was necessary was the elaboration of new norms by which literary phenomena could be evaluated.

Two major obstacles stood in the way. First, the country had not settled its identity or finalized its civilizational choices. For decades (centuries, if one adds the colonial to the Soviet past) Ukrainian society and culture had been pressed into a Russian paradigm. When the collapse of the Soviet system turned Ukraine towards Europe and democracy, the inscription of the Ukrainian literary canon into the European might have become part of Ukraine's reorientation towards Europe and, more broadly, the democratic world and its civil, cultural, moral, and legal values. But Ukraine followed a zigzag path towards democracy. In culture no less than in politics, intentions to integrate with Europe often degenerated into opportunistic rhetoric or half-baked plans. The reassessment of the literary canon was among the projects that suffered. Research into Ukrainian literature had been conducted, in the main, either in Ukraine itself (in isolation from external contexts), or in North America, where a diaspora had established scholarly institutions and a tradition of scholarly activity. There was less European input into Ukrainian literary studies and the result was a certain disproportion: in contrast to Ukrainian-North American cooperation, collaboration with Europe in the humanities was fragmentary and inconsistent. It is in this context that interpretive paradigms of Ukrainian culture need to be reconsidered. The American contribution to the study of Ukrainian literature in the West has been paramount, to say nothing of its role in the modernization of literary criticism in Ukraine itself. However, an urgent need remains for further comparative research that would take into account literatures such as the Polish, the German, or the Italian, all of which had an impact on Ukrainian literature and at times confronted problems analogous to those that Ukrainian literature faced – problems, in particular, of identity and nation-building.

The second obstacle to a post-Soviet reassessment of Ukrainian literature is a phenomenon characteristic of culture under authoritarianism, especially in Eastern Europe. In colonial circumstances literature is often a space of national self-assertion and political discussion. When oppression by the regime ends, the reconsideration of literature follows one of two interpretive models: the civic and the aesthetic. In Ukraine these have, with considerable simplification, been labelled the "neo-populist" and the "postmodern." The former focuses on ways in which the literary process affirms national values and pays less attention to the aesthetic dimension of literature. The latter places the aesthetics of modernism in its Western variant at the centre of its judgments, frequently imposing predetermined templates upon literary phenomena and marginalizing their sociopolitical content. These approaches have sometimes overlapped and at times clashed; a synthesis between them, balancing the aesthetic and the historical, might yield an image of Ukrainian literature as part of European literary evolution – for, as noted above, problems of history and identity are essential to the cultures of the Old Continent.

In first twenty years of Ukraine's independence much was done to reassess Ukrainian literature and establish its genealogical links to the culture of the modern world. But many aspects of the Ukrainian past remain controversial, and the resulting polemics impair education, hinder society's understanding of its culture, and complicate the representation of this culture to others. Among such contentious phenomena are the Sixtiers, dissident intellectuals of the 1960s. Their opposition to the Soviet regime and world view laid foundations for broader protest movements on the eve of the fall of the USSR and, more generally, for the European turn in Ukrainian culture and the democratization of Ukrainian society.

Both of the above-mentioned interpretive models are in evidence in histories of the Sixtiers movement. At the beginning of the 1990s, when culture was dominated by a yearning to negate Soviet realities, a conception of the Sixtiers based on an oversimplified opposition of culture and politics took root. Tired of the unrelentingly ideological perspective on society and culture under the Soviet regime, many writers and intellectuals, especially those of the younger generation, aimed for a complete separation of politics from culture and envisaged the latter in the spirit of the idea, condemned in Soviet

times, of "art for art's sake." They viewed the Sixties movement as a purely
political phenomenon that contributed nothing to aesthetic innovation. Typical
of this attitude was the book *Bunt pokolenia* (Revolt of a Generation), which
reflected, favourably but exclusively, on the political aspects of the Sixties'
activity.[1] Equally revealing was the debate over one of the key poets of the Sixtiers, Vasyl' Stus. His heroic biography – his uncompromising stance against
the regime and death while imprisoned – enabled many Ukrainian scholars to
inscribe him into a "martyrological" canon, while their Western counterparts
sought to disaggregate the political and aesthetic dimensions of his oeuvre.[2]
Both approaches are legitimate, but the marginalization of either would impov-
erish understanding of the poet's work. To this day, no synthetic vision has
been proposed.

The Sixties were also an object of dispute among their fellow writers in
the diaspora. The Prague School poet and cultural critic Ievhen Malaniuk,
proscribed in the USSR, welcomed the movement as a link to the "Executed
Renaissance" of the 1920s and as an innovative manifestation of protest that
raised hopes for the survival of Ukrainian literature in an oppressive system.[3]
The poets of the New York group, especially Bohdan Boichuk in his autobiography,[4] on the other hand, accused the Sixties of encroaching upon their
territory in Ukraine and depriving the group of readers and critics there.[5] The
reality was simpler and even less edifying: in the USSR the Sixties were subject to persecution, while the writings of the New York group were prohibited.
There were minimal relations between the two groups, and they could only
perceive one another through the aberrant prism of distorted information. With
the coming of independence and the possibility of direct communication, it
was the Soviet system's code of alienation that was triggered rather than a
desire for dialogue and unprejudiced analysis.

In Ukraine itself, attempts to come to terms with the Sixties have led to
intergenerational conflicts. In keeping with their idea of the transmissibility of
culture, the Sixties respected and felt solidarity both with their predecessors,
the intellectuals of the "Executed Renaissance," and with younger writers.
This younger generation, on the other hand, adopted an ironic attitude towards
the patriotism of their antecedents: in 1992, for example, a poem of Oleksandr Irvanets's exhorted its audience to "Love Oklahoma," parodying Volodymyr Sosiura's "Liubit' Ukrainu" (Love Ukraine, 1944), for which Sosiura
had been accused of bourgeois nationalism in the early 1950s. Literature on
so-called "civic themes" encountered hostile criticism in younger literary circles. But when it became clear that neither genuine independence nor democracy had established themselves in Ukraine, the younger generation once again
blamed the Sixties, this time for the failure of their politics.[6] Such tensions

were indicative of the instability of the border between culture and politics in Ukraine, a state of affairs typically encountered in post-totalitarian societies.

2004, the year of the Orange Revolution, was a watershed year for the country. The all-too-brief period of its victory and the subsequent reversal of its achievements showed how incomplete and vulnerable the democratization of post-Soviet Ukraine (and independence itself) had been. As the question of the responsibility of intellectuals has again arisen with unprecedented urgency in the spheres of culture and politics, so the phenomenon of the Sixtiers has acquired a new significance. A similar revival of interest had happened once before in the late 1980s and early 1990s: in the years of *perestroika* and early independence the Sixtiers found themselves at the epicentre of intellectual and political opposition.[7] Recent studies see the dissent of the 1960s as the manifestation of a new-style "resistance movement,"[8] some analyses have moved away from the view of the cultural and political dimensions of the Sixtiers movement as mutually exclusive,[9] and several autobiographies have cast it in a more nuanced light.[10]

Europe: A Theme Shared by the Sixtiers and the Literature of the "Executed Renaissance"

Europe and the participation of Ukrainian culture in the European are motifs that link the "Executed Renaissance" to the Sixtiers movement. In both the 1920s and the 1960s a cluster of related topics came to the fore: Europe, individual freedom, freedom of artistic expression, an open and inclusive identity for Ukrainians, human and minority rights, language as vehicle for spiritual values, and the correlation between tradition and modernity.

The Ukrainian "European discourse" of the 1920s, drawing inspiration from the political philosophy of Mykhailo Drahomanov, Ivan Franko, and Mykhailo Hrushevs'kyi, saw national liberty as inextricably linked to political and social freedom. It prioritized the rights of the person over those of the nation and promoted self-determination for the national minorities of Ukraine. The cultural discourse was dominated by Drahomanov's view of Ukrainian culture as a natural part of the European and by his conviction that a European orientation in future would guarantee the maintenance of Ukraine's cultural identity.[11]

These postulates re-emerged in the so-called "literary discussion" of 1925–8, a debate between Europe-oriented writers and those who chose the Russian and Soviet vector or, as Mykola Khvyl'ovyi saw it, between an elite intellectual literature and "red graphomania."[12] The discussion anchored the idea of Europe in Ukrainian cultural criticism and literature, anticipating its later reactivation in émigré circles and, more systematically, by the Sixtiers.

The main advocates of a European Ukraine were, in the 1920s, Mykola Zerov, Mykola Khvyl'ovyi, and Dmytro Dontsov. Zerov saw Ukraine as part of a Europe founded on the culture of the Ancients. In contrast to Russia, he polemically asserted, "in Ukraine nobody cut through windows [to Europe, as Peter I was said to have done in Russia]; here the tendrils of European culture penetrated everywhere through a thousand barely visible clefts and fissures; they were absorbed gradually and imperceptibly, but through all pores of the social organism."[13] In Khvyl'ovyi's polemical pamphlets the *Homo Europaeus* was the citizen of a modern, Faustian "psychological Europe" of doubt and quest, of questions rather than answers. It was a Europe that over the centuries had refined the "ideal of the civic person."[14] Dontsov posed the confronting question, "Russia or Europe?" and, like Zerov, interpreted Ukraine's journey towards its European heritage as a return *ad fontes*.[15] He envisioned Europe as antithetical to Russia with its hostility towards the democratic order and its messianic ideologies – from Moscow as the Third Rome to communism. For Dontsov Europe was a world view welcoming of change and marked by an active will to life; its adoption would save Ukraine from the stagnation and backwardness of Russia.

In the 1920s the stylistics and poetics of Ukrainian literature were reformed with an eye to Europe, as would again be the case in the 1960s. There was conscious adoption of European models but there were also spontaneous affinities. These were visible in the poetic innovations of Pavlo Tychyna that resisted classification into any of the extant literary movements, in the futurism of Mykhail' Semenko, the prose of Mykola Khvyl'ovyi and Valerian Pidmohyl'nyi, the dramaturgy of Mykola Kulish, the stage innovations of Les' Kurbas, the graphic art of Heorhii Narbut, and the monumental paintings of Mykhailo Boichuk and his school. Some poets – Mykola Zerov, Maksym Ryl's'kyi, and other "Neoclassicists" – held to traditional forms of strophe, metre, and rhyme while radically rejuvenating theme, metaphor, and style. The expressionist neo-baroque of Mykola Bazhan resonated now with the tradition of Verhaeren, now with that of Rilke; the mystical and mythological poetry of Bohdan Ihor Antonych recollected García Lorca, and echoes of Ungaretti could be heard in the minimalism of Volodymyr Svidzins'kyi.

How did this heritage of the 1920s reach the Sixtiers? Most of it was inaccessible; parts were altogether unknown or known only fragmentarily. Many works of the 1920s were proscribed; as for such "permitted" authors as Tychyna and Bazhan, only those of their works that celebrated the Communist Party or Soviet ideology were published. Europe was interpreted as a bourgeois entity inimical to "developed socialism." Nonetheless, the Sixtiers initiated the return into circulation of some of the forbidden works – the poetry of Antonych, Semenko, Ievhen Pluzhnyk, and some of Tychyna's early oeuvre.

The Sixtiers of Ukraine and the Dissident Movements of Eastern Europe

The protests of Ukrainian intellectuals and defenders of rights began in the mid-1950s, when there were still occasional outbursts of armed resistance against the Soviet occupation in Western Ukraine. The Ukrainian intelligentsia mounted the Soviet Union's first consolidated antiregime protests against the background of Khrushchev's ostensible de-Stalinization and of the flirtation with Russia by a largely left-leaning Western intelligentsia. The Ukrainian intellectual elite pursued the democratic transformation of society at a time when the democratic world itself neither understood nor supported it (in contrast to its later championing of Solidarity in Poland). In Russian dissident circles, as well as support, Ukrainian intellectuals encountered instances of national prejudice (such as Iosif Brodskii's explicit Ukrainophobia). While the Sixtiers' dissent resembled that of analogous movements in Eastern Europe, their predicament was more complex. Russia, Poland, and other countries of the Soviet bloc were "visible" to the West: the names of Solzhenitsyn, Sakharov, and Brodskii had worldwide resonance, while Ukraine fell into a shadow zone between Russia and Poland. A certain solitude, then, characterized the Sixtiers movement.

Furthermore, in Ukraine the opposition confronted not only Sovietization, but also an exceptionally burdensome colonial heritage that Sovietization reinforced. Any movement in Ukraine that sought to defend or develop national identity came up against accusations of "nationalism" not only from the Russian but often also from the Western side. This phenomenon distinguished Ukrainian dissent from that of other East European countries whose right to self-determination the West acknowledged. In Ukraine even such basic activities as the defence of language rights were deemed "nationalist." Of all the countries of the communist camp, ideological pressure on intellectuals in Ukraine was the most intense and aggressive.

In Eastern Europe, too, the image of Ukraine did not often correspond to realities. Emblematic was Milan Kundera's view of Eastern Europe and Russia as two mutually opposed entities in which it was inconceivable that similar processes could occur. On the barricades of Budapest, Prague, and Warsaw, the author claimed, intellectuals were sacrificing themselves for Europe and for freedom, something impossible in Moscow or Leningrad.[16] To the east of Warsaw, in Kundera's mind, there stretched only a limitless homogeneous "Russia" of which Ukraine was an undifferentiated part. Only the Polish intellectuals of the post-war period understood the specificity of the Ukrainian situation in depth. Jerzy Giedroyc developed a theory of the fall of the USSR consequent upon a revolt of intellectuals in Ukraine, Belarus, and Lithuania, former lands of the Polish-Lithuanian Commonwealth. A confederation of free states would arise in Eastern Europe; integration with a democratic Western Europe would follow.[17] No less important was the discourse of historical memory among Polish intellectuals and the desire to neutralize past conflicts through the "priority of the extended hand" and the acknowledgment of mutual historical culpability.[18] In Polish sources Ukraine figured as a European historical reality that contributed to the evolution of Polish statehood.[19] This attitude is still in evidence today: despite unpromising political developments in Ukraine, Poland remains the most consistent advocate of its neighbour's European integration.

The Sixtiers: Names and Contexts

It is traditional to regard literature as the centre of Ukrainian cultural life in the 1960s. But in the Sixtiers movement, as in the 1920s, literary innovation took place in a broader context: an atmosphere of change and aesthetic and civic challenge pervaded all art forms and branches of the humanities. Literary innovations often took shape under the influence of the visual arts or historiography, cinema reinterpreted literature, and music was inseparable from poetic experimentation. Rights activists were also literary critics, while artists and scholars joined lawyers and journalists in their political battles. In short, cultural life was interwoven with political struggle and was imagined as a new form of moral presence in the world.

The term "Sixtiers" refers only in part to a generation. It is true that the Sixtiers, in the main, were born between 1930 and 1940. But among their number were the translator Hryhorii Kochur, born at the beginning of the century, as well as the rights activist Valerii Marchenko, born after the Second World War. It was not age that was decisive but moral membership of a group of like-minded people. There was a narrower and a broader circle of Sixtiers, but even the core members make for a long list.[20]

In Kyiv, the Sixtiers movement was centred in three locations: the apartment of one of its founders, the essayist and poet Ivan Svitlychnyi, who subsequently endured a long term of imprisonment that left him incurably ill; the studio of the painter Alla Hors'ka, murdered in unexplained circumstances in 1970; and the home in Irpin' near Kyiv of the translator Hryhorii Kochur, older than the main Sixtiers cohort, who returned to translation after years of exile.[21] While the three centres attracted dissidents of differing professional profiles, focusing, respectively, on public commentary, the arts, and translation, the Club of Ukrainian Youth played a consolidating role. Its Kyiv branch, "Suputnyk," was headed by Les' Taniuk (1938–2016), and its Lviv counterpart, "Prolisok," by Mykhailo Kosiv (b. 1934).

The Sixtiers emerged during Khrushchev's "Thaw," which for the Ukrainian intelligentsia was brief: already in 1962–3 they were harassed by the censors and accused of "formalism" and "bourgeois nationalism." They were subjected to waves of arrests in 1965 and 1972. Tiutiunnyk would commit suicide, Stus would die in a prison camp, and Chornovil would be killed, in already independent Ukraine, in a car accident that remains unexplained. Some Sixtiers, though not imprisoned, would have their works banned for many years. Others would succumb to pressure and adopt official views. At the start of the 1970s the movement gradually lost its coherence, but its cultural and political heritage would inspire the protests of the 1980s that brought Ukraine to independence in 1991.

The Sixtiers' Concept of Europe

Artists exist, to paraphrase Albert Camus, midway between the beauty without which they cannot live and the human society they cannot escape.[22] This image accurately reflects the thinking of the Sixtiers. They undertook a philosophical reconsideration of the condition of the human being deprived of freedom. They sought to create a new ontology of the twentieth-century person entrapped in totalitarianism. Their writings for the first time tore through the curtain of provincialism that had descended over Soviet Ukrainian literature, mired as it was in ideological and pseudofolkloric cliché.

Ideologically the Sixtiers were unified by their orientation towards Europe, with which their central themes were associated: liberty, free choice, language as an image of the world, and the humanist tradition of culture. But this orientation was not directly articulated everywhere. For some of the Sixtiers Europe was a rationally adopted political concept, for others it was a cultural centre of gravity or the object of creative intuition. Europe was understood as Ukraine's spiritual homeland and the source of democracy, without which an independent Ukraine was unthinkable. Ivan Svitlychnyi put it in words that retain their relevance today: "With democracy, there will be a Ukraine, without democracy there will be no Ukraine."[23] Meanwhile, Ukrainian lawyers worked on a constitutional framework for Ukraine as a state based on the rule of law – on the transformation of the "Beria Reserve," as Valentyn Moroz put it, into an open society.

"In the mirror of the West," Ievhen Sverstiuk wrote, "the Sixtiers first saw their historical role, their face, projected onto the field of the unending struggle for humanity and human rights, for inalienable human values."[24] According to Sverstiuk, "the return to the universal human values trampled by the East and neglected or forgotten by the West" generated for the Sixtiers an ideal space of European civilization within which Ukraine's return to Europe, or Europe's return to Ukraine, could take place on an intimate, almost domestic level: "when at last we were visited by our belated guest Exupéry, or Hemingway, Remarque, Faulkner, or Camus, they came to us as if to their own home."[25] The passage echoes the tonality of Czesław Miłosz's *Rodzinna Europa* (Native Europe). Sverstiuk understood Europe, free of division into East and West, as a common homeland from which Ukraine had been forcibly excised; yet he invoked the opposition, familiar in Western discourse, of East and West as civilizational categories. The totalitarian "East" was associated with imperial and Soviet Russia as an unassailable despotism, the democratic "West" with triumph over dictatorship and timeless human values.

The reference to Hemingway was symptomatic. "Portraits of Hemingway hung on the walls of intellectuals' apartments and his books were bestsellers. Perhaps his individualistic variant of unaccommodated humanism was close to our own view of truth, relative and dispossessed and alienated from its sources. It was good to be quiet with Ernest," Sverstiuk wrote.[26] As an American intimately connected to Europe, a member of the *génération perdue*, a First World War volunteer, a habitué of libertarian Paris, a participant in the war for a republican Spain, and a man who put aside a writer's career to report from the inferno of the Second World War, Hemingway with his stoicism, moral steadfastness, and commitment to action was psychologically congenial for the Sixtiers.

It is no accident that the Sixtiers are sometimes called "children of the war." In their childhood and youth most experienced the Nazi and Soviet occupations as intersecting catastrophes of Ukrainian history. Their genealogy encompassed the "European night" of the twentieth century, to use Camus's phrase, from which arose a new understanding of the human person, of liberty, choice, and struggle.

The philosophical source of the Sixtiers' world view was existentialism in its French variant with its emphasis on the individual being of the person, the problem of freedom as the prerequisite of moral choice, and the question of responsibility for such choices. Camus's notion of the obligation to struggle for liberty, his calls for human solidarity in the "absurd rebellion," and his vision of totalitarianism as the embodiment of existential evil enjoyed the Sixtiers' profound respect. Naturally, at the time the Sixtiers' access to existentialism could only be fragmentary and mediated. Poland and the Ukrainian diaspora were conduits for Western culture. Polish translations and overseas publications were transported, often clandestinely, from Poland, the United States, and Canada. The publishing house "Na hori" (On the Hill), founded in 1955 in Germany by Ihor Kostets'kyi and his wife Elisabeth Kottmaier, was an important literary source, bringing out editions of Dante, Shakespeare, Baudelaire, Verlaine, Novalis, Eliot, Wilde, Claudel, Anouilh, Jiménez, Lec, and others.

Soviet criticism interpreted existentialism as a profoundly "bourgeois ideology of the imperialist epoch." Mykola Bazhan's introduction to Sartre's memoirs, *Les mots* (Words), welcomed the fact that the "French intellectual" had broken through "the gloom of petit bourgeois narrow-mindedness [...] to the goal pursued by the Soviet people."[27] But censorship was selective, and some authors were permitted due to their communist sympathies (e.g., the younger Sixtiers met Sartre and Simone de Beauvoir during their 1961 visit to the USSR). The theatre of the absurd was a familiar concept and the term took on emblematic significance in a Soviet environment. The above-mentioned Russian translation of *Les mots* appeared in 1966; its analysis of the creative process was important for the Sixtiers. Camus's novel *La Peste* (The Plague) and his short stories were published, but not his plays or essays, notably *Le Mythe de Sisyphe* (The Myth of Sisyphus) or *L'Homme révolté* (The Rebel), perhaps the works to which the ethos of the Sixtiers was closest.

These connections point not to borrowings or cryptic quotation from the existentialists, but to similarities of theme, ideas, and aesthetic experience. The revolt of the Sixtiers was in the first instance neither political nor aesthetic, but existential; it was part of the "philosophical tension" of post-war Europe. The catastrophe of the Second World War proved not to be the last: Stalinist dictatorship soon cast another shadow over Europe. The Sixtiers emerged during an epochal crisis that unmasked the world as alien to the aspirations of the individual. Rationalist philosophical systems that purported to know the world and secure its progress had failed. Every new embodiment of "progress" led to new forms of ruin. Great discoveries of the human intellect became means for the destruction of the planet. Human beings in this contemporary world, their hope and despair, the loss and renewal of meaning in their lives, the problem of choice – these themes grounded the new historical consciousness that the Sixtiers introduced into Ukrainian culture.

The Sixtiers understood the plague of Camus's novel as a metaphor of the two totalitarianisms. The idea that the world is divided into the plague and its victims, and that the main task was not to side with the plague, became axiomatic for them. Lina Kostenko called this the Sixtiers' imperative.[28] Stus spoke of his affinity with Camus. Intellectuals thought of themselves in the role of Camus's Dr Rieux, tending the victims of the plague but also warning that even should the plague subside its microbe would never die.

It is a commonplace of descriptions of the Soviet system that it aimed for the destruction of national cultures. In fact the regime constructed a complex system for dismantling culture as a form of humanist reflection on the world in all of its key dimensions: historical memory, identity, morality, and religious and emotional experience. For that reason access to Western culture, and especially Western humanities scholarship, was blocked throughout the sphere of influence of Soviet ideology. Western twentieth-century philosophy, anthropology, linguistics, history, sociology, and psychology were filtered through censorship, and what was allowed through was adapted to the needs of the regime. A perverse child of the Enlightenment tradition, the regime imposed the rule of pragmatism, utilitarianism, and cynicism; it repressed imagination and critical thinking and demanded mechanical obedience to instructions from above, eliminating from society's intellectual life the pluralism of Western thought.

The Sixtiers movement constituted a complex and many-sided intellectual coup against these Soviet realities. It grew into an endeavour to reclaim space for a humanist vision of the world, to affirm human subjectivity against the primitive providentialism of Marxism, and to reinstate in human beings the will to live and to transform reality. The breadth of the movement's mission is another reason why efforts to erect an opposition between the political and the aesthetic in the Sixtiers movement are not merely mistaken but contrary to its very nature. For in the tranquility of the study no less than in the courtroom, at poetry readings no less than in prisons, the object at stake in the Sixtiers' collisions with the regime was the human being and its right to sovereign existence in historical and cosmic time.

At various times translation had great significance for the rapprochement of Ukraine and Europe. It was Panteleimon Kulish (1819–97) who first identified translation as one of the main building materials for a Ukrainian national literature. He did so at a time of systematic prohibitions of the use of the Ukrainian language, including a ban on translations into Ukrainian in 1892. Translation was a powerful vehicle of Europeanization during the "Executed Renaissance"; its master theoretician and practitioner was Mykola Zerov, an accomplished translator of Latin, French, and Russian poetry. In the 1960s translation was a gateway to the free world and a means of returning to Ukrainian culture its estranged civilizational heritage. Translation enabled indirect protest through texts from other cultures. It was also a means of enriching the Ukrainian language thematically and lexically, for it exercised the conceptual, synonymic, and stylistic treasures of the authentic language in the face of its standardized and Sovietized counterfeit. In the 1960s members of the older generation made important contributions to translation. They included Maksym Ryl's'kyi (1895–1964), Mykola Bazhan (1904–83), Vasyl' Mysyk (1907–83), and Borys Ten (1897–1983). Zerov had translated Virgil's *Aeneid* while in a concentration camp; Borys Ten translated the *Iliad* and the *Odyssey* after his return from exile. Bazhan's near contemporary Hryhorii Kochur, an inmate of prison camps for many years, bridged two generations of translators. Kochur and Mykola Lukash, who knew eleven and twelve languages respectively, were the most accomplished translators of the time; the latter's translations included works by Boccaccio, Cervantes, Goethe, Flaubert, Apollinaire, García Lorca, and Julian Tuwim.[29] There was much emphasis on translations of modern literature, though these were difficult to publish. Some translators specialized in particular literatures: Anatol' Perepadia translated from the French a wide panoply of authors, his last work being a monumental edition of Montaigne. Ol'ha Seniuk translated from the Scandinavian languages, Ievhen Popovych from the German (his emphasis was on philosophical texts and the novel; on the eve of his death he was working on Rilke and Heidegger). Poets, too, created luminous translations: Stus rendered Goethe, Rilke, and Celan; Lina Kostenko the poems in Hesse's *Das Glasperlenspiel* (The Glass Bead Game) and poetry written in Polish, Czech, Hebrew, and Georgian; Ivan Svitlychnyi translated French lyrical poetry. A key element of the "European project" of the 1960s, translation did more than aesthetically and linguistically enrich the Ukrainian cultural sphere with infusions from other cultures: it was an organic part of the renascence of Ukrainian culture itself.[30]

The Poetry of the Sixtiers: The Integration of the Discourse of Europe into Ukrainian Culture

Of the arts, it was poetry that in the 1960s exercised the most influence on society. Poetry readings attracted enormous audiences. Forbidden poetry, reproduced in carbon copies or even written out by hand, rapidly reached its readers.

The Sixtiers movement began with notable poetic debuts: Lina Kostenko's *Prominnia zemli* (Rays of the Earth, 1957), Ivan Drach's long dramatic poem *Nizh u sontsi* (Knife in the Sun, 1961), and, in 1962, Mykola Vinhranovs'kyi's *Atomni preliudy* (Atomic Preludes) and Vasyl' Symonenko's *Tysha i hrim* (Silence and Thunder). In 1965, the year of the first arrests of dissident intellectuals, Vasyl' Stus's first collection *Kruhovert'* (Whirlpool) was refused publication. The same fate befell his second collection, *Zymovi dereva* (Winter Trees), which was then published in Brussels in 1970. These years marked the peak of the Sixtiers movement. After the second wave of arrests in 1972 it began to decline.

Poets who espoused divergent poetics and differed in temperament, origin, and literary formation were united by a new vision of literature and of Ukraine in the world. In this vision Europe was an anthropocentric civilization, the opposite of the state-centred system of the Soviet regime. Three features linked the philosophy of the poets among the Sixtiers to Europe: their affirmation of the subjectivity of the human person, their approach to history, and their victory over the tyranny of "Soviet language." The person, time, and the word: these were the three grounds on which the Sixtiers challenged the system. There were others: the urbanity and intellectualism of their poetry, their psychologism and irony, their invocation of the theme of ecology, their formal experimentation, their word plays, and their metrical innovations. A new type of love lyric was born: passionate, intimate, and characterized by a refined eros and a complex dialectic of emotions. But these aspects of the poetry were secondary to the foundational three.

The personal quality of this poetry constituted a breakthrough of European discourse into Ukrainian literature. Emphasis on the subjectivity of the human being, and through the human being of language and nation, accompanied the creation of a new intellectual and aesthetic code and the assertion of the priority of freedom, which was inextricably linked to ideas of consciousness, choice, conscience, individual responsibility, and the Other. This new code was in the spirit of European philosophy of the twentieth century and in opposition to the Marxist materialist conception of liberation. Like other totalitarianisms, the Soviet system laboured to depersonalize the human being and to standardize the spiritual, material, moral, and aesthetic dimensions of human life. The "Soviet person" could possess nothing except what was in common. Ugly living conditions, a lack of aesthetically pleasing objects, and the endless hunt for essential items in chronically short supply were also elements of the education of *homini sovietici*, who were denied choice even in the clothes they wore and who experienced humiliating dependence in every aspect of their everyday existence. And these were trifles relative to the psychological burdens that the system imposed: fear of repression and the consequent readiness to conform, to participate in denunciations, and to abandon moral constraints.

Against this, poetry posited human beings of a new kind: independent, conscious of their own dignity, and confident of their inalienable right to disagreement and to their own voice. With the Sixtiers the "I," unrepeatable and unique, entered Ukrainian literature. This "I" had experienced the catastrophes of the world; recognizing the vulnerability and solitude of human existence, it harbored a tragic world view but accepted moral responsibility for its being in time. Yet this was also an attractive, youthful "I" that, armed with abrasive irony, craved rejuvenation and transformation; its spontaneous desire for rebellion evolved into a consciousness of its right to rebel.

The works of the Sixtiers consistently gave flesh to a sense of personal self and insisted, in the spirit of Heidegger, on the self's unmediated "being-in-the-world." This presupposed a definition of the relations between the "I" and the "Thou." For the regime the collective was an end in itself, the individual but a means to that end. The Sixtiers radically altered that relationship. The person became the end in itself, and the collective (also in its broad sense as the state) no more than a means for the existence of the individual. The collective, therefore, had no right to exercise mechanisms of repression; on the contrary, its obligation was to protect the individual, guaranteeing its essential freedoms. This conception was the basis of the demands for democratic transformation and the rule of law that the Sixtiers explicitly and consistently formulated in their letters of protest and their critical essays.

The poetry of Symonenko, Stus, Lina Kostenko, Drach, and Vinhranovs'kyi rejected the collectivist Soviet "we." Poetry defended the inner world of the individual and affirmed its absolute value. The formal equivalent of this centrality of the "I" was different for each poet. Symonenko's style was straightforwardly emotive, that of Drach was surreal, Lina Kostenko's philosophical, Stus's hermetic, and Vinhranovs'kyi's dreamlike. Symonenko's lines were emblematic:

Ти знаєш, що ти – людина?
Ти знаєш про це чи ні?
Усмішка твоя – єдина.
Мука твоя – єдина.
Очі твої – одні.[31]

(Do you know that you are a person?
Do you know this or not?
Your smile is unique.
Your suffering is unique.
Your eyes are unique.)

The horizon of this "I" was not of this earth; it was cosmic. As Drach put it:

Я – переклятий ворогом не тричі
(Рубцями ран закутана душа),
Дивлюся зорям в мерехтливі вічі.[32]

(Cursed more than thrice by enemies
[My soul is swathed in the scar tissue of wounds],
I gaze into the shimmering eyes of stars.)

Or Lina Kostenko:

З неба, гір і свободи собі збудувала дім я.
Небосхил для людини –
                                  якраз відповідна стеля.

Піднімеш думку – і не розіб'єш їй тім'я.[33]

(I built myself a house of sky, of mountains and of freedom.
For a human being the horizon
                                  is just the right ceiling.
If you lift up your thought you won't break its head.)

The horizons of being opened out to infinity: "U syn'omu nebi ia vysiiav lis" (I sowed a forest in the azure sky), one reads in Vinhranovs'kyi,[34] and in Stus, "Nam ie de ity – na khvyli, na zemli – / shliakhy – mov obrii – daleki i prozori" (There are places where we can walk: on waves, on the Earth; / the roads are as distant and transparent as the horizons).[35]

On the one hand there was the cosmic span of the human subject that reached passionately for the horizons of being. On the other hand, there was an illusion-free understanding of the dramas of human existence – and of Ukraine. Camus's idea that "we all carry within us our places of exile"[36] was close to the Sixtiers' sense of themselves. For Stus life was imprisonment and alienation from an intolerable reality: the persona of a poem titled "Meni zdaiet'sia, shcho zhyvu ne ia" (It Seems to Me That It's Not I That Live) has become "Ochuzhilyi / v svoiemu tili" (A Foreigner / in his own body).[37] "Tsvyntar" – cemetery – is a frequent word in the Sixtiers' poetry. *Veselyi tsvyntar* (The Cheerful Cemetery) is the title of one of Stus's collections; the lyrical subject is surrounded by "tsvyntar dush" (a cemetery of souls).[38] For Symonenko "Na tsvyntari rozstrilianykh iliuzii / Uzhe nemaie mistsia dlia mohyl" (In the cemetery of illusions executed by firing squad / There is no more room for graves),[39] while Lina Kostenko asks, "De dumka epokhy, vesela i pechal'na?" (Where is epoch's idea, cheerful and sad?) and responds, "Poïkhala u zakrytomu poïzdi. / Pokhovana na tsvyntari movchannia" (It has departed in a sealed train. / It is buried in the cemetery of silence).[40]

The Sixtiers discovered for themselves the "extreme situation," to invoke Karl Jaspers's term "Grenzsituation," that confronted them with the problem of choice. Choice, the awareness of which was accompanied by a certain fatalism, was a moral imperative: it was necessary stoically to refuse the system's alien offerings in order to elect one's own life, even if it was tragic: "Blahoslovliaiu tvoiu svavoliu, / doroho doli, doroho boliu" (I bless your random tyranny, / O path of fate, O path of pain),[41] Stus would write, or, in another place, "Spodob mene, Bozhe, vysokoho krakhu!" (Render me the honour, O God, of a grand failure!).[42] For Lina Kostenko the poet is Sisyphus:

А ми йдемо, де швидше, де поволі.
Йдемо угору, і нема доріг.
І тінь Сізіфа, тінь моєї долі...
І камінь в прірву котиться з-під ніг.[43]

(And we walk on, here faster, there more slowly.
We walk uphill, and there are no paths.
And there is the shadow of Sisyphus, the shadow of my destiny...
And the stone rolls into the abyss from beneath my feet.)

The price of choice was high: loss of freedom and sometimes of life itself. But by restoring a sense of ethical behaviour the Sixtiers challenged the anonymous dictatorship of the lowest common denominator. They confronted collective lack of responsibility with the agony of individual conscience. "Tse shcho, na vsikh podilene sumlinnia? / [...] Ni, tse na vsikh pomnozhena vyna" (What's this – a conscience divided among all? [...] No, it's guilt multiplied by everyone), Lina Kostenko proclaimed.[44]

For the Sixtiers freedom was the only state of being befitting human dignity. For Stus freedom was achieved through a final loss of illusions: "Utracheni ostanni spodivannia. / Nareshti – vil'nyi, vil'nyi, vil'nyi ty" (Lost are your last expectations. / At last you are free, free, free).[45] For Lina Kostenko the situation of the banned poet meant excluding oneself from an intolerable reality:

Я пішла як на дно. Наді мною свинцеві води.
Тихі привиди верб обмивають стежку з колін.
Захлинулась і впала, як розгойданий сполох свободи,
як з німої дзвіниці обрізаний ворогом дзвін.[46]

(It is as though I have sunk to the bottom. Above me are leaden waters.
Quiet ghosts of willows wash the path from my knees.
I have choked and fallen, like the swung-about tocsin of freedom,
like a bell cut by an enemy from a silent bell tower.)

The bell that sinks in an icy river is inaccessible to hostile bell-ringers. There were choices like this in the Sixtiers' personal destinies: Stus chose prison in order to be free of the system. Lina Kostenko spoke through silence during her sixteen years of non-publication.

The work of the Sixties may be viewed through the prism of Camus's *L'homme révolté* (The Rebel, 1951). The plague of Hitlerism had retreated, but the plague of Stalinism had returned. Rebellion for Camus was more than a possibility or a choice – it was a duty. Camus's credo, "I rebel, therefore I am" and the idea of "metaphysical rebellion" formed the existentialist basis of the Sixties' philosophy. Only rebellion possesses reality, based as it is on one's free choices; it transforms the personality and the surrounding reality. As Lina Kostenko put it,

> А вранці повстану. Обуренням серця,
> веселим азартом очей і ума.
> На вікнах розсиплеться сонячне скерцо
> і рух засміється над скрипом гальма.[47]

> (In the morning I shall rebel. With outrage of heart
> and joyous wager of eyes and mind.
> A sunlit scherzo will spill over the windows
> and movement will laugh over the squeal of brakes.)

Similarly Drach:

> Ми чорні гори перегорнем,
> Ми вдарим серцем в мур зажур,
> Ми розквитаємося з горем
> на рівні вічних партитур![48]

> (We shall overturn black mountains,
> We shall ram our heart into the wall of despondence,
> We shall settle our accounts with grief
> at the level of eternal musical scores.)

It was a case not only of "I rebel, therefore I am," but also of "I rebel, therefore we are." The only real form of connection among people, according to Camus, is solidarity in rebellion against the absurdity of the world and the imperfection of human life. The rebels' transformation of the ethical code transforms "I" into "we." The ethos of solidarity creates a new kind of community able to be embodied as a people, a society, a state. The Sixties saw themselves as being in solidarity with all oppressed nations: in Ukraine especially Jews and Crimean

Tatars, but also all peoples of the USSR, not to mention the Hungarians in 1956 or the Czechs in 1968. The individual and the collective met at the point of ethical duty. This meeting could be with one's own nation or with others; it could cross generations and forms of experience. "Spasybi vam za smutok planetarnyi, / Moi premudri i nerozumni liudy. / Spasybi vam za te, shcho ia – vash brat" (Thanks for this planetary sadness, / My wise and foolish folk. / Thanks for the fact that I'm your brother), wrote Drach.[49] "My – tse ne bezlich standartnykh 'ia,' / A bezlich vsesvitiv riznykh" (We are not a myriad of standard "I's," / But a myriad of different universes), proclaimed Symonenko.[50] Stus wrote of the solidarity of a "handful": "horstka nas. Malesen'ka shchopta / lyshe dlia molytov i spodivannia" (a handful of us. A tiny cohort / only for prayers and expectations).[51] Vinhranovs'kyi celebrated the utopian promise of community:

Прощальний час надій прощальних!
Ми тут. Ми є. Ми – всі. Ми – гурт.
Єднаймося! Ми є той грунт
Подій майбутніх, вирішальних.[52]

(It's time to take our leave of parting hopes!
We are here. We are. We are all of us. We are a team.
Let us unite! We are the ground
Of future events, decisive ones.)

The Sixtiers inaugurated a new understanding of time and of history. Historical themes were important in their poetry and prose, which not only offered an alternative to official historiography but also altered the method of reflecting on history. Official history represented time as the immobile, solemn time of the system, indifferent to the individual and remote from the concrete flow of life. The Sixtiers fashioned a subjective, personalized, existential time that undermined "Soviet history" from within, opening up the unrepeatability and unique value of every moment of human life. It was no accident that Drach's collection of 1967 and Kostenko's of 1980 bore the titles, respectively, *Balady budniv* (Ballads of Everyday Life) and *Nepovtornist'* (Unrepeatability). Drach revealed the phantasmagorical in the everyday, Kostenko the "deathless touch upon the soul" ("bezsmertnyi dotyk do dushi") of the most fleeting moments of human life. At the same time Lina Kostenko's historical works (especially her novels in verse *Marusia Churai* and *Berestechko*) and Vinhranovs'kyi's (the novel *Nalyvaiko* and his historical poems), as well as the prose of Valerii Shevchuk, linked history to the problematic of the present while also rethinking Ukrainian history as part of the history of Europe.

Most importantly – again, in contradiction of official history – history in the works of the Sixtiers was the history of turning points, moments of *kairos*, whose agents were human beings. As the human being became the subject of history, so the future became the locus of human choice and decision, challenging intellect and conscience. This turn was a triumph over the determinism of a system that had dragooned history into a ruthless Marxist spiral.

The title of Stus's collection *Palimpsesty* (Palimpsests, 1986) was emblematic of the Sixtiers' understanding both of history and of language: it is necessary layer by layer to read the texts that become visible one beneath the next in order to get to the primary, authentic word. "Dusha tysiacholit' shukaie sebe v slovi" (the soul of millennia seeks itself in the word), said Lina Kostenko.[53] The new vision of history became possible through a new awareness of language, not as a resource serving regime ideology but as a symbolic representation of the world, a way of organizing one's picture of being.

Thanks to this new sense of language the Sixtiers renewed the communicative dimension of culture. The Soviet system had created a language in which words no longer carried their primary meanings. "Liberty" meant prison, "internationalism" was xenophobia, "progress" was degradation, and the "decay of the West" was its florescence. Lina Kostenko called this "vid'oms'ki shabashi fiktsii" (witches' sabbaths of fictions).[54] Loneliness beset individuals who were unable to express themselves or to communicate, and for whom Orwellian doublethink and newspeak had become self-protective habits. The Sixtiers confronted such "words" with the Word that craved rejuvenation, reconstruction, and the rediscovery of its meanings. The poet, wrote Lina Kostenko, was "alkoholik strachenoi suti, / ïï Sizif, alkhimik i murakh" (an alcoholic of lost essence, / its Sisyphus, its alchemist and ant).[55]

Likewise, the Sixtiers posed the question of their homeland in a new way. "Homeland" was one of the central motifs of Soviet ideological rhetoric. This abstract "wide native land" had no inner boundaries and cultivated the "person of new formation" as a creature without memory or connection to roots. Against an uncritical formal love for a "measureless Fatherland" was ranged a love for a home for which one had chosen to suffer and that housed the stratified memory of generations. In such a home, as Lina Kostenko put it, "Smutok nashchadkiv – iak tanets' bdzholy, / tanets' bdzholy do bezsmertnoho polia" (The sadness of successors is like the dance of a bee, / the dance of a bee for its undying field);[56] in this home "halaktychnyi Kyïv bronzoviie / u merekhtinni naidorozhchykh lyts'" (the bronze of a galactic Kyïv / looms in the shining of beloved faces).[57] From this perspective the concrete homeland – the habitat, the familiar and intimate space of belonging – opened for the human person the cosmic dimension of being.

The writer is fated to oppose all forms of oppression. Poems are "smertel'ni platsdarmy / samotn'oï bytvy z derzhavamy, / z chasom, / z samym soboiu" (lethal bridgeheads / in the lonely battle with states, / with the times, / with one-self).[58] It was in this sense that the rebellion of the Sixtiers was less a political than, in the words of Václav Havel, an "existential revolution," an inalienable part of the protest movement of East European intellectuals, for whom "antipolitical politics" was but "one of the ways of seeking and achieving meaningful lives, of protecting them and serving them."[59] And just such a revolution is the source of democracy, insofar as it contributes to the moral renewal of society by reviving the link between the "I" and the "human community" – through the discovery in oneself of a yearning for truth and the dimension of infinity.

Notes

1 Bogumiła Berdychowska and Aleksandra Hnatiuk, eds., *Bunt pokolenia: Rozmowy z intelektualistami ukraińskimi* (Lublin: Uniwersytet Marii Curie-Skłodowskiej, 2000), transl. into Ukrainian by Roksana Kharchuk as *Bunt pokolinnia: Rozmovy z ukraïns'kymy intelektualamy* (Kyiv: Dukh i litera, 2004).

2 Marco Carynnyk, "Poetry and Politics," *Studia ucrainica* 4 (Ottawa: University of Ottawa Press, 1988), 23–31; Marko Pavlyshyn, "Kvadratura kruha: Prolehomeny do otsinky Vasylia Stusa," in *Kanon ta ikonostas* (Kyiv: Chas, 1997), 157–74; Iurii Sherekh, "Trunok i trutyzna: Pro 'Palimpsesty' Vasylia Stusa," in *Porohy i zaporizhzhia* (Kharkiv: Folio, 1998), 2: 105–35.

3 Ievhen Malaniuk, "Malorosiistvo," in *Knyha sposterezhen'* (Kyiv: Atika, 1997), 226–7; Leonid Kutsenko, "Ievhen Malaniuk nad riadkamy poezii Liny Kostenko," *Den'* 48, 19 March 2005, http://day.kyiv.ua/uk/article/cuspilstvo/ievgen-malanyuk-nad-ryadkami-poeziy-lini-kostenko.

4 Bohdan Boichuk, *Spomyny z biohrafii* (Kyiv: Fakt, 2003).

5 Bohdan Boichuk, "Istoriia mozhe staty elementom hordosti, tvorchosti i natkhnennia," interview with Nadiia Tysiachna, *Den'* 237, 26 December 2008, http://day.kyiv.ua/uk/article/kultura/bogdan-boychuk-istoriya-mozhe-stati-elementom-gordosti-tvorchosti-y-nathnennya.

6 The article "Smert' shistdesiatnytstva" (The Death of the Sixtiers Movement) by the politician Oles' Donii was symptomatic: it accused the Sixtiers of unwillingness to resume the role of "civic activists." *Dzerkalo tyzhnia* 6, 10 February 2001, http://gazeta.dt.ua/SOCIETY/smert_shistdesyatnitstva.html.

7 Iurii Kurnosov, *Inakomyslennia v Ukraïni (60-ti–persha polovyna 80-kh rokiv)* (Kyiv: Instytut istoriï NANU, 1994); Heorhii Kas'ianov, *Nezhodni: Ukraïns'ka intelihentsiia v rusi oporu 1960–80-kh rokiv* (Kyiv: Lybid', 1995); Borys Zakharov, *Narys istoriï dysydents'koho rukhu v Ukraïni (1956–1987)* (Kharkiv: Folio, 2003).

8 Osyp Zinkevych and Oles' Obertas, *Rukh oporu v Ukraini: 1960–1990. Entsyklopedychnyi dovidnyk* (Kyiv: Smoloskyp, 2010); Oles' Obertas, *Ukraïns'kyi samvydav: Literaturna krytyka ta publitsystyka (1960-i–pochatok 1970-kh rokiv)* (Kyiv: Smoloskyp, 2010).

9 Dmytro Drozdovs'kyi, *Kod maibutn'oho: Filosofiia ukraïns'koho shistdesiatnytstva* (Kyiv: Vsesvit, 2006); Roman Korohods'kyi, *Brama svitla: Shistdesiatnyky* (Lviv: Vydavnytstvo Ukraïns'koho Katolyts'koho Universytetu, 2009) and *Do bramy svitla: Portrety* (Kyiv: Dukh i litera, 2016); Liudmyla Tarnashyns'ka, *Ukraïns'ke shistdesiatnytstvo: Profili na tli pokolinnia* (Kyiv: Smoloskyp, 2010) and *Siuzhet doby: dyskurs shistdesiatnytstva v ukraïns'kii literaturi XX stolittia* (Kyiv: Akademperiodyka, 2013).

10 Ievhen Sverstiuk, *Bludni syny Ukraïny* (Kyiv: Znannia, 1993); Mykhailyna Kotsiubyns'ka, *Moï obriï*, 2 vols. (Kyiv: Fond "Ukraïna," 2009); Korohods'kyi, *Brama svitla*; Iryna Zhylenko, *Homo feriens* (Kyiv: Smoloskyp, 2011); Lina Kostenko, "U maibutn'oho slukh absoliutnyi," interview with Oksana Pakhl'ovs'ka, Ivan Dziuba, *Ie poety dlia epokh* (Kyiv: Lybid', 2011), 98–203; Ivan Dziuba, Lina Kostenko, and Oksana Pachl'ovs'ka, "*Harmoniia kriz' tuhu dysonansiv...*" (Kyiv: Lybid', 2016).

11 See Drahomanov's "Malorossiia v ee slovesnosti" [1870] and "Chudats'ki dumky pro ukraïns'ku natsional'nu spravu" [1891], in Mykhailo Drahomanov, *Vybrane* (Kyiv: Lybid', 1991), 5–45 and 461–558, respectively.

12 Myroslav Shkandrij, *Modernists, Marxists and the Nation: The Ukrainian Literary Discussion of the 1920s* (Edmonton: Canadian Institute of Ukrainian Studies, 1992).

13 Mykola Zerov, "Ad fontes," in *Tvory v dvokh tomakh* (Kyiv: Dnipro, 1990), 2: 585.

14 Mykola Khvyl'ovyi, "Ukraïna chy Malorosiia?" in *Novely. Opovidannia. "Povist' pro sanatoriinu zonu." "Val'dshnepy." Poetychni tvory. Pamflety* (Kyiv: Naukova dumka, 1995), 673.

15 Dmytro Dontsov, *Rosiia chy Ievropa? ta inshi eseï* (Kyiv: Dakor, 1992), 19.

16 Milan Kundera, "The Tragedy of Central Europe," *New York Review of Books*, 26 April 1984, 33–8.

17 Jerzy Giedroyc, *Emigracja ukraińska: Listy 1950–1982*, ed. Bogumiła Berdychowska (Warsaw: Czytelnik, 2004).

18 Józef Łobodowski, "Przeciw upiorom przeszłości," in *Nie jesteśmy ukrainofilami: Polska myśl polityczna wobec Ukrainców i Ukrainy*, ed. Paweł Kowal, Jan Ołdakowski, and Monika Zuchniak (Wrocław: Kolegium Europy Wschodniej, 2002), 231–92.

19 Andrzej Sulima Kamiński, *Historia Rzeczypospolitej wielu narodów, 1505–1795: Obywatele, ich państwa, społeczeństwo, kultura* (Lublin: Instytut Europy Środkowo-Wschodniej, 2000).

20 They include the poets Vasyl' Stus (1938–85), Vasyl' Symonenko (1935–63),
Lina Kostenko (b. 1930), Ivan Drach (b. 1936), Mykola Vinhranovs'kyi
(1936–2004), Iryna Zhylenko (1941–2013), Ihor Kalynets' (b. 1939), and
Vasyl' Holoborod'ko (b. 1945); the prose writers Valerii Shevchuk (b. 1939),
Hryhir Tiutiunnyk (1931–80), Volodymyr Drozd (1939–2003), Ievhen Hutsalo
(1937–95), and Iurii Shcherbak (b. 1934); the essayists and rights activists Ivan
Dziuba (b. 1931), Ivan Svitlychnyi (1929–92), Nadiia Svitlychna (1936–2006),
Viacheslav Chornovil (1937–99), Iryna Stasiv-Kalynets' (1940–2012), Ievhen
Sverstiuk (1928–2014), Mykhailo Osadchyi (1936–94), Semen Gluzman (b.
1946), Mykhailo Horyn' (1930–2013), Bohdan Horyn' (b. 1936), Valentyn Moroz
(b. 1936), Leonid Pliushch (1939–2015), the founders of the Ukrainian Helsinki
Accords Monitoring Group Mykola Rudenko (1920–2004), Levko Lukianenko
(b. 1928), and Ivan Hel' (1937–2011), as well as three who died in exile: Valerii
Marchenko (1947–84), Oleksa Tykhyi (1927–84), and Iurii Lytvyn (1934–84);
the historians Mykhailo Braichevs'kyi (1924–2001), Olena Kompan (1916–86),
Olena Apanovych (1919–2000), Iaroslav Isaievych (1936–2010), Iaroslav
Dashkevych (1926–2010), Iaroslav Dzyra (1931–2009); the literary historians
Volodymyr Krekoten' (1929–95), Dmytro Nalyvaiko (b. 1929) and, again, Valerii
Shevchuk, as well as the literary critics Ivan Dziuba, Roman Korohods'kyi
(1933–2005), and Mykhailyna Kotsiubyns'ka (1931–2011); the philosopher
Vasyl' Lisovyi (1937–2012); and the linguists Oleksandr Mel'nychuk (1921–77),
Vasyl' Nimchuk (b. 1933), Oleksandr Ponomariv (b. 1935), Hryhorii Pivtorak (b.
1935), and Ivan Svitlychnyi. The Sixtiers movement contributed to modernization
in most of the art forms: in the visual and plastic arts – Alla Hors'ka (1929–70),
Teodoziia Bryzh (1929–99), Halyna Sevruk (b. 1929), Liudmyla Semykina (b.
1924), Opanas Zalyvakha (1925–2007), Heorhii Iakutovych (1930–2000), Ivan
Marchuk (b. 1936), Ivan Ostafiichuk (b. 1940), Liubomyr Medvid' (b. 1941), and
Bohdan Soroka (1940–2015); in cinema – Serhii Paradzhanov (1924–90), Iurii
Illienko (1936–2010), Leonid Osyka (1940–2011), Ivan Mykolaichuk (1941–87);
in music – Lesia Dychko (b. 1939), Myroslav Skoryk (b. 1938) and the so-called
"Kyiv avant-garde" or "bastard children of Anton Webern," comprising Ievhen
Stankovych (b. 1942), Valentyn Syl'vestrov (b. 1937), Leonid Hrabovs'kyi (b.
1935) and Volodymyr Huba (b. 1938), and in popular music – Volodymyr Ivasiuk
(1949–79). Translators played a notable role as "Europeanizers": Hryhorii Kochur
(1908–94), Mykola Lukash (1919–88), Ol'ha Seniuk (b. 1929), Ievhen Popovych
(1930–2007), Anatol' Perepadia (1935–2008), Iurii Lisniak (1929–95), Dmytro
Palamarchuk (1914–98), and Andrii Sodomora (b. 1937).
21 Lina Kostenko, "U maibutn'oho slukh absoliutnyi," *Vybrane* (Kyiv: Dnipro,
1989), 147–8.
22 Albert Camus, *Discours de Suède* (Paris: Gallimard, 1958), 13.

23 Quoted in Ivan Dziuba, "Dusha, rozplastana na plasi," in Ivan Svitlychnyi, *Sertse dlia kul' i dlia rym* (Kyiv: Radians'kyi pys'mennyk, 1990), 17.
24 Ievhen Sverstiuk, "Shistdesiatnyky i Zakhid," *Bludni syny Ukraïny*, 32.
25 Ibid., 28.
26 Ibid.
27 Mikola Bazhan, "Nelegkii put'," Zhan-Pol' Sartr, *Slova* (Moskva: Progress, 1966), 22.
28 Kostenko, "U maibutn'oho slukh absoliutnyi," *Vybrane*, 147.
29 Oleksandr Skopenko and Tetiana Tsymbaliuk, eds., *Frazeolohiia perekladiv Mykoly Lukasha: Slovnyk-dovidnyk* (Kyiv: Dovira, 2003); Borys Cherniakov, *Mykola Lukash: Biobibliohrafichnyi pokazhchyk 1953–2005* (Kyiv: Krytyka, 2007); Leonid Cherevatenko, ed., *Nash Lukash*, 2 vols. (Kyiv: Vydavnychyi dim "Kyievo-Mohylians'ka Akademiia," 2009–11).
30 Maksym Strikha, *Ukraïns'kyi khudozhnii pereklad: Mizh literaturoiu i natsiietvorenniam* (Kyiv: Fakt, 2006).
31 Vasyl' Symonenko, "Ty znaiesh, shcho ty – liudyna?" in *U tvoiemu imeni zhyvu* (Kyiv: Veselka, 1994), 59.
32 Ivan Drach, "Nizh u sontsi," in *Protuberantsi sertsia* (Kyiv: Molod', 1965), 122.
33 Lina Kostenko, "Vyrlooke sontse," in *Vybrane*, 142.
34 Mykola Vinhranovs'kyi, "U syn'omu nebi ia vysiiav lis," in *Z obiiniatykh toboiu dniv* (Kyiv: Veselka, 1993), 26.
35 Vasyl' Stus, "Ne odliuby svoiu tryvohu ranniu," in *Tvory u chotyr'okh tomakh, shesty knyhakh* (Lviv: Prosvita, 1994–99), 1: 152.
36 Albert Camus, *L'homme révolté* (Paris: Gallimard, 1951), 372.
37 Stus, "Meni zdaiet'sia, shcho zhyvu ne ia," *Tvory*, 1, bk. 1: 155.
38 Stus, "Iak strashno vidkryvatysia dobru," *Tvory*, 1, bk. 1: 177.
39 Symonenko, "Prorotstvo 17-ho roku," *U tvoiemu imeni zhyvu*, 61.
40 Kostenko, "Vyrlooke sontse," *Vybrane*, 142.
41 Stus, "Uzhe Sofiia vidstrumenila," *Tvory*, 3, bk. 1: 153.
42 Stus, "Hoidaiet'sia vechora zlamana vit'," *Tvory*, 3, bk. 1: 28.
43 Kostenko, "Tin' Sizifa," *Vybrane*, 180.
44 Kostenko, "Duma pro brativ neazovs'kykh," *Vybrane*, 514.
45 Stus, "Utracheni ostanni spodivannia," *Tvory*, 1, bk. 1: 178.
46 Kostenko, "Ia pishla iak na dno,"*Vybrane*, 198.
47 Kostenko, "Hotychni smereky nad baniamy bukiv," *Vybrane*, 62.
48 Drach, "Protuberantsi sertsia," *Protuberantsi sertsia*, 11.
49 Drach, "Nizh u sontsi," *Protuberantsi sertsia*, 140.
50 Symonenko, "Ia...," *U tvoiemu imeni zhyvu*, 144.
51 Stus, "Iarii, dushe. Iarii, a ne rydai," *Tvory*, 1, bk. 1: 163.
52 Vinhranovs'kyi, "Nich Ivana Bohuna," *Z obiiniatykh toboiu dniv*, 255–6.

53 Kostenko, "Skifs'ka Odisseia," *Vybrane*, 442.

54 Kostenko, "Hotychni smereky nad baniamy bukiv," *Vybrane*, 62.

55 Kostenko, "Marnuiu den' na poshuky nezrymoi…," *Vybrane*, 187.

56 Kostenko, "Zatinok, sutinok, den' zolotyi," *Vybrane*, 15.

57 Stus, "Sosna iz nochi vyplyvla, mov shchohla," *Tvory*, 3, bk. 1: 32.

58 Kostenko, "Velyki poety ne vmiiut' pysaty virshiv," *Vybrane*, 175.

59 Václav Havel, "In Search of Central Europe: Politics and Conscience," *Salisbury Review* 3, no. 2 (1985): 37.

Waiting for Europe: Public Intellectuals' Visions and Political Reality on the Eve of the Euromaidan

OLA HNATIUK

In the years of Ukraine's independence one of the most important subjects of public debate in Ukraine has been the country's European orientation and its need for integration into the European Union.[1] In the course of this debate there has been a significant shift in the position of public intellectuals. Between the Orange Revolution of 2004 and the revolution of 2013–14 known as the Euromaidan that ended the presidency of Viktor Yanukovych and toppled his government, intellectuals grew disappointed with the European Union's neglect of Ukraine's European aspirations, just as they increasingly came to reject Ukrainian internal politics.

In 2004 Viktor Yushchenko's main declared aim during his presidential campaign was to integrate Ukraine into the EU. Throughout his presidency the Ukrainian and EU flags were displayed side by side next to the presidential headquarters and residence. These EU flags disappeared on 26 February 2011, the day of Viktor Yanukovych's presidential inauguration. This change was symbolic of the new president's realpolitik. There had been only one period during which Ukraine's foreign policy was oriented more towards the European Union than towards Russia: the first months of the Yushchenko presidency.

This introductory statement should not imply that the following discussion will be a(nother) "chronicle of the Orange defeat," to quote the subtitle of a book by Mykola Riabchuk, one of Ukraine's best-known public intellectuals.[2] In contrast to Riabchuk, I want to focus attention not on the political elite but primarily on those public intellectuals in Ukraine who were the most active advocates of the country's European orientation. My analysis takes cognizance of the changes after 2004 which, on the one hand, influenced and transformed Ukrainian political discourse on Europe and, on the other, changed the attitude of Ukrainian citizens towards integration into the EU.

There is a correlation between social attitudes and the activities of public intellectuals. Public intellectuals are part of society, and their withdrawal from the public space into Internet social networks from the mid-2000s onward made it easier to manipulate public debate. Their ambiguity as far as EU integration was concerned, combined with the findings of research into attitudes of Ukrainians in recent decades, leads me to my thesis that in the years preceding the Euromaidan public intellectuals in Ukraine adopted a strategy of passivity. I shall begin by using sociological data to look at the attitudes of Ukrainians to EU integration during the first decade of the twenty-first century. I shall then examine the role of public intellectuals in shaping public opinion in Ukraine. These considerations will allow me to analyse the attitudes towards Europe of key figures in Ukrainian intellectual life and to conclude with some general remarks.

Attitudes towards EU Integration

In the decade commencing in 2000 support for Ukraine's integration into the EU decreased by almost 20 per cent, while disapproval of EU integration increased by almost 30 per cent. In the course of the Yushchenko presidency a paradoxical situation emerged. While the elite favoured entering a community of more highly developed states, the population at large cooled towards Europe: in 2008 support for Ukraine's integration into the EU was 17 per cent less than it had been in 2006. At the same time support for the idea of union with Russia and Belarus remained steady at 60 per cent.

However, a comparison between the percentages of people who supported and who rejected EU integration in 2004–5 and in 2009 shows that the change of attitudes during the second half of the decade was not as significant. A poll conducted in April 2011 suggested that 51.2 per cent of Ukrainians supported European integration.[3]

A comparison between this poll and another in which people were asked to identify the most desirable direction for Ukraine's international relations indicated increasing interest in a close relationship with Russia (52.5 per cent in November 2009 and 46.3 per cent in May 2010, while in April 2005 it had been 34.9 per cent) and decreasing interest in a partnership with the EU (26.5 per cent in May 2010 and 23.8 per cent in November 2009, while in April 2005 it had been 39.6 per cent).[4] Another public opinion poll conducted in December 2009 inquired into public support for integration into the EU and into the Eurasian Economic Community (EurAsEC). It revealed a similar tendency: 58 per cent of respondents supported EurAsEC and 51 per cent the EU.[5] Analysts concluded that such parallel support for EurAsEC and for EU integration provided evidence that public opinion was split. Moreover, this split then appeared to be permanent. According to data published in 2011 by the Institute of Public Affairs (Poland), those who favoured an orientation towards either EurAsEC or the EU, together with those who were undecided, made up approximately two-thirds of Ukraine's population.[6] Data published in 2012 by the Razumkov Centre showed a different picture – support for EurAsEC had decreased.

Intellectuals and Public Debate

Ukrainian public intellectuals are the most prominent group in Ukraine who actively support a European orientation for the country.[7] After the Orange Revolution some of them believed that they had succeeded in transmitting their ideas to the public and that the revolution itself was the best evidence of their impact.[8] However, their impact on public opinion is hard to measure, and the very existence of public opinion in Ukraine was regarded by some as problematic.[9] Such prominent public intellectuals as Yuri Andrukhovych, Oksana Zabuzhko, Yaroslav Hrytsak, and Mykola Riabchuk pointed out that they had limited impact on public opinion and political debate.[10] Even more radically, Heorhii Kas'ianov argued that there was no such phenomenon as a public intellectual in Ukraine.[11] On a similar note, Oleksandr Boichenko sarcastically referred to public intellectuals as "superfluous people."[12] Some public intellectuals, for instance Mykola Riabchuk and Heorhii Kas'ianov, argued that the proper places for serious debate on issues of public concern are conferences and other instruments of academic life.

Some analysts attributed this weak position of public intellectuals to the weakness of Ukrainian media and their dependence on the Russian media market, which continued to dominate Ukraine's information space.[13] However, this fragility of the Ukrainian media was not the only and most likely not even the most crucial reason for the aforementioned changes in public attitudes. In my opinion, this state of affairs was the outcome of a number of significant domestic factors that cannot be reduced to the combination of a totalitarian legacy and a postcolonial syndrome. (The latter view was espoused by Mykola Riabchuk, who argued that postcolonial elites are inherently weak, persisting as they do in their orientation towards the empire.)[14]

When public intellectuals are excluded from such mass media spaces as television debates, this cannot be explained by the gravitation of elites to an "old colonial center" or its postimperial successor. During the period under discussion political television shows in Ukraine – programs geared towards entertaining rather than informing – occupied the media space that in other circumstances could have served as a platform for serious political discussion among members of the intellectual elite. Paradoxically, while such television shows as "Svoboda slova" (Freedom of speech) were widely criticized for being poor in quality and failing to adhere to codes of journalistic conduct, they succeeded in promoting their style as a certain norm. Consequently, political television shows began to offer little by way of serious debate. This situation was of advantage as much to owners of television stations as to the ruling authorities: the former reaped commercial benefits from it, while the latter exploited it as a safety valve. (Media owners and politicians, incidentally, were often the same people.)

One of the factors that can contribute to the degradation of public debate is the responsiveness of mass culture to political manipulation. Already in 1930 Jose Ortega y Gasset described this phenomenon in detail in his work *La rebelión de las masas* (The Revolt of the Masses). Increased censorship beginning with the presidential elections of 2010[15] was another important factor contributing to the elimination of intellectuals from the public media landscape.[16] In addition, it became a common practice among political television show moderators to reduce the pool of invited guests to a particular cohort of politicians and political analysts dependent on political parties or oligarchs. Consequently, a nationwide audience could witness the simulacrum of a debate in which the place of public intellectuals was taken by persons who used their academic titles and formal positions in supposedly independent research institutes to manipulate the public. One can describe this state of the affairs using Viktor Shklovskii's metaphor of the "Hamburg score": because medieval circus owners displayed only their most popular circus giants, the giants had to meet in a Hamburg tavern once a year to establish among themselves their true hierarchy of strength. Ukrainian media owners, like these circus owners, preferred to show popular stars and pretend that they did so in response to the taste of the mass audience.

How did Ukrainian public intellectuals express their positions if they had been effectively banned from public debate? They used genres (blogs, social networks, e-news portals) made possible by new electronic media technologies. Some were also columnists in the print media. However, quality magazines and the analytical press had low circulations and their popularity could not be compared to that of TV debates.[17] For instance, in 2011 the national newspaper *Den'* (The Day) had an official circulation of 62,000 and the analytical *Dzerkalo tyzhnia* (Weekly Mirror) a mere 31,000. (In reality these circulations were even lower than the official data suggest.) By contrast, in Poland the circulations of the nationwide *Gazeta Wyborcza* (Electors' Gazette) and the weekly *Polityka* (Politics) were 400,000 and 140,000 copies respectively, although Poland's population is about nine million less than Ukraine's. Not only were the circulations of both of the aforementioned Ukrainian publications outstripped by those of the Russian-language tabloids and magazines that dominated the Ukrainian market, they were also small compared to the circulation figures of the regional press, which enjoyed wide popularity. For example, the circulation of *Molodyi bukovynets'* (The Young Bukovynian), a newspaper from the smallest Ukrainian *oblast'*, amounted to 53,000 copies, the Lviv daily newspaper *Vysokyi Zamok* (High Castle) distributed 100,000 copies, and *Ekspres* (Express), the regional tabloid for Western Ukraine, circulated around 500,000 copies. Ukrainian readers often preferred the regional press to national newspapers.[18]

Such a situation contributed to the further atomization of a public opinion that was already divided on many issues and, consequently, to the fragmentation of Ukrainian society. It promoted deeper regional rifts and acted against the formation of nationwide public opinion. Furthermore, Ukrainian editions of the Russian press helped expand the pan-Russian information sphere to Ukraine, in accordance with Kulyk's and Riabchuk's aforementioned theses concerning the pervasiveness of Russian domination of the media. In sum, there was little chance that a true discussion forum and a space for politicians and intellectuals to exchange opinions could emerge on the pages of the Ukrainian press.

Let us compare the circulation of some of the respected Ukrainian print periodicals, such as *Dzerkalo tyzhnia* or *Den'*, with the most popular Internet publications, such as *Ukraïns'ka Pravda* (Ukrainian Truth), *Polit.UA*, *Zaxid. net*, or even Internet portals such as *Istorychna pravda* (Historical Truth) that appealed to a narrow band of intellectual users. (*Istorychna pravda*, according to its editor-in-chief Vakhtanh Kipiani, had 30,000 visiting users.) Comparison between the readership of the printed and electronic press shows that in Ukraine even marginalized newspapers had more readers than the e-media. Yet public intellectuals clearly preferred to place their publications in the e-media,[19] a shift dating back to 2004–5. The Internet gave a voice to even the most marginalized and exotic minorities who previously had no chance of a public presence. This shift, however, reinforced the dominant tendency towards the fragmentation of the public sphere. Research into Internet communication and social networks has demonstrated that active communication between bloggers grows in proportion to the similarity of the sources being used. The kind of communication encouraged by the Internet thus contributes to a deeper fragmentation of a national audience, and at the same time to the further polarization of already disparate viewpoints.[20]

Between 2000 and 2011 the number of Internet users in Ukraine increased almost tenfold. However, this rate of increase was low in comparison with Germany, where it was three times higher, and Poland, where it was twice as high.[21] Internet users in Ukraine were concentrated predominantly in Kyiv and other large cities with populations of over a million. The majority of them were young people aged between fifteen and twenty-nine who used the Internet primarily for leisure, self-education, and social networking, and less as a source of information about current political events.[22] These facts further suggest that the impact of the Internet on public debate is rather limited.

In certain respects new media technologies facilitated the free expression of opinion, since authors using them were not (normally) subject to word limits or censorship. On the other hand, Ukrainian public intellectuals now operated mainly within the new Internet-based media, and their absence from media outlets with the largest outreach, such as the most popular television channels, significantly reduced their already limited influence.

Public Intellectuals and Their Attitudes

In the early 2010s two issues of importance for Ukrainian intellectuals were subject to public debate: the assessment of Stepan Bandera, the controversial leader of one branch of the Organization of Ukrainian Nationalists during and after the Second World War, and the purported differences between Ukraine's West and East. While these were issues of importance to Ukraine's internal political life, they were also connected to Ukraine's European debate.

The debate on the place of Bandera in the heritage of the national movement started in January 2010 and lasted for a year. The last decree of Viktor Yushchenko's presidency conferred upon Stepan Bandera the title of Hero of Ukraine.[23] The debate revealed how ambiguous the nation's feelings about Bandera's legacy were. Many Ukrainians who took part in the discussion regarded Bandera and the Ukrainian nationalists of the period from the 1920s to the 1940s as an important part of the history of the Ukrainian national movement, and their activities as steps anticipating the achievement of independence in 1991. The totalitarian heritage of Organization of Ukrainian Nationalists was omitted from this perspective. In its resolution deploring Yushchenko's decree, the European Parliament added a European dimension to the debate.[24] Public intellectuals treated this declaration as a show of support for Viktor Yanukovych, the new Ukrainian president, and proof of the European Parliament's lack of support for Ukraine's democratic opposition. Moreover, the parliament's insistence that Ukraine adhere to common European values was criticized as an application of double standards.[25] Many questioned the parliament's right to make such statements when it had repudiated "Ukraine's European dream."[26] Mykola Riabchuk argued that Ukrainian nationalism should not be judged by the same criteria as Polish or Russian nationalism. Yaroslav Hrytsak maintained that Ukrainians saw Bandera not as a fascist but as the leader of a national liberation movement.[27] Thus the Bandera debate revealed an inconsistency in the views of Ukrainian public intellectuals: they appeared not ready to reject the burden of the nationalist movement, and at the same time they declared their esteem for European values.

The dispute about internal contradictions within Ukraine (I shall call it "the debate on the two Ukraines," adapting the title of Riabchuk's well-known book),[28] which had lasted more than a decade, intensified after the presidential elections of 2010. In the mid-2000s the prevalent belief had been that Ukraine as a country was unified rather than divided. Hrytsak, summing up his discussion of "two Ukraines" with Riabchuk, gave his readers the following advice: "if you are watching TV or reading a newspaper and see a program or a text about the inexorable and insurmountable linguistic, cultural and political incompatibility of Ukraine's two parts, you can just switch to another channel or jump to the next text. Life is too short to waste time on old jokes."[29] But by 2010–11 most public intellectuals were convinced that the split between two different orientations (to simplify, the pro-European and pro-Russian) was one of Ukraine's main obstacles on the road to joining the EU. Some of them believed that the partition of Ukraine would help citizens in the Western part of the country liberate themselves from a "Donetsk occupation regime" and realize their "European dream."

In the next part of my analysis I shall examine three variations of a project for modernizing Ukrainian identity that Yuri Andrukhovych, the pre-eminent writer-intellectual in the Europe-oriented part of Ukrainian public discourse, proposed at intervals of more or less five years. The first emerged in 2000–1, the second in 2004–5, and the third in 2010–11. The first was characterized by a slight shift from an open identity model based on the notion of an open society towards a closed identity model that endorsed a society based on ethnic values. The second displayed a pendulum-like oscillation between these models, and the third was marked by an ultimate transition to the closed identity model under the banner of a farewell to political illusions. Although this project as described here has Andrukhovych as its author, he was not alone in championing it. On the contrary: it attracted many supporters.

I would like to place this project into the context of a number of key events in the Ukrainian politics of the time: first, the murder in 2000 of the journalist Heorhii Honhadze, the disclosure of recordings that appeared to link the then president, Leonid Kuchma, to this event (the so-called Cassette Scandal) and the "Ukraine without Kuchma" campaign; second, the falsified elections of 2004 that resulted in mass protests memorialized as the Orange Revolution, and the rise to power of two political parties: Yushchenko's "Our Ukraine" and the "Yulia Tymoshenko Bloc" (known as BYuT); and, third, the election as president in 2010 of Viktor Yanukovych of the Party of Regions. It is useful to recollect some of the slogans associated with each of the presidents of Ukraine during this period: Leonid Kuchma's so-called multivector policy, as well as his statement that "nobody is waiting for us in Europe"; Viktor Yushchenko's catchphrase "Ukraine's European choice"; and, finally, Viktor Yanukovych's promise of "Ukraine for the people" that ostensibly signalled a focus on internal policies with the aim of "implementing European standards of living and social security."

Two international events had a strong effect on Ukrainian attitudes towards the EU. On 1 May 2004 EU membership increased by ten states and the new EU members were incorporated into the Schengen area, resulting in the introduction of a new visa regime. In public discourse these events generated a number of new expressions, including "united Europe" (and the "fresh members" within it), as well as "the new Iron Curtain" or "Velvet Curtain," the latter articulating the consequences of the EU and Schengen-area enlargement for Ukraine. The first phrase masked an inner contradiction: although the enlargement of the EU appeared to be a further unification of Europe, the countries that did not join the EU remained "outside Europe." The expression "whereas in Europe" began to denote a divergence and an opposition; it became an element of mapping, a gesture that unconsciously placed Ukraine outside Europe.

Just as important as these two events were official EU statements on which the Ukrainian media commented widely: the European Neighbourhood Policy declaration of February 2005, which Ukraine was given in lieu of a prospect of EU membership, and the European Parliament's above-mentioned resolution on Ukraine of February 2010. There was a widespread view that the very phrase "Neighborhood Policy" could not compete with the traditional notion of the "brotherhood" that, many believed, linked Ukraine to Russia and rendered Ukraine's displacement "back to the USSR" inevitable.[30]

In my book *Farewell to Empire*,[31] analysing the European discourse in Ukrainian intellectual debates of 1990–2001, I observed in those debates a curtailment of the liberal discourse and a shift to the right, as well as a tendency to endorse a closed-identity model. This trend was noticeable even among those intellectuals who advocated a European or a Central European identity for Ukraine. The metaphor of a "besieged fortress" in Yuri Andrukhovych's essay "Little Intimate Urban Studies," published in 2000, reflected a change in his Central European project. The essayist proposed the notion of a Central European identity as an attractive alternative to a (post-)Soviet identity and, at the same time, as a way of modernizing a traditional closed ethnic identity. While intellectuals actively debated the issue of Ukrainian identity, this project of a renewed identity did not evolve into a model of open identity, Andrukhovych's initial declarations notwithstanding. Instead, it was replaced by a closed-identity model oriented towards identity homogenization through the exclusion of others.

However, the influence of the Orange Revolution of 2004 interrupted this drift in Andrukhovych's writings. The sense of victory (which did not last long) convinced the essayist that intellectuals had successfully managed to convey European ideas to the broad public. For Andrukhovych as well as for many political observers the events of the Orange Revolution symbolized the triumph of the European idea. Yet disillusionment was not long in coming: despite President Yushchenko's declarations, and despite unprecedented European public support for Ukraine's aspirations, there emerged no clear prospects for Ukraine's joining the EU. The reformers in Ukraine did not receive even symbolic support,[32] and pro-European attitudes rapidly gave way to an orientation towards the EurAsEC. Awareness of this defeat took root in 2005–6, as resentment towards the EU came to dominate Ukrainian public discourse.

In his essay "Atlas: A Meditation," written in August 2005, Andrukhovych tried to defend his understanding of Central Eastern Europe, which he defined as a territory "between the Russians and the Germans and, after 1 May 2004, the space between Russia and the EU." Central Eastern Europe seemed to him to have started "drifting eastward across Ukraine"; the greatest challenge lay in a Ukraine divided by the Dnipro, while Russia appeared as a different (other) continent. Andrukhovych's bitterness was explicit: "future historians will define as the gravest sin of EU enlargement […] the division of my Central Eastern Europe and its further fragmentation and allocation to different centers; and among these centers at least one, Moscow, is in fact no center any more, however insistently it pretends otherwise."[33] The essayist was equally straightforward when he called the failure to offer European prospects to Ukraine a betrayal. He attributed this failure, on the one hand, to the mercenary nature of Eurocrats and their "reluctance to anger Russia" and, on the other, to double standards. Twenty years after Milan Kundera's famous essay "The Tragedy of Central Europe" Andrukhovych repeated Kundera's claim: the West had betrayed its own European values in Central Europe under pressure from a civilizational "other." The essayist did not directly account for the EU's refusal to give Ukraine any hope of membership, blaming a collection of Western stereotypes concerning Ukraine and a civilizational clash with the East. In other words, he perceived Ukraine's exclusion from the EU as the consequence of external, not internal, factors.

If we compare this perspective with the outcomes of opinion polls, we shall be surprised by the difference between the opinions of Andrukhovych and the public. Ten times fewer respondents attributed Ukraine's failure to secure prospects for EU membership to geopolitics or cultural differences than to the economic situation or to corruption.[34]

It is worth remembering that "Atlas: A Meditation" was written nine months after the Orange Revolution and eight months after an unprecedented personal success for Andrukhovych: his address to the European Parliament in Strasbourg. At that time he had spoken of EU enlargement as an expansion of European values, a cultural phenomenon that had occurred during the 2004 elections in Ukraine. He also emphasized the need to offer European prospects as the most effective means of backing "the European choice of Ukraine":

> Europe has expanded by those Ukrainian regions where Viktor Yushchenko has won. After December 26 – I sincerely believe this – it will expand by the whole of Ukraine. [...] What do "we" expect of "you"? First of all, ladies and gentlemen, a clear rebuttal of what Mr. Kuchma's propaganda machine has spent the last decade trying to prove: that nobody is waiting for us in Europe; [and a rebuttal of] what Mr. Yanukovych based his whole campaign upon: that in Europe they dislike us and sneer at us – that for Europe we are aliens. Ladies and gentlemen, I am convinced that Kuchma and Yanukovych lied to us. Although I am merely a writer, I do have some eccentric wishes of my own. I would like to hear Europe clearly say that Kuchma, Yanukovych and their public relations people are wrong: that Europe awaits us; that Europe cannot do without us; that Europe without Ukraine will not be completely fulfilled.[35]

In essays written after 2006 Andrukhovych expressed his feelings of personal defeat and betrayal by the EU. These works, addressed directly to the European audience, carried such provocative titles as "Europe: My Neuroses" and "Europe is Not Yet Dead." In the former Andrukhovych took issue with Günter Verheugen, the vice-president of the European Commission, who in an interview with the German newspaper *Die Welt* (20 February 2006) ruled out further EU enlargement to encompass countries of the former USSR. In the latter essay Andrukhovych defined the EU as a "special project of psychological compensation: a union of postimperial losers who have not managed to become superpowers on their own." True Europe, the Europe of values, had revealed itself in Ukraine, and formal borders had little importance for feeling European:

> One might assume, extravagantly, that Europe is wherever the local inhabitants imagine themselves to be in Europe or, even more extravagantly, consider themselves to be Europeans [...]. The Orange Revolution unexpectedly reanimated the whole ethical and worldview conglomerate that is traditionally referred to as "European values." In other words, the victory, though shaky and tenuous, of the Ukrainian revolution toward the end of 2004 was in fact a victory of Europe *with a little help from the Ukrainian people*. For in the course of those few weeks toward the end of 2004 *the Ukrainian people* through their every action, individual and collective, transformed those rhetorical European values into real ones.[36]

Andrukhovych also strongly objected to the seemingly innocent habit, common in daily conversation, of identifying Europe with the EU.

Ukrainian intellectuals resented the EU for refusing to grant European prospects to Ukraine as well as for introducing visa requirements for Ukrainians travelling to the new member states, and expressed their resentment in more[37] or less[38] emotional forms.

It is instructive to compare Andrukhovych's views with the attitudes of Ukrainians at large. A study by Natalia Panina shows that, in October 2006, a time close to the period when Andrukhovych wrote his essays, Ukrainians declared an extraordinarily high level of trust in the European Parliament (much higher than in Germany, France, and the United Kingdom). At the same time Panina detected a very low degree of civic activity among Ukrainians (only 2 per cent of the country's citizens were members of non-governmental organizations). While Ukrainians were unwilling to participate in organizations that might influence the governance of the country, they were ready to trust and support new authorities. Consequently, they quickly became disillusioned with these new authorities "when they did not receive everything and at once."[39] Panina also noted that the high level of support for European integration mainly reflected people's desire to have a high standard of living and did not necessarily correlate with a belief in European values or in a market economy; indeed, she quoted data showing that anti-free-market attitudes were growing concurrently with the geopolitical orientation towards the East. In addition, Ukrainians turned out not to be ready to ban political parties that rejected democracy.

The juxtaposition of social attitudes attested by sociological data against Andrukhovych's vision as a public intellectual (the views of Oksana Zabuzhko as articulated in *Let My People Go*, not analysed here, are not dissimilar) leads to an obvious conclusion: political realities were remote from the visions born of the euphoria of the Orange Revolution. Of course, without such faith any great movement, particularly a revolution, would have been impossible.

The fall of illusions came in 2010, after the Party of Regions came to power in Ukraine. Andrukhovych's Central European project and the metaphor of "two Ukraines" now took on a different shape – one that many called "separatist." In July 2010, when Andrukhovych declared this shift during an interview,[40] Hanna Herman, a high-ranking adviser to President Yanukovych, entered into heated polemics with him, asserting that a famous writer was propagating in the West the idea of "the possibility of changing the borders of the united Ukraine."[41] Oksana Zabuzhko, a writer and public intellectual no less critical of the new government than Andrukhovych, also rejected his view, though from a different perspective.[42] According to Andrukhovych's vision, Ukraine, deprived of unnecessary makeweights like the Crimea and the Donbas, would be a more successful country capable of internal reforms. More importantly, this Ukraine would be immune to Russia's influence, as it would belong to Europe rather than the "Russian world." A further provocative statement by Andrukhovych appeared in the *Frankfurter Allgemeine Zeitung*, flashily titled "Please Watch My Country!"[43] Reactions to the Andrukhovych-Herman debate included Oleksandr Boichenko's feuilletons, full of black humour: "Back in the USSR," "Together, But Not with Them," and "Tabachnyk Above All."[44] Boichenko's scepticism did not allow for the exposition of a straightforward vision of his own "ideal Ukraine": "Sometimes I think I would like to support the two-Ukraines plan and protect at least the Europe that exists, for example, in Lviv, from the Asia that presses upon it, for example, from Donetsk. But as soon as I have thought this, I begin to think something else: it's one thing to look like Europe in the context of Donetsk, and quite another in the context of Europe. Having fenced itself off from Asia with a state border, might Lviv not find itself in the role of the new Donetsk of Europe?"[45]

Among more analytical responses was Taras Vozniak's essay "Vacillations of an Electoral Pendulum, or Preparations for the Abolition of the Ukrainian Project?" Vozniak expressed alarm that "disregard for any *Ukrainian* substance of the *Ukrainian* state in *Ukraine* has reached monstrous proportions. If events continue to develop at the same pace as now, Ukraine will inevitably lose its identity."[46]

The rhetoric of exclusion and the references to an ethnonational model of identity that replaced a previous open identity model have obvious implications. In contrast to the situation that emerged in the aftermath of the Euromaidan, in the Ukraine of 2011 no political force stood for the division of Ukraine, but there were groupings that advocated ethnic nationalism and used antidemocratic slogans. No doubt the third version of Andrukhovych's project grew out of the deep disappointment that he voiced in July 2010: "Five years ago I believed that my vision of this country, which I shared with many, would triumph. I could not imagine that in 2010 this vision would suffer such a crushing defeat. It is wrong to speak of a lost battle. It is the war that is lost. And the consequence of a lost war is occupation. In Ukraine there is already an expression for it: 'inner occupation.' We have been occupied from within, by means of presidential elections and parliamentary machinations."[47]

In the course of 2010, the notion of "internal occupation" was incorporated into right-wing political discourse. It became part of the rhetoric of the right-wing party "Svoboda" and other political groups further to the right.[48] The oxymoron "internal occupation" is also used, surprisingly, by some serious political observers.[49] Intellectuals who used the term were concerned about the situation in Ukraine, and justifiably so: reports of human rights violations and denial of freedom of speech in Ukraine left no doubt that the situation was alarming. Yet intellectuals were hardly unaware of the danger of using the term "inner occupation" to describe a situation brought into being by elections that were recognized as fulfilling OSCE norms. To speak of "inner occupation" in this context meant to deny the validity of democratic processes. It was self-contradictory to advocate democratic values and at the same time reject the results of legitimate elections.

Throughout 2010 and 2011 Andrukhovych voiced his concerns about Ukraine's future many more times,[50] believing that he, as a writer and public intellectual, should say what others pass over in silence. He did not reserve his critical treatment for the Ukrainian political elite alone, taking aim, as well, at the EU establishment and its Eastern policies.

Conclusions

Finally, I should explain the title of these reflections – "Waiting for Europe." Yes, it does suggest passivity on the part of intellectuals. It should be clear that I have in mind passivity not as a lack of activity but as a deliberate strategy. In social terms – and here I refer to the second part of my article – we witnessed intellectuals withdrawing from the space of public debate, and that space subsequently becoming fragmented. The departure of intellectuals from public forums and their turn to the new media was one of the expressions of this strategy of passivity – a deplorable one, for maintaining the public sphere is at least partially the responsibility of intellectuals. Public intellectuals were and still are the main promoters of the European idea in Ukraine; the diminution of their role in society, combined with prevailing distortions in the forums of public debate, weakened their influence and thereby that of the European discourse. In such a situation their hopes to be heard both inside and outside of the country seemed to be wishful thinking.

The title of Andrukhovych's appeal, "Please Watch My Country!," best reflected this strategy of passivity. After the election of Yanukovych as president it was published in ten European languages. In the political world, opposition politicians such as Borys Tarasiuk, a tireless critic of both Ukraine's foreign policy and Europe's Ukrainian policy, exemplified this strategy of passivity. Ukraine appeared to lack a political message that could be understood by both Ukrainians and foreigners. Oleksandr Boichenko once joked that he did not know how European politicians could understand their Ukrainian colleagues in translation if he himself did not understand them in the original. In the spirit of his witticism one can say that no knowledge of a foreign language or cultural code guarantees such understanding. If thoughts were expressed, in

European languages and with reference to European values, that contradicted those very values, there could be no hope for Ukraine of understanding or support from Europe. Ukraine's waiting for Europe had become a "Waiting for Godot" – an attitude learnt, fittingly, from the theatre of the absurd.

May 2011

Notes

1 This chapter was first written in April 2011 as a kind of afterword to my book, *Pożegnanie z imperium: Ukraińskie dyskusje o tożsamości* [Farewell to Empire: Ukrainian Discussions of Identity] (Lublin: UMCS, 2003); translated into the Ukrainian as *Proshchannia z imperiieiu* (Kyiv: Krytyka, 2005). While the chapter reflects upon the situation of intellectuals in Ukraine prevailing at the beginning of the Yanukovych presidency, developments up to 2015 have underscored the continuity of some of the fundamental problems of Ukraine's internal politics that are discussed here, and of the country's geopolitical predicament.

2 Mykola Riabchuk, *Uliublenyi pistolet pani Simpson: Khronika pomaranchevoï porazky* (Kyiv: K. I. S., 2009).

3 "Does Ukraine need to join the European Union? (recurrent, 2002–2011)," Razumkov Centre, http://www.razumkov.org.ua/eng/poll.php?poll_id=387. See also data delivered by SOCIS in September 2010: 47.1 per cent of citizens would vote for integration of Ukraine with the EU and 24.9 per cent would be against it (www.socis.kiev.ua). Another sociological study of Ukrainian society during the independence period paints a picture that is only slightly different: support for EU integration decreased from 56 per cent in 2000 to 41.4 per cent in 2011, and disapproval of EU integration increased from 9.6 per cent in 2000 to 20.5 per cent in 2011 (*Ukraïns'ke suspil'stvo: 20 rokiv nezalezhnosti. Sotsiolohichnyi monytorynh* [Kyiv: Instytut sotsiolohii, Natsional'na Akademiia Nauk Ukraïny, 2011], 2: 162).

4 These polls were conducted by the Razumkov Centre and Il'ko Kucheriv's Democratic Initiatives Foundation (www.razumkov.org.ua).

5 The poll was conducted by Democratic Initiatives and the Ukrainian Sociological Service on 12–26 December 2009 (http://dif.org.ua). See also data delivered by the Institute of Sociology of the National Academy of Sciences of Ukraine: a Western orientation for Ukraine's foreign policy was preferred by only 16.4 per cent of respondents, while 53.3 per cent favoured an Eastern orientation (*Ukraïns'ke suspil'stvo*, 2:29).

6 Joanna Konieczna-Sałamatin, *Coraz dalsi sąsiedzi? Wizerunek Polski i Polaków na Ukrainie* (Warsaw: Instytut Spraw Publicznych, 2011).

7 For extensive discussions of the world views of intellectuals in Ukraine, see my *Pożegnanie z imperium*, as well as relevant chapters in Larissa M. L. Zaleska

Onyshkevych and Maria G. Rewakowicz, eds., *Contemporary Ukraine on the Cultural Map of Europe* (Armonk, NY: M. E. Sharpe and Shevchenko Scientific Society, 2009).

8 See, e.g., Andrukhovych, "Evropa: Moï nevrozy," *Krytyka* 10, no. 5 (2006): 29–30 (Andrukhovych's acceptance speech, delivered on 15 March 2006, at the ceremony conferring upon him the Leipzig Book Fair Prize for European Understanding), and Oksana Zabuzhko, "Publichnyi intelektual v Ukraïni," in *Let My People Go* (Kyiv: Fakt, 2005), 114.

9 See the interviews in the series "Intelektual'nyi prostir Ukraïny" published on the website *Polit.ua* at the end of 2010 and the beginning of 2011 (http://polit.ua).

10 Iurii Andrukhovych, "U teperishnii Ukraïni rezhymovi vdalosia znachnoiu miroiu marhinalizuvaty publichnykh intelektualiv," *Polit.ua*, accessed on 8 September 2016, http://dialogs.org.ua/ru/periodic/page21833.html; Oksana Zabuzhko, "My prodovzhuiemo zhyty na ruïnakh odnoï z naistrashnishykh totalitarnykh imperii," *Polit.ua*, accessed on 30 April 2011, http://polit.ua:8080/print/articles/2011/03/25/zabuzhko.html; Iaroslav Hrytsak, "Zrada intelektualiv," *Zaxid.net*, http://zaxid.net/blogs/showBlog.do?zrada_intelektualiv&objectId=1102830, and his "Intelektual ta vlada," *Krytyka* 9, no. 10 (2005): 2–4; and Mykola Riabchuk, "Na poliakh ukrainskoi intelektual'noi zhizni," *Polit.ua*, accessed on 30 April 2011, http://polit.ua/articles/2010/11/23/Riabchuk.html.

11 Georgii Kas'ianov [Heorhii Kas'ianov], "Vlast' i intelektualy – eto protivopolozhnosti," *Polit.ua*, accessed on 30 April 2011, http://polit.ua/articles/2010/11/10/kasianov.html.

12 Oleksandr Boichenko, "Zaivi liudy, tobto intelektualy," *Ukraïns'kyi zhurnal* 1 (2011): 22–3.

13 For a detailed account of this domination see Volodymyr Kulyk, *Dyskurs ukraïns'kykh medii: identychnosti, ideolohiï, vladni stosunky* (Kyiv: Krytyka, 2010), 177–408.

14 Riabchuk, "Na poliakh."

15 In a poll conducted by the Sociological Rating Group on 6 November 2011 45 per cent of respondents said that they believed that freedom of speech had been curtailed (www.ratinggroup.com.ua). See also the detailed report of the Kharkiv Human Rights Protection Group (http://www.khpg.org/index.php?id=1298305884).

16 Oksana Zabuzhko, "Publichnyi intelektual v Ukraïni," 113.

17 *Ukraïns'ke suspil'stvo*, 2: 124–5.

18 Ibid., 2: 125.

19 Yaroslav Hrytsak said of his essay "Movchannia ne po-evropeis'ky," "On *Zaxid.net* it has been read by 8000 persons, and more than 100 have commented on it," accessed on 30 April 2011, http://zaxid.net/home/showSingleNews.do?movchannya_ne_poyevropeyski&objectId=1066324#comAnch.

20 See, for example, Eric Lawrence, John Sides, and Henry Farrell, "Self-Segregation or Deliberation? Blog Readership, Participation, and Polarization in American Politics," *Perspectives on Politics* 8, no. 1 (2010): 141–57; Eszter Hargittai, Jason Gallo and Matthew Kane, "Cross-ideological Discussions among Conservative and Liberal Bloggers," *Public Choice* 134, no. 1 (2008): 67–86.

21 *Ukraïns'ke suspil'stvo*, 2: 123 and 2: 448.

22 See the results of polls of Internet users in Ukraine in *Obozrevatel'*, accessed on 4 May 2011, http://watcher.com.ua/2011/02/03/ukrayinska-internet-audytoriya-za-2010-r-zrosla-na-29-doslidzhennya-gemius/, http://watcher.com.ua/2011/04/14/pronyknennya-internetu-sered-doroslyh-zhyteliv-ukrayiny-stanovyt-35/, and http://watcher.com.ua/2011/04/15/mayzhe-10-mln-ukrayintsiv-schodnya-zahodyat-v-internet/. I am grateful to Vakhtanh Kipiani for these references.

23 For details of the debate see Tarik Amar, Ihor Balyns'kyi, and Iaroslav Hrytsak, eds., *Strasti za Banderoiu* (Kyiv: Hrani-T, 2010).

24 Resolution RC-B7-0116/2010 of 17 February 2010 concerned the European aspirations of Ukraine in the context of the imminent presidential elections. One of its twenty-one sections stated that the European Parliament "deeply deplores the decision by the outgoing President of Ukraine, Viktor Yushchenko, posthumously to award Stepan Bandera, a leader of the Organization of Ukrainian Nationalists (OUN) which collaborated with Nazi Germany, the title of 'National Hero of Ukraine'; [and] hopes, in this regard, that the new Ukrainian leadership will reconsider such decisions and will maintain its commitment to European values." "European Parliament Resolution on the Situation in Ukraine," accessed on 21 July 2013, http://www.europarl.europa.eu/sides/getDoc.do?language=EN&reference=RC-B7-0116/2010.

25 Oleksandr Boichenko, "Moia rezoliutsiia z pryvodu sytuatsiï v Ievroparlamenti," in *Aby knyzhka* (Chernivtsi: Knyhy XXI, 2011), 249–51.

26 Hrytsak, "Klopoty z pamiatiu," in *Strasti za Banderoiu*, 353; Boichenko, "Moia rezoliutsiia," 252.

27 Hrytsak, "Klopoty z pamiatiu," 346.

28 Mykola Riabchuk, *Dvi Ukraïny: Real'ni mezhi, virtual'ni hry* (Kyiv: Krytyka, 2003). See also my analysis of this text in *Pożegnanie z imperium*, 245–51.

29 "Dvadtsiat' dvi Ukraïny," in *Strasti za natsionalizmom*, ed. Iaroslav Hrytsak (Kyiv: Krytyka, 2004), 228.

30 Halyna Iavors'ka and Oleksandr Bohomolov, *Nepevnyi obiekt bazhannia: Ievropa v ukraïns'komu politychnomu dyskursi* (Kyiv: Vydavnychyi dim Dmytra Buraho, 2010), 65–77.

31 Hnatiuk, *Pożegnanie z imperium*, esp. 173–285..

32 Two years earlier, responding to the question, "What is your advice for EU policy towards Ukraine," the historian Natalia Yakovenko said, "What I would like to change is the [EU's] view of Ukraine, which should be seen not as one of the EU's

'neighbours,' but as a potential candidate for EU membership. Naturally, between a potential and a real candidate there lies a chasm of requirements that Ukraine is not yet able to fulfil. But if Ukraine were treated as a potential candidate, this would help overcome Ukrainian society's ambivalence concerning its orientation and would decisively increase the number of supporters of a 'European choice,' and this in turn would help advance reforms and change." Oleksandr Sushko and Nataliia Parkhomenko, eds., *Ievropeis'ka intehratsiia Ukraïny v otsinkakh lideriv ukraïns'koho polítykumu, biznesu ta suspilstva* (Warsaw: Fundacja Stefana Batorego; Kyiv, Mizhnarodnyi Fond Vidrodzhennia, 2003), 187.

33 Iurii Andrukhovych, "Atlas: Medytatsii," *Krytyka* 10, no. 1–2 (2006): 10.

34 A poll conducted by the Razumkov Centre on 17–24 December 2008 showed that 70.4 per cent of respondents saw the level of economic development as the main obstacle to Ukraine's European integration. Almost as many (64 per cent) named · the high level of corruption as a major obstacle, and only 7.4 per cent believed that geopolitical circumstances, i.e., Ukraine's close ties with Russia, played a role.

35 Iurii Andrukhovych, "Vriatuvaty prokliatu Ukraïnu," *Ukraïns'ka pravda*, 15 April 2004, accessed on 30 April 2011, http://www.pravda.com.ua/articles/2004/12/15/3005387/; my emphases.

36 Iurii Andrukhovych, "Shche ne vmerla Evropa" (speech delivered on 24 November 2006 at the Kyiv conference "Europe: Past and Future. Vision and Revision"), *Krytyka* 11, no. 1–2 (2007): 8–9. In the original Ukrainian text the phrases shown here in italics appeared in English.

37 Oleksandr Boichenko, recalling the Polish writer, Marek Hlasko, wrote: "Even in my state of indignation I wish Europe no ill. I would like to come to an understanding with her. A few of Putin's tanks on the Champs Elysees, a few looted shops ... could greatly facilitate this process." Boichenko, "Soiuz ievropeis'kykh radians'kykh respublik," *Ukraïns'kyi zhurnal* 2 (2009): 19.

38 Mykola Riabchuk, for example, asserted that "in the last decade denizens of the West added new phobias to their natural disinclination to share their hard-earned shashliks with who-knows-whom: above all, fear of militant Islamists and their terrorist Jihad ... The 'East' has become for the West not merely an external problem, but an internal one as well." Riabchuk, "Ievroshashlyk: kil'ka retseptiv," in *Sad Metternikha* (Lviv: Klasyka, 2008), 278.

39 Natalia Panina, "Ukraïns'kyi profil' na evropeiskomu tli," *Krytyka* (2006), 11.

40 The UNIAN news agency published the interview under the headline, "Andrukhovych: If the Orange forces win, Crimea and the Donbas should be allowed to secede" (accessed on 8 September 2016, http://www.unian.net/ukr/news/news-387844.html). In subsequent interviews the writer claimed he had been misunderstood.

41 BBC, "Intelektual'nyi 'separatyzm': Herman vs. Andrukhovych," 4
August 2010, accessed on 30 April 2011, http://www.bbc.co.uk/ukrainian/
news/2010/08/100803_herman_andrukhovych_oh.shtml.

42 Asked for her view of Andrukhovych's proposal that Ukraine separate from the
Donbas, Zabuzhko answered, "I gave my opinion on Yuri's wish to be at the
centre of attention at all costs, even if the world should be on fire, ten years ago
when he published his awful 'anti-Kyiv' essay 'An Intimate Little Urban Study.'"
Oksana Zabuzhko, "XXI stolittia bude stolittiam 'zhinochykh fashyzmiv,'"
Ukraïns'ka pravda, accessed on 9 September 2011, http://life.pravda.com.ua/
interview/2010/09/27/61220/. See also Natalia Vlasenko, "Stariiuchyi radians'kyi
18-richnyi khlopchyk – Zabuzhko pro Andrukhovycha," Gazeta.ua, 8 August
2011, http://gazeta.ua/articles/culture/_stariyuchij-radyanskij-18-richnij-hlopchik-
zabuzhko-pro-andruhovicha/393812.

43 Juri Andruchowytsch [Andrukhovych], "Bitte beobachten Sie mein Land!"
Frankfurter Allgemeine Zeitung, 11 August 2010, http://www.faz.net/aktuell/
feuilleton/buecher/autoren/juri-andruchowytsch-in-der-faz-bitte-beobachten-sie-
mein-land-1608799.html. The text was reprinted in many European newspapers.
Russian media reported about it in ten languages as a sensation.

44 The feuilletons were published in Ukraïns'kyi zhurnal, Post-postup and Kraina.
The entire collection appeared in 2011 as Oleksandr Boichenko, Aby knyzhka.

45 Oleksandr Boichenko, "Lviv: Sutsil'na ambivalentnist'," Zaxid.net, 21 January
2008, accessed on 8 September 2016, http://artvertep.com/print?cont=4942;
emphases in the original.

46 Taras Vozniak, Retrospektyvna politolohiia: Epokha Ianukovycha (Lviv: Ї, 2010),
73; emphases in the original.

47 Andruchowytsch, "Bitte beobachten Sie mein Land!"

48 The definition of "internal occupation" that appeared on the official website of
Svoboda and was then copied by Ukraïns'ka pravda was as follows: "In general,
inner occupation is the coming to power of a minority group whose social position,
consciousness and interests contradict those of the majority … In Ukraine it rests on
the remains of the former empire and is supported by revanchists in the Kremlin"
(Iurii Noievyi, "Vnutrishnia okupatsiia," accessed on 8 September 2016, http://www.
pravda.com.ua/columns/2010/06/8/5115764/). The author claimed that a "regime of
internal occupation" had come into being immediately after the fall of the USSR. A
creature of the post-communist nomenklatura, it was now supported by activists of
Our Ukraine (aligned with Yushchenko) and BYuT (the Yulia Tymoshenko bloc). He
implied that only one political movement, Svoboda, could confront this "regime." The
phrase "internal occupation" was probably first used by the "Tryzub" organization,
which, together with Svoboda and UNA-UNSO, organized demonstrations using the
slogans "Down with the internal occupation! Long live the national revolution!"

49 Taras Vozniak, for example, has stated that "the minority that voted for the government now in power has entirely usurped everything in my country. For that reason I cannot refer to the situation in my country as anything other than an occupation." See Vozniak, "Promova na tradytsiinomu sviatkuvanni 'Mezha roku' i vruchenni nahorod seredovyshcha 'Ï,'" 15 December 2010, accessed on 30 April 2011, http://www.ji-magazine.lviv.ua/seminary/2010/mezha_roku_2010.htm#1.

50 See, for example, Iurii Andrukhovych, "Ukraïny cherez 20 rokiv ne bude," *Polit.ua*, 8 September 2016, http://dialogs.org.ua/issue_full.php?m_id=21977, and "Utrata nezalezhnoï Ukraïny ie nadzvychaino real'noiu," *Deutsche Welle, Ukraine*, 5 May 2010, http://www.dw.de.

Epilogue. The EuroRevolution: Ukraine and the New Map of Europe

SERHII PLOKHY

The Ukraine Crisis, as the Russian annexation of the Crimea and the hybrid war in Donbas became known in international media, began in late December 2013 with a group of young Kyivan urbanites, many of them students, camping on the Maidan (the Independence Square in downtown Kyiv) to protest against the refusal of the Ukrainian government to sign an Association Agreement with the European Union. The protests became known as a EuroRevolution, or Revolution of Dignity. As government forces attacked the protesters, hundreds of thousands of Ukrainians showed up on the streets of their capital to voice their disapproval of the authorities' actions. It was the largest political rally in history sparked by a foreign policy decision, as well as a manifestation of belief in the transforming power of the European Union and its institutions at the very time when trust in those institutions inside the Union was at one of its lowest points. The Kyiv protests led to a change of government in Kyiv and provoked Russian aggression against a West-leaning country. Thousands were killed and wounded and millions of Ukrainians citizens were displaced as a result of the conflict. Despite the war and unprecedented pressure from Russia, the new Ukrainian government signed an Association Agreement with the EU and embarked on a series of reforms, viewing the country's future as linked to the family of European nations, either within the European Union or in close alliance with it.[1]

The vision of Ukraine as an integral part of Europe and a future member of the European Union took off in Ukraine in the aftermath of the Orange Revolution of 2004, one of whose main slogans was "joining Europe." The leader of the revolution, Viktor Yushchenko, declared in his inaugural address in January 2005, "Our path to the future is the one now being followed by United Europe. We belong to the same civilization as its peoples; we share the same values."[2] President Yushchenko and his numerous supporters were in for a disappointment. The leaders of the European Union, troubled by its internal problems and preoccupied with the difficulties accompanying the two waves of eastward expansion in 2004 and 2007, were not eager to consider any new members. Moreover, Ukraine was far behind its western neighbours who had joined the Union in bringing its legal and economic system up to EU standards. The Yushchenko years became known as a period of "Euroromanticism," but they left some important marks on the identity of Yushchenko's countrymen. They also put Ukraine on the mental map of Europe. Western media coverage of the Orange Revolution familiarized the publics of English-speaking countries with the names "Kyiv" and "Ukraine."

When the pro-European protests began in Kyiv in November 2013, Ukraine was no longer an unknown country in Eurasia. Whatever the Western public thought about Ukraine's pro-EU aspirations, few questioned its European credentials, and many sympathized with the protesters' demands for closer ties with the European Union. Ukrainian resistance to Russian aggression only enhanced these attitudes. The Ukrainian protesters' belief in Europe as a model for reform in their own country and the ability of the member countries of the European Union to stand by Ukraine in its time of trouble surprised the Russian leadership and dramatically affected EU-Russian relations. It also launched a process that could lead to the political and cultural redefinition of Europe, which until recently has been delimited in the minds of most Europeans by the borders of the European Union. The role of Ukraine in this process is yet to be fully studied and explained.

The Lure of Central Europe

In February 2011 a Kyiv tourist firm called *KievClub* offered its clients a sweet Valentine's Day deal. Advertised as a "romantic weekend in the heart of Europe," it cost only £660 per couple and included a round-trip airfare from Luton airport near London, accommodation in a three-bedroom apartment in downtown Kyiv, and "meet and greet parking." Only twenty years earlier Kyiv, the city in the "heart of Europe" that British tourists were being invited to visit, had been regarded by many in the West as part of Russia and thus not European at all. *KievClub* is not the only firm luring Western clients to the capital of Ukraine by calling it the heart of Europe. The same advertising strategy is employed by *Studio Kiev*, which offers visa support, lodging, language courses, and medical insurance to visitors, and *Kiev Apartments*, which advertises on Facebook, as do many other tourist and real-estate firms in Kyiv. What do the authors of the Kyiv ads mean when they call their city the "heart" of Europe? Whether their British clients know it or not, they are referring to the geographic centre of the continent (or, rather, subcontinent). Once the guests arrive, they can find tour guides who will be happy to bring them to a globe-crowned column on Kyiv's main street that they call the midpoint of Europe.[3]

There was nothing absolutely new or unexpected in the attempts of the Ukrainian businessmen to present their country to the world as a nation at the centre of Europe. This tactic had been used for decades by East European intellectuals and politicians whose nations were left out of the prosperous, democratic West European core. In 1950 Oskar Halecki, a Polish émigré historian living in the United States, offered a version of the European historical and cultural map that redrew the boundaries of Central Europe so as to include Poland in its eastern subdivision. The term "East Central Europe" – the counterpart to "West Central Europe," which included Germany – gained currency in Western academic discourse. In the early 1980s, Milan Kundera, a Czech writer living in Paris, published an essay that not only put his country (along with Poland and Hungary) in the centre of Europe but also defined it as part of the European West. Kundera's assumptions were fully reflected in his title, "The Stolen West or the Tragedy of Central Europe." The essay, translated in 1984 from its French original into English and published in the *New York Review of Books*, became one of the most influential late Cold War texts shaping the views of educated Westerners about the Soviet-occupied lands of Europe on the eve of the collapse of Soviet power in the region.[4]

Both Halecki and Kundera sought to modify an established mental map of Europe that placed Germany and areas immediately south and east of it at the centre of the continent. In the second half of the nineteenth century, Otto von Bismarck had turned a newly united Germany into the hub of European diplomacy; then, at the dawn of the new century, his countrymen declared Dresden the geographic centre of Europe. It was the territories around that centre to which German political thinkers such as Friedrich List and Friedrich Naumann gave the name *Mitteleuropa*, a German-dominated area between Germany in the west and Russia in the east. Writing in the midst of the First World War, Neumann rejected the idea of German imperial rule and military occupation of the region but never clearly defined the form that German predominance was to take. Despite strong misgivings about German plans in the region, the idea of a federal organization of *Mitteleuropa* soon took root among the leaders of peoples struggling against Austro-Hungarian rule. In October 1918 Thomas Masaryk created in the United States a Mid-European Democratic Union composed of representatives of twelve European nations that sought to promote regional economic cooperation as an initial step towards federalization. The Union did not last long, but its creation showed that *Mitteleuropa* was not only a German idea: its non-German inhabitants were also prepared to imagine themselves as part of a separate grouping between France and Russia.[5]

The defeat of the Kaiser's Germany in the First World War, the disintegration of Austria-Hungary, and the diminution of the Russian Empire dramatically changed the situation in the region. The elites of the newly independent countries were now in search of a common new identity but wanted nothing to do with the now discredited name of *Mitteleuropa*. The new states of the region settled for the name of Eastern Europe, despite its implication that this "other" Europe was less than fully civilized. An even worse alternative presented itself: Hitler's attempt to create a German *Lebensraum* in the lands earlier defined as *Mitteleuropa* led to a disastrous world war that completely discredited the older German term. But the idea of a mid-European unity did not disappear completely. Masaryk's vision lived on as an ideal after Eastern Europe was overrun by the Red Army and subjected to rule from Moscow. East European intellectuals were now eager to distance themselves as much as possible from the communist East and associate themselves with the democratic West. As soon as the Berlin Wall fell and Moscow began the gradual withdrawal of its troops from the region, the leaders of Poland, Czechoslovakia, and Hungary met in the Hungarian castle of Visegrád and created a Central European alliance to promote integration with their western neighbours – the European Union and NATO. By 2004 their dream had come true: all of them (Czechoslovakia now divided into the Czech Republic and Slovakia) had joined Western institutions, shedding the legacy of Soviet occupation and the civilizational stigma of Eastern Europe.[6]

Is it fair to say, then, that the Ukrainians are simply following in the footsteps of their western neighbours, trying to sell themselves to the European West as a central and thus indispensable part of Europe that was forgotten, if not betrayed, by its rich western cousin? Yes and no. Yes, in the sense that this was exactly the argument employed by some Ukrainian political leaders and intellectuals in the years following the Orange Revolution. No, in the sense that the Ukrainians are using a different map to make their case. This is not the Germanocentric map of *Mitteleuropa*, even though both Naumann and Halecki regarded parts of Ukraine as components of Middle or East Central Europe, and the practical realization of Naumann's vision led to the German occupation of Ukraine in 1918. Ukrainian leaders, intellectuals, and business people have something else in mind when they claim a central position for their country on the map of Europe. Their mental map can be found in atlases used in schools from Tokyo in the east to San Francisco in the west – with Kyiv, of course, somewhere in the centre. Their Europe does not end at the eastern borders of the European Union or even at the western borders of Russia but extends all the way to the Urals. Such a perspective greatly changes how one defines the centre of the European subcontinent.[7]

The map of Europe used by Ukrainian proponents of European integration is a product of the Enlightenment, and it is as confusing and contradictory as the legacy of the Enlightenment itself. That era produced not only the fathers of the American Revolution but also a cohort of "enlightened despots." The latter included Catherine II, who proclaimed that the Russian Empire, with its vast Asian possessions going all the way to the Pacific, was a European state. Although this definition was unpalatable to Europeans, Russia eventually got its way. After the partitions of Poland – a development welcomed by Voltaire, who believed that, along with Russian troops, civilization and order had finally arrived in that forsaken part of the world – few European rulers or their cartographers dared challenge the claim. They rejected the age-old tradition that began with Strabo, who had placed the eastern boundaries of Europe on the river Tanais, or Don, and redrew the map of Europe by moving its boundaries eastward, all the way to the Ural Mountains. According to the Russian promoters of the change, that was where Russia proper ended and its colonies began.

While European geographers agreed to move their border eastward, the "map of Europe on the mind of Enlightenment," to use Larry Wolff's phrase, remained largely the same. Strabo's map of Europe fitted West European self-perceptions much better than that of Catherine's geographers, and it persisted in the minds of educated European elites for generations to come, no matter what map they had studied in school. This disjunction of the physical, political, and cultural geographies of Europe persisted for most of the twentieth century. It is only if one thinks in Strabo's terms that Dresden can be imagined as the geographic centre of Europe, while Hungary, Poland, and Czechoslovakia are consigned to Eastern Europe.[8]

It appears that Ukrainians treat the Enlightenment-era map of Europe much more seriously than their West European counterparts. They were instructed by generations of teachers that their country was located at the geographic centre of Europe. It was on the territory of today's Ukraine, near the town of Rakhiv (N47°57'46", E24°11'14"), that in 1887 Austrian geographers placed the first known landmark indicating the geographic centre of Europe. In so doing, the Austrians were claiming European centrality for themselves. The Soviets, who took control of the area in 1945, followed suit. The Ukrainians are now doing likewise, but the field has become crowded in the meantime: the Czech Republic, Slovakia, Hungary, Lithuania, Estonia and, last but not least, Belarus have all made similar calculations to boost their European credentials. Politics were part and parcel of all the "discoveries" of the centre of Europe. The French did the calculation for Lithuania when that country was about to leave the Soviet Union, and the Russians confirmed the findings of the Belarusians at a time when Belarus had become an international outcast, counting only the Russian Federation and Venezuela as friendly nations.[9]

Politics are not solely to blame for present-day confusion with regard to establishing the centre of Europe. The complex geography of Europe is also a factor. All recent attempts to "discover" its geographical centre have been undertaken on the basis of a map that goes all the way to the Urals, but calculations differ depending on whether islands are counted and, if so, which ones. There seems to be general agreement among geographers, whatever their political and cultural biases, that the centre of Europe is located somewhere along a line extending through Lithuania, Belarus, Ukraine, and Moldova and bisecting the continent. This line is located east of the countries that make up what is now known as Central Europe. However naive and inaccurate the definition of Kyiv as the centre or heart of Europe (it lies more than 500 km northeast of Rakhiv), it is not completely arbitrary and reflects certain geographic realities that Ukrainians are now trying to turn to their political, economic, and cultural advantage.

While maps and visions of Europe remain diverse, it would appear that Ukrainians are intent on reminding their western counterparts not only about the existence of the "other" Europe but also about its "other" centre. Its self-serving character aside, the *KievClub*'s definition of Kyiv as the heart or centre of Europe not only points to a real problem with the European geographical imagination but also pushes the boundaries of European identity. Irrespective of its authors' wishes, it undermines the Western (and "Orientalist," in Edward Said's sense) vision of the centrality of Western Europe for the geographic, if not cultural, understanding of the subcontinent.

The Shadow of *Mitteleuropa*

In the early 1990s the distinguished French geographer Michel Foucher, one of the world's leading experts on borders and frontiers, put forward his vision of the new Europe that had just emerged from the geopolitical turmoil caused by the fall of the Berlin Wall, the unification of Germany, and the disintegration of the Soviet Empire. In the atlas of "Middle and Eastern Europe" that he produced in 1993, Foucher proposed a concept of Middle Europe (*Europe médiane*) that differed from the *Mitteleuropa* of Friedrich Naumann or Thomas Masaryk. While reminiscent of Oskar Halecki's East Central Europe, it also included the Balkans. Foucher's Middle Europe was characterized by "an intermediate geopolitical situation between the West and the USSR or Russia; a current state of historic transition between these two organizing centers: territorial and political legacies imposed by the East, but modernization henceforth impelled by the West."

The region was largely made up of countries that were under communist control before 1989. Its northern part consisted more or less of those states that now define themselves as belonging to Central Europe: Germany, Poland, the Czech Republic, Slovakia, Hungary, Slovenia, and Croatia. Its southern part included the Balkans, with the sole exception of Greece. According to Foucher, the region "overflowed toward Ukraine and Belarus." Foucher included in Middle Europe those parts of Ukraine and Belarus that belonged to Poland before 1939. Judging by some of the maps, he also included Moldova. By 2007, fourteen years after the atlas appeared, the eastward expansion of the "West" as defined by its political, economic, and military institutions, such as the European Union and NATO, had largely swallowed up Foucher's "Middle Europe." It certainly continues to exist as a historical concept but makes less and less sense in terms of contemporary geopolitics. Still, the area between the "West" – defined in political, institutional, and military terms – and Russia has not disappeared altogether. It has simply moved east towards the countries that Foucher considered to be on the margins of Middle Europe in 1993: Ukraine, Belarus, and Moldova.[10]

This eastward geopolitical shift of the last decade of the twentieth century and the first decade of the twenty-first has also brought Foucher's "Middle Europe" to the region where the continent's centre has been located since the Enlightenment-era revision of Strabo. This is also the region through which Europe's cultural dividing line has run ever since the eleventh century, when the Christian world split into East and West. When the Roman legates excommunicated the patriarch of Constantinople, who responded in kind, the church was divided, leaving the princes of Kyiv on one side and the Polish, Hungarian, and German kings on the other. It soon became apparent that the differences between the two parts of the Christian world were not limited to questions of church jurisdiction, clerical celibacy, or the *filioque* controversy about the procession of the Holy Spirit. The split reinforced already existing differences in relations between church and state: an autonomous if not fully independent church in the West, and a church subservient to the state in the East. These differences turned out to be crucial for the subsequent development of social and political structures. In the West, the existence of a Roman-dominated church often independent of state power helped build autonomous institutions. In the East, the Byzantine legacy of a state-controlled church left little scope for autonomous bodies of any kind. The limited impact of the Reformation on the Orthodox world further contributed to the growth of differences in religious and political culture between the Christian East and West.

The map of Eastern and Western Christendom in Samuel Huntington's bestselling *Clash of Civilizations* shows the boundary between them passing generally along the geographic axis of Europe, with Lithuania, Poland, Slovakia, and Hungary on one side of the divide and Ukraine, Belarus, and Moldova on the other. Indeed, Huntington's line runs through Ukraine, Belarus, and Romania, assigning the western parts of those countries to the sphere of Western civilization. The map allegedly indicates the eastward extent of Western Christianity ca. 1500. In reality, it more or less follows the Soviet-Polish border before 1939. But it was not the geopolitical border of interwar Europe that the cartographers had in mind as they struggled to recreate the realities of pre-Reformation Europe. Their main problem was that of turning the relatively broad Christian frontier, which is not easily mapped, into a clear line. What any such line fails to reflect is the existence of institutions and entire regions that were neither eastern nor western or, alternatively, both eastern and western. One such institution has been the Uniate Church established on the Catholic-Orthodox border in the late sixteenth century, a product of the Catholic Counter-Reformation and the Orthodox need for reform. The Uniate Church was thus Orthodox or Eastern in ritual and tradition but Western in jurisdiction and dogmas. With strong Polish support, it became the dominant church in most of Ukraine and Belarus by the mid-eighteenth century. It was wiped out by the tsars once they took possession of those lands after the partitions of Poland.[11]

The tsars wanted to abolish a church controlled from Rome that had the potential to corrupt the Orthodox world with Western values, the most dangerous of which was independence of church structures from the imperial authorities. The destruction of church institutions independent from the state and linked to the West was also the motive of Joseph Stalin: in 1946, soon after Roosevelt and Churchill agreed at Yalta to the Soviet incorporation of Western Ukraine and Western Belarus, Stalin oversaw the incorporation into the Russian Orthodox Church of the Uniate (Greek Catholic) Church, which had survived in the Western Ukrainian lands ruled from Vienna and then Warsaw. What Stalin tried to achieve, apart from pursuing the goal of the tsars, was to turn the chaotic religious and civilizational frontier into a clearly defined and easily policed cultural and political border. He shipped hundreds of thousands of Roman Catholic Poles to Poland and turned millions of Greek Catholic Ukrainians and Catholic Belarusians into pro forma Orthodox. The resulting outcome was a dream come true for modern map-makers. Finally there was a line that could be drawn not only between Eastern and Western Christianity but also between Eastern and Western civilization. Collapsing religious, national, political, and other frontiers into borders turned out to be a favourite project of modernizing states and societies. Stalin was simply its most brutal and most successful practitioner.[12]

The borders imposed by Stalin had been taken over and reinforced by the European Union. If in the past it was the Soviets who built walls like the one in Berlin, and Westerners who wanted to tear them down, we now see a reversed situation. It is the proponents of Western values who are surrounding their world with walls, from the US-Mexico border to the strictly policed boundaries of the European Union. Keeping out the "barbarians" (generally associated in the public mind with such negative phenomena as illegal immigration, terrorism, and the smuggling of drugs and weapons) while admitting the products of their labour has been a basic task of the European states for decades. During the Cold War they did not have to worry about their eastern borders and could indulge in rhetoric about the free flow of people and ideas. With the fall of the Berlin wall and the eastward shift of the EU borders, the rhetoric has changed: it is no longer about walls but about frontiers and neighbourhoods. But the frontiers of the EU are not regarded in Brussels as open contact zones; rather, they are seen as outer defensive lines, like those of the Roman Empire. The EU is involved beyond its borders and present in its neighbourhood, but one of its reasons for being there is to provide neighbouring governments with incentives to help police the approaches to Fortress Europe. This approach has been an important aspect of EU policy in Ukraine, where, in return for future liberalization of the visa regime, the Ukrainian government was expected to take on the task of policing the perimeter of the European Union. With EU financial assistance and expertise, it has been reinforcing its border controls and promising to take back, process, house, and deport illegal aliens who have managed to cross its territory into the EU.[13]

The fact that the European Union came so close to Ukraine but stopped at its borders not only caused severe dislocations in the post-Soviet economics of the region but also dealt a stunning blow to the self-identification of the Ukrainian elites. Ukraine was now cut off not only from Poland but also from Lithuania – with which it had had long-standing cultural and religious ties. The victory of Solidarity in the Polish elections of 1989 not only triggered the implosion of the Soviet outer empire in what was then known as Eastern Europe but also sent a powerful signal to Vilnius, the capital of the Soviet republic of Lithuania – across a border that did not exist before 1939. The start of Soviet disintegration is often correctly associated with the Baltics. It is important, however, to remember that of the three Baltic countries it was Lithuania, with its close traditional connections to Poland, Belarus, and Ukraine, that began the process. In December 1989, a few months after the victory of Solidarity in Poland and a few weeks after the success of the Velvet Revolution in Czechoslovakia and the fall of the Berlin wall, the Lithuanian communists broke with Moscow, and in March 1990 Lithuania became the first Soviet republic to proclaim its independence.

Ukrainians in Western Ukraine, which had been part of Austria-Hungary before 1918 and part of Poland before 1939, first voted for independence in March 1991. They confirmed their choice, together with Ukrainians from the centre and east of the country, in December 1991, effectively putting an end to the Soviet Union. By that time, the Greek Catholic Church – the most vivid institutional embodiment of the East-West frontier – had emerged from the catacombs and renewed its activity with the help of Pope John Paul II and the reluctant "blessing" of Mikhail Gorbachev. The Moscow-controlled church in Ukraine split in two, with one of the new churches proclaiming its independence of Moscow. The Stalin-imposed cultural border crumbled, and the frontier came back into the everyday lives of Ukrainian citizens. They could now travel not only to Russia but also to Poland, Hungary, Czechoslovakia, and Romania. Then came the expansion of the European Union, which shifted Foucher's Middle Europe to the east and promptly built a visa fence to separate the old Middle Europe from the new one.[14]

The Transformation of the European Frontier

After the European Union admitted all of Ukraine's western neighbours into its ranks in 2007 and the Russo-Georgian war of 2008 put an end to Ukraine's aspirations to join NATO, Ukraine found itself in the centre of a redefined European geopolitical space, but not in the way envisioned by proponents of Ukraine's European integration. That centre is a proverbial "no man's land" between the extended but enervated European Union and the shrunken but resurgent Russian Federation. Optimists in Kyiv began to speak of the new opportunities that this situation afforded their country, which could serve as a bridge (more prosaically, an intermediary) between Europe's east and west. Sceptics, for their part, deplored the de facto buffer status of Ukraine, which they considered all but abandoned by the West (for them, this term meant not so much Western Europe, always reluctant to recognize Ukraine, but the more enthusiastic United States, especially during the tenure of George W. Bush). Despite their differences, both groups in Kyiv recognized the new "in between" reality of Ukraine's geopolitical situation. Even those who before the events of the EuroRevolution believed that the European Union and the United States had relegated Ukraine to the Russian sphere of influence admitted at the time that Ukraine had some power to define its future role between the newly expanded West and the somewhat diminished but increasingly resurgent East.[15]

The tight spot in which Ukraine has found itself during the last few years was a long time in the making. After the Ukrainian referendum of 1991, in which more than 90 per cent of voters supported independence and issued a death certificate to the Soviet Union, the country's elite envisioned a bright future for the newly independent state. To be sure, Russia remained a powerful, chaotic, and aggressive neighbour, but the Kyiv authorities believed that they could ally themselves with the countries of the former Eastern Europe in an Intermarium – an alliance linking the nations between the Baltic and Black Seas, as envisioned by Polish politicians during the interwar years. But times had changed, and Kyiv was in for a disappointment. Having learned the hard lessons of 1939, the new Poland teamed up with Hungary and Czechoslovakia to create not an Intermarium but an alliance meant to accelerate the integration of all three countries into Atlantic structures. Moreover, the countries of the former Eastern Europe (where Russian troops still remained in the early 1990s) avoided dealings with Ukraine so as not to upset Russia, whose leadership wanted to keep Ukraine in the Russian-dominated Commonwealth of Independent States. As Ukraine's western neighbours underwent economic restructuring and began preparing to join the European Union, and while President Clinton pushed through a decision to integrate the region into NATO, the most farsighted among the Ukrainian elites saw the writing on the wall: they might well be left out of the integration process and find themselves obliged to face Russia on their own. In the 1990s Ukraine managed to develop a pluralistic political system that profoundly differed from the much more authoritarian Russian and, especially, Belarusian models, but it was mired in corruption and slow to undertake necessary legal and economic reforms.

Relations with Russia were not all doom and gloom at that time. Boris Yeltsin's Russia allowed Ukraine to distance itself from its former metropolis, and by the end of the 1990s it had signed an agreement recognizing the borders of the newly independent state. The change came at the dawn of the new millennium. The Russia of Vladimir Putin took a much more aggressive stand towards its western neighbour, seeking to interfere in Ukrainian elections and use energy agreements to force Ukraine to join Russia-led economic structures, including the customs union of Russia, Belarus, and Kazakhstan. But Russia's meddling in the Ukrainian presidential elections of 2004 backfired. Massive fraud in favour of a pro-Russian presidential candidate set off the Orange Revolution and brought to power Western-oriented politicians led by Viktor Yushchenko. The new administration tried to enhance its cooperation with the EU and get an invitation to join it at the very time when the Union expanded to the western borders of Ukraine. Poland, Slovakia, and Hungary were admitted into the Union in 2004 and Romania in 2007, but Yushchenko did not manage to crash the European party. Tired of expansion, the EU decided to sort out its constitutional problems. The Ukrainian legal and economic reforms promised by Yushchenko stalled, and he became involved in an endless feud with his prime minister, the charismatic Yulia Tymoshenko. Once the European Union declined to consider Ukraine as a potential member, and American resolve to support Ukraine's pro-Western orientation faded with Barack Obama's arrival in the White House, Russia emerged as the likely victor in the geopolitical competition for Ukraine.[16]

The victory seemed all but complete in January 2010, when Ukrainian voters cast their ballots for the new president of Ukraine. Yushchenko's popularity was at an all-time low. The Ukrainian elites seemed to realize the futility of their efforts to gain support from the West, and the two main presidential candidates, Yulia Tymoshenko and Viktor Yanukovych, tried to outbid each other in showing loyalty to Russia. Yanukovych won and, shortly after taking office, signed the Kharkiv Accords, which prolonged Russia's lease of the Sevastopol naval base until 2042. Ukraine renounced its plans to join NATO, and the government abandoned the Yushchenko administration's contention that the Great Famine of 1932–3 had been a genocide – a claim that Moscow considered anti-Russian. The opposition protested, but the Yanukovych government silenced its critics through a combination of political pressure, criminal prosecutions, and outright bribery. Russian-style authoritarianism had made its way into democratic Ukraine with a swiftness that few would have predicted. On the big geopolitical issues, however, the new Ukrainian government remained as unaccommodating towards Russia as the old one. It never renounced its long-term intention of joining the European Union; refused to join the customs union with Russia, Belarus, and Kazakhstan despite strong Russian pressure; and continued to stay away from the Russia-led Tashkent Collective Security Treaty Organization. In a gesture full of irony if not political cynicism, Yanukovych put his main political opponent, the former prime minister Yulia Tymoshenko, in jail for selling out Ukraine's economic interests to Russia by signing a gas deal disadvantageous to Ukraine with Vladimir Putin.

At a time when Poland, Ukraine's strongest advocate in the European Union, had all but given up on its indecisive, chaotic, and corrupt neighbour, accepting the notion that Ukraine was part of the joint "EU-Russian neighborhood," the Ukrainian government showed signs of resilience that no one expected of it. The reasons for this sudden turn away from Russia are quite simple. Ukrainian big business did not want to be swallowed up by even bigger Russian business. It also needed access to Western technology, markets, and capital. The Yanukovych government, widely regarded as representing the interests of Ukrainian steel barons and oil and gas traders, needed the EU not only for economic but also for political reasons – as a lever against Russia. It was for these reasons that the government of President Yanukovych came close to signing the Association Agreement with the EU in November 2013, backing off only in response to increased Russian pressure and the Russian promise of a financial bailout for the struggling Ukrainian economy. This change of course cost Yanukovych and his government dearly as the Maidan protests removed him from power and opened the door for Ukraine's closer ties with the European Union.[17]

Ukraine is certainly the largest but not the only player in the area between Russia and the EU, the others being Ukraine's neighbours Moldova and Belarus. Students of geopolitics in the EU and North America have taken note of the appearance of this new region between the two major economic and military groupings of contemporary Europe, but they are not sure what to call it or what to make of it. Is it a geopolitical fluke – a group of countries that have little in common and thus lack a shared identity or future – or has something more substantial taken place in that part of the world, a development that has its preconditions and, consequently, something of a future? Some observers were not sure whether this grouping should even be defined in European terms, as calling it "European" might antagonize Russia and produce unreasonable expectations among the local elites of future membership in the EU. The term most often used to define the region is "the New Eastern Europe." There are a number of problems with this definition, the most obvious being that the region cannot remain "new" forever.[18]

Moldova, Ukraine's neighbour to the west, is another country that for a long period of time had been neither here nor there. Ukrainians constitute more than 8 per cent of Moldova's population of 3.5 million and are the country's largest ethnic minority. Moldova, which does not belong to the EU, is arguably even more chaotic, corrupt, and economically inefficient than Ukraine. But it, too, has managed to remain democratic and has also refused to join Russia-led economic and military alliances. Some observers of the region consider Ukraine and its foreign policy not only in relation to Moldova but also to its northern neighbour, Belarus. This "last European dictatorship," a country of 10 million that went authoritarian even before Russia turned away from democracy, often issued official pronouncements that made it appear more Russian than Russia itself. For years President Aliaksandr Lukashenka, who badly needs cheap Russian oil and gas, was able to get them from Russia in return for political loyalty in the international arena. Belarus joined a union with Russia in 1996 and takes part in all major Russian integrationist activities. Since 2006, however, a number of disputes over the price of oil and gas have rocked Belarusian-Russian relations. More than once Lukashenka made public attacks on his Russian allies, and they paid him back in kind. In 2014, Lukashenka refused to recognize the Russian annexation of the Crimea and moved towards establishing closer relations with the EU. In Moldova, pro-European parliamentarians ensured that in June 2014 their country signed an Association Agreement with the EU along with Ukraine and Georgia, ratifying it a few days after the signing.[19]

The events of the EuroRevolution and the signing of the Association Agreement in June 2014 have changed the dynamic of talks on visa-free travel of Ukrainian citizens to the countries of the European Union. In May 2015, the European Union issued a statement favouring a visa-free regime for Ukraine and Georgia. Two years later, in May 2017, the European Council approved visa-free travel for Ukrainians. In the Ukrainian case the major obstacle had been the ongoing conflict in the Donbas. By annexing Crimea and launching a hybrid war in Eastern Ukraine, Russia turned a good part of the Ukrainian-Russian border into a military front line. It comes as no surprise that Russian aggression has made many Ukrainians who used to look at the West with suspicion into proponents of closer ties with the European Union. If in February 2014 36 per cent of Ukrainians supported their country's joining the Russia-led Eurasian Union, that number fell to 12 per cent in June 2015. The proportion of those who wanted to join the EU grew from 41 per cent in February 2014 to 67 per cent in June 2015. These numbers, however, reflect not only the change in the attitudes of the Ukrainians but also the loss by the Ukrainian state of the Crimea and parts of the Donbas – where pro-Russian sentiment was traditionally stronger than in other parts of Ukraine.[20]

The Ukraine Crisis has forced many to start rethinking the map of Europe as it has existed for generations in the minds of Western elites and the public at large. In June 2015 only 1 per cent of those polled in the countries of the EU questioned Ukraine's right to join the Union; 31 per cent believed that Ukraine has the right to do so as a European country, and another 30 per cent believed that membership of the EU would help Ukraine to defend its sovereignty against Russian aggression. Ukraine has come a long way in redefining the map of Europe in the imagination of its own citizens, but the same process seems to be beginning to the west of its borders. Both processes are far from over. Neither are they irreversible.[21]

Notes

1 Andrew Wilson, *Ukraine Crisis: What It Means for the West* (New Haven, CT: Yale University Press, 2014).
2 "Promova prezydenta Ukraïny Viktora Iushchenka na Maidani," *Ukraïns'ka Pravda*, January 23, 2005 http://www.pravda.com.ua/articles/2005/01/23/3006391/
3 "Romantic weekend in the heart of Europe!," http://www.klubkiev.com/index.php/romantic-weekend; "The Center of Europe," http://www.tripfilms.com/Travel_

Video-v64305-Kiev-The_Center_of_Europe-Video-Embed.html; Kiev Studio, http://crytek.com/career/studios/overview/kiev; "Kiev Apartments," http://www. facebook.com/Kiev.Apartments.Rent. All sites accessed February 2011.

4 Oskar Halecki, *The Limits and Divisions of European History* (New York: Sheed and Ward, 1950); Milan Kundera, "The Tragedy of Central Europe," *New York Review of Books* 31, no. 7 (26 April 1984): 33–8.

5 Friedrich Naumann, *Mitteleuropa* (Berlin: Reimer, 1915); Peter Bugge, "The Nation Supreme: The Idea of Europe, 1914–45," in *The History of the Idea of Europe*, ed. Pim den Boer at al. (London: Routledge, 1993), 60–70; Bo Stråth, "Mitteleuropa from List to Naumann," *European Journal of Social Theory* 11, no. 2 (May 2008): 171–83.

6 See the official portal of the Visegrád group at http://www.visegradgroup.eu/main. php. On the origins of civilizational bias in Western treatments of Eastern Europe, see Larry Wolff, *Inventing Eastern Europe: The Map of Civilization on the Mind of the Enlightenment* (Stanford: Stanford University Press, 1994).

7 On the treaty of Brest-Litovsk, which brought German and Austro-Hungarian troops to Ukraine, see John Wheeler-Bennett, *Brest-Litovsk: The Forgotten Peace, March 1918* (London, 1938; repr., New York: Norton, 1971). On the German and Austro-Hungarian visions of Ukrainian statehood, see Mark von Hagen, *War in a European Borderland: Occupations and Occupation Plans in Galicia and Ukraine, 1914–1918* (Seattle: Herbert J. Ellison Center for Russian, East European, and Central Asian Studies, University of Washington, 2007) and Timothy Snyder, *The Red Prince: The Secret Lives of a Habsburg Archduke* (New York: Basic Books, 2008), 99–120.

8 On the "Russian revolution" in European cartography, see Vera Tolz, *Russia: Inventing the Nation* (New York: Bloomsbury, 2001), 155–61.

9 N. Gardner, "Pivotal Points: Defining Europe's Centre," *Hidden Europe* 5 (November 2005): 20–1; "Dilove: The Center of Europe," http://www.castles.com.ua/dilove.html.

10 Michel Foucher, ed., *Fragments d'Europe – Atlas de l'Europe médiane et orientale* (Paris: Fayard, 1998), 55, 60.

11 Samuel P. Huntington, *The Clash of Civilizations and the Remaking of World Order* (New York: Simon and Schuster, 1996), 157. On the establishment of the Uniate (Greek Catholic) Church, see Borys Gudziak, *Crisis and Reform: The Kyivan Metropolitanate, the Patriarchate of Constantinople and the Genesis of the Union of Brest* (Cambridge, MA: Harvard Ukrainian Research Institute, 2001).

12 On the liquidation of the Greek Catholic Church, see Bohdan R. Bociurkiw, *The Ukrainian Greek Catholic Church and the Soviet State, 1939–1950* (Edmonton: Canadian Institute of Ukrainian Studies Press, 1996).

13 See articles on the website of the European Union Border Assistance Mission to Moldova and Ukraine (EUBAM), http://www.eubam.org.

14 On the fall of the Soviet Union, see Ronald Grigor Suny, *The Revenge of the Past: Nationalism, Revolution and the Collapse of the Soviet Union* (Stanford: Stanford University Press, 1993); John B. Dunlop, *The Rise of Russia and the Fall of the Soviet Empire* (Princeton: Princeton University Press, 1993); and Serhii Plokhy, *The Last Empire: The Final Days of the Soviet Union* (New York: Basic Books, 2014).

15 Andrii Portnov, "Nova Skhidna Evropa iak 'blizkaia zagranitsa' Rosiï?" *Krytyka* 15, no. 1–2 (January–February 2011): 7–8.

16 For overviews of Ukrainian domestic and foreign policies since independence, see Bohdan Harasymiw, *Post-Communist Ukraine* (Edmonton: Canadian Institute of Ukrainian Studies Press, 2002); Jennifer D. P. Moroney, Taras Kuzio, and Mikhail Molchanov, *Ukrainian Foreign and Security Policy: Theoretical and Cooperative Perspectives* (Westport, CT: Praeger, 2002); Arkady Moshes, "Ukraine between a Multi-vector Foreign Policy and Euro-Atlantic Integration: Has It Made Its Choice?" PONARS Policy Memo (Helsinki, 2006), https://www.gwu.edu/~ieresgwu/assets/docs/ponars/pm_0426.pdf.

17 Wilson, *Ukraine Crisis*, 38–65.

18 Daniel Hamilton and Gerhard Mangott, *The New Eastern Europe: Ukraine, Belarus and Moldova* (Baltimore, MD: Center for Transatlantic Relations, Johns Hopkins University, 2008); Svante E. Cornell, *The New Eastern Europe: Challenges and Opportunities for the EU* (Brussels: Centre for European Studies, 2009); Andrii Portnov, "Nova Skhidna Evropa iak 'blizkaia zagranitsa' Rosiï?"; Serhii Plokhy, "The "New Eastern Europe": What to Do With the Histories of Ukraine, Belarus and Moldova?" *East European Politics and Societies* 25, no. 4 (November 2011): 763–69.

19 "EU Signs Pacts with Ukraine, Georgia, and Moldova," *BBC*, 27 June 2014, http://www.bbc.com/news/world-europe-28052645; "Lukashenka Says 'We Can't Be Dicing Up' Europe's Borders Again," *Radio Free Europe*, 14 July 2015, http://www.rferl.org/content/belarus-lukashenka--russia-ukraine-borders/26628861.html.

20 Cynthia Kroet, "EU approves visa-free travel for Ukrainians," *Politico*, 11 May 2017, http://www.politico.eu/article/eu-approves-visa-free-travel-for-ukrainians/; "V ES khotiat 53% ukraintsev, v Tamozhennyi Soiz – 28%," *24kanal*, 5 April 2014, http://24tv.ua/news/showNews.do?v_es_hotyat_53_ukraintsev_v_tamozhenniy_soyuz__28&objectId=429597&lang=ru; Katie Simmons, Bruce Stokes, and Jacob Poushter, "Ukrainian Public Opinion: Dissatisfied with Current Conditions, Looking for an End to the Crisis," *Pew Research Center*, 10 June 2015, http://www.pewglobal.org/2015/06/10/3-ukrainian-public-opinion-dissatisfied-with-current-conditions-looking-for-an-end-to-the-crisis/.

21 Anastasiia Zanuda, "Shcho dumaiut' ievropeitsi pro Ukraïnu ta ïï vstup v IeS," *BBC Ukraine*, 24 June 2015, http://www.bbc.com/ukrainian/politics/2015/06/150624_europians_ukraine_az.

Index

Adler, Emma, 308–9
Adler, Victor, 305–6, 308
Adorno, Theodor, 364
Aheieva, Vira, 41, 278
Aizenshtok, Iarema, 224
Aksakov, Ivan, 248
Aksakov, Sergei, 220, 241, 248
Alain de Lille, 108
Albert the Great, 108
Aleksandrovych, Volodymyr, 92–3, 98–100
Aleksei (tsarevich), 183
Aleksii (metropolitan), 58
Alexander II (tsar), 252, 260, 263
Alexander the Macedonian, the Great, 191
Alighieri, Dante, 24, 270, 399
Allende, Isabel, 367
Ambrose of Milan, Saint, 108
Améro, Constant, 251
Anacreon, 207
Anderson, Benedict, 300
Andrássy, Gyula, 303
Andreev, Leonid, 277
Andrew of Crete, Saint, 82
Andrew the Fool, Saint, 73, 80, 82–5, 92–4, 96, 99
Andrew, Saint (Apostle), 51, 82

Andrukhovych, Yuri (Iurii), 13, 35, 286, 416, 420–6, 428, 430–2
Anne, Saint, 74
Anouilh, Jean, 399
Anselm of Canterbury, Saint, 108
Antonii (Anthony) of the Caves, Saint, 58, 198–200
Antonovych, Volodymyr, 334
Antonych, Bohdan Ihor, 291, 394
Apanovych, Olena, 411
Apollinaire, Guillaume, 401
Aquinas (Saint Thomas Aquinas), 108
Aristophanes, 22, 385
Aristotle, 22, 104
Arp, Jean, 380
Arsenios the Greek, 166
Ashcroft, Bill, 285, 287, 291, 297
Askochenskii, Viktor, 204–5
Athanasius, Saint, 183
Augustine, Saint, 108
Averintsev, Sergei, 204
Averröes, 380
Ávila, Hernando de, 159–63, 176
Azadovskii, Mark, 229

Bab, Julius, 358
Babel, Isaac, 363
Bachyns'kyi, Iuliian, 33

Bacon, Francis, 380
Badeni, Kasimir, 306–7
Bahalii, Dmytro, 334
Bahr, Hermann, 305, 309
Bakhtin, Mikhail, 8, 378
Balanchine, George, 375
Balzac, Honoré de, 262, 380
Bandera, Stepan, 419, 429
Baranets'kyi, Pavlo, 114
Baranovych, Lazar, 48–9, 51, 56–8, 64, 67–9, 107, 113–14
Barbara, Saint, 184, 206
Barbusse, Henri, 342
Baronio (Baronius), Cesare, 104, 110
Baudelaire, Charles, 11, 276, 284, 296, 309, 399
Bazhan, Mykola, 380, 388, 394, 399–401
Beaumarchais, Pierre-Augustin Caron de, 381–2
Beauvais, Vincent of, 111
Beauvoir, Simone de, 399
Beckmann, Johann, 107
Belinskii, Vissarion, 28, 30, 240, 323, 337
Bellarmino, Roberto, 61, 104, 110
Benzon, Thérèse, 258
Bercé, Yves-Marie, 142, 144, 148
Bestuzhev, Aleksandr, 237
Bezkhutryi, Iurii, 379, 388
Bida, Konstantyn, 117
Bielski, Marcin, 103, 109
Bilets'kyi, Oleksandr, 22–3, 360, 385
Bilozers'kyi, Vasyl', 222
Bilozir, Ihor, 242
Bilyts'kyi, Zhdan, 102
Bisaccioni, Maiolino, 143
Bismarck, Otto von, 303, 435
Bleau (Blavius), John, 107
Bloom, Harold, 283, 285, 288, 291, 297–9
Boccaccio, Giovanni, 24, 275, 379, 401
Bodians'kyi, Osyp, 216, 220, 235–6, 241–2, 244–5, 333

Boehme, Jakob, 37
Boethius, Severinus, 109
Bogoliubskii, Andrei, 80, 82, 94
Boichenko, Oleksandr, 416, 425–6, 430–1
Boichuk, Bohdan, 392, 409
Boichuk, Mykhailo, 394
Bojanowska, Edyta, 9, 245, 247, 337
Bonfini, Antonio (Antonius Bonfinius), 111
Borets'kyi, Ivan, 24, 36
Borgia, Cesare, 353
Borovyk, Teodozii, 110
Borovykovs'kyi, Levko, 29, 214
Borovykovs'kyi, Volodymyr, 334
Botero, Giovanni, 104, 106, 110
Braichevs'kyi, Mykhailo, 411
Bratkovs'kyi, Danylo (Daniel Bratkowski), 25
Breuer, Josef, 364
Briusov, Valerii, 310
Brodskii, Iosif, 395
Brodziński, Kazimierz, 230–1, 241
Brogi Bercoff, Giovanna, 6–7, 66–70, 111, 115, 118, 203
Brown, Peter, 152
Brueghel, Jan (the Elder), 380
Brutus, 233
Bryzh, Teodoziia, 411
Bulgakov, Sergei, 97
Burevii, Kost', 384, 389
Burliuk, Davyd, 375
Burns, Robert, 29, 326, 328
Bush, George W., 442
Buzhyns'kyi, Havryïl, 62
Byron, George Gordon, 19–20, 28–9, 328

Caesar, Julius, 172
Caesar of Heisterbach (Caesarius Heisterbacensis), 73, 111
Calepinus, Ambrose, 188
Callistus, Nicephorus, 109
Camus, Albert, 397–9, 404, 406
Capgrave, John, 173

Cartagena, Juan de (Ioannis de Carthagena), 111
Caruth, Cathy, 368
Casimir, John (king), 146
Cassiodorus, 109
Catherine II (tsarina), 30
Catherine of Alexandria, Saint, 159–60
Cato the Elder, 195
Cato the Younger, 195
Čelakovský, František, 230
Celan, Paul, 401
Cervantes, Miguel de, 270, 401
Chaadaev, Petr, 238
Chaplenko, Vasyl', 214
Charcot, Jean-Martin, 364
Charles X (king), 153
Charnets'kyi, Stepan, 284
Chateaubriand, François-René de, 270
Chaucer, Geoffrey, 24, 379
Cheremshyna, Marko, 285, 306
Cherniak, Ievhen, 8, 346–7
Choniates, Nicetas, 109
Chornovil, Viacheslav, 397, 411
Chrysostom, John, Saint, 93
Chulkov, Mikhail, 243
Chuprynka, Hryhorii, 331
Churchill, Winston, 440
Chyzhevs'kyi (Čyževs'kyj), Dmytro, 22, 24, 37
Cicero, 65, 70, 109, 159
Cichoński, Jan Pawel, 159
Cichowski, Mikołaj, 110
Clarke, John, 158
Claudel, Paul, 399
Clinton, Bill, 443
Conrad, Joseph, 380
Constantine (emperor), 51, 172–3
Cornelius a Lapide, 111
Cornelius Nepos, 64
Crantius, Albertus (Albert Krantz), 112
Croce, Benedetto, 212
Crummey, Robert, 137, 145

Curtius, Ernst Robert, 206
Cyril, Saint, 69, 327
Čyževs'kyj, Dmytro. See Chyzhevs'kyi, Dmytro
Czarnocki, Adam. See Dołęga-Chodakowski, Zorian (pseud.)

Dal', Vladimir (pseud. Vladimir Luganskii), 219, 236–7, 241
Danilevskii, Nikolai, 341, 376
Danylevs'kyi, Oleksandr, 337
Danylo Romanovych (prince), 93
Dashkevych, Iaroslav, 411
Daszyński, Feliks (pseud. Szczęsny), 308
De Molinari, Gustave, 260
Dems'ka-Budzuliak, Lesia, 278
Denikin, Anton, 361
Dentu, Edouard, 252
Descartes, René, 380
Dewald, Jonathan, 155
Diaghilev, Sergei, 375
Dickens, Charles, 380
Di Mauro, Giorgio, 248
Dmitriiev, Oleksandr, 345
Döblin, Alfred, 340
Dobrovský, Josef, 244
Dołęga-Chodakowski, Zorian (Adam Czarnocki), 229–31, 241
Domontovych, Viktor (pseud.). See Petrov, Viktor
Donii, Oles', 409
Dontsov, Dmytro, 36, 312, 332, 335, 394
Dos Passos, John, 340
Dostoevskii, Fedor, 258
Dosvitnii, Oles', 380
Dovzhenko, Oleksandr, 343
Drach, Ivan, 401, 403, 406–7, 410
Drahomanov, Mykhailo, 30–3, 36–7, 304, 312, 329–30, 332, 393
Drozd, Volodymyr, 411
Dryden, John, 275
Duccio di Buoninsegna, 74–5

Duhamel, Georges, 342
Dukes, Paul, 152
Dunning, Chester, 137, 145
Duns the Scot, John, 111
Durand, Émile, 252, 257
Dychko, Lesia, 411
Dziuba, Ivan, 410–11
Dzyra, Iaroslav, 411

Ekaterina Alekseevna (Marta Elena
    Skowrońska, tsarina), 179
Eliot, Thomas Stearns, 295, 399
Elliott, John, 136–9, 142, 149–51
Epiphanios, 73, 80, 82–3, 92–3, 96
Eremin, Igor', 22
Erikson, Kai, 368
Estreicher, Karol, 68
Eusebius of Caesarea, 109
Eustachius, Saint, 160
Exter, Alexandra, 375, 387

Faulkner, William, 398
Fedor (tsar), 57–8
Fedoruk, Yaroslav (Iaroslav), 152–3
Fed'kovych, Iurii (Osyp-Iurii),
    223, 288
Feodosii (Theodosius) of the Caves,
    Saint, 58, 198–200
Fichte, Johann Gottlieb, 228, 380
Filians'kyi, Mykola, 331
Flaubert, Gustave, 401
Flavius, Joseph, 110
Florovsky, Georges, 199, 207
Forster, Robert, 140, 145–6, 148
Fortunato, Venanzio, 109
Foucault, Michel, 37, 366
Foucher, Michel, 438–9, 442
France, Anatole, 380
Franko, Ivan, 11, 30–1, 33, 36, 274, 280,
    283, 289, 296, 298, 300–12, 314–16,
    342, 393
Franz Joseph (emperor), 262
Freeze, Gregory, 173
Freud, Sigmund, 310, 364

Frost, Robert, 146
Fussel, Paul, 363

Gabriel, Archangel, 164
Galiatovs'kyi, Ioannikii, 12, 48, 56, 103,
    105–14, 117
Galileo Galilei, 380
García Lorca, Federico, 394, 401
Gay, Peter, 304
Gedimin (prince), 48
Gellner, Ernest, 11, 300–1, 313
Gessner, Conrad (Conradus Gessnerus), 112
Giedroyc, Jerzy, 395
Gizel', Innokentii, 108, 110, 113
Glinka, Sergei, 26
Gluzman, Semen, 411
Goethe, Johann Wolfgang, 11, 215, 228,
    283, 285–93, 297–8, 376, 380, 401
Gogol', Nikolai (Mykola Hohol'), 12,
    231, 234–5, 237–9, 241, 245–8, 283,
    319, 322–9, 333–4, 337, 345, 374,
    377, 379–80, 383, 386
Goldfaden, Abraham, 255–6
Goldstone, Jack, 136–7, 142, 144, 149
Golitsyn, Vasilii, 54
Gorbachev, Mikhail, 442
Górnicki, Łukasz, 258, 267
Goszczyński, Seweryn, 27
Grabowicz, George, 6, 8, 227, 283,
    365–6, 377
Grabowski, Michał, 20, 29
Granofsky, Ronald, 366
Grech, Nikolai, 228
Greene, Jack, 140, 145–6, 148
Gregory of Tours, Saint, 111
Griffiths, Gareth, 285, 287, 291, 297
Grillparzer, Franz, 286
Grimm, brothers (Jacob Grimm and
    Wilhelm Grimm), 29, 230
Grosz, George, 341, 346, 349, 352
Guagnini, Antonio, 109

Habermas, Jürgen, 211
Hafiz, 380

Halecki, Oskar, 435–6, 438
Hanka, Václav, 227, 237
Haşedeu, Alexander, 238
Havel, Václav, 8
Hegel, Georg Wilhelm Friedrich,
    227, 380
Heidegger, Martin, 401, 402
Hel', Ivan, 411
Hemingway, Ernest, 398
Herder, Johann Gottfried, 9, 214, 227–8,
    230, 237, 240
Herman, Hanna, 424–5
Herolt, Johann, 111
Herzl, Theodor, 305, 308, 315
Hesse, Hermann, 401
Hillis, Faith, 231
Hitler, Adolf, 312, 436
Hnatiuk, Ola, 12–13, 415, 429
Hobsbawm, Eric, 137–8, 140–1, 143–4,
    155–6
Hoffmann, Ernst Theodor Amadeus,
    379–80, 388
Hohol', Mykola. See Gogol', Nikolai
Holoborod'ko, Vasyl', 411
Homer, 22, 172, 195, 241
Honhadze (Gongadze), Heorhii, 420
Horace, 195, 215
Hors'ka, Alla, 396, 411
Horyn', Bohdan, 411
Horyn', Mykhailo, 411
Hrabovs'kyi, Leonid, 411
Hrebinka, Ievhen, 212, 216
Hrinchenko, Borys, 36
Hrushevs'kyi, Mykhailo, 39, 121, 145,
    155–6, 393
Hryn, Halyna, 7, 387
Hrytsak, Yaroslav (Iaroslav), 11, 416,
    419–20, 428
Huba, Volodymyr, 411
Hulak-Artemovs'kyi, Petro, 212, 215,
    217, 224, 247
Hundorova, Tamara, 8, 41, 278, 285–7,
    291, 296–8
Huntington, Samuel, 439–40

Hutsalo, Ievhen, 411
Hynes, Samuel Lynn, 362

Iakutovych, Heorhii, 411
Ianovs'ka, Liubov, 278
Ianovs'kyi, Iurii, 343, 355, 363, 380
Iaroshevyts'kyi, Ilarion, 166–7,
    174–5
Iaroslav (prince), 23
Iasyns'kyi (Jasyns'kyj), Varlaam
    (metropolitan), 49, 54, 62, 111, 165,
    167, 169, 177, 179, 183–4, 198, 202,
    204, 207
Iats'kiv, Mykhailo, 331
Iavors'kyi, Matvii, 143
Iavors'kyi, Stefan, 54–6, 59–65, 70–1,
    106, 111–12, 168
Ibsen, Henrik, 11, 275–6, 284, 309
Ievshan, Mykola, 335
Illienko, Iurii, 411
Ilnytzkyj, Oleh, 12, 336
Iohansen, Maik, 349, 374, 389
Ionas (metropolitan), 58
Irvanets', Oleksandr, 392
Isaievych, Iaroslav, 67, 121, 441
Isherwood, Christopher, 340
Iurynets', Volodymyr, 345, 356
Ivan Alekseevich, Prince, 171
Ivanov, Viacheslav, 380
Ivasiuk, Volodymyr, 411
Izdryk, Iurii, 35

Jagić, Vatroslav, 304–5
James, Henry, 250–1, 265–6
Jan Skala of Dubravka (Joannes
    Dubravius), 112
Janion, Maria, 248
Jansen, Jakob, 173
Jaspers, Karl, 404
Jiménez, Juan Ramón, 399
Joannes Dubravius (Jan Skala of
    Dubravka), 112
John Chrysostom, Saint, 93
John Paul II (pope), 442

John the Forerunner, Saint, 73, 82
John the Theologian, Saint (Apostle),
    73, 82
Jones, William, 224
Joyce, James, 340
Judeus, Michael, 109
Jünger, Ernst, 11, 363–4,
Justinian the Philosopher, 109–10

Kalynets', Ihor, 411
Kal'nofois'kyi, Afanasii, 47, 48, 105–7,
    111–12, 116, 118
Kamen, Henry, 140, 144–5, 147
Kamenka, Eugene, 148
Kapral', Myron, 121
Karadžić , Vuk, 29
Karamzin, Nikolai, 235
Karmans'kyi, Petro, 11, 283–91, 298,
    331
Kas'ianov, Heorhii, 416
Katkov, Mikhail, 321
Kentschynskyj, Bohdan, 152–3
Khmel'nyts'kyi, Bohdan, 11, 25, 36,
    136–7, 141, 144–51, 155–7, 239
Khomiakov, Aleksei, 242
Khotkevych, Hnat, 276, 331
Khrushchev, Nikita, 395, 397
Khvyl'ovyi, Mykola, 8, 11, 319, 322,
    336, 341–7, 349, 351–4, 356–61,
    363–5, 368, 370, 372–6, 378–82,
    385, 387–8, 393–4, 410
Kichura, Meletii, 284
King, John, 363
Kiossev, Alexander, 41
Kipiani, Vakhtanh, 418
Kireevskii, Petr, 229, 239
Kiukhel'beker, Vil'gel'm, 237
Kobryns'ka, Nataliia, 274–6, 278
Kobylians'ka, Ol'ha, 276, 278, 331
Kochanowski, Jan, 65, 168, 258
Kochanowski, Piotr, 110
Kochur, Hryhorii, 396, 401, 411
Kompan, Olena, 411

Konashevych-Sahaidachnyi, Petro,
    51–3, 104, 158
Kontzen, Adam, 111
Konys'kyi, Oleksandr, 223
Kopitar, Jernej, 237
Kopylenko, Oleksandr, 343, 348
Kopystens'kyi, Zakharii, 104
Koriak, Volodymyr, 343
Korohods'kyi, Roman, 411
Korona, Marek, 109
Kosach, Larysa. See Ukraïnka, Lesia
    (pseud.)
Kosiv, Mykhailo, 396
Kosov (Kosiv), Syl'vestr, 47–51, 107,
    165
Kostenko, Lina, 399, 401, 403–8
Kostets'kyi, Ihor, 398
Kostomarov, Mykola, 212, 214, 231,
    238, 320, 333–4
Kotliarevs'kyi, Ivan, 20, 212–15, 217,
    219–20, 377, 384–5
Kotsiubyns'ka, Mykhailyna, 411
Kotsiubyns'kyi, Mykhailo, 278, 368
Kottmaier, Elisabeth, 398
Kozachyns'kyi, Emanuel, 58
Kozak, Stefan, 231
Koznarsky, Taras, 234
Kraevskii, Andrei, 325
Krantz, Albert (Albertus Crantius), 112
Kratochvil, Alexander, 11
Krekoten', Volodymyr, 411
Krleža, Miroslav, 290
Krokovs'kyi (Krokovius), Ioasaf, 7,
    182–6, 190–1, 193, 196–200, 202–7
Kromer, Marcin, 109
Kropyvnyts'kyi, Marko, 278
Krylovs'kyi, Amvrosii, 121, 125
Kuchma, Leonid, 420–1, 423
Kulish, Mykola, 394
Kulish, Panteleimon, 19, 29–30, 32, 36,
    39–40, 220–2, 326–30, 333, 353–4,
    386, 400
Kulyk, Volodymyr, 380, 418

Kundera, Milan, 395, 422, 435,
Kurbas, Les', 385, 394
Kurkov, Andrei, 35
Kvitka-Osnovianenko, Hryhorii, 212–13,
    216–20, 222, 236–7, 324–6, 328,
    374, 377, 380

Lachmann, Renate, 298, 368
Lactantius, 108
Lami, Giulia, 10
Landos of Crete, Agapios, 166
Lang, Fritz, 340, 356
Langer, Lawrence, 365
Lathoud, R.P.D., 90
Lazarevs'kyi, Mykhailo, 220
Le, Ivan, 343
Lec, Stanisław Jerzy, 399
Łęczycki, Mikołaj, 106
Léger, Fernand, 375
Lenin, Vladimir, 144, 346, 365
Leo I (emperor), 72
Leonardo da Vinci, 380
Lepkyi, Bohdan, 11, 283–91, 298, 331
Lermontov, Mikhail, 20
Leroy-Beaulieu, Anatole, 252, 257
Levyts'kyi, Iosyf, 298
Lippomano, Lodovico, 109
Lipsius, Just, 65
Lisniak, Iurii, 411
Lisovyi, Vasyl', 411
List, Friedrich, 435
Liubchenko, Arkadii, 343–4
Liublinskaia, Aleksandra, 136
Lorris, Guillaume de, 275
Losyts'kyi, Mykhailo, 113
Louis XVI (king), 332
Lucan, 195
Lueger, Karl, 306
Lukash, Mykola, 401, 411
Lukashenka, Aliaksandr, 445
Lukianenko, Levko, 411
Luts'kyi, Ostap, 284, 296
Lypyns'kyi, Viacheslav, 145

Lytvyn, Iurii, 411
Lyzohub, Andrii, 220

Machiavelli, Niccolò, 352–3
Macpherson, James, 227
Madame de Staël (Germaine de Staël), 228
Maecenas, Gaius, 53, 55, 191
Maeterlinck, Maurice, 11, 284, 309
Maioli, Simone (Simon Maiolus), 112
Makhno, Nestor, 361
Maksymovych, Mykhailo, 214, 217, 220,
    229–36, 238–9, 241–2, 333
Malaniuk, Ievhen, 392
Malczewski, Antoni, 27
Malevich, Kazimir, 375
Mallarmé, Stéphane, 310
Mamontov, Iakiv, 331
Mark Anthony, 195, 233
Marchant, Jacques (Iacobus Marchanus),
    111
Marchenko, Valerii, 411
Marchuk, Ivan, 411
Marcian (emperor), 72
Marcus Antonius, 195
Marker, Gary, 166, 179–80, 184, 198,
    206–7
Markevych, Mykola, 337
Markovych, Opanas, 221–2
Marx, Karl, 138, 304
Masaryk, Tomáš (Thomas), 305,
    435–6, 438
Matisse, Henri, 375
Maupassant, Guy de, 276–7
Maxentius (emperor), 159, 172
Maximus, Valerius, 109–10
Mazepa, Ivan, 7, 28, 49, 51, 53–6, 62,
    66–8, 114, 159, 165–7, 169, 172–3, 175,
    177, 183–4, 197, 202, 205, 288, 327
Medvid', Liubomyr, 411
Meller, Vadym, 387
Mel'nychuk, Oleksandr, 411
Menshikov, Aleksandr, 61
Mercator, Gerhard, 107

Meredith, George, 380
Merriman, Robert, 138, 140, 147
Metaphrastes, Simeon, Saint, 109, 166
Methodius, Saint, 327
Metlyns'kyi, Amvrosii, 212, 214, 235–6, 244
Michael, Archangel, 164
Mickiewicz, Adam, 29, 125, 231, 247–8, 307, 309
Miczyński, Sebastian, 109
Miechowski, Justyn, 110
Miechowski, Maciej, 101
Miliaieva, Liudmyla, 83, 92, 94–5
Miliukov, Pavel, 332
Miłosz, Czesław, 398
Milton, John, 215
Mirabeau, Honoré, 332
Mohyla, Petro, 36, 46, 51, 53, 103–7, 110–14, 158–9, 165, 167, 176–7, 182–5, 191, 202–4, 207
Mohylians'kyi, Mykhailo, 8, 349–51, 354
Molière (Jean-Baptiste Poquelin), 385
Montaigne, Michel de, 380, 401
Moote, Alanson Lloyd, 140, 145–6
Mordovtsev, Danylo, 212
Moroz, Valentyn, 397, 411
Morris, William, 375
Morrison, Toni, 361, 367
Moschus, John, 109
Moser, Michael, 9, 298
Mosquera de Figueroa, Cristóbal, 161, 170, 176
Münster, Sebastian, 107
Musil, Robert, 344
Mykhailyn, Ihor, 310
Myklashevs'kyi, Mykhailo, 175
Mykolaichuk, Ivan, 411
Myrnyi, Panas, 223
Mysyk, Vasyl', 400

Nadezhdin, Nikolai, 237–8, 240
Nalyvaiko, Dmytro, 38, 411

Nanni, Giovanni (Joannes Annius Viterbiensis), 112
Napoleon Bonaparte, 26, 254, 380
Narbut, Heorhii, 394
Narezhnyi, Vasilii, 237
Natal'ia Alekseevna (tsarevna), 180
Naumann, Friedrich, 435–6, 438
Nechui-Levyts'kyi, Ivan 10, 223, 269–81, 330–1, 335
Nestor, 52
Newton, Isaac, 380
Nicholas I (tsar), 233–4, 253
Niemcewicz, Julian Ursyn, 27
Nietzsche, Friedrich, 11, 18, 276, 284, 296–7, 355, 380
Nijinsky, Vaslav, 375
Nikephoros, 73
Nikonenko, Arkhyp, 220
Nimchuk, Vasyl', 411
Nordau, Max, 276, 282
Novalis (Friedrich von Hardenberg), 380, 399
Numa Pompilius (king), 195

Obama, Barack, 444
Obydovs'kyi, Ian, 55
Offenbach, Jacques, 271
Oleh (prince), 52
Olesnyts'kyi, Ievhen, 307
Oles', Oleksander, 277, 331
Olivares, Gaspar de Guzmán, Count-Duke of, 142, 149
Origen, 108
Orikhovs'kyi, Stanislav (Stanisław Orzechowski), 51
Orlyk, Pylyp, 54–5, 168
Ornovs'kyi, Ivan (Ian), 54, 114, 168
Ortega y Gasset, Jose, 417
Ortelius, Abraham, 107
Orzechowski, Stanisław (Stanislav Orikhovs'kyi), 51
Orzeszkowa, Eliza, 255
Osadchyi, Mykhailo, 411

Ossoliński, Jerzy, 149
Ostafiichuk, Ivan, 411
Osyka, Leonid, 411
Ovid, 109

Pachlovska, Oxana, 8, 390
Pachovs'kyi, Vasyl', 283–5
Palamarchuk, Dmytro, 411
Panina, Natalia, 424
Paradzhanov (Parajanov), Serhii, 411
Parente, James, 160
Pavlychko,Solomiia, 41, 269, 278
Pavlyk, Mykhailo, 33, 36
Pavlyshyn, Marko, 9, 291
Percy, Thomas, 28
Perepadia, Anatol', 401, 411
Pernerstorfer, Engelbert, 306
Pertsev, Nikolai, 83
Peter, Alekseevich. *See* Peter I
Peter (metropolitan), 58
Peter I (tsar), 30, 54, 56, 59–63, 167,
    171–3, 179, 183–5, 198, 394
Petrarch, Francesco, 24, 300
Petrenko, Mykhailo, 214
Petricius, Sebastian, 109
Petrov, Nikolai, 203–5, 207
Petrov, Viktor (pseud. Viktor Domon-
    tovych), 343, 347, 349, 351–4, 359
Pétrovitch, Michel, 260
Petryts'kyi, Anatol', 374, 387
Philip II (king), 163
Picasso, Pablo, 375
Piccolomini, Enea Silvio (Pope Pius II), 112
Pidmohyl'nyi, Valerian, 8, 343, 347,
    351, 354–5, 394
Pierio, Valeriano (Valerianus Pierius), 112
Piero della Francesca, 74, 76
Pincus, Steve, 141, 154
Pindar, 22
Pivtorak, Hryhorii, 411
Plato, 22, 162, 206
Plautus, 385
Pliny, 109

Pliukhanova, Maria, 82
Pliushch, Leonid, 411
Pliushch, Oleksii, 276
Plokhy, Serhii, 13, 74
Plutarch, 109, 110
Pluzhnyk, Ievhen, 394
Pochas'kyi, Sofronii, 105
Pogodin, Mikhail, 233, 239, 247
Pokors'kyi, Opanas, 175
Polidorus, Vergilius (Vergil Polydore),
    112
Polishchuk, Valerian, 343, 346, 349
Polotskii, Simeon, 56–7, 64
Polycrates, 195, 207
Polydore, Vergil (Vergilius Polidorus), 112
Pompey (Pompeus), 52, 195
Ponomariv, Oleksandr, 411
Popovych, Ievhen, 401, 411
Porshnev, Boris, 138, 144, 152
Potebnia, Oleksander, 334
Potii, Ipatii, 103
Pritsak, Omeljan, 23
Prokofiev, Sergei, 375
Prokopovych, Feofan, 62–3, 68, 106–7,
    111–12
Propertius, 198
Przerwa-Tetmajer, Kazimierz, 296
Psellus, Michael, 23
Pugachev, Emel'ian, 140, 145–6, 148
Pushkin, Aleksandr, 20, 29, 231
Putin, Vladimir, 430, 443–4
Putsko, Vasyl', 93
Pylypenko, Serhii, 343
Pylypiuk, Natalia, 7, 184, 191
Pymonenko, Mykola, 334
Pypin, Aleksandr, 229

Quinet, Edgar, 228

Rabb, Theodore, 136, 141
Rabelais, François, 378
Radyvylovs'kyi, Antonii, 56
Radziwiłł, Mikołaj Krzysztof, 110, 118

Raeff, Marc, 145
Rahoza, Mykhailo (metropolitan), 102
Rambaud, Alfred, 252, 257, 262
Raphael, Archangel, 164
Raphael (Raffaello Sanzio), 376
Ratmirova, Olena, 278
Remarque, Erich Maria, 11, 362, 398
Remy, Johannes, 233–4
Repnina, Varvara, 220
Reusner, Elias (Reusnerus), 106
Reynoso, Francisco de, 160
Riabchuk, Mykola, 414, 416, 418–20,
    430
Rice, Eugene, 191
Richelieu (Armand Jean du Plessis,
    cardinal), 142, 149
Rilke, Rainer Maria, 394, 401
Riurik (prince), 48
Roberts, Michael, 143
Rolland, Romain, 342
Romanos the Melodist, 80–2, 88, 91–6
Roosevelt, Franklin Delano, 440
Rostovskii, Dymytrii, Saint. See Tuptalo,
    Dymytrii
Rozdolsky, Roman, 155
Rubens, Peter Paul, 380
Rudenko, Mykola, 411
Rulin, Petro, 279
Rutherford, Andrea, 240
Rutkowski, Jan, 155
Ryleev, Kondratii, 26
Ryl's'kyi, Maksym, 331, 394, 400
Rzewuski, Henryk, 20

Sacher-Masoch, Leopold von, 258
Šafárik, Pavel, 29, 231, 236–7, 245
Sahaidachnyi, Petro. See Kona-
    shevych-Sahaidachnyi, Petro
Said, Edward, 438
Saint-Exupéry, Antoine de, 398
Sakharov, Andrei, 395
Sakharov, Ivan, 229, 236

Sakovych, Kasiian, 23, 38, 52–3, 104,
    158, 174, 177
Samoilovych, Ivan, 49, 114
Sarbiewski, Maciej Kazimierz, 50, 57,
    166
Sartre, Jean-Paul, 399
Saunders, David, 229
Savva, Spiridon, 58
Schiller, Friedrich, 228, 376
Schlegel, August Wilhelm, 228
Schlegel, Friedrich, 228
Schönerer, Georg, 306
Schorske, Carl, 312
Schuhmeier, Franz, 306
Scott, Walter, 28–9, 230, 270, 326,
    328–9, 353
Sękowski, Józef (Osip Senkovskii), 236–7
Semenko, Mykhail', 331, 343, 349, 394
Semykina, Liudmyla, 411
Senchenko, Ivan, 380
Seniuk, Ol'ha, 401, 411
Serafimovich, Aleksandr, 363
Sergios (patriarch), 72
Ševčenko, Ihor, 18, 38, 40
Sevruk, Halyna, 411
Shakespeare, William, 29, 233, 328, 353,
    376, 380, 399
Shamrai, Ahapii, 233
Shcherbak, Iurii, 411
Shcherbakivs'kyi, Danylo, 83
Shchurat, Vasyl', 310, 315
Shevchenko, Taras, 20, 29–30, 36–7,
    219–20, 222, 257, 263, 283, 303–4,
    325–8
Shevchuk, Valerii, 281, 407, 411
Shevyrev, Stepan, 231, 233, 235, 238
Shklovskii (Shklovsky), Viktor, 417
Shkurupii, Geo, 355
Siedina, Giovanna, 7, 167, 202
Sienkiewicz, Henryk, 20, 36
Sigismund III (king), 174
Sigonio, Carlo (Carolus Sigonius), 112

Simonek, Stefan, 310
Siniavskii, Andrei, 365
Singer, Isidor, 306, 308–9
Sirenius, Szymon, 109
Sismondi, Jean Charles, 228
Skarga, Piotr, 23, 36, 57, 109–10, 163, 165–6, 172
Skoryk, Myroslav, 411
Skovoroda, Hryhorii, 238
Skowrońska, Marta Elena (Ekaterina Alekseevna), 179
Słowacki, Juliusz, 27
Smirnov, Sergei, 185
Smirnova, Engelina, 98
Smirnova-Rosset, Aleksandra, 337
Smotryts'kyi, Meletii, 23, 25, 36, 104, 107, 116
Soares, Cypriano, 167
Socrates, 109, 162
Sodomora, Andrii, 411
Sof'ia Alekseevna (tsarevna), 54
Solov'ev, Sergei, 242
Solzhenitsyn, Aleksandr, 365, 395
Somov, Orest, 26, 237, 247
Sophronius, 109
Soroka, Bohdan, 411
Sosiura, Volodymyr, 392
Sotnikova, Marina, 83
Sozomenos, 109
Spengler, Oswald, 341–2, 345, 349, 376
Spivak, Gayatri, 285, 291, 297
Sreznevskii, Izmail, 212, 214, 224, 229, 234, 236, 239, 241
Staël, Germaine de (Madame de Stael), 228
Stalin, Joseph, 34, 341, 440–2
Stankovych, Ievhen, 411
Starowolski, Szymon, 110
Staryts'kyi, Mykhailo, 279
Stasiv-Kalynets', Iryna, 411
Statius, Publius Papinius, 195
Stavrovets'kyi, Kyrylo Trankvilion, 102

Stecchetti, Lorenzo, 284
Steensgaard, Niels, 138, 148
Stefanyk, Vasyl', 33
Sterne, Laurence, 380
Stone, Lawrence, 150
Strabo, 437, 439
Stravinsky, Igor, 375
Strikha, Edvard, 380, 384, 389
Struk, Danylo Husar, 283
Struve, Petr, 321, 332–3
Stryjkowski, Maciej, 102, 109
Studyns'kyi, Kyrylo, 304, 314
Stus, Vasyl', 392, 397, 399, 401, 403–5, 407–8, 410
Sue, Eugène, 270
Surius, Laurentius, 57, 109
Susha, Iakiv, 110
Sverstiuk, Ievhen, 377, 397–8, 411
Sviatogorets, Stefan, 109, 117
Svidzins'kyi, Volodymyr, 331, 394
Svitlychna, Nadiia, 411
Svitlychnyi, Ivan, 396–7, 401, 411
Swift, Jonathan, 380–2
Syl'vestrov, Valentyn, 411
Symonenko, Vasyl', 401, 403–4, 407, 410
Sysyn, Frank, 10
Szporluk, Roman, 240

Taine, Hippolyte, 270
Taniuk, Les', 396
Tarasiuk, Borys, 426
Tarnawsky, Maxim, 10
Tasso, Torquato, 110
Ten, Borys, 400
Ternovskii, Filipp, 64
Tertullian, 108
Thomas Aquinas, Saint, 108
Tieck, Ludwig, 380
Tiffin, Helen, 285, 287, 291, 297
Tissot, Victor, 10, 249–64, 266, 268
Titus (emperor), 195

Tiutiunnyk, Hryhir, 397, 411
Tolstaia, Anastasiia, 220
Tolstoi, Fedor, 220
Tolstoi, Lev, 258, 309
Tolstoi, Petr, 61
Tovkachevs'kyi, Andrii, 332–4
Trakl, Georg, 290
Trevor-Roper, Hugh, 138, 141, 148
Trithemius, Johann, 111
Trommler, Frank, 344
Tsertelev, Nikolai, 214, 229–32,
    234, 241
Tuptalo, Dymytrii (Dmytro Tuptalo;
    Dymytrii Rostovskii), Saint, 48–9,
    58–61, 63–5, 67, 70, 106, 111,
    165–6, 169, 171–2, 174, 180
Turgenev, Ivan, 222, 256, 258
Turobois'kyi, Iosyp, 7, 62, 184–5, 189,
    191, 195, 197–8, 202, 205, 207
Tuwim, Julian, 401
Tychyna, Pavlo, 34, 331, 394
Tykhyi, Oleksa, 411
Tymchenko, Ievhen, 129
Tymoshenko, Yulia, 420, 431, 444
Tzvi (Zevi), Sabbatai, 109

Ukraïnka, Lesia (Larysa Kosach), 10, 33,
    36, 278–81, 283
Ungaretti, Giuseppe, 394
Uriel, Archangel, 164
Urosh V (king), 58
Uvarov, Sergei, 233–4

Valuev, Petr, 213, 336
Vasyl'kivs'kyi, Serhii, 334
Velychko, Samiilo, 113
Velychkovs'kyi, Ioan, 177
Venelin, Iurii, 238
Venevitinov, Dmitrii, 237
Verdensis, Ioannes (John of Werden),
    111
Vergara Ciorda, Javier, 158–9

Verhaeren, Émile, 394
Verheugen, Günter, 423
Verlaine, Paul, 296, 310, 399
Viazemskii, Petr, 230, 237, 241
Vico, Giambattista, 376
Vierus, Johannes (Johann Weyer), 112
Vinhranovs'kyi, Mykola, 401, 403–4,
    407, 410
Virgil, 55, 109, 167, 213, 400
Viterbiensis, Joannes Annius (Giovanni
    Nanni), 112
Vogüé, Eugène-Melchior de, 258
Volodymyr (prince), 23, 51–2, 58, 83
Voltaire (François-Marie Arouet), 437
Voragine, Jacopo (Iacobus) de, 111
Voronyi, Mykola, 274, 284, 296, 331
Vossius, Gerhard, 112
Vovchok, Marko (Mariia Markovych), 9,
    213, 221–3
Vozniak, Taras, 425, 432
Vrangel', Petr, 361
Vynnychenko, Volodymyr, 277–8, 344,
    349, 355–6
Vyshens'kyi, Ivan, 24
Vyshnevets'kyi, Mykhailo, 102
Vyshnia, Ostap, 346, 359

Wagner, Richard, 309
Webern, Anton, 411
Werden, John of (Ioannes Verdensis),
    111
Weretelnyk, Roman, 278–9
Weyer, Johann (Johannes Vierus), 112
Wilde, Oscar, 276, 310, 399
Winckelmann, Johann Joachim, 380
Wiśniowiecki, Jeremi, 149, 151
Władysław IV (king), 145–6, 149
Wolf, Karl Hermann, 306
Wolff, Larry, 261, 437, 447
Wujek, Jakub, 110
Wyclif, John, 173
Wysocki, Szymon, 111

Yakovenko (Iakovenko), Natalia, 12, 180, 429
Yanukovych, Viktor, 242, 414, 419–21, 423–4, 426–7, 444–5
Yeltsin, Boris, 443
Yurkevich, Myroslav, 153, 155
Yushchenko, Viktor, 414–15, 419–23, 429, 431, 433–4, 443–4

Zaborowski, Tymon, 27
Zabuzhko, Oksana, 35, 416, 424, 428, 431
Zagorin, Perez, 141–2, 147–8
Zaleski, Józef Bohdan, 27
Zalyvakha, Opanas, 411

Zamojski, Jan, 52, 165
Zborovs'ka, Nila, 278
Zelins'ka, Lidiia, 279
Zema, Valerii, 117
Zeno of Citium, 195
Zerov, Mykola, 342–3, 356, 394, 400
Zhadan, Serhiy (Serhii), 35, 286
Zhivov, Viktor, 68
Zhukovskii, Vasilii, 21, 29
Zhylenko, Iryna, 411
Zinoviiev, Klymentii, 39
Zonaras, 109
Zweig, Stefan, 308
Zwinger (Zwingerus), Theodor, 112